THE FINANCIAL TIMES

GLOBAL
GUIDE
TO
INVESTING

'Only the FT has the contacts and the clout to pull together a list of contributers of this calibre . . . this handbook covers a lot of ground and does so with immense credibility.'

Business Age

'Eminently readable – full of analytical insights and personal anecdotes from investors who have consistently stayed ahead of the pack.

Whether you are a professional advising clients or a private investor seeking to create or preserve personal wealth, this book is a must. Even if you have not got a penny to invest, this book will repay your time with a cornucopia of entertaining anecdotes and fascinating insight into the thoughts and behaviour or people who make more than just a living in the serious world of investment.'

Simon P. Duffy, Group Finance Director, Thorn EMI

'Unquestionably the world's definitive work on investments.'

Rupert Hambro

'Anyone with a real interest in investment will want a copy of *The Financial Times Global Guide to Investing*. James Morton has succeeded in securing some fascinating contributions from some of the investment industry's leading practitioners. The result of his efforts is a compendium that you can either dip into at leisure or treat as a longer term serious read.'

Nigel Hurst-Brown, Deputy Chairman, Mercury Asset Management

'The great and the good of the investment industry have been brought together in one massive tome. It is a book packed with wisdom which will appeal to both the novice and the most experienced and cynical investor.'

Investor's Chronicle

'An indispensable book. Morton has assembled all the stars in the financial firmament. Read it and reap.'

Gretchen Morgenson, Senior Editor, Forbes

'Financial changes are sculpting the shifts in the nature of political economies creating unstable and unrealiable capital flows. *The Financial Times Global Guide to Investing* is an indispensable book to aid in navigating financial markets.'

**Steven H. Nagourney, Chief Investment Strategist,
Lehman Brothers' Private Client Group**

THE FINANCIAL TIMES

GLOBAL
GUIDE
TO
INVESTING

The secrets of the world's
leading investment gurus

Edited by
JAMES MORTON

FT
PITMAN
PUBLISHING

LONDON · WASHINGTON · SINGAPORE · HONG KONG · MELBOURNE

PITMAN PUBLISHING
128 Long Acre, London WC2E 9AN

A Division of Pearson Professional Limited

First published in Great Britain 1995
Reprinted 1995

© James Morton 1995

British Library Cataloguing in Publication Data
A CIP catalogue record for this book can be obtained
from the British Library.

ISBN 0 273 61414 2

Typeset by Pantek Arts, Maidstone, Kent.
Printed and bound in Great Britain by
Biddles Ltd, Guildford and King's Lynn

*The Publishers' policy is to use paper manufactured
from sustainable forests.*

CONTENTS

Creating a Portfolio

Part 2 BUILDING BLOCKS OF SUCCESSFUL INVESTING

Interpreting Investment Indicators

Utilizing Investment Strategies to Increase Profits

CONTENTS

Part 3   SELECTING WINNERS IN THE MARKET
The UK

Global Markets

Part 4 INVESTING IN SPECIAL INDUSTRIES

Part 7 LEARNING FROM LIVING LEGENDS

The Top Ten Global Investors of the 1990s

FOREWORD

The vast quantity of wisdom contained in this book will make it abundantly clear to the reader that there are many ways of becoming a successful investor. Some experts read balance sheets, some plot price charts, others attempt to predict the beneficiaries of economic or financial developments. Still others use computer power to crunch enormous quantities of data and pick out anomalies. One or two (fortunately not mentioned here) try astrology.

But the very first challenge for the investor is to assess his or her own objectives: the balance of risk and return, of growth or income, that will offer hope of financial reward but will also allow the investor to sleep at nights. Investors have to analyze themselves before they can profitably analyze the markets.

Beyond that, it is crucial to focus effort in a productive way. Many markets are, in a general sense, 'efficient'. That is an academic word describing markets that are driven by widely available information and where prices are set fairly – which is not to say that the markets never make mistakes but that an investor without access to private information or without special insights will find it impossible, on average, to outperform.

For many private investors, however, merely keeping up with the stock market is a considerable feat. All too often people are sucked in near the market highs but sell out, disillusioned, near the bottom. The sections about strategy and market timing should be read carefully. The markets can be treacherous, but the investor is often his own worst enemy.

The best rule, in my view, is to stick where possible to what you know about and are interested in. Special information – not the same as insider information – may be crucial. This comprehensive guide sets out the amazing range of opportunities, but selection and timing are crucial to investment, and in the end they are *your* responsibility.

Barry Riley, Investment Editor, *Financial Times*

ACKNOWLEDGEMENTS

First and foremost I want to thank my wife, Ellen, without whose help *The Global Guide to Investing* would never have been completed. This book is dedicated to her for all the sacrifices that she had to make in order that I could finish this work. Editing *The Global Guide* on top of managing an investment fund during the day has spilled over into many late nights and consumed almost every weekend during the first half of 1995. She could not have been more understanding nor more supportive of my goal to produce an investment book, which would be the most comprehensive of its kind ever published. Her encouragement and enthusiasm has been indispensable to me. I hope you will agree that the results are worthwhile and we have succeeded in producing a truly unique volume in the annals of investment publication history.

So many people have supported the development of this book that it is not possible to give proper recognition to all the help given so generously. It is only thanks to the assistance of many busy senior executives within the financial community in the City and on Wall Street that the *Financial Times* has been able to assemble the greatest collection of talent ever to write for one book on investing. I would like to single out the contribution of Bill Broadbent, Senior Vice President/Private Client Services of Lehman Brothers in New York, whose rolodex reads like a who's who of the top names in the investment community and who was instrumental in securing the participation of a number of the most eminent investors featured in the *Global Guide*.

My Publisher, David Sharp, deserves special thanks. He conceived the concept and stayed the course through the execution, sorting out numerous problems along the way. Without his consistent dedication and encouragement the *Global Guide* would be a much less important work. I also want to thank Richard Stagg who helped in many aspects of the preparation of this book, and many other people at Pitman who laboured long and hard to bring this book to publication on schedule. I particularly want to mention Sally Green and Kim Whiting, who have been more than helpful throughout.

Thanks also to Richard Koch, Managing Partner of Odyssey, who was instrumental in convincing me that the task was not as huge as it seemed, even though it was. Had I realized quite how much work was involved, it is doubtful if this book would ever have been started. This book could not have been completed without the support of my partner at Chelverton, Matthew Cartisser, who was very tolerant of the sizeable slice of my time diverted from our business during a nine-month period.

I also want to pay tribute to Claire Powell, who is the very model of a modern working mother and who proved to be much better organized than I was in tracking the progress of the 140 individuals who contributed to this book; and to my secretary Sylvia Nash, who ended up having to do much more work on the *Global Guide* than either of us expected.

With apologies in advance to anyone overlooked, because there are bound to be some, I also want to express my thanks to:

Madeleine Alatas	Joint Managing Director	Corporate Finance Advisory
Henry Bellingham	Member of Parliament	
Charles D. Blackmore	Chief Operating Officer	Fleming Martin
David Coleman	Chief Economist	CIBC Wood Gundy
David Curling	Director	Williams de Broë
Robert Davies	Director	Wexford Capital
Justin Dowley	Director – Corporate Finance	Morgan Grenfell
Philip Ehrman	Director	Invesco
Mark Evans	Director	Credit Lyonnais Securities
Michael Franklin	Finance Director	Chelverton Properties
Philip Franklin	Marketing Manager	Regent Fund Management
Louise Hatch	Associate Director	Ludgate Communications
David Kiddie	Director	Lloyds Investment Managers
Ann Knight	Managing Director of Research	Paine Webber
David Leathers	Director	Abingworth
Chien Lee	Director	Scottish & Eastern Investment Services
David Lowes	Director	Robert Fleming
Rolf Mæhle	Vice President Public Affairs	Kværner Group
Andrew Martin-Smith	Executive Director	Hambro Investment Management
Deryck C. Maughan	Chief Executive	Salomon Brothers
Tom McConnell	General Partner	New Enterprise Associates
Michael Montague	Chairman	Montague Multinational
Paul Myners	Chairman	Gartmore Investment Management
Thomas Nilsson	Managing Director	Investor (UK)
Paul Nix	Director	M&G
Blake Nixon	Executive Director	Guinness Peat Group
Richard Orders	Managing Director, Investment Banking	Barings Asia Pacific
William H. Page	Assistant Product Manager	Wellington Management Company
Paul Parshley	Senior Vice President	Lehman Brothers
Richard Pease	Director	Jupiter Tyndall
Robert Power	Director	Hambrecht & Quist
Nigel Pilkington	Director	Consulta
John Scotcher	Vice President	Citibank Private Bank
David Simpson	Director	Ludgate Communications
Tim Steele	Director	Cazenove
Ian Stewart	Director	Savills
Marc Sylvain	Managing Director, European Customer Services	Fidelity Investment Management
Andrew Tidbury	Barrister at Law	
Jonathan Tinker	Director	Richard Ellis Structured Finance
Jim Torrey	Managing Director	Torrey Capital LP
Julian Treger	Managing Director	Active Value Advisors
Cees van de Giessen	Director	Rabobank, Guernsey
Henrik von Platen	Senior Vice President	Samco Services
Devina Walter	Investment Manager	Henderson Administration
Alan Yarrow	Managing Director	Kleinwort Benson Securities

THE EDITOR

James Morton is a Director of Chelverton Investment Management and manager of the Chelverton Fund. The Chelverton Fund specializes in micro-cap stocks investing on behalf of high net worth individuals in equity markets around the world. His twenty years in the financial services sector spans commercial banking, corporate finance and investment management, and embraces some sixteen separate countries. Before Chelverton, James was a Director of Samuel Montagu Inc. and worked at Arthur Young, Bain & Citibank. He sits on the Board of Directors of several public and private companies in the UK, US and France. James has a BA in law from Cambridge, an MBA from Stanford Business School and an MA in Third World economics from the Stanford Food Research Institute. When not managing money or writing books James likes to read investment newsletters from around the world.

INTRODUCTION

No one person has a monopoly on wisdom in the investment business. Even the greatest minds struggle to become experts on more than a small corner of such a complex subject. It follows that no single individual is qualified to author a book that covers the broad spectrum of the world of investing. The solution: get investment professionals to write specialist sections on defined topics which are most relevant to investors in the mid-1990s. We set out to track down systematically the best investment minds in the world today. The result: *The Financial Times Global Guide to Investing* contains valuable and practical insights from the largest group of top talent in the investment community ever assembled in one book.

The impossibility of catering in full to every topic included, let alone including every deserving topic, means no reader will find answers to all their questions. Look at the other side of the ledger. The selection process may appear a tad idiosyncratic, but the choices were driven by one overriding consideration. Pick articulate and knowledgeable people. Find the very best. Do not compromise on quality. Select only leading experts and issues that really matter.

In every category throughout the book, we found winners willing to share the secrets of their success, helping the individual investor to negotiate the maze of the investment world. Nobody knows more about value investing than the firm of Tweedy Browne, and no organization has applied the principle with greater rigour and more success over the last 25 years. M&G have made an art form of investing in recovery stocks. T. Rowe Price virtually invented the concept of investing for growth and its Growth Stock Fund was a pioneer with a remarkable record. Nick Knight of Nomura has made more controversial calls more correctly on the direction of stock markets the world over than anyone else in the field. Geraldine Weiss is a doyenne of the investment profession whose focus on the use of dividends as an approach to stock picking makes her the acknowledged expert world wide. When it comes to real estate, who has not heard of Savills? Who better than the chief executive of the Institute of Financial Planners, David Norton, to offer advice on how to use financial advisors?

We have gone around the globe to seek out the top talent in every major country. That is why Deutsche Bank has written the section on Germany, Crosby Securities on Hong Kong, and Banque Bruxelles Lambert on the Benelux. A director of Salomon has penned the section on government securities. Vanguard Wellington contributed the section on US equities. Hambrecht & Quist provided the material on venture capital. On emerging markets, Dr Mark Mobius boldly goes where no other investor has gone before.

Anyone who thinks that making the right investment decision is a non-trivial issue should ponder this statistic recently published by the *Dick Davis Digest*. If you took a dollar and invested it in gold 188 years ago, your investment would be worth $15 today. If you had invested a dollar, instead, in long-term US Government Bonds, that dollar would be worth $5,700. But if you had invested the same dollar in the US stock market, you would now have $955,000. If you can get over that, think about what $955,000 might be if you had picked above average performers. The very best investment professionals seem capable of doing this on a consistent basis, even though the random walk theory of efficient markets remains compulsory reading in the rarefied world of our establishments of higher education. That is one reason we prefer to profile advice from practitioners.

Not many people who read this book are likely to live to be 188, even with the most optimistic scenario for medical advances. A more reasonable proposition is that your grandchildren could enjoy benefits of smart investment decisions today and the difference in their level of gratitude could be of the same order of magnitude. Look at the calculus on a smaller scale. The difference between £1,000 invested at 5 per cent over 25 years and the same sum invested at 6 per cent is £905. That does not seem such an irrelevancy: rather the reverse. It is the most powerful argument I have ever heard as to why the average investor should be willing to spend a little time each week learning more about how to make better investments. Reading *The Financial Times Global Guide to Investing* is a good place to start. In these pages you will find many ways to improve investment skills and returns, none more so than in the insights of our top ten global gurus.

Everyone loves a winner, and all investors can learn from people who are successful at making money. Arguably there is no better teacher than the experience of those few individuals who, year after year, manage to outperform the market, overcoming the handicaps of commissions, spreads, currency crises and back office costs. We have endeavoured to find the ten we feel have the greatest span of collective wisdom to offer the private investor. Some are household names. Sir John Templeton pioneered the whole concept of global investing. There is no one who has done more to make the world of investing a smaller place. Michael Price at Mutual Series has achieved an extraordinary record of risk adjusted return for his investors through his unique, three-pronged approach.

No one else knows the world of the media like Mario Gabelli. He has coined the term, 'the interactive couch potato'. Dr Martin Zweig is a technical investor without peers. What he does not know about markets is not worth knowing and the record of his funds reflects his deep understanding of the dynamics of the markets. Sir Ron Brierley is the ultimate survivor whose nose for value makes him the global equivalent of Warren Buffet.

We have has also profiled some who may not be celebrities in 1995, but are achieving such outstanding results that they will be household names in the next decade. Michael Aronstein somehow manages to move effortlessly between asset classes, achieving extraordinary results from short and long positions all along the asset spectrum. Canadian Peter Cundill has turned in truly outstanding performance while retaining a pure value approach. Dr

Marc Faber, 'Doctor Doom', transplanted from Switzerland to Hong Kong, finds ways to make money when all around are losing theirs. Robert Lloyd George opened up China long before that country was popular, and has results followers can only emulate. Christopher Mills is the London investor whose performance has won more awards than any other UK fund manager this decade. These are the stars of tomorrow.

But where does that leave the rest of us? Well, investing would be a funny old game if the consequences were not so serious. What should the average punter make of a business where people think spreads are sexy, where otherwise intelligent professionals go on random walks, or where a bunch of dart throwing chimpanzees regularly pick better stocks than seasoned investment managers. Don't despair. There are a few fundamental truths to give us all one up on the chimp. Remember the simple rules are also the easiest to forget.

1 *What if your investment falls by 20 per cent?*
  You will need to make a profit of 25 per cent the next year just to break even. A sobering proposition. Which is why so much advice focuses on managing risk and minimizing losses. Start with a couple of basic premises. Recognize mistakes early and cut your loss, but leave market timing to traders.

2 *It is essential to stay invested.*
  How essential? Well, research into stock market performance in the US during the 1980s showed that, if you were out of the market just 40 days during the decade, your annual rate of return plummeted from over 17 per cent to a measly 3.9 per cent. Staying invested means you will lose money at times. Loosing money is painful. Always. Without exception. There is great merit to market timing. If you get it right. Robert Prechter manages to do this. Most lesser mortals always miss the mark. Being out of the market when it is going up – which it does tend to do over time – is even more painful.

I am not advocating that you buy something and then forget about it. You cannot afford to neglect your investments. Yesterday's winner can all too quickly turn into tomorrow's horror story, even so-called widow and orphan investments, if such a category still exists. Bonds, stocks, real estate, commodities, all have been subject to extraordinary volatility over the last ten years; but cash can never be more than a short-term repository until you decide where to put your money to better use. If you cannot give your investments the time they deserve, give them to a professional who can, to manage for you.

I have learnt much more in the last nine months talking with and listening to the talented and successful people who have contributed their time to the *Global Guide to Investing* than in the rest of my 20–year career. My main challenge has been to make sure that all their collective wisdom survived the editor's pen. Each section contains valuable information and guidance from people who put their reputations and careers on the line every day. They have to be right to stay on top; and so the people who take the time to read this book will earn an edge. No one except the proof editor and yours truly are ever likely to read *The Financial Times Global Guide to Investing* cover to cover. Not every section is relevant to every investor, but there is something here for everyone who invests. Select sections which can help you the most and start there.

Let me end this introduction by sharing a few personal thoughts on investing. Any individual, with a minimum amount of application, can follow this approach. My style, shamelessly plagiarized from the greatest who have gone before, contains a blend of Peter Lynch meets Graham and Dodd with a dash of John Neff thrown in for good measure. Even though Chelverton's area of special expertise is micro cap stocks, we follow a relatively defensive approach which can be used across the board in equity and bond markets.

- Invest only in companies you can understand. If you violate this rule, you will be in automatic violation of all the rest, because analysis may lead you to the wrong conclusion.
- Buy assets at below true market value. This is especially important for convertible and debt instruments. Do not get confused by the balance sheet. Never forget that, if book value and actual value are the same, it is a rare coincidence.
- Don't worry about this year's profits. Focus on the underlying earnings power of the operations, and then never buy a stock trading above five times the potential pre-tax profits two years out.
- Do worry about cash flow. Companies often come back from an interruption to earnings, but a cash crunch kills more often than not.
- Too much debt means someone other than management is in charge of the company. That is normally bad for business and the value of the shares. Let the experts make money from over-leveraged businesses. Remember there are likely to be more losers than winners in a restructuring, and the average investor is usually to be found in the losing camp.

No one style works best for everyone, and the *Global Guide* will examine many different ways for investors to make money. The last golden rule is to stick to whatever rules work well for you. Find your own personal comfort zone and do not venture outside. My experience has been that investments which adhered to these guidelines produced pleasing results but, whenever I strayed beyond my area of competence, I usually came a cropper.

The objective of the *Global Guide to Investing* is to give its readers ideas and tools to manage investments better. You should find what you need in these pages to do just that. I want you to make more money in 1996 than you would have before buying this book. Take advantage of what is on offer in these pages and the purchase of the *Global Guide to Investing* should prove to be one of the best investments you ever make. Let me wish you all success possible in your investing future!

James Morton
September 1995

PART

1

AN
INTRODUCTION
TO INTELLIGENT
INVESTING

Surveying the Investment Spectrum

CASH

Tony Plummer

*Tony Plummer is a Director of **Hambros Bank Ltd** and is currently responsible for the Investment Management Division's strategy on global bond markets. He has been involved with financial markets since 1976 and is the author of* Forecasting Financial Markets.

***Hambros Bank Ltd** is the principal subsidiary of **Hambros plc**. It is a leading international merchant bank and has over 150 years of history in London. Hambros Bank is engaged in all aspects of international and domestic banking, investment banking, investment management, corporate finance, and leasing and asset finance. It is one of the market leaders in cash management services.*

Introduction

Cash is the amount of money, available at very short notice, which is either awaiting some other use or is specifically being used for savings. It need not be held physically in notes and coins. It can refer to the amount of money available in a bank or building society account. In today's modern financial markets, cash can also be held in short-term interest-bearing assets. These assets are effectively cash because they can be used without serious delay.

Cash as an Investment

Of all the various reasons for holding cash, the one that is least understood – and the one that is most often ignored – is that of investment itself. There are two main reasons why cash becomes available for investment. The first is that cash is not immediately required for other purposes. The second reason is that conditions are, for some reason, not deemed right for committing funds to bonds, equities or commodities.

This highlights the main advantage of cash, within the context of investment. It is relatively safe, because its nominal capital value will not change. If a person or institution holds cash, the only capital risk relates to the safety of the place where it is deposited: if the cash is held in a financial institution, the risk concerns the viability of the financial institution itself; if the cash is held under the mattress, the risk concerns those of theft and fire in the house! However, leaving aside these 'systemic' risks, cash is to all intents and purposes free of 'market', or investment, risk.

Unfortunately, holding cash is not without a cost. If risk is reduced, so is the likely return. Where assets are held in cash, the prospects of capital gain are necessarily reduced. Indeed, if cash is held in the form of notes, coins or non-interest bearing bank deposits, such as current accounts (often called 'sight' deposits in the USA), then there is no interest income either. Consequently, many investors regard cash as being a 'non' investment: that is, instead of being regarded as an important part of an investment portfolio, cash is often treated as being a necessary evil.

> **many investors regard cash as being a 'non' investment: that is, instead of being regarded as an important part of an investment portfolio, cash is often treated as being a necessary evil.**

In truth, however, cash is as much an investment vehicle as are equities and bonds. In modern economies, large cash amounts need not be held in non-interest bearing form. It is possible to place cash with a financial institution, or in a marketable financial asset, in the knowledge that it can be returned to the depositor/ investor at very short notice. The investment thus has the dual advantages of capital security and a known return. Interest-bearing cash is an ideal asset for risk-averse investors.

The Structure of 'Cash'

The definition of cash in today's highly sophisticated financial markets is to some extent a subjective one. From one perspective, cash can only be defined as money which is accessible at no more than one day's notice, with no capital loss. From another perspective, however, cash may be thought of in terms of the length of time before it is actually needed. Investors who are bearish on equity or bond markets, may regard cash as being financial instruments which will mature within three months. From yet another perspective – that is, those of the financial markets themselves – 'cash' instruments are generally those with a maturity date of one year or less, which can be liquidated at short notice.

It must be stressed that a long maturity date does not necessarily make an asset illiquid. Cash assets fall into two broad categories – namely fixed deposits with a financial institution (such as banks or building societies) and negotiable money market instruments (which are usually issued by, or guaranteed by, a financial institution). Fixed deposits are deemed to be of an illiquid nature insofar as the deposit-taking institution assumes that the deposit will be held until maturity. It is sometimes possible for an investor to 'break' the deposit and retrieve the money early. However, the financial institution will almost certainly demand a penalty in recompense for the costs involved. Fixed deposits can therefore only be regarded as 'cash' if they are of a very short maturity.

Most cash assets are, therefore, marketable or 'negotiable'. This means that they can be sold into a secondary market to realize a capital sum. Normal settlement of such sale varies depending on the type of instrument. Often settlement is on the same day as the transaction; sometimes it is the next business day after the transaction; and only very rarely is it as long as seven calendar days. Even in the latter case, it is often possible to arrange settlement for a different, mutually convenient, day if necessary. Accordingly, investments in negotiable cash instruments enable an investor to purchase (say) a one-year asset on a one-year view of liquidity requirements; but the investor retains the ability to liquidate the asset if circumstances change. Because of this flexibility, the yield on such assets is generally slightly lower than those on fixed deposits of a corresponding maturity.

Within the category of negotiable money market instruments is an asset which is a hybrid between a short-dated maturity and a long-dated maturity. This asset is known as a floating rate note. The coupon on these instruments is fixed for short periods of time and is then changed to reflect market conditions at the end of that period.

The ability to buy and sell negotiable short-dated instruments creates a very flexible maturity structure within the cash markets. In principle it is possible to buy instruments today with a maturity date on any business day within the next twelve months. Indeed, it is possible to buy instruments forward, in the future, with the subsequent maturity date occurring on any business day within twelve months after forward date. This gives the cash market great range and depth and allows for the calculation of a yield curve.

The yield curve basically aligns a yield with each date in the future and enables the investor to see the return which will be received by buying a negotiable cash instrument and holding it to maturity date. Subject to the usual qualification relating to credit risk, this return is guaranteed in nominal terms.

Cash Market Instruments

There is a variety of instruments which an investor can use. The most common ones – but not all of them – are shown in the list below. In principle, the instruments may be split into two categories: those issued with an original maturity date of one year or less, and those issued with an original maturity date of more than one year. The latter are 'bonds', and are covered in subsequent sections of *The Global Guide to Investing*.

Original maturity of one year or less

1 Fixed deposits ('Depos') Deposits with a bank or savings institution (such as a building society in the UK) which have a fixed maturity date.
2 Treasury Bills ('T-bills') Issued by governments, at a discount to nominal value. There is no coupon. High quality, very liquid. Generally issued for three months. Some countries (e.g. USA) issue for periods up to one year.

3 Bills of Exchange ('Acceptances') Available only in the UK. Loans to companies, guaranteed (i.e. 'accepted') by a bank. Fixed maturity, but very marketable. Can be sold to the Bank of England.
4 Certificates of Deposit ('CDs') Technically, proof of ownership of a bank deposit. Fixed maturity date, but marketable. Very liquid.

For any given period to maturity, the yield may vary with the quality of the issuer and the liquidity of the issue. Short government paper usually yields less than commercial paper. Negotiable instruments usually yield less than fixed deposits. A simple example of the differences is shown in the table below, which compares yields in four countries, across three basic types of market instrument, as at end March 1995.

3-Month Yields (%) On:	Sterling	Dollars	Deutschmarks	French Francs
Fixed Deposits	6-9/16	6-3/16	4-15/16	7-31/32
Certificates of Deposit	6-1/2	6-1/8	4-7/8	7-15/16
T-Bills	6-7/32	5-7/8	N/A	7-5/8

Investor Considerations

Most investors have cash balances which either have a short life expectancy because they will be needed for something else, or must be readily available to deal with unforeseen events. It is arguable that there is a range of instruments and maturities which can increase the return on this money, without seriously jeopardizing either the capital value or its availability.

An investor faced with a cash surplus has three factors to consider. First, are interest rates expected to go up or down? If rates are expected to rise, then there is almost no better alternative to keeping the money in a call, or overnight, deposit account. There is, of course, always the question as to whether the forthcoming rise in interest rates is already discounted by the markets. Are market rates already sufficiently higher than officially administered rates, such as base rates? If so, then consideration may be given to investing cash resources in longer-dated assets, such as Certificates of Deposit. The same considerations apply if the potential investor thinks that interest rates are coming down. Then, trying to 'lock-in' a yield of (say) 8 per cent for a given period will be more valuable than rolling money on an overnight deposit at 8 per cent.

There are three major considerations with respect to the qualities of an asset.

1 the **security**;
2 its **liquidity** in terms of marketability; and
3 its initial **yield**, or return, in relation to expected future market yields.

The security of an asset relates to credit-worthiness. Each borrowing institution is rated on the basis of a number of criteria, including credit risk, legal protection offered to debt holders, country risk, and industry risk. Ratings are made separately on short-term debt with an original maturity of twelve months or less, and on long-term debt with an original maturity of more than twelve months.

The liquidity of an asset relates directly to its marketability. This is usually reflected in the width of the spread between the bid price and the offer price of an asset: the lower the spread, the higher the marketability; and conversely. There are a number of factors at work here, depending on the type of instrument. Generally, these are: (a) the credit rating of the asset, because lower-rated assets will be less popular; (b) the number of market-makers who deal in the issue, since prices will tend to have a higher bid-to-offer spread if there are only a small number of market-makers involved; and (c) especially in the case of bonds, the size of the original issue, because larger issues are more tradeable. Obviously, these factors are closely related. Usually the most liquid assets will have the combination of a high credit rating, a large number of market-makers, and a large outstanding issuance. Such assets, however, tend to be tightly held as they approach maturity. Large deals may be difficult to transact in shorter maturities, and the purchase yields will be below that of other assets.

Finally, the yield is the return that the investor will obtain if the asset is bought and held to maturity. If the asset has to be sold before the maturity date, the proceeds may be higher or lower than the price paid. There is thus a **market** risk. For very short-dated instruments, this risk is minimal. For longer-dated maturities, the investor needs to be aware of, and plan for, the possibility of the market moving the wrong way. Very risk-averse investors should avoid longer maturities.

Services to Investors

Managing cash assets in such a way as to increase yield, without jeopardizing unnecessarily the nominal capital value, is a sophisticated but potentially very lucrative exercise. The simple rule of thumb is that **active** management becomes practicable if the cash is available for more than one year and is of a size that can command the standard dealing rates in the market – e.g. £1 million in the UK, $5 million in the USA, DM10 million in Germany. However, the amount of information and management time required is often beyond the resources of the individual investor, and smaller dealing sizes may not command the fine rates necessary for yield enhancement.

The smaller retail investor might, therefore, consider using **money market funds**. These funds, of which there are a large number, are professionally managed. They work on the principle that a multitude of small sums from investors can be combined to take advantage of the better yields which accrue to larger amounts. In addition, an active approach to managing the assets may be adopted by the manager.

Money market funds are attractive because the alternative deposit rates offered by banks to small investors are often so much lower than the rates offered to large depositors. In the UK, for example, small depositors can receive 1 per cent less than large depositors. Consequently, small investors can place cash in a money market fund and still benefit, provided the annual management charges are less than 1 per cent. ♀

GOVERNMENT BONDS

Michael Saunders

*Michael Saunders joined **Salomon Brothers International Ltd** in October 1990. He is a Director and the UK Economist with particular responsibility for the coverage of the UK gilts market.*

***Salomon Brothers** is a major dealer in government securities in New York, Tokyo and London, and is a member of major international equity and financial futures exchanges throughout the world. With one of the largest capital bases in the United States securities industry and its extensive market distribution capabilities, **Salomon Brothers** is a leader in marketing securities for governments and high-grade primary issues.*

Bonds generally are considered a relatively safe investment, because they lack the risk associated with equity dividends. However, in practice, it is possible to make or to lose significant amounts by getting the bond markets right or wrong.

Returns from the world's major bond markets have varied significantly in recent years, both in local currency terms and allowing for exchange rate movements. Common currency returns are shown expressed here in terms of the US dollar, but the ranking would hold regardless of currency used. Only the absolute returns would differ.

The scale of choices available to bond investors has widened considerably in recent years, as more countries have opened up their markets to overseas investors. Moreover, the size of each individual country's bond market generally has risen, because of rising public debt levels. The nominal level of outstanding bond issues in the world's 21 major bond markets (including non-government bonds) rose from just over $10,000 billion at the end of 1988 to $16,306 billion at the end of 1993. The figures for end 1994 are not available, but probably are near $18,000 billion, that is, about 80 per cent up on the 1988 level.

In local currency terms, UK gilts were the top performing market in 1992, with a 18.58 per cent return. Contrast that with returns expressed in US dollar terms where they were near the bottom of the list because of sterling's sharp fall.

Table 1.1 Bond Market Rankings and Returns in Local Currency

1992 Ranking	Return %	1993 Ranking	Return %	1994 Ranking	Return %
UK	18.58	Italy	28.75	Austria	0.02
Netherlands	15.37	Spain	28.49	Italy	−0.91
Belgium	14.29	UK	22.00	Belgium	−1.19
Germany	13.03	Denmark	21.26	Germany	−1.84
Sweden	12.04	Sweden	21.11	Japan	−2.67
France	10.98	France	20.88	US	−3.36
Japan	10.81	Australia	17.40	Spain	−3.66
Italy	10.78	Canada	16.68	Denmark	−3.79
Australia	9.92	Netherlands	15.83	Netherlands	−4.49
Canada	9.50	Germany	14.32	Canada	−4.50
Spain	8.02	Japan	14.04	Sweden	−4.74
Denmark	8.00	Austria	13.99	France	−5.67
US	7.21	Belgium	13.08	Australia	−6.47
Austria	NA	US	10.69	UK	−6.89
World Index	10.5	World Index	14.77	World Index	−3.27

Source: Salomon Brothers International Limited

Table 1.2 Bond Market Rankings and Returns in US Dollars

1992 Ranking	Return %	1993 Ranking	Return %	1994 Ranking	Return %
Japan	10.84	Japan	27.58	Belgium	12.22
Netherlands	8.58	UK	19.54	Austria	11.80
Belgium	7.64	Australia	15.69	Germany	9.98
US	7.21	France	13.15	Japan	8.88
Germany	5.94	Denmark	12.02	Netherlands	7.43
France	4.27	Canada	12.01	Denmark	7.43
Denmark	1.82	Italy	11.08	Canada	6.90
Australia	−0.27	US	10.69	Australia	6.88
Canada	−0.42	Netherlands	8.51	Sweden	6.81
UK	−4.12	Germany	6.70	Spain	4.61
Spain	−9.42	Austria	6.06	Italy	4.57
Sweden	−12.22	Belgium	4.00	France	4.37
Italy	−13.88	Spain	3.61	UK	−1.54
Austria	NA	Sweden	2.90	US	−3.36
World Index	5.53	World Index	13.27	World Index	2.34

Gilts continued near the top of the list in 1993, in both local currency terms and dollar terms, but were among the worst performing market in 1994. If an investor had selected the top performing countries in 1992, 1993 and 1994, then the cumulative return in dollar terms would have been 58.7 per cent. With the worst market each year, an investor would have lost 14.4 per cent.

Clearly, it is impossible to specify at the time of writing which bond markets will look most attractive at the time of reading. The markets may have moved to the extent that those which currently look attractive will already have produced the desired return. So the approach of this article is to lay out the principles to be considered in choosing among markets.

Economic and Policy Background

The first issues to be considered are the economic and policy background, particularly the inflation outlook. Most bonds have payments that are fixed in nominal (cash) terms for the life of the bond. Hence, the real present value of these payments – and thus the value of the bond – is inversely related to the expected path of inflation. Moreover, higher inflation usually is associated with rising short-term rates, increasing the attractions of leaving money on deposit. So rising inflation, or expectations of higher inflation, usually imply poor bond returns.

In some countries, particularly the UK, investors have the choice of index-linked bonds. With these, both the coupon payments and redemption value are indexed to consumer prices, thereby approximately offering a guaranteed real yield if the bond is held to maturity. Index-linked bonds may be more attractive than fixed interest bonds if inflation is expected to rise.

Index-linked bonds may be more attractive than fixed interest bonds if inflation is expected to rise.

Although economists disagree about the weight attached to different factors in causing inflation to rise, one major factor is the extent to which the economy's growth rate creates capacity pressures. Economic growth faster than the growth of the economy's productive capacity usually is followed eventually by rising inflation. The ability of the economy to grow rapidly will be greater if it starts from a depressed position. Nevertheless, bonds almost always react badly to signs of strong growth, because of the suspicion that higher inflation will follow. The economy's highly interest sensitive sectors usually are the first to turn up, or down, in each economic cycle. Thus, indicators such as housing starts, car sales, credit growth, money supply and asset prices (e.g. housing and property) are key. Few countries have all-encompassing measures of capacity use, so investors need to focus on indicators such as unemployment and the trade balance.

When an economy comes close to full capacity, the trade balance usually starts to deteriorate, as imports meet an increasing share of any further rise in demand.

Apart from the cyclical position, investors need to take account of the country's policy framework. Even if cyclical factors will keep inflation low in the near term, how likely is it that inflation will stay low in the medium term? Over time, countries with independent central banks that are charged with aiming for low inflation usually have been more successful than countries where short-term interest rates are set by politicians. As a result, a growing number – including France, Denmark and Spain – have made their central banks independent in recent years. Other countries – including the UK, New Zealand, Sweden and Canada – have introduced specific inflation targets that provide a clear and visible policy constraint. Investors need to judge how solid the framework is as a bulwark against policy slippage.

The third aspect of the economic backdrop is fiscal policy and the political situation. Loose fiscal policy not only boosts growth, and therefore adds to risks that cyclical pressures will push inflation higher. Fiscal expansion also hits the market by increasing the supply of government bonds. Experience tells us that unpopular governments, or governments that face elections, frequently loosen fiscal policy with tax cuts or public spending increases, and this might hit the country's bonds. Thus, investors need to consider whether this is a risk. In extreme conditions, a country's fiscal position may be so bad that the government can only finance it by paying high yields, and the resultant rise in debt service costs compounds the fiscal deficit. A few countries, Greece, Italy, Sweden, Canada and Belgium have public debt levels in excess of 100 per cent of that country's annual GDP, and may be at risk from such a scenario.

Valuations

The extent to which bond yields are affected by inflation means that investors should compare yields with current and expected inflation rates, that is, look at the real yield. Over the ten years 1985–94, bond yields in the US, Germany and Japan – the world's three biggest economies – have, on average, been 4.2 per cent above their inflation rates. As of April 1995, average real yields on those three markets are in line with that 10-year norm. Such real yields are high compared to the averages of the 1950s, 1960s and 1970s. However, if a 4 per cent real yield is a fair guide to the global benchmark, then investors should only aim for smaller or riskier markets if they offer a decent premium.

There are variants on measuring real yield against consumer price inflation. Occasionally, inflation rates may be affected by indirect tax hikes, giving a temporary boost to prices that will fade. The UK's Retail Price Index includes floating mortgage rates, and therefore perversely shows inflation rising when policy makers raise interest rates in order to keep inflation low. Alternatively, inflation in a particular country may temporarily be boosted by import prices or commodity prices. In order to track the extent to which inflation is being pushed up on a durable versus temporary basis, it may make sense to compare yields against wage growth.

It is not always the case that a bond market with an unusually high real yield is more attractive than a different market with a lower real yield. Higher yields may reflect higher risks of rising inflation or that a country's fiscal position is unsustainable. For instance, at the end of 1994, real yields on Italian government bonds were well above those on US government bonds. However, with rising inflation and a large budget deficit in Italy, US bonds have outperformed through the first five months of 1995.

Translating Choices into Actions

Personal investors can choose between buying bonds directly, or bond unit trusts. Funds have the advantage of offering professional management, but incur extra charges. If an investor is buying directly, care should be taken to ensure that the bond is a reasonably liquid issue, in which prices will be continuously available without too wide a bid-offer spread. Investors also need to select the maturity of the bond or range of maturities that are available to each bond fund. Fixed-interest bonds range in maturity from a few months to 22 years (at present) in UK gilts and up to 30 years for US Treasuries. The price of shorter dated bonds usually is less volatile than that of longer dated bonds, rising by less in a bull market and falling by less in a bear market. A risk-averse investor therefore should stick to shorter dated bonds, of less than five years to maturity. Longer dated bonds usually have a slightly higher yield to compensate for their greater volatility. Finally, if overseas diversification looks attractive, an investor needs to decide whether to accept currency risk or hedge the exposure back into the investor's base currency. As the bond returns data highlight, currency movements frequently can add, or detract, significantly, from bond market returns. ♀

CORPORATE BONDS
Dr Fred Huibers

*Dr Fred E. Huibers, BA, MBA, PhD joined the **Robeco Group**, the largest independent fund management group in Europe in 1989 as a portfolio manager. He moved to **Rabobank's** Head Office in Utrecht, The Netherlands in 1994 as Head of Asset Management.*

In addition, Dr Huibers teaches at Tilburg University in The Netherlands. He has written a book on the returns generated by investing in Initial Public Offerings of both private and public sector companies in the UK, Canada and Singapore which is published by Eburon, Delft.

Many investors in the global bond markets limit their choice to government bonds. After all, debt paper issued by sovereign governments is considered to be safer as governments have the ability to increase taxation in order to meet their obligation to bondholders. In addition, the sheer volume of debt issued by governments implies that the bond investor can almost always find a fixed-income instrument issued by some government with the characteristics which he is looking for. Finally, government bonds tend to dominate most fixed-income markets in terms of total value of the bond market and are thus most prominent in the minds of investors.

As is shown in Table 1.3, on average, approximately 60 per cent of the total value of the fifteen largest bond markets in the world is taken up by government bonds. Thus, by focusing their investment decisions in the fixed-income markets exclusively on government bonds, many investors ignore a quite large section equal to 40 per cent of the market. In some of the markets, such as the bonds denominated in DEM, DKK, CHF and SEK, government bonds actually make up less than 50 per cent of the total market.

Clearly, then, bonds issued by institutions other than governments make up a substantial part of the world's largest bond markets. Because the bulk of the bonds issued by non-sovereign debtors are issued by corporations, these fixed-income instruments are called corporate bonds.

Not only the (relative) size but also the structure of these corporate bond markets – in terms of the characteristics of the main debt issuers – varies from one market to the next. In Table 1.4, an overview of the structure of the world's largest corporate bond markets is given.

The corporate bond markets of the world's largest bond markets fall into four broad categories. Corporate bonds make up a relatively small portion of the southern European bond markets denominated in ITL, FRF and ESP. The second category consists of corporate bonds denominated in GBP, CAD and ECU which are predominantly Eurobonds. Banks dominate the corporate bonds in the third category which consists of bonds in JPY, DEM, BEF, NLG, DKK and the SEK. Finally, the corporate bond market denominated in USD, CHF and AUD is characterized by a high degree of fragmentation in terms of the number of issuing institutions.

Private placements are frequently used to sell corporate bonds denominated in DEM, NLG and CHF. If the value of the corporate bonds which have been sold by way of private placement are added to the volume of publicly sold bonds, the total value of the corporate bond markets denominated in DEM, NLG and CHF increases by 25 per cent, 80 per cent and 30 per cent respectively.

Table 1.3 Fifteen largest bond markets and the relative sizes of the market for government bonds and corporate bonds

Currency	Total size* (billion USD)	Government bonds (%)	Corporate bonds (%)
USD	7,547.2	68.4	31.6
JPY	3,044.0	59.3	40.7
DEM	1,590.8	39.2	60.8
ITL	780.7	81.4	18.6
FRF	748.6	73.6	26.4
GBP	436.6	64.6	35.4
CAD	393.0	67.1	32.9
BEF	301.3	57.0	43.0
NLG	227.5	63.5	36.5
DKK	227.4	32.1	67.9
CHF	200.7	16.3	83.7
SEK	186.4	33.5	66.5
ECU	144.6	34.1	65.9
ESP	144.4	73.6	26.4
AUD	106.1	65.4	34.6
Total	16,079.3	62.4	37.6

*end of 1993; *Source:* Salomon Brothers international bond market analysis August 1994

Thus, global fixed-income investors have a menu of different corporate bonds to choose from. Corporate bonds often have a higher yield than government bonds with the same time to maturity, because bonds issued by corporations are usually riskier than bonds issued by sovereign governments. By adding corporate bonds to a portfolio of government bonds, investors can increase the average yield of their holdings.

Corporations have limited resources in terms of cash flow and financial reserves from which to pay interest on their debt. Both the magnitude of the cash flow and the value of the assets of the corporation vary over time according to the prevailing business conditions. A severe recession might force a corporation to default on its debt,

By adding corporate bonds to a portfolio of government bonds, investors can increase the average yield of their holdings.

leaving bondholders scrambling to recuperate at least part of their investment. Sovereign governments, on the other hand, are always able to increase taxation in order to increase their revenues. Purchasers of government bonds (at least of the governments issuing debt on one of the fifteen largest bond markets) do not have to worry about the risk of a government going bankrupt.

Table 1.4 Structure of the fifteen largest corporate bond markets

USD	fragmented: no specific category of corporate issuer dominates market
JPY	banks dominate; convertible bonds frequently used by corporations
DEM	banks (Deutsche Bank, Dresdner Bank and Commerzbank) dominate; non-financial corporations rely mostly on bank financing; private placements important
ITL	relatively small corporate bond market; disproportionate use of floating rate instruments
FRF	government dominates bond market: as privatization of banks, insurance companies and car companies progresses, corporate bond market receives growth stimulus
GBP	most corporate loans in Eurobond market
CAD	approximately 50% loans in Eurobond market
BEF	banks (BBL, Generale Bank and KB) dominate
NLG	commercial banks (ABN AMRO, ING and Rabobank) dominate; private placements important
DKK	traditionally about 75% of bond market issues are mortgage banks. Share has fallen due to real estate crisis in Denmark
CHF	fragmented corporate bond market; private placements important
SEK	mortgage banks (Urban Mortgage Bank Group, Spintab of Swedbank) dominate
ECU	all Eurobonds; initiated in 1981; stagnation of issue volume since European Monetary System crisis of 1992
ESP	utilities and banks dominate relatively small corporate bond market
AUD	fragmented corporate bond market

Source: IRIS research papers; G Van Breukelen

The low default risk of government bonds is reflected in the top rating which these bonds receive by internationally renowned credit rating agencies such as Standard & Poor's and Moody's. The rating system used by Standard & Poor's, for example, varies from AAA for a bond with a minimal default risk through AA, then to A, BBB, BB, B, CCC, CC, C and D in increasing order of riskiness. An investment in a bond with a rating below BBB is considered speculative. All government bonds denominated in the currencies of the fifteen largest bond markets are rated by Standard & Poor's as either AAA or the slightly lower AA rating for Italian, Canadian, Belgian, Danish, Swedish, Spanish and Australian government bonds.

While there exist some AAA-rated firms such as the Swiss bank UBS and the Dutch Rabobank Nederland, most bonds issued by corporations get a lower rating than government bonds. Therefore, in order to be compensated for the risk of default, purchasers of corporate bonds demand a risk premium in the form of a higher yield. The question, of course, is if purchasers of corporate bonds are adequately compensated for the higher default risk on their investments. The results of statistical studies conducted by both Standard & Poor's and Moody's, indicate that there is reason to believe that indeed corporate bondholders are compensated.

Table 1.5 First year default risk (%)

Rating	1981	1982	1983	1984	1985	1986	1987	1988	1989	1990	1991	1992	1993
AAA	0.00	0.00	0.00	0.00	0.00	0.00	0.00	0.00	0.00	0.00	0.00	0.00	0.00
AA	0.00	0.00	0.00	0.00	0.00	0.00	0.00	0.00	0.00	0.00	0.00	0.00	0.00
A	0.00	0.45	0.00	0.00	0.00	0.19	0.00	0.00	0.18	0.00	0.00	0.00	0.00
BBB	0.00	0.36	0.34	0.72	0.00	0.34	0.00	0.00	0.58	0.83	0.52	0.00	0.00
BB	0.00	4.27	1.19	0.58	1.55	1.32	0.38	1.38	0.70	3.17	2.50	0.00	0.33
B	2.44	3.25	3.40	3.85	5.80	8.68	3.34	3.86	3.40	9.12	12.29	8.19	2.48
CCC	0.00	17.65	0.00	17.65	12.50	25.00	8.20	21.82	26.42	29.17	32.81	20.00	11.76

Source: Standard & Poor's Rating Services – Creditreview of 2 May 1994

Table 1.5 shows the risk that a US issuer defaults one year after he has issued a rated bond.

While AAA or AA-rated bonds (the category to which the earlier mentioned government bonds belong) carry a minimal default risk, this is not the case for the lower-rated bonds. The default risk seems to increase in recessionary periods such as periods starting in 1982 and 1989. The lower the rating of the bonds, the higher the risk of default.

Table 1.6 shows the average risk premium that 10-year AA, A and BBB-rated US corporate bonds carry compared to AAA-rated 10-year US government bonds. The difference between the yield of a lower-rated bond and that of a comparable top-rated government bond, is referred to as the yield spread.

Table 1.6 Difference between the yield of below AAA-rated US corporate bonds and AAA-rated US governments bonds

Yield spread (%)	AA	A	BBB
1960s	0.14	0.29	0.64
1970s	0.28	0.56	1.08
1980s	0.40	0.93	1.45
1990	0.13	0.50	1.03
1991	0.24	0.53	1.03
1992	0.23	0.48	0.84
1993	0.15	0.35	0.71

Source: Moody's Investor Service, Corporate Credit Research

Not surprisingly, the lower the rating of the corporate bond, the higher the spread. But is the yield premium or spread high enough to compensate for the higher default risk of the corporate bond relative to that of a government bond?

The results of the studies by the credit rating agencies do indeed suggest that investors receive more than adequate compensation. According to Moody's (Table 1.6), buyers of BBB-rated US corporate bonds received a yield premium of 0.64 per cent, 1.08 per cent and 1.45 per cent in respectively, the 1960s, the 1970s and the 1980s. If attention is turned to more recent history, the yield premium of BBB-rated US corporate bonds in 1990, 1991, 1992 and 1993 has been, respectively, 1.03 per cent, 1.03 per cent, 0.84 per cent and 0.71 per cent. According to the results of a study by Standard & Poor's (Table 1.5), an investor who holds a BBB-rated US corporate bond for a period of one year after the bond has been issued, runs a default risk of 0.83 per cent (1990), 0.52 per cent (1991), 0.00 per cent (1992) and 0.00 per cent (1993).

The numbers indicate that the reward (i.e. the yield premium) is larger than the risk (i.e. the risk of default within one year after purchase of the corporate bond). The 'extra' reward over risk for the years 1990, 1991, 1992 and 1993 equals 0.20 per cent, 0.51 per cent, 0.84 per cent and 0.71 per cent respectively. Thus, investors who held a diversified portfolio of US corporate bonds did better than investors who only invested in comparable US government bonds, even after adjusting returns for the higher default risk of corporate bonds. If the risk/reward ratio of corporate bonds issued in earlier periods (such as the 1980s) is examined, similar conclusions can be drawn.

Why do corporate bonds in the world's largest bond market seem to reward investors so handsomely? Part of the answer may stem from the fact that many corporate bonds are less well-known by many investors because of their relatively small issue size. Thus, similar to the 'small firm-effect' which occurs in most of the world's equity markets, the under-researched corporate bonds offer an attractive risk/reward ratio to investors.

By adding corporate bonds to a fixed-income portfolio, investors may enhance returns without running commensurate risks. This is particularly true for individual investors who usually can afford to deal in smaller corporate bonds and can profit from the attractive returns offered by corporate bonds. 🔌

By adding corporate bonds to a fixed-income portfolio, investors may enhance returns without running commensurate risks.

EQUITIES

Nicholas Knight

Nicholas Knight is Deputy Managing Director and Head of Strategy at **Nomura Research Institute (Europe) Ltd.** *He has been ranked in the top three for UK equity market forecasting by* Institutional Investor *and seventh in the* Nikkei Financial Daily's *annual analyst's survey for Japanese equity market strategy. He joined* **Nomura** *from* **Drexel Burnham Lambert**, *where he was Managing Director of Research. Between 1983 and 1988 he was Head of Strategy at* **James Capel** *and was rated in the top three for equity market forecasting in surveys by* **Extel, Greenwich Associates** *and* Institutional Investor.

Nomura Research *is an independent subsidiary of* **Nomura Securities**, *with offices in Japan, South East Asia, USA, and Europe. Serving a broad international client base, it provides both macro-economic and stock specific research, analysis and forecasting.*

The short introduction to the issue of equities as an asset class is that over the long term, they easily out-perform both bonds and cash. According to a study by BZW, UK equities have returned a real compound return of 7.7 per cent per annum since 1919, as compared to 1.8 per cent real for bonds and 1.4 per cent real for cash. The power of compound interest translates into massively different total returns over the period. The most suitable advice for most investors would put a large part of the City out of business – 'buy and hold' and 'pound cost average'. Translated into plain English, buy a little every month and never sell!

An old adage reminds us, however, that a stock market is only a market of stocks, and in reality, clever stock selection and timing the entry and exit from the market carefully can dramatically enhance returns. In the eleven years since the FTSE was created, for example, the UK equity market has risen by 206 per cent; if one had been out of the market in 1989 – the best year – this return falls to 127 per cent. Conversely, if one had been lucky enough to miss out the worst year – 1990 – this return rises to 246 per cent. Much more dramatically, had one invested in the top ten best performing FTSE shares each year since 1984 the average gain per annum is a mouth-watering 44 per cent. Investing in the ten worst FTSE shares on the same basis, however, and one would have lost 27 per cent per annum.

Some might think that being lucky enough to buy the right stocks at the right time all the time is just too good to

Some might think that being lucky enough to buy the right stocks at the right time all the time is just too good to be true – and they would be right.

be true – and they would be right. Most academic literature suggests that it is extremely difficult for investors to perform significantly better than the market (hence the rise of 'index trackers', funds designed to replicate the performance of the market at the lowest cost). Notable exceptions exist, of course, Warren Buffet being probably the most famous example of a genuine long-term investor capable of consistently out-performing the market by looking through the vagaries of the economic cycle. For those investors incapable of looking quite so far ahead, however, it is vital to understand the way the market moves in the shorter term, particularly during the course of a complete economic cycle.

Whilst in the very long run, therefore, the ability of equities to out-perform cash and bonds is driven by the growth in their earnings and dividends over time, shifts in valuation can be much more important in the short term. The Price Earnings Ratio (PER), therefore, the most common form of valuing corporate earnings, is nothing more than the stock price divided by the earnings and represents the number of years the stock has to be held before the company has delivered earnings equal to the current share price; fluctuations in this 'multiple' is the biggest determinant of the total return from equities in any one year more often than not.

Examination of the underlying data shows that shifts in the relative contribution to the total return derived from the yield, earnings and a shift in the PER is far from random, as a simple 'cycle' tying the stock market and economic data together illustrates. This cycle breaks down into four distinct periods – Recession, Recovery, Boom and Slowdown – the characteristics of which can be broadly defined as follows:

- Recession: GDP and/or earnings growth is negative but multiple expansion offsets the fall in earnings so the stock market rises.
- Recovery: GDP growth and earnings growth are positive and the multiple, in the early stages at least, rises; stock prices rise.
- Boom: GDP and earnings growth are positive but the multiple falls by an offsetting amount, leaving the prices effectively flat to down.
- Slowdown: GDP and earnings growth are positive, albeit the rate of growth is slowing, but the multiple falls more than the earnings rise, thereby making the Index fall.

The key insight provided by this approach is that the stock market acts as a discounting mechanism, going down, for example, in the Slowdown period, in anticipation of the forthcoming Recession. The market is efficient indeed. The multiple falls so far in advance of the earnings decline that prices actually bottom before the emergence of negative earnings growth. Typically, and paradoxically perhaps, the best part of the overall return over the past quarter of a century has been made in periods of Recession and subsequent Recovery; Boom periods have yielded little and outright losses are sustained in the Slowdown.

This concept of the stock market as a discounting mechanism is explained by the interaction between the multiple and interest rates on the one hand and interest rates and the economic cycle on the other. Interest rates thus represent the discount rate for calculating the net present value of future earnings; in so far as rates rise, therefore, the multiple (the numbers of years of current earnings represented by the current share price) falls.

Interest rates tend to move – more or less – pro-cyclically with the real economy; so do corporate earnings fairly obviously. The actual impact on stock prices thus depends on the interaction of forces that work in opposite directions as the economic cycle unfolds; downward pressure on valuations as the economy recovers (and interest rates rise) versus, at the same point in the cycle, upward pressure on earnings. Seen in this context the movement of the market through the cycle can be explained by the following rearrangement of the normal PER.

Recession: PE+ > E- = P+

Recovery: PE-/+ < E+ = P+

Boom: PE- = E+ = P=

Slowdown: PE- > E+ = P-

With three out of the four phases positive to neutral for stock prices, it   is easy to see why it is that bull markets tend to be fairly long drawn out affairs with bear markets typically being characterized as 'nasty, brutish, and short'!

Perhaps the best way of further explaining these concepts is to provide concrete examples.

The evolution of the UK equity market through the last cycle is a good one. It is a matter of historical record, in our opinion at least, that the last bull market began in September 1990 and ended in February 1994, with the FTSE rising by 77 per cent over the period from just under 2,000 to just over 3,500. In the context of our analysis, therefore, 1990 was clearly the Slowdown year, followed by Recession in 1991–2, Recovery in 1993, and, more controversially, Boom in 1994. Table 1.8 on page 24 contains the percentage change in the FTSE in these years.

The early stages of this bull market cycle fit the theory perfectly. Under the impact of higher interest rates, the PER fell away through 1990 ending up at under 10x historic by September. This effectively discounted a recession, even though economists were still forecasting further strong growth. Taking data from Consensus Economics Inc the expectation for 1991 GDP growth in the UK as at September 1990 was only just below +2 per cent. Incredible as it may sound, this collapsed to –2.1 per cent twelve months later, yet the market rose 25 per cent over the same period as interest rates fell as the 'unforecast' recession suddenly started to emerge.

As an aside, this period also illustrates why it is that retail investors (and indeed, many professionals) routinely sell the bottom and buy the top of the market; they forget the inverse correlation between interest rates and valuations. A good rule of thumb, therefore, is to remember that the actual attractions of cash are the inverse of the perceived attractions of cash. As the market bottomed, short rates were a mouth-watering 15 per cent; unit trusts experienced net redemptions in August 1990 of nearly £500 million, with a further £317 million in the following month. To put this into context, there had been net redemptions in only five months of the previous decade, March 1990 being the previous biggest monthly outflow at just £19 million.

By the first quarter of 1994, at the very top of the bull market as short rates fell to multi-year lows of 5.25 per cent, net sales were running at record levels, peaking in March at just under £1,400 million. The previous highest monthly inflow, believe it or not, was September 1987 (£1,159 million), the very month prior to the October 1987 crash!

In terms of market timing, the man in the street is almost invariably a contrary indicator. Remembering this rule will almost certainly stand investors in good stead looking forward.

It is important to stress that our framework of cyclical analysis seems to be generally applicable to most equity markets; one could show equally persuasive examples from markets as diverse as France to Japan. In the latter, for instance, the market was clearly driven higher in 1986–7 by the decline in the long bond yield from 6.2 per cent to 2.8 per cent; the PER thus rose from 35x to over 75x, driving the Nikkei up by over 100 per cent (from 12,881 to 26,646) before the crash intervened in late 1987. That was only a very temporary interruption of the bull trend, with the market all but doubling again between October 1987 and December 1989. This time, however, the driving force of the market was strong earnings momentum unleashed by the strength of the economy generated by the prior period collapse in interest rates. Even though long rates retraced dramatically, dragging down the PER, the sharp rise in corporate earnings was more than sufficient compensation.

Looking forward over the next couple of years, the first requirement is to locate the phase of the economic cycle which most accurately describes the position of the major economies, and then to interpret what implications this has for interest rates at both ends of the yield curve. Fit the valuation and earnings cycle to the latter, and some broad conclusions should fall out quite easily.

Table 1.7 shows, the recent evolution of the major G7 economies since 1990.

It is clear that the world economy, which was unusually unsynchronized in the early years of the decade has finally come together in large measure in the direction of very strong growth. Led by the US, and to an increasingly large extent South East Asia, Europe in particular surged in 1994, and, following the stimulus to growth provided by the Kobe earthquake of January 1995, there is every likelihood that Japan will follow suit in 1996.

Table 1.7 GDP Growth Actual and Forecast

	US	Japan	Germany	France	UK	Canada	Italy
1990	0.8	5.2	5.0	2.3	0.6	–0.5	2.2
1991	–1.2	4.4	3.6	0.8	–2.4	–1.7	1.4
1992	2.6	1.5	1.6	1.4	–0.4	0.7	0.9
1993	3.0	0.1	–1.9	–0.9	1.9	2.2	–0.7
1994	4.0	0.8	2.3	2.4	4.0	4.2	2.3
1995(F)	3.1	1.9	2.6	3.1	3.2	3.8	2.9
1996(F)	2.3	3.3	2.8	2.9	2.8	3.0	2.8

At a very minimum, therefore, it seems appropriate to place the world economy in 1994–5 in 'Recovery' mode and in many respects the 'Boom' profile appears more appropriate for, as the economies have recovered, so interest rates have risen, the resulting downward pressure on valuations robbing equity markets of any earnings-driven upside potential.

After 'Boom' comes the 'Slowdown'. This is already indicated to a certain extent by the growth forecasts shown in Table 1.7. Our guess is that these forecasts will be shown to be significantly over-optimistic, and that the negative implications of this for corporate earnings will more than offset any eventual decline in interest rates; negative returns are thus likely in 1995 if not 1996. It is important to understand quite how difficult it is to achieve what the Fed and others are currently forecasting, i.e. a soft-landing for the world economy. Note, for example, that the US economy has grown in the 2–3 per cent range in only four of the past twenty-five years, and none of those years were consecutive! Even Japan, the one economy which might be expected to buck this trend, is unlikely to escape, either because the good news is already priced into the market or because the recovery does not materialize because of the strong yen. 'Recession' is likely to provide the next buying opportunity for equities – 1997 looks like the target date. ♀

Table 1.8 Annual Change in Main Stock Market Index

	US	Japan	Germany	France	UK	Canada	Italy
1990	–4.3	–38.7	–21.9	–24.1	–14.3	–18.0	–24.9
1991	20.3	–3.6	12.9	16.3	15.1	7.9	–1.7
1992	4.2	–26.4	–2.1	5.2	14.8	–4.6	–12.1
1993	13.7	2.9	46.7	22.1	23.4	29.0	38.8
1994	2.1	13.2	–7.1	–17.1	–9.6	–2.5	2.1
1995*	10.3	–15.6	–7.2	0.1	2.4	0.9	2.2

*to 20 April

CONVERTIBLE BONDS AND OTHER EQUITY LINKED SECURITIES

Peter Everington

*Peter Everington is the Managing Director of **Regent Fund Management Ltd**, a Hong Kong based investment company with US$ 2.5 billion under management. Peter has been in Hong Kong for 11 years. He previously worked for **GT** and **Thornton**, both companies that specialized in Asian investing.*

***Regent** is focused primarily on Asian equity and equity linked markets and manages a number of 'undervalued asset' funds that specialize in securities such as CBs, GDRs and closed-end funds. **Regent** also manages two Asian hedge funds that are among the first such funds dedicated to the region.*

A convertible bond, or CB, is exactly what the name implies: a bond paying a fixed rate of interest that is convertible into the common shares of the issuing company at the option of the buyer, and at some pre-determined date in the future. By way of illustration, let us suppose that shares of the 'Hong Kong Rickshaw Co' are trading at $8 and the company pays an annual dividend of 20 cents, or 2.5 per cent, based on the current share price. The company wishes to expand its fleet of motorized rickshaws and decides to issue a CB with the following terms. The CB carries a coupon of 5 per cent and is convertible at $10 per share any time in the ten years up to 2005, when the bonds will be redeemed for $100. However, at any time you may convert your bond into ten shares, being the $100 bond divided by the $10 conversion price.

The difference between investing in the company's shares versus the CBs can be summarized as follows. If the company does well, its earnings and dividends will rise and so, too, will its share price over time. If the shares rise to $40 by 2005 and the dividends rise steadily to $1.10 per share, then the equity investor will have earned a capital gain of 400 per cent as well as total dividends of $6.50 or 81.25 per cent, giving a total return of 481.25 per cent. If we assume that the bond holder waits until the last moment to convert the bonds, then the return will have been 50 per cent in interest and 300 per cent in capital gain, for a total return of 350 per cent.

If, on the other hand, the business fails to grow, so earnings and dividends remain the same and the share price is still languishing at $8 in 2005, then the equity investor will have seen a meagre return of 25 per cent by way of dividends (ten years at 20 cents a year), while the bond holder will have earned an interest return of 50 per cent. Neither will earn any capital gain. If we assume, however, that rickshaws go completely out of fashion, earnings decline steadily to the point where dividends fall to zero by 2005, and the shares fall to just $2, then the positions are as follows. The equity investor will have earned a total dividend return of just $1.10 or 13.75 per cent, while suffering a capital loss of 75 per cent, giving a total return of –61.25 per cent. The CB

Chart 1.1 CB Theory

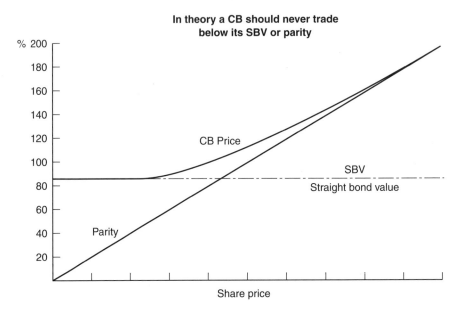

In theory a CB should never trade below its SBV or parity

Source: Regent Pacific CB Hedge Fund – Regent Fund Management Ltd

investor will have earned 50 per cent interest return and cashed in the bonds for $100 at expiry for a total return on investment of +50 per cent.

This illustration demonstrates the essence of investing in CBs. The investor sacrifices a part of the potential gain in return for carrying a lower level of risk. In effect, a CB is simply a straight bond with a long-term option, or warrant, attached. (See section on options and warrants starting on p 54.) These two elements of the CB can be valued separately with the value of the bond known as the 'Straight Bond Value' or SBV, and the equity value being referred to as the 'parity'. By convention, CBs are priced in percentage terms, with most US$ CBs being issued in units of $5,000, so that a price of 120 per cent would correspond to US$ 6,000. As the price of the underlying share rises, the CB will trade more on the basis of its equity value or 'parity' but, as the underlying share price falls, the CB will trade more on the basis of its 'straight bond value'. In theory, as illustrated by Chart 1.1, a CB should never trade below either its SBV or parity. In practice, some CBs occasionally do.

To the extent that a CB trades like a straight bond, it will be subject to the normal macro influences affecting interest rates generally, such as inflation expectations and overall credit conditions while, at the micro level, the CB will also be affected by the credit rating of the issuing company. To the extent that a CB trades like equity, it will be subject to macro issues affecting the relevant equity market as well as conditions facing the company itself such as growth prospects, management capabilities, etc. Since it is possible to assess the bond and equity option elements of a CB separately, it is possible to work out a the-

Chart 1.2 CB Practice

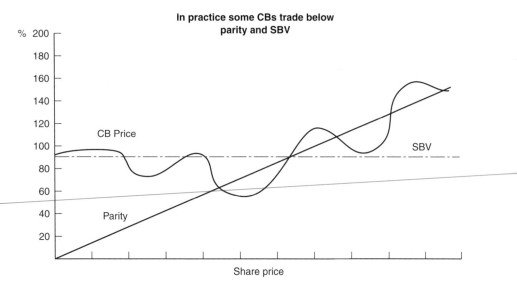

In practice some CBs trade below parity and SBV

Source: Barings Securities

oretical fair value. Unfortunately, the process is highly theoretical and depends heavily on computers. That said, most major international securities companies have capabilities in this area and the layman can often start by asking to be supplied with regular print-outs of parity sheets. It is not necessary to understand all the intricacies of the models, just as it is not necessary to understand fully how a car works to be able to drive. Some knowledge of the basic principles is essential. In particular, it is important to be able to think both in terms of investing in bonds as well as in equities.

In practice, the typical CB investor is an equity investor who wishes to lower his/her overall risk profile. That is a reasonable approach to take, except that one should always realize that the baseline straight bond value will fluctuate with interest rates so, in 1994, for example, CB investors were clobbered both from declines in equity markets worldwide as well as sharp falls in bond markets. The other factor most often ignored is that the total size of a company's CB issue normally will be significantly smaller than the value of the shares outstanding. As such, the CB will be less liquid than the underlying shares; an issue that tends to be ignored in good times, but which gives rise to a liquidity discount at times of tight credit conditions.

In practice, the typical CB investor is an equity investor who wishes to lower his/her overall risk profile.

Because the CB is a hybrid instrument, there are occasions when pricing can be distorted. Normally, the CB market will comprise some balanced mix of equity oriented investors operating alongside fixed interest oriented investors. On occasion, extreme moves in either equity or bond markets will lead to a mass exodus by that class of investor leaving the CB market, and this results in the whole market being distorted, in pricing terms, towards only one side of the equation. While this is, in some sense, a problem, it can also be a source of great opportunity, as it implies periods of inefficient pricing. This is exacerbated by the fact that, whereas the basic CB is a simple instrument, in practice many variables can be added to differentiate CBs. Conversion dates and terms can be varied; conversion is sometimes limited to discrete rather than continuous periods; investors are sometimes given the right to 'put' the CB back to the issuer and, occasionally, issuers have the right to force the conversion of a CB via a 'call' feature that kicks in if the underlying equity trades continuously above a certain level. Sometimes the CB is issued in one currency, whereas the underlying equity can be in another currency, which gives rise to a foreign exchange risk that can be either fixed or variable.

The size of the respective CB markets as at the end of 1994 in US$ billions was as follows:

Country	Stock Market Capitalization US$ bn	CB Market Capitalization US$ bn
USA	4,400	61.9
America excl USA	1,059	9.4
Europe	2,923	74.8
Japan	3,709	398.0
Asia/Pacific excl Japan	1,626	21.0
TOTAL	13,717	565.1

Additional to the above are the other equity linked markets such as those for Global Depository Receipts (GDRs). The GDR market is much smaller than the CB market, but is an important feature of the emerging Asian markets since many of these have restrictions on foreign investment. A GDR is a security issued by a depository, typically a bank, against an underlying holding of another security. The GDR is directly exchangeable into the underlying security, subject to certain restrictions. In the USA, many GDRs have been issued against foreign securities so as to make those securities effectively available to US citizens or institutions which would otherwise be prohibited or restricted from investing. In Asia, countries such as Korea, Taiwan, India and China impose tight restrictions on foreign investors, typically in the form of quotas. Certain companies have then been authorized to issue GDRs overseas, with the GDRs only becoming convertible into their underlying securities at such time as the markets open up more fully to foreign investors.

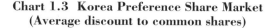

Chart 1.3 Korea Preference Share Market
(Average discount to common shares)

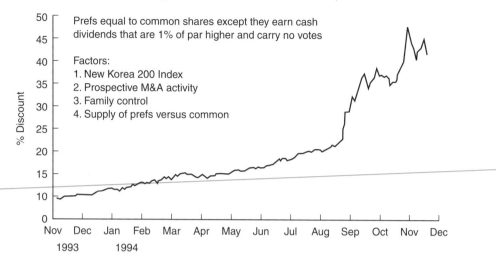

Source: Tong Yang Securities

Because foreign investment restrictions in Asia are being continuously lifted, and because the underling equity markets are developing at such a rapid pace, the CB and GDR markets in Asia are frequently mis-priced and thereby offer numerous opportunities.

By way of example, in Korea, most CBs and GDRs are convertible into 'preferred' rather than 'common' shares once conversion is allowed. Korean preferred shares have no voting rights but, instead, enjoy a marginally higher dividend entitlement than the common shares. In 1994, two events led Koreans to abandon preferred shares en masse. Firstly, a new Korean Composite 200 share index was announced as the intended benchmark for the forthcoming index futures market due to commence full trading at the end of 1995. This index did not include preference shares. Secondly, the timetable for financial deregulation in Korea anticipates that merger and acquisition activity will be allowed some time in 1996. Koreans have concluded that such activity is likely to be frenetic and that voting rights will become critical. As a result, in late 1994, the entire preference share market in Korea collapsed to an average discount as high as 50 per cent relative to the common share market, as shown in the accompanying chart.

While this was devastating to the Korean offshore CB and GDR markets, this results in the situation where an investment in Samsung Electronics, for example, can currently be purchased at a 1995 PE ratio of 6x through the common share market or 3x through the preferred share market. Given that Samsung Electronics is undoubtedly destined to become one of the world's top five electronics companies within the next few years, this looks to be attractive.

At the same time, the inefficiency of these markets can be evidenced by the fact that, again in Korea, the Hankuk Glass GDR in May 1995 was trading at a 19 per cent discount to its underlying security, despite the fact that the instrument is already fully convertible and the time necessary to purchase, convert and sell the instrument can be cut to less than 20 days. That is an incredibly high discount for 20 days of market risk in such a security, and suggests that the market is being mis-priced.

In summary, CBs can be purchased by the risk averse investor as a safer way of accessing equities, so long as it is realized that a price is being paid for that risk reduction. However, for the more diligent investor, the rapidly emerging equity linked markets in Asia and South America in particular, are often too small, as yet, to have attracted the full attention of the big institutions. The resulting pricing anomalies can often give rise to opportunities for low risk arbitrage or simply a cheaper way to access a particular company or market. Finding such opportunities is more a question of common sense rather than heavy duty statistical analysis. ♀

UNIT TRUSTS

Julian Tregoning

*Julian Tregoning is Director of Latin American Operations for the **Flemings** Group. Prior to that, he had been with the **Save & Prosper** for 27 years, ending as Executive Director responsible for investment products, with particular emphasis on Unit Trusts and Personal Equity Plans. He has represented **Save & Prosper** on the Executive Committee of the Association of Unit Trusts & Investment Funds, of which he was Chairman from April 1993 to May 1995.*

Amongst other duties he sat on the Takeover Panel, is on the European Committee of British Invisibles and is a Member of the General Meeting of the Fédération Européenne des Fonds et Sociétés d'Investissement (FEFSI).

A unit trust is quite simply an investment vehicle which allows private investors who may lack the time, capital or expertise required to build their own portfolio, access to a full set of investment options. By pooling resources and investing in a wide range of securities, usually equities or bonds, unit trusts offer private investors a cost-effective way of reducing the inherent risks and

Actively managed funds (being the vast majority) can provide the benefits, in terms of actual returns, of the resources and expertise of experienced investment professionals.

administrative burden connected with investment of this kind. Furthermore, actively managed funds (being the vast majority) can provide the benefits, in terms of actual returns, of the resources and expertise of experienced investment professionals.

Unit trusts, unlike their sister vehicles, investment trusts, are a true form of trust in that each has an independent trustee (usually a major bank) acting to safeguard the rights of the unitholders and the assets of the fund, who ensures it is managed appropriately and within the terms of the strict legislation which applies to them under the provisions of the Financial Services Act 1986. A unit trust is divided into equal portions called units. The prices are calculated regularly (in practice, usually every day) by the manager. Prices thus reflect the actual market value of the assets of the fund at any given time, rather than being determined by supply and demand as in the case of the shares of an investment trust.

Two prices are quoted for unit trusts. The higher (offer) price is the price investors pay to buy units; when they sell units back to the managers (there being no secondary market for unit trusts), investors receive the lower (bid) price. Unit trust managers must be prepared to buy and sell units in their funds at any time.

There are certain restrictions on the investment powers of unit trust managers, designed to ensure both sufficient diversification of risk and that funds' portfolios are easily realizable. This then allows managers to buy and sell units at any time. Most funds invest mainly or wholly in company shares although UK equity trusts can hold up to 35 per cent of their assets in government bonds. Within strict limits, funds can use futures, options and forward currency contracts for the purposes of efficient portfolio management and/or to reduce risk. All such transactions must be approved in every case by the trustees. Additionally, there are a small number of specialist unit trusts which do not invest in securities. These are money market funds, derivative funds and property funds.

The great advantages of unit trusts are the ease with which investors can buy and sell their holdings.

The great advantages of unit trusts are the ease with which investors can buy and sell their holdings, the significant reduction in risk which they can provide, the expert investment management which over the long term has provided most investors with far better returns than those offered by building society accounts and finally the safeguards provided by the Financial Services Act legislation and the presence of independent trustees.

Unit trusts now offer investors a huge range of choice with over 1,400 funds currently available in the UK. This is a far cry from January 1934 when Save & Prosper, then called the Trust of Insurance Shares Ltd, launched its first fund, Scotbits, to invest in the shares of UK banks and insurance companies. Investors can now choose between investing in the UK or overseas, blue chip or smaller company funds, regional or single country funds, developed or emerging market funds, equity or bond funds, income or growth or even balanced funds. The ideal portfolio mix depends on the requirements of individual investors and their tolerance to risk. It remains the case that investors seeking higher returns must in most cases accept a correspondingly higher level of risk. The old adage about not being for widows or orphans certainly applies to specialist funds such as the recently launched emerging markets funds which by their very nature will behave in a far more volatile fashion than a fund investing in, say, UK gilts. I certainly would advise investors to choose a geographically diversified portfolio and to take a minimum five-year view on the investment, making sure they keep sufficient 'rainy day funds' on deposit to meet short to medium term needs.

Income is a priority for many investors seeking a better return than those offered by building society interest rates. Again, investors should be made aware that higher levels of income usually imply at the very least reduced prospects for capital growth. Fund managers now have the option to charge their annual management fees (typically around 1.5 per cent) to the capital account rather than the income account and this may have the effect of boosting income levels at the cost of restraining capital growth or possibly causing a degree of capital erosion. Furthermore, by their very nature, higher yielding shares which equity income funds would naturally hold, tend to offer less chance of capital growth since substantial proportions of the underlying corporate earnings are paid out in dividends instead of being ploughed back into long-term investment. However this new flexibility does mean funds can be managed in a manner to meet the specific requirements of the investor, be they income or growth, conservative investment or a more risky approach.

Unit trust investment is increasingly and correctly being seen as a vital part of financial planning by the UK adult population and 1987's introduction of Personal Equity Plans (PEPs) with their attendant tax advantages, has played a major role in this. UK taxpayers can invest £6,000 into a general PEP each tax year and although the tax advantages apply to various types of security, the vast majority of plans hold unit trusts. UK investors holding unit trusts within a PEP can receive all income distributions free of tax and investment gains are free from the potential burden of capital gains tax. PEPs have naturally proved extremely popular, with around £15 billion having been invested in general plans by the end of the 1993–4 tax year. There is currently close to £100 billion invested in UK unit trusts overall, illustrating how important unit trusts and unit trust PEPs now are. A tried and tested means of generating superior longer term returns for investors, I hope and firmly believe unit trusts will continue to grow over the coming years.

INVESTMENT TRUSTS

Ernest J. Fenton

Mr Fenton is Director General of **The Association of Investment Trust Companies**, *which represents over 90 per cent of investment trusts and provides a range of information about them and their performance. For details, write to The Private Investor Helpdesk, AITC, Durrant House, 8-13 Chiswell Street, London EC1Y 4YY.*

A Scottish chartered accountant, Mr Fenton has spent most of his career in the City with stockbrokers **W. Greenwell & Co** *as research partner and, latterly, as Chairman and Chief Executive of the successor company,* **Greenwell Montagu** *Stockbrokers. He became Director General of the AITC in 1993.*

Not long ago investment trust companies were still seen as a vehicle for institutional investment that was almost irrelevant to private investors. The few individual shareholders who had discovered them were just as keen to keep them exclusive as travellers are to stop others invading their jealously guarded favourite village or beach.

But all that has changed. In 1994, 45 new companies raised £3.9 billion. Investment trusts are the most numerous group of companies listed on the London Stock Exchange and between them manage over £45 billion. They are widely recognized both as an ideal introduction to the stock market for private investors and as one of the most versatile methods of providing exposure to specialist markets.

What are investment trusts?

Investment trusts are public companies listed on the London Stock Exchange but, instead of manufacturing goods or owning shops, their principal business is to invest funds according to a predetermined investment policy. They are 'closed-end'; they have a fixed number of shares in issue at any time, the price of which fluctuates according to supply and demand. Their shares are bought and sold in exactly the same way as those of other listed companies. They are the oldest form of collective investment: the first investment trust, Foreign and Colonial, was created in the 1860s and is today the second largest among the 330 listed in London. The largest is 3i, a constituent of the FTSE 100 Index.

The Association of Investment Trust Companies in the UK divides its 300 members into twenty different categories, which fall broadly into six groups:

- General trusts with an international portfolio
- Trusts investing in specific geographical areas, e.g. North America, the Far East or single countries

- Trusts investing in specific market sectors, either globally or in the UK: such as smaller companies, natural resources, privatization stocks or biotechnology
- Trusts aiming to generate high income
- Trusts aiming for capital growth
- Trusts with a split capital structure, enabling sophisticated financial planning.

Advantages

Investment trusts provide professional management in an enormous range of specializations, and their closed-end structure makes them the perfect vehicle for less liquid markets, such as emerging economies or venture and development capital.

When you buy in the secondary market there is no front-end charge as with many mutual funds. The market-maker's spread in popular trusts will be low, and there are management-run schemes for buying and selling the shares that are very much cheaper than the average stockbroker's commission of around 1.75 per cent. So they are cheap to buy.

Annual management costs – paid by the trust, not by the shareholder – have traditionally been very low in comparison to any other UK-pooled investment. They can be as low as 0.2 per cent for a large international general company, rising to around 1.5 per cent for a geographical specialist or emerging market fund, where research and dealing costs are expensive.

There are also tax advantages. The company pays no tax on capital gains within the fund. All the management costs can be set against corporation tax, in contrast to a self-managed portfolio where there is no tax allowance for the costs of buying and selling, researching

All the management costs can be set against corporation tax.

and maintaining records. If you are a UK resident you can also hold most investment trust shares in a Personal Equity Plan, protecting them from all income and capital gains tax.

Flexibility helps risk management

Investment trusts carry the same risks as any equity-based investment – markets rise and fall and share prices fluctuate. Because they are a basket of investments they spread risk. They can also manage risk through their structure, creating different classes of share as well as debentures and other forms of loan stock.

About 10 per cent of the funds under management are in split capital trusts offering anything from two to five different types of share, each with a different level of risk and a different investment objective. At one extreme, zero dividend, preference and stepped preference shares offer a low risk investment with a predetermined return. At the other, capital shares offer the potential for a high capital return at winding up but also the possibility that the shares will be valueless at the end of the trust's life.

Warrants

Investment trust companies dominate the warrant scene in the UK and there is a lively market in many issues. Warrants have become popular in recent years as part of a new issue package, designed to counteract the problems of the share price falling to a discount to net asset value. Serious private investors, prepared to follow progress very closely, can give a hefty fillip to their portfolio performance with investment trust warrants by exploiting the gearing inherent in this market.

Growth

The investment trust sector is the only part of the British stock market where the volume of shares in private hands has been steadily increasing for the past ten years. The institutions have not left the field – indeed, many who fifteen years ago predicted the demise of the investment trust are now among the most enthusiastic holders. This means there is real shareholder power, in contrast to some other types of collective investment.

Investment trusts have their place in every type of portfolio.

Investment trusts have their place in every type of portfolio, whether as part of the UK indices, or providing specialist exposure to a particularly attractive market. 🌑

MUTUAL FUNDS

John Rekenthaler

John Rekenthaler is the Publisher of Morningstar Mutual Funds and Morningstar No-Load Funds and the editor of Morningstar's Morningstar Investor. These publications have a combined circulation of approximately 100,000. John helps monitor the day-to-day work of 24 analysts. Prior to his current position, John was Associate Editor of Morningstar's Mutual Fund Sourcebook, and Editor of Morningstar Mutual Funds.

Morningstar Mutual Funds reviews 1,500 stock and bond mutual funds. Each fund report contains nearly 1,000 data items, including detailed performance, risk and portfolio analysis, and a 400-word analysis of the fund's strategy and prospects.

In the past 15 years, open-end mutual funds have taken several countries by storm. From near obscurity in 1980, mutual funds have ballooned to approximately $4 trillion, making them larger in aggregate than any global equity market save that of the United States. Such size gives funds great power to move markets. In 1994, several US mutual funds helped to trigger Mexico's currency crisis by selling large chunks of Mexican debt.

Aiding the mutual fund industry's growth has been its unique capital structure. Unlike equities, closed-end funds, limited partnerships, and other competing entities, open-end mutual funds continuously offer (and redeem) shares, so that they need not re-register to expand their investment pools. Such flexibility permits popular funds to expand their asset bases very rapidly. For example, the largest mutual fund, the United States' Fidelity Magellan, swelled from $4 billion in assets in 1985 to $40 billion ten years later.

> **Unlike equities, closed-end funds, limited partnerships and other competing entities, open-end mutual funds continuously offer (and redeem) shares, so that they need not re-register to expand their investment pools.**

The drawback to funds' flexibility is that it restricts their list of potential investments. Because funds must reprice their assets frequently so as to be able to sell and purchase their shares at current market value, most emphasize easily priced items. That rules out real estate and other tangible goods, limiting funds to financial assets. Therefore, with the exception of cash funds, mutual funds react poorly to bouts of inflation.

Mutual funds show much variety. Most funds, naturally enough, invest broadly in their sponsoring country's securities, but others specialize by emphasizing certain foreign investments, or even by focusing on a particular industry. The effect in combination can be quite striking, as evidenced by the existence of such peculiarities as Asian Infrastructure, Continental Europe Small Company, and Global Health Care portfolios.

Unfortunately, most of these products are not readily available to any single country's investors. For various reasons, including tax, regulatory, and other barriers, mutual funds are rarely sold across national boundaries. Even fund companies that have dodged such barriers by establishing expatriate operations have had difficulty cracking the code of local customs. Consequently, mutual funds remain primarily national, rather than international, products.

When a global mutual-fund market is finally created, it will likely resemble that of the United States. The US market has transformed over the past three decades from a relatively homogenous arena to a bewilderingly complex marketplace that features more than 8,000 publicly offered funds. Sponsoring companies span the gamut from huge, diversified financial services firms to boutique money managers to (literally) retirees working out of their bedrooms. Their funds may be sold through the mail, with no sales charge, or through various sales forces, and they may be sold to retail or institutional customers.

The most popular funds in the US are simply cash substitutes, termed money-market funds. These funds, created when banks and other savings institutions were required by law to quote artificially low payment rates, command about 30 per cent of all US fund assets and invest in very short-term interest-bearing securities. With rare exception, they have performed precisely as promised, causing neither scandal nor excitement.

Next along the risk spectrum lie bond funds, which account for 35 per cent of industry assets, and are distinguished from money-market funds by owning securities with average maturities exceeding 90 days. Morningstar divides bond funds into 14 categories with distinct objectives: four varieties each of government, corporate and municipal, and two types of international bond funds. Because most investors favour high-grade funds, the government- and municipal-bond objectives possess four-fifths of all bond-fund assets.

When used as they should be, as side dishes by more aggressive investors to diversify their portfolios, and as income-generating investments for retirees seeking current spending money, bond funds have considerable merit (particularly those with annual expenses of less than 0.75 per cent). Unfortunately, many first-time fund buyers purchase bond funds as cash substitutes when US short-term interest rates are low. Such buyers tend to head for the exits the first time they encounter a bear market, causing the fund industry some ill will.

The final 35 per cent of industry assets reside in equity funds. Most popular are growth funds, which seek growth of capital, and growth-and-income funds, which aim for a mix of capital appreciation and dividend income. Virtually all of the industry's largest stock funds pursue one of those two objectives. Rounding out the domestic-stock fund mix are bolder small-company, aggressive-growth funds, and yield-oriented equity-income funds.

Remaining stock-fund monies are devoted to international and industry-sector funds. While international-stock funds only account for one-quarter of the industry's equity-fund assets, they have greatly expanded their market share in recent years. Particularly popular have been emerging-market funds. Industry-sector funds, on the other hand, have grown more unevenly, flourishing during bull markets but losing assets rapidly during difficult times due to the inconstancy of their investors.

> **Particularly popular have been emerging-market funds.**

Fund consumers in the US are bombarded with a deluge of information regarding their investments, ranging from daily listings in the newspapers to voluminous quarterly reports in all major business magazines. Such articles tend to combine total-return statistics on their funds with features such as portfolio-manager interviews, market predictions, and so forth. Consumers also encounter more sophisticated materials presented by companies specializing in fund research, including risk/reward measures.

The most famous of these is Morningstar's, which rates all mutual funds but money-market funds. Half of Morningstar's rating is derived from the fund's expense-adjusted total returns, and half from a risk score that is derived from the fund's past performance. Specifically, Morningstar considers each month in which a fund's total returns fail to match that of a risk-free asset (US Treasury bills) to be a 'losing' month and stashes the amount of this underperformance in a loss column. Eventually, the figures in each fund's loss column are totalled and compared with those of other funds sharing the same broad category (stocks, taxable bond, tax-free bond, and a catch-all category termed 'hybrid').

The difference between the fund's return and risk scores, as determined over the trailing three-, five-, and ten-year periods, is used to calculate the overall Morningstar rating. Ten per cent of funds in each broad category receive the top, 5-star rating and 10 per cent the bottom, 1-star rating. The other 80 per cent receive one of Morningstar's middle three ratings. Such ratings are recalculated each month.

Table 1.9–1.12 summarize the best risk-adjusted performers over the last five and ten years as of March 1995 for taxable bonds and general equity funds. We have edited out unusual vehicles such as single date redemption bonds which are suitable for special investment objectives only and omit industry select equity funds as too narrow, though it is interesting to note the prevalance of two sectors – healthcare and information technology among top performers.

Table 1.9 Taxable Bonds (5 Years through 31 March 1995)

Fund	Performance (%)	Risk	Risk-Adjusted
FPA New Income	10.76	0.58	0.76
Fortress Bond	13.20	1.65	0.66
Invesco Select Income	9.90	0.76	0.62
PIMCo Total Return Instl	10.43	0.91	0.62
Strong Advantage	7.54	0.17	0.55

Table 1.10 Taxable Bonds (10 Years through 31 March 1995)

Fund	Performance (%)	Risk	Risk-Adjusted
FPA New Income	11.14	0.69	0.67
Invesco Select Income	10.39	0.83	0.45
Managers Bond	10.74	1.03	0.37
MAS Fixed-Income	10.92	1.09	0.36
Vanguard Short-Term Corporate	8.67	0.44	0.31

Table 1.11 Stock Funds (5 Years through 31 March 1995)

Fund	Performance (%)	Risk	Risk-Adjusted
AIM Aggressive Growth	26.14	1.29	3.60
Oppenheimer Main St Income & Growth A	24.33	0.82	3.47
Twentieth Century Giftrust	24.01	1.59	3.07
PIMCO Advisors Opportunity C	23.31	1.36	3.07
MFS Emerging Growth B	23.49	1.45	3.01

Table 1.12 Stock Funds (10 Years through 31 March 1995)

Fund	Performance (%)	Risk	Risk-Adjusted
Twentieth Century Giftrust Investors	24.45	1.55	3.30
GAM International	22.94	0.83	3.07
Fidelity Advisor Equity Growth	18.77	1.09	1.51
Fidelity Contrafund	18.00	0.83	1.43
Templeton Foreign 1	17.31	0.66	1.31

In these tables, performance is the annualized rate of total return (not adjusted for effects of entry or exit sales charges). Risk is Morningstar risk score for the period, set on a scale such that the average fund has a score of 1. Finally, risk-adjusted subtracts the risk score from the performance score (not shown; we just set the performance figures on a scale such that average fund has 1). A higher risk-adjusted number is better. By definition, the average fund has a risk-adjusted score of 0.00. ♟

CLOSED-END FUNDS

Thomas Herzfeld

*Thomas J. Herzfeld is Chairman and President of Miami-based **Thomas J. Herzfeld Advisors Inc** (an SEC registered investment advisory firm), **Thomas J. Herzfeld & Co Inc** (a stock brokerage firm), and **Herzfeld/Cuba**, which is the investment advisor to **The Herzfeld Caribbean Basin Fund**, a recently formed closed-end fund and the first investment company formed to invest in Cuba and the Caribbean Basin.*

Thomas J. Herzfeld is considered the leading expert in the field of closed-end funds. He is the author of the first, and for many years the only, textbook on the subject, The Investor's Guide to Closed-End Funds *and* Herzfeld's Guide to Closed-End Funds.

What is a Closed-end Fund?

One of the best ways to define a closed-end fund is to state what it most definitely is not: a closed-end fund is not a mutual fund which, by its very nature, is open-ended, continually offering new shares for sale to the investing public. Mutual funds operate differently, basing their purchase price on the net asset value per share (NAV) – the total net assets of the fund divided by the number of its outstanding shares.

Closed-end funds, on the other hand, do not sell new shares endlessly. Closed-end funds issue a fixed amount of stock which, with the exception of splits or additional offerings of stock, essentially always has the same number of shares outstanding.

Another important factor which differentiates closed-end funds from mutual funds is that an investor can purchase a mutual fund only from the fund itself or its agents and, when he sells the shares, the fund redeems them. Closed-end funds are bought or sold in the open market. Shares in closed-end funds are not redeemed at their net asset value, like shares in open-end funds, but are bought and sold at the price the general market places on them – net asset value, above net asset value (a premium), or below net asset value (a discount).

Why Discounts Occur and How We Take Advantage of Them

The first question is, 'Why do closed-end funds sell at discounts from their net asset value per share?' The answer is complicated, because different factors influence different types of closed-end funds, and because they do not always sell at discounts. Some have a history of selling at premiums during bull markets, illustrating a key point, namely that discounts change. In rising markets, the discounts tend to shrink and premiums can exist. In declining markets, the discounts tend to be greater.

Since the market price of the fund is determined by the forces of supply and demand and the supply is relatively fixed, the price is more a function of investor demand. Demand for shares of closed-end funds has, historically, not been strong. Brokerage firms rarely recommend them, except at the initial offering when they receive an underwriting fee of up to 8 per cent.

A further reason for lack of demand for closed-end funds is that, theoretically, when purchased at NAV, the yield on a closed-end fund compares unfavourably with the yield investors would receive if they purchased the identical stocks held by the fund in the open market, because there are expenses associated with the operations of an investment company to be paid by the

What is generally overlooked is that funds get favoured tax treatment

fund before distributing the dividend income to shareholders. What is generally overlooked is that funds get favoured tax treatment and that, through its trading and long-term investments, a fund can make profits to offset expenses. Also overlooked is the fact that, when the fund is selling at discounts to the NAV, dividend yield is greater than could be obtained by buying the same stocks in the open market.

There is a seasonal effect. Some of the best trades can be made buying in the latter part of the year when discounts tend to be at their widest because year-end tax selling generally causes an unusual supply of fund shares to come onto the market, depressing prices to wider discounts.

Another variable influencing the discount is the pace of new issues of closed-end funds. The primary purpose of closed-end funds – diversification – has stayed essentially the same. The first closed-end fund created by King William I of The Netherlands in 1822 was designed to provide a means of capital diversification (as well as a way to invest in foreign government loans). In the past decade the number of such new issues has increased dramatically. The US industry has grown from $8 billion to $130 billion. When supply grows faster than existing demand, discounts occur.

Under ideal conditions, I buy a fund when I believe:

- the market will rise
- its portfolio is concentrated in groups likely to demonstrate relative strength
- its discount from NAV is likely to narrow.

Conversely, I consider selling a fund when:

- a general market decline seems likely
- the portfolio no longer appears concentrated in attractive areas
- the discount from NAV is unlikely to narrow further.

(It should be noted that, to trigger a buy or sell decision, not all conditions must be met.)

Generally, I try to buy a fund when it is trading at a discount to NAV at least five percentage points wider than its own average discount, based on a six-month moving average. Under ideal circumstances, the shares should also be trading at a discount wider than the average for similar funds. I would buy a fund at a 20 per cent discount if its average discount is 15 per cent and the average discount of similar funds is less than 15 per cent. This fund would be a candidate for sale if the discount narrowed to 10 per cent.

In determining whether to buy, hold, or sell, you must consider general shifts in the average discount of all closed-end funds. When the average discount is narrowing, I

Try to buy a fund when it is trading at a discount to NAV at least five perentage points wider than its own average discount, based in a six-month moving average.

41

buy at more aggressive discounts. For instance, if the average discount of the funds in The Herzfeld Closed-End Average slides by two percentage points, I would adjust my buy targets to more aggressive levels. The general narrowing and widening of closed-end discounts are akin to the expansion and contraction of price-earnings ratios on common stock.

The Herzfeld Closed-End Average (THCEA)

The Herzfeld Closed-End Average measures the share price of 17 US closed-end funds that invest principally in US equities. The following is a list of the funds:

The Adams Express Company
Baker, Fentress and Company
Bergstrom Capital Corporation
Blue Chip Value Fund Inc
Central Securities Corporation
The Charles Allmon Trust Inc
Engex Inc
The Gabelli Equity Trust Inc
General American Investors Company Inc
The Inefficient-Market Fund Inc
Liberty All-Star Equity Fund
Morgan Grenfell Small Cap Fund Inc
Royce Value Trust

Chart 1.4 The Herzfeld Closed-End Average (THCEA)

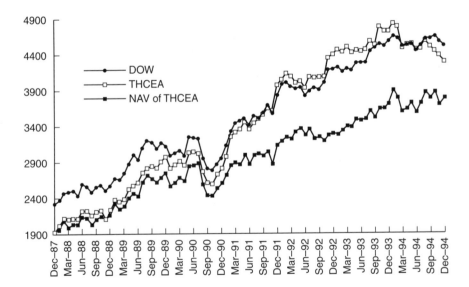

The Salomon Brothers Fund Inc
Source Capital Inc
Tri-Continental Corporation
The Zweig Fund Inc

All funds are listed on either the New York or American Stock Exchanges. The average was established with, at year end 1987, the funds weighted approximately equally. We pegged THCEA at the same level as the Dow. THCEA therefore gives an excellent comparison, at all times, of how closed-end funds as a group are moving, compared with the Dow. A corresponding Herzfeld Closed-End Average by net asset value of the same group of funds and the average discount from net asset value of the group are also published weekly in Barron's, with the Dow Jones Industrial Average presented for purposes of comparison.

Chart 1.5 The Average Discount of the Herzfeld Closed-End Average

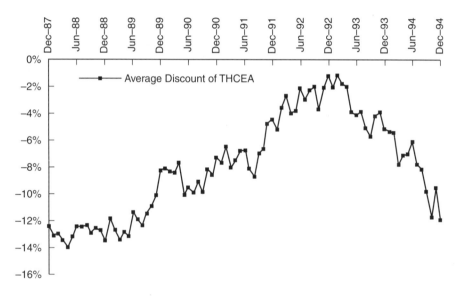

The Herzfeld Single Country Average (THSCA)

This average measures the share price of 25 US traded closed-end funds that invest principally in equity securities of foreign countries. The following is a list of the funds:

ASA Limited
The Austria Fund Inc
The Brazil Fund Inc
The Chile Fund Inc

The Emerging Germany Fund Inc
The First Australian Fund Inc
The First Philippine Fund Inc
The France Growth Fund Inc
The Germany Fund Inc
The India Growth Fund Inc
The Italy Fund Inc
Jardine Fleming China Region Fund Inc
The Japan Equity Fund Inc
The Japan OTC Equity Fund Inc
The Korea Fund Inc
The Malaysia Fund Inc
The Mexico Fund Inc
The Portugal Fund Inc
The ROC Taiwan Fund
The Spain Fund Inc
The Swiss Helvetia Fund Inc
The Taiwan Fund Inc
The Thai Fund Inc
The Turkish Investment Fund Inc
The United Kingdom Fund Inc

These funds are also listed on either the New York or American Stock Exchanges. The average was established at the end of 1989 with all the funds weighted approximately equally. THSCA is designed to show how closed-end single country fund share prices are moving. ♀

Chart 1.6 The Herzfeld Single Country Average (THSCA)

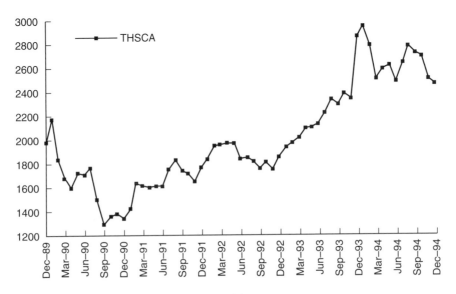

FUND RATING

Peter Jeffreys

*Peter Jeffreys has over 25 years investment experience, training initially with **M&G Securities**, then as Deputy Head of Research and Member of the Stock Exchange with stockbrokers, **Colegrave & Co**, and then managing unit trusts and offshore funds with **Schlesinger** and **Fidelity**. He is Co-founder and Managing Director of **Fund Research Limited**, an independent firm dedicated solely to analyzing investment funds.*

The Fund Research rating process is based on a combination of quantitative assessment and qualitative appraisal. However, compared with purely quantitative services such as those provided by Micropal in the UK and Morningstar in the US, Fund Research places emphasis on the qualitative aspect of its research. Not uncommonly, some four- and five-star quantitative rated funds do not even pass Fund Research's screening, let along get rated. Qualitative appraisal is derived from in-depth interviews with fund managers, chief investment officers, analysts and others associated with the investment process within fund management houses, and is designed to avoid the dangers which can arise from risk-adjusted quantitative re-rankings, turning mediocre or poor funds into highly rated 'stars'.

The starting point for the Fund Research rating process is, nevertheless, quantitative assessment, but aimed at consistency of performance as distinct from absolute returns. The firm's universe of funds embraces UK authorized unit trusts, London listed investment trusts and offshore funds, both open and closed-end, registered in Luxembourg, Jersey, Guernsey, Dublin, Bermuda, Cayman, Hong Kong and other 'offshore' centres. For specialist emerging markets research, the universe extends to US mutual funds and New York listed, closed-end single country funds.

Quantitative Assessment

Quantitative assessment is based on multiple, discrete period performance comparisons as distinct from single period, cumulative comparisons which Fund Research has found to be unreliable and anti-predictive in terms of future performance results. By breaking down historical performance into a number of separate measurement periods, the firm is able to assess fund manager skills at varying stages of the stock market cycle.

Development of the 'Consistency Ratio' which measures relative performance within geographical/type sub-sectors is central to the quantitative process. Funds are ranked by weighted percentile performance to produce a screen for further analysis. In essence the screen seeks to identify those funds

45

having mid-second quartile or better performance over the prior five years, placing emphasis on the most recent three years. Quantitative risk analysis based on historical standard deviation is then undertaken to refine further the list of funds selected for rating consideration.

Qualitative Appraisal

The next, and most important, stage in the rating process – qualitative appraisal – is undertaken after quantitative screening. Managers of the funds passing this screen are contacted for face-to-face interviews. These are conducted by a team of two and, wherever possible, are held in the manager's own office.

Qualitative appraisal addresses all aspects of fund management:

- Corporate: seeking to identify the investment culture, process, disciplines and resources of each management group
- Fund manager: seeking to identify personal skills, experience, stability and flair
- Fund: analysis of risk characteristics, charging structure and other relevant points

This part of the process probes behind performance results to determine whether or not these were achieved by luck or judgement, whether as part of a disciplined investment process or by unstructured 'feel'.

Interviews last between one and two hours, but are prefaced and followed by intensive ancillary research. Portfolio activity is carefully analysed, not just by degree of portfolio turnover, but also by motive; for example, was turnover initiated by design of disciplined sales procedures, or by virtue of random trading opportunities.

Fund manager 'flair' is an important part of the appraisal process but is analysed against the background of the fund management group employing the manager, by reference to the type of fund under review (aggressive or conservative, single country/sector specific, or internationally diversified/multi-disciplined) and by the stage of the market cycle against which performance prospects will need to be considered.

Rating methodology

The final stage in the rating process is to combine the quantitative assessment, as determined by the 'Consistency Ratio', with the numerical values ascribed to the qualitative appraisal. As noted previously, emphasis is placed on the qualitative appraisal; 60 per cent of the total 'score' derives from the qualitative analysis.

Funds are rated single 'A' to 'AAA' depending on the combined results. There is, of course, differentiation between 'A' and 'AAA' rated funds, but the margin is frequently modest. In general terms, only 15 per cent to 20 per cent of funds within a sector attain rated status: an 'A' rated fund equates to good, 'AA' excellent, 'AAA' superior. But, importantly, as an element of the rating reflects historical results, it may sometimes be necessary to view an 'AAA' rated with a degree of circumspection. Although Fund Research is at pains to point out that its ratings are not predictive devices, the end result is a statement of anticipated superior results over the medium and long term.

Funds deriving AAA status do change each year, but some shine through. Those that have been awarded the highest rating in each of the last five years represent a broad cross-section of geographical markets and asset categories. Examples include: Perpetual Far Eastern Growth, run by Scott McGlashan; (Kathryn Langridge, who runs the other Perpetual Asian Fund, and whose section appears on page 414 also earns AAA); GT US and General, run by Soraya Betterton; and Newton Income, run by Robert Shelton.

Conclusions

Approximately 25 per cent of the 3,000 plus funds monitored pass the quantitative screen of above mid second quartile relative performance. Of these, some two-thirds (approximately 15 per cent of the total) achieve rated status The degree of comfort and reassurance derived from a more complete rating process is immeasurably greater for investors and advisers alike than if based upon simple quantitative rating systems. ♊

HEDGE FUNDS

Leo van der Linden

*Leo van der Linden is an Executive Director at **Goldman Sachs International** in London. He has worked for **Goldman Sachs** since 1987 in the investment banking and equities divisions. He is currently responsible for the firm's prime brokerage activities in Europe. These activities include the financing of hedge funds, the facilitation of short sales and the settlement, custody and monitoring of hedge funds' assets and liabilities.*

Unlike other investment categories described in this book, no unambiguous definition exists for what a hedge fund is or does. Hedge fund managers are different from traditional asset managers not because of the assets they invest in but because of the investment styles that they deploy. Traditional

47

asset managers will aim to outperform a pre-specified index such as the S&P 500 or the FT-SE-100. In addition they are usually remunerated based on the total assets under management. Hedge fund managers on the other hand are typically not measured on a relative performance basis but on an absolute basis. They normally will receive 15-20 per cent of any outperformance above the previous period's performance or the short -term money market rates. Hence their investment style is more in line with the financial incentives of their investors.

Obviously investors do need to feel comfortable with the inherent conflict of interest in such an arrangement. The hedge fund could bet the store on an all-or-nothing trade with the chance of participating in the upside. A long track record, proper due diligence and a large investment by the manager in the fund itself, can help in assessing this risk.

Various types of hedge funds are listed below. Leverage may be applied in all categories.

Type	Description
Market Neutral	Long and short securities in roughly equal proportions in the <u>same</u> market(s). Outperformance is created by owning assets that appreciate in value and selling assets that depreciate in value.
Securities Arbitrage	Long underpriced convertibles and/or warrants, short the underlying shares or futures.
Macro	Long and short assets in <u>different</u> markets. Outperformance is created by taking directional bets on individual securities (technology stocks for example) or markets (bonds, currencies or commodities for example).
Event Arbitrage	Long and short securities involved in take-over situations based on the likelihood of a take-over being completed at the proposed terms and conditions and by taking a view on the relative values of the acquirer and acquire.
Distressed Securities	Purchase debt and/or equity securities of companies in re-organization and bankruptcy.

Background on the Growth of the Sector

The earliest hedge funds can be traced back to the 1950s in the US There are two main reasons why there are still more hedge funds in the US than anywhere else. First, the percentage of individual investors participating in the equity markets directly is roughly 51 per cent versus 12 per cent for the UK and 10 per cent and 2 per cent for France and Germany respectively. Hence the potential supply of funds that aspiring hedge fund managers can draw upon has always been much larger in the US. Second, the US market has started shifting its pension plans from defined benefits to defined contributions. Instead of receiving a pension that is predetermined upon retirement according to a specific formula, employees now receive an annual contribution to their individual pension plan that they need to invest themselves. As a result, the money management business has become much more competitive, because the investment choices of individuals have a direct impact on their own future net worth. For example, US based employees of Goldman Sachs must determine how their own pension contributions are invested. One of the 22 investment vehicles that they can invest in is a hedge fund.

Which Funds Have Done Well?

It is difficult to compare the performance of hedge funds because the asset classes that they invest in and the leverage that is being utilized are so diverse. In addition, no benchmark exists against which their performance can be measured on a consistent basis. Besides, it is statistically difficult to prove that past performance is a predictor of future performance. The size of the hedge fund however can be viewed either as a proxy for other people's confidence in the management or as a proxy for the marketing skills of the fund.

It is difficult to compare the performance of hedge funds because the asset classes that they invest in and the leverage that is being utilized are so diverse.

TASS (London 0171-233 9797) and MAR/Hedge (New York 212-213 6202) are two organizations that track the performance of hedge funds. They both sell their performance data bases.

How can you Participate?

US investors

Not only do hedge funds have different investment styles, they also have different legal structures from the traditional mutual fund industry. In the US many hedge funds are structured as limited partnerships. LPs are only allowed to have 99 or fewer (qualified) investors in them. The advantage of the LP structure is that the fund does not have to register as a public company and comply with all the onerous SEC reporting requirements for a publicly quoted fund. The minimum investment size with the more well-known funds can be quite high ($100,000 – $5 million).

Alternatively, if you are looking to participate in more than one hedge fund or if you do not meet the minimum requirements the most effective way to invest may be through a Fund Of Funds ('FOF'). FOFs invest in multiple hedge funds on your behalf. LPs and FOFs are not allowed to advertise to the general public in the US. A big advantage for investing in a FOF is that the asset allocators spend a great deal of time performing due diligence on the managers.

Non-US investors

Most non-US hedge funds are set-up as off-shore investment vehicles. The general philosophy is that the fund should legally be based in a jurisdiction where there is minimal taxation such as the Cayman Islands, BVI, Bermuda, Isle of Man, Dublin or Curaçao. It is up to the individual investor to report all investment activities to his or her relevant tax authorities. As these off-shore funds are not regulated by the US securities laws there are no limitations on the number of investors that can participate. As mentioned above, minimum investments could be $100,000 and upwards. Again, if you do not have a great deal of time available for monitoring your investments in various hedge funds, or if you cannot get into closed US LPs or if you do not meet the minimum investment criteria you may want to participate through the FOFs.

Even though the legal and technical barriers to entry for new hedge fund managers are minimal, their biggest obstacle is effective marketing and distribution. Therefore, we expect many of the traditional fund managers in the US and in Europe to start offering high performance and/or alternative investment vehicles in the near future, because they can capitalize on their distribution strength.

Are Hedge Funds Suitable for Individual Investors?

You should evaluate your decision based on three parameters. First, what is the overall risk profile of the hedge fund? This can be expressed as the average performance over various periods relative to the volatility of that performance. Second, what is the overall risk profile of your portfolio and can this hedge fund investment be a good addition to your risk/performance objectives? Third, how easy is it to get out of the fund when you want to? There is a fair amount of work involved in assessing all three items as no two hedge funds are the same. If you identified the right ones, however, the returns could be phenomenal. 🔔

ANNUITIES

Peter Quinton

Peter Quinton is Managing Director of The Annuity Bureau. London based,
The Annuity Bureau is the only independent company in the UK to specialize
solely in annuities. It offers a personalized service to people approaching
retirement or seeking investment opportunities by quoting, arranging and
advising on the best annuity available in the UK marketplace.

Many people assume that their annuity is more or less a fixture. They will retire at a particular age, whereupon they will exchange their pension fund for a regular income from the life office.

Yet the annuity should be regarded in exactly the same way as any other asset, yielding a return which can be measured against competitive investments – and they can be bought by anyone with money to invest. Furthermore, the amount of choice now available in terms of annuity type, provider and choice of benefits, gives the investor who is looking for income a wide scope for maximizing his return.

An annuity is either bought with pension fund monies – a 'pension annuity', or with the investor's own savings – a 'voluntary' or 'purchase life annuity'. The pension annuity is normally taxed as earned income and the income from a voluntary annuity is only partly taxable. The reason for this is that part of the income from the voluntary annuity is treated as a return of the original capital that was invested. Naturally, the tax implications depend on the fiscal policy of the country concerned.

Rates for both the pension and voluntary annuities vary according to the individual's circumstances. Annuity rates rise with age; the effective yield can go as high as 16 per cent per year. Because of their lower life expectancy, men command higher annuity rates than women of the same age. Enhanced rates under 'impaired life' annuities are also available for those with serious illnesses and shortened life expectancy.

The rates of return vary considerably between countries and also across providers. Variants between countries are normally due to the underlying investment. In the UK annuity yields are closely associated with the yield on 15-year government high coupon gilts. Variants between providers in the same country, reflect more the individual company stance to their investment strategy and mortality tables and their own mortality experience based on previous annuity clients.

In the UK, the best and worst rates offered on a conventional pension annuity can differ by more than 25 per cent

> In the UK, the best and worst rates offered on a conventional pension annuity can differ by more than 25 per cent at any one time.

at any one time. Rates constantly fluctuate, and the ranking of the top providers is therefore constantly changing. Companies will also position themselves in specific markets. For example, they might be extremely competitive for single life female annuity purchases but not for male counterparts. It is important for all pension annuity purchasers to be aware of the availability of the 'open market option', which means that investors can shop around for the best annuity rates on the market.

Table 1.13 Personal Pension Annuity Rates as at 29 March 1995

Male age 55		Female age 50	
Annuity Supplier	Annuity	Annuity Supplier	Annuity
(Month's movement 0%)		(Month's movement 0%)	
Equitable Life	£7,710.00	Norwich Union	£6,962.28
MGM Assurance	£7,536.72	MGM Assurance	£6,871.92
Generali	£7,523.43	Prudential	£6,768.12

Male age 60		Female age 60	
Annuity Supplier	Annuity	Annuity Supplier	Annuity
(Month's movement −0.7%)		(Month's movement −1.4%)	
Equitable Life	£8,394.72	Norwich Union	£7,610.28
Generali	£8,188.90	MGM Assurance	£7,538.16
RNPFN	£8,169.96	NPI	£7,520.82

Male age 70		Female age 70	
Annuity Supplier	Annuity	Annuity Supplier	Annuity
(Month's movement −2.6%)		(Month's movement −2.9%)	
RNPFN	£10,869.60	RNPFN	£9,384.86
Equitable Life	£10,600.56	Equitable Life	£9,147.72
Canada Life	£10,482.12	NPI	£9,129.18

Joint Life – 100% Spouse's Benefit

Male 60/Female 57		Male 65/Female 63	
Annuity Supplier	Annuity	Annuity Supplier	Annuity
(Month's movement −0.01%)		(Month's movement −0.4%)	
Norwich Union	£7,008.72	MGM Assurance	£7,436.64
MGM Assurance	£6,999.12	Norwich Union	£7,391.28
Prudential	£6,823.08	Equitable Life	£7,270.56

All payments are monthly in arrears, without a guarantee period and without escalation. Rates are as at 29 March 1995. Figures assume an annuity purchase price of £75,000 after paying tax free cash of £25,000 and are shown gross. RNPFN annuities are available only to those in the nursing and allied professions. Figures supplied by The Annuity Bureau Ltd.

Table 1.13 illustrates the position in the UK as of March 1995.

The open market option is not universally accepted. While it exists in the UK, the normal practice throughout the rest of Europe is for the annuity to be provided by the insurance company running the pension scheme. However, the option is available in some other countries like Australia and South Africa.

Annuity rates are linked closely to long-term gilts. UK rates are about 11 per cent, as of February 1995, which is higher than building society and bank interest rates and current inflation. When you take into account the income tax advantages of the voluntary annuity, this is an extremely attractive secure investment.

For investors seeking a constant income from their capital, a life annuity offers a guaranteed rate of return, regardless of what happens to interest rates, for the rest of the investor's life. The annuitant gets complete peace of mind and is not affected by unpredictable returns.

There are many types of annuities. The standard and most common is the fully guaranteed product. However, purchasers are free to choose the type to suit their own risk profile. A with-profits annuity allows the annuitant to share in the future performance of that company's with-profits fund. Naturally, there is a risk that if the company does not perform sufficiently then his or her income will fall. The income is therefore not guaranteed and will fluctuate according to the annual fund performance.

Similarly, a unit-linked annuity, through which the annuitant's fund is invested in units linked to stock market funds run by the provider, can be even more prone to fluctuation. The size of each pay-out varies according to the market value of the units at the time of redemption and is therefore vulnerable to market forces. While both these types of annuity involve a degree of risk, an investor who envisages strong equity performance may consider this chance worth taking.

All types of annuity offer a wide range of benefits which allow them to be tailored to suit the individual's circumstances. For instance, to combat the effects of inflation the annuitant may wish to have an annuity which escalates annually at either a fixed percentage per year or in line with the retail price index. The starting rate for such an annuity is significantly lower than for a level annuity of the same purchase price. In general for a 65-year-old male, it takes approximately seven years for the income of an annuity rising at 5 per cent per year to equal that of a level annuity, and a further seven years before the total payments made under both annuities are equal. This assumes that both annuities cost the same and that all the other benefits are equal. With the escalating annuity the longer the investor lives, the greater the gain. So the choice between level and escalating annuity depends on the investor's assessment of life expectancy and future inflation.

It may however be more cost effective for the disciplined saver to buy a level annuity, investing the difference between the income received, and the notional income which would be received from an escalating annuity, into an investment such as a bank or building society, and to use this capital to offset future inflation. Furthermore, the capital value of the deposit will not be lost when the annuitant dies as is normally the case with an annuity.

It is in fact the loss of capital on death which is the conventional annuity's main weakness. To counteract this, protection for a partner can be obtained by purchasing spouse's benefits, so that the income stream is extended if they outlive the annuitant. Investors can also buy a guarantee period, which means that the annuity will be paid for a minimum length of time even if they die before that period is up. Another option is to purchase a life policy which is bought in conjunction with an annuity to return the capital on death, but the cost of this cover will vary tremendously from country to country making it worthwhile, for example in South Africa, but not nearly as attractive in the UK.

While the choice of product specification and product provider, together with the surrounding tax environment, differs around the world, the fundamental principles in considering an annuity as an income paying investment are the same. Dependent on individual circumstances and attitude to risk, it is possible to use the annuity to acquire a highly favourable income structured to the investor's needs. And the range of annuity products available is becoming wider all the time. ♀ •

WARRANTS AND OPTIONS

Andrew McHattie

Andrew McHattie is the author of the **Pitman/Financial Times** *book,* The Investor's Guide to Warrants. *He has also edited the* Warrants Alert *newsletter since 1989, published by the* **McHattie Group in Bristol.**

When investors first discover warrants and options they commonly react in one of two ways. Some investors recoil in horror at the perceived risk; others embrace what they regard to be an excellent opportunity to enhance their profits while using the very same skills and analysis which they have already been using to invest in shares. The key difference is education. Of course instruments which exaggerate market movements and give a rollercoaster ride can be frightening if they are not understood, but if investors can make a small investment in time and education then these derivatives can be powerful allies in the quest for high profits. If shares are a saloon model, then warrants and options are sports cars for more adventurous investors. And as those who drive them will know, sports cars are much more fun.

What are Warrants and Options?

Markets around the globe offer a diverse range of warrant and option markets, from London Traded Options to US LEAPS (Long-Term Equity Anticipation Securities), from UK investment trust warrants to Spanish bank basket warrants and Japanese bond warrants. It is this latter market which is the most established and in some ways the most notorious, but wherever you are seeking to invest you will almost certainly have the choice to invest in warrants and options if you wish.

Both types of derivative carry the right (but not the obligation) to buy an underlying security at a fixed price at a specified time or times in the future. The difference between warrants and options is principally one of longevity. Whereas the maturity of options is generally less than one year, warrants can be launched with lives as long as fifteen years, although the typical maturity will fall more between two and ten years. The other main difference is that when subscription rights are exercised, with warrants the shares will generally come from the company, and with options the shares will come from other investors. An exception in both cases is that some warrants and options are exercisable for cash.

Achieving a basic understanding

The terminology commonly applied to these instruments may be new to many investors, but it is not difficult to grasp. It is, however, essential. A good basic understanding of these technical indicators will enable you to select warrants and options which offer the best potential for gain.

Always check the conversion terms first. These specify the price at which the warrant or option may be exercised, the date on which this can take place, and any other features or restrictions which may apply. Without this basic information you cannot hope to make an informed judgement.

Intrinsic value is often the first stop for the 'value' investor with little knowledge of warrants or options. This is the value which the instrument would have if it were to be exercised immediately. For example, if a share is trading at 150p and an option carries the right to buy that share at 100p, then the option must have an intrinsic value of 50p. In practice though, neither warrants nor options will trade simply at their intrinsic value, because investors are willing to pay more for the benefits which warrants and options confer. Investors expecting the underlying share price to rise will pay a 'premium' for the right to buy those shares at a fixed price in the future. The introduction of future expectations explains the most elementary quandary which can confront investors new to warrants and options. Why pay for the right to buy shares at 125p a year from now when they can be bought today for 100p? The answer is of course that the shares may be well above 125p in a year's time, but the warrant or option holder will still have the right to buy them at that fixed price. It is from this that the 'premium' or 'time value' arises.

So what is this advantage which investors are prepared to pay a premium for? The answer is gearing, which is calculated simply by dividing the share price by the warrant or option price:

Example: Share price 100p; option exercisable at 90p; warrant price 20p
Gearing = 100/20
         = 5 times

Using this example, £1,000 invested in these options confers rights over £5,000 worth of shares – a benefit which may be exploited in two distinct ways. On the one hand, a speculative investor can gain much more exposure from a given investment, so that if the shares rise by 40 per cent to 140p then the options will be worth at least 50p (share price of 140p less exercise price of 90p) – a rise of 150 per cent, implying much more profit for a given outlay. On the other hand, a more cautious investor can achieve the desired equity exposure at a much reduced outlay, achieving the same return from just one-fifth of the cash. Which approach you adopt depends upon your investment aims and also the market conditions.

When seeking value you would normally look for high gearing, some intrinsic value, a low premium, and a long maturity date. The ideal warrant or option will combine all of these features with a strong fundamental position to drive the price.

Profit potential

When you have the right warrants or options in your portfolio they can be a great bull market instrument. The majority of warrants around the globe are 'call' warrants which carry the right to buy and benefit from rising prices. Among the wide range of options, however, most markets offer a large number of 'put' options which carry the right to sell at a fixed price in the future and enable investors to benefit from falling prices. Again, these options can be used for speculative or for hedging purposes.

Investment for speculative profit can be hugely rewarding if your judgement is correct, and the returns can dwarf those from equities. One prominent example from the UK is the travel company Airtours which benefited from the end of the Gulf War in 1991, coupled with the collapse of one of its principal competitors. Airtours shares took off from 170p to 812p in the first ten months of 1991 – a rise of 378 per cent which would make most fund managers cheerful. Until, that is, they consider the opportunity from the warrants which flew from 10p to 590p over same period, making a rise of no less than 5,800 per cent. The warrants rose more than fifteen times as much as the shares.

It is true that rises of that magnitude happen rarely, but gains are far from isolated. In 1993, again in the UK, the average listed equity warrant rose by 222 per cent. It is not surprising that these profits attracted a whole new generation of private investors to begin trading in warrants. Many made some money, lost it again when the market declined, and decided to withdraw. Whilst this is understandable, it seems short-sighted. Investors should learn about the instruments and then stick with them, because a well-informed investor armed with technical information ought to fare well over a long period, if only because of the huge price anomalies which occur as 'fair-weather' investors move in and out of the markets.

Risk

The risk attached to warrants and options is often exaggerated. Unlike futures contracts, where you may be required to stake huge underlying sums and you can lose more than you invest, most investors in warrants and options will not face these daunting prospects. Warrants and options are commonly used by a wide range of investors who would not consider themselves cavalier. Yes, warrants and options are more volatile and do carry a higher risk than ordinary shares, but these instruments can be used for hedging as well as for straight speculation.

Warrants and options are commonly used by a wide range of investors who would not consider themselves cavalier.

If warrants and options are used in conjunction with interest-bearing securities such as gilts or treasuries then they can actually reduce risk, and the same is true for portfolio management. Take, for example, a fund manager with ten million dollars in Hong Kong blue chip shares. Fearing a short-term fall in the market, the manager could sell securities, incurring dealing costs and, of course, sacrificing considerable gains if wrong. A better alternative may be to buy highly geared put options on the Hang Seng Index, which are listed on Amex and a wide range of other markets. These should gain in value if the market falls, ameliorating losses on the shares. Should the market gain, then the fund suffers a reduction from the falling price of the put options, but still rises in total value.

	Scenario A	Scenario B	Scenario C
	Fund is unhedged and left unaltered	Fund is unhedged; manager sells $2m blue chips	Fund is hedged; manager sells $500,000 blue chips and buys put options geared 10 times
Market falls 20%	Fund value falls 20% to $8m	Fund value falls 16% to $8.4m	Blue chips fall 20% to $7.6m. Options gain 200% to $1.5m; fund value $9.1 m.
Market rises 20%	Fund value rises 20% to $12m	Fund value rises 15% to $11.6m	Blue chips rise 20% to $11.4m; option premium is lost; fund value $11.4m

By using put options instead of selling blue chips, the fund manager improves his position. The fund stands to lose $700,000 less if correct about the market falling, and will only sacrifice $200,000 in gains if wrong. By using options, it is possible to tilt the odds in your favour. The key point is that the risk with warrants and options may be relatively high, but it can be both quantified and controlled, which makes it acceptable in most circumstances.

The main exception to this rule occurs when investors write, or sell, options. While the buyer of an option pays a premium and has a limited loss, the seller receives that premium, but incurs an unlimited liability. Options will usually be written by an investor with a hedged position in the underlying stock, and few investors will wish to write 'naked', or without cover. This is probably the most speculative approach to dealing in derivative markets, and one which should only be undertaken by confident investors able to scrutinize the market continuously.

The Analysis of Warrants and Options

Risk can also be reduced, of course, by careful analysis. Option analysts tend to place considerable emphasis upon chart indicators, largely because they are trying to forecast short-term fluctuations rather than looking at the long-term when fundamental factors are of paramount importance. With warrants the technical factors are important, but those with longer maturities push the focus much more on to the likely performance of the underlying security.

Warrants and Options in the Context of a Portfolio

Advisers are often warned of the need for prudence, and not to encourage enthusiastic investors to put too much of their portfolios at risk. The possibility of loss must be an important consideration, and the value of warrants and options can fall to zero. Around 5 to 10 per cent of assets is usually regarded as acceptable, largely to add 'spice' to portfolios. That said, the percentage which should be allocated to warrants and options really cannot be specified, and depends upon a number of variables including (i) risk preference; (ii) extent of knowledge and understanding; (iii) whether the objective is to hedge or speculate; (iv) the market conditions; and (v) the type of warrants and options. Clearly an investment of surplus funds by an option expert who is partly hedged in long-dated instruments with intrinsic value in bullish market conditions is far easier to justify than a nervous private investor putting his life savings into speculative short-dated call options in a bearish market. At the final reckoning, it's your choice. You can, within reason, choose your level of investment and your level of risk so that they are commensurate with your objectives. The rewards are, of course, less certain but, with careful selection, warrants and options have a proven worth in enhancing international portfolio returns. ♀

PRIVATE COMPANIES
William Eccles

*William Eccles is a Director of **Foreign & Colonial Ventures**, a leading UK investor in private companies, which manages funds of approximately £200 million. He joined **Foreign & Colonial** after working at **Alta Berkeley Associates**, a London based venture capital partnership. He is involved in making, monitoring and disposing of unquoted investments and has a number of private company directorships. He has written numerous articles for the investment press.*

*   **Foreign & Colonial Ventures** specializes in equity investment in established unquoted companies in the UK with a size of between £5 million and £50 million. It has made around 100 such investments in the last 15 years.*

An ancient business

Investment of one person's money in the skills and enterprise of another is a practice as old as the formation of the money economy, predating the invention of the limited liability company by centuries and of quoted equity markets by even longer. Private company investment can legitimately claim to be one of the longest established of all investment types. Venerability does not, however, guarantee safety and such investment has often proved to be a highly risky business. The risks associated with private companies can be mitigated and exceptional returns are available, but perhaps more than in any other asset class the quality of the people to whom investors' money is entrusted is paramount, whether they are the managers of the companies themselves or the managers of funds investing in them.

Private company investment can legitimately claim to be one of the longest established of all investment types.

A hidden market

Private companies account for a very significant proportion of economic activity even in countries where there are highly developed stock markets. For example, in the UK there are 2,100 quoted companies. By contrast, ignoring the smallest companies of which there are hundreds of thousands, there are approximately 100,000 companies with turnover of over £1 million. Inaccessible to the great majority of investors is a large population of companies, many of which are dynamic and fast-growing. Both to gain a balanced exposure to countries' economies and to seek higher returns than are available from conventional quoted markets, investors have paid increasing attention to the private company sector in the last fifty years.

The informal and the formal markets

Before 1945 nearly all investment in private companies was conducted by individuals directly backing managers. Private individuals investing on their own account remain a significant source of capital, but in the last fifty years a more formal market has also developed. Professional managers have established funds focusing on private companies which provide investors with a means of gaining a diversified and closely managed exposure to the sector.

By its nature, it is impossible to measure how individuals have fared with direct investment in private companies but there are statistics available for the formal market. In looking at long-term returns from private companies it is appropriate to focus on the US market as it is the most highly developed and longest standing. The UK market has developed rapidly since about 1980 and is the most advanced in Europe. Elsewhere there is little formal investment.

A comparison of different asset classes in the US between 1945 and 1994 shows that the risks associated with private company investment or 'venture capital', have been justified by superior returns. A composite analysis prepared by Morgan Stanley showed a 14 per cent annualized return during the period for venture capital. Venture capital investments outperformed all other main asset classes except Japanese and emerging market equities. Volatility of returns has also been high and the gap between the best and worst performers in venture capital is frequently greater than in other asset classes. Once again, this demonstrates that the choice of manager is key.

Types of investment

Private company investment can be divided between young, small, often high technology companies (true 'venture capital') and established, generally profitable companies of all sizes and across all sectors (so-called 'private equity'). Contrary to popular belief, only a small proportion is directed at small, fast-growing but often loss-making and highly risky technology companies. The great majority is invested in less risky and perhaps less exciting companies through management buy-outs and by providing capital to enable companies to expand or make acquisitions. Returns from private equity have proved more consistent and predictable than from true venture capital and there is a greater requirement for funding.

The investment process

Professional investors in private companies have a very different task from mainstream fund managers investing in quoted companies. The investment process is far more lengthy and the level of ongoing contact with investee companies is far greater.

One of the most powerful advantages of private company investment is that there are no insider trading rules to restrict research. The only limits to investigation into private companies are time and cost. Managers of private company funds exploit this advantage by conducting extensive inquiries into companies' management, markets, history and forecasts before they invest. They frequently commission accountants' reports and consultants' studies to supplement their own research. They also spend considerable time with the managers of prospective investee companies, assessing their strengths and recruiting to fill any gaps in management teams. Whereas a quoted fund manager may take a few hours deciding whether to invest in a public company, it is typical for private company investment decisions to take many man months. Venture capital firms generally expect their professional staff to average only two to three investments each year.

> **One of the most powerful advantages of private company investment is that there are no insider trading rules to restrict research. The only limits to investigation into private companies are time and cost.**

Monitoring and selling private company investments

As well as being able to investigate potential investments exhaustively, private company fund managers generally retain extensive rights after they have invested. They frequently take board seats or nominate outsiders to represent them. Whether as directors or through formal rights negotiated as a condition of investing, their consent is generally required for any significant corporate decisions such as increases in borrowing or acquisitions. They often approve company budgets and almost invariably receive monthly accounts and performance reports to enable them to monitor progress and to take prompt action if agreed targets are not met.

Successful investments in private companies generate returns for investors from a combination of profit growth, multiple expansion and gearing. Profit growth needs no explanation. Relative price earnings multiples for private companies fluctuate, but they are generally around 25 per cent lower than for their quoted counterparts. For this reason managers frequently realize their investments through stock market flotation, but if investments are not suitable for the stock market or conditions are unfavourable managers will look for trade buyers. Finally, private companies with strong and predictable cash flows will often be bought using higher levels of debt than are commonly found in quoted companies, providing equity investors with significantly geared returns.

Diversification and risk

In assessing investments, private company fund managers make extensive use of financial modelling to project potential returns. The most common measure is the compound annual growth rate of investments or internal rate of return (IRR). Target IRRs vary with the level of interest rates and returns from quoted markets. For investments at the lower end of the risk spectrum, for example in management buy-outs of large private companies, the target IRR will typically be in the range of 15 to 25 per cent over the yield on a long gilt. For investments in high technology start-ups, the target rate of return may exceed 50 per cent per annum.

Investment in private companies is labour intensive both when investments are being considered and after they have been made. Very often this results in funds with fewer, larger investments than in quoted company funds. This reduces diversification, but the corresponding increase in risk is mitigated by private company fund managers' greater knowledge of and influence over their investee companies. Private company investment does, however, suffer from the disadvantages of liquidity and scale when compared with investment in large quoted companies. Investments typically have a life of between three and five years before which they can be difficult or even impossible to sell and they are generally in relatively small companies which have limited management resources and product ranges. As we have seen, they may also be highly geared. For these reasons private company fund managers must achieve medium-term returns significantly higher than those available from large quoted companies in order to attract investors.

The investment choice

For investors seeking an exposure to private companies there is a wide range of different managers and funds, particularly in the UK and the US, from which to choose.

Investment Trusts

These are UK funds, structured as quoted companies which are exempt from capital gains tax. There are over 20 investment trusts in the UK which focus on private companies. As quoted companies themselves, they offer liquidity to investors, there is no minimum investment, and their performance can be relatively easily compared with other funds and asset classes. In the five years to 31 December 1994, two of the investment trusts in the sector (Pantheon International Partnerships & Foreign & Colonial Enterprise Trust) were in the top seven performers of all investment trusts (measured by Micropal). This sector has been rewarding for investors compared to broader market indexes.

Chart 1.7 Foreign & Colonial Enterprise Trust five-year performance

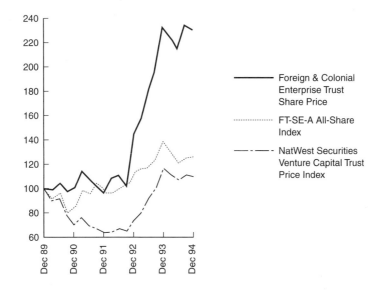

In the UK there are no retail unit trusts and in the US no mutual funds focusing on investment in private companies. This is because private company investment is illiquid in the short term and unit trusts and mutual funds need to maintain liquid portfolios to meet redemptions.

Private funds

Specialist private funds, most frequently structured as limited partnerships, are numerous in both the UK and the US These are designed for institutional and high net worth individuals and often have a substantial minimum investment of around £500,000 or $1,000,000. Limited partnerships generally draw

63

down investors' commitments over two or three years as investments are made and distribute the proceeds as investments are realized.

Tax privileged investments

UK tax law in 1995 provides three tax privileged routes into private company investment. The first is the Enterprise Investment Scheme. This is designed primarily for so-called 'Business Angels' who can invest up to £100,000 each year through the scheme and who can enjoy income and capital gains tax benefits whether or not they are involved in the management of their investee companies.

The second route is through Venture Capital Trusts. These are a new type of investment trust and offer similar, if slightly less generous, tax benefits to the Enterprise Investment Scheme. Venture capital trusts are highly regulated and focus on investments in relatively small trading companies.

The third route is through Personal Equity Plans (PEPs). Investments in PEPs are exempt from capital gains and income tax. UK tax payers can invest up to £9,000 each year in qualifying equities and related instruments. Some of the investment trusts described in the earlier sections (including Foreign and Colonial Enterprise Trust) qualify for PEPs.

Conclusion

Whichever route is taken, the private company sector of the investment market is increasingly recognized as offering diversification and attractive returns. Frequently, it can also offer a high level of intrinsic interest as investors follow the fortunes of the small and dynamic companies they have backed. For these reasons many sophisticated investors now have commitments to the sector of between 2 per cent and 10 per cent of their portfolios. ♀

LLOYD'S

Nigel Sidebottom

Nigel Sidebottom is Managing Director of **GVG Asset Management** *and a director of* **Gerrard Vivian Gray** *Stockbrokers. He is a specialist on the Investment Trust Sector. In 1991, he set up GVG's Investment Trust Management Service providing managed portfolios of investment trusts for private investors designed to meet a variety of investment objectives. For those with specific interest in the Lloyd's Insurance Market, a managed portfolio of Lloyd's funds is one aspect of these services.*

Mention Lloyd's as a possible investment and many people would throw up their arms in horror. Reports of the enormous losses that individuals have incurred on the Lloyd's insurance market have not been restricted to the business pages. Stories of individual hardship have hit the front pages and the popular press. But how many people, I wonder, realize that the Lloyd's insurance market, when taken as a whole, returned a profit for every year of account between 1948 and 1987 with the exception of only three years? The problems started in 1988 with a spate of catastrophe claims and an acceleration of pollution and asbestosis claims on policies which had been written in earlier years with no protection against 'long-tail' liabilities. These problems were exacerbated by the so-called 'London Market Excess of Loss spiral', whereby syndicates sought to limit their risk by taking out reinsurance but were unaware that, like a game of pass the parcel, the same risk was returned to them through a spiral of reinsurance. Syndicates heavily exposed to Excess of Loss business carried the heaviest losses.

Individuals investing in Lloyd's, Lloyd's Names, carry unlimited liability and this is why the financial consequences for those exposed to the loss-making syndicates were so severe and led Names to leave the market in droves. Over 32,000 Names were actively underwriting in 1988. By 1993 this number had fallen to under 20,000 and is still falling. With names leaving, the capital base of the market was under threat. To ensure survival the Lloyd's membership voted in October 1993 to allow the entry of corporate capital. Corporate capital, by its nature, must have limited liability; a corporate investor cannot lose more than the value of its shareholders' funds. This singular fact provided individuals with the opportunity, for the first time, of investing in the Lloyd's insurance market, with limited liability, by becoming shareholders in the companies providing corporate capital. Before examining the attractions of corporate capital it may be helpful to explain the general workings of the Lloyd's insurance market.

Lloyd's has been operating for over 300 years. It has a dominant position in the insurance of complex risks, such as marine, aviation, catastrophe and reinsurance.

Lloyd's is not an insurance company. It is a market regulated by the Council of Lloyd's and offering central administration services. Its members, both individual Lloyd's Names and the new corporate members, conduct their business in syndicates. Each member will normally, on the advice of a Members' Agent, underwrite on a number of syndicates.

A syndicate is a group of members for whom insurance business is accepted by an underwriter employed by a Lloyd's Managing Agent. That underwriter will tend to specialize in a particular type of risk. Members of a syndicate will make a profit if the premium income received by the syndicate, plus any investment returns on that premium income, exceeds the cost of managing the syndicate and any claims made on the policies underwritten. It is when the claims exceed the income received that the syndicate then faces a loss and the members of that syndicate will be required to provide the capital to cover that loss.

A member will need to deposit capital with Lloyd's generally in the form of a portfolio of stocks or shares, and will be permitted to underwrite up to a certain level of premium income which will be defined by a multiple of the value of the member's funds at Lloyd's.

The principal attraction of Lloyd's is that it offers a means of making one's capital work twice. In the first case capital can be invested in stocks and shares to produce the capital growth and dividend income which one would expect from such a portfolio. At the same time, that portfolio can be used as security for underwriting insurance risks through syndicates and making a further return on one's capital if those syndicates are profitable.

A corporate member operates in exactly the same way. Typically a corporate member will be structured as an investment trust. It will raise a sum of capital which it then invests in a portfolio of equities or fixed interest securities. These investments are held with Lloyd's to enable the corporate member to underwrite up to two times the value of it's deposit through a range of Lloyd's syndicates. Profits from underwriting will be passed through to shareholders in the form of dividends. In addition, just like an investment trust, the income received from investments will also be passed through to shareholders as dividends and the share price is likely to rise as the asset value of the trust increases. If the Lloyd's Fund makes losses from underwriting these will be covered by drawing down capital thereby reducing the net asset value of the fund which in turn is likely to cause the share price to fall.

The Lloyd's corporate capital funds offer a number of important attractions to shareholders which would not be available to someone participating in Lloyd's as an individual Name;

- First and foremost they offer limited liability. A shareholder in a Lloyd's corporate capital fund has no liability beyond the amount that has been invested in the company.
- The rules governing corporate capital are designed to prevent exposure to the long-tail liabilities from pollution and asbestosis which have caused much of the problems of the past. Whilst it cannot be said with certainty that there will be no 'leakage' of these claims it is intended that the ongoing liabilities are ring-fenced from corporate capital.
- The rules governing corporate capital also require that each corporate member conduct their underwriting through a minimum of five subsidiary underwriting companies such that there is a measure of protection against losses incurred in one subsidiary from impacting on another.
- The investor in the fund obtains professional management both of the investment portfolio and of the syndicate selection. Most funds provide a broad spread of risk in relation to both the investments and the syndicates.
- Many of the corporate capital vehicles are quoted on the Stock Exchange offering investors the chance to sell the shares if they decide that they no longer wish to be involved in the Lloyd's insurance market. In contrast a Lloyd's Name cannot escape from syndicate participation midway through a year and even at the end of the year will need to wait for a further three years before knowing the full extent of their potential profit or loss.

Taken together these facts mean that many of the benefits and attractions of the Lloyd's insurance market can be obtained through purchasing shares in Lloyd's corporate capital funds without taking on the risks which are faced by Lloyd's Names with unlimited liability.

The first tranche of Lloyd's funds were launched in November 1993. With few exceptions these companies were all quoted and were generalist, i.e. they participated in the range of syndicates operated by a variety of managing agents and covering different sectors of the markets. Some of the trusts directed their investment portfolios solely towards equities and others focused most on bonds. The largest fund, London Insurance Market Investment Trust, opted for an investment portfolio designed to track the top 350 UK equities and insurance exposure spread across 100 syndicates.

1994 saw a further tranche of issues, both quoted and unquoted, several of them 'dedicated' to the syndicates of just one managing agent.

Corporate capital can now offer potential investors a choice ranging from a broad exposure to the Lloyd's market or a focused investment in the syndicates of a particular managing agency. The Lloyd's corporate capital funds provide access to the Lloyd's insurance market to a wide range of individuals and institutions for whom it was not previously an option. Private investors with capital resources too small to qualify as individual Lloyd's Names can put just a few thousand pounds into a Lloyd's fund. Trusts, pension funds, charities and

Table 1.14 Quoted Lloyd's Corporate Capital Funds

	Market Cap(£m) April 1995	Lloyd's Adviser	Investment Manager
Issued to participate in the 1994 year of account			
Abtrust Lloyd's	21.90	Bankside	Abtrust
Angerstein	54.00	Stacebarr	Natwest
CLM Insurance	75.66	Sedgwick	BZW
Delian Lloyd's	43.31	R. F. Kenshaw	Foreign & Colonial
Finsbury Underwriting	26.10	Wren	Finsbury
HCG Lloyd's	54.76	Conning Grimstone	PDFM
Hiscox Select	27.60	Hiscox	Morgan Grenfell
London Insurance Market	266.00	Fenchurch	HSBC
Masthead Insurance	35.42	Murray Lawrence	Hambros
New London Capital	43.20	Chartwell	Mercury
Premium Trust/Premium			
Underwriting	25.61	Wellington	Martin Currie
Syndicate Capital	23.34	Insurance Analysis	John Govett
Issued to participate in the 1995 year of account			
Euclidian	18.40	Indemnity Insurance	Abtrust
Kiln Capital	25.62	R.J.Kiln	Mercury
Matheson Lloyd's	19.75	Jardine Lloyd's	Swiss Bank
Wellington U/Writing	17.42	Wellington	Mercury

companies can also acquire shares in these corporate capital funds when previously they would have been excluded from participation in the Lloyd's market.
    Performance to date has varied, as can be seen below.

Table 1.15 Lloyd's Trusts – Performance to 30 April 95

	Value at Launch (p)†	Value at 30 April 95	+/– %
Abtrust Lloyd's*	100	78.2	–21.8
Angerstein*	100	82.7	–17.3
CLM	100	85.0	–15.0
Delian Lloyd's	100	79.0	–21.0
Finsbury Underwriting	100	82.5	–17.5
HCG	100	80.5	–19.5
London Insurance Market	100	92.5	–7.5
Masthead	100	82.0	–18.0
New London Cap	100	69.0	–31.0
Premium Underwriting/Premium Trust** £10 units		£7.57	–24.3
Syndicate Cap*	100	72.3	–27.7
Hiscox Select	100	89.0	–11.0

* Price includes package of 1 ordinary share and 1/5 of a warrant.

** Each unit represents six shares of Premium Trust and four shares of Premium Underwriting. Price is the value of a reconsituted unit.

† Most trusts were launched in November 1993 so performance represents an 18 month period.

The doors to a realm of investment, previously the preserve only of wealthy individuals, have been thrown wide. At the same time much of the risk has been removed making Lloyd's an investment option worthy of serious attention. ♀

CURRENCIES

Stephen Baxter

Stephen Baxter is a Director – New Products (Global Money Markets and Foreign Exchange) for Barclays Bank plc. He is responsible for world-wide marketing of new products in Barclays Global Money Markets and Foreign Exchange. The group focuses particularly on investment products in these markets, including an advanced new range of guaranteed offerings. Before joining Barclays, Mr Baxter worked for 15 years in financial services at Andersen Consulting, where he was a Partner.

Currencies may not, at first, seem an obvious means of making medium-term investments. Yet investment in currencies has grown strongly over the past 5–10 years. Many investors are looking at alternatives to traditional stock market or fixed income investments. The foreign exchange market is the largest and most liquid of the financial markets, with an estimated $1 trillion traded every day. Although it is a highly efficient market with thin spreads, there are good opportunities for profit by professional traders supported by powerful computer systems.

The foreign exchange market is the largest and most liquid of the financial markets.

From an investor's point of view, there is the potential to earn excellent returns. The investor can benefit from the trading profits of a successful trading strategy as well as earning interest on the underlying currency positions. Currency investments can also offer a good means of diversification from more traditional forms of investment. They have a low correlation with stock and bond indices. Currency investments can therefore be combined with traditional investments to construct a lower risk overall portfolio. These advantages can, in some cases, also be combined with the safety of a guaranteed minimum return, underwritten by a bank.

Trading Managers

Most currency investments are managed by specialist advisors – Commodity Trading Advisors (CTAs) – trading managed accounts on behalf of clients. The term Commodity Trading Advisor is something of a misnomer, as CTAs trade mostly foreign exchange accounts and financial futures: trading of tradi-

Chart 1.8 Growth of the Managed Accounts Industry

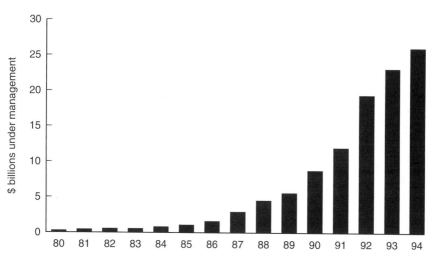

Source: Managed Account Reports

tional commodities (which was the starting point for many CTAs in the 1970s) now represents only a small part of their business. However, the name continues.

The CTA industry has grown sharply over the past 10 years, as shown in Chart 1.8.

There are now more than 400 Commodity Trading Advisors, the majority of which are in the United States. The industry has now grown to some $25 billion worldwide, and about 30 per cent of this business is trading foreign exchange on behalf of clients.

Returns

A managed foreign exchange account can earn highly attractive returns. Account growth for foreign exchange advisors has averaged about 20 per cent over the past 10 years, with some achieving very much higher returns, although performance over the past 18 months has been disappointing (as a result of trendless markets). The average performance for CTAs trading exclusively foreign exchange is shown in Chart 1.9.

Chart 1.9 Performance of CTAs trading foreign exchange – Industry Average

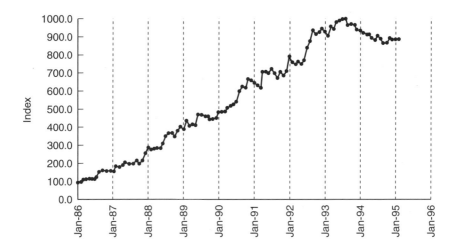

Risks and Rewards

In looking at any new investment, an investor must also consider the risk that he is prepared to take in relation to the potential reward. A key indicator in assessing this is the **Sharpe Ratio.** This compares the average return of the

Chart 1.10 Comparison of annual rate of return and standard deviation

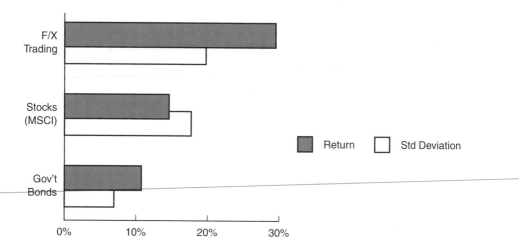

account (over the risk-free interest rate) with its risk (or volatility). A high **Sharpe Ratio** means that returns are high in relation to the risk taken. Looked at in this way, foreign exchange managed accounts compare favourably with investments in equities (the Morgan Stanley Capital Index) or government bonds (the J.P. Morgan Global Government Bond Index) over the period 1986–94, as shown in Chart 1.10.

Correlation with other Investments

Another factor to consider is performance correlation with other forms of investment. This is a measure of the extent to which different types of investment move together in response to external conditions. In setting up a balanced portfolio, managers like to choose investment classes with low correlation to each other. This has the effect of reducing the overall risk while maintaining returns.

One of the principal advantages of currency investment is its very low correlation with other forms of investment. When compared with equities or government bonds, the currency investment has a low (or even negative) correlation. It can therefore form an extremely attractive component of a balanced investment portfolio.

The correlation between the returns of CTAs trading foreign exchange over the period 1986–94 and the returns from stocks (MSCI index) and government bonds (JPM Global Government Bond Index) are shown in Chart 1.11. This shows that CTAs trading foreign exchange have almost no correlation with stock market returns (and a low correlation with bond markets).

Chart 1.11 Correlation between Foreign Exchange CTAs and other Investments

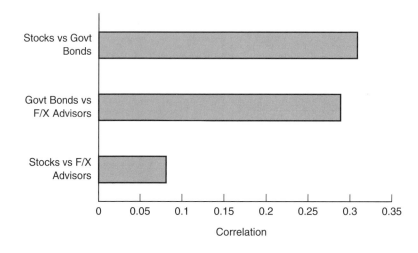

Trading Styles

Every Commodity Trading Advisor will tell you what is special about his trading style. In practice, about 80 per cent of them employ trend-following techniques and therefore produce broadly similar results. A good CTA will have some additional value to offer.

Trading styles used by CTAs fall into several categories:

- *Trend following.* This normally uses a computer model to identify trends in the market and follow them. This style, or a variant of it, is used by the majority of CTAs. Trend followers have normally performed well over the past 20 years, but have had disappointing results over the past 18 months in the absence of long-term market trends.
- *Contrarian.* This is the opposite of trend following. The CTA is looking for opportunities when trend followers have overrun underlying market values.
- *Fundamental.* This is where the CTA is making trading decisions on the basis of external economic data, evaluating the respective strengths of the currencies.
- *Arbitrage.* This is where the CTA is trading on price differences in the markets.

In practice, it is often best to choose a combination of CTAs offering differing trading styles: this offers further diversification and a corresponding reduction of risk.

Fees

There is considerable variation in fees charged by CTAs. Fees typically consist of:

- a management fee, based on the amount of the client deposit. This typically ranges between 0 and 4 per cent per annum of the client funds invested.
- a performance fee, based on trading profits. This typically ranges from 10 per cent to 30 per cent of the profits made (net of management fees and interest)

CTAs' fees are high in relation to fees for more traditional forms of fund management. However, against this it should be borne in mind that their published returns are generally net of all management and performance fees.

How to Invest

There are several ways in which an individual can invest in currencies. These vary considerably in terms of risk, convenience and flexibility These are, in decreasing order of risk, as follows.

Margin Trading

Some banks offer a facility whereby an individual can trade foreign currencies on a 'margin' basis at near market rates. The individual lodges margin with the bank (to meet potential losses) and is then allowed to trade directly on the foreign exchange markets up to specified limits. As all trading decisions are made by the investor, this is for experts only.

Commodity Trading Advisors

CTAs generally offer managed account services to private investors. The investor places money on account, which is then traded by the CTA. The investor specifies the maximum trading positions that may be taken by the CTA: this is meant to limit the risk, although the investor is liable for all profits or losses made – and these may theoretically exceed the original amount invested. CTAs will normally only accept high value investors – minimum account size of $1 million is not uncommon.

The main difficulty is choosing CTAs. The quality of CTA performance is quite variable, although the sales talk may be similar. Also, as many CTAs are in the United States, it is more difficult for investors from other parts of the world to select a CTA. Choice of good CTAs requires good understanding of performance data, trading style and risk control systems. Again, this is difficult for the individual investor to evaluate unless he is an expert.

Multi-Advisor Facility

This is a facility offered by some banks (including Barclays) and Commodity Pool Operators (CPOs). It enables an investor to spread his investment between a selection of CTAs that have been selected by the bank (or CPO). Although the choice of CTAs remains with the investor, the bank will normally be able to provide comparative data on the CTAs, which can be used to make the selection.

A Multi-Advisor Facility gives an investor the advantage of being able to diversify a portfolio between different CTAs with different trading styles, thus reducing the overall risk of the investment. This is also likely to be backed up by a risk management system which monitors CTAs' trading positions and closes them out if specified positions or stop loss limits are exceeded. The investor is, therefore, provided with a degree of diversification and safety, although it should be noted that he is still directly liable for trading profits or losses made by the CTAs.

Currency Funds

A variety of funds have been set up to enable a wider range of investors to participate in the currency markets. These are generally more accessible to the investing public, as they have a lower minimum investment requirement and are normally backed by a guarantee that limits potential losses. However, they offer less flexibility in choice of trading manager and investment may be required for a fixed term.

The best potential for investor returns is offered by a fully traded currency fund. This means a fund that is able to use the full range of trading activities offered by a CTA (e.g. take both long and short positions in the spot and forward markets). It does not mean funds where the principal is simply converted into a selection of currencies on the spot market and occasionally switched by the manager.

It is important for the investor to look closely at terms of any minimum return offered and the assumptions on which target returns are projected. In general, the lower the minimum return, the higher the target return should be. However, many guaranteed funds are inefficiently structured, meaning that investor returns are diluted unnecessarily.

The main points for the investor to watch are as follows:

1 What is the level of risk? Some traders are highly speculative; others adopt conservative trading strategies. Risk will also depend on the level of leverage allowed by the fund manager. The primary measure of risk is the expected volatility (or standard deviation) of the returns.

2 What is the guaranteed minimum return offered to the investor? Some funds offer no guarantees; others offer return of principal plus, perhaps, interest (which will be at less than the market deposit rate). It is not necessarily best to choose the fund with the highest minimum return, as this is likely to have a lower target return.

3 What is the target return? What Sharpe Ratio does this assume? Looking at the CTAs' track records, how often has this Sharpe Ratio been achieved in the past? How does it compare with the Sharpe Ratios on which target returns for other funds have been calculated. (A higher assumed Sharpe Ratio may not be better as it means that the CTA has to perform better to achieve the target return).

4 How many CTAs are trading the fund? What trading styles do they use? How well diversified are they? What track records do they have?

5 What is the quality of the underlying guarantee? Who picks up the bill if a CTA exceeds his limits in an adverse market move? Does the investor have any residual risk if the guarantor is unable to pay?

6 What is the investment term? Is early redemption allowed? If so, when?

7 What fees are charged?

Summary

Currencies are increasingly being recognized as an alternative form of investment. They have a low correlation with equities and bond investments, and thus represent an effective means of diversification. There are now a variety of vehicles, including guaranteed funds, through which private investors can participate in the market. ♀

COMMODITIES

David James Hutchins

David James Hutchins is a director of M&G Investment Management Limited. He has been in the investment industry for 13 years and currently manages three funds: M&G Commodity and General Unit Trust; M&G Gold and General Unit Trust and The Vanguard Specialized Gold Portfolio.

M&G Group, one of the largest and most successful investment companies in the United Kingdom, launched Britain's first unit trust in 1931. At the end of September 1994, funds under management totalled approximately £13.8 billion.

Commodities, even in their broadest sense, represent one of the smaller investment sectors. However it is arguably one of the most interesting, most volatile, most intriguing, and most misunderstood investment sectors, often driven as much by sentiment, as by fundamentals. It is also unquestionably a

It is also unquestionably a sector that offers the potential for exceptionally high returns for a degree of risk.

sector that offers the potential for exceptionally high returns for a degree of risk. However it is very important that one always remembers and understands the risk itself. On the broadest definition, commodities encompasses not only the precious and base metals, but also a range of soft commodities such as coffee, cotton, orange juice, pork bellies, soybeans, sugar, and wheat, as well as oil and gas.

Much has been written about commodities as a great diversification tool and numerous studies far too voluminous to repeat in this article, highlight a desirable negative correlation to stocks and bonds and a positive correlation to inflation. So when inflation spikes up, and stocks and bonds suffer, commodity returns actually improve. However there is an important distinction that must be made between physical commodities and an investment in commodity shares. For under most scenarios, commodity shares behave firstly as shares and secondly as commodities, so the correlations are not always perfect. Regardless of this, many investors still view commodity stocks as an inflation hedge, while unfortunately, many other investors only involve themselves in the speculative end of the market. Consequently, they often base their investment decision upon market gossip or a 'tip' from a friend, and not upon the actual fundamentals, hence the speculative reputation that commodities markets generally have.

A perfect example of fundamentals versus speculation was the performance of De Beers, a major producer and marketer of diamonds, and Southern Era, a high profile diamond exploration stock in Canada during 1993 and 1994. The excitement of a potential new exploration discovery of diamonds led to a spectacular move in the share price of Southern Era; however this quickly evaporated when exploration results began to disappoint. Contrast this with the performance of De Beers over the same period, which was nowhere near as exciting. Given the diversity and high quality of its business, its share price performance was not as vulnerable to a single piece of bad news. Oscar Wilde's advice is probably relevant to speculative mining situations: he once said that a mine was nothing more than a hole in the ground, owned by a liar!

Investment in physical commodities is rarely possible for the private investor due primarily to storage problems and charges. For instance, an investor buying gold bullion in the UK must pay VAT at the ruling rate (currently 17.5 per cent), so there is obviously little incentive to do that, almost regardless of how bullish one is for the gold price. While in other commodities, dealing in the futures market, for the uninitiated, brings with it the added risk of possibly being forced to take delivery of a consignment of say oil, wool, or wheat. Obviously this is an area best left to the professionals. Additionally, with many of the soft agricultural commodities, the ability to forecast the weather is probably the single most important factor determining price, as we saw with the spectacular performance of coffee in 1994, following damaging frosts in Brazil.

Ultimately however, most commodity prices fluctuate with supply and demand and their abundance or otherwise can be affected as much by climatic

Chart 1.12 De Beers Share Price Performance

De Beers (S A Rand, 1993-94)

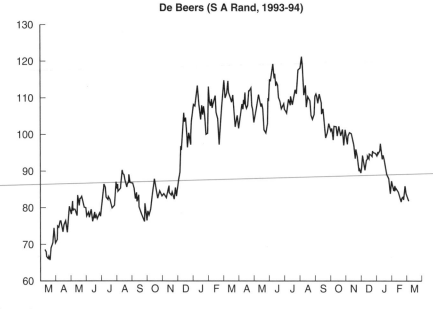

Source: Datastream

Chart 1.13 Southern Era Share Price Performance

SOUTHERN ERA (C$ 1993-94)

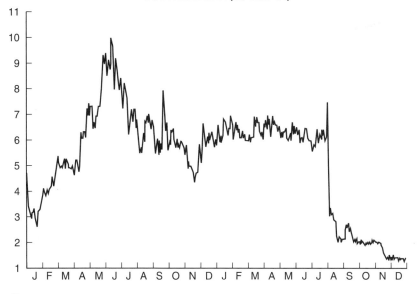

Source: Datastream

considerations as we have seen above, as by political ones. Take for example the former Soviet Union exporting metals at distressed prices as in 1993, with the sole objective of earning much needed hard currency. Across a broad range of commodities, supply side imbalances may even out because the events affecting them are unconnected. In contrast, the demand side is more likely to reflect the state of the global economy.

Mining is essentially a very simple business. Mineralized rock, or ore, is extracted from the ground and processed to produce a concentrate, which is further processed to produce finished metal. At all times, like any other company in any other industry, managements are always looking at ways to reduce costs and improve margins. This inherent gearing, is, in my view, one of the attractions of investment in commodity shares over the investment in the physical metals, for any improvement in the underlying price of a commodity flows straight through to the company's bottom line. Witness Chart 1.14 which not only shows the impact of higher nickel prices on Inco's earnings, but also graphically illustrates the cyclical nature of commodities.

Chart 1.14 Inco Earnings & LME Nickel Cash Price

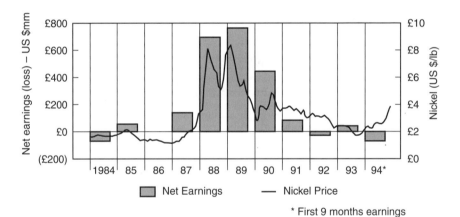

Net Earnings   — Nickel Price

* First 9 months earnings

Source: First Marathon Securities Limited

Given the cyclical nature of the commodity markets, it is clear that timing is probably the most crucial issue in any investment decision in this area. In that regard, the following chart of US interest rates and the relative performance of aluminium stocks against the Dow Jones Index is particularly helpful in trying to second guess the bottom of the cycle. As you can see, the correlation is excellent, with the aluminium stocks outperforming the market as interest rates rise. This is what one would expect, for a rising interest rate environment signifies a strong economy which would be indicative of increased metal usage.

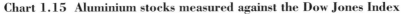

Chart 1.15 Aluminium stocks measured against the Dow Jones Index

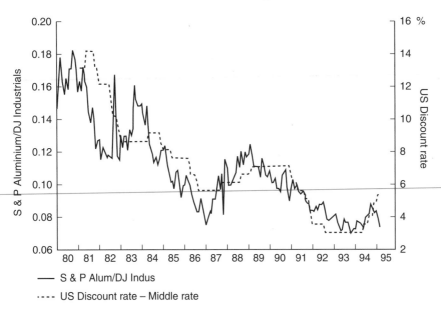

Source: Datastream

The importance of timing is also obvious from the chart of Inco's earnings. There are only three years of good earnings out of a ten-year period and the earnings' growth clearly came from the commodity price improvement. So in this instance, Inco is certainly a hostage to fortune of the nickel price, as it is a single product company. This is not always the case and many major mining companies have undertaken major diversification, in an effort to smooth out the effects of the cycle.

As I have already mentioned, mining is basically a simple business and like any industry group, it has its well-managed companies, and it has its badly managed companies. As a simple rule of thumb, when analysing mining companies, I am attracted to those companies that are not reliant solely upon commodity price improvement to show earnings growth (such as Inco), but those that can achieve real cost savings or can show organic growth, either through increased production or new projects. Bearing in mind that a mine is a wasting asset, it is also important that a mining company continues to replace the reserves that it mines each year. Hence exploration is the life blood of any mining company and a company's exploration spend can be equated to a pharmaceutical company's spend on research and development. Just like an industrial company, the exploration budget must be ongoing, and realistic in relationship to the company's production levels and cash flow.

79

The universe of mining stocks worldwide is quite extensive, particularly when you consider that the capitalization of the FT Global Gold Mines Index is roughly equal to the market capitalization of British Telecom and Guinness (only a telephone call and a glass of beer!). It is largely concentrated in the resource rich countries of Australia, Canada and South Africa and there is a clear distinction between the large 'majors', and an even more extensive list of speculative 'juniors'.

We have already seen the impact of exploration news on a company's share price, with the earlier example of the Canadian diamond exploration stock, Southern Era. Local knowledge is of particular advantage in these types of situations and any investment in such a speculative stock should only be made with money an investor can afford to lose. If, however, the temptation proves too great and you happen to become involved in a very speculative situation, the important thing is always to remember to sell; although this is often much easier said than done. Therefore a disciplined approach is most necessary and the best idea is probably to sell part of any holding into a rising market so as to at least recover all or part of the investments' initial cost. That way you still have an involvement and interest in the stock, but you have also successfully limited your downside. Additionally it is always worth remembering, that the lead time from exploration to discovery to actual production is normally a couple of years and during that time the company will often need to raise additional capital. Against that background and with the exploration upside removed, the share price generally tends to under-perform.

At the other the end of the spectrum, a long-term investment in one of the leading mining companies can prove quite profitable. Witness the ten year chart of RTZ Corporation, relative to the FT-SE-100 Index and the Commodity Research Bureau Index. Due to its diversity of mining interests both by commodity and geographically and its strong management team, RTZ has been successfully able to weather previous commodity cycles. In fact the management of RTZ is not just highly regarded in the mining industry, they are also seen as one the better management teams within UK industry in general. Similarly, the strong management team at Barrick Gold Corporation in Canada, have, with the help of a world class ore body, created one of the world's leading gold companies in only ten years. As Chart 1.17 shows, Barrick has convincingly outperformed both the gold price and the Dow Jones Industrials Index over those years. It should be said, however, that the performance of Barrick, as a gold stock, is probably the exception and not the rule, but it does prove quite categorically, that selective investment in the gold sector can indeed be very profitable.

If there is any middle ground for the private investor in the commodities sector, it lies with the variety of collective investment schemes available. These include dedicated energy, gold, or broadly based commodity unit trusts, offered by many of the leading investment houses in the United

Chart 1.16 RTZ measured against FT-SE 100 and CRB Indexes

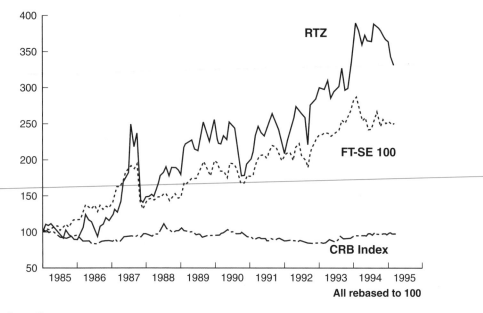

Source: Datastream

Chart 1.17 Barrick Gold measured against Dow Jones Index and Gold price

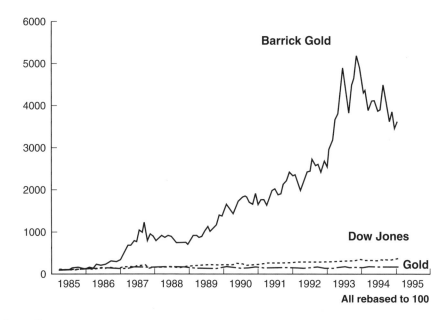

Source: Datastream

Kingdom. This range includes two funds managed by M&G Investment Management Limited, the M&G Gold and General Fund, and the M&G Commodity and General Fund. Other products in the market place include a range of closed-end investment trusts, the majority of which were only launched in 1994. The investment trusts differ from the unit trusts, in that they are generally capable of investing in the physical commodities as well as the equities. However, I would always be reluctant to buy into any of these investment trusts, unless they were selling at a discount to their net asset value. For the

If there is any middle ground for the private investor in the commodities sector, it lies with the variety of collective investment schemes available.

private investor, these collective schemes have their attractions, as they are professionally managed, and are therefore able to invest in a wide range of international companies, both large and small. Thus they can effectively diversify their risk and gain exposure to a wide variety of companies, which are then monitored on a continuous basis.

In the final analysis, the commodity sector is ultimately high risk for high reward. This should not deter private investors, but it should make them cautious. The most efficient investment route is therefore a collective scheme of some sort, as it ensures that all the investor's eggs are not in one basket. If this approach is too timid for an individual who thinks we are on the verge of the next Poseidon boom, my only advice would be: 'Don't forget to sell.' ♀

REAL ESTATE

Yolande Barnes

Yolande Barnes is Head of Residential Research at Savills. and has ten years experience in property research having worked previously at Healey and Baker as an office and industrial real estate analyst. The department analyses all aspects of the residential property market, undertakes regular surveys on the housing market, publishes surveys and quarterly bulletins and has built up extensive databases. It also undertakes bespoke research for clients.

Savills is a well-known and respected public company, with a national and international network of subsidiaries and associates, which specializes in a wide variety of real estate functions including estate agency and consultancy.

Introduction

Investment in international real estate can take a huge variety of forms. Different countries have different laws and practices which can often be quite complex. To cover the subject would require a whole book, if not a series of volumes. This section therefore aims to cover just direct property investment as it applies primarily to the UK and to the individual investor.

Options for the Individual Investor

Direct investment can be problematic for the individual. There are three main features which make it so: 'lumpiness', management obligations and illiquidity.

'Lumpiness'

'Lumpiness' relates to the minimum size of real estate holding that it is possible to buy at any one time. Even the wealthy investor, if investing directly in bricks and mortar, will find it difficult to spread risk across a portfolio of different types of property. Consequently, the luxury of investing, in the commercial sector, across a wide diversity of prime properties is confined to large investment fund managers and institutions. Residential property generally has a lower unit price and may therefore be a more suitable medium for the smaller investor.

Management Obligations

Direct property investment carries with it a need for management. Real estate investments are subject to the external forces of the elements as well as wear and tear from occupants. Leases may also carry certain obligations on the part of the landlord. Generally, commercial property is freer from management obligations than residential, because most commercial buildings are let under full repairing and insuring leases so that responsibility for the fabric becomes the tenant's. Residential property on the other hand, has a reputation for being time-consuming and costly. The services of a managing agent need to be taken into consideration when calculating net yields.

Illiquidity

Illiquidity is a feature of all sectors of the property market. Individual properties cannot be traded in the same way as stocks and bonds. Transactions can be both time consuming and costly. The average sale of a residential property, for example, takes about six months to completion and longer in poor markets. For this reason, it is generally considered advisable to view real estate as a longer-term investment.

For those who are willing to try something new and perhaps involving higher, or at least unquantified, risk, experiments are now being made with various property derivatives and synthetic instruments. Some of these, such as the London FOX property futures, have already failed. Others however, such as Property Index Certificates have had limited success but it must be remembered that such vehicles constitute a tiny and very immature investment market at present.

The Advantages of Real Estate

Ironically, some of the features of real estate which are viewed by some as disadvantages can also be advantageous to certain types of investor. The fact that single buildings are expensive may be a positive feature for a very large fund because all management effort can be concentrated in one building.

There is also evidence to suggest that the illiquidity of property means that its price is less volatile. This is evidenced by the fact that the price of property derivatives and asset-based property companies, which are freely traded, fluctuate much more than the value of the underlying asset.

Similarly, the longer-term nature of property as an investment medium is an advantage for those seeking the prospect of steady income and capital growth in the more distant future. High trading costs can then be offset by the fact that the property will be held for a long period of time and not traded frequently. Some analysts would also argue that real estate is a good long-term hedge against inflation as its value tracks or, in the case of residential property, can exceed the cost of living.

Chart 1.18 opposite shows data of residential property prices since the middle of the last century compared with average earnings and the cost of living. House prices over the past 140 years have out-paced inflation and tended to lag behind earnings growth.

Obviously, the data must be viewed with caution, due to its unreliability prior to 1955, especially the house price estimates. House prices have matched or out-grown inflation in nine of the fourteen decades. The last time that house prices rose more slowly than inflation was during the Second World War. One feature to note is the exponential growth following the Second

> **Some analysts would also argue that real estate is a good long-term hedge against inflation as its value tracks or, in the case of residential property, can exceed the cost of living.**

Chart 1.18 House Price Growth, Cost of Living and Earnings compared (1855–1995)

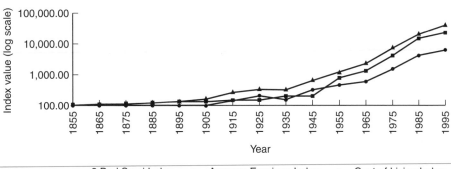

Sources: CSO, Nationwide BS, Savills Residential Research

World War, which coincides with a rapid increase in owner-occupation as a form of tenure in the UK. Consequently, residential values tend to be governed by occupiers rather than investors.

The main feature of any type of property as a direct investment is that it combines the prospect of capital growth with regular rental income. This income can be used to service debt and thereby gear the investment to maximize capital growth if so desired.

In the case of commercial property, if a building is let on a long, institutional lease on a good covenant (i.e. to a good tenant) this income can be quite secure. Yields available vary according to property type and over time. Rental income can compare favourably with gilt yields, although as can be seen from Chart 1.19 overleaf, this varies according to the type of property investment in question and fluctuations in gilts over time.

Components of growth

Returns on property investment are made up of two components: rental income and capital growth. These elements work together in different ways depending on the type of investment medium chosen. While rental income for all types of property is dependent on levels of occupier demand, the capital value can be dependent on levels of either investor demand or owner-occupier demand. In the case of residential property, capital values are almost always set in the owner-occupier market while, in the case of commercial property, capital values are dependent on the rental income generated by the property and set by investor sentiment and the yield that investors are prepared to accept.

Chart 1.19 Comparison of gross yields for prime central London residential property against Gilts (1985–1994)

Source: Savills Residential Research

The capital value of commercial property tends to rise when there is widespread expectation of rental rises. Investors are willing to accept a lower yield on an existing rental stream and pay more. When expectation of rental growth is low, investors look for higher yields and capital values fall. As well as investor perception on future rental levels, the yields available in other investment media will also govern what yield is applied on a given property. Yields also vary according to the perceived level of risk associated with property investment in relation to other media.

Rents

Rental levels for any type of property will vary according to occupier demand. Different factors govern the level of demand in different sectors. Put very simplistically, consumer spending levels will govern retail demand, service sector employment rates will affect demand for offices, manufacturing and distribution levels will drive demand for industrial buildings and the number of households requiring shelter will govern demand for housing.

In the residential sector, demand for rental accommodation, as opposed to owner-occupied housing, will tend to depend more on the number of temporary households or short-term employees in an area as well as other complicating factors such as the availability and cost of financing owner-occupation. Increasing demand is also coming from younger households who are delaying house purchase but need an alternative form of accommodation in the meantime. Only time will tell if the average age of first-time house buyers will now be permanently raised or whether it is a temporary phenomenon resulting from falling nominal house prices and resulting disillusionment.

All of the above factors have strong regional and locational components. Rental demand will vary according to where a property is situated. Similarly, demand will vary from sector to sector: from the most expensive properties to the cheaper.

Capital Growth

The components of capital growth for residential property are extremely complicated and experts disagree on exactly what they are. It is probable that many of the factors which influence prices actually change over time or produce different effects in different combinations. For example: whilst it is widely accepted that rapidly rising interest rates precipitated market falls in 1989, the same high level of interest rates in 1985 did not have the same effect. It seems probable that the personal mortgage sector and credit gearing, had a part to play. When gearing was relatively low in 1985, interest rates were not critical; when gearing was high in 1989, interest rates became a critical factor.

Yields

Gross

Gross yields on residential property are usually expressed as the annual rent as a percentage of capital value. These gross yields vary enormously, from 2.5 per cent for large, remote, rural period country houses to 25 per cent for small flats and bedsits in locations where rental demand is high and supply scarce. Across the UK, average yields stand at around 9 per cent gross as of April 1995.

Net

An investor needs to be aware of how ongoing costs such as management, maintenance, agents fees etc. will reduce the rental income. The buying costs, solicitors and surveyors fees and so on, as well as the cost of initial refurbishments will also push up the capital costs. The combined effects of these factors typically reduce a gross yield of 9 per cent to 7 per cent net.

Commercial Property

General

The issues related to investment in commercial property, and companies whose main assets are commercial property, are examined in more detail on p 483. A brief outline of past performance is given in Chart 1.20 so that some comparison may be made with other investment types.

Chart 1.20 Comparison of Total Returns: Property vs Equities
(1985–1994)

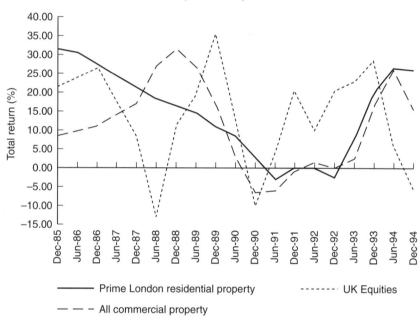

Source: Savills Residential Research

Retail

Retail property takes a variety of forms, from small high street shops in provincial towns to large, out of town shopping complexes. Generally speaking, the health of the sector is dependent on consumer spending levels which governs the demand for retail selling space. Demand, however, is subject to locational differences and will also differ between sectors. Consequently, rental levels for large out-of-town supermarkets could be growing whilst rental levels for small boutiques in town centres are falling.

Offices

Office property is perhaps less diverse than retail but varies greatly in terms of quality and, consequently, in let-ability. The health of the sector is dependent on service sector employment levels. The potential investor will need to consider the current and likely future demand from local businesses in a particular location, the prospects for the local economy and also the age, suitability and life-span of the building in question.

Industrial

The term industrial property covers a variety of building types and can include factory units, distribution warehousing, storage facilities and accommodation for high-tech industries with a variable office component. Some industrial buildings are very flexible and can accommodate a variety of functions.

Important considerations to be taken into account by investors in industrial sheds and warehouses include: the strength of the local manufacturing sector and, in the case of warehousing especially, the suitability of the site for distribution and its accessibility to transport links. Investors should note that industrial property can have a shorter life-span than other commercial property due to physical deterioration. Equally, industrial property will usually be cheaper to rebuild and replace than offices or retail.

Residential Property

History of Sector

Residential investment in the UK is not generally widespread. Most dwellings (66.4 per cent) are owner-occupied either outright (25 per cent) or with a mortgage (42 per cent). A large proportion of UK housing stock is owned and let by local authorities (20 per cent) or housing associations (3.7 per cent) and both of these types of landlord let in the social housing sector at lower-than-market rents. Only the remaining 9.7 per cent of stock is let by private landlords. There are pockets where higher proportions of stock are held and let by private landlords, most notably central London with approximately 30 per cent.

The UK differs dramatically from other countries in its lack of rented housing in the private sector. The table below shows international comparisons with other industrialized economies.

Country	% Privately Rented
United Kingdom	10
The Netherlands	15
France	18
Australia	20
Sweden	21
Canada	23
Italy	25
United States	33
Portugal	36
Switzerland	67

There is a desire amongst government policy makers to see the private rented sector expanded. This has broad cross-party support as there is a widespread belief that the rush to owner-occupation in the late 1980s was bad for the country's economy and has led to more widespread social problems such as repossessions, negative equity and labour immobility.

The Private Rented Sector

The 1988 Act

The experience of these private landlords differs widely according to the type of tenancy and the degree of rent regulation applied to it. Research by the Joseph Rowntree organization has found an increased level of investor satisfaction with the new forms of tenure.

Tenancy Type	Yield
Pre 1988 letting (regulated)	4.4 per cent
Post 1988 letting (open market rent)	9.2 per cent

The table above illustrates how rental returns have been enhanced where properties are let after the 1988 act. Clearly, the ability to charge market rents and the new types of tenancy have made residential investment more attractive to the private investor.

Owner Occupation as Investment

Another option for residential investors is to occupy the property. Obviously, rental income is foregone, although the household will save on what might otherwise have been spent in rent or mortgage. The main purpose would be capital growth which has been high in the past. However, the experience of the early 1990s shows that capital values can go down as well as up and so the timing of purchase may be critical.

There are two main advantages of this type of investment: first, there will be a saving on capital gains tax when it comes to sale as owner-occupied properties in the UK are, in most cases, exempt. Second, owner-occupation offers the opportunity for a high level of gearing through mortgage borrowing which is usually less expensive and more widely available and in larger quantities than other types of loan.

The disadvantages of owner occupation as an investment are that the risk cannot be diversified through a portfolio of properties of different types in different locations. Liquidity is also likely to be even more of a problem than it would be with let properties as there is a personal cost in moving whenever property is sold. Ultimately owner-occupation is not a suitable investment medium if used solely for that purpose.

Opportunities in Development

It is possible for an investor to achieve capital uplift through improvement, refurbishment or redevelopment of a property. In these cases, detailed advice should be sought as to what suits the local market best, how much development will cost and how much added to the value of the original building or site. Development profit may then be taken by the investor either by selling the property or in the form of an enhanced rental yield.

Conclusions

For those investors who want to buy direct property as an investment, there are two main methods of acquisition. The first is to use estate agents to provide details of properties for sale. This course is likely to provide the widest choice of properties as most are sold by this means. However, it should always be remembered that the agent's responsibility is primarily to the vendor, not the purchaser.

Those with more knowledge and experience may also like to try auctions. This may be especially popular amongst residential investors as fully let properties with ready-made income streams can be found and may be acquired at lower prices than properties in the mainstream, owner-occupied market.

Whatever the method of acquisition, this section has shown some of the advantages and disadvantages of real estate as a direct investment for the individual investor. For those inspired by it, there is more homework to be done but there will also be that satisfaction at the end of the day of owning an investment which can provide attractive returns, diversify a portfolio and is much more interesting to look at than stock and bond certificates. ♀

Creating a Portfolio

MAKING AN INVESTMENT PLAN

Victor Cazalet

Victor Cazalet leads a team of over nine investment professionals dedicated to managing the assets of high net worth private investors. Prior to joining **Lazard Brothers Asset Management (LBAM)** *in 1992, the greater part of his career had been spent with* **Morgan Grenfell Asset Management.**

LBAM *is the wholly owned subsidiary of* **Lazard Brothers & Co Limited,** *the London based merchant bank.* **Lazard Brothers** *is one of the three major* **Lazard** *houses, the other two being based in New York and Paris.* **LBAM** *offers a comprehensive range of investment management services to UK and international clients. Private investors constitute over 20 per cent of* **LBAM's** *funds under management.*

Investors who want to succeed in increasing the value of their invesments will want to think carefully about a precise plan to meet distinctly personal objectives. Investment professionals, like those at LBAM have been through this process countless times and find that, while no two investors are exactly the same, there are some general guidelines which apply again and again.

Before we meet a prospective new client, we try to find out from the introducer or from the individual the type of product they are looking for and the sort of investment advice they are seeking. At this first meeting, the single most important requirement is for the investment manager to come away with a clear view of the prospective client's objectives. The starting point, of course, is to assess the existing holdings. The next, and more important issue is whether the current spread of investments is right for the client, given their unique circumstances and requirements. That means we need to know their views on such matters as:

- risk and volatility
- time horizons
- income requirements
- preferred base currency
- currency exposure
- performance benchmark
- administration details.

It is never easy to explain risk and volatility without worrying the client about the potential downside of any individual investment or of the portfolio as a whole. Nonetheless it is vital that this issue is addressed early on. It is our experience that the more cautious clients, however much they may be assured that over the longer term equity investments have shown a superior return over cash and/or bonds, may prefer an exposure to bonds and cash of somewhere between 25 and 50 per cent in the expectation that the probability of significant falls in the value of their portfolio will be somewhat less.

Clearly the astute investment manager will have anticipated weaknesses in equity markets but it is rare indeed, even ill advised, for a portfolio of equity investments to be wholly liquidated in anticipation of falls in markets. It is probable that the client will, from time to time, suffer losses which need to be carefully addressed when discussing the investment strategy. There is nothing more upsetting for the client and destructive of mutual confidence than for the investment manager to underestimate the extent to which capital preservation alone is the client's objective. It is permissible to err on the side of conservatism for a higher risk client but never to take risks for a conservative client.

Client's investment objectives may change over time, not always in reaction to changing market circumstances. On retirement, for instance, the emphasis may change from capital growth to income generation. The simplest way of achieving this is to decrease the equity content in favour of fixed interest investments which typically will yield more. Otherwise it would be possible to switch a proportion of the existing equity holdings into higher yielding stocks, such as utilities.

At the official reporting periods, usually quarterly or half-yearly, we remind clients of their portfolio objectives using the phraseology enshrined in their investment management agreement. If they set parameters for exposure in certain markets or investment categories, these may be revisited to ensure that they remain comfortable with the way their portfolio is being managed. In practice we have found that the investment objective rarely changes, although in a number of instances after a volatile experience guidelines may be tightened.

We tell clients that our house style has been established to provide them with a portfolio consisting largely of equity investments, well spread across sectors and markets and intended, at a minimum, to retain purchasing power in their base currency over the medium to longer term. We find that is the best balance for a majority of portfolios. Again we need to establish at an early stage the client's time horizon. Demanding short-term targets unsettle investment managers and, in reality, are unlikely to be met. When we are set targets we try to establish that the money will be with us over an economic cycle of something between three and five years, thus ensuring that the good years outnumber the down years so that we have a reasonable chance of meeting the client's requirements. Generally, clients will tell us that they are looking to the longer term.

Income requirement is one issue which needs to be established before finalising an investment plan. Some investors never touch income allowing it to accumulate within the portfolio. Others rely on the income generated by their portfolio for living expenses. So long as it is entirely clear what their requirements are there will be no problem. The trouble arises when clients require both income and capital growth, as performance tables will confirm that portfolios orientated towards income will produce lower overall returns over the medium to long term. Many high growth economies, particularly in the Far East, produce little or no income and as a consequence it can take some persuasion to achieve the sort of exposure we think clients should have in these markets. Of course such exposure can be offset by fixed interest or convertible holdings, but only to the extent that the client's capital growth requirement is not compromized. Our clients increasingly look to overall return which, if we assume that the treatment of income and capital for tax purposes is broadly neutral, must be the more sensible attitude.

The question of base currency and currency exposure has become more complex in recent years. High net worth clients may spend time and money in two or more countries. Trying to work out where their liabilities are, which is only one aspect of the question, can therefore be difficult. As the investment business becomes more international, base currencies or, more accurately, the currency in which we account for our client, may be a matter of convenience and have no further implications for the management of the portfolio. We have found that international clients who will tend to have their money based offshore give us that most difficult brief of all: 'make money for us wherever and in whatever currency'. In other words, they only want exposure to markets and currencies that are appreciating.

During the 1980s and 1990s, turmoil in currency markets had a greater impact on the international financial scene and portfolio returns than hitherto. Clients expect the manager to have definite views on the short, medium and long term as far as the major currencies are concerned which is a considerable challenge in an area of investment that is notoriously difficult to predict over any term. Efforts by central banks to stabilize currencies are often unsuccessful and attempts to create fixed exchange rates over the medium term have equally been unsuccessful. We try to establish with our clients in which currencies they think, in which currencies they are most likely to be spending their money and then slant the portfolio accordingly. Particular care has to be taken when the brief is to create an international portfolio of equities but the base currency of the client appreciates against other major currencies and would typically only constitute a small proportion of the portfolio. A sound plan has to address this problem up front. Hedging techniques can be used but it raises the question as to whether an international portfolio was the right choice in the first instance. Once a currency benchmark has been set and agreed, then the task of the investment manager will be that much clearer, though it may be at the expense of true international diversification.

Increasingly, the question of performance benchmarks is raised by potential clients. No investment plan is complete without a clear sense of the appropriate benchmarks. It is our hope that performance league tables of private investor portfolio investment managers will not be treated in the sacred way that they are in the institutional pension fund market. The management of private investors' assets is a subtler and more personal business than that of large institutional funds. It is our belief that clients will continue to choose their investment advisors for a variety of reasons and not only for performance. Our clients continue to concentrate on their portfolios retaining their purchasing power by increasing in total value in excess of the rate of inflation.

97

One or a combination of indices may be appropriate for comparison and every effort is made to outperform these relevant indices.

There are other aspects of the client's financial affairs which may be of greater interest for us to know than for the client to tell us. In order to comply with the regulations in the UK, investment advisors should have a clear understanding of the clients' financial circumstances. These details may not always be forthcoming but it certainly helps in formulating an individual investment strategy if we have an overall feel for the client's spread of assets. The best plan has to start with a complete financial inventory. Most clients will have some property interests as well as other possessions which may be of considerable value. It is only in very rare circumstances that we find ourselves managing an investment portfolio that constitutes the great majority of our clients' assets.

If asked to advise whether a client should split his portfolio between two or more managers, our first consideration will be size: if split in two, would each half be sufficient to command the sort of service that the client wants? For larger amounts of $10m or more, there may well be a strong case for splitting. Clients may choose to split their portfolio between what they perceive as a higher performance, higher risk manager and a more conservatively inclined investment house. That decision should only be taken after a proper plan is in place.

Investment management for the private investor becomes increasingly complex but the confidence between client and manager remains vital. An agreed plan is the cornerstone on which that confidence can be built. ♀

UNDERSTANDING RISK AND VOLATILITY

Professor David Wilkie

Professor David Wilkie is a Partner of **R. Watson & Sons**, *part of* **Watson Wyatt**, *the leading actuarial consultancy, which is particularly strong on investment consultancy to pension fund trustees. David Wilkie is a prolific author of actuarial papers on investment and other topics.*

The future is uncertain, but it is uncertain in a predictable sort of way. We do not know what the weather will be like in a month's time, but we do know what the climate is like. We know roughly how warm the summers will be and how cold the winters.

So it is with investments. If we buy shares when the index is at 3,000, we know that it is most unlikely to go down to 300 or up to 30,000 in the near future; but we would be surprised if it remained within ten points of 3,000 for more than a day or two.

In the London Stock Exchange daily price changes in the share index, either up or down, of up to 1 per cent are common, changes of over 3 per cent are newsworthy and changes of over 10 per cent are almost unheard of – though 19 October 1987 is a date engraved on the memory of anyone who was involved with stock markets at that time. What is true of a share index is true for individual shares, but the shares of any one company may well change by more than the market index.

As with shares, so also with interest rates. Changes of $1/4$ per cent or $1/2$ per cent in Bank Base Rates are the common size of step, and one does not expect them to change more frequently than three or four times a year. The sequence formed in the United Kingdom by Bank Rate, Minimum Lending Rate, and Bank Base Rates is recorded since 1 January 1797 and there were 738 changes between that date and 2 February 1995. The longest run when it was unchanged was 25 years from 1797 to 1822, and the year in which there were most changes was 1873, when Bank Rate changed 24 times.

The prices of long-term government stocks change almost continuously when the markets are open. But for bonds the typical size of fluctuation is less than for shares. Over the course of a year, the accumulated changes can easily mean a rise or fall in share prices of up to 20 per cent in a year, and a rise or fall of the prices of long-term bonds of up to 10 per cent. A change of 50 per cent either way for shares is exceptional, though 1974 and 1975 were such exceptions, and a change of over 30 per cent for bonds is also exceptional.

Thus, while the future is uncertain, many risks are measurable, especially the sort of risks where the cumulative effect is the result of a large number of small changes. Statistical methods allow one to make some estimates of the variability that might occur in the future, even though, in the event, only one outcome will happen.

There is a different type of risk for an individual, in that certain events may happen at specific times and not at others. Most people do not know in advance when they will die. For each of us this is a single final event. But for an insurance company deaths of policy holders are sufficiently frequent for considerable averaging out to occur. The same sort of averaging out applies to portfolios of shares. Shares individually are more risky than the market. A reasonably well spread portfolio is less risky than individual shares, and not much more risky than the market. The majority of the benefits of diversification can be obtained with as few as 20 shares.

The majority of the benefits of diversification can be obtained with as few as 20 shares.

How should the individual investor approach this bewildering world of predictable uncertainty? One needs to understand the types of risk, what one means by risk, and how it can be measured.

Different investment vehicles carry different types of risk. The building society deposit gives a generally safe guarantee of one's capital, but provides an interest rate that can be varied at the building society's discretion from time to time. The capital is guaranteed but the income is variable. A long-term gilt guarantees interest payments and a redemption amount. The income is fixed but the value of the capital is variable. Ordinary shares provide both sorts of uncertainty. Both income and capital are variable.

The sort of risks that an individual can undertake depend on the purpose of the investment. If you are saving for retirement, you wish to get an income that will give you the purchasing power that you might hope for, so an investment that is likely to keep pace with inflation is a good match. Index-linked stocks should suit such individuals better than conventional fixed interest stocks. Of course, you may make an assessment that inflation will be higher or lower than the market expects and decide that one stock will do much better than the other. Then you are backing your hunch rather than reducing your risk.

Ordinary shares are often described as 'a hedge against inflation', and in the long run they generally are, but there is a lot of variation in the meantime. The value of an ordinary share depends on the value of the company, which in turn depends on its earnings. These in turn depend on turnover and profit margins. For most companies turnover is related to current prices, so a rise in the general level of prices results in an increase in turnover. This may not be directly translated into higher profits. If inflation is high, wage increases may also be high, interest rates may be high, taxation may be raised and the government may introduce dividend controls. However, in due course higher inflation works through into higher profits and then also higher dividends.

If you buy a share with an initial yield of 4 per cent gross, you can expect, in the first year, a 4 per cent return. In addition, dividends may rise with inflation. If you expect inflation to be about 4 per cent per year then the total growth in your investment can be expected to be about 8 per cent per year (the initial 4 per cent plus growth of 4 per cent). If you think dividends will grow by 1 per cent more than inflation, then you can add 1 per cent to your expected return. But it is unreasonable to assume that you will be able to sell your share on a much better rating, ie at a much higher multiple of the dividend than when you bought it.

What have dividends done in relation to retail prices over the years? Adequate records go back to the early 1920s. Between 1923 and 1993 share dividends grew at 5.7 per cent per annum compound, and share prices by almost the same. This was 1.2 per cent higher than inflation, which was 4.5 per cent over the same period.

If we measure from 1979 to 1994 we get much better figures. Inflation was 6 per cent, dividends grew by 9.5 per cent and share prices rose by 13.4 per cent, but part of the growth of shares was because the dividend yield changed from 6.9 per cent at the end of 1979 to 4 per cent at the end of 1994, an increase in the value of shares of 70 per cent simply as a result of re-rating. It would be optimistic to imagine that this can happen again, so that dividend yields fall to 2.3 per cent, but this is what a crude projection of past share price performance would imply.

The main reason why shares have been a much better investment than bonds since the Second World War is that inflation has turned out to be much higher than investors were expecting during the 1940s or 1950s. Bonds, at that time, were not priced to allow for the inflation that has occurred. Bonds now allow for, perhaps, 3 per cent to 4 per cent real return, and 4 per cent to 5 per cent future inflation. Share prices allow for much the same but, in addition, there may be a modest growth of dividends in real terms, so that shares may be expected to give 1 per cent return better than bonds, with greater uncertainty.

How it will turn out over future decades will depend very much on whether inflation, in fact, averages the 4 per cent to 5 per cent implied by current bond yields. It might be much lower. The present Government hopes that it will. But no government lasts for ever. It might be much higher again. The uncertainty of future inflation is the main risk investors face. ●

DETERMINING AN ASSET ALLOCATION APPROACH

Stephen Lowe

Stephen Lowe is a Director and the Head of Macroeconomic Research at Gartmore Investment Management. He is also a member of Gartmore's Global Policy Committee. His previous career includes broking at Rowe and Pitman and fund management with Mercury Asset Management.

Gartmore is one of the six largest managers of UK pension funds. It also manages portfolios, investment trusts and unitised vehicles for UK and international investors. At the end of 1994, Gartmore managed almost £21 billion, predominantly in equities. Nations Gartmore, the company's joint venture in the United States with Nations Bank, began trading in 1995.

With a plan you can set about investing to achieve your objectives. You need to decide what you will invest in, otherwise known as asset allocation. Clearly, the allocation appropriate to a policeman in Leeds to meet school fees over the next ten years will be very different from that appropriate to a high-earning 36-year-old divorced expatriate stockbroker in Hong Kong making alimony payments to ex-wives in Cannes and Singapore, with a long-term goal to retire to his Palm Springs condo and keep the sum of his age and his golf handicap to seventy.

Asset allocation is not the same thing as stock picking or portfolio management. But it is an essential first step in the investment process and one which may very well have the biggest influence on your eventual returns. Only an exceptionally risky portfolio is likely to diverge far from the stock market as a whole. The performance of the chosen investments within an asset category is likely to be determined by the fortunes of that category. Whether you own UK equities or gilts is more important than whether you own Marks and Spencer or Boots.

Bear in mind when considering your approach that timing stock markets is extremely difficult. Sanford Bernstein of New York calculated that for a US investor who had tried to guess at the start of each quarter between 1980 and 1991 whether equities or cash would do better and had been right two-thirds of the time, the resulting return from this policy of aggressive switching between equities and cash would only just have matched the 16.7 per cent return from a portfolio which stayed fully invested throughout, riding the peaks and troughs.

If the investor had been right half the time – statistically a more likely result given that few investors appear to have made a fortune trading index futures – then the resulting returns would have fallen 4.0 per cent below the 16.7 per cent annualized return of the fully invested portfolio. (These calculations assume 'index' returns and do not take into account trading costs, not to mention tax liabilities.) You might well conclude that it would be best to have a fixed allocation of assets, with equity investment in index-tracking funds and without attempting to time markets by changing your asset mix.

Effectively, a lot of institutional portfolios are run like this. Obviously, it is vital that the fixed asset allocation determined at the outset is appropriate for the duration of the plan. For most investors with an objective of maximizing wealth over an indefinite, but probably long (15 years plus) time horizon, the fixed allocation should be 100 per cent equities.

There is a danger in becoming too risk averse for older people. A 60-year-old still has a life expectancy exceeding ten years and even an 85-year-old may see no need to liquidate the equities in an estate. Only if you envisage a strong possiblity of the need to liquidate your capital within a short period of a decade or so, should you be seriously considering a sizeable allocation to bonds. This will obviously be related to the cushion of surplus savings you have, your own age and state of health and that of your dependants. There is no need to own bonds in a longer-term fixed plan because the lower volatility of a mixed equity/bond portfolio brings no true benefit, while lowering prospective real returns.

That is because in the very long run, bonds should not produce returns as high as equities. If they did, businesses would cease to expand using share capital and would focus on repaying debt with their profits. This does of course happen periodically during economic cycles, particularly when real interest rates are high, but it isn't a sustainable condition of a society seeking to improve the real standard of living through economic growth.

Indeed bonds are a dangerous asset to consider for any long holding period relative to equities. Suppose you had been sitting on a UK equity portfolio in 1936. If the prospects of a world war had prompted you to want to sell, you would have been right. As you can see from Table 1.16, real returns to UK equity investors were negative for the next 17 years. But what if you had switched into gilts, 'for safety'? As the BZW 1995 Gilts-Equity study shows, you would still be showing a negative real return on your year end 1936 gilt portfolio!

Table 1.16: Cycles in Real Returns from:

Duration	UK Equities	% Real Return pa	Duration	Gilts	% Real Return pa
1 yr	1919	+38.8	2 yrs	1919–20	–16.7
1 yr	1920	–36.7			
8 yrs	1921–28	+25.6	16 yrs	1921–36	+12.2
3 yrs	1929–31	–9.4			
5 yrs	1932–36	+24.0			
16 yrs	1937–52	–0.1	57 yrs	1937–94	–0.2
2 yrs	1953–54	+32.6			
3 yrs	1955–57	–4.4			
2 yrs	1958–59	+49.9			
7 yrs	1960–66	–0.2			
6 yrs	1971–72	+13.0			
4 yrs	1973–76	–18.2			
1 yr	1977	+40.2			
2 yrs	1978–79	–1.7			
10 yrs	1980–89	+15.3			
1 yr	1990	–14.7			
3 yrs	1991–93	+17.8			
1 yr	1994	–6.8			

Sources: BZW/Gartmore (- gross returns)

International bonds are also unlikely to fit into most approaches: it is easy to fall into the trap of owning a weak bond market in a country whose currency is in decline. Most equity markets, by contrast, are inversely correlated with their currencies – with notable recent exceptions being Canada, Australia and Italy.

While most investors with no ambition or desire to manage their asset allocation actively should invest in equities, for some investors other assets may be appropriate. Those who have lower return objectives or who pay high taxes may decide to own index-linked bonds where these are available. To a UK higher-rate tax payer, these have offered a prospective real return of between 2 per cent and 3 per cent for much of the 12 years of their existence as an asset class.

Index-linked yields should continue to move in a band 1.5 per cent above or below UK equity dividend yields, as they have over the past decade. Near the higher end of this range, it may well make sense to regard index-linked as fundamentally attractive in relation to equities, offering a particularly good return relative to their lower risk, but such value has rarely been seen. Most of the time, however, index-linked gilts offer the certainty of a 2 to 3 per cent real return with the high probability that this return will be exceeded by equities. This is because corporate profits and dividends rise in real terms with the growth of the economy, which has been and can reasonably be expected to continue at the rate of 2 to 2.5 per cent over the longer term. If equities yield more than index-linked gilts and if dividends rise a little faster than inflation, in line with real economic growth, then it is obvious that the difference between the index-linked yield and the dividend yield effectively being earned by an equity portfolio will widen dramatically over time.

Whatever the final approach taken to asset allocation, whether fixed or active, your investments must make sense in value terms. You cannot rely on historic data and theory alone. It is true that equities should outperform other asset categories, but if their value at the time of investment is nonsensical, they probably won't. If all investors believed that equities must outperform, they would bid prices up to levels which would defeat the proposition.

With a fixed approach to asset allocation, you need look at value only once, at the point of your initial allocation decision. If your local equity market is priced rationally – which most are, for much for the time – then it should be offering a 6 per cent real prospective return to a non-taxpaying investor. Note the persistency of the $6^{1}/_{2}$ per cent level of real returns to US equity investors over long periods throughout the past two centuries, and how consistently this has been superior to bonds by a wide margin. You can also see from Table 1.17 that local equities have provided a return of 5 to 8 per cent in real terms to UK, US and Dutch investors. All three equity markets have generally been priced to yield 3 to 5 per cent from current dividends, with 2 to 3 per cent real economic growth in prospect.

The German stock market has delivered returns in a far more erratic fashion and bond returns have been much more competitive. But this market may be the exception that proves the rule, for the German stock market's dividend yield was well below 3 per cent at the start of 1987, 1961 and 1972, which all initiated periods of poor real equity returns. Following the Wirtschaftswunder post-war years, the German economy has grown at approximately 2.5 per cent, so it isn't surprising that equity returns have been inadequate when the market was bought on dividend yields well below 3 per cent.

Table 1.17: Real Returns to Local Investors in:

USA
Comparative Real Returns on Equities and bonds, % pa

	Bonds	Equities	Inflation
1802–1992	3.4	6.7	1.3
1802–1870	4.8	7.0	0.1
1871–1925	3.7	6.6	0.6
1926–1992	1.7	6.6	3.1

Source: 'Stocks for the Long Run', by Jeremy J. Siegel (thanks to Smithers & Co)

	Stocks	UK Bonds	Cash
1986–94	9.0	5.9	5.4
1976–94	10.1	5.5	3.3
1966–94	6.5	1.6	1.7
1956–94	6.7	0.9	1.7
1946–94	6.4	(0.4)	0.7

Source: BZW

	The Netherlands		Germany	
	Equities	Bonds	Equities	Bonds
1987–91	12.6	2.3	0.1	2.5
1977–91	12.0	4.1	5.9	3.9
1967–91	6.8	2.1	4.8	3.6
1957–91	5.4	1.4	5.7	3.6
1947–91	6.1	0.5	N/A	N/A

Source: BZW

If your local equity market does offer the prospect of 6 per cent real returns you may decide to look no further. The experience of US, UK and Dutch investors tends to confirm that a strong (Dutch) or weak (British) local currency is of no particular consequence to a local investor.

So why do we at Gartmore, and other managers of pension money, invest clients' funds in other assets? For a start, clients have a lower risk tolerance than our hypothetical investor. Most trustees wish to protect capital from the shorter run fluctuations which are an inevitable risk of a 100 per cent local equity allocation.

Table 1.16 illustrates the big dipper of equity returns. In the four years following 1972, returns from UK equities were a negative 18.2 per cent in real terms annually! Our passive 100 per cent local equity investor would have stuck to his guns and profited from this panic with his dividend income being reinvested at cheap prices. If he had been investing since 1949, his real annual return after 25 years would have been 8.6 per cent at the end of 1971. By the end of 1974 it would have declined to 2.4 per cent. But by the mid 1980s it would have recovered to 7.0 per cent.

A pension fund trustee or life insurance office might look at a wobble such as occurred between 1972 and 1975 with less equanimity. The trustee may need to make annual cash contributions which may well increase when rates of return have been below expectation, and so is keener to diversify investment in order to reduce the fluctuations in real value.

So how to diversify? Using cash is dangerous. Even a relatively small cash position as 'insurance' can prove to be ballast. A basic rate taxpayer in the UK would have subtracted nearly 0.6 per cent, or 15 per cent of his total portfolio's real return from equities, by keeping 10 per cent of it in the building society. Over long periods, Tables 1.16 and 1.17 show cash has persistently produced real returns much inferior to equities, despite the odd year of spectacular outperformance. The problem is that it is difficult to anticipate those periods of outperformance and even harder to invest your cash in equities after a fall.

Investing overseas is more sensible. Of course, if you decided in your planning that liabilities in other currencies needed to be met in your objectives, you will want to integrate them into your asset allocation. So, for example, if Singapore dollars represent 25 per cent of your future liabilities and planned wealth objective, then a 75 per cent UK equity/25 per cent Singapore equity portfolio may be a sensible allocation for a UK resident.

As you can see from Table 1.18, a US investor would have benefited with higher returns from overseas diversification in 1970. A UK investor however would only have received the benefit of diversification smoothing the fluctuations in his portfolio's value: despite a chronically weak sterling, UK equities outperformed most other equity markets and the combined MSCI World Index in terms of one currency.

Table 1.18: MSCI Stock Market Indices in US dollar terms (Jan 1970 to April 1995)

Hong Kong	4115.9	France	681.5
Japan	3216.6	UK	649.3
Singapore	2547.4	**The World**	**647.1**
Switzerland	1243.1	USA	475.4
Netherlands	1046.2	Canada	360.6
Germany	752.4	Australia	280.1
	Italy	189.4	

Source: Morgan Stanley Capital International
(1 Jan 1970 Base = 100)

It simply isn't possible to predict with any degree of certainty whether investors will reap enhanced returns from overseas investment in the next 25 years. A lot depends not only on the future direction of the local currency, but also on the course of other overseas equity markets and the choice of overseas equities. A very big decline in the US dollar's value in terms of the yen has failed to offset the effects of a deep bear market in Japanese equities since 1990. More subtly, US equities have consistently outperformed many other equity markets in dollar terms despite a weak dollar since 1988, so even if your judgement of a currency's value is proved correct, the consequences of deciding to allocate your portfolio to equity markets in accordance with that view may not produce the results you were looking for.

Overseas equities as a class were the best asset for a UK investor to own in 43 per cent of calendar year periods between 1974 and 1994. If it is possible to buy an 'index' of international equities, then the investor should certainly consider this as a relatively effortless means of diversification. It may or may not be a better performing asset class over the longer run, but it certainly smoothes out the ride from a local equity market held in isolation. If an overseas equity index approach doesn't appeal or is impractical, active selection of overseas equities might. It is important here to select markets which are rationally priced to enjoy superior returns from superior economic growth. Ideally, you are looking for equity markets which promise higher returns and a low correlation with your local market.

Overseas equities as a class were the best asset for a UK investor to own in 43 per cent of calendar year periods between 1974 and 1994.

From Table 1.19 we can see that the 18 per cent annual return in £ sterling terms over the five years to December 1994 has been compensation for the 7.2 per cent monthly volatility of the IFC Composite Emerging Markets Index. Additionally, a relatively low 0.57 correlation with the UK Equity market helped smooth fluctuations in a UK investor's global portfolio value.

Table 1.19: International Equity Markets for a UK based Investor 1984–94

Category	% Total Annual Returns in £ Terms				Monthly Volatility in £ Terms over		Correlation with UK Equities over	
	3 Yrs	5 Yrs	7 Yrs	10 Yrs	5 Yrs	10 Yrs	5 Yrs	10 Yrs
UK	13.4	9.7	13.4	14.8	4.7	5.3	1.00	1.00
Europe ex UK	17.0	6.7	15.0	16.3	4.7	5.2	0.74	0.62
Pacific ex Japan	25.7	16.0	20.6	15.3	6.5	7.5	0.66	0.64
Emerging Markets (IFC)	24.9	18.0	N/A	N/A	7.2	N/A	0.57	N/A

Sources: Datastream/Gartmore

International diversification is probably a good idea notwithstanding the risks. A local investor can never know for certain whether the experience of a US-based investor between 1970 and 1995 will be repeated. If the dollar was overvalued in 1970, so might the D-mark or the yen be overvalued now. Perhaps UK equity investors have not suffered from the undignified decline of an overvalued pound because the UK economy was more 'open' and the UK stock market contained a good number of companies with strong international operations. If this accounts for the difference between the US and UK experience, then Japanese investors may have a particular reason to look overseas, given their country's relatively 'closed' economy and the relatively puny overseas earnings of their corporate sector.

An active approach to asset allocation could theoretically have paid off handsomely. At Gartmore, our UK Pension Fund Management has pursued a relatively aggressive policy of active asset allocation. The benefit over a

12-year period has been calculated to average out at 1.0 per cent per annum, in a range over rolling three-year periods of 0.5 per cent to 1.6 per cent. In other words, a Gartmore managed fund enjoyed a 1.0 per cent higher return than the average UK Pension Fund monitored by the WM Company. To put this into context, this 1.0 per cent is a return in excess of total annual fund returns in the order of 14 per cent (in nominal, not real terms).

A simple 100 per cent local equity market allocation is by no means as risky or as unimaginative as it might look, provided that the valuation at the time of investment is rational. A two-thirds local one-third international approach also makes a lot of sense and can be adhered to for investors willing to accept more risk of falling short of acceptable local returns for the prospect of lower interim portfolio volatility and potentially superior long-term returns.

If you decide to take an active approach to your asset allocation, set yourself fixed ranges outside which you will not be tempted to stray. For example, a minimum of 50 per cent in UK equities, a maximum 20 per cent in non-equity assets or a maximum time limit of 18 months below 90 per cent in equities. The use of cash and bonds is not advisable as asset categories for long-term investors in search of real wealth maximization. Another glance at Tables 1.16 and 1.17 should be enough to convince investors that very astute timing would have been needed to take advantage of the short periods of superior returns from gilts and cash. The considerable taxation implications of a policy of switching are also daunting for the taxpaying investor. A properly implemented fixed asset allocation policy stands as good a chance as an imperfectly managed active asset allocation approach of producing a satisfactory return.

MEASURING PERFORMANCE

Dan Macfie

Dan Macfie has wide-ranging experience of performance analysis, both as a consultant and over 30 years spent in research and commercial roles in industry, most recently as technical director of the chemicals Division of Alcan ranked equal top in the aluminium world. He has specialized in identifying and measuring critical performance criteria and forecasting and monitoring returns on capital investment. He is the author of **The Investor's Guide to Measuring Share Performance** ***published by Pitman/Financial Times in May 1994. With the book is a floppy disk containing spreadsheets with examples of the calculations.***

Investors need to know how their investments have performed in the past, in order to improve their performance in the future. Performance should be measured and compared with appropriate standards, to determine whether it has been satisfactory. Just as scientists use hypotheses to make predictions, so investors use investment policies to guide purchase or selling decisions.

Many books have been written recommending a wide variety of policies to private investors. They range from the simplest, such as the sale of shares whose price has fallen by more than 10 per cent in four days or less, to more complicated formulae, requiring a detailed analysis of the company accounts and the share price, yield and P/E ratio over the last ten years. Often investors take short-cuts, by combining a limited amount of technical analysis with a review of the financial press. Some investors will delegate one level of decision making by investing only in investment and unit trusts, while others will use delegation to its maximum by employing someone to manage their portfolio. Such delegation, if anything, increases the need to monitor performance.

Unfortunately, investment strategies recommended to private investors, in contrast to scientific hypotheses, are not generally tested to validate their effectiveness. In other words, they are unproven. It is recommended that investors should assess the effectiveness of the investment policy they use, by measuring their own investment performance. A quantified assessment of the performance of each of the investor's separate holdings and the overall portfolio is required. The performance is derived from share price movements and dividends, but is only useful if this information is analysed in depth. The mistake should not be made, by the way, of regarding the performance of the company as being parallel to that of the investor's share holding.

The full benefit of calculating performance criteria is only realized if they are compared with appropriate benchmarks and targets. Investors will only buy a share if they think it is going to do better than average. This attitude is quantified in the UK by choosing the FT-SE-A All-Share Index as the target for equity investments. The performance of a share can be better understood by comparing it with that of the relevant sector, but sector performance is not an appropriate target.

An investor would not consider a share a good investment if it seriously under-performed the All Share Index, even though it was above average in its sector.

An investor would not consider a share a good investment if it seriously under-performed the All Share Index, even though it was above average in its sector. The three-month inter-bank interest has been chosen as representative of deposit rates.

Techniques for measuring performance can be used equally well in any country, the only change required being the choice of standards. Americans might use the Dow Jones Industrial Average or S&P 500 in place of the FT All Share Index, and Germans the Dax. Comparison of the performance criteria for investments in different countries are broadly valid, since they are expressed in real terms.

The performance criteria chosen for calculation range from the most empirical, the P/A ratio for individual shares, to the most fundamental, the real return on the capital invested in the portfolio.

Individual Shares – Short-term Performance

When the price of a share moves in line with most other shares on the market, even though the absolute price level might move up or down, the relationship of the price (P) to the All Share Index (A) will remain the same. The P/A ratio will be constant. On the other hand, if the price of a particular share falls at a time when the market as a whole is stable or prices are rising, the investor should certainly consider selling. For share price movement to be meaningful the price of the share divided by the All Share Index, i.e. the P/A ratio, should be monitored instead of the price itself.

The term 'relative strength' has been used by some authors for the ratio of the price to the All Share Index, but others have defined it as the ratio of the current price to the average price over some specified period of time. The term P/A ratio has been chosen because it is specific and self-explanatory.

Chart 1.21 Share price rebased to 1.0 CH 28 Jan 1994

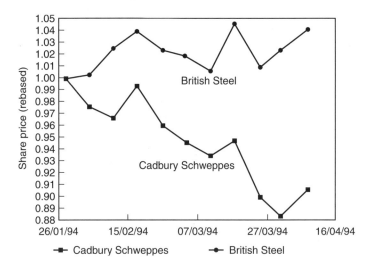

An example, based on the share prices of Cadbury Schweppes and British Steel, will make this clear. Chart 1.21 shows the price trends of the two shares. Conventional wisdom would indicate that Cadbury Schweppes was showing signs of weakness, and should have been considered for sale, while British Steel was maintaining its position and should have been held. The P/A ratios (see Chart 1.22) present a different and more meaningful picture. They indicate that Cadbury Schweppes tracked the All Share Index, whereas the British Steel shares performed significantly better. Consideration should therefore have been given to purchasing British Steel and holding Cadbury Schweppes. The P/A ratios nine months later, at the end of 1994 and before the Cadbury Schweppes rights issue, were 1.26 for British Steel and 0.93 for

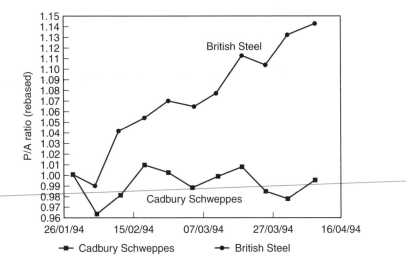

Chart 1.22 P/A ratio rebased to 1.0 CH 28 Jan 1994

Cadbury Schweppes. (This analysis leads to the conclusion that the techniques of Chartism could be improved by charting the P/A ratio instead of the price.)

Individual Shares – Medium and Long-term Performance

All the criteria used to measure performance have to be expressed in real terms after correction for inflation. This is essential, particularly when comparisons are being made between equities and fixed interest investments. An increase in the rate of interest on a deposit account from 6 per cent to 12 per cent might seem advantageous to the investor, until account is taken of the fact that the rate of inflation increased from 2 per cent to 10 per cent over the same period of time. The real rate of return has halved, even though the apparent rate has doubled.

The performance of an individual share can be assessed by measuring the real growth rate of the price and the yield, in aggregate the real rate of return, and comparing the figures with appropriate targets. The relevant criteria for a selected list of privatization shares are shown in Table 1.20.

The target figures show the real rates of return that would have been achieved if the shares had tracked the All Share Index. The actual real returns take into account the bonus shares received in British Airways, Anglian Water and Scottish Power. Comparing the actual and target real returns, it is seen that these shares have performed significantly better than the All Share Index, in contrast to British Steel.

111

Table 1.20

Company	Purchase Date	%Real Return pa to 5 April 95 Actual	Target
British Airways	Feb 1987	15.2	5.6
British Steel	Nov 1988	3.7	8.1
Anglian Water	Dec 1989	14.9	5.9
Scottish Power	June 1991	11.7	8.6

The figures are calculated with dividends or interest net of tax, as received by the private investor The calculations are easily adjusted to allow for tax at a rate appropriate to the owner of the portfolio.

Performance figures can be calculated over a range of time-periods so that any trends can be identified. Chart 1.23 shows the 13-year performance of Marks & Spencer to 5 April 1995. The chart also shows the real return that would have been obtained by investing in a bank savings account. An investment in the shares from 31 March 1982, the base date for the calculation of capital gain tax to 5 April 1995 would have given a satisfactory real return of 11 per cent per annum. The performance of the shares matched the target over the first five and the last two years and improved on it over the middle years. The real return from the shares was well in excess of the savings account, which was 3 per cent over most of the period, falling to 2 per cent over the last two years.

Chart 1.23 % Real Return per annum to 5 April 1995

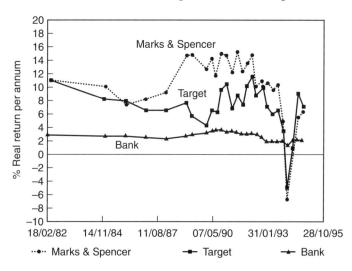

Portfolio Performance

The ultimate test of an investor's ability is the performance of the whole portfolio. The chosen criteria for assessing performance are the same as those for individual shares. The simplest approach is to average the chosen criteria for the individual investments. To be valid, however, the performance of the portfolio must be calculated to give more weight to the performance of larger holdings. The calculation must also take account of the timing of purchases and disposals.

Most investors will want to know the performance of the different types of asset contained in the portfolio as well as the performance of the whole portfolio. Appropriate categories could be ordinary shares, investment trusts, unit trusts, PEPs, fixed interest stocks and deposit accounts. The methodology of the performance calculations are identical, whatever the category.

The performance of an equity portfolio can be expressed as follows: 'the real returns per annum over the past four, three, two and one year (s) were 12 per cent, 11 per cent, 5 per cent and –10 per cent, compared with targets of 10 per cent, 8 per cent, 6 per cent and –9 per cent respectively. Over the same periods a savings account would have shown a real return of 3 per cent, falling to 2 per cent per annum'.

PART 2

BUILDING BLOCKS OF SUCCESSFUL INVESTING

Interpreting Investment Indicators

Market Related Indicators

Market Valuation Indicators
Earnings Estimates
Technical Gauges
Initial Public Offerings
Liquidity
Futures Indexes as Equity Benchmarks
The Importance of the TED Spread

MARKET VALUATION INDICATORS

Anthony Mulliner

*Anthony Mulliner is an Equity Strategist with **Cazenove & Co.**, which he joined in 1990. Prior to this he had been head of Equity sales with **Scrimgeour Vickers** and, in all, has 15 years experience of equity sales.*

***Cazenove & Co.** is a member of the London Stock Exchange, and the only major stock broking firm to have remained an independent partnership. **Cazenove** is the UK's leading corporate broker, acting for over 330 UK and Irish companies, as well as some 120 overseas companies. In addition, there are five other areas of business: institutional broking, syndication, international, fund management and money broking. The firm employs 870 people in 11 financial centres worldwide.*

Introduction

When a share is purchased, the owner acquires the right to all the future income streams, represented by dividends. In order to put a valuation on those future income streams, they are discounted back to the present day at a suitable discount rate, normally taken to be the long-term interest rate. Therefore, critical to any valuation of a share is its potential earning stream, from which dividends can be declared, and the relevant long-term interest rate used to put the appropriate current value on those streams.

Investors able to forecast more accurately than the consensus hope to achieve superior returns. The most common approach involves calculating the price-earnings ratio by dividing the share price by current earnings per share, and comparing and contrasting with other shares. More recently, with the debate over what are the correct earnings for a company, investment analysts have focused on cash flow per share as a more consistent and universal comparison. Other indicators compare equity valuations with other financial assets, especially with the bond market. This is particularly appropriate in the UK equity market, where institutional investors manage 'balanced funds', a combination of equity, bond, property and cash assets. These indicators highlight not only absolute valuations, but also relative valuations across asset classes.

Price-earnings ratio

This is the most commonly used indicator employed by investors to assess value. Investors calculate price-earnings ratios for a number of years and then attempt to forecast at least two years into the future. Depending on a number of factors, including growth rate, type and cyclicality of business, financial strength, competitive position of the industry, future prospects, management and comparison to similar companies, investors can decide whether the calcu-

Chart 2.1 FT-SE Total Non-Financial PER

Source: Datastream

lated price-earnings ratio is appropriate. By necessity, these assessments are very subjective and lead a number of commentators to question the viability of this approach.

Most investors take a short cut by assuming that the market is far more efficient in putting the appropriate weightings on the various influences on a company's price-earnings ratio. Instead they look for discrepancies between similar companies and they look for divergence away from long-term averages. The obvious opportunity is to sell when price-earnings ratios are relatively high and buy when they are low. A number of studies have shown that a low price-earnings ratio increases the prospects of a good return from equities. As Chart 2.1 illustrates, the price-earnings ratio of the UK equity market has moved between a low of 4 in 1975 and a high of 23 in 1972. At the very least, as the market approaches either of these levels, interesting investment opportunities are suggested.

A number of studies have shown that a low price-earnings ratio increases the prospects of a good return from equities.

Dividend yield

The second most common valuation approach involves measuring the dividend yield of an equity or of the market. The dividend yield is calculated by dividing the gross dividend per share by the share price. This should be more relevant to an investor because, while earnings influence dividends, it is only dividends that investors actually receive. Like the price-earnings ratio, the dividend yield of a share or the market is viewed in the context of similar shares and in relation to its trading range. Buying when yields are high and selling when they are low would appear to be appropriate policy over the long-term.

Dividend yield ratio

A more useful indicator used by investors involves comparing equity market yields to bond market yields. This relationship hints at the competitive impact of interest rates. Bond yields are used as the effective long-term interest rate. When bond yields are high, the economic environment for equities is hostile. With high interest rates, saving becomes more attractive than spending. The cost of capital for companies increases, shrinking the potential return from any project. As a result the risk of investing in equities increases, making bond yields more attractive. Once again, this indicator is used relative to its trading range.

Chart 2.2 FT-SE Total Non-Financial Dividend Yield

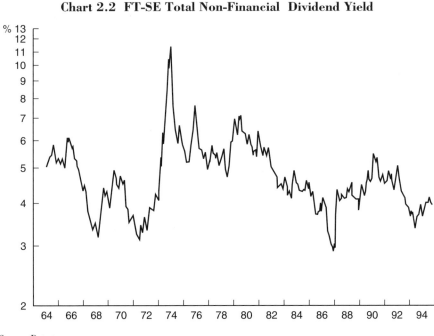

Source: Datastream

A word of caution is required in interpreting this indicator. Inflation can distort the relationship of equities to bonds. Equities have proved, over time, to be a far better preserver of value during times of inflation. As a result, investors have expected to receive a significantly higher yield for investing in bonds during periods of inflation to cover the risk of losing real purchasing power. During most of the 1980s, bonds have yielded over twice the yield of equities. Whenever this ratio has approached the bottom of its trading range, commentators have argued that equities were cheap in relation to bonds. However, as governments accept the desirability of low, controlled inflation, the dividend yield ratio is being reassessed.

Why should bonds have to yield such a premium over equities if inflation is not the problem it has been in the past? Therefore, there is an argument for adjusting the trading range of the dividend yield ratio to levels approaching parity, last seen in the 1960s when inflation was subdued.

Equity yield premium to index-linked yield

Since the introduction of index-linked bonds the relationship of equity yields to the yield on index-linked bonds has received a lot of attention. Index-linked bonds are a promise by the issuer (the Treasury) to offer a guaranteed real return. The historical performance of equities suggests that they offer a real

122

Chart 2.3 UK 20 year/FTA500 I

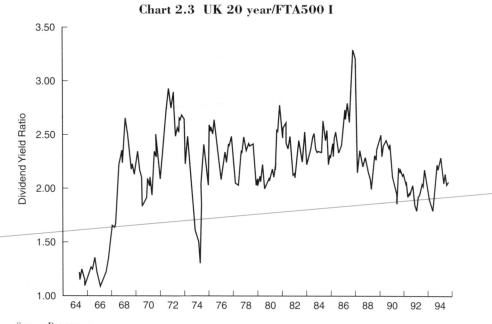

Source: Datastream

Chart 2.4 Equity Yields vs Index Linked Bond Yields

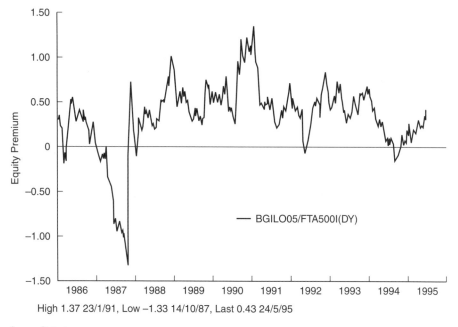

High 1.37 23/1/91, Low −1.33 14/10/87, Last 0.43 24/5/95

Source: Datastream

123

return over time. Given this similar characteristic, with an appropriate premium for the greater risk inherent in equities, the relationship is watched for wide divergence from the long-term average of 0.5 per cent. At the beginning of the economic cycle, investors will have great expectations for earnings growth, and therefore for dividend prospects, hence the ratio will tend to show little or no premium. As the cycle progresses the traditional yield premium of equities over index-linked bonds should be rebuilt. The size of the premium will dictate the relative attraction of equities, in terms of risk, to index-linked bonds.

Earnings/yield ratio

Most investors look at price/earnings alone. However, increasingly a comparison is made to bonds. It is argued that comparing equity dividend yields to bond yields is unfair, as it ignores the impact of retained earnings in growing the company which, in turn, influences future dividend streams. The earnings yield, which is the reciprocal of the price/earnings ratio, is used to judge whether equities or bonds are attractive relative to one another, in a similar manner to straight dividend yields.

Price to cash flow

With the recent debate over what actually constitutes a company's earnings and the numerous ways of computing earnings per share (actual, normalized or FRS3), investors have sought other means to produce a normalized number with which to carry out comparative analysis. Cash flow analysis is the life blood of any business and the currently accepted definition, derived from the US, is EBITDA: earnings before interest, tax, depreciation and amortization. It produces a number which makes comparisons more meaningful and in particular, in ignoring taxation, makes international comparison more meaningful. This measure of valuation has greater influence in the US than in the UK. However, with the continued diversification by US investors overseas it is expected to take on greater significance. Again, like all the other ratios discussed, comparisons are usually made within sectors and with similar companies to draw profitable conclusions.

Market to book value

This indicator compares the value of the assets of the business to the current value of the company, as measured by the share price. The indicator has limited use in the UK, being primarily reserved for the net asset values of the property sector. Investors are looking for significant discounts to book value to indicate value or significant premiums to indicate overvaluation. This indicator's greatest support comes from corporate finance departments, where it is used heavily in valuations during corporate activity. As a result, its popularity tends to increase during these times. Market to book value, though, has numerous critics who question its value, particularly as a result of the recession, when companies recorded huge write-offs and, coupled with several accounting changes, severely reduced book values, so making comparisons between companies and sectors extremely difficult.

Summary

All these indicators are attempts to answer the question of equity market valuation. Individually, they have limited use, as they address only one facet of equity valuation. Taken together, particularly where they confirm a message about valuation, these indicators have use. However, they should form part of a comprehensive analysis of a market's fundamentals, including the attractions of international equities and other asset classes. Markets are dynamic, changing their emphasis on what is considered important in valuation. Investors should also not underestimate the impact of accounting and taxation changes in assessing these ratios in relation to historic trading ranges, as highlighted by the historic relationship between equity and bond yields. ●

EARNINGS ESTIMATES

Justin Willey

*Justin Willey trained with stockbrokers **Bell Lawrie White** as a private client Investment Advisor and later as an Investment Analyst. In 1991 he joined **Edinburgh Financial Publishing** to start* The Estimate Directory, *a digest of stockbrokers' forecasts and recommendations.* The Estimate Directory *now covers many thousands of companies in Europe, Asia-Pacific, Latin America and elsewhere, and has a world-wide readership.*

What do Equity Market Analysts do, and why do they do it?

Before using any information in investment decisions it is important to consider its source and the motivation of those providing it. In the most part research is provided by stockbrokers to fund managers as a service to encourage the fund manager to use them. The stockbroker is not paid directly for the research but receives commission on the share transactions (if acting as agent) or may make money on the transaction itself (if acting as principal or market maker). It is clearly in the interests of stockbrokers to encourage clients to deal with them more frequently, however, any analyst who compromised the quality of research in order to do so would be unlikely to command respect for long. In some markets, particularly the US, a number of stockbrokers charge directly for their research and make a point of emphasizing their independence, however, the practice is rare in the UK.

Within the research department of the stockbroking firm individual analysts will specialize in particular market sectors, such as banks, chemicals, food manufacturing, and so forth. They are likely to have studied their particular sector for a number of years and know the companies and personalities in their industry well. Despite Nigel Lawson's 'teenage scribblers' jibe, a recent survey of company finance directors in the UK showed that 58 per cent of them believed that most analysts understood their companies 'extremely well' or 'very well'. Of the same group, only 4 per cent believed that financial journalists had the same level of understanding. (Source: Annual Broker Survey 1994/ Consensus Research International.)

a recent survey of company finance directors in the UK showed that 58 per cent of them believed that most analysts understood their companies 'extremely well' or 'very well'.

This level of knowledge is built up from the study and analysis of published financial statements, visits to companies, discussion with board members and senior employees, study of industry trends and, in many cases, personal experience of working within the industry.

The result of all this effort, and very considerable expense, is published in a variety of ways. These include individual discussions with and presentations to institutional clients, short or in-depth studies on individual companies (with detailed financial forecasts of profit and loss accounts and balance sheets), detailed surveys of whole industries, summaries of forecasts and recommendations for a whole market.

How can the individual investor benefit from analysts' forecasts?

There is an important difference to be grasped when considering the uses of brokers' estimates. This is the difference between what a forecast tells one about the prospects for a company in comparison with its industrial sector or the market as a whole, and the very short term effect of the forecasts or recommendations themselves on share prices.

Important changes of opinion by widely respected analysts can have an immediate effect on share prices. An example occurred in April 1995 when several analysts voiced concern over the future performance of Cable & Wireless's subsidiary, Mercury. At the same time they came to the conclusion that fears over future pressure on call prices in the mobile telephone market were exaggerated. As a result they recommended their clients to switch holdings from Cable & Wireless into British Telecom and Vodafone (both companies with substantial mobile phone interests). These recommendations came out on 20 April and the effect on the company's share price can clearly be seen below.

Chart 2.5 Share Price Movement

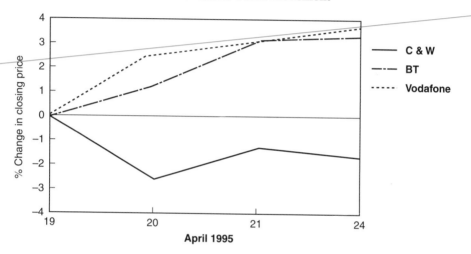

It is difficult for private individuals to take advantage of this kind of information as the effects are felt in the market very quickly and the investor is unlikely to be aware of the information until most of the share price movement has happened.

The real area of interest to the individual investor is what forecasts tell one about the longer-term outlook for companies. When considering a company, one must remember to look not only at past and expected future performance but also to what extent the share price already reflects those factors. In this area, analysts' forecasts can help tremendously. The price-earnings ratio (PE) and earnings per share (EPS) growth are well established measures in investment analysis. They are particularly helpful if calculated from forecast figures (e.g. prospective PE) as they give an informed guide to future share price performance, which is, after all, what actually matters. Individual indicators alone can be misleading. For example, a company may have a low PE (based on the reported EPS) not because the shares are cheap, but because the share price has fallen in anticipation of poor results. Similarly a company may have excellent forecast earnings growth compared with others in its sector, but a high forecast PE compared with other similar companies, which shows that any expected good news is already in the price.

Dividend forecasts are also useful information. First, as an aid to choosing shares with the aim of obtaining a certain level of income, or obtaining income growth. Second, as a measure of an analyst's view of the long term optimism of the company's management. Companies are unlikely to increase dividends if they do not believe that they will be able to maintain the higher payout level.

Analysts' estimates are available to investors in a number of forms. Publications such as *The Estimate Directory* provide comparative forecasts from different analysts (sometimes as many as twenty or thirty) for each company. The spread of forecasts in itself is quite instructive. If the forecasts and recommendations are similar, one will gain confidence in the accuracy of the forecasts, but it is more likely, in these circumstances, that the share price already values the company fairly. If however there are widely differing opinions, there is more uncertainty, but perhaps greater investment opportunity. For example, in a certain company where all analysts may be forecasting dividend increases, even if the estimated amount of the increase varies, this is a positive sign. If, however, half of the analysts forecast an unchanged dividend while the other half forecast dividend cuts, one can be sure that there is some uncertainty about the company's ability to maintain dividend payments. Publications also frequently include forecasts for whole sectors and countries derived from individual company forecasts which makes the task of comparing one company with its sector or market much easier.

Some other publications, rather than giving a breakdown of the individual analyst's forecast for a particular company, give a consensus of those forecasts. This is useful for seeing an overall picture of the expected trends for a particular company, but does not give any indication of how much spread of opinion lies behind the consensus.

Here, in summary, and no particular order of importance, are some guidelines for making use of analysts' forecasts:

- Do remember that it is not forecasts themselves that move share prices, but the market's reaction to forecasts and published results.
- Do try to establish to what extent the forecasts are already reflected in the share price. Use PE in conjunction with EPS growth and dividend yield in conjunction with dividend growth.
- Do look at forecasts for individual companies in the context of forecasts for their competitors and their industry sector as well as for the market as a whole.
- Do consider the spread of forecasts and the level of uncertainty in the market that such a spread represents.
- Do remember that analysts' forecasts can be wrong and market conditions can change.
- Don't look at individual indicators in isolation. Consider the relationship between them.
- Don't forget the value of common sense in using forecasts, as in all aspects of investment. ✎

TECHNICAL GAUGES

James B. Stack

James B. Stack is President of Stack Financial Management, and Editor of the InvesTech Market Analyst and the InvesTech Mutual Fund Advisor. Formerly a Project Manager for IBM Research, he holds a number of domestic and international patents. Jim was one of only a handful of advisors credited by the media as having warned subscribers to exit the market before Black Monday. He foresaw this recent bull market with the famous 'Toro Toro' issue, published ten days before the January 1991 blast off.

InvesTech presents a unique blending of monetary and technical analysis leading to specific stock and mutual fund recommendations. InvesTech's mutual fund portfolio has outperformed the Wilshire 5000 Index by 39 per cent over the past eight years, and has earned Hulbert's number one rating for risk-adjusted return during that period.

While global stock exchanges have existed for centuries, 'technical analysis' as a tool for the average investor has thrived over a much shorter period. It was around the turn of the century when Charles H. Dow proposed a theory (the '*Dow Theory*') which recognized that once established, a market trend tends to continue; and that confirmation by multiple indexes was a logical first step to identifying that trend.

Particularly since the 1960s, the technical approach to market analysis has been greatly expanded in both scope and credibility. The technical tools available for today's investor or analyst are limited only by innovation and historical data. Such indicators and tools include moving averages, trend lines, relative strength, and numerous other gauges which measure momentum, valuation, sentiment, leadership, breadth (participation), or monetary policy.

Yet for the most part, such indicators are not used to 'forecast' stock prices as much as identify the major market trend and measure risk. In other words, it could be said that the true objective of technical analysis is to determine whether or not the ingredients of a healthy bull market are present – and to watch out for possible warning flags before a major decline or bear strikes.

Moving averages (momentum)

Day-to-day gyrations in stock market indexes often mask the overall trend. And many an investor has been whipsawed or fooled into making the wrong decision by a one- or two-day stampede in the stock market. A moving average is one method to help smooth out the daily bounces to reveal the longer-term trend.

Chart 2.6 S&P 500 Index

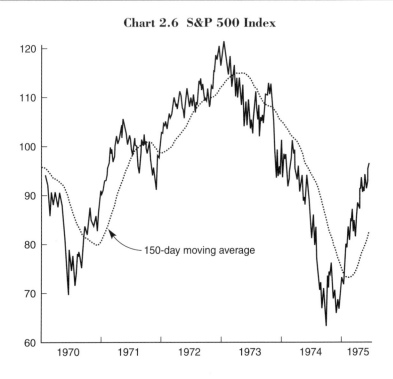

The most popular moving averages are the 39-week, 200-day, and 150-day averages. Constructed by averaging many days or weeks of a market index's closing value, a moving average is usually plotted or graphed along with the underlying index. For example, the 150-day moving average for the S&P 500 Index is calculated by adding the past 150 days of closing prices for the S&P 500 Index together, then dividing the result by 150.

If the market index is above the long-term moving average, it can generally be concluded that the stock market is in an uptrend. Conversely, a market index below its moving average is usually destined to fall further.

The value to one's portfolio can be explained by a simple example. Suppose that as an investor, you decided to stay fully invested only when the S&P 500 Index was above its 150-day moving average – confirming the stock market was in a general uptrend. In this case, whenever the S&P 500 Index dipped below its 150-day moving average, you would move your portfolio to the safety of T-bills or a money market fund. How might your portfolio have performed when compared to someone who remained fully invested all the time?

Based on the S&P 500 Index, such a strategy would have virtually doubled an investor's return over the past 40 years. A $10,000 investment, instead of growing to $562,058 with a buy-and-hold strategy, could be worth $1,060,613 using this simple timing technique. Of course, to avoid the commissions and tax consequences of more frequent trading, an investor would have to use a no-load 'index fund' in a tax-deferred retirement account.

Of greater importance, is the 'safety' that this simple moving average introduces to portfolio management. An investor using a buy-and-hold strategy over that 40-year period would have suffered a 20 per cent loss in seven different bear markets (*with two of those losses exceeding 35 per cent!*). In contrast, using that 150-day moving average to know when to sit safely on the sidelines, you would have avoided every one of those losses. Your worst loss would have been 15 per cent on just one occasion.

So a moving average can prove to be a valuable tool in 'managing risk' as well as improving profits in one's portfolio.

Leadership

Of course, it only seems logical that a strong, advancing bull market should see almost all stock market averages moving higher. That requires a large number of industry sectors and individual stocks to take part. For that to occur, there generally must be broad participation (breadth), as well as good leadership. Yet leadership has typically been one of the more difficult bull market attributes to measure.

One such gauge of leadership looks at the number of stocks hitting new yearly highs (and the number hitting new yearly lows) reported in most daily financial newspapers. A healthy, long-term bull market should see an increasing number of stocks hitting new highs during subsequent rallies that carry the major indexes to new highs. If not, a divergence is developing. In that case, leadership is narrowing which could be a precursor to a market correction or something worse – a bear market.

Just as the number of stocks hitting new yearly highs or 'upside leadership' can be used to confirm a bull market, it's highly unusual to see a major bear market strike without first developing strong 'downside leadership'. This is available in the daily number of stocks hitting new yearly lows. An aging bull market will often see an increasing number of stocks hitting new yearly lows even as market averages manage to bounce to new highs. That's a sign to build up cash and prepare for at least a 5-to-10 per cent correction. And as a general guideline on the New York Stock Exchange, by the time you see over 50 stocks hitting new yearly lows every day for more than a week, odds have risen dramatically that trouble and a probable bear market lie just around the corner.

Breadth

As mentioned earlier, a solid bull market is one in which many stocks, industries, and indexes are taking part. But as a bull market matures, investors

131

start to become more nervous and more selective. Fewer stocks take part in market advances. And there's a general decay in participation. The market develops a case of *bad breadth* (sic).

Although sophisticated models exist for tracking breadth, one of the oldest and most reliable gauges is the traditional Advance-Decline Line. It is calculated each day, by subtracting the total number of stocks which closed lower from the total number of stocks closing higher. That day's net calculation is added to the previous summation – and so on. Because the Advance-Decline Line's trend is more important than the absolute value or number, this calculation may be started at any point in time:

Chart 2.7 Advance-Decline Line and DJ1A (1985–7)

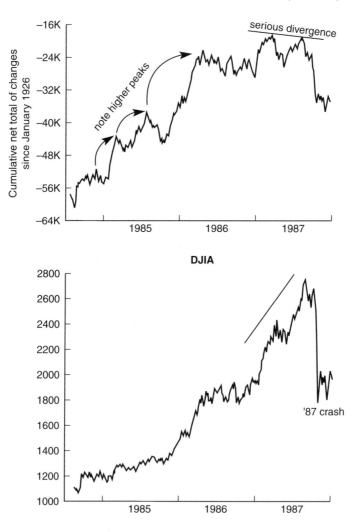

Advance-Decline Line = [Advancing Issues – Declining Issues] + previous value

The merit of the Advance-Decline Line lies in warning of market 'tops' or periods of high risk. It does this through a series of nonconfirmations or divergences. For example, when overlaid on the graph of a major stock market index (i.e. S&P 500 Index), the A-D Line will usually hit new 3, 6, or 12-month highs at the same time as the market index. However, danger lurks when the stock market continues to frolic at new highs, but at the same time this A-D Line is lagging far behind or in a downtrend.

For example, look at the big bull market of the mid-1980s shown in Chart 2.7.

You'll see the Advance-Decline Line moved upward with each subsequent peak higher than the last. However by the summer of 1987, the A-D Line was diverging as it failed to hit new highs when the Dow Jones Industrial Average was hitting new highs. This was a classic technical warning flag that appeared prior to the 1987 crash.

Similarly, in the more recent 1990 bear market (Chart 2.8), you'll notice that breadth measured by the Advance-Decline Line was deteriorating for almost a year before the market's final peak in July of 1990.

Chart 2.8 Advance-Decline Line and DJ1A (1989–90)

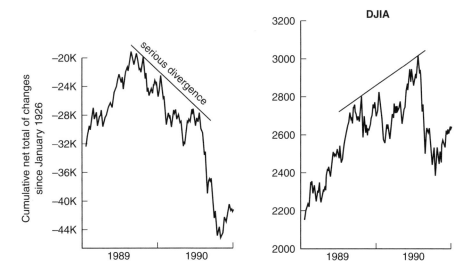

133

Like many technical tools, 'breadth' also has an inherent weakness. Historically, the Advance-Decline Line has usually provided little or no early warning of market bottoms. In other words, it often bottoms at the same time as major market indexes. As such, extra care should be taken to limit its use in anticipating the end of a bear market.

The gauges described here are but a few of those commonly used in technical analysis. With such esoteric names as 'On-Balance Volume', 'Speed-Resistance Lines', 'Stochastics', and 'McClellan Oscillator', many other technical indicators are beyond the scope of this discussion. Yet knowing about, and understanding even several of the more basic tools can often help the average investor make better decisions and reduce portfolio risk. ♀

INITIAL PUBLIC OFFERINGS

Claudia E. Mott

*Claudia Mott is a .First Vice President of **Prudential Securities Inc** and Director of Small-Cap Research. Ms Mott joined **Prudential Securities** in 1986 and provides investors with quantitative research in the form of stock valuation and topical studies. She was voted to* Institutional Investor *magazine's annual research all-star team in 1991, 1992, 1993 and 1994, ranking first in the small company category for the past two years. Ms Mott's research has been published in* The Journal of Portfolio Management *and* The Journal of Investing, *as well as in* The Wall Street Journal.

The initial public offering (IPO) market is one of the more popular areas for investors looking to invest in small cap stocks. However, analysis of the performance of IPOs issued over the past three years indicates that this is a very difficult area in which to make money. In addition, many of the major peaks in the small-cap market have occurred when the IPO market is at its hottest.

It **Pays To Buy At The Offer Price**. Analyzing the performance of more than 1,500 initial public offerings (IPOs) that came to market in the US in 1991, 1992, and 1993 shows that a significant difference exists between the performance achieved by investors able to buy at the offer price and that of investors who buy after the first day of trading. This conclusion is in synch with previous studies done in the 1980's. On average, an IPO gains 10.9 per cent on its first day of trading, beating the market by the same margin. Over the first week of trading, the average issue is up 11.0 per cent. The average return for issues bought after the first day was a meagre 0.1 per cent.

Table 2.1 Buying IPOs at the Offer is the Way to Play the Game

| | Average Return From Offer Price | | | | | | |
	1 Day	1 Week	1 Month	3 Months	6 Months	1 Year	2 Years
Overall	10.9	11.0	13.7	20.7	24.6	27.3	46.8
1991	11.1	10.8	17.4	29.4	30.6	23.9	46.8
1992	9.9	10.1	10.9	11.7	19.0	29.6	
1993	11.6	11.7	14.1	24.2	27.7		

| | Average Return From First Day Close | | | | | | |
	1 Day	1 Week	1 Month	3 Months	6 Months	1 Year	2 Years
Overall	0.1	2.2	8.5	11.8	15.3	33.5	
1991	−0.2	5.8	16.5	16.4	11.1	33.5	
1992	0.2	0.7	1.6	8.4	18.2		
1993	0.1	1.5	10.2	12.2			

Through 31 December 1993

Sources: Securities Data Corp, Prudential Securities Inc

Chart 2.9 It pays to buy IPOs at the Offer Price

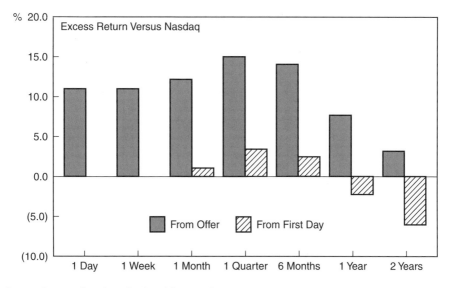

Sources: Securities Data Corp, Prudential Securities Inc

But The Outperformance Is Short-Lived. As can be seen in Chart 2.9, the excess return for new issues peaks at three months and falls off sharply after a year or two (two-year returns are 1991 issues only). The excess-return pattern based on the first day of trading is even more disillusioning. Performance peaks with a 3.3 per cent excess return after an issue is public for one quarter and actually becomes negative after a year.

As Time Goes On, It's Harder To Pick The Winners. Investors who can't get stock at the offer price have less than a 50 per cent chance of picking a winner if they buy the day after, and the odds don't improve over time. Investors buying at the offer have better than a 75 per cent chance of beating the market over the following week, but many stocks fall quickly thereafter. Outperformers drop to 64.2 per cent for one-month returns and to 61.2 per cent at one quarter, and it goes downhill from there.

There Is No Relationship Between Size Of Deal And Performance. Big deals don't produce the best returns, nor do the smallest. Returns don't get progressively better as size increases or decreases. It appears that the relationship is purely random. IPOs from $20 to $40 million have the best returns for the first four time periods from the offer date, but they do not maintain the lead over the long run.

The Nasdaq Gets The Deals. The Nasdaq got almost 80 per cent of the IPOs during this period. The NYSE captured 18.6 per cent and the American Stock Exchange (AMEX) had 2.4 per cent Interestingly, the best performance is from those stocks listed on the NYSE, although the Nasdaq IPOs start off with much better returns in the shorter time periods. At the six-month, one-year, and two-year intervals, the NYSE issues beat the market by 14.1 per cent, 17.0 per cent, and 15.9 per cent, while the Nasdaq excess returns were 13.8 per cent, 6.0 per cent, and 1.6 per cent, respectively.

Which Leads To Speculative Excess And Corrections. Historically, the relationship between IPOs and the direction of the market has been closely correlated. When the market is doing well, investors appetite for deals is strong and companies take advantage of the favourable financing environment. But things get ahead of themselves. As the IPO calendar gets more and more active, the market gets frothy and typically experiences a major correction. The term 'frothy' can be measured in many ways, i.e. the number of deals reaching new highs, the fast run-up in prices of hot deals, the number of deals oversubscribed or the deteriorating quality of the companies coming public.

Over the past dozen years, there have been three periods when the IPO market has been extremely active and Nasdaq reacted with a nasty correction (Chart 2.10). The first was 1983, which ended an eight-year run in small-cap stocks. The crash of 1987 brought to an end the second period of hot IPO activity, and the most recent occurred in late 1993.

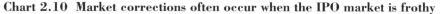

Chart 2.10 Market corrections often occur when the IPO market is frothy

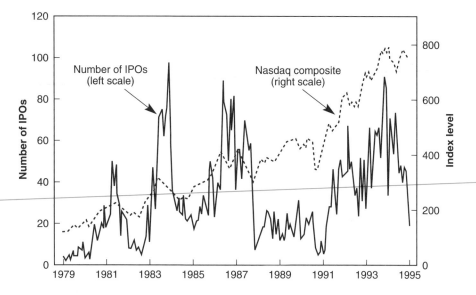

Sources: Securities Data Corp, Prudential Securities Inc

The IPO Market Is Not For The Faint Of Heart. All this evidence would indicate that investors should be cautious when investing in IPOs. While there is money to be made in new issues, investors unable to acquire stock at the offer price have the deck stacked against them. ☻

LIQUIDITY

Robin Aspinall

*Robin Aspinall is Chief Economist and Strategist with the London stock-broking firm of **Panmure Gordon & Co**, where has gained a reputation as an iconoclastic forecaster of the equity market. His experience includes several years in a specialist economic forecasting consultancy and in industry. He is a keen advocate of the use of technical analysis.*

It seems natural to suppose that markets respond to economic fundamentals such as growth and inflation. For example, you would imagine that, during a period when profits and dividends are growing rapidly, the equity market should perform well. Yet there are endless examples of periods when economic and market performance have diverged markedly. Economic performance can only translate into market performance when there are the funds available to drive prices higher. Hence, in the end, there is only one factor that determines market performance. And that is liquidity.

Liquidity is usually thought of as the proportion of investable funds that is held in cash. If the investment community has unusually high cash balances, it clearly has the ability to move significant funds into the markets. Hence, high liquidity levels are taken as a bullish sign for the markets. The difficulty is that information about institutional liquidity is often not readily available. Official government data tend to be incomplete and rather out of date, while the industry's own data are either confidential or expensive to obtain. But, in a sense, such information, useful though it is, is not completely necessary to form a liquidity-based view about the market.

On the well-founded basis that investors are most prepared to commit themselves to a market when prices are rising, you can be sure that the longer a rising trend has been in place, the lower liquidity reserves will be. And, conversely, a bear market trend contains within it the mechanics of its own reversal, because you can be sure that, while prices are falling, liquidity is increasing. It is exactly for this reason that 'contrarian' thinking is so effective: the time when investors are most bearish is, almost by definition, when they are most liquid and, therefore, most able to push prices up.

Bearish or bullish sentiment is not, of course, the sole determinant of liquidity levels. Cash yields its own return; so, when interest rates are high, it is quite legitimate to expect investors to run higher cash balances. It follows that the behaviour of interest rates can have a profound influence on markets. In this sense liquidity is best considered as an element in investor portfolios. When interest rates are high, investors are happy to keep a large proportion of their portfolios in interest-bearing deposits (loosely referred to as 'cash'). As interest rates fall, cash becomes less attractive and a portfolio shift away from cash and into equities and bonds is likely.

It is conventional to think that falling interest rates are good for the equity market because of the benefits to growth and profits. While these economic consequences are certainly important to the longer-term performance of the markets, it is the liquidity effects that dominate movements in the short term. There has been no better example of this than the experience of 1993 and 1994. When the US Federal Reserve cut interest rates aggressively in the early 1990s it began a process which culminated in the largest portfolio shift from cash that the world has ever seen. With official interest rates as low as 3 per cent (and investor deposit rates still lower), investors began to shift their funds away from cash and into the financial markets. In 1993, this became a flood, with net transfers into mutual funds (the US equivalent of the UK's unit trusts) easily exceeding $300 billion. That was the equivalent of 5 per cent of US GDP!

Much of that liquidity flowed out of the United States and into the financial markets of the world. (In the process, the dollar weakened considerably, demonstrating how important liquidity is to the currency markets as well.) This 'wall of money' produced spectacular gains in global markets ranging from Hong Kong equities to Swedish bonds. At the time, attempts were made to 'explain' the market movements in terms of economic fundamentals. 'Emerging markets' and 'convergence' of bond market yields were two of the more popular pseudo-economic rationalizations for a process that was actually being fuelled by the weight of money.

Portfolio shifts can be enormously powerful – and this one certainly was – but they are accompanied by an equally powerful certainty: they always come to an end. When they do, market prices, which have been artificially boosted by this injection of liquidity, return to reality. Indeed, it will normally be the case that the withdrawal of liquidity support will cause market prices to overshoot on the downside, just as they overshot on the upside previously.

When the influx of US liquidity came to an abrupt end in early 1994, the consequences for the world's markets were severe, producing, for instance, the worst performance by the gilt market in almost forty years. For the equity markets, the poor performance seemed especially dismaying. After all, every measure of real economic performance – growth, profits and dividends – outstripped even the most optimistic expectations. Economics and liquidity were pulling strongly in opposite directions. Of course, liquidity won. The chart presents the example of the Hong Kong equity market, whose performance – like so may others – was utterly dictated by US liquidity (reflected here in the M1 measure of US money growth).

It has always been the case that investors who are particularly bullish can borrow funds for investment purposes. This form of 'negative liquidity' was instrumental in the 1929 Wall Street Crash, when investing on 'margin' was rife. ('Margin' investment is when investors borrow funds against the security of the shares they are buying. If share prices fall, the debt exceeds the value of the shares, and the resulting 'margin call' can lead to forced selling of shares

Chart 2.11 Hang Seng Index against US M1 growth

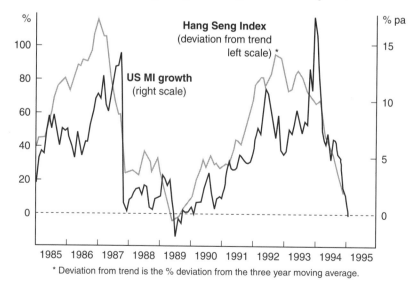

* Deviation from trend is the % deviation from the three year moving average.

Source: Panmure Gordon

and exaggerated market weakness.) Whilst this form of 'negative liquidity' plays a relatively minor role today, it was certainly true that many investors and investing institutions were prepared to borrow in order to participate in the stock market boom of 1986–7. The consequence was inevitable.

Yet, in another form, margin investment has taken on a dramatically increased significance. The futures markets allow investors to take on large exposures to the financial markets for relatively small initial margin. Hence, any attempt to assess liquidity merely on the basis of cash balances can grossly underestimate the true extent of investor exposure: a quite small adverse market movement can quickly absorb what appears to be a comfortable cushion of liquidity. It was the increased use of derivative instruments such as futures and options which added to the distress of 1994, causing crippling losses not just for the aggressive 'hedge funds' but also for many traditionally conservative fund managers, companies and local authorities.

Since liquidity is essentially a portfolio phenomenon, it is important to recognize that for any one market, funds held in other markets are just as much a source of potential inflows as are cash holdings. Hence, for example, the intention of US pension fund managers to diversify their equity and bond holdings away from the US and into international markets provides a huge potential source of 'liquidity' for non-US markets. (But, beware: this source of liquidity behaves as perversely as any other. International funds tend to flow into markets when they are rising, exaggerating the upward moves; they do not act as a protection in weak markets.)

Similarly, the enormous portfolio shift from UK Gilts into equities during the decades of the 'cult of the equity' fuelled the extraordinary out-performance of equities during that time. Now that the portfolio shift is reversing – thanks partly, but not solely to impending legislation on pension fund liquidity – the UK equity market represents a large source of potential liquidity for the gilt market. Which means that gilts can look forward to enjoying an extended period of liquidity-induced out-performance. ♀

FUTURES INDEXES AS EQUITY BENCHMARKS

Gary L. Gastineau

Gary Gastineau is Senior Vice President, New Product Development, with the American Stock Exchange. Formerly he was head of global equity derivative research at S.G. Warburg & Co Inc, and was Director of Customer Risk Management Research at Swiss Bank Corporation. Mr Gastineau is the author of The Options Manual, *the* Dictionary of Financial Risk Management *and numerous journal articles. In addition, he serves as a Practitioner Director for the Financial Management Association, and is on several editorial boards. He is an Adjunct Professor at The Center for Technology and Financial Services at the Polytechnic University.*

One of investment management's leading cottage industries is the creation, maintenance and advocacy of portfolio benchmark indexes. Whether an investment manager specializes in equity, fixed income, currencies, commodity futures or real estate, he knows his performance will be compared with the performance of a benchmark index.

The dominant benchmark for US equity portfolios is the Standard & Poor's 500, with the S&P MidCap 400 and the Russell 2000 often used for medium- and small-capitalization stocks, respectively. Three organizations – Morgan Stanley Capital International, Goldman Sachs-Financial Times Actuaries and Salomon Brothers – publish proprietary national, regional and global benchmarks for equity portfolios. While the US market components of these global equity benchmarks do not seriously challenge the benchmark roles of the S&P and Russell indexes, they were until recently the only well-constructed indexes for many markets outside the United States.

In recent years, some markets have introduced new stock indexes to serve as the basis of stock index futures trading. With the growth in stock index futures volume, these new indexes have come to dominate public and media attention. Not surprisingly, they have also begun to be used as portfolio benchmarks.

Growth of Stock Index Futures

Stock index futures trading began with the S&P 500 contract on the Chicago Mercantile Exchange in 1983 and has spread to nearly all the world's major equity markets. Today, single-country stock futures indexes cover more than 95 per cent of the world's publicly traded equities. A listing of these futures indexes appears as an appendix to this chapter.

The indexes underlying non-US stock index futures contracts differ from the proprietary benchmark indexes. In most markets, stock index futures contracts have been based on new indexes that generally meet high international standards for index computation and maintenance. A few traditional indexes, such as the venerable NIKKEI 225 Stock Average in Japan and the broad-based Australian All-Ordinaries Index, underlie stock index futures contracts. These indexes have not been wholly satisfactory for futures trading, however. Japan appears to be moving to the new NIKKEI 300 index, a capitalization-weighted index. The diversity of the All-Ordinaries Index has contributed to the relatively high cost of futures trading in Australia. User preferences for capitalization weighting and underlying stock liquidity have led most futures markets to create or adopt capitalization-weighted indexes based on actively traded stocks. The new indexes include the FTSE 100 (UK), the CAC 40 (France) and the DAX (Germany).

A single-country futures index may account for less than 70 per cent or more than 95 per cent of the market value of the country's publicly traded stock. These indexes are increasingly accepted as representative of the national market. Even though some media organizations have created their own equity indexes, virtually all published reports on a national equity market's performance include a reference to the performance of the country's leading futures index.

Despite the public's focus on the new futures indexes, many users of traditional portfolio performance benchmarks have stayed with the proprietary benchmark families. The proprietary benchmarks often provide greater breadth within a national market than the corresponding futures index. In the continuing competition for benchmark users, however, indexes underlying actively traded futures contracts have some important advantages over the proprietary benchmark indexes. The pressure to change is growing.

> **Despite the public's focus on the new futures indexes, many users of traditional portfolio performance benchmarks have stayed with the proprietary benchmark families.**

For the most part, futures indexes comprize highly liquid, actively traded issues, whereas some of the securities in benchmark indexes trade 'by appointment only.' In some cases, benchmark index weightings are not adjusted for corporate cross-holdings or control blocks of stock, casting doubt on claims that the benchmarks are more useful or more representative of markets than the corresponding futures indexes. The futures indexes are usually less subject to distortion from cross-holdings and control blocks, if only because all their underlying stocks trade more actively than many of the benchmark index components. Stock index arbitrageurs and multiple market makers, may of whom trade whole index portfolios, enhance the liquidity of the futures indexes.

Indexes and Investment Management

The leading determinants of the performance of an asset allocator are the weightings of market sectors (equities, fixed income, currencies, etc.) and country allocations. Futures indexes can approximate the performance of proprietary equity benchmark indexes closely enough that most asset allocators will be indifferent between the future indexes and the proprietary benchmarks. This is not to say that the futures contracts will track the proprietary benchmarks exactly, or that the two types of indexes are perfect substitutes for one another. However, the differences between the two usually favour the futures indexes.

If an investor is engaged in cross-border diversification primarily to take advantage of low correlations between different countries' stock returns, the indexes underlying the futures contracts provide highly satisfactory substitutes for the slightly broader-based proprietary benchmark indexes.

Proprietary index vendors provide country weightings for their regional and global composite indexes. The user of futures indexes can use proprietary index country weightings as a frame of reference or, alternatively, develop a customized country weighting scheme. In an appropriate combination, the futures indexes serve as highly satisfactory regional or global benchmark indexes.

Not only are the futures indexes as useful as the proprietary benchmarks for most purposes, but they have some important advantages.

1 The stocks in the futures indexes are usually the **most liquid** and widely held issues in their markets.
2 The introduction of futures contracts almost invariably increases **the relative liquidity** of the stocks in the underlying futures indexes – individually, in portfolios, and in the index as a whole. This futures-induced liquidity is more important in some markets than in others, and it is probably more important to cross-border investors than to domestic investors.
3 Looking to the future, **stocks in an index underlying a futures contract should outperform the average stock in their national market.**

The latter point is worth a more detailed explanation.

The Importance of Being in the Index

Observers of the impact of indexation and the growth of stock index futures markets often note that stocks in popular indexes perform better simply because of their index membership. The most obvious examples of the advantage of index membership are provided by stocks that have been selected for addition to or removal from an index. For example, stocks removed from the S&P 500, the NIKKEI 225 or even the Morgan Stanley Europe, Asia and Far East (EAFE) index have dropped sharply, whereas stocks added have risen sharply upon announcement of the changes. Stocks in the NIKKEI 225 but not in the new NIKKEI 300 performed poorly, while stocks slated for inclusion in the NIKKEI 300 outperformed the rest of the market when their selection was announced. The effects of inclusion or exclusion can be so disturbing that index sponsors have adopted policies to minimize disruptions to the market stemming from changes in index composition.

There is substantial reason to believe that being part of an index is especially important in a period when indexation and futures trading are growing. Figure A illustrates the results of a study by Martingale Asset Management and BARRA that measures the value of membership in the S&P 500 during a period when both indexation of portfolios and stock index futures trading were growing rapidly in the United States. Separating the effect of indexation from the effect of futures trading is not possible, but the implications for newer futures markets outside the United States are important. Whatever the cause of the outperformance by S&P 500 'members', Chart 2.12 shows an extra 4.0 per cent average return per year attributable to index membership

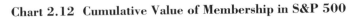

Chart 2.12 Cumulative Value of Membership in S&P 500

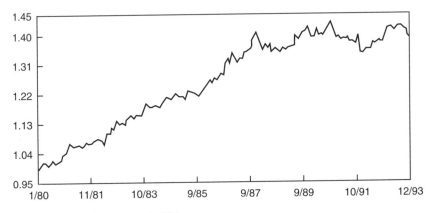

Source: Martingale Asset Management, BARRA

from 1980 through 1987. Allocation of the credit for this outperformance between the growth of portfolio indexation and the growth of futures probably does not matter in drawing international implications.

The 4 per cent average outperformance attributable to index membership in Chart 2.12 does not mean that S&P 500 outperformed other indexes by an average of 4 per cent per year or even that the average S&P 500 stock outperformed the average non-member by 4 per cent. The appropriate interpretation is that, on average, two stocks similar in all respects except for index membership would have shown the indicated performance difference during that period.

So far, there is little evidence that membership in non-US futures (or benchmark) indexes has carried a value comparable to the value of S&P 500 membership in the 1980s. However, as indexation and futures trading grow in importance, the advantage of membership in non-US stock futures indexes is likely to grow.

One caveat seems in order: the membership effect is not open-ended. Just as the relative performance associated with S&P 500 membership has been erratic since the end of 1987, the futures membership effects in any country is likely to be important for a few years and lead to a relatively permanent higher valuation for index member stocks.

Conclusion

Like index managers and asset allocators, active investors in international markets should keep the futures-index-membership effect in mind when they make stock selections. Given a choice between two otherwise equally attractive stocks, the investor may conclude that the futures index stock is the more appealing.

Both active managers and indexers should find futures indexes more meaningful than proprietary benchmarks as gauges of performance. Portfolio beneficiaries will want to measure their managers against the futures indexes. Most of the stocks in a futures index are also in the broader benchmarks, but all the stocks in the futures indexes should have both the growth of indexation and the liquidity of futures markets working for them.

On balance, futures index stocks and futures index derivatives deserve attention from both active and passive investors. Unless the broader composition of some proprietary benchmark index is particularly important, the dominant stock futures index in a national market should be the benchmark of choice for cross-border equity investors.

Appendix
Stock Indexes Underlying Futures Contracts

Country	Index	Type	Number of Stocks in Index	Primary Exchange
Australia	All-Ordinaries Share Price Index (SPI)	Cap Weighted	280	Syndey Futures Exchange
Austria	Austrian Traded Index	Cap Weighted	19	Austrian Futures & Options Exchange (OTOB)
Belgium	Bel 20 Index	Liquidity and Cap Weighted	20	Belgian Futures and Options Exchange CV/SC (BEL-FOX)
Brazil	IBOVESPA Stock Index	Liquidity Weighted	48	Bolsa de Mercadorias & Futuros (BM&F)
Canada	Toronto 35 Stock Index	Modified Cap Weighted	35	Toronto Futures Exchange (TFE)
Chile	IPSA Index	Liquidity and Cap Weighted	40	Santiago Stock Exchange
Denmark	KFX Stock Index	Cap Weighted	20	FUTOP Market-Copenhagen Stock Exchange and Guarantee Fund for Danish Options and Futures
Finland	Finnish Options Index (FOX)	Cap Weighted	25	Finnish Options Market
France	CAC 40 Stock Index	Cap Weighted	40	Marche a Terme International de France (MATIF)
Germany	German Stock Index (DAX)	Cap Weighted Total Return	30	Deutsche Terminboerse (DTB)
Hong Kong	Hang Seng Stock Index	Cap Weighted	33	Hong Kong Futures Exchange Ltd (HKFE)
	MSCI Hong Kong Index	Cap Weighted	39	Singapore International Montary Exchange Ltd (SIMEX)
Ireland	ISEQ Index	Cap Weighted	64	Irish Futures & Options Exchange (IFOX)
Italy	MIB 30 Index	Cap/Price Weighted	30	Italian Stock Exchange
Japan	Nikkei 225 Stock Average	Modified Price Weighted	225	Osaka Securities Exchange Singapore International Monetary Exchange Ltd (SIMEX)
	Tokyo Stock Price Index (TOPIX)	Cap Weighted	1st sect	Tokyo Stock Exchange
	Nikkei 300 Stock Index	Cap Weighted	300	Osaka Securities Exchange
Netherlands	Dutch Top 5 Index	Cap Weighted	5	Financiele Termijnmarkt Amsterdam NV (FTA)
	Amsterdam EOE Index (AEX)	Modified Cap Weighted	25	Financiele Termijnmakt Amsterdam NV (FTA)

145

New Zealand	NZSE 40 Capital Share Price Index	Cap Weighted	40	New Zealand Futures & Options Exchange Ltd (NZFOE)
Norway	OBX Index	Cap Weighted	25	Oslo Stock Exchange
South Africa	All Share Index	Cap Weighted	157	South African Futures Exchange (SAFEX)
Spain	Index Bolsa Espana (IBEX 35) Stock Index	Cap Weighted	35	Meff Renta Variable
Sweden	Swedish OMX Stock Index	Cap Weighted	30	OM Stockholm AB The London Securities & Derivatives Exchange (OMLX)
Switzerland	Swiss Market Index (SMI)	Cap Weighted	22	Swiss Options and Financial Futures Exchange (SOFFEX)
United Kingdom	FTSE 100	Cap Weighted	100	London International Financial Futures Exchange (LIFFE)
United States	S&P 500 Stock Index	Cap Weighted	500	Index and Option Market Division of the Chicago Mercantile Exchange (IOM)
	S&P MidCap 400 Index	Cap Weighted	400	Index and Option Market Division of the Chicago Mercantile Exchange (IOM)
	Russell 2000 Stock Price Index	Cap Weighted	2000	Index and Option Market Division of the Chicago Mercantile Exchange (IOM)
	Major Market Index	Price Weighted	20	Index and Option Market Division of the Chicago Mercantile Exchange (IOM)
	NYSE Composite Index	Modified Cap Weighted	all NYSE	New York Futures Exchange (NYFE)
	Value Line	Price Weighted	1600-1650	Kansas City Board of Trade (KCBT)
	Wilshire Small Cap Index	Cap Weighted	250	Chicago Board of Trade

THE IMPORTANCE OF THE TED SPREAD

Galen Burghardt

*Galen Burghardt is Senior Vice President at **Dean Witter Institutional Futures**. Previously, he was Executive Vice President for **Discount Corporation of New York Futures** and Vice President/Financial Research for the **Chicago Mercantile Exchange**. Mr Burghardt has taught economics at **Amherst College**, and worked at the **Federal Reserve Board** in Washington, DC. He is the lead author of* The Treasury Bond Basis, *and* Eurodollar Futures and Options: Controlling Money Market Risk. *He also teaches a course on financial futures and options for the **University of Chicago Graduate School of Business**.*

The Treasury market underpins the entire dollar fixed income market. Yields on Treasury bills, notes, and bonds are the standards against which every other yield is compared. Treasury bills, notes, and bonds are the hedging tool of choice for many securities dealers and corporate treasurers who are exposed to the risk of changing bond yields.

146

Just because everything is priced against Treasuries, though, does not mean that the spreads between private and government yields are fixed or even stable. Rather, the difference between the yields on private debt and the yields on Treasuries can fluctuate wildly and widely. And when it does, the effects are either devastating or exhilarating for those involved.

Proxy for the credit spread

The main reason for the spread between private and Treasury securities is the difference in credit quality. So far, the US Treasury is viewed as the premier credit in the dollar market. Banks and corporations, on the other hand, do

not have the same unlimited access to US taxpayers' wallets and purses. As a result, investors extract a premium to compensate them for the possibility of a default.

A widely used measure of the credit differential between private and Treasury paper is the spread between three-month LIBOR and three-month Treasury bill rates, which is known widely as the TED (Treasuries versus Eurodollar) spread. A history of this spread from 1970 through 1994 is provided in Chart 2.13

Chart 2.13 History of the TED Spread, 1970–1995
(3-month LIBOR less 3-month Treasury bill rate)

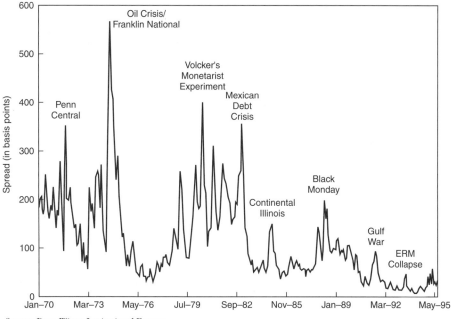

Source: Dean Witter Institutional Futures

147

This history of the TED spread shows two things quite clearly. One is that the spread is sensitive to financial crises or events that may be precursors of financial crises. Beginning with the Penn Central bankruptcy in the early 1970s and ending with the collapse of the European rate mechanism (ERM) in September of 1992, the spread has widened sharply in response to each shock to the financial system.

It is also plain from this history that the financial world appears to have become less skittish over the years. In the early 1970s, the combination of the oil crisis and the failure of Franklin National added 450 basis points or so to the spread. In contrast, the collapse of the stock market (Black Monday) in October 1987 was good for only 100 basis points. The Gulf War added 60 or 70 basis points, and the utter collapse of the European rate mechanism (ERM) in September 1992 contributed a mere 20 or 30 basis points to the spread.

Why the market's response to financial shocks is less extreme now than what it once was may be due in part to experience. Central bankers (the Federal Reserve included) are fond of describing financial markets as fragile. Our experience suggests otherwise. Even a cataclysm like the stock market collapse in 1987 did not bring the world to an end. And if the single biggest one-day drop in stock prices does not bring the apocalypse, it is hard to know what would. To be sure, central banks have contributed a great deal to the robustness of financial markets. They have learned a lot about the importance of monetary policy and the management of interest rate crises over the decades, and it seems that central banks now spread a calming influence (when they want to) over the markets at large. Also, central banks have shown themselves unwilling to let large banks fail. Since Eurodollar rates reflect the rates paid by large, high-credit banks in the London market, the diminishing responses to financial shocks may reflect a growing appreciation for this fact.

> **Why the market's response to financial shocks is less extreme now than what it once was may be due in part to experience.**

The risk is still there

Although the swings in the TED spread are smaller than they once were, financial markets are much, much bigger. Securities dealers often find themselves underwriting billion dollar bond offerings in which the value of a basis point swing in the bond's spread over Treasuries is worth more than $1 million. In such a world, a dealer can ill afford to be caught off guard. Even the comparatively small 30 basis point widening of the spread in the face of the collapse of the ERM cost banks and securities dealers several billions of dollars – at least for the duration of that particular crisis.

But help is at hand

Fortunately for anyone who is exposed to risk in the TED spread, the futures markets provide a highly useful hedging tool. And, for those who want to pit their skills against the market, the hedging tool can be used as a trading tool.

In particular, futures on three-month Treasury bills and on three-month LIBOR are traded at the Chicago Mercantile Exchange. By futures market convention,

Treasury bill futures price = 100.00 – *3-month Treasury bill rate*
Eurodollar futures price = 100.00 – *3-month LIBOR*

By construction, then, the difference between the Treasury bill futures price and the three-month Eurodollar futures price is equal to the TED spread, or the spread between three-month Eurodollar rates and three-month Treasury bill rates. As a result, anyone who stands to lose money if a financial crisis causes the spread between bank and Treasury paper to widen can protect themselves by buying the TED spread – that is buying Treasury bill futures and selling Eurodollar futures.

Although the TED spread typically is thought of as a spread between two three-month rates, the Eurodollar market has developed to a point where one can trade or hedge changes in the spread between Eurodollar yields and Treasury yields with horizons as long as ten years. One can, for example, buy a five-year Treasury note and sell a suitably constructed strip of Eurodollar futures with expirations ranging out to five years. The resulting position will capture the effects of any change in the five-year credit spread between bank and Treasury paper. ♀

Economic Indicators

Index of Leading Economic Indicators

Employment and Unemployment

Inflation: The New Disinflation of the 1990s

Interest Rates and Asset Allocation

Savings

Money Supply: The Global Money Rule

Capacity Utilization: The Impact on Financial Markets

The Foreign Exchange Market

Housing Market Data

INDEX OF LEADING ECONOMIC INDICATORS

Allen Sinai

*Allen Sinai is the Chief Global Economist at **Lehman Brothers** and Adjunct Professor of Economics and Finance, **Lemberg School, Brandeis University**.*

***Lehman Brothers** is a global investment banking firm with offices in New York, London, Hong Kong, Tokyo and forty one other financial centres.*

For investors in any major financial market, how the US economy is likely to behave can be an important ingredient for investing and investment strategy.

From the position of the US economy in the business cycle can flow much information on prospects for Federal Reserve monetary policy, interest rates, profits and the equity market, and the dollar. Non-US markets often take their cue from the US, so that monitoring which stage of the business cycle the US is in and where a turning point might occur is essential.

The business cycle has much to do with how different categories of investments perform, has regular and systematic relationships with the ups and downs of interest rates and stock prices, and for the timing of shifts from bull to bear markets and vice-versa.

How can an investor determine where the US economy is in its business cycle and how can that knowledge be of help for investments?

Index of Leading Economic Indicators (LEI)

One overall business cycle indicator is the Index of Leading Economic Indicators (LEI), a summary measure designed to indicate the future path of business activity as the economy progresses through a business expansion, its peak, the recession, trough, recovery, then the next expansion, and so on.

The LEI contains 11 components, economic time-series that in the past have had a highly reliable relationship with the stages of the business cycle as defined by the National Bureau of Economic Research (NBER). Research on business cycles by the NBER dates back to the 1920s when, through the examination of hundreds of economic time-series , the business cycle and its stages were defined and determined. Of course, with modern high-speed computers, the various economic time-series that make up the LEI can now be culled from thousands of candidates. Selection is by regularity of the lead time for the particular indicator with respect to the turning points of business cycle peaks and troughs. There is also a set of coincident indicators used to determine how the economy is performing at the current time. And, there is a lagging indicator that follows turns in economic activity. The ratio of coincident-to-lagging indicators also has some information content on the business cycle.

The components of the LEI may be divided into several main categories: Financial Indicators, Labour Market Indicators, and Production-side components. The Financial Indicators include:

1   S&P500 Common Stock Index (0.023 weight)
2   M2 Money Supply (1982 dollars) (0.158 weight) and Building Permits-Housing (0.012 weight);

Labour market indicators would be:

3   Average Workweek in Manufacturing (0.156 weight) and
4   Average Initial Unemployment Insurance Claims (0.015 weight)

Production-side components are:

5   Vendor Performance (0.015 weight)
6   Contracts and Orders for Plant and Equipment (0.012 weight)
7   Changes in Sensitive Materials Prices (0.405 weight)
8   Change in Manufacturers Unfilled Orders for Durable Goods (0.158 weight) and
9   Value of New Orders for Consumer Goods (0.033 weight).

There is also a component related to the consumer

10 The index of consumer expectations from the University of Michigan Consumer Sentiment Survey (0.013 weight).

The LEI as constituted has had a reliable relationship in forecasting the turning points of the economy and the magnitude of its change can be used to determine how strong, moderate or weak business activity might be.

By and large, the LEI has tended to forecast recessions and recoveries well and to roughly approximate the pace of economic activity in between peaks and troughs. Percentage changes in the index are used to determine its forecasts. The rough rule-of-thumb is three consecutive declines of the LEI as a recession signal and three straight rises for a recovery.

All but one of the nine post-World War II recessions have been indicated in advance, to a greater-or-lesser degree. The LEI has given some false signals of recession – in 1951, 1962, 1966, 1978, 1984 and 1987. A signal for the 1990–91 recession actually showed up in early 1989, only to be followed by increases in the LEI, then declines beginning two months before the downturn.

All recoveries were signalled, although in some instances with hardly any lead time. The lead times for recession, in months, have varied from zero to nine; for recovery, zero to three.

Chart 2.14 GDP Growth vs. Leading Economic Indicators
(percent change qtr. to qtr.)

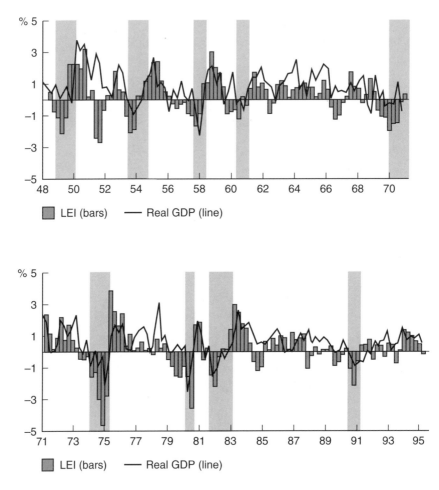

LEI (bars) —— Real GDP (line)

Sources: The Bureau of Economic Analysis, Lehman Brothers Global Economics

Investor Implications

The use to investors of the LEI is advance knowledge, with some degree of confidence, on how the economy will be behaving some months into the future. Recoveries tend to last from six to twelve months, sometimes longer. Recoveries and expansions have been anywhere from eight to 106 months. Roughly speaking, financial markets behave in certain ways, depending on the state of the business cycle.

Typically, in mid-recession, the stock market begins to rise, a 'bull' market. As the economy approaches a peak, the stock market peaks and then declines, entering into a 'bear' market. In recession, interest rates, short and long term, move downward. Monetary policy is tightened in the later stages of expansion and is eased not long after a recession. After a trough, most often about a year or so, interest rates tend to rise.

> **The use to investors of the LEI is advance knowledge, with some degree of confidence, on how the economy will be behaving some months into the future.**

In the recent cyclical episode spanning 1990 to 1993, which extended over recession, recovery and expansion and was well signalled by the LEI, the US equity market performed as might have been expected, given the LEI.

From 1989 Q2 to 1989 Q4, the LEI declined, signalling a coming recession. By mid-1990, a recession had begun, lasting until March 1991. By then, the LEI was rising again, starting a sequence to signal recovery.

The equity market, as measured by the S&P500 Index of Common Stocks, declined 8.2 per cent between the fourth quarters of 1989 and 1990. Between the fourth quarter of 1990, about the mid point of the recession, and fourth quarter 1991, suggested as a time of economic recovery by the LEI the equity market rose 22.1 per cent.

Knowledge of the LEI as the markets relate to the business cycle should be an ingredient in the thinking of all investors, US and worldwide. Market movements in the US correlate well, with some lags, to those of major industrialized country financial markets. For investors, the LEI needs to be watched as an ingredient to strategy. ♟

EMPLOYMENT AND UNEMPLOYMENT

Romesh Vaitilingam

Romesh Vaitilingam is a freelance writer and consultant, numbering among his clients the Boston Consulting Group, Pearson Professional, and the Centre for Economic Policy Research. He is the author of The Financial Times Guide to Using the Financial Pages *(FT Pitman Publishing, Second edition, 1994) and* The Financial Times Guide to Using Economics and Economic Indicators *(FT Pitman Publishing, 1994), books designed to help investors interpret financial and economic information.*

Most of us agree that the high unemployment that pervades many countries of the developed world is not a desirable phenomenon. So why is it that news of an increase in the jobless figures, noticeably in the US, is often greeted enthusiastically by the markets with stock and bond prices surging in response to lengthening dole queues?

At the individual firm level, a BT or an IBM, for example, might temporarily improve their profitability and perhaps raise their share prices by laying off workers. But there are broader connections between labour markets and financial markets: how do they operate, and how might the global investor successfully interpret changing patterns of work without necessarily condoning the reality of vast numbers of people without it?

The obvious place to start is with the conventional view of how figures on jobs interact with those for inflation, interest rates and the stock market. The levels of employment and unemployment are some of the most contentious and widely reported economic indicators, and, unlike many indicators, they provide a broad picture of the economy, typically encompassing the manufacturing, retail, service and agricultural sectors. If the majority of players in a market believe that shifts of such prominent indicators have regular and predictable effects, frequently those expectations will become self-fulfilling prophecies.

Employment data cover not only jobs; they are also an essential guide to personal incomes, wages and unit labour costs, as well as being the basis for measuring gross domestic product by income and often for assessing inflationary pressures. The standard theory in this case is that a high and/or rising jobless rate implies low or falling inflation. This in turn indicates low interest rates and thriving bond and stock markets. Such an analysis of the economy sees employment moving in line with the series of economic fluctuations described by the business cycle.

In a recovery and boom, for example, increased demand for goods and services raises the demand for labour to produce them. If there are unemployed and appropriately skilled workers available to meet that demand, they will be employed; if there are not, there will be upward pressure on wages. The latter outcome inevitably leads to rising inflation and the likelihood of central bank action on interest rates to choke off demand and slow down the rate of output growth. In this way, there is perceived to be a trade-off between inflation and unemployment.

In the US, employment has indeed been rising and falling with the business cycle since at least the mid-1970s. Thus, for investors in American markets, high levels of employment on 'non-farm payrolls' or falls in the overall unemployment rate are usually considered to be dangerous. Bond prices, for example, might fall on the announcement of growth in employment, particularly in the later stages of a recovery or boom when unemployment is relatively low. At such times, traders tend to fear the further tightening of monetary policy, meaning higher interest rates and lower bond prices.

Similarly, the possible combination of higher wage and capital costs (from higher inflation and interest rates) might lead to diminished profitability for American firms with implications for their future dividend payments and prospective share prices. The widespread anticipation of a decline in the stock market can then actually cause the decline to happen.

Over the past 25 years, the civilian unemployment rate in the US has ranged from a low of around five per cent in 1973–4 through a high of a little below ten per cent in 1989. These indicators correspond very roughly to an interest rate peak in 1974 and a stock market trough at the end of that year, to an interest rate trough and market peak in 1983, as well as to further interest rate highs and a market mini-crash in 1989.

But while the American labour market has been largely 'pro-cyclical', unemployment in the countries of the European Union, in contrast, has soared to an average of 8 per cent. And it has pretty much remained there, even in buoyant periods when the economic brakes have had to be put on to prevent inflation accelerating. In these countries, a decline in the unemployment rate is more likely to be good news for business, boosting incomes, increasing demand for companies' output, and generally having a positive effect on consumer confidence. Such results should enhance the prospects for corporate profitability and encourage higher share values.

What's more, falling unemployment, after a long period in which human resources have been squandered, might be indicative of an economy repositioning itself for future success. While some share of the unemployment total is cyclical, another portion is structural: there is a mismatch between available jobs and the people who might fill them.

An economy where structural unemployment is in decline, where perhaps jobs in traditional manufacturing industries are being replaced by jobs in services or high-tech industries, and workers are being effectively retrained, is bound to be a strong economy. Its new companies, as well as existing companies in such sectors as media, telecommunications and support services, are likely to be good investments, and you can also expect to gain from an appreciating exchange rate.

So, in the short-term, the impact of falling unemployment can be bad for share prices, especially if the economy is 'overheating'. Falling unemployment is, after all, characteristically a lagging indicator of the business cycle. But longer term, depending on the sectors and regions in which you are invested, more jobs should mean better returns on your portfolio.

And you should always be aware of labour market data shifting dramatically in response to seasonal changes in the demand for labour, or simply as a result of statistical redefinitions. 1980s Britain, for example, witnessed no less than thirty changes to the definition of unemployment all but one of which reduced the total. The most important change was in 1982, when the count of the unemployment was shifted from those registering at job centres to those claiming unemployment benefits at social security offices, removing from the total 190,000 job seekers not entitled to benefit. By late 1986, this and other redefinitions had reduced the unemployment rate from 14.3 per cent under the old system of calculation to 11.6 per cent on the new basis.

You should also be careful when comparing national statistics since official definitions of unemployment differ from one country to another. In Germany, for example, the unemployment rate is defined as the proportion of the civilian labour force, excluding the self-employed, that is actively seeking work through registration at employment offices. In contrast, Britain's rate is the number of benefit claimants as a percentage of the total labour force, including all employees, claimants, the self-employed, HM Forces and people on government training schemes. Many other countries base their calculations on survey data, a system that is usually more accurate than register or claimant counts.

Finally, there remains the question of how seriously you should take any of these employment statistics in an age when the fundamental nature of work is changing so dramatically. The decline of the 'job for life', the rise of service industries driven by portable human skills, and the emergence of the 'telecommuter' and the 'portfolio worker' who spans a number of careers in his or her working lifetime, all point to a new understanding of what work is all about. What they mean for global asset markets is as yet anybody's guess. ●

INFLATION: THE NEW DISINFLATION OF THE 1990S

Stephen S. Roach

Stephen Roach is Chief Economist and Director of Global Economic Analysis at **Morgan Stanley & Co.,** *Incorporated, a global investment banking firm headquartered in New York. Mr Roach manages* **Morgan Stanley's** *worldwide team of economists located in New York, London, Paris, Hong Kong and Tokyo. He is widely quoted in the financial press and his work has appeared in academic journals, books, congressional testimony, and on the op-ed pages of* The Wall Street Journal, The New York Times, The Washington Post, *and* The Financial Times. *Before joining* **Morgan Stanley** *in 1982, he was vice president, economic analysis, for the* **Morgan Guaranty Trust Company.** *Prior to that, he served six years at the* **Federal Reserve Board** *in Washington DC. He has also been a research fellow at the* **Brookings Institution.**

There's something new and important brewing on the US price front that could have profoundly positive implications for the financial markets. The squeeze is finally on in America's vast service sector, that segment of the US economy that accounts for fully 57 per cent of all items contained in America's Consumer Price Index (CPI). In the past, inflation trends were dominated by shifts in the prices of commodities, where pricing is determined by the interplay between the forces of supply and demand in the goods-producing segment of the economy. By contrast, the impacts of service sector inflation were far more muted – not surprising for a sector that has long been relatively immune to the forces of the business cycle.

But that was then, The service sector has now joined the fray in shaping an important breakthrough on the US inflation front. No, it's not just the annual ritual of the now-familiar airline price war. Medical care inflation is finally waning. There are some early signs that once excessive college tuition hikes are beginning to wane. Moreover, cable-TV rates are falling, advertising costs are on the downswing, long-distance telephone charges continue to decline, and new financial services are proliferating without any attendant pricing pressures.

These, and many other trends, are all part of the new mosaic of disinflation in the 1990s. Nor are these developments a mere coincidence. At work is a veritable sea change confronting services, transformed by the powerful confluence of deregulation and globalization. Facing such intense competition for the first time ever, countless service companies have embarked on a massive wave of restructuring. The result has been a new and long overdue outbreak of cost-cutting in America's chronically inefficient service sector. Indeed, our estimates reveal that unit labour costs in the service sector were rising at only a 2.5 per cent annualized rate through the end of 1994. That's less than half the 6.5 per cent pace recorded at comparable stages of the past four business cycle upturns – an encouraging sign that the service sector of the 1990s has finally broken the mould of its long-standing complacency on the cost front.

Since services are the most labour-intensive segment of the US economy, this extraordinary compression of labour cost pressures is the essence of the case for further unwinding of inflationary pressures. But there's more to the story than just heightened efforts at cost control. Indeed, also at work are the powerful forces of process re-engineering, increased technology leverage, and aggressive outsourcing strategies – the new mega-trends of the 1990s that increase the chances that the rebound in service sector productivity is here to stay after two decades of near stagnation.

Renewed productivity enhancement in services is really the key to America's next leg of disinflation. Indeed, as the manufacturing sector powered back up the efficiency curve in the latter half of the 1980s, the service sector languished in a quagmire of near stagnant productivity and experienced a sharp relative deterioration of cost and inflationary pressures. But now that's beginning to change. Nor is the recent improvement in service sector productivity solely attributable to the cyclical forces of economic recovery. Indeed, our calculations suggest that the pace of productivity change in services over the past four years is nearly double the 0.9 per cent rate that would have been expected from this relatively sluggish recovery.

There are early signs that these productivity improvements are already beginning to pay a dividend in the form of reduced inflationary pressures in services. Relative to peak rates reached in early 1991, overall services inflation has already slowed from 6.2 per cent to about 3 per cent – nearly two percentage points below the pace reached at a comparable stage in the disinflationary recovery of the 1980s. While the unwinding of service sector inflation has been broadly based, a residue of pricing pressures remains concentrated in three segments of the service sector: medical care, education, and transportation – categories that collectively account for 57 per cent of the total consumer services budget (excluding the so-called imputed rent on shelter). And yet, slowly but surely, the trend is now changing in each of these categories as well.

Indeed, left to its own devices, medical care inflation edged below 5 per cent in early 1995, the lowest pace in 20 years. The inflation rate for the professional services component of healthcare – the direct charges of doctors and physicians that account for nearly 60 per cent of CPI-based medical service outlays – has been reduced to just 4.8 per cent, down nearly four full percentage points from gains three years ago. Maybe just the threat of Washington's intrusion into this area has been enough to trigger the inevitable shakeout that holds the key to cost control and disinflation in healthcare.

There is similar ground for tentative optimism in education inflation. The American Council on Private Education estimates that tuition increases for private colleges and universities has slowed to a 7 per cent rate – still double the overall US inflation rate but down sharply from runaway gains of nearly 13 per cent in the early 1980s. Finally, there can be no mistaking the potential for disinflation in transportation. In this era of deregulation, an average transcontinental air ticket probably costs 30 per cent less today than it did a decade ago. As a result, inflation of purchased transportation slowed to just 2.6 per cent in 1994, literally half the gains of just $2\frac{1}{2}$ years ago and far below the 8.4 per cent peak increases in the late 1980s.

A service sector that stays the course of improved productivity enhancement offers a unique opportunity for disinflation in the 1990s. That's because America's first leg of disinflation actually occurred without the full participation of the service sector – particularly astounding, since services comprize fully 56 per cent of all items in overall CPI-based measures of inflation. Indeed, while the goods component of inflation has run at about a 2 per cent rate so far in the 1990s – less than half the nearly 7 per cent gains of the 1970s – services inflation has still averaged about 4.5 per cent so far in the current decade; that's a deceleration of only about one-third from the excessive 7 per cent pace of the 1970s and an inflation rate that remains more than double what's still evident in the goods sector. In our view, that is now about to change.

So how does it all play out? While there is no instant gratification in the realm of service sector disinflation, I believe that services inflation is headed to a $2\frac{1}{2}$ per cent rate in the latter half of the 1990s, a bit more than one percentage point below the current rate. The precise timing of this outcome depends largely on when the next business cycle occurs. That's because recession can play the role as a catalyst to the forces of disinflation – spurring companies to maintain market share by passing through cost reductions. Assuming the U.S. economy peaks at some point in the 1996–7 interval, the disinflationary potential of the subsequent downturn should reach full force in 1998–9.

Whatever the cyclical outcome holds for the US economy, it is our strong conviction that the die of further disinflation is now cast. Emerging from the latest wave of restructuring are increasingly vibrant service industries of great scope and diversity – industries that now have the opportunity to become dominant players in the global economy, ushering in an era of renewed job creation. The icing on the cake is an overall inflation rate that has the clear potential to fall about a full percentage point from the lows of the early 1990s – moving down to the rarefied zone of 2 per cent at some point before the turn of the century.

For the financial markets, the next leg of disinflation would be a true bonanza. A US economy that stays the course of productivity revival offers opportunity for steady expansion of corporate profit margins – the essence of a sustained earnings revival that guarantees a most constructive underpinning for the stock market. A critical by-product of this outcome is the likelihood of a long overdue reversal of the deterioration in relative prices in the service sector, with marginal pricing leverage shifting back to the cyclically-sensitive goods-producing segment of the economy, a conclusion that would have important implications for leadership in the stock market. And for the US bond market, the next leg of disinflation is stuff of the mother of all rallies – the force that might well hold yields on long Treasuries well below 6 per cent. Who could ask for more?

> **For the financial markets, the next leg of disinflation would be a true bonanza.**

While the macro play in the financial markets is compelling, there are also some specific investment themes that emerge from the breakthroughs in the service sector. First and foremost, service sector disinflation is about white collar productivity enhancement. The primary facilitators of such efficiency improvements are twofold – outsourcers and information technology producers. Outsourcers enable companies to jettison costly in-house functions that are supplementary to a company's core mission, enabling managers to repurchase staffing and data processing as cost and demand considerations dictate. As such, clear beneficiaries of the outsourcing strategies of productivity enhancement will include the temporary hiring companies (such as Manpower, Kelly and Olsten) and the data processing vendors (such as EDS, Xerox, IBM and First Data).

The technology play on white-collar productivity is mult-dimensional. In particular, it benefits those companies which provide the tools that facilitate back office consolidation, (e.g. mainframe producers such as IBM and Amdahl and network providers such as Novell) empower sales workers with increasingly sophisticated point-of-sales computing devices, (e.g. AT&T [NCR] and Micros Systems) and achieve a streamlining of mid-managerial ranks through the advent of new telecommunications networks (e.g. AT&T, MCI and Sprint) and increasingly powerful real-time transactions tracking systems. Needless to say, however, the technology play is even more basic than implied by specific white-collar productivity strategies, providing opportunities for a host of producers, including, but not limited to, the chip producers, (e.g. Intel and Motorola), workstation vendors, (e.g. Compaq and Sun) and software developers, (e.g. Computer Associates and SAP). In short, the sky's the limit for high-tech companies as the US economy enters the new disinflation of the 1990s. ♀

INTEREST RATES AND ASSET ALLOCATION

Edward M. Kerschner

*Mr Kerschner is Managing Director of **PaineWebber Inc** and, as Chairman of the firm's Investment Policy Committee, is the Chief Investment Officer, providing investment strategy advice to the firm's clients. He is also a member of the Board of Directors of **PaineWebber Inc**. He began his investment career in 1974 with **Cowen & Co** and joined **PaineWebber** in 1982. Mr Kerschner has been recognized by* Institutional Investor *magazine with positions in its All American Research Team for both portfolio strategy and quantitative analysis. The* Wall Street Journal *ranked Mr Kerschner's asset allocation advice first among the twelve major brokerage firms for 1993. Mr Kerschner's advice also ranked number one in 1987 (the first year the ranking was published), 1990 and 1991, and second in 1992 .*

***Paine Webber Group Inc** is the parent of **PaineWebber Inc**, the major operating subsidiary and one of the leading financial services firms in the US. With 283 offices worldwide and a capital base of $3.5 billion, **PaineWebber** is one of the strongest independent firms in its business.*

Why do interest rate movements lead to fluctuations in stock prices? Quite simply, because changes in interest rates (i.e., expected returns) cause investors to alter their asset allocation among stocks and fixed income instruments.

The first investment decision is the allocation of resources among financial assets: stocks, bonds and cash equivalents. This is done even before one chooses specific instruments within each asset. How do you select among assets? In fact, you do not decide in any absolute sense if stocks are cheap, or bonds are cheap, or cash. What you do is compare the relative attraction of one asset with the others. If in fact all are cheap, you buy the cheapest, and if none are cheap, you select the least costly. What you compare is the **expected** rate of return from each asset.

In the PaineWebber Asset Allocation model, first the expected market return for each asset is calculated. For the fixed income markets, where the price is known and future payments (the coupon) are known, the expected rate of return is the yield to maturity at a given price.

What may cause the yield to maturity (i.e., interest rate) to fluctuate? Nominal interest rates are the sum of a real interest rate and an inflation expectation. Real interest rates are driven by supply and demand factors. For example, an increased personal savings rate will typically cause real rates to fall because the supply of investment funds is increased. Alternatively, a larger government budget deficit will typically cause real rates to rise because of an increased demand for investment funds. As for expectations about inflation, some of the key factors driving investors' perceptions of pricing pressures include real GDP growth, capacity utilization, the foreign exchange rate and labour productivity. Fast, real GDP growth, and tight capacity utilization typically lead to increased inflationary pressures because there is increased demand for a limited supply of output. Conversely, a strong currency typically leads to lower inflationary pressures because imported goods are now cheaper, while improving labour productivity means that more output is being produced for a given amount of inputs, thereby keeping wage gains moderate.

As for stocks' expected return, the information available in the marketplace is not as accommodating as it is in the fixed income market. While we know the price of the stock market, we do not know the market's expectation for future payments (individuals). Yes, the currect dividend is known, but unlike a bond where the coupon is a contractual guarantee, the dividend is simply an implicit 'best efforts' promise. And that best effort includes a promise of future growth in that dividend.

At PaineWebber, the expected return from stocks is calculated from our proprietary survey of institutional investor expectations of dividends, earnings and growth rates – a unique data base we have developed over the past years. This is a model based upon actual data of expectations as they existed, not a model working on perfect hindsight. We have been surveying a broad sample of instituational investors, not as to their forecast for retun but as to what are their forecasts for fundamentals, for the equity market in aggregate. Based upon the actual expectations as they existed at each point in time, and the price of the market (S&P 500) at that point, the implicit expected rate of return for the stock market is calculated.

Now we can compare the expected return of the stock market to the expected return – the yield – from US Government issue Treasury bonds. What we want to know is how much more return is received for taking the risk of investing in stocks as compared with the safety of investing in bonds – or what is the 'equity risk premium'?

The PaineWebber Asset Allocation model subtracts the yield at each point in 10-year T-bonds form the corresponding expected return on the S&P 500 and calculates the equity risk premium versus T-bonds at each point in time. The average risk premium over the past 20 years is also calculated (Chart 2.15). So, by definition, whenever the actual risk premium is above the average risk premium, an investor receives an above-average return or premium to be in stocks relative to T-bonds, and therefore stocks are relatively attractive. When the risk premium is below average, an investor receives a below average risk premium to be in stocks, and therefore stock are unattractive relative to T-bonds.

Chart 2.15 Risk premium: Stocks versus bonds

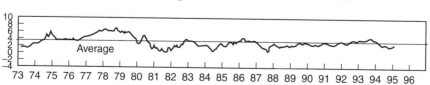

161

We then translate the risk premium series into a probability series of stocks outperforming T-bonds. To do so, we simply use the cumulative normal distribution function. The average risk premium corresponds to a 50 per cent, or neutral, probability. As the risk premium goes above average and the attraction of stocks increases correspondingly, the probability of stocks outperforming T-bonds increases: as the risk premium goes below average, the probability decreases (Chart 2.16).

Chart 2.16 Probability of Stocks outperforming Bonds

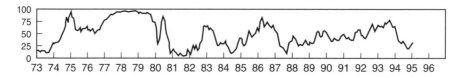

In addition to the risk premium relationship analysed between stocks and T-bonds, we analyse in exactly the same manner the relationships between stocks and US Government thirteen-week Treasury bills. Now if we know the probability that stocks outperform bonds is 75 per cent and the probability that stocks outperform cash is 70 per cent, what is the probability that stocks outperform both bonds and bills? Well it's not the average, 72.5 per cent, nor is it the product, 52.5 per cent. It's a little more complicated than that.

It is a type of Bayesian probability. (Recall that Bayes Theorem enables us to do the following: if we know the probability of A [stocks] outperforming B [bonds], **and** we know the probability of B [bonds] outperforming C [cash], then we can calculate the probability of A [stocks] outperforming **both** B [bonds] and C [cash].) But the maths aside, the answer is 62 per cent. If the probability that stocks outperform bonds is 75 per cent and the probability that stocks outperform cash is 70 per cent then the probability that stocks outperform both bonds and cash is 62 per cent. And that in theory would be the suggested equity weighting in a balanced account: 62 per cent.

If, for example, there was a 100 per cent probability that stocks outperform both bonds and cash, one would be 100 per cent in stocks. A sure thing is a sure thing. That's what 100 per cent means. If there was a 0 per cent probability that stocks outperform both bonds and cash then one would be 0 per cent in stocks. With a 62 per cent probability that stocks outperform both bonds and cash then one would be 62 per cent in stocks.

By combining these probabilities an asset weighting strategy is developed. These 'theoretical' asset weightings are for an unconstrained portfolio, i.e., where each asset – stocks, bonds and cash – can range from a 0 per cent to 100 per cent weighting (Chart 2.17). The weightings for any given 'real world' account (i.e. an account with narrower ranges) can also be calculated.

Chart 2.17 Probability of Top Performance ('theoretical' asset weightings)

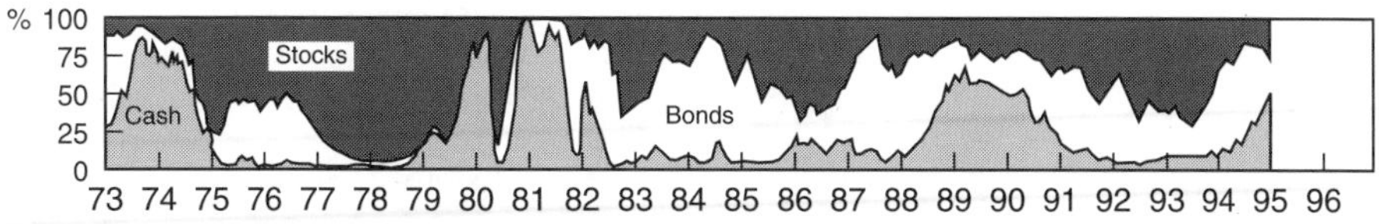

Looking at an unconstrained portfolio, a portfolio that would have followed these weightings would have outperformed each of the underlying assets. The total annual rate of return for the 22 years from 1973 through 1994 is 13.0 per cent, versus 7.5 per cent for cash, 8.5 per cent for bonds and 10.8 per cent for stocks.

SAVINGS RATE

Keith Wade

Keith Wade studied at the London School of Economics before joining the ***Centre for Economic Forecasting*** *at the London Business School. He joined* ***Schroders*** *in 1988 and became Chief Economist in 1992.*

Schroders *is a leading international investment banking and fund management group with a well established presence in key financial centres across the world.*

The term 'savings' tends to be used very loosely with some commentators referring to flows into bank and building society accounts, while others use it to describe total savings in the economy as a whole. In this section we are concerned with the broader measure, and define savings as income which is not spent on consumption. Two measures are of interest to investors.

Personal savings

The first, and one of the most commonly quoted, is the personal sector savings ratio, defined as personal income minus consumption expenditure as a percentage of personal income. This is a net measure of saving as it is equal to total cash flows into financial and real assets, minus borrowing. The latter counts as negative savings as it enables people to consume more than their income. In the UK, for example, personal sector saving exceeded £54 billion in 1993, and with disposable income of £460 billion, this gave a savings ratio of just under 12 per cent. The sector increased its funds available for investment to £75 billion through borrowing and other sources. This was then invested, primarily in dwellings (£26 billion) and pension funds and life assurance schemes (£30 billion).

		£bn			£bn
		Personal sector sources as uses of funds (1993)			
		– where it comes from and where it goes			
	Income	460.2	Investment in:		
minus	Consumption	405.8	Dwellings		25.9
equals	**Saving**	54.4	Liquid assets		15.0
			Gilts		5.3
plus	Borrowing	16.6	Equities		0.6
plus	other	4.6	Life and Pension funds		30.0
			other		2.1
			Total investment		78.9
			bal. item		−3.3
equals	**Total sources**	75.5	**Total uses**		75.5

Source: Financial Statistics, CSO

The breakdown of flows into different financial assets is driven by people's short-term need for liquidity, and longer-term aims such as retirement. The allocation between interest-bearing deposits and equities can be influenced by changes in interest rates and tax-concessions which alter the relative attractiveness between the two, but the total tends to be quite stable as it is dominated by contractual savings. This means that although only a small proportion of personal savings are directly invested in equities, the amounts held indirectly through life assurance and pension funds are far greater. Pension funds in particular, hold a large proportion of their assets in equities as these tend to grow in line with the economy, and so provide the best match with future wages and salaries, to which pensions are linked.

Another consequence of this large stable element in personal savings is that fluctuations in the savings ratio tend to be driven by changes in borrowing. For example, the increase in the UK savings ratio in recent years largely reflects a decline in borrowing as households reined in their expenditure.

the increase in the UK savings ratio in recent years largely reflects a decline in borrowing as households reined in their expenditure.

National savings

The second measure which investors focus on is national savings. This represents savings by all sectors of the economy and so includes savings by the corporate and government sectors as well as the personal sector. In practice the government sector normally dissaves (i.e. it is a net borrower) and so national savings are less than private. This broad measure can be determined either by adding up net savings from each sector, or by subtracting consumption (both personal and public) from national income. In the UK in 1993 private sector savings were £114.8 billion (£54.4 billion from the personal sector with the remainder coming from the corporate sector), offset by dissaving of £30 billion from the government sector, to leave total national saving of £84.8 billion.

Savings and financial markets

National savings are important because they represent the capital available for financing the economy's investment expenditures on items such as roads, buildings, plant and machinery. The public and private sectors bid for funds to finance their projects which are then channelled from the flow of national savings via banks, the stockmarket and other intermediaries. To see the link between savings and financial markets it is best to think of capital like any other commodity, with supply and demand being brought into equilibrium by changes in real interest rates. The level of real interest rates then underpins the valuation of financial markets. From this perspective an increase in savings provides more funds to the economy and reduces real interest rates, boosting the value of financial markets. Conversely if the demand for funds rises, say because firms decide to increase their capital expenditures, real interest rates will be bid up causing financial markets to weaken.

To see how this works in practice we can trace out the effects of a change in savings on financial markets. Imagine that households become more concerned about the future and decide to save more – let's assume they direct a higher proportion of their income into the stockmarket. If borrowing is unchanged, the savings ratio of both the personal sector and the economy as a whole should rise. The initial effect of this would be to boost equity prices as more money chases the same amount of stock. Higher equity prices reduce the cost of raising capital and encourage companies to increase investment. In this way an increase in savings is matched by an increase in investment and the economy returns to equilibrium with a lower real interest rate.

This outcome is likely to be reinforced by macroeconomic policy changes as the authorities may reduce short-term interest rates in response to an increase in savings, in order to try to offset the fall in consumption and support growth.

International savings

From the perspective of an individual country this analysis needs to be modified to allow for the fact that the international capital markets allow a country to lend or borrow overseas. Savings and investment do not need to balance within an economy as any difference can be made up, either by borrowing capital from abroad or by lending overseas. In theory this means that countries can break free of their domestic savings constraints and by borrowing abroad raise their investment. In practice though there are limits to how much international investors are prepared to lend an individual country, as they need to be convinced that the borrowing is put to productive use so that the debt will be repaid in the future. If international capital was being used to make up a fall in domestic savings, and so was effectively financing consumption rather than investment, then there would be no increase in future growth and the increase in debt to overseas lenders could eventually become unsustainable. This would be reflected in an increasing current account deficit, and is likely to culminate in an exchange rate crisis, as international funds curtail or start to withdraw their investments.

Therefore, there are limits to how much a country can rely on international borrowing without creating strains on its exchange rate. This means that countries are largely dependent on their domestic savings to fund the bulk of their investment expenditure, and it has been notable that economies with high savings rates

economies with high savings rates also have high rates of investment.

also have high rates of investment. This has been one of the factors behind the rapid growth in the Far Eastern economies in recent years, and a feature which has attracted international investors to those capital markets.

The UK's recent experience provides an insight into how fluctuations in savings and investment affect interest and exchange rates and, therefore, financial markets. During the late 1980s an investment boom meant that the demand for capital in the UK out paced national savings by a considerable margin (see chart). To fill the gap, the UK had to attract funds from abroad and, consequently, domestic interest rates rose sharply, with adverse effects on financial markets. While it was argued, at the time, that the rise in investment would be self-financing, as it would raise the UK's long-run growth rate, much of the capital went into speculative property developments rather than more productive uses. Furthermore, although national savings were relatively stable during the period, the inflow of funds was also being used to finance consumer spending as private savings fell sharply. Eventually the increase in interest rates pushed the economy into recession, investment was cut back significantly, and private savings rose.

This allowed interest rates to fall as the gap between savings and investment closed. Thereafter, national savings and investment both fell in response to the weakness of the economy. On the savings side, this was due to a sharp increase in government borrowing which more than offset the increase in personal saving, as higher unemployment drove up public expenditure and falling activity slowed tax receipts. On the demand side, restructuring in the corporate sector led to a further reduction in the demand for capital.

Chart 2.18 UK National Savings and Investment

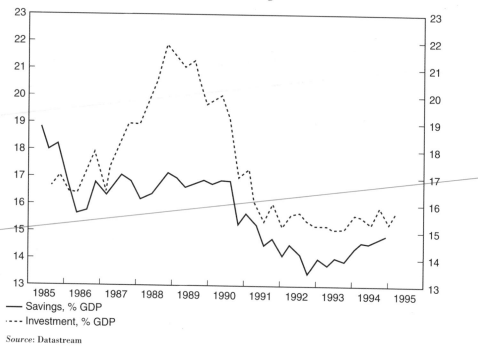

— Savings, % GDP

···· Investment, % GDP

Source: Datastream

Another consequence of international capital markets is that real interest rates are set to equalize global, rather than local, savings and investment. Consequently investors look at savings on a world scale. From this perspective recent trends have not been favourable for financial markets as, according to the IMF, global savings have fallen by about 4 percentage points of world GDP since the 1970s. This has added to upward pressure on real interest rates, and is evidenced by the increased gap between bond yields and inflation. This decline has been largely attributed to the increased absorption of private savings by the government sector, and is reflected in the increase in budget deficits. Consequently, one of the most persistent issues in the financial markets is whether these deficits can be reduced on a sustainable basis, a development which would ease the pressure on global savings and real interest rates. ♇

MONEY SUPPLY: THE GLOBAL MONEY RULE

Jonathan Wilmot

Jonathan Wilmot is Chief Global Strategist at CS First Boston in London, and author of the 'Market Focus', which now has a readership of over 5000 in 45 *countries. In addition, he works with the firm's New York hedge fund coverage group. He was International Economist at **Bank of America** and **Merrill Lynch** before joining **CSFB**.*

***CS First Boston** is a leading global investment banking and securities firm working in close co-operation with **Credit Suisse**. Through 32 offices in 21 countries, **CS First Boston** provides comprehensive financial advisory and capital-raising services and develops and offers innovative financial products for a broad range of clients.*

A Monetarist Credo

There are almost as many types of monetarism as of Christianity. On the evangelical wing are those who advocate, passionately, that central banks should follow simple rules, not discretion, in setting monetary policy. Specifically, they should adopt a constant growth rule for the money stock to prevent accelerating inflation or deflation. Or, if inflation is already high, then target a gradual but inexorable decline in money growth, preferably announced in advance, aimed at grinding inflation down to zero. Once inflation expectations have ceased to become a significant factor in economic and financial decisions, the central bank should keep them there by following a constant money growth rule indefinitely.

In the late 1970s, when inflation really was public enemy number one, such ideas became very influential. They were seen as vital insurance against the stop-go cycles that had, by then, led the world economy into a stagflationary morass. This philosophy was clearly articulated in the Thatcher government's Medium Term Financial Strategy: it was common currency in the US during the early Reagan years, and still has strong echoes in the Bundesbank.

Out of Favour

Financial deregulation and structural change during the past dozen years, however, played havoc with the simple money rule approach. In most of the G7 nations, targeted money aggregates have fluctuated more or less wildly, have been frequently rebased, redefined or changed, and have not been reliably predictive of inflation or real growth trend. The current fashion leans more towards direct targets for inflation or exchange rate pegs against another, more credible, currency. Yet, ironically, since the several global recession of 1981–2, the results of this shift to eclecticism have been sustained disinflation with moderate growth. Discretion rules, OK?

Resurrection?

Not quite. Simple monetarism is all but dead at the national level, but seems to have resurrected itself, largely unnoticed, at a global level. In contrast to the erratic national swings, GDP-weighted G5 money growth has shown modest cyclical variations around a steadily declining trend since 1980. In the light of this gentle trend decline in global money growth, it becomes less surprising that inflation (and G5 bond yields) are at, or around, 25-year lows.

Of course, this conclusion is subject to certain caveats about which national money aggregate to use as constituents of the G5 total, but that total is generally less prone to major distortions than the underlying national series themselves. In Chart 2.19, we have selected national aggregates so as to minimize the bias created by well-documented structural changes in each country's financial system. In the next section, we examine more closely the theoretical basis for this 'mysterious' monetary regularity suggested by our G5 series.

Chart 2.19 G5 Money Supply and Inflation: Annual Percent Change

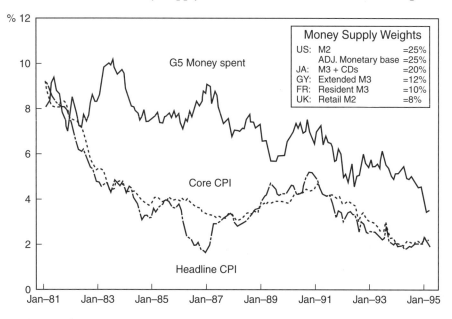

McKinnon on Currency Substitution

For a long time, Professor McKinnon advocated setting a stability oriented rule for combined money growth in the major industrialized countries, preferably linked to fixing exchange rates at Purchasing Power Parity levels for internationally traded goods. A central consideration behind McKinnon's proposal is that it would help avoid international money demand shocks from having destabilizing effects on national output and prices. For example, suppose that (non-resident and resident) holders of the main international reserve currencies decided to hold more yen and fewer dollars. The US money supply would fall and the Japanese money stock would rise, but with little or no direct implication for domestic output and inflation. If the Bank of Japan responded by tightening, and the Fed by easing, policy might become needlessly inflationary in the US and deflationary in Japan. Moreover, the policy response would, itself, tend to accelerate the shift of international reserve holdings out of dollars and into yen, inviting further instability. A joint money target would help avoid such mistakes, since the acceleration in Japan would (roughly) offset the slowdown in the US.

The Invisible Anchor

Alternatively, and this is what has happened in practice, use of discretion by national central banks inadvertently produces the more stable global pattern advocated by believers in monetary rules. Particularly if international money demand shocks (shifts between the major reserve currencies) are quite large and frequent compared to domestic shocks, one would expect to see a pattern of rather erratic domestic money growth with rather stable global growth.

A vital enforcing mechanism is the process of competition between the major (reserve) currencies, a process which has great power in today's closely integrated and deregulated financial markets. It is both quick and cheap for international investors to switch their money out of countries which appear to be pursuing imprudent policies, disrupting that country's financial markets, depressing (real) money growth and sending an eloquent signal to national policy makers to take remedial action. Free capital flows between the major currencies thus help to maintain disinflationary discipline for the system as a whole, an under-appreciated benefit. (A similar process of competition probably also played a key enforcing role under the nineteenth century gold standard, when global capital markets were also very open and closely integrated.) And so long as open capital markets endure, low world money growth will probably continue to provide an effective – though invisible – anchor for the global system.

No Utopia . . .

None of this should be taken to mean that we have somehow arrived, half unwittingly, at a kind of global monetarist Utopia. Far from it. Hindsight suggests, for example, that global monetary policy was eased rather too much in 1986, and perhaps again in early 1988 and 1993. G7 exchange rates have not been stable, nor has policy co-ordination based around wide target zones for currencies been a durable success. (Though note that the US dollar trade weighted exchange rate has been effectively maintained at a rather steady, and mildly undervalued level, since the Louvre Accord of February 1986.) Moreover, improvements in the supply side responsiveness of the global economy due to deregulation and intensified competition in world goods and labour markets have also played a key role in the disinflationary process, without which improved monetary discipline at the global level might have proved politically unsustainable.

Damping the Cycle

The next step in the analysis is to examine how G5 money interacts with cyclical fluctuations in world output, commodity prices and inflation, and to ask what recent trends might imply going forward.

Part of the rationale for pursuing a stable or gradually declining trend for money growth is that it will, almost automatically, short circuit both inflationary booms and deflationary slumps. Chart 2.20 shows the relationship between G5 real money growth and industrial production, the most cyclical component of output.

The progressive dampening of cyclical fluctuations in output shown above is highly suggestive. Accelerations or decelerations in real money tend to lead

Chart 2.20 G5 Real Money Supply and Industrial Production Annual Percent Change

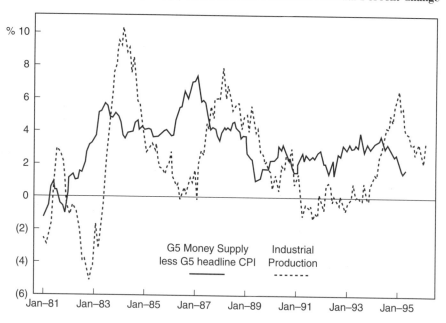

171

the major fluctuations in economic activity with somewhat variable lags, the response to monetary stimulus apparently taking longer to show up than the response to restraint.

Transmission Mechanisms

The causal chain goes roughly as follows. Suppose G5 money growth remains relatively stable in the face of a slowing or recessionary trend in real growth. With a short lag, (non-oil) commodity prices and wage inflation will start to fall, allowing real money growth to accelerate just as the transactions demand for money is slowing. In the real economy, consumers will be trying to improve their balance sheets by borrowing less and delaying purchases of durable goods. Companies will be doing the same by reducing inventories, deferring investment and reducing labour costs. Falling money and credit demand foster lower short-term interest rates and free up liquidity for investment in financial assets, with bonds initially outperforming equities. As the process unfolds, real interest rates will fall steeply (to historically low levels), but with yield curves tending to steepen as short-term rates fall faster than long rates. Equity markets will begin to revive as earnings stop falling and multiples expand in response to lower real rates. Housing activity and purchases of consumer durables will also have begun to revive in response to falling real rates.

At first, this process merely stabilizes the economy but, before too long, businesses switch from de-stocking to a dynamic inventory re-building phase. Commodity prices pick up, industrial output recovers strongly, and so does money and credit demand. Suddenly there is no surplus liquidity available to support asset prices and a savage phase of liquidation unfolds in the bond markets, driving real yields sharply higher. Yield curves typically steepen further as long rates rise ahead of short rates. The strong cyclical revival in productivity allows inflation to keep falling for a while, even while corporate profit margins are rebuilt. Equities handsomely outperform bonds as corporate earnings shoot up, but P/E multiples tend to fall. Corporate investment and hiring also starts a trend recovery.

At first, the economic recovery is immune to the tightening of monetary conditions and higher real rates. Inflation stops falling and can be expected to trend upwards if, and when, margins of spare capacity and labour have shrunk sufficiently. Short-term rates start to catch up with the rise in bond yields, yield curves typically start to flatten and real money growth starts to decelerate. However, once the dynamic inventory building phase comes to an end – usually around a year to 18 months from the cyclical trough – industrial output growth tends to moderate rather quickly to a more sustainable pace. At this point, G5 bond yields will begin to drift down again in real terms, as nominal yields fall and/or inflation rises. If (core) inflation picks up only briefly (as in 1984–5 and, so far at least, in 1994–5), then yield curve flattening will accelerate as long rates fall and short rates stabilize. If inflation trends persistently higher (as in 1988–90), the underlying trend towards yield curve flattening will be driven by short rates rising faster than long rates. In due course, slower output growth, or rising costs, or both, will usually squeeze corporate profit growth, eroding business confidence and pre-figuring a slow-down in business hiring and investment. Eventually, consumer confidence will also buckle, as income and job prospects weaken and the (OECD) economies as a group, will slide towards zero growth, or even recession. At this point, the process has come full circle and the basic sequence starts all over again.

The Bottom Line

The less world money growth accelerates during recessions and contracts during expansions, the less prone the world economy will be to extremes of inflation or slump, and the more naturally and quickly self-damping the cycle will be. Thus, the persistent, and largely unnoticed, decline in both the level and volatility of G5 money growth over the past dozen years is of great importance. Moreover, it seems that trends in G5 money, production and inflation explain the major trends in world bond, equity and commodity prices extremely well, frequently over-riding or intensifying national trends.

> **it seems that trends in G5 money, production and inflation explain the major trends in world bond, equity and commodity prices extremely well,**

In an increasingly well integrated world capital market, cycles in global asset prices seem to be rather more synchronized than the differences in national economic and policy conditions might lead one to expect. Successful asset or liability management decisions – even for those with little off-shore exposure – depend more and more on an ability to put national trends into the right global context. ♀

CAPACITY UTILIZATION: THE IMPACT ON FINANCIAL MARKETS

Geoffrey Dicks

Geoffrey Dicks joined NatWest Markets as Chief UK Economist in October 1993. Before that he spent 17 years at London Business School, where he was

Associate Professor of Economics and Head of Forecasting. He was Editor of London Business School's Economic Outlook *and* Exchange Rate Outlook.

NatWest Markets is the corporate and investment banking arm of NatWest Group.

Inflation is never far from the nerve centre of financial markets. But the analytical framework is constantly shifting. Go back thirty years and the focus was the Phillips curve, emphasizing the trade-off between wages and unemployment; twenty years ago it was OPEC and exploding oil prices. In the early Thatcher years domestic monetarism flowered; by the mid-1980s the exchange rate was key and entry into the ERM was seen as the permanent solution to the UK's endemic inflation problems.

Now, apparently, we are all 'gapologists', analysing inflation in terms of the 'output gap', defined as the production shortfall relative to what would be obtained if the economy were on trend, operating at 'normal' or sustainable levels of output – demand relative to (potential) supply in other words. The idea is that inflation waxes and wanes in direct proportion to the degree of capacity utilization. When output is above trend and capacity utilization is high (or even excessive), inflationary pressures should be rising, and vice versa when output is below trend – the existence of an output gap helps curb inflation.

The Bank of England, in its quarterly *Inflation Report*, is a typical exponent of the practice. It regards inflation as the complex product not just of the output gap, but also the rate that output is growing relative to trend and relative to the growth of capacity. It is not just the size of the output gap but also the speed with which it is closing that is seen as important. Note that the inflation analysis has two stages: the measurement of the output gap and the relationship between the output gap and inflation. The OECD in its *Economic Outlook* provides estimates of the output gap for the main economies.

Defining capacity

The economy's capital stock has two dimensions: physical and human. In the long term, to compete in world markets the quality of human capital is all important. Ultimately an economy like the UK's only resource is its people. We neglect their education and skills at our peril, especially as it is clear that other countries, particularly the dynamic economies of the Pacific Rim, are pouring resources into educational attainment.

In the short term human capital is limited by the supply of labour – the number of people, the hours they work and their skill base. Falling unemployment and/or an increase in hours worked suggest that the output gap is narrowing and that wage pressures may re-emerge (the Phillips curve trade-off). Even at relatively high levels of unemployment (localized or even general) skill shortages may appear.

In terms of physical capacity, we can distinguish between technological limits, which suggests absolute constraints, and economic capacity which is something of a movable feast. In the short term supply can be increased by working the existing capital stock more intensively. Putting on an extra 'night-shift' is an obvious example. It is also the case that the quality of new capital is streets ahead of what it replaces so that the normal cycle of replacement investment increases capacity, improves the underlying supply position, and improves labour productivity even where total output is not growing. The level of manufacturing output today is not very much higher than the level of 20 years ago, whereas employment in manufacturing in that period has virtually halved – from around eight million to today's four million plus. The consequent improvement in labour productivity owes much to qualitative changes in the capital stock as well as to improvements in human capital.

Measuring capacity

The concept is easily stated, more difficult empirically. Obvious problems include taking account of capital scrapping when measuring the overall level of capacity. There is also a clear distinction between manufacturing industry, where capacity limits have a clear meaning, and the service sector, where it is difficult enough to measure output. How, for example, should we measure the capacity of the retail sector or the financial services sector?

Chart 2.21 Change in Fed Funds vs Capacity Utilization

(1993 – 1995)

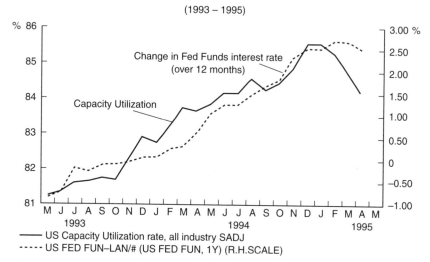

———— US Capacity Utilization rate, all industry SADJ
- - - - - US FED FUN–LAN/# (US FED FUN, 1Y) (R.H.SCALE)

Source: Datastream

In some economies, such as the US, there are official measures calculated by the Federal Reserve of capacity and hence the degree of capacity utilization for the industrial sector. Indeed casual observation suggests that US monetary policy may well have been driven in 1994 by this measure – the Fed funds rate of interest rose from 3.5 per cent to 6 per cent as capacity utilization rose from 82.5 per cent to above 85 per cent.

In the UK in contrast there is no official measure, and calculations of capacity and the output gap rely on survey data and economists' estimates. The main source for the former is the CBI survey of manufacturing industry, in particular the questions on the number of firms working below capacity and the existence of skilled or other labour shortages. It was clear from the middle of 1994 onwards that a sharp drop in the number of firms reporting below-capacity working was followed by an increase in the number of firms expecting to raise prices and thence by a pick-up in the official measure of producer price inflation.

It was noticeable that, in the new monetary regime, which gives the Governor of the Bank of England a greater public role in the formulation of monetary policy, the first increase in base rates, following the drawn-out relaxation of policy after ERM withdrawal, came in September 1994. This followed shortly after the CBI survey reported above-average levels of capacity utilization for the first time in four years, but before the low point in retail price inflation. Early action on rates contrasts sharply with the experience of the late 1980s when, despite very high levels of capacity utilization, the first tightening of monetary policy was delayed until June 1988.

Chart 2.22 CBI Capacity Utilization

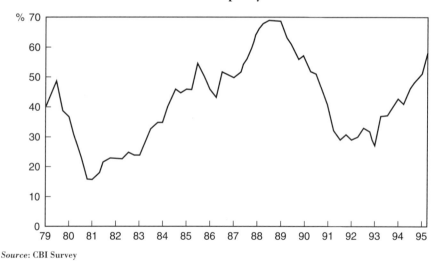

Source: CBI Survey

Relative shifts

The above concentrates on the macroeconomic picture, where the implications are clear. A large output gap, low levels of capacity utilization, implies little or no inflationary consequences and easy money, and vice versa high levels of capacity utilization point either to rising inflation or, if the authorities are concerned to avoid such an outcome, a tighter policy stance in general and higher interest rates in particular, with immediate repercussions for bond and currency markets. Indeed, forward-looking markets, seeing a rise in capacity utilization, will probably anticipate higher inflation or monetary tightening by pushing yields higher at the short end and, even more so, at the long end. Fixed income investors need to monitor developments and move shorter down the curve to minimize the risk of capital loss at the longer end, especially when capacity pressures are rising rapidly.

While equity markets may in large part take their lead from other markets, there is also a microeconomic angle. If the relative supply-demand position diverges across different sectors of the economy, the ability of firms to raise prices and thence profits may also diverge. This should then give rise to relative share price shifts which need to be taken into account in the investment decision. There could hardly be a more obvious example in the present UK conjuncture than the divergence between the buoyant, export-oriented, manufacturing sector, which is operating at high levels of capacity utilization, and the housing sector. The latter, exposed to the domestic consumer, who is facing rising taxes and interest rates, is struggling to raise operating levels and has suffered a major investment downgrade in consequence. ♥

THE FOREIGN EXCHANGE MARKET

Neil MacKinnon

Neil MacKinnon is Chief Currency Strategist with Citibank, America's biggest commercial bank and the premier operator in the world's foreign exchange market. He has been consistently voted the best forecaster and researcher in the foreign exchange market over the past few years and took the top spot in Euromoney's Annual Foreign Exchange Survey *for 1995. Before joining* Citibank *he was an economist with* Her Majesty's Treasury. *He is the author (with Paula Neal) of 'Economics – A Guide for the Financial Markets'.*

The turnover of the world foreign exchange (FX) market is estimated to be $1 trillion per business day with about 25 per cent of that total going through the London market. It is estimated that only 5 per cent of total turnover actually relates to traded goods. Financial liberalization and deregulation during the 1980s has led to an explosive increase in cross-border portfolio flows. The exchange rates which account for most of the turnover are US dollar/Deutschmark, sterling/US dollar, and US dollar/Japanese yen.

For international investors, making the right decision on the currency is crucial to maximizing total investment returns. As Japanese investors have found to their dismay, miscalculating the direction of the US dollar has cost trillions of dollars in lost returns over the past decade. Likewise, corporate treasurers working for multinational industries need to ensure that future receivables and payments are not subject to loss through unexpected currency movements. Of course, there are varieties of financial instruments available such as options which allow fund managers, corporate treasurers and other fx users to hedge their foreign exchange risk.

So what determines exchange rate movements? A popular, though misguided, approach is to use the concept of purchasing power parity (PPP). Essentially, this says that the value of the exchange rate will equate the cost-of-living between the two economies. For example, if inflation is at a higher level in the US compared to the UK, the value of the US dollar will decline relative to the pound to compensate for the loss of purchasing power. In the interim, the US dollar will be regarded as 'overvalued' and sterling 'undervalued'. At equilibrium, PPP will be achieved. Popular variants on this approach include *The Economist*'s Big Mac Index which compares the price of a Big Mac hamburger in the US with the price in other international locations. With the Big Mac being a standardized global product, so the argument goes, one is able to derive a PPP exchange rate.

Strictly speaking though, the theory of purchasing power parity as first expounded by the eighteenth century Scottish economist and philosopher David Hume is based on tradable goods. McDonald's hamburgers are not actually tradable goods as most of the cost reflects local rents, wages and distribution charges. Nevertheless, PPP remains popular as it gives a quick guide to 'valuation'. The problem is that PPP is not much use for short-term currency forecasting. In the modern fx market, exchange rates depend on a lot more than just relative rates of inflation. The modern portfolio theory of exchange rates includes such factors as budget deficits and debt/GDP ratios, relative economic growth rates, politics, etc.

It is probably best to think of the exchange rate as being the share price of a country. If ICI, say, have a board of directors that is competent and pursues policies which increase ICI's profits, other factors being equal, then ICI's share price will go up. Likewise with the exchange rate. If a government (the board of directors) pursues policies that deliver 'good' things such as steady economic growth, low inflation, reasonable budget deficits, etc. then investors will want those countries' 'shares' i.e. the exchange rate will go up. That is why higher interest rates do not guarantee that an exchange rate will go up. High interest rates produce unemployment and recessions – not good for the 'share price' and therefore not necessarily good for the currency.

If we look at the recent case of the US dollar, many pundits have been caught wrong-footed and have failed to predict the US dollar's slide. Why? Many have then argued that the US dollar was 'undervalued' – many estimates put PPP at DM 1.70 and JPY 145. However, the dollar bulls failed to take account of America's transition within a decade from being a creditor to the world's biggest net debtor. Japan and Germany, on the other hand, are the world's leading creditors. America also has a widening current account deficit (the US owes more to foreigners than it receives) and is also experiencing a capital outflow. The main reason why the US dollar fell in the 1994–5 period is due to investor concern over America's ability to discharge its external liabilities. Of course, the bail-out package for Mexico in early 1995 was the biggest in IMF history. The pumping of a never-ending supply of US dollars into Mexico is seen by investors as undermining America's traditional role as 'first spender of first resort and last lender of last resort'.

In times of financial stress e.g. Orange County, Mexico, Barings, credit quality is paramount and investment decisions are based on the 'safety first' principle. In this environment, 'hard' currencies preferred by these are few and far between – the Deutschmark, Swiss franc and Japanese yen. Why are they termed 'hard'? Because, during the period of floating of exchange rates (1973 onwards) these select currencies have exhibited long-term uptrends. Why? Because the central banks of those countries have pursued anti-inflation policies over a long-time period and delivered inflation rates below that of their competitors. The 'soft' currencies such as the US dollar and sterling have exhibited long-term downtrends reflecting erratic anti-inflation policies and a track record of exchange rate devaluation (the US dollar in 1971, when it broke the link with gold, sterling in 1931, 1946, 1967 and 1992). You can see this in Chart 2.23 overleaf.

Of course, the politicians and the bureaucrats would like to believe that the foreign exchange market is full of short-term speculators who create unwanted volatility and instability. More often than not though, it is economic policies rather than the market itself which are the source of instability. In other words, if you get the economic policies right, you'll have no problems with the exchange rate. But if you look at the problem through the wrong end of the telescope and believe that simply by fixing the exchange rate everything else will be OK, you are asking for trouble.

The ERM is a case in point. Like most fixed or semi-fixed exchange rate systems from the Gold Standard onwards, the ERM was ill-equipped to deal with recessionary situations. The real problem with the ERM in the 1990–3 period was one of interest rate misalignment rather than exchange rate misalignment. Countries that have unemployment rates at double-digit levels (i.e. most of Europe) cannot possibly sustain interest rates at double-digit levels. If they try to (as many countries did for a short time), it is only a recipe for a full-blown economic slump. That is why the markets knew the ERM was

Chart 2.23 US Trade Weighted Exchange Rate (1975–1995)

Source: Datastream

doomed to failure. Contrary to conventional wisdom, most of the currency selling was not done by 'speculators' but by genuine investors such as corporate treasurers and fund managers looking to protect their balance sheets. The desire to fix exchange rates still remains. Stage 3 of the EMU timetable looks to fix exchange rates for all time despite the fact that many countries have economic structures which respond differently to economic shocks. In other words, Greece is not Germany. Time will tell whether history repeats itself as tragedy or farce.

As far as the relationship between currency movements and financial markets are concerned, an international investor's total return in shares, bonds or money market instruments can be significantly affected by the exchange rate. For example, although the Dow Jones share index reached record highs in early 1995, the index in yen terms made a four-year low. The weakness of the US dollar at that time provided little incentive for Japanese investors to put funds in the US market.

Of course, movements in currencies can have a material effect on the direction of markets themselves. For example, during the ERM crises of 1992 and 1993, currency devaluation allowed interest rates to drop. The fall in borrowing costs as well as the cheaper currency (which improves exporters' profit margins) pushed European equity markets up. Bond markets also went up as short-term interest rates fell. Normally, currency devaluation can push inflation up (as import prices rise) , but high levels of unemployment in Europe, together with substantial excess capacity, meant that inflation stayed low – a plus for bond markets.

Those economies that continued to have exchange rate targeting as the centrepiece of economic policy and raised interest rates to defend weak currencies found that they suffered capital flight, much to the detriment of their bond and equity markets. Indeed, there is a close correlation in some cases with the yield gap (measured as the difference between the ten-year yield on the benchmark domestic government bond and the yield on the ten-year benchmark German bond). A wider yield gap is associated with a weaker domestic currency (and a stronger Deutschmark) reflecting international investors' exit from the domestic bond market.

Chart 2.24 German Trade Weighted Exchange Rate (1975–1995)

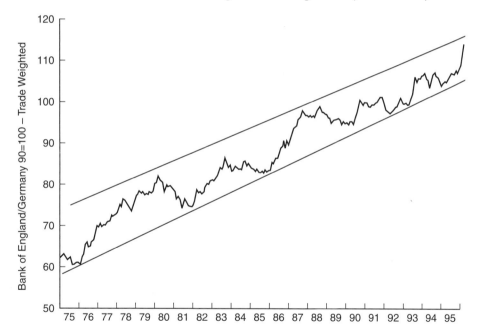

Source: Datastream

Table 2.2

	Equity Prices	*Bond Prices*	*Interest Rates*
Currency Appreciation	Down	Up	Down
Currency Depreciation	Up	Down	Up

Conversely, currency appreciation can be bad for equities (as it reduces exports), especially for open economies like the UK, where a substantial proportion of company profits are generated overseas. For the bond market, currency appreciation contains a silver lining as it reduces import costs and, therefore, helps to subdue inflation pressure. Typically, some central banks use currency appreciation as an opportunity to reduce short-term interest rates.

Table 2.2 summarizes the usual direction of markets in response to currency movements. ◓

HOUSING MARKET DATA

Robert Thomas

*Robert Thomas is the Housing and Building Society Analyst at **UBS** and is a recognized authority in the field, being frequently quoted in the financial press. Prior to joining **UBS**, he was an economist at the **Bank of England** specializing in the housing and mortgage markets.*

***UBS** is the merchant banking arm of the **Union Bank of Switzerland**, with a wide range of activities including bond and equity trading, corporate finance and commercial banking.*

Perhaps reflecting our national obsession, there are a plethora of data on the housing market in the UK. These data cover all aspects of housing from the rate of construction of new dwellings to right-to-buy public sector housing sales to lump sum mortgage repayments. These data can be placed in three main categories.

1 Residential construction activity data
2 General housing market data
3 Mortgage market data

Housing data are unusual in that their impact can be both very specific and very general. Specific because the activities of numerous companies are closely related to the well-being of the housing market. For instance, housing starts and completions data provide a good guide to activity amongst the housebuilders as a whole. And general because the importance of the housing market is such that its data form a key part of the jigsaw of information that give rise to a view of the macro-economy. While each country compiles different data, and housing elsewhere plays a greater or lesser role relative to the total economic picture than in the UK, relationships which hold in this country exist in most mature countries.

General

General macroeconomic data affect securities markets through two main channels – the information directly reveals something about the state of the economy which in turn affects company performance and profitability. But there is another equally important route for general macroeconomic data – in its signal of future policy changes. The overheating of the housing market was one of the most prominent factors cited by the chancellor in mid-1988 as an indication that policy was too loose. For those with a monetarist bent, rapid growth of mortgage lending is a signal of excess liquidity, feeding directly into the calculation of the M4 lending figures, the balance sheet counterpart to sterling M4 or 'broad money'.

Specific

Of all sectors the fortunes of the housebuilders are those most inexorably linked to the well-being of the housing market. Data on housing starts and completions provides information on builders' activity in aggregate. A number of other sectors are highly dependent on activity in the housing market, including DIY and builders merchants, and manufacturers of carpets and household durables. Sales in these sectors tend to show a strong correlation with housing turnover as a house move is often the trigger for purchases of new carpets, white goods and DIY expenditure.

The relationship between new housing construction and certain building supply sectors is self-evident. If new permit applications are rising and more construction of new houses is in the offing, can demand for bricks, window frames and other structural members be far behind? New housing usually means new roads and infrastructure – great for sand and gravel suppliers. Behaviour and the consequent purchasing pattern varies across countries only to the extent that local conditions, lifestyles and architectural preferences affect the choice of materials used in residential building. Results of specific companies will also reflect the differing point in cycles across countries. This market is more international than you would expect. UK investors wanting international exposure might look to Bardon if they are bullish on the US, but RMC if they prefer prospects in Europe.

Housing and the wider economy

First we will look at which factors influence housing market activity and then consider the ways in which the housing sector feeds back on the economy in general.

Housing is an endogenous element in the broader economy; this means that it is both affected by and affects the rest of the economy. The importance of housing as a determining influence in the economy is well

Housing is an endogenous element in the broader economy; this means that it is both affected by and affects the rest of the economy.

known but common sense would suggest that the main influences are from the economy to housing rather than the other way around.

Housing is not a particularly large part of the overall economy. As a proportion of GDP, residential investment has fluctuated around 2 to 3 per cent, one of the lowest proportions in the industrialized world, reflecting Britain's slow household formation rate which in turn reflects our stable overall population. To this could be added housing related demand which covers white goods, carpets, estate agents' and solicitors' fees and housing maintenance costs.

Looking at household expenditure patterns gives a different picture. Although we do not invest as much in the housing stock as other nations, the cost of housing is high which is reflected in the proportion of household income going on housing costs. A large proportion of this expenditure relates to servicing mortgage debt. Here Britain is exceptional, with much higher levels of mortgage debt than other countries. More than 80 per cent of this debt is at variable interest rates which is also an exceptionally high proportion.

Thus the main influence of the housing sector on the broader economy is through its effect on the personal sector's spending decisions. This occurs through the wealth effect generated by changes in the market value of the housing stock, through changes in disposable household income (after receipt and payment of interest) generated by fluctuations in interest rates and through equity extraction which gives households a cheap source of funds to finance extra expenditure.

Chart 2.25 House Prices and Disposable Incomes Adjusted for Inflation

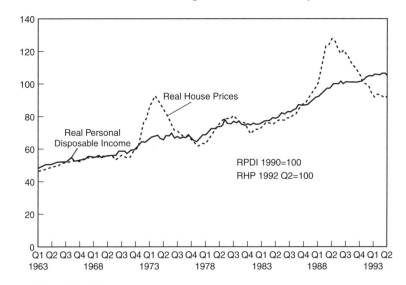

Sources: RPDI – The CSO
House Prices – Dept of the Environment, Halifax BS (post 1983) series

Unlike most other asset markets housing exhibits a relatively predictable cyclical pattern. Since the start of the 1960s, recessions in the economy have always been associated with a fall in real house prices, upswings with rising real house prices. Additionally the housing market has tended to lag the cycle in the wider economy. The underlying trend in house prices also appears to be predictable, as house prices have risen in line with incomes in the longer term.

The Future

How does one set about making predictions about the housing market? First, it is useful to separate the trend from any cyclical pattern. Over the last 30 years the trend in UK house prices has been set by household incomes as Chart 2.25 above shows. But house prices are more cyclical than incomes, and this additional cyclicality is strongly linked with the economic cycle, so that the house price/income ratio tends to rise in upswings and fall in recessions. And this process occurs with a lag – the bottom of a typical housing slump is some way into the recovery in the general economy. As a result, the low level of the house price/income ratio in the mid 1990s is not unsurprising, particularly given the severity of the housing recession of the early 1990s but it does point to a robust recovery as confidence rises. To put numbers to this, it should be expected that house prices will rise faster than nominal incomes in the latter stages of the recovery. If nominal incomes rise by 5 per cent per annum (which would seem something of a minimum), this probably points to house price inflation of 5 to 10 per cent until the next recession takes hold.

What Does a Strong Housing Recovery Mean for Securities Markets?

The forward looking nature of modern securities markets means that expectations of events move securities prices long before the events come about. It is therefore difficult to make precise predictions about the impact of a housing recovery on the market in general or on specific stocks. Consider housebuilders, whose share prices rose sharply following sterling's exit from the Exchange Rate Mechanism in September 1992 on the widely-held believe that looser monetary policy would stimulate a recovery in the housing market. Although the recovery in housebuilders' profits occurred, early signs of a slowdown in new building caused share prices to slip back. So it is advisable for investors to think beyond the immediate cyclical condition of the economy and consider each share price against a longer-term background. ●

Political Indicators

THE IMPACT OF POLITICAL DEVELOPMENTS

Steven Bell

*Steven Bell is Chief Economist of **Deutsche Morgan Grenfell**, the investment bank and asset management company. He studied economics at the London School of Economics and Stanford University and has published several books and articles on financial economics.*

Governments can and do have important effects on financial markets. Political events influence markets in three broad ways: by making a change of government more likely, by causing an existing government to change its policies or by causing investors to seek safe havens. The first two of these are relevant because they imply changes to economic policy, the third reflects movements in the attitude to risk by investors which are often the result of changes to the economic background. It is precisely because governments can have a powerful influence on the economy which make their actions so relevant. The following sections discuss the role of political factors for monetary, fiscal and other policies together with some discussion of what constitutes political stability and country safe haven status.

Political influences on monetary policy

Markets increasingly take a negative view of political influences on monetary policy. Interest rates are the key mechanism for controlling inflation and higher interest rates are unpopular. If governments are involved, therefore, the fear is that monetary policy will be too loose resulting in a rise in inflation and ultimately higher nominal interest rates.

For this reason, markets generally prefer the central bank to be independent of political control. Independence can only be a matter of degree; it is conferred by national governments which, in turn, can take it away. Institutional arrangements can be put in place which make it difficult for politicians to influence monetary policy. In recent years there has been a clear trend towards making more central banks independent. The Bundesbank was established as an independent central bank, as was the US Federal Reserve. Under the terms of the Maastricht Treaty participating countries must have independent central banks and this has duly been done in all EU member countries save the UK and Greece.

Perhaps the most spectacular change in central banking arrangements has been in New Zealand, where the Reserve Bank is independent and has an explicit inflation target. This began when a tight monetary policy aimed at reducing inflation was adopted in early 1985. As inflation started to come down in 1987, general discussion about the ultimate target began with the 0 to 2 per cent target adopted

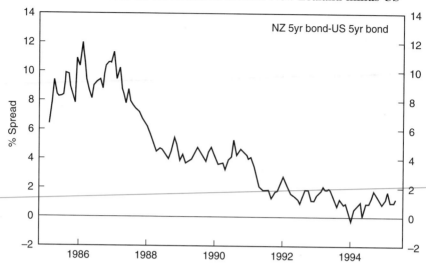

Chart 2.26 Yield on Government Bonds: New Zealand minus US

Source: Bain & Co, New Zealand

Chart 2.27 New Zealand Inflation

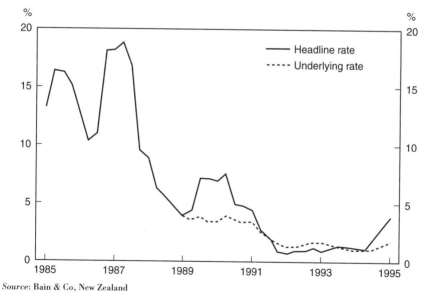

Source: Bain & Co, New Zealand

informally by early 1988. The target was not adopted formally until the first PTA (Policy Targets Agreement) was signed in March 1990, at which time the target was 0 to 2 per cent by 1992. The result has been a dramatic improvement in absolute and relative inflation performance in New Zealand.

Even in those countries where the central bank is independent, appointments to its governing body are normally made by the government. Attention therefore tends to focus on whether new appointments are likely to be hawks (tough on inflation) or doves (soft on inflation). Where hawkish appointments are made, long-term interest rates tend to fall as inflation expectations decline but if a tightening of monetary policy becomes more likely, short-term interest rates tend to rise. The currency normally benefits but the stock market may go down as a result of higher exchange rates and short-term interest rates.

Where the central bank is under government control, the scope for political influence is much greater. Markets fear that politicians will be reluctant to raise interest rates where necessary or may cut them when they should not and will be sensitive to suggestions that this might occur. Indeed there are situations where government controlled central banks seem to get the worst of all worlds: when they have a good economic case for reducing rates (or not raising them) the market suspects that political influences are at work.

Political factors and fiscal policy

Fiscal policy is relevant for a number of reasons and constitutes a significant conduit for political influences. An expansionary fiscal policy, by reducing taxes or raising government expenditure, stimulates the economy. This is good for equities, particularly those stocks which benefit directly but raises fears of overheating and inflation which may offset these effects. Interest rates typically rise but the impact on the exchange rate is unclear. This is because a rising fiscal deficit tends to widen the deficit on the balance of payments current account, offsetting the impact of higher interest rates. In practice, a sustained fiscal expansion will initially boost a currency but ultimately depress it.

Within a given budget deficit, the balance between taxation and spending is also relevant. High spending and high taxation countries tend to have lower rates of growth and higher rates of unemployment which can debilitate economic performance. When a country has a serious fiscal deficit problem, the size of the outstanding debt relative to national income becomes relevant. In extreme circumstances, a government may have difficulty funding its fiscal deficit by issuing bonds and attempt to use central bank finance. This is the modern equivalent to printing money. If the central bank is independent or its statutes prevent it from lending to central government, this route will not be possible. Weak governments, often but no longer exclusively left-wing, are more likely to allow debt ratios to rise significantly. High budget deficits and high debt/income ratios tend to be associated with current account deficits, inflation, high nominal interest rates and declining currencies.

The traditional classification of governments into left- and right-wing is no longer as useful as it once was. Following the collapse of communism and the rise of new classical economic theory which suggests that higher budget deficits do not affect the economy, there have been many cases of left of centre governments pursuing a very prudent fiscal policy and vice versa. The big deterioration in the US fiscal position occurred under President Reagan, while President Clinton has taken action to reduce the deficit. Similarly, left of centre governments in Norway and New Zealand have turned their fiscal deficits into surpluses.

It is no longer, therefore, assured that a switch to a right-wing government will result in a more prudent fiscal policy. However, it is still the case that left of centre governments are more likely to raise taxes and in some countries, notably the UK, right-wing governments have a better record on fiscal policy.

> **It is no longer, therefore, assured that a switch to a right-wing government will result in a more prudent fiscal policy.**

Other policy factors

Apart from the broad stance of fiscal policy at the macroeconomic level discussed above, there are a myriad of other ways in which microeconomic aspects of fiscal policy can influence the market. One area of particular concern in recent years has been withholding tax on government bonds. Where this is introduced, or the rate increased, foreign investors tend to move out of the markets. The ill-judged introduction of withholding tax by Germany in 1989 had a serious negative influence on the bond market.

The move to a single currency within Europe has created a very specific route for political influences on the markets. Although most political parties within most European countries are in favour of EMU, the strength of their conviction varies substantially. In addition, leaders of certain political parties have promised referendums on the issue which raise fears in the market that the result may be negative. The effects are normally seen on the interest rates and currencies of weaker countries. Were, Italy for example, to become a member of EMU, its interest rates would fall markedly and the stability of its currency would be more assured. Similar arguments apply, to a lesser degree, to other members of the EU whose prevailing interest rates are generally above those in Germany. In the UK, the Conservative Party is deeply split over its attitude to Europe and evidence of this split widening tends to depress the exchange rate and raise long-term interest rates. Were EMU to be implemented, national monetary policy would cease and political factors would be considerably diluted in member countries.

189

What constitutes a safe haven?

Safe haven countries attract international investment funds in times of great uncertainty. A safe haven country may therefore offer returns that are relatively low but secure. What are the characteristics of a safe haven country? The world's leading industrial power and reserve currency normally has clear safe haven status. Before the last World War, this position was occupied by the UK, now it is the US. As a result, the US dollar has safe haven status in times of international turmoil. The Gulf War in August 1990 and the Soviet coup a year later both saw a sharp rise in the US dollar. In each case, the dollar's rise was temporary, because the political events were temporary or, at least, had temporary economic effects.

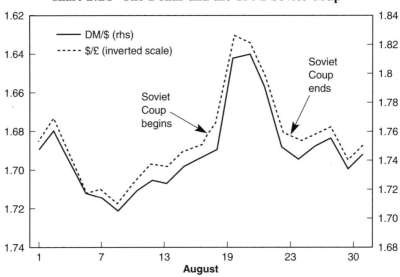

Chart 2.28 The Dollar and the 1991 Soviet Coup

Source: Deutsche Morgan Grenfell

Yet the safe haven status of the dollar has been undermined in the last decade or so by persistent current account and fiscal deficits in the US. This has resulted in one of the basic principles for safe haven status being violated: a strong currency. Indeed low inflation and prudent fiscal policy are normally the hallmarks of a safe haven. For these reasons, Germany is increasingly being regarded as a safe haven. This is in marked contrast to the situation which prevailed before the collapse of the Soviet Union, when Germany experienced outflows and currency weakness in times of turmoil. Switzerland, although no longer the great financial power that it once was, retains safe haven status due to its long track record of political neutrality coupled with the more traditional safe haven virtues of low inflation and sound financial

190

policies. When the Deutschmark strengthens for safe haven reasons, the Swiss franc often strengthens further.

War and Civil Disturbance

The above discussion relates mainly to mature developed countries. These countries are, in most cases, militarily secure and enjoy robust political institutions. In emerging markets civil disturbance can threaten weak political institutions and war can be financially catastrophic. Yugoslavia, for example, has defaulted on all financial obligations. Leading indicators of civil disturbance are high inflation and recession. Countries with ethnic tensions and income inequality are prone to civil disturbance. Former communist countries were often free of civil disturbance or were able to suppress it quickly. Some totalitarian regimes in the Middle East, Africa and Asia, are in a similar position today. Yet, in each case, pressure for democratization increases over time, a transition which can cause considerable difficulty.

Oil producers have a special role in this context because of their influence on the oil price. Many OPEC members have domestic political problems and are frequently involved in international disputes. The oil price has been declining in real terms since 1980 but the problems of the major producers will continue to affect world markets, perhaps increasingly so.

In South America, several countries have made the transition to liberal democracy. In some cases, such as Argentina, this has been followed by tough policies which have virtually eliminated inflation. This puts strain on any system, including a democracy. Having survived this process, the political risk premium diminishes. It is notable that, when Mexico's finance crisis struck in December 1994, many expected Argentina's currency board system which ties the peso to the US dollar, to collapse. Yet it survived the Mexican crisis.

Conclusion

Political events are a crucial influence on financial markets. As in all influences on market prices, the effect depends on the degree to which they are unanticipated. A general election won by the clear favourite will leave markets undisturbed on day one. Thereafter, the markets will move as policies are implemented that differ from expectations. Many of the political 'shocks' discussed – the Gulf War, German withholding tax, Soviet coup – had large, but temporary, effects on markets and there is a tendency for markets to over-react to such events. But it would be a mistake to conclude that this is a reliable rule. Investors who sold New Zealand bonds in 1987 on that basis would have lost heavily. In analysing and interpreting political developments, the investor must decide which are temporary and which permanent. This is one of the fundamental questions in all investment analysis. ◉

Taking the Temperature

The Put/Call Ratio
Bulls vs Bears: Advisor Sentiment
Purchasing Managers' Surveys

THE PUT/CALL RATIO

Ralph Bloch

*Ralph Bloch is a Senior Vice President at **Raymond James** who does technical analysis of the equity markets and individual stocks. Bloch's weekly column is published in the 'Mansfield Stock Chart Service', and he was an original contributor to* The Encyclopaedia of Stock Market Techniques. *His investment career began 36 years ago with **Merrill Lynch**, and he has been writing weekly commentaries since 1962. He is a former Chairman of the Ethics Committee of Market Technicians.*

*Founded in 1962, **Raymond James Associates** is the eighth largest brokerage firm. With a combined total of more than 2300 account executives throughout the US and Europe, it provides financial services to more than 400,000 individual and institutional client accounts, and is listed on the NYSE.*

Definition: the Put-Call Ratio is a sentiment indicator, all of which are contrary opinion indicators. One of the most difficult approaches in the stock market is to try and statistically verify what consensus thinking is and then have the wherewithal to do the exact opposite. Difficult, but almost always fruitful.

The P-C ratio is calculated by dividing the number of puts on a daily basis by the number of calls for the OEX (Standard and Poor's Option Index). These are the people making direct bets on the direction of the overall market as opposed to merely an individual issue. P-C ratio readings are available on the half hour by calling the CBOE (Chicago Board Options Exchange). The OEX P-C ratio can work during a lengthy trend (up or down) and also literally on a day-to-day basis. The pattern of high P-C ratios during the current powerhouse uptrend has continued in 1995 into the end of April, which is when this was written. The market has run some 700 points since early December and the P-C ratios are so high that it's startling. All through 1995 they fought the rally and actually exploded on days that were in minus territory.

The advent of options rendered ineffective a couple of indicators on which most technicians relied. Some still use Specialist Shorts, Short Interest Ratio, and Odd-Lot Shorts. I do not, simply because these tools are no longer 'clean'. In other words, these segments of the investing world can 'hedge' their positions, which makes it difficult to get a true 'read' on their thinking. In the old days a Short Interest Ratio (total number of shorts on NYSE divided by the daily average volume) of 2.0 or higher was almost an automatic buy signal after a sharp decline. In recent years I have seen ratios over 5.0 without a response from the market.

These old tools have been replaced and improved upon by the Put-Call Ratio. This is far better and far more sensitive, on a day-to-day basis, than any indicator in our technician's bag of tricks. I have seen it work beautifully on an intra day basis. The following will attempt to show a few periods of relatively recent origin that highlight this indicator's value from a longer-term view, and other occasions where it has indicated a direction change coming from a very short-term perspective of one to two days.

Possibly the most significant and dramatic example of how this indicator kept me long for virtually the entire run was the drama of 1987. It also evinced the shift in sentiment – from Bearish (high P-C ratios) to acceptance of the rally (low ratios) in late July–August 1987 – via falling ratios that got me out.

The first two days of 1987 posted institutional buying 'stampede' figures. The Put-Call Ratios were very high for that period. These levels have changed in recent years as more investors and traders are utilizing options. On 9 January 1987, I put out a special wire stating that the P-C ratio had become very high – 62 per cent – having started the year in the 35 per cent range. That morning the market had opened 8 points lower and the bears bought puts in size into what turned out to be the seven-month bull run of some 700 points. By 2:00 p.m. that day the market was plus 13 points – a good example of an intra day call. The rally continued and the bears grew ever confident that the market was either (i) wrong or (ii) had moved so high, so fast that it *had* to come down. So, on 19 January 1987, the P-C ratio absolutely exploded to 95 per cent, and I advised my firm not to go short. By early August of the same year, the P-C ratio began to drop from the higher levels established earlier. On 5 August 1987, for example, it fell from 72 per cent to 47 per cent – a dramatic one-day shift. I stated at the time that I would be a short seller if it fell any further. After a few days of higher readings, it dropped to a very low 37 per cent on 11 August 1987.

By late August, the market was falling sharply and the P-C ratio, via puts, should have been exploding if traders were going to benefit by going short. In actuality, they were viewing the sell off as an opportunity to buy the market. After seven months of shorting rallies into a powerhouse up trend, they were now finally buying calls just as the killer bear market was starting. My 21 August 1987 weekly report was titled 'Sell New Highs'. The market went on to score a new high which proved to be the peak. This call was the direct result of the shift from scepticism of the rally from January through August 1987 (high P-C ratios) to acceptance of the rally in August (low P-C ratios). A perfect call for the P-C ratio. We will add that this new behaviour pattern remained as the market fell for quite a while.

Let's shift to the 10 per cent drop from early February 1994 to the market's intra day low of 3,520 on 4 April 1994. As the market was falling, the P-C ratio didn't really rise to significant levels (as might have been expected) which would have indicated a bottom was forthcoming. In other words, 'they' had remained relatively sanguine during February and March as the DJI fell from intra day 4003 to 3800 in early March. There was a 100-point rally into late March and then prices fell off a cliff, eventually landing at 3,520. P-C ratios finally began to explode after a 500-point drop, rising to a whopping 196 per cent at 11:00 a.m. on 29 March 1994, just days from the absolute low. On 3 April 1994 the P-C ratio was 181 per cent at 11:00 a.m. – the day before the low. They sat and watched the market fall all those points before they got bearish, then did so smack into the bottom!

Just a few words on how to interpret changes in the OEX P-C Ratio. One of the things I'm always on guard for is a change in a well-established pattern of trading. Why, because such changes are almost always meaningful and prepare you for possible direction changes in the overall market. Therefore, if we have seen continued high levels of scepticism from 4 April 1995 to the end of April 1995 we have to be on guard for a shift in this picture – similar to August 1987. If I were to see falling P-C ratios, that would mean that, after fighting the rally for one year, they are now starting to accept it (having been wrong for at least 700 points). I would become an aggressive seller if I saw readings in the mid 70 per cent range (into still rising prices) for several days. If low readings persisted as the market fell, I would get even more bearish. Such action would mean that they are viewing the start of a drop as opportunity to 'buy' – after doing the opposite for at least one year.

In the limited space available we've tried to illustrate how my favourite indicator fared during a rising market and how well it served me during a falling market. There are, I assure you, a myriad of other occasions when it served the believer extremely well. I will make a startling statement – it has rarely failed. ♀

ADVISOR SENTIMENT

Michael Burke

*Michael Burke has been the Editor of **Investors' Intelligence** since 1982. This publication has been ranked second in market timing as measured by **Hulbert Rating Service** for the last five and seven years, and has been consistently in the top three for mutual fund advice since 1987. Mr Burke appeared on the* Forbes *Honour Roll in 1995 and is a winner of the* Value Line *Stock Picking contest. He is a regular guest on CNBC.*

Chartcraft, *which publishes the* Investor's Intelligence, *provides analytical market timing services, one of which is the widely used* Sentiment Index.

Investors' Intelligence Sentiment Index measures the bullishness among investment advisory newsletter writers in the US like Joseph Granville, James Dines and Martin Zweig. Most brokerage firm newsletters have a bullish bias, so all but a handful of the 130 we track are by private non-brokerage companies or individuals.

The Composition of the Index

The *Sentiment Index* was started in 1963 by Abraham W. Cohen. The original idea was that if a large majority of 'experts' were bullish, the market would go up; if a large majority were bearish, the market would go down. We quickly found out that the opposite was true.

Starting with about 50 newsletters, Cohen would read each one and decide if the writer was bullish, bearish, or looking for a correction. Bullish letters were openly telling you the market was going up, or were suggesting a number of stocks to buy. Bearish letters were those telling you the market was going to go down, or recommending short sales or a very low percentage invested position. Newsletters looking for a correction were those who were long-term bullish, but short-term bearish. A letter writer who said 'we like General Motors, but would only buy it if it dropped three points from current levels,' would be in the correction camp.

Determining the status of the letter writers is, of course, judgemental, but Cohen tried to be constant in his treatment. Since many of these writers will often hedge, be vague, or even contradictory, someone else reading these same letters might differ in their opinions of the status. Fortunately, the vast majority are very clear as to what they are thinking, so the difference would not be major, and probably no more than 5 per cent or so.

The orginial idea was that if a large majority of 'experts' where bullish, the market would go up; if a large majority were bearish, the market would go down. We quickly found out that the opposite was true.

In addition to Cohen, over 30 plus years, only Michael Burke, Rayne M. Herzog, and John E. Gray have judged the status of the newsletters. We have always tried to keep the survey as consistent as possible.

There is also a fourth category, neutral. With the Dow Jones average at 3,800, they might be saying, 'buy if it goes above 3,900, sell if it drops below 3,700.' There are always a few of those and we exclude them from the total count.

Letter writers tend to be trend followers, so very often during upmoves there are more bullish advisors than bearish ones and, during market downmoves, there are more bearish ones than bullish ones. At major turning points, however, we often find too many bulls or too many bears. Extreme readings often come before the actual peak or low in the market so don't expect to find the most bulls at the very top, or most bears at the very bottom.

Lessons from History

At the end of April 1965 the percentage of bulls reached 67.3 per cent, the highest reading seen since the inception of the index two years earlier. About a month and a half later a sell-off started that dropped the DJIA down around 13 per cent in July. Readings of over 60 per cent bulls indicate a lot of optimism among advisors and a cautious attitude should be adopted. In 1965 at the July lows we saw two consecutive readings of more bears than bulls. In bull markets, corrections often end with a week or two of more bears than bulls. The market usually rises very quickly when this happens. After the turnaround in July 1965 the market upmove saw the percentage of bulls rise to 64.4 per cent by October. The DJIA peaked in February 1966.

1966 was a bear market year. During the decline we saw more bearish advisors than bullish ones for 19 weeks in a row, the eighth longest streak of net bears in our history. The end of such streaks has always been followed by good gains in the market. The average advance in the DJIA has been 29 per cent over a nine-month period. The most recent streak, the longest in our history was 45 weeks, ending on 3 March 1995.

Previously, the seven longest streaks ranged from 19 to 40 weeks. The ending of very long streaks with more bears than bulls is a very bullish development. When everyone is so pessimistic for so long it means that there is lots of money on the sidelines that will usually find its way into the market at higher levels. Long periods of too many optimists are usually followed by above average market drops.

An important market top was made from the end of 1972 to December 1973. Eight readings of bulls over 61.1 per cent took place in that time frame. In January, Barron's had a now famous cover story titled 'Not a Bear Among Them', as they interviewed a number of analysts regarding their outlook for 1973. The disastrous bear market that followed saw the DJIA drop almost 50 per cent from high to low, while the broad-based line index of stock prices dropped around 75 per cent from its 1968 peak to its December 1974 low.

During the 1974 decline we saw 13 weeks in a row with over 59 per cent bears each week. From the start of this very, very high reading of bears the DJIA dropped from 80 per cent to 577 at its final low in December 1974. Critics point to that period as one in which the sentiment readings did not work, and on a short-term basis they were absolutely correct. On a longer-term basis, however, that was only one of two periods that you could have bought with the DJIA below 700.

Bear markets normally end with the percentage of bears over 55 per cent. Any time the percentage of bears goes over 59 per cent, a down move below

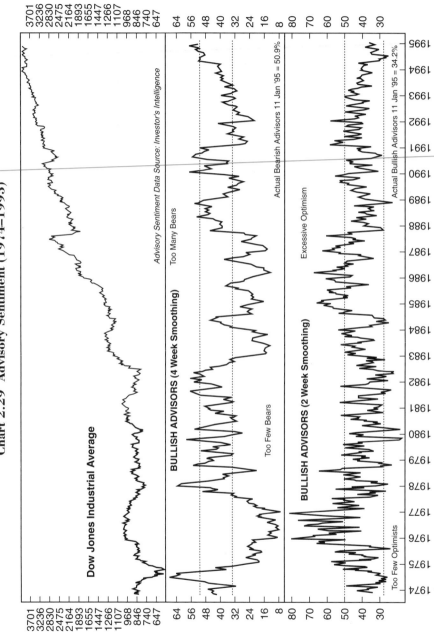

Chart 2.29 Advisory Sentiment (1974–1995)

197

59 per cent in the bears makes the market a buy. This happened in December 1994 when we saw back-to-back readings of 59.1 per cent and 59 per cent and the DJIA, as of the third week of March 1995, is up around 450 points.

Some of our other rules are: bull market peaks are preceded by readings of bulls over 60 per cent, but good corrections can start with readings over 50 per cent. Another rule is when the percentage of bulls and bears are both very high, with very low correction reading, expect the market to go sideways for around five weeks. The market then goes in the opposite direction the advisors go during the sideways movement. For instance, if we see a reading of 46 per cent bulls, 44 per cent bears, 10 per cent correction and the market goes sideways while the bulls go up to 50 per cent and the bears go down, look for the market to go down. If, during the consolidation, the bears go up over 50 per cent while the bulls go down, look for the market to go up.

Advisory sentiment, though extremely important, is only one of the elements needed to establish overall market sentiment. In our work we also use put/call ratios, short interest ratios, and insider sales/purchase readings to give us an overall total sentiment picture. ☻

PURCHASING MANAGERS' SURVEYS

Chris Williamson

Chris Williamson is an economist responsible for running the monthly UK Survey of Purchasing Managers conducted by NTC Research and for producing the Report on Business, *in which the survey findings and analysis are published, on behalf of the Chartered Institute of Purchasing and Supply. NTC is one of the UK's largest specialist providers of business research and information.*

Purchasing Managers' Surveys have been conducted in the United States Since 1930 by the National Association of Purchasing Managers (NAPM) and in the United Kingdom since 1991 by their sister organization, the Chartered Institute of Purchasing and Supply (CIPS). The speed by which the survey findings are processed means that hard data, not forecasts or indications of intentions, are available often months ahead of equivalent government statistics. The surveys therefore provide the first indication each month of the state of the manufacturing economy.

Around 300 questionnaires are sent around mid-month to purchasing managers, on which they state whether their company's situation has improved, deteriorated or not changed compared with the previous month for eight different categories. These categories are new orders, output, employment, suppliers' delivery times, stock levels of items purchased, stock levels of finished goods, the quantity and prices of goods purchased.

An index is then calculated for the eight categories monitored. These indices vary between 0 and 100 per cent. An index reading above 50 per cent signals an improvement in conditions compared with the previous month; below 50 per cent signals a deterioration. An index of exactly 50 per cent signals no change. Each index is seasonally adjusted.

The Purchasing Managers' Index (PMI), the most important single piece of information derived from the survey, is a weighted average of the first five categories listed above. The size of each weight is determined by each component's ability to lead the economic cycle. Thus, new orders, which drives all of the other categories, is assigned the greatest weight. Stock levels, which tend to lag in the economic cycle, are assigned the lowest weight. When the PMI exceeds 50 per cent this indicates overall growth in the manufacturing economy compared with the previous month. A reading below 50 per cent indicates contraction.

Furthermore, because conditions in manufacturing industry tend to change ahead of conditions in the economy as a whole – whether they be improvements or deteriorations in performance – the survey also acts as a leading indicator as to the performance of the economy as a whole. Research in the US and UK has found that the PMI and associated indices are closely correlated with comparable official data series, although the relatively short data run of the UK survey can lead to only tentative conclusions. By plotting the NAPM (US) index against US gross domestic product (GDP), a close correlation is seen between the two series.

> **Research in the US and UK has found that the PMI and associated indices are closely correlated with comparable official data series**

Chart 2 30: NAPM Index and US GDP Growth

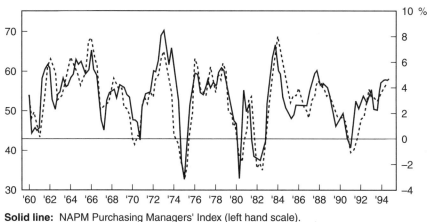

Solid line: NAPM Purchasing Managers' Index (left hand scale).
Dotted line: US Gross Domestic Product, annual % change (right hand scale).

This quite clearly demonstrates the PMI's usefulness as a timely guide to future GDP figures, which suffer the disadvantages of being published only on a quarterly basis, are subject to long delays before publication and are often revised significantly. Consequently, the NAPM Index is widely regarded as one of the most important and eagerly awaited economic indicators in the US. Recognition of the usefulness of the UK equivalent is growing rapidly.

The Prices, Output, New Orders and Suppliers' Delivery Times Indices are probably the other most valuable individual measures to watch. The New Orders Index provides the first indication of change in activity levels, while the Suppliers' Delivery Times Index provides important evidence of over-heating in the economy. The index tends to lengthen as suppliers become busier, the first signs of manufacturers reaching filll capacity. The Output Index provides a reasonably accurate advance indication of official manufac-turing output data.

Chart 2.31 CIPS Output Index and UK Manufacturing Growth

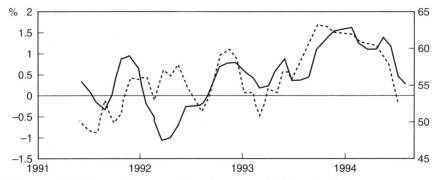

Solid line: CIPS Output Index, 3 month moving average (right hand scale).
Dotted line: Manufacturing output, 3 month on 3 month % change (left hand scale).

The Prices Index is closely watched as an early warning indicator of the build up of inflationary pressures. This has been noted by the Bank of England:

"The February CIPS Survey [released 1 February 1995] showed that a season-ally adjusted positive balance of 76 per cent of purchasing managers reported that prices had risen during the month. The CIPS measure has tracked input prices fairly closely over the past three years, but has risen much more sharply in recent months. It is possible that the CSO [official] index is not as sensitive to price discounting as the CIPS index; if the CIPS measure has detected a pick-up in prices as discounts have been withdrawn, this could soon be reflected in an increase in official input prices."

The Bank of England Inflation Report, February 1995

200

On 16 February 1995, a full two weeks after the release of the CIPS data, official UK figures showed the biggest annual increase for 10 years in manufacturers' fuel and raw material costs.

Chart 2.32: CIPS Prices Index and Government Producer Input Prices

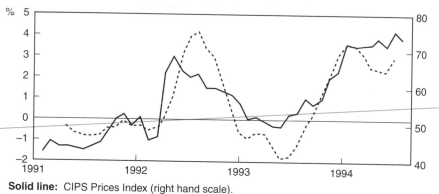

Solid line: CIPS Prices Index (right hand scale).
Dotted line: Manufacturing input prices, 3 month on 3 month % change (left hand scale).

The surveys are able to provide such an accurate and timely picture of the economy because the surveys are simple, therefore fast to compile and collate, and because purchasing managers comprise an ideal survey base. Purchasing executives tend to have access to information denied to other managers. They must anticipate the needs of a growing business as soon as expansion becomes possible and, conversely, they must cut spending when business turns down. The companies are carefully selected to ensure that the survey panel composition closely resembles each manufacturing industry's contribution to Gross Domestic Product.

The UK survey findings first started moving financial markets in 1994, largely due to concerns at the time regarding inflation. The CIPS survey findings are frequently referred to in the minutes of the Bank of England and Treasury monthly monetary meetings. As such, any indication of a build-up of inflationary pressures – either through manufacturers' costs rising sharply, or the manufacturing economy growing faster than its long-term potential – may affect interest rate decisions. Shares and gilts have both been affected in the past, as has the value of sterling:

"UK government bonds dropped sharply through key psychological levels, dragged down by fears of rising inflation . . . Inflation fears were triggered by the UK purchasing managers' index for June, which showed a sharp rise in manufacturing activity and strong price pressures. . . . London equities were hit hard by heavy falls in British government bonds on news of a sharp rise in the Purchasing Managers' Index for June."

Financial Times 1 July 1994

Conversely, a year later the survey reinforced suspicions of slower growth and reduced markets' fears of inflation, leading to a strengthening of the value of sterling

"DECLINING ORDERS SUGGEST RECOVERY IS SLOWING DOWN
The purchasing managers' index indicated that one in seven manufacturers reported that they reduced output in May, with the biggest drop among component manufactures."

"The results appear to give further ammunition to Mr Kenneth Clarke, UK chancellor, following his decision to leave interest rates unchanged last month."

"Signs of weakness in the purchasing mangers' index prompted a rally in interest rate markets, with the September short sterling contract closing 13 basis points higher at 93.10."

Financial Times 2 June 1995

The survey findings are published in both countries on the first working day of the month in the *Report on Business*. In addition to the index numbers, the reports summarize important anecdotal evidence from the questionnaires, providing an insight into why the indices may have moved in a direction which was not anticipated. A detailed list of items which were in short supply or changed in price is also included, providing information on the feeding through of price rises from commodities to manufactured inputs within each sector of manufacturing. ☻

VALUE RELATIONSHIPS

Michael Lenhoff

Michael Lenhoff graduated with a PhD in economics from the London School of Economics in 1975. He is head of the research department at Capel-Cure Myers Capital Management and is also portfolio strategist responsible for making recommendations on the firm's asset allocation. Capel-Cure Myers Capital Management Limited is an independent investment management house which provides a full range of international investment services to private clients, unit trusts, pension funds and charities.

Can portfolio managers recognize value? Are they able to exploit it? The attempt to do so happens, for many professional investors, to be an instrumental part of active portfolio management. But is it a credible approach or merely the pretext for a talking shop?

Our analysis offers empirical support for a value-based philosophy to investment in the UK equity market. We find there is a correction mechanism at work. This correction – upwards following an undervalued situation and downwards following an overvalued situation – represents a separate and distinctive force from the influence of interest rates and corporate fundamentals on the equity market.

These findings have prescriptive and somewhat paradoxical implications for asset allocation. We shall see how the analysis can lead to an aggressive allocation to the equity market when, on the face of it, the economic background appears least favourable for equities; and how it can lead to a defensive stance when economic conditions appear most favourable for equities.

Measuring Value in the UK Equity Market

What is not widely appreciated is the extent to which value influences the equity market and how this influence differs from other key factors which 'drive' the equity market such as interest rates and corporate fundamentals like dividends or earnings growth. But what is value? A high dividend yield? A low price-earnings ratio or low gilt-equity yield ratio? We argue that the investment merits of the equity market should not be judged on the basis of the dividend yield or the price-earnings ratio or the gilt-equity yield ratio alone. For example, one might think that a high dividend yield denotes a cheap market. But if interest rates are expected to remain at historically high levels and corporate dividends are expected to grow at a slower rate than usual, an historically high dividend yield is warranted and the market is not cheap.

What is relevant for the determination of value is the difference between say the actual dividend yield and its warranted level, i.e., that level which is theoretically justified by the prospects for interest rates and corporate fundamentals such as dividend payouts. Chart 2.33 shows estimates of what this difference (expressed as a percentage of the actual yield itself) has been historically for the UK equity market.

Overreaction as Sine Qua Non for Value

While it is not the intention here to explain why periods of over or under valuation arose and persisted when they did, it is curious that for most of the eight-year period spanning 1976 through to 1984, the tendency of the UK equity market was toward undervaluation. For much of the period, interest rates were at historically high levels and real dividend growth stagnated. The combination of these factors would have had the effect of keeping up the warranted yield. With the equity market deserving of a low rating for such a prolonged period the natural persuasion of investors may have

In 1994, interest rates were historically low and real dividend growth was accelerating. The combination, had it been sustained, would have warranted an historically low dividend yield.

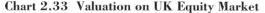

Chart 2.33 Valuation on UK Equity Market

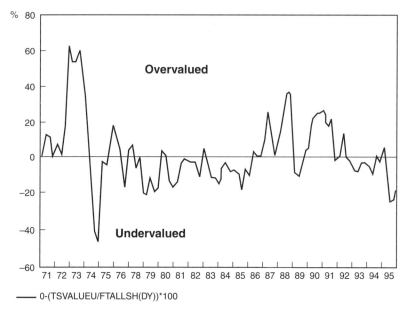

── 0-(TSVALUEU/FTALLSH(DY))*100

Source: Datastream

been biased towards overreaction. This would have pushed market yields above warranted levels and so sustained the tendency toward undervaluation.

Which brings us to last year. 1994 was a good example of when the dividend yield did not have to be unusually high for the equity market to be considered undervalued. If anything, the dividend yield was unusually low even after the US Federal Reserve's change in monetary policy induced global bear market conditions. In 1994, interest rates were historically low and real dividend growth was accelerating. The combination, had it been sustained, would have warranted an historically low dividend yield. What changed after the Federal Reserve raised interest rates were expectations about future interest rates and real dividend growth worldwide. The trauma in equity markets led to overreaction and overreaction produced the degree of undervaluation for the UK that is illustrated in the chart.

Our conclusion is that value is created by overreaction. Yield may be driven to critical levels by over-zealous buyers or fervent sellers but, by itself, yield need not be historically high (low) for the equity market to be undervalued (overvalued). Value can exist even when the dividend yield is below the historical average.

Correcting for Overreaction

We are arguing that value is created by overreaction due to changes in the expectations for interest rates and corporate fundamentals. What may be the warranted dividend yield in one quarter need not be warranted in another quarter. The reappraizal and induced rerating of the equity market invariably leads to overreaction which in turn generates an over or undervalued situation.

Chart 2.34 combines our estimate of the time series for the historical valuation of the UK equity market with the actual changes that took place in the aggregate index (the FT-SE-A All Share Index). The chart shows an inverse relationship between the valuation in one quarter and the percentage change in the equity market over the following four quarters. The series for the changes in the price index has been shifted back by one full year in order to illustrate this inverse pattern. Generally, a period of overvaluation is followed by a negative price change and a period of undervaluation by a positive price change. In other words, the response to an overreaction in one period is a correction in the aggregate price index in another period.

Chart 2.34 Valuation and Price Changes

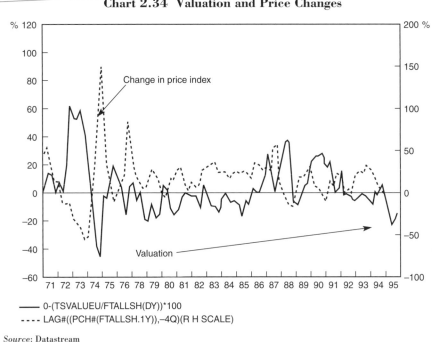

0-(TSVALUEU/FTALLSH(DY))*100
LAG#((PCH#(FTALLSH.1Y)),–4Q)(R H SCALE)

Source: Datastream

Quantifying the Influence of Value

Does this process of correcting for overreaction lend itself to quantification? An econometric analysis indicates it does. Indeed, it shows that three factors are largely responsible for explaining the behaviour of the UK equity market. These are contemporaneous changes in long-term interest rates, 'earnings momentum' – namely the rate of change in corporate earnings growth, and valuation as illustrated in Chart 2.34. The results are summarized in Table 2.3.

205

Table 2.3 Percentage Impact on UK Equity Market of a 100 Basis Points Change In:

1. Long term interest rates	−9.3
2. Earnings momentum	+1.0
3. Valuation	+4.3

These results are interesting in several respects. First, they indicate the over-whelming importance of changes in long-term interest rates on the UK equity market. Second, they show that while corporate fundamentals are not unimportant, it is only earnings momentum – the rate of change in corporate earnings growth – which is important and not earnings growth itself. Third, and perhaps most novel of all, there is a correction mechanism at work in the UK equity market where overreaction is the key.

This correction mechanism is sustained by perceptions of the warranted dividend yield which are themselves conditioned by expectations of interest rates and corporate dividends. These expectations are subject to revision and this in turn alters investors' notion of the warranted dividend yield. By its very nature, the induced rerating of the equity market produces overreaction and a subsequent correction.

The correction in the equity market – up following the case of a yield premium and down following the case of a yield discount – is quite separate from the effects of changes in long-term interest rates and earnings momentum. While the initial impact of overreaction is of less importance than changes in long-term interest rates, it is of more importance than earnings momentum.

Implications for Tactical Allocation to Equities

The estimates in Table 2.3 imply that the ideal position for the equity market is one where value is present, where long-term interest rates are declining and where earnings momentum is positive. Is there a particular stage in the economic cycle where, by some happy coincidence, this ideal position is to be found?

Figure 2.35 depicts four phases of an economic cycle. It combines two of the three factors shown to affect the behaviour of the equity market, namely changes in long-term interest rates and earnings momentum. Phase I is where the trend of long-term interest rates remains downward, reflecting say the monetary policy regime of the central bank, and where earnings growth is positive. Such features are associated with an economic recovery and during this phase corporate earnings growth tends to accelerate. There is thus a momentum gain.

Phase II is the maturing or expansionary stage of the cycle. Here the trend of long-term interest rates is upward, reflecting say the shift in the monetary policy regime of the central bank, and corporate earnings continue to grow. Often however the earnings growth slows down. There is thus a momentum

206

loss in this phase. In Phase III, long-term interest rates continue to rise, reflecting an increasingly tight monetary policy regime, but earnings begin to decline and the loss in earnings momentum acquired in Phase II is sustained. We have labelled this stage the terminal phase because of its association with the end of the cycle. Stagflation, that uneasy combination of slow or stagnant growth and rising inflation, is likely to be found in this stage of the cycle.

Finally, Phase IV is where the trend of long-term interest rates is downwards, reflecting once again the shift toward relaxation in the monetary policy regime of the central bank. In this stage of the cycle corporate earnings continue to decline, but the rate of decline decelerates. Thus there is a momentum gain. These characteristics tend to be symptomatic of recession.

Of course, the cycle need not progress from one phase to the other in the counter clockwise direction indicated. The progression could proceed from recovery to expansion and then back to Phase IV which, as indicated, extends to the case of a slowdown or growth pause. Such a progression might be called the soft landing in contrast to the hard landing where the progression is from mature expansion to the overheating conditions and/or stagflation implicit in the terminal phase of the cycle and then to recession.

Chart 2.35 The Economic Cycle

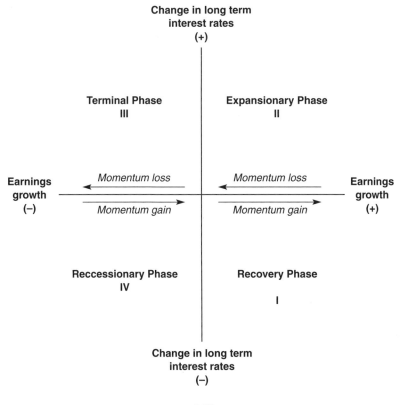

207

This highly stylized representation fails to capture in detail every aspect of the economic cycle but the salient features which it describes help illustrate the main point of the exercise which is to demonstrate when an aggressive (defensive) stance on the UK equity market is most desirable. Such a framework might be extended to other equity markets, particularly those which are more liquid than others (for example the United States, Germany, France) and where there is some recognizable relationship between valuation criteria on the one hand and the relevant economic background as identified for the case of the UK on the other (the notable exception is likely to be the idiosyncratic Japanese equity market). In the case of the US, for instance, there is much evidence that the prices for common stocks vary inversely with dividend yields in preceding periods. Such behaviour is consistent with our notion of overreaction and suggests that the kind of framework developed for the United Kingdom may well apply elsewhere.

Recall that the estimates in Table 2.3 imply that the ideal position for the equity market is one where value is present, where long term interest rates are declining and where earnings momentum is positive. Chart 2.35 indicates that the latter two are characteristic of the recessionary and recovery phases of the cycle, namely Phases IV and I. Although value can be created at any time, it tends to be prevalent in and around recessions which would take in the latter stages of Phase III, all of Phase IV and the early stages of Phase I. Phase IV, the recessionary phase, is thus the one stage of the economic cycle where the likelihood is greatest that all three factors identified in Table 2.3 will unite to provide the most favourable backdrop possible for the equity market.

In Phase III interest rates rise, earnings decline and in the process suffer a momentum loss. The analysis leads to the paradoxical conclusion that investors ought to be more committed to the UK equity market when economic fundamentals such as economic growth and corporate profits seem least attractive, and less committed to the UK equity market when the economic fundamentals appear most attractive.

Prospects for the UK Equity Market

Where does this analysis lead? What does it suggest about where the market will be over the course of the next two years? And what commitment should investors have to the equity market?

In the framework of Chart 2.35, the UK economy is approaching the mature expansionary phase of the cycle. This warrants a less aggressive allocation to the equity market than would be the case in the recession or recovery phases of the cycle. However, in the latter stages of 1995, long-term interest rates are expected to fall. This backdrop combined with a deceleration in earnings growth is comparable to the soft landing conditions that form part of Phase IV. As such a more aggressive approach to the equity market would be warranted at the time.

As Chart 2.33 shows, value existed throughout most of 1994. This suggests that there should be some correction during 1995. All things considered, the bottom line is an expected rise in the UK equity market of some 15 per cent from end 1994 levels. For 1996, we expect long-term interest rates to continue declining but earnings growth to undergo a further loss of momentum (though earnings will be growing). The combination should be good for another 12 per cent rise.

Utilizing Investment Strategies

ACTIVE ASSET ALLOCATION

Steven L. Bakovljev

Steven Bakovljev has enjoyed a varied career in the City since 1977. He has experience of securities sales, trading, research and fund management, and has had the benefit of working for British, Japanese, and American companies. Until May 1995, he was Chief Investment Officer responsible for investment strategy with **INVESCO Asset Management,** *London. He has since started his own fund management company,* **Alnista Capital Management,** *featuring funds which aim at positive returns rather than index comparable returns.*

Experts and professionals are renowned for overcomplicating their stock in trade due to the difficulty in determining the key ingredients which will provide a simple solution to a seemingly simple problem. Investment is no exception.

This article will endeavour to provide some pointers for making 'common sense' decisions, although these are neither exhaustive nor foolproof. My efforts will concentrate on establishing the environment and price at which different asset classes are attractive, and leave for others in this book to help with pinpointing the timing of switches between them. The scope is limited to the three primary asset classes in which investors place their free liquid savings; cash, bonds and equities.

Cash

The attraction of cash is the capital security it offers over both the short and long term. It is unfortunately regarded by many as a non-investment, a residual, a cop out. This is a big mistake. The dash for cash following the crash of 1987 is typical of investors who undergo a complete about turn when reminded that financial markets are and will always be cyclical, and that 'normal' valuations and ranges are not only durable, but that they reassert themselves with a vengeance. The greatest attraction of cash is that bonds and equities tend to move in the same direction, so when times get rough, it really is the store of value which ultimately enables you to acquire long-term assets at a lower cost.

The major disadvantage of cash is the inherent instability of its return. Many savers in the UK will recall the colossal decline of deposit rates during the early 1990s, as base rates sank from 15 to 5.25 per cent between 1991 and 1994. Savers who had budgeted a satisfactory income return watched mesmerized as the high yields slipped through their fingers. They were left scrambling for higher income, higher risk products at less attractive prices than had been available just a short time before.

Chart 2.36 UK Yield Curve
Bond yield less cash rate

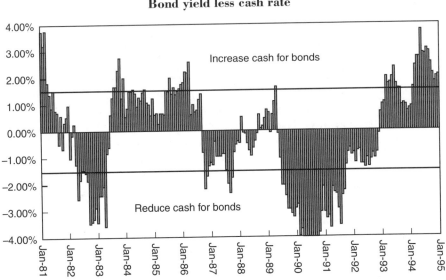

Sources: Bloomberg Financial Markets, Datastream

So, what general measures can we apply to gauge the attraction of cash as an investment?

The yield curve : when cash yields are 1.5 per cent <u>higher</u> than bond yields, the peak in interest rates is approaching. The typical investor is mistakenly inclined to sit on cash. This is a good time to accumulate bonds to lock-in high yields as cash rates are likely to drop. Conversely, when cash rates are 1.5 per cent <u>lower</u> than bonds, this is a better time to accumulate cash (see Chart 2.36).

The economy : strong economic growth pushes interest rates higher – accumulate cash. Weak growth leads yields lower – reduce cash.

In conclusion, cash is at its most attractive when the return it offers is low with a tendency to rise, not when it is high with a decline in prospect. From an asset allocation standpoint, the former condition coincides with high bond and equity markets, while the latter is more typical of depressed financial markets. Shifting into or out of cash in these circumstances should not be too difficult, although the greed and fear syndrome tend to get the better of us all. It usually means having the courage to switch to a lower yielding, more volatile asset; a counterintuitive decision.

cash is at its most attractive when the return it offers is low with a tendency to rise, not when it is high with a decline in prospect.

Bonds

The time to acquire bonds and fix the interest income is when there are prospects of falling rates. Just as cash is threatened from lower interest rates, bonds are threatened by rising inflation eroding your real capital value. This is why bonds have not been a popular investment in the UK or other countries which have been prone to high inflation. Inevitably, the means by which to best judge the attractiveness of bonds revolves around prevailing and prospective inflation.

> **Just as cash is threatened from lower interest rates, bonds are threatened by rising inflation eroding your real capital value. This is why bonds have not been a popular investment in the UK or other countries which have been prone to high inflation.**

Bond yields reflect the relationship between the demand and supply of credit in the economy. The most common error is the belief that government financing in bond markets is the best reflection of the demand for credit in the economy and, therefore, an overwhelming influence on the level of bond yields. From my experience, the inverse is closer to the truth, since the private sector of the economy is the biggest borrower. Governments tend to borrow heavily when the economy is weak and private sector borrowing slows.

The measures of bond market attraction are to some extent a mirror image of cash valuation;

The yield curve: as explained above, a good rule to follow is when bond yields are materially <u>lower</u> than deposits, buy bonds, and vice versa.

The economy: strong economic activity is bad news for inflation, credit demand and therefore bonds. Weak activity is good news since inflation subsides, private sector credit weakens, and bonds benefit.

Real bond yield: the satisfactory yield offered by a 10-year gilt-edged bond is 3~5 per cent in excess of inflation. A reasonable measure of the attraction of bonds is the degree to which current real yields deviate from this range (see Chart 2.37). Gilts become a low risk investment when the real yield exceeds 5 per cent, and increasingly high risk investment below 3 per cent.

Equities

Rules of thumb for equity evaluation proliferate to infinity. At risk of over-simplifying, I have narrowed down three factors which go a long way to explain the potential for the equity market. These are; profits, interest rates and the risk premium. The future level of the equity market may be defined as follows:

Chart 2.37 UK Real Bond Yield
(10 year Gilt less RPI)

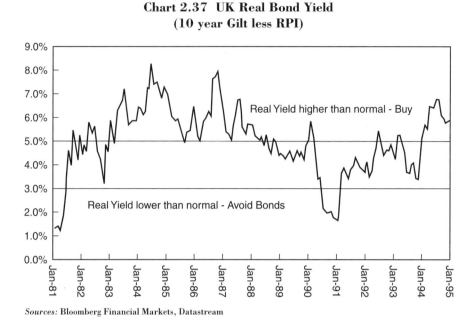

Sources: Bloomberg Financial Markets, Datastream

$$\text{Profits} \times (\, 1 \, / \, \text{Bond Yield} - \text{Normal Risk Premium}\,)$$

Naturally, this is easier said than done, but the method below will help to arrive at a reasonable estimate of value and therefore price direction.

- **Profits** Economists and strategists are often quoted in the media with their profits forecasts (earnings per share or EPS). Unfortunately, most people, especially industrialists, confuse the market direction with the direction of profits. This is wrong. Bear in mind that is only part of the answer.

- **Bond yield** Estimates and forecasts are widely available. I have chosen 10-year government bonds due to their universal availability, a prerequisite for global asset allocation. The reason why bond yields are so important is that they are a dominant influence on the price earnings ratio (P/E) of the equity market, and therefore provide the framework in which to judge the multiple we should apply to profits to estimate an appropriate equity market level. High bond yields lead to low P/E multiples, and low bond yields to high P/E multiples.

- **Risk premium** My definition of risk premium is the historic difference between bond yields and earnings yields (1 / P/E). For the UK market, earnings yields have been on average 3 per cent lower than bond yields since 1980. The risk premium can and does occasionally move significantly

Table 2.4

	EPS	Bond Yield	Risk Premium	Effective P/E	Market Level
Today	150	8.0%	–3%	20.00	3,000
Example 1	175	9.5%	–3%	15.38	2,692
Example 2	135	7.0%	–3%	25.00	3,375

from normal bounds. The most dramatic example was the run-up to the crash of 1987 when bond yields reached 10.32 per cent while earnings yields were on a lowly 5.65 per cent, a difference of 4.67 per cent.

From here, the estimation of the market potential may be calculated as in Table 2.4 above.

Example 1 assumes a rise in EPS of 16.6 per cent from 150 to 175 and higher bond yields (9.5 vs 8 per cent). As a result, the effective P/E becomes 15.38 (1 / 9.5 per cent – 3 per cent). The expected market level is then 175 times 15.38 which is 2,692. Similarly, Example 2 assumes a fall in the EPS of 10 per cent (from 150 to 135), but a drop in bond yields to 7 per cent. As you can see, this combination results in a higher market level as the P/E has risen to 25 times.

For global asset allocators like myself, we are all looking at variants of the above calculations, even though every one of my peers may have a slightly different approach. What makes our task particularly interesting is the application of these formulae to many different markets, where the tendency, trend and predictability of some of these factors can vary enormously. Further, the margin for error in any of the projections is very limited. Don't take my word for it, try some of the maths above with small variations, and you will soon find that the difference between choosing a winner and an also-ran can be very small.

In conclusion, I urge you to follow rule number one in any 'how to invest' manual. Do your homework! Do not be misled into hearing and reading only that which suits your original idea. If you shop around for opinions, you will find every shade of grey. Not every one of them can be correct. Try some of the ideas I have mentioned above, and always remember that investment is about the future, not the past. Just because markets have gone up, or interest rates have fallen, does not meant that they will continue in the same direction. Finally, using simple rules of thumb will help you to remove the emotion from your decisions. Following the herd is a wonderful, safe, warm feeling, Sadly, it seldom adds to the bank balance.

You have been warned. Good luck. ♀

Technical/Chartist

Technical Analysis: A Conceptual Introduction
Technical Analysis: Some Practical Applications
Japanese Charting Techniques: Candlestick and Kagi Charts

TECHNICAL ANALYSIS: A CONCEPTUAL INTRODUCTION

Elli Gifford

Elli Gifford is a Director of **Investment Research of Cambridge Ltd,** *the oldest established technical research house in Europe. She was previously a Director of* **Rudolf Wolff,** *one of the world's largest metal broking houses and specializes in technical analysis of international markets, including stocks, currencies and financial and commodity futures. She is Editor of* **Investment Research's** Cambridge Futures Charts *and* Global Trends. *She is also the author of the recently published* The Investor's Guide to Technical Analysis, *published by Pitman, the definitive work on this subject currently available in the UK.*

Technical analysis is a subject which has recently attracted the attention of academics from mathematicians to rocket scientists and is now the basis for generating trading signals in dealing rooms around the world. It is the analysis of price behaviour in financial markets – as against the fundamental analysis of the value of the underlying assets that that price represents. Share prices not only reflect 'value', but also the hopes and fears of those in the market. This emotional element can allow periods of over enthusiasm or panic to develop which cause prices to move well away from their 'value', sometimes for protracted periods of time. As price and value often differ, analysis of the economic background and the balance sheet alone is insufficient to allow an investor to time market commitments well. Price analysis is needed to get the timing right.

As price and value often differ, analysis of the economic background and the balance sheet alone is insufficient to allow an investor to time market commitments well. Price analysis is needed to get the timing right.

Much technical analysis as it is used today has developed from the work of Charles Dow, a nineteenth century economist who edited the *Wall Street Journal*. He recognized it was the action of the people in the marketplace that caused prices to change, rather than the news itself. Dow had noted that his Industrial Average would stop rising and start to fall once investors' expectations had been fulfilled, some time before the *Journal* carried evidence that the economy had peaked. And, likewise, prices would stop falling and start to rise once those with money in low-earning deposits had enough confidence to enter the market to buy relatively high yielding blue chips. This would occur some time before improvements in trading conditions were evident. This introduced the now well-recognized concept that markets discount future events.

Technical analysis is effectively based on market psychology; it recognizes that people make prices and, in that the emotional makeup of the human does not change. If a certain set of circumstances recurs, traders will react in a similar manner to how they did in the past; and the resultant price move will likely be much the same in extent. The 1929 and 1987 market crashes were extreme examples of this. Technical analysts monitor price charts whose plots trace these patterns and trends and, using past experience as a guide, make predictions.

A price trend will normally form as a series of 'building blocks' which are broadly sideways movements subsequently resolved by prices moving outside the range. The 'building blocks' represent periods when prices are in equilibrium. Rallies peter out as earlier highs are neared since buyers do not wish to pay more than they have had to do previously. Reactions stall as the lows are approached. Sellers are unwilling to accept less. This activity occurs the vast majority of the time and technicians refer to these periods as bouts of consolidation, with the price region around the highs being called resistance and that around the lows, support.

These levels are critical – with prices paying particular attention to them if they represent all-time extremes or round numbers, such as 100. These numbers cause re-examination of the fundamentals, and put a stop to an impulse buy (or sell). Sudden enthusiasm – or renewed fear – allows the range to be abandoned.

This sharp move will eventually attract profit-taking or 'bottom picking' and will reverse. However, the fall (or rise) will likely be stemmed as the price area in which the earlier resistance (or support) is approached as people will recognize that prices have moved sharply from this area before and the price is now looking 'cheap' or 'dear'. It is this change of perception of value that allows trends to form.

This 'step and repeat' performance forms a trend which can be monitored by a straight line or, more usefully, a parallel trend channel that encompasses both the highs and the lows, allowing an assessment of where the inclined support and resistance lies. Such phenomena occur frequently when a semi-logarithmic grid is used. This form of scaling forces price plots to show in terms of percentage change and it is a very effective way of monitoring longer-term trends. Not only do convincing channels form but the volatility of one market can be compared to another at a glance.

A popular way of assessing where the trend lies is by the use of moving averages. At their simplest they are the sum of the last 'n' closing prices, divided by 'n'; they are called 'moving' averages since the calculation is repeated as each day ends. Frequently more than one average is used. A common combination is the use of the 50-day moving average to monitor the medium-term trend and the 200-day to delineate where the long-term trend lies. A bull market is identified when a short-term moving average is rising above a longer-term one, and a bear market is in place when the opposite is the case. Not only should support and resistance be found in the region of the averages, their distance from one another is a useful indication of how over-bought or oversold the market may be. In short-term trading (when, say, 5 and 10 or 10 and 20-day moving averages may be used) traders often treat a bullish crossover as a buy signal and a bearish one as a sell. In that moving averages necessarily lag price moves, this discipline ensures that the position is retained for as long as the trend lasts and not abandoned on an aberrational price move that causes a panic sale.

Pattern analysis assists in gauging how far a price move may go. The shapes that develop within trends are called continuation patterns and, once the price exceeds its earlier boundaries, the subsequent move can be estimated by mea-suring the depth of the consolidation and extrapolating this amount in the direction of the price break. Continuation patterns take several different shapes; the most common is the rectangle – basically a broadly sideways trend – but sometimes triangles and, occasionally, diamonds form and the move once these have been resolved can be very fast indeed.

It is a common misunderstanding that, once a price trend is breached, it will reverse. This is a dangerous assumption to make since trends frequently slow in their later stages, causing a breach, before they resume, albeit at a slower pace. Reversal is signalled when the last reaction low in an uptrend – or the last rally peak in a downtrend – is breached, when the more famous technical patterns, such as the head and shoulders top, form.

The long-term monthly range chart, chart 2.38 shows several interesting technical properties:

1   A reversed head and shoulders pattern allowed the downtrend to turn round in early 1989. Its upward prediction was fulfilled in four months.

2 & 3   These patterns are triangles, strong continuation patterns within trends. Their upward predications (made by measuring their bases) were fulfilled with ease.

4   This pattern is a relatively uncommon continuation pattern – a diamond. It is an energetic one and the prediction from it is made by measuring its depth and extrapolating this distance up from the point of breakout. It is a formation you would not expect to find in a downtrend.

5   The chart is plotted on a semi-logarithmic grid which has allowed the six-year uptrend to be defined within parallel lines. This trend has now been breached, opening up the possibility it may be reversed.

Chart 2.38 Marks & Spencer Monthly Range

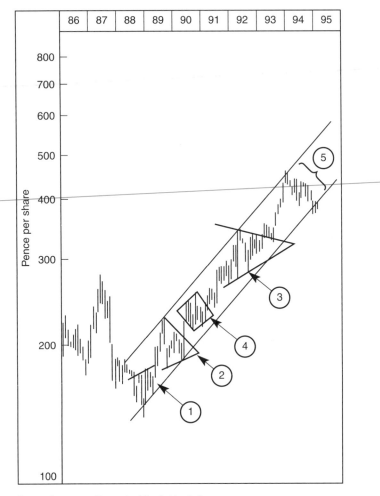

Source: Investment Research of Cambridge Ltd

Over the long term it is the market's assessment of fundamental factors that allows bull and bear markets to form. However, there comes a stage when judgements among those in the market increasingly begin to differ. This shows on a price chart as a wide band of argument which often continues long enough to break even the longest trend. There is then a growing likelihood that, eventually, this argument will be won by the opposite forces to those that previously have prevailed. In that people, ever-cautious, turn bearish more quickly after a bull market than they turn bullish after a bear market, basing patterns often take very much longer to form than tops.

The head and shoulders reversal, together with all technical patterns, takes its name from its shape; it looks like a human head and shoulders in silhouette.

It is a pattern which has a high degree of success in fulfilling price predictions once it is resolved. It forms in an energetic manner, usually after a very fast trend. The argument is excited; if it is a head and shoulders top the first sign a reversal could be seen is when, after a reaction, prices move into new high ground but the move is accompanied by lower volume and the new highs are not retained. Prices ignore the support from the previous rally peak and the fall extends to the last reaction low. The bounce from this support is often relatively short-lived and accompanied by even lower volume still. Once the line joining the reaction lows is breached the fall can be anticipated to extend by the height of the head and shoulders itself. This is measured from the head down to the neckline – the name given to the line joining the reaction lows. The reversed head and shoulders forms in the same way – but upside down.

Chart 2.39 Marks & Spencer Daily Range

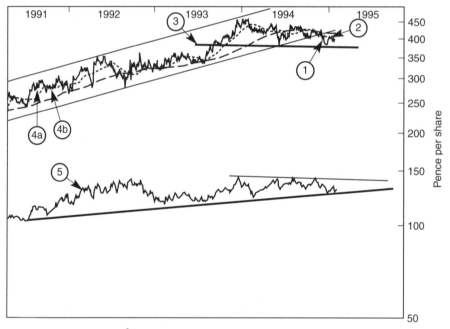

Source: Investment Research of Cambridge Ltd

While Chart 2.38 shows the long-term price history of Marks & Spencer, Chart 2.39 shows the recent developments on an amplified time scale – it is plotted daily. The techniques employed by technical analysts are the same, whatever the periodicity of the chart.

1   The breach of the parallel trend channel shows up clearly here.

2   It is interesting to note the late 1994 rally found resistance from the back of the lower trend line. It is the nature of support that, when

broken, it reverses its role and becomes resistance – whether it is horizontal support or, as in this case, inclined. The same happens with resistance too; once breached, it becomes support.

3   This is the neckline to the potential multiple top. While prices hold over the mid-1994 reaction low, this long uptrend will stay in place. But a breakdown would signal falls to 275p at least – measured from the January 1994 highs to the neckline at 370p, and extrapolated down. It is interesting to note that the neckline is virtually coincident with the 1992–3 highs which are offering support. This is the top of the triangle seen in Chart 2.38 (pattern 3).

4 (a)&(b)   These are the 50- and 200-day moving averages, used to define the medium- and long-term trends. During the early part of the chart, they identify an uptrend but, since June 1994, they have been in bearish sequence, implying a top pattern could soon firm. However, a breach of the neckline is required to confirm this. Note how the averages gave misleading signals when prices moved sideways during 1992.

5   The relative strength line is a ratio of the price of Marks & Spencer to the FT-SE Actuaries All Share Index. It remains in an uptrend – albeit a slowing one – still, suggesting a breakdown in price is not a foregone conclusion.

More common reversal patterns are double, triple or multiple tops and bottoms which form in a similar way to the head and shoulders but are usually less energetic and predictions from them may be less accurate. Indeed, although they are more common, they can be considered more 'difficult', since they frequently are indistinguishable from the rectangle (the most common continuation pattern) until the last moment, when the neckline is breached.

Clues that a trend may be vulnerable to reversal can often be gained from the indicators with which technical analysis now abounds. Most are calculations based on the price and many measure the speed with which price change occurs. In that a trend often slows before it is reversed these momentum indicators give early warning of an imminent trend change.

A generic term for the measurement of the rate of price change is 'momentum' and one of the simplest oscillators carries this name. It is the differential between the price now and that 'n' periods ago, where 'n' is usually half the length of the cycle observed. It forms similar shapes to the price itself and oscillates either side of a zero line. There are two main signals that momentum can give: when it rises or falls to levels from which it, and prices, have previously reversed it is warning that the market move is overextended and a reaction or rally is due. The other, equally important, signal is seen if the price moves through a previous extreme but momentum fails to do so too – it has not 'confirmed', it has diverged. If such divergence occurs when momentum is in an area identifying overextension then serious alarm bells ring.

Chart 2.40 FT-SE 100 Index & Momentum

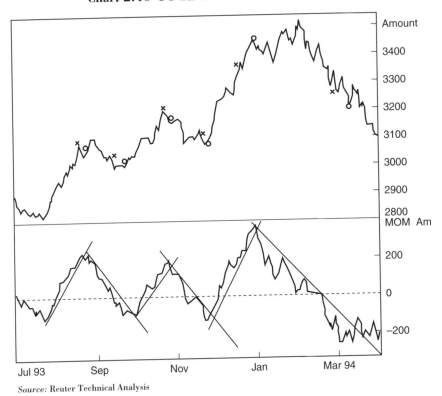

Source: Reuter Technical Analysis

Additionally, a simple technique is to monitor momentum's trend; its breach can give very early warning indeed.

The momentum indicator in the bottom window highlights periods when the market is overbought or oversold and thus prone to reversal. The points where the indicator reaches overextended levels from which it has reversed previously are marked with crosses on the price chart. The circles highlight the price levels when the trends in momentum were broken – pinpointing prices very near the absolute extremes, in most cases. These indicators should take on the same shape as the price curve. When they do not do so – for example, when the moves into new high ground in early 1994 by the price were not confirmed by momentum – alarm bells ring. This signals the likelihood the new highs in price will not be sustained. But sometimes these signals can be very premature. The downtrend in momentum was broken in early March, but prices continued falling until June. This chart additionally highlights the point that overbought and oversold levels alter according to the market background. While the market was in an uptrend, +200 was overbought and –100 oversold. Now a downtrend is in place, –200 is oversold and +100 overbought.

There are hosts of indicators and oscillators in use today. Broadly speaking, their interpretation is based on the general rules outlined for analysing momentum itself. However, any analysis of the stock market would be incomplete if mention of one of the most frequently used indicators – relative strength – were not made. It is the ratio of the share price to a market index; its plot rises or falls when the share performs better or worse than the market itself. A share's trend may be vulnerable if, following a bout of outperformance, the relative strength line sinks back. It could be warning of switching into another sector or share. In the opposite circumstances a bull signal can be given.

A trend goes on until it stops; when it is reversed. These matters and the assessment of overbought and oversold conditions and warning signals from oscillators should all give the investor a greater insight into market developments – and the ability to time commitments better. ♀

TECHNICAL ANALYSIS: SOME PRACTICAL APPLICATIONS

Robin Griffiths

*Robin Griffiths is Chief Technical Analyst at **James Capel**, where he heads up the Technical Analysis department and publishes regular newsletters with global coverage of 32 markets. Prior to joining Capel he was a Partner in **WI Carr** and **Grieveson Grant**, where he authored the* Amateur Chartist Newsletter. *He was Chairman of the British Society of Technical Analysts from 1988 to 1990 and is now a Fellow. He was the Chairman of the International Federation of Technical Analysts for three years, and remains a Director.*

***James Capel** is owned by the **Hong Kong and Shanghai Bank** and has offices in most major financial centres. It is known for good research in most markets and deals primarily in equities.*

The theory of technical analysis is inherently interesting as an academic subject, but most people will concentrate on it with far greater attention if they think it is going to make them money. There are several ways in which it can do this and, curiously, the least important of them is the apparently most obvious, namely that it will help make better forecasts of the future in financial markets. It is possible to use technical analysis to make good forecasts and draw out a map of how the chart should look as time goes by, but we also get signals that are more analogous to traffic lights. We may not know when they will go red or green but the action to take on these signals can be set out as a rule based system. Used in this way technical analysis is a discipline that responds without emotion to changing market conditions, and can make far more money than any ability to forecast might imply.

It is probable that very small fluctuations in market prices are random, or at least not easily distinguishable from a random walk, which amounts in practice to the same thing. However, the longer term moves have a significant

Chart 2.41 Schumpeter's model

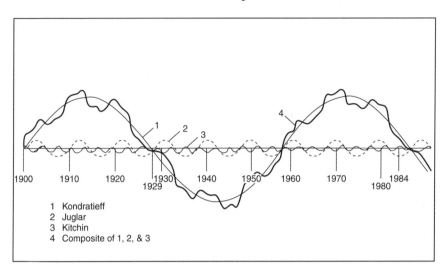

1 Kondratieff
2 Juglar
3 Kitchin
4 Composite of 1, 2, & 3

tendency to trend that is far higher than the laws of chance allow for. Forecasts are therefore made by recognizing and extrapolating those trends into the future. The longest trends are driven by underlying economic factors. Economists have long ago recognized different lengths of cycle in activity and, back in the 1930s, Schumpeter published the model shown in Chart 2.41. This puts together three cycles, one very long term named after Kondratieff, a decadian rhythm after Juglar, and the normal cycle documented by Kitchen. The composite complicated line is the result of these interacting, and is the reality that stock markets try to discount. The shape of the stock market chart will relate to this model, only always be in front of it in time.

Chart 2.42 shows a map that was first published by Charles Dow. The heavy bell-shaped curve represents the prime trend for the market through one Kitchen wave in the economy. Superimposed on it are smaller fluctuations of intermediate length and very short-term duration. The complete cycle averages four and a quarter years, although individual cycles have been as short as three and as long as five years. The intermediate surges and setbacks last three to nine months, and the short-term fluctuations from one to six weeks. Monitoring where one is on this basic model, and then extrapolating into the future, is part of the process of forecasting.

This model is frequently distorted from the normal shape, but only to a limited extent and always for a reason. Understanding these factors, and the cause and effect they will have, is the next step. In practice most markets tend to trend upwards through time as they are based on growing economies, giving a skew to the map. This has the effect of making the up part of the move last longer and be larger than the down. On average, markets trend up for 32 months, hardly ever for less than 20 months, and only rarely for as long as 44 months. On the

Chart 2.42 Market Cycle Model

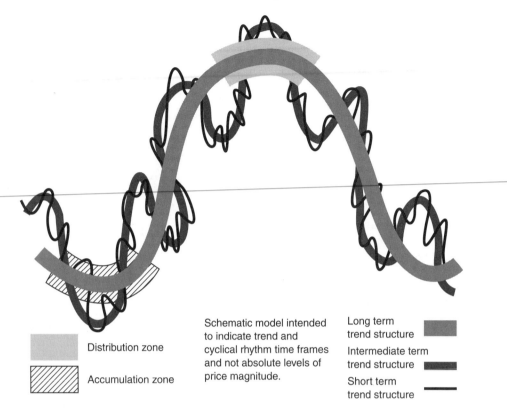

Distribution zone

Accumulation zone

Schematic model intended
to indicate trend and
cyclical rhythm time frames
and not absolute levels of
price magnitude.

Long term
trend structure

Intermediate term
trend structure

Short term
trend structure

downside the average duration is about 14 months. This shape is often called the Elliott Wave, and is covered in greater detail on pages 525–533.

In the presence of a strong secular uptrend the model will be distorted favourably. This is a trend that persists longer than one cycle of four years, and is almost always driven by a rapid compound rate of growth of GNP. The Far East markets tend to behave like this and smaller emerging markets could be expected to. In the case of individual stocks, the key driving variable behind such a trend would be rapid growth of dividends and earnings per share. Some companies have such a business franchise that this run can last for over a decade. Xerox is a good example The main difference is that it will change the normal shape of a bear into more of a plateau shape. Chart 2.43 shows this. The initial fall in the bear will be small, and the normal bear rally goes to a new all-time high. It will only be the final decline in the bear that looks and feels like a negative trend at all.

Chart 2.43 Bear Market with Secular Uptrend

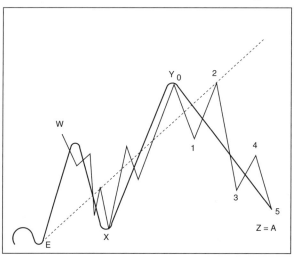

In a secular downtrend the distortion goes the other way as shown in Chart 2.44. The normal cycle is depressed into the flat shape shown. This was our forecast for Japan. It was made several years in advance and is the exact shape that has been traced out in real time on the chart for both the Nikkei Index and the Topix Index.

Chart 2.44 Distortion for Secular Downtrend

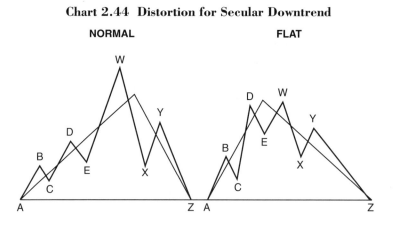

It becomes possible to build up a road map for the overall stock market and then for the major stocks within it, which helps to indicate what to buy and sell, and when to trade. Of course in practice not all sectors and stocks move together, but rather in sequence. In a normal cycle it is often the most interest-rate sensitive groups which move up first. The action will be taken up in time, progressively through groups that are co-incident with the economy, and ending with the heavy engineering sectors which tend to lag.

The analyst needs a filtering system to monitor where different stocks are on this cycle. Moving averages of the price are one method. As a price starts to advance it will first meet Charles Dow's description of an uptrend. The pattern on the chart will become one of rising highs and lows. If this persists, then the price will cut up through a short-term moving average, a 25-day average would be useful. Then, if the rise is to last longer, it will cut a 50-day and finally the long-term or 200-day moving average will be

Of course in practice not all sectors and stocks move together, but rather in sequence. In a normal cycle it is often the most interest-rate sensitive groups which move up first.

cut. A computer can quickly scan large lists of stocks to rank in descending order those that have risen upwards through these various averages. It can also calculate the rates of rise of the trends and compare these to the rate of rise in the underlying general market index. In this way the stocks can be compared and ordered, both as to their position in the road map but also to their current, actual and relative performance. This enables a useful buy and sell list to be compiled and a diagrammatic forecast of what to expect from each stock price.

At this stage the skills and discipline of the technical analyst have become a semi-quantitative technique for sector and stock selection. Obviously by using the same methodology for different markets in the global context then market or asset allocation decisions can be made.

The principle of confirmation is important as it builds confidence in the forecast. On any chart the actual price move should be confirmed by relative strength, but extra confirmation can come from the sequence. At the start of the cycle only the leading stocks in the leading market start to rise. The majority are still declining. Later, many stocks in the lead market will be performing well and some in the second market. Lagging markets will still look negative. At the very end of this sequential development, when most stocks of laggard markets look strong, the lead stocks in the lead market will have topped out and be declining again. A good analogy is of a train on a rollercoaster track. Typically the USA is the engine of the world economy. The UK tends to come close behind, then core European markets, then Pacific region and, lastly, emerging markets. The sectors that lead in the US cycle often tend to be the very same ones that lead in their own domestic markets when each starts up. This fact gives an increased ability or confidence when forecasting later events in the progression.

There is another aspect to confirmation and this comes from indicators. There are many but they all fall into categories. Firstly, the monitoring of the numbers of stocks that are advancing or declining in price. The actual number in proportion to the total number of stocks in the market, and the ratio of advances to declines itself are important. Some advances may just be random movements in price, and so it is vital to determine how many of these are trending. The ratio and the number of uptrends to downtrends is therefore the second type of indicator. The amount and time duration of these moves is then measured. The stock can be said to be overbought or oversold if it has deviated too far from its trend line. It can be overdue on time as well. These indicators help us get a better feel for where the stocks are on the bell curve road map that is our forecast.

Accurate knowledge of where they have been, and where they are now, is a good guide to where they will be going in future. The first two steps in this trio are the very essence of what technical analysis is all about. ◗

JAPANESE CHARTING TECHNIQUES: CANDLESTICK AND KAGI CHARTS

John Murphy

John Murphy is president of JJM Technical Advisors, Inc. (Oradell, New Jersey). He has authored two best-selling books, Technical Analysis of the Futures Markets *(which has been translated into four languages) and* Intermarket Technical Analysis. *He has written articles for various publications including* Barron's *and* Technical Analysis of Stocks and Commodities, *for whom he is a contributing editor. Mr Murphy is also the technical analyst for* **CNBC-TV**.

Japanese charting techniques have gained immense popularity among western technical analysts during the 1990s. The most popular technique is called the candlestick chart. The use of candlesticks is so widespread that virtually every charting software program on the market now includes them. The main attraction of the candlestick chart is that it presents the same data as the Western bar chart (open, high, low, and closing prices) but in a more useful visual format. Candlesticks can be combined with other traditional technical indicators, such as the moving average. While nothing is lost, therefore, much is gained.

As an example, Chart 2.45 is a weekly candlestick chart of the Dow Jones Industrial Average covering the period from early 1994 into the spring of 1995. Each bar includes a thin portion (the shadow) which measures the weekly price range. The fat portion of the bar (the real body) is the difference between the open and the closing prices. If the close is above the opening, the wide portion is white (bullish). If the close is below the open, the wide portion is black (bearish).

Candlesticks reveal bullish and bearish patterns that aren't as apparent on the Western bar chart. The preponderance of white bars in early 1995, for example, reveals a bullish bias in the market. Candlestick charts are also commonly used on daily price charts to study shorter time periods.

Chart 2.45 Weekly Candlestick Chart of Dow Jones Industrial Average (1/94–3/95)

Chart created using MetaStock by EQUIS International

Another type of Japanese chart is called the kagi chart. The kagi is similar to Western point and figure charts, but with valuable refinements. Chart 2.46 is a 50-point kagi chart of the Dow Jones Industrial Average from early 1993 to the spring of 1995. The direction and thickness of the kagi lines are important. To reverse direction, prices must trend in the opposite direction by a predetermined amount (in this case, 50 points). The line thickens when a prior high is penetrated (bullish), and thins when a prior low is violated (bearish).

Chart 2.46 50 Point Kagi Chart of the Dow Jones Industrial Average (1/93–3/95)

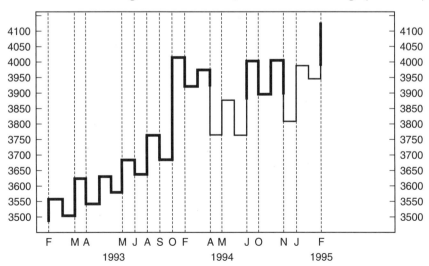

Chart created using MetaStock by EQUIS International

231

Chart 2.46 shows thick (bullish) kagi lines during 1993 as the market trended higher, a neutral mixture of thick and thin lines during the consolidation of 1994, and a thick (bullish line) in early 1995 as the uptrend resumed.

Stock traders should be aware of one minor problem. Candlestick charts require an opening price to be constructed properly. Since newspapers usually don't print individual stock openings, that data must be obtained from a computer data vendor. In addition, candlesticks can't be applied to open-end mutual funds which provide only closing net asset values. Any market entity (including stocks and mutual funds) can, however, be analysed with the kagi chart. For a more in-depth study of Japanese charting methods, including both candlestick and kagi charts, the best single source is *Beyond Candlesticks: New Japanese Charting Techniques Revealed* by Steve Nison. Mr Nison is credited with introducing Japanese charting to the West in his first book, *Japanese Candlestick Charting Techniques* (1990). ♀

MARKET TIMING

Dan Sullivan

Dan Sullivan, Publisher of The Chartist *and* Chartist *Mutual Fund Timer investment letters, has built one of the most impressive long-term performance records in the investment advisory business. He has published* The Chartist *newsletter since 1969. He combines a stock picking strategy based on relative strength with a market timing approach which reduces market risk. The basic element of his investment strategy is capital preservation.*

One of the most frequently debated subjects in the investment community is the question of which approach produces the best performance results – buying and holding an investment or trading an investment in and out of the market based on a timing strategy.

Timing signals for entry and exit points can be generated using a variety of approaches. Among the different methodologies used are: trend following, seasonality, pattern recognition, cycles and artificial intelligence. One of the most common is trend following. An example of trend following is to use a 39-week moving average crossover of a popular market index like the Dow Jones 65 Stock Average. The crossover must be confirmed by a similar index composed of a small number (three to five) of popular growth or aggressive growth (non-specialized) mutual funds. A shorter moving average is an option which produces more trades but also increases the possibility of whipsaws (a buy followed rather quickly by a sell). Extensive trade-off studies are needed to optimize a desired result. Other potential indices include advance/decline lines, new highs/new lows, interest rates etc. These indices can be used individually or in combination. While *The Chartist* methodology is proprietary, we do use a basic trend-following approach in combination with other technical factors.

The buy and hold strategy has long been promoted as the best method over a technical approach to accumulate wealth. Various academic studies have supported the 'random walk hypothesis' which essentially says that equity returns are not predictable and, therefore, trying to time the market is fruitless. In other words, equity price movements are random and do not trend. The mutual fund industry, of course, supports this view when marketing to individual investors. Their ultimate wish is that you buy their shares and hold them forever. This would make their lives much simpler.

Their arguments for buy and hold are supported by:

1 The compound annual return on common stocks with dividends reinvested from 1926 through the present averages about 10 per cent.

2 Risk is reduced over time. Over 20 years the worst outcome for stocks was +3.1 per cent compounded per year. Over a 10-year holding period the worst outcome over the last 67 years was −0.9 per cent, which occurred during the great depression.

3 Markets are efficient and random and cannot be timed according to academic studies.

Despite the litany of voices that urge buy and hold and to buy dips, at *The Chartist* we strongly subscribe to timing.

For a timing methodology to be successful markets need to trend. The very fact that labels have been applied to major market trends, i.e. 'bull and bear', acknowledges the existence of these cycles. In fact, over the past 95 years for the US stocks, there have been 30 bull or bear markets. Keep in mind that there are different definitions of what constitutes a bull or bear market. For our purposes we have adopted the definition provided by Ned Davis Research Inc. A bull market is defined as a 30 per cent rise in the Dow, or a 15 per cent rise after 155 days. A bear market is a 30 per cent drop or a 15 per cent drop after 145 days.

Chart 2.47 overleaf provides a composite picture of the 95-year history of the Dow, starting with the first year of the twentieth century. From the low to the high, the average gain is 84.7 per cent over a 24.1-month period. The declining portion of the trend consumes an average of 14.1 months and leaves investors with a loss of 31.9 per cent. The total cycle, from one low to the next low, takes 38.2 months. The rising portion of the Dow consumes 63.1 per cent of the cycle with the declining portion taking 36.9 per cent of the cycle (It is interesting to note that the 'Timer Methodology' is invested in equity and mutual funds approximately 70 per cent of the time and is invested in risk-free money market funds 30 per cent, closely matching the bull and bear trends.)

The Dow 30 , the senior index, has the longest history to show these trends. If you use data for other US equity indices which have a broader stock representation, like the S&P 500, the Wilshire 5000, the Russell 2000 or the Value Line Index, a similar pattern evolves.

Chart 2.47 95 year Dow Summary

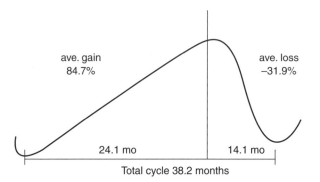

ave. gain
84.7%

ave. loss
−31.9%

24.1 mo   14.1 mo

Total cycle 38.2 months

There is little doubt from the evidence that markets, indeed, do trend. The only question that remains is, 'Are there viable technical tools to measure and evaluate trend changes for purposes of switching between equities and money market mutual funds?' To answer this question we point you to a recent study by William Brock, Josef Lakonishok (University of Wisconsin) and Blake LeBaron (University of Illinois), who have presented a report in the *Journal of Finance*, Volume XLVII, Number 5, December 1992, which refutes earlier conclusions.

Their study utilized the Dow Jones Industrial Average from 1897 through 1986. Their paper tested two timing strategies, moving averages and trading range breaks. They found that their moving average methodology produced a 12 per cent annualized gain during buy periods whereas, during sell periods, the Dow declined at a 7 per cent annual rate. While the moving average method produced the best performance, the trading range break also produced positive returns, which is in sharp contrast to, and refutes, the random walk hypothesis. They have reported, of course, what common sense told us all along: that prices of stocks do move from undervaluation to overvaluation in a rather rhythmic pattern. This evidence strongly supports the idea that markets trend and gives viability to the idea of market timing.

prices of stocks do move from undervaluation to overvaluation in a rather rhythmic pattern. This evidence strongly supports the idea that markets trend and gives viability to the idea of market timing.

One common buy and hold argument uses the S&P 500 compound annual return for the ten-year period from 1980 to 1990 of 17.6 per cent. A $10,000 investment grew to $50,591. If, for instance, through timing, an investor was out of the market for just a few of the following **BEST** days, the return would have suffered considerably.

234

Table 2.5

Missed Best Days	Return Fell to	$10,000 Investment
0	17.6%	$50,591
10	12.7%	$33,055
20	9.6%	$25,009
30	6.9%	$19,488
40	4.4%	$15,382

Obviously, a buy and hold strategy during such a dynamic period was a far superior approach based on this evidence. What if timing caused you to be out of the market for just 40 of the best days in this 10-year period? Instead of increasing your investment by $40,000, you would have realized only $5,000.

However, what is NOT presented is: **What if you missed the WORST days?** The story is dramatically different, as evidenced by Table 2.6.

Table 2.6

Missed Worst Days	Return Rose to	$10,000 Investment
0	17.6%	$50,591
10	26.6%	$105,764
20	30.5%	$143,253
30	33.8%	$183,891
40	36.9%	$231,225

Now let's examine what happens **if both the BEST and WORST days are missed.** This is more representative of our timing methodology, since we cannot always be on the right side of the market when these days occur. An astute investor should focus on trying to be on the right side of the market MOST of the time, not ALL of the time.

Table 2.7

Missed Both Best/Worst Days	Return was	$10,000 Investment
0	17.6%	$50,591
10	21.1%	$67,833
20	21.4%	$69,532
30	21.4%	$69,532
40	21.3%	$68,962

By missing both the 40 worst and best days, the ending value of $68,962 was 45 per cent better than the buy and hold ending value of $50,591. (The above data is courtesy of Ned Davis Research Inc.)

The preceding analysis of missed days does not portray how a particular timing system performs relative to buy and hold, but it does show the effect on performance by not being in the market on the days of significant gains and losses. Any useful timing system is devised to be out of the market and safely in money funds during long-term declines, thus satisfying our number one goal of capital preservation. We can then re-enter the market when our long-term model indicates the odds are favourable for a significant market increase.

The significance of avoiding the down cycles can be seen in a study by John Liscio (*The Liscio Report*). He asked the question, 'How much time did it take on average for someone with $10,000 in stocks at the beginning of the average bear market (at least a 20 per cent decline in the Dow) to catch up with some-one who held $10,000 in cash?' The answer was an average of 2.6 years to make up all of the lost ground. However, if you include the interest an investor could have earned in three-month Treasury bills by sitting out the bear market, the waiting time was a staggering 7.5 years.

Bull markets tend to end when fewer and fewer stocks are participating in the move. A good indication would be a new 52-week high in a popular average and seven days before or after the new high, the number of declining stocks is greater than advancing stocks. Confirming this event would see at least a third of the stocks listed on the exchange declining for two consecutive days when one of those days shows an advance/decline ratio <.25 or if, after the 52-week high, four out of the next seven-day period record declining issues greater than one-third of the stocks listed on the exchange.

At market bottoms, typically there is broad participation where, for two consecutive days, advancing issues exceed one-third of the issues on the exchange and one of those days shows four times more stocks advancing than declining, or a single day of nine times advancing issues over declining issues. Another confirming event would see four days out of seven when advancing issues exceed declining issues.

The debate between buy and hold and use of a timing methodology will doubtless continue on ad infinitum. Both approaches have merit, particularly if you follow them religiously. Buy and hold works well if you have the luxury of a 30-year time horizon and the beneficial effect of compounding working for you. If you can withstand the inevitable bear markets, accompanied by the depreciation in values, then you have a strategy you can live with.

The Chartist Timer Methodology, on the other hand, will be out of the market about 30 per cent of the time. It, too, will have some anxious moments as the market rises and the momentum model is in a negative mode. It appears that the train is leaving the depot without you. Instead of the fear generated by large losses in a buy and hold strategy, we experience the greed factor of seeing a market rise. However, if it is a strong market, rest assured the Timer Methodology will sense this major trend change and put us on board.

A successful timing strategy provides results superior to a buy and hold approach. Buy and hold exposes the investor to 100 per cent of the market risk. The emotional pressures exerted by the market often lead to poor investment decisions. Sadly, it is an all too frequent occurrence for investors to let greed and fear influence their investment judgement. A disciplined timing strategy, on the other hand, will help reduce the emotional impact of the market. Timing can accomplish the following:

- Capital preservation
- Capital appreciation
- Avoids bear markets
- Reduces risk
- Reduces stress
- Provides a consistent and disciplined approach to the market.

In our opinion, timing combines the best of both worlds; the opportunity to participate in the long-term growth of equities at a lower risk level than buy and hold. ✑

In our opinion, timing combines the best of both worlds; the opportunity to participate in the long-term growth of equities at a lower risk level than buy and hold.

RECOVERY INVESTMENT

Richard Hughes

Richard Hughes, who has managed the Recovery Fund at M&G for the last seven years, was trained by David Tucker. M&G is the UK's leading Unit Trust Manager. It is an independent, quoted company, founded in 1931. The M&G Recovery Fund was managed from inception by David Tucker until his retirement in 1988. Richard Hughes wishes to acknowledge his debt to David Tucker for many of the ideas which are expressed in this article.

Fifty years ago, that master of the art of investment, John Maynard Keynes, observed that there was nothing so potentially disastrous as to pursue a rational investment policy in an irrational world.

Similarly inspired, perhaps, M&G decided in 1969 to launch a unit trust whose declared policy would be wholly irrational: to buy those shares that others were selling, to invest in companies that most people thought were going to fail and generally to follow an investment strategy regarded as highly speculative by the standards of the day.

We called it the Recovery Fund. The public largely ignored it and its initial subscription was a paltry £200,000. Nearly 26 years later, on 12 December, 1994, an initial investment of £1,000 had grown to £102,400. The average annual compound growth rate of 19.9 per cent net over the Fund's life is well ahead of both the rate of inflation over the same period of 8.7 per cent and the net return from the FT Stock Exchange All-Share Index of 13.2 per cent. It is the best performing unit trust out of all the UK unit trusts which have been in existence since 1969. That, in itself, suggests there is a lot to be said for the recovery approach to investing.

The Fund has never invested in successful, well managed companies such as Marks and Spencer, Sainsbury's or Shell. The Fund invests in companies which are experiencing difficulties such as making losses, weak balance sheets, frauds, natural disasters, or a specific industry downturn.

How do we select investments? We do not act until after the bad news is widely known. This will encourage selling of the shares to a low level. We then analyse the source of the problem and assess its seriousness in the context of the group as a whole. The next stage is to identify a solution to the problem. The three most common solutions are new management, an injection of capital and the passage of time. The final stage is to analyse what the share price might be once the problems have been solved. The investment will only be successful if the gap between the current share price and the potential share price is sufficiently high. As a rule of thumb, I invest when I think the shares can double over a three-year period.

There are three other factors which help performance. Firstly, a wide spread of holdings is needed to minimize the impact of failure. Secondly, a contingency plan in case the management cannot solve the problem, and thirdly, there are some obvious failure candidates. If these can be avoided the Fund's success ratio can be much improved.

How do we identify shares which can double over three years? An accurate assessment of the reward that can be achieved compared with the risks is a central consideration. I look at companies where the annual turnover is much greater than the market capitalization. I also like companies where the depreciation charge is large in relation to market capitalization. This signals the importance of cash flow. It is negative cash flow rather than losses which drive companies into receivership. There must be a viable business capable of prospering once indifferent management is removed. I am less attracted to high gearing than was my predecessor, David Tucker. We have been living with very high real interest rates for quite some time and this looks likely to continue making life far more difficult for heavily geared companies.

I look at companies where the annual turnover is much greater than the market capitalization. I also like companies where the depreciation charge is large in relation to market capitalization.

The ideal company is one where management has changed, a rescue rights operation is necessary and the existing shareholders are thoroughly fed up. Granada, a leisure company with interests in television, television rental, motorway services, catering and computer maintenance, which had a rights issue at 140p in May 1991, was a good example. The Recovery Fund's purchase had quadrupled in value within three years as Gerry Robinson, the new chief executive, quickly improved shareholder returns by concentrating on margin improvements, reducing over-manning and inflated pay scales in the television company and boosting efficiency together with selected price increases in other divisions. Chart 2.48 shows how spectacular the effect of a recovery can be on a company's share price.

Chart 2.48 Granada Group (from 30 Dec 1988 to 5 Apr 1995: weekly)

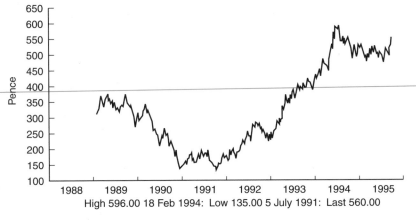

High 596.00 18 Feb 1994: Low 135.00 5 July 1991: Last 560.00

Source: Datastream

Such share price behaviour is not restricted to the UK. The Fund has benefited from the recovery at Philips, the Dutch conglomerate. Following a change of management, the shares have risen from Dfl20 to Dfl50. In the USA Texaco was a spectacularly successful investment from the time it filed for Chapter 11 protection in April 1987. The shares soared from US$30 to US$65.

The policy on diversification of risk is simple. We restrict investment in the riskiest stock to 1 per cent of the Fund. Two casualties of the recession in the early 1990s were Lowndes Queensway, a retailer of furniture and carpets, and Davies and Newman, which was the holding company for Dan-Air, a long established airline providing both charter and scheduled flights. The losses were painful but did not decimate the Fund.

The contingency plans usually centre around asset disposals. The majority of our holdings are in the industrial sector where companies have tangible assets. In the service sector the assets go up and down in the lift and can leave very easily.

How can obvious disasters be avoided? We always buy voting shares and we avoid companies where there is a majority shareholder. In both cases outside shareholders have no power to make changes if things go wrong.

How can obvious disasters be avoided? We always buy voting shares and we avoid companies where there is a majority shareholder.

The Recovery Fund avoided a number of disasters in the UK stock market during the late 1980s and early 1990s, stocks such as British and Commonwealth, Polly Peck, Coloroll, Brent Walker, Maxwell Communications, etc. A fundamental principle is not to invest in a company where all that has happened is that the share price has fallen, however sharply. The old stock market adage of not catching a falling knife held true in all the above cases. The management was either not changed or changed far too late to save the company in each case. The people responsible for the mess are seldom the right people to lead the company out of trouble.

Will the recovery principle remain valid? In my view definitely yes. I believe that there will always be companies managed by incompetent or over ambitious people. This will lead to poor performance and investors will panic and sell the shares when the bad news is made public. There will also always be managers who are looking for a challenge and willing to tackle recovery stocks. Once they can demonstrate a turnaround then other investors will notice and drive the share price up strongly, at which point the recovery manager makes his excuses and leaves. ♀

VALUE INVESTING

Christopher H. Browne, William H. Browne,
James M. Clark, Jr., John D. Spears
General Partners, Tweedy, Browne Company LP

Tweedy, Browne is recognized as the leading exponent of value investing. The partnership's managed account composite has achieved a phenomenal 17.9 per cent compound annual total rate of return net of fees from 1 January 1975 to 31 December 1994. An investor who had put in $10,000 at the start of the period would now have a holding worth $271,158.

'Confronted with the challenge to distill the secret of sound investment into three words, we venture the motto, MARGIN OF SAFETY', *The Intelligent Investor*, Benjamin Graham.

Most professional equity investors claim in theory to buy 'value' regardless of what they may do in practice. After all, it would be foolish to say that one's investment selections represent anything else. However, upon closer examination there are far fewer true practitioners of value investing than the number who claim adherence to the faith.

Those who, in our opinion, are true value investors may hold different stocks as a result of differences in approach at the margin. However, their particular biases are still firmly grounded in a common philosophical principle that from time to time discrepancies exist between the market price of stocks and the true underlying value of the business. Value investors dispute the efficient market hypothesis of modern portfolio theorists, and believe that stock prices are often wrong as an indicator of underlying corporate net worth. They see investment opportunities created as a result of discrepancies between stock price and net worth. In their view, common stock is an ownership interest in a business, not a piece of paper to be traded based on price momentum. They do not concern themselves with the unknowable, but rather concentrate their analysis on quantitative facts that offer real evidence of value. For instance, a true value investor does not waste his intellectual energy trying to decide whether the Federal Reserve Board will raise interest rates next week or month; he takes little interest in the impact of politics on securities markets and could care less whether the general trend in the market has been up or down. Most would not know the meaning of the terms 'beta' or 'r²' or the 'standard deviation of returns'. Instead, they are focused on underlying business value, and its relation to stock price.

For well over a quarter of a century, the partners of Tweedy, Browne have been investing their clients' money, as well as their own, utilizing an approach that derives directly from the investment principles first set forth and practised by the late Benjamin Graham. Author of *Security Analysis* and *The Intelligent Investor*, widely recognized as the father of modern investment analysis, Graham developed a set of simple common sense principles for investment that have served us and other practitioners of this philosophy very well over the years. Having professionally suffered through the depression with no small amount of hardship, Graham paid great attention to risk and carefully distinguished investment from speculation. In the words of Graham, 'An investment operation is one which upon thorough analysis promises safety of principal and an adequate return. Operations not meeting these requirements are speculative.'

The basis of Graham's thinking and our investment decision-making process is the existence of a two-tier price structure for the shares of publicly traded corporations. First, there is the stock market value; the price most recently at which the shares have traded. Second, there is the intrinsic value on a per share basis of the business, which is the value of that share in the event the company was sold or liquidated. The essence of investing is to exploit discrepancies between price and value to find a bargain.

Our research seeks to appraise the intrinsic value of a share of stock by estimating its acquisition value, or by estimating the collateral value of its assets and/or cash flow. We believe the process is in many respects closely related to credit analysis as we are seeking collateral net worth in excess of the cost of our investment. Once an estimate of intrinsic value has been determined, the decision to buy or sell a security is made by a comparison of its current price to its estimated intrinsic value. Investments are made when stock prices are at significant discounts to their estimated intrinsic values, usually 40-50 per cent. Graham referred to this discount as '. . . an investor's margin of safety'. He insisted on a significant discount or margin of safety.

A security purchased at prices which are 50-60 per cent of intrinsic value is backed by corporate net worth which is nearly twice the cost of the investment. Although security prices can fluctuate dramatically in the short run, this collateral value provides protection against permanent capital loss. As these bargains become recognized by other investors, their security prices are often bid up to levels approaching or exceeding their intrinsic value, thus eliminating their margin of safety. At which time, they would be sold back into the market's enthusiasm, and the proceeds would be invested in another bargain with an acceptable margin of safety. These principles result in a contrarian approach to investment, forcing the purchase of securities in generally declining stock markets and, conversely, forcing sales as stock markets or individual companies rise in price.

One of the many unique and advantageous aspects of value investing is that the larger the discount from intrinsic value, the greater the margin of safety and the greater potential return when the stock price moves back to intrinsic value. Contrary to the view of modern portfolio theorists that increased returns can only be achieved by taking greater levels of risk, value investing is predicated on the notion that increased returns are associated with a greater margin of safety, i.e. lower risk.

While our process does allow us to unearth undervalued stocks, we usually do not know how or when a gain from a particular stock will occur. In fact, sometimes we lose money on a particular stock even though it appears to be undervalued. However, we do know that there are profit producing occurrences in a diversified portfolio of undervalued securities such as a general rise in market prices, special dividends, tender offers, mergers, recapitalizations, spinoffs, purchases of shares by raiders, and corporate share repurchases. An integral part of our and Graham's approach has been the diversification of holdings within portfolios. Not only does diversification reduce risk, it also increases the probability, through the workings of the '...law of large numbers', that a return will be realized from the entire portfolio.

Two obvious examples of undervaluation are a closed-end mutual fund whose share price is significantly less than the market value of its investment portfolio, or a company whose shares are priced at a large discount to the company's cash after the deduction of all liabilities. These types of easy-to-understand bargains do appear in the stock market recurrently. However, it cannot be said with certainty that a clear-cut bargain investment will produce excess investment returns, and it is impossible to predict the pattern, sequence or consistency of returns for a particular investment. It can only be stated that repeated investment in numerous groups of bargain securities over very long periods of time has produced excess market returns with less risk of permanent capital loss.

Warren Buffett confirmed this when he studied the records of a number of successful practitioners, including ourselves, whose investment approaches derived from Ben Graham. Speaking at the 50th anniversary of the writing of Graham's book, *Security Analysis*, Buffett used these superior records, including his own, to statistically dispel the notion of modern portfolio theorists that investors who seem to beat the market consistently are merely lucky. This speech, entitled The Superinvestors of Graham and Doddville, was reprinted in the Columbia Graduate School of Business magazine Hermes, Fall 1984.

In recent years, with advances in computing capabilities, including the historical analysis of financial data and security returns, numerous academic studies have been performed on fundamental investment criteria and characteristics that produced results better or worse than the stock market averages. We have compiled descriptions of 44 such studies in a booklet entitled, *What Has Worked In Investing*. Our choice was not selective; we merely included most of the major studies we have seen through the years. Approximately one-half are based on US stocks, and the rest are based on stocks outside the US Interestingly, geography had no influence on the basic conclusion: US and non-US stocks performed similarly based on similar financial criteria. The overall conclusion is that stocks with the following characteristics provide the best returns over long periods of time:

- Low price in relation to book value; i.e., what the company itself has paid for its own assets.

- Low price in relation to earnings. Included within the broad, low price-to-earnings category are two additional related characteristics: high dividend yield and low price-to-cash flow. Dividends and cash flow are largely a function of earnings.

- Insider purchases of the company's stock; i.e. purchases of the company's stock by officers, directors or the company itself.

- A significant decline in the market price.

- Small market capitalization.

While this conclusion comes as no surprise to us, it provides empirical evidence that Ben Graham's principles of investing, first published in 1934 in *Security Analysis*, do work.

One might logically ask that if the empirical evidence exists to show value investing provides superior returns, why hasn't the philosophy been adopted by most professional investors, thus narrowing the spreads between price and value and eliminating its advantage as a methodology? Graham's teachings have been around for over 50 years, and while he has a significant number of loyal disciples, the group of 'pure practitioners' has remained rather modest in size. The fact is that being a contrarian requires a level of courage and independent thought that is rare in even the most disciplined of individuals. Unfortunately, to their financial detriment, investors often seek refuge and comfort in conventional thinking. As Warren Buffett has reminded us, an investor pays an awfully high price for a cheery consensus.

From our early days as Ben Graham's broker to the last 25+ years as value investors, the discipline of investing in stocks priced at significant discounts to

243

real business value has increased our wealth and the wealth of our clients. Fortunately, and to our way of thinking, logically, it has also generated returns in excess of stock market indices over a long period of time. In caring for our wealth and the wealth of our clients, we are not persuaded that there is a more sensible course to follow. ♀

CLASSIC GROWTH INVESTING

David Testa

M. David Testa is a Managing Director of T. Rowe Price Associates. He is Director of Equity Investing, Chairman of the T. Rowe Price Growth Stock Fund and Chairman of Rowe Price-Fleming International and the T. Rowe Price International Funds.

T. Rowe Price was founded by Mr Price in 1937 and became one of the leading proponents of the growth stock style of investment.

The concept of investment in growth companies as a distinct and appropriate style of equity investing seems to emerge only in a maturing economy. Talk to an investor in Asia today about stock selection criteria and you will find growth assumed to be an integral element of any stock selection approach. Once an economy matures, however, and the average corporation's fortunes are no longer assisted by the strong tail wind of vigorous underlying demand, then the ability of a company to generate autonomous growth becomes a primary differentiating characteristic. Thus, it is no accident that growth stock investing emerged as a distinct approach in the United States during the Great Depression of the 1930s, in the writings of Mr Price and a few of his contemporaries. Not surprisingly, the dominant investor focus at that time was on income and security of principal, even in the selection of equity securities. Mr Price argued for a shift in focus to growth of earnings and dividends as a superior approach to gaining income and securing principal over a lifetime of investing in the face of economic uncertainty and the inevitable ravages of inflation.

Since the 1930s, the growth style of investing has grown tremendously in popularity, and its adherents have developed a bewildering array of rules and variants on the theme when it comes to implementation. However, at the root of all these approaches lie a few simple premises:

1   As a company's earnings per share of stock grow, the company can afford to pay a rising dividend on that stock, and its price in the market will tend to rise over time in reasonable relationship to its trend of earnings and dividends.

2   A company whose earnings are growing faster than the average of other companies and the nominal rate of economic growth on a secular basis is

considered a growth company (even if its pattern of earnings performance is somewhat cyclical).

3   When bought at a reasonable price, shares of such a company will deliver a satisfactory and perhaps superior return to the shareholder without the need to trade the shares until above average growth is no longer likely.

Assuming they can identify and price these companies with even a moderate degree of success, this approach offers investors a number of distinct advantages:

1   The number of decisions can be greatly reduced as shares, once purchased, tend to be held for years. As a result the pressure on timing and judgement is less than in more trading-intensive investment strategies.

2   For an investor facing capital gains taxes it is a great advantage to choose investments which can be held indefinitely, deferring realization of gains, instead of a higher turnover strategy which generates current tax liabilities before capital is redeployed into the next investment opportunity.

3   The pressure on the pricing process is less intense since, unless a gross error has been made, a growing stream of earnings and dividends will eventually deliver a positive rate of return. In contrast, the passage of time provides no rescue for a poorly timed investment in a cyclical or mature company.

4   A portfolio of such investments will generally produce a rising level of nominal and real income as dividends on the underlying holdings grow, potentially overwhelming any immediate disadvantage in yield at the time of purchase.

The challenge for the investor who wishes to realize these advantages then becomes one of identifying companies which will achieve sustainable, above average growth, whose stock is not already selling at prices which reflect their superior prospects. A complex treatise could be written on either subject, but prospective growth stock investors would do well to focus on a few basic concepts which underpin any successful approach:

1   Companies which sustain above-average earnings growth for long periods of time generally do so through the organic process of selling a growing stream of units of a product or a service. A high level of profitability on capital employed in the business is usually present and is an important indicator of the sustainability of above-average growth. Less sustainable approaches involve managed gains achieved through above-average price increases, cost cutting, consolidation of other companies, or accounting changes.

2   Identifying industries at the forefront of a process of secular change can be one of the easiest ways to zero in on companies with the potential to achieve sustained organic growth. The strong tail wind a company enjoys by operating in what Mr Price called 'fertile fields for growth' can make even an average company in such an industry into a growth company.

245

A good example can be found in the above-average growth and returns available from virtually all US airline shares when jets were introduced into their fleets. Fares were maintained or even increased while costs declined, service was improved and passenger miles growth accelerated. The same concept can be applied in international investing by seeking out companies operating in the more dynamic regions of the world.

A good example can be found in the above-average growth and returns available from virtually all US airline shares when jets were introduced into their fleets.

3 Over longer periods of time, quality of management will be the greatest differentiator in the results of companies within an industry and can even lead to above-average performance by a company operating in a less attractive field. Identifying and monitoring quality of management by assessing their vision, style, depth, and accomplishment is a vital step in building and monitoring any growth portfolio.

Growth investing adherents are sufficiently numerous today that it is rare for an investor to identify a promising company which is not known as such to other investors. For example, leading drug companies such as Merck, Glaxo or Hoffman La Roche are broadly held by growth investors. Technology companies such as Intel, Motorola or Ericsson have long been seen as leading and benefiting from the rapid pace of change in computers and communications. Even less recognized companies such as Rentokil, which is transforming the economic equation in pest control in the UK, are broadly followed by financial analysts.

Successful timing of choices from a broad list of recognized alternatives may be the key to acceptable returns. The investor's objective should be to buy into such a company when its short-term performance is depressed for transitory reasons. A marvellous example of such timing was Warren Buffets' purchase of a large holding in Coca-Cola in the early 1980s during a period of sub-par financial performance by the company and in the midst of confusion generated by an ineptly handled new product introduction. Few investors will time their entry into a stock as exquisitely as that, but as long as they avoid purchasing their shares when a growth company or industry is at a peak of investor infatuation, they are likely to achieve satisfactory returns over time.

Inevitably, assessing the fairness of a stock's price is a relative decision. Various rules of thumb have been proposed such as the current notion that a stock is fairly priced if its price to earnings ratio is below its growth rate. These 'rules' may have some utility, but generally are overly simplistic. An investor's choice among alternatives can be improved by keeping various trade-offs in mind:

1 The higher the profitability of a company at a given growth rate the better since it indicates the company's ability to finance continued growth and pay dividends.

2 Theoretically, each unit of higher growth should accrue a larger valuation premium, but sustainability is also critical and is likely to be more suspect as the growth rate rises. Hence, investors should factor in their judgement on sustainability and may wish to moderate their enthusiasm as evidenced in the increments of valuation they would pay per additional unit of growth.

3 Absolute and relative growth stock pricing is very sensitive to the rate of inflation and to the returns on competing investment instruments such as bonds. As inflation and interest rates rise (or fall), growth company valuations contract (or expand) more rapidly than for the market as a whole, and premiums for incremental units of growth become increasingly compressed (or extended).

Successful sale decisions are often the hardest part of growth stock investing. The standard answer is to recommend sale when signs of maturity or failure to maintain superiority are discerned. For example, the airline stocks bought when passenger jets were first introduced should have been sold once jets became pervasive in airline fleets and price competition re-emerged. Unfortunately, it can be easy to see such signs in temporary problems or setbacks that are driving stock prices lower, in fact creating the best opportunities for new or additional purchases.

the airline stocks bought when passenger jets were first introduced should have been sold once jets became pervasive in airline fleets and price competition re-emerged.

Patience, common sense and an ability to take a contrary view at moments of extreme optimism are the investor's best defence in deciding whether to hold or sell a portfolio company. A permanent and significant negative change in a company's operating environment or a change for the worse in company management are signals which should focus investor attention on the need to sell the stock. A wildly inflated price springing from excessive investor optimism may also provide sufficient incentive to reduce or eliminate a holding. Fortunately, experience indicates that a reliable selling strategy is somewhat less vital to a growth investor's overall success than is the case for a more trading oriented investment style. The powerful compounding of successful selections tends to compensate for mis-timed dispositions. If anything, selling good companies prematurely is a bigger potential problem than missing appropriate sale opportunities.

Long-term investment in the shares of dynamic business enterprises probably has underpinned most of the world's great fortunes in the post-agricultural era. Even Mr Graham, the great teacher of value investing, owed more of his investment success to his long-term holdings in GEICO than to adherence to his fundamental approach. However, classic growth investing is not a panacea for investors. Successful implementation requires patience, hard work, attention to continuing developments, intelligence and common sense. ♀

MOMENTUM

William H. 'Beau' Duncan, Jr

Mr Duncan is the founder, Chairman & Chief Executive Officer of Duncan-Hurst Capital Management, a San Diego, California based manager of over U.S.$1 billion in emerging growth small-cap and medium-cap growth equities for institutional clients. The firm also manages hedged growth equity portfolios which include an offshore mutual fund for individuals and institutions. Mr Duncan has been involved in equity portfolio management and research for over 25 years.

The theory of momentum investing is similar to one of Newton's Laws which states that once an object is set in motion it stays in motion until stopped, and when an object is stationary, it tends to remain that way until something moves it. In a similar fashion, a corporation having fundamental problems will probably continue with those problems longer than expected, and a corporation which has experienced faster growth will probably continue that rapid growth longer than expected. Whatever the factors causing the change in corporate momentum (e.g. changes in management, new products, changes in competition), those factors will remain in effect longer than expected.

There exists a continuum of investment styles from value investing, to growth at a price, to momentum investing. First of all, let me establish that no style is superior to the next, and each style attempts to capture a different part of the typical cycle of stock movements. Each style has its strong points and weak points. A stock price movement may be divided into several stages: (1) late decline and basing, (2) early breakout, (3) growth, (4) topping, (5) early decline. As a general rule, momentum investing is involved with stages 2-5. Value is involved with stages 1-3, and growth at a price using stages 1-4. One can also divide the price cycle between beginning, middle and end. Momentum investors buy late and sell late, but the middle part of the price cycle may be quite extended in price movement and duration. Value investors take profits early but a large part of the price move could be missed if earnings estimates are raised for several quarters, or even years. What looked like an expensive stock, was really a cheap stock because estimates were too low.

248

Every style uses earnings surprise to some extent, but momentum investing has more dependence on this. When a corporation turns momentum from negative earnings growth to positive earnings growth, the analysts following the stock tend to be surprised as corporate earnings come in above expectations. Therefore, valuation tends to be less important for momentum investing than other styles, since the estimate will constantly be changed (hopefully higher after a stock is bought and lower when a stock is sold). Momentum investing takes advantage of the surprise in earnings to boost the stock price, watching the factors involved which may cause earnings estimates to be raised (or lowered in the case of a sale or a short). With regard to the timing of the purchase or sale, momentum investing waits for the turn in fundamentals to be established. By waiting for the turn, momentum investors are closer to the stock price movement which discounts the turn in fundamentals, resulting in more 'live' money in the portfolio. By the same token, the stock may have already moved somewhat, so the momentum investor will be paying some 'insurance' to be right a higher percentage of the time. As explained earlier, problems may persist longer than expected, so the price of being early is 'dead' money – a period which many times is longer than expected.

Portfolio turnover tends to be higher for momentum investing, because the change in momentum causes a shift in the compounding effects of revenues and earnings per share. The discounting mechanism is very sensitive to the change in growth expectations, and the stock will overshoot in valuation in both directions – at the top when expectations are very high, and at the bottom when expectations are the lowest. Since pure momentum investors tend to buy stocks with higher valuations and therefore higher growth rates, they are at risk to a bigger change in valuation from high to low. The momentum investor knows these trends last longer than expected in both directions, and he tends to buy and sell more often due to subtle changes in expectations, whereas the value investor will ignore small fluctuations.

Momentum investing is more of a dynamic analysis – looking for changes in growth rates and the factors causing those changes, whereas value investing tends to be more of a static analysis while not ignoring the factors causing the change in fundamentals, but placing less emphasis on them. Also, momentum investing waits for a change in fundamentals before acting (at the risk of being late) while value investing places more weight on absolute valuation (probably buying earlier, but at the risk of being too early).

A prime example of the benefits of momentum investing is Cisco Systems. When the company went public in 1990 at $1 per share (adjusted for splits), there were many sceptics about the stock because the valuation was high, even though the company was the key provider of routers for corporate computer networks, a market with substantial growth prospects. However, the company kept dramatically beating revenue and earnings estimates over a period of three years, and the stock went up 35 times. While there were many bulls on routers, few analysts predicted how rapidly the company would grow to a $1 billion revenue run rate from a very small base.

As a general rule, momentum investors tend to traffic in technology, health care, and specialty retail sectors, because the earnings growth rates are higher. From time to time, however, sectors with slower growth (like regional banks) or cyclicality (like energy) could be momentum candidates, as long as some change in fundamentals causes an acceleration in earnings growth. ♀

ROTATIONAL STRATEGY: AVOIDING THE FASHIONABLE

Dan Bunting

*Matheson Securities is a member of The Securities and Futures Authority and of the London Stock Exchange. The ultimate parent company is **Jardine Matheson Holdings Limited**, the multinational trading and services related company. Dan Bunting, Investment Strategist in London, joined **Matheson** in 1988 following 15 years' research experience with a number of large broking firms. **Matheson Securities'** research embodies, where appropriate, the contrary view, which in turn may involve longer-term perspectives and a greater concentration on intrinsic risk/reward valuation than is perhaps usual elsewhere.*

Technical or chart analysis receives excellent coverage earlier in this volume, and indeed there can be few practitioners who are not to some degree familiar with 'heads and shoulders', 'double tops' and the like. We are careful students of such items, not least because they can save the fundamental analyst from horrendous errors of timing. Nonetheless we would express one reservation, namely that classical chart analysis does seem inclined to emphasize the fashionable. The indicators have an intrinsic tendency to become more bullish when a share has been going up for a while. Then on the slightest setback one is liable to be told that 'the pattern has aborted'.

Overbought/oversold indicators

In consequence, we have acquired a predilection – on a sort of 'belt and braces' basis – for a conceptually different type of chart; the **overbought/ oversold** indicator. This reinforces the most fundamental of all investment disciplines, namely the need to buy what is out of fashion and sell what is in. It is hard work. One must of necessity analyse a

This reinforces the most fundamental of all investment disciplines, namely the need to buy what is out of fashion and sell what is in.

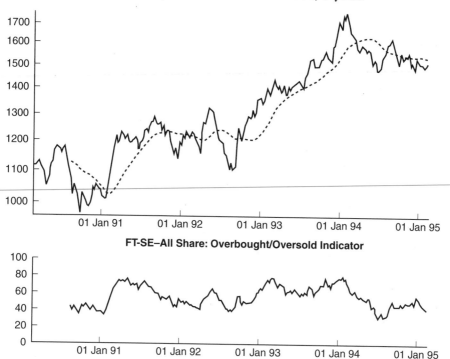

Chart 2.49 UK FT-SE All Share Index, 5 years

company when the share is oversold, and find out whether or not there really is reason to believe that its fortunes are catastrophically deteriorating – but then again what should one expect? If profits were to be made simply by looking at pictures who would be working for a living? The approach is particularly applicable to overall markets and individual stocks which are market leaders, in that it is really very rare that one such animal fundamentally changes its spots. In other words, the vast majority of extreme share price movements are attributable to the fevered moods of the market (reminiscent of that American saying; 'Wall Street has infallibly signalled ten out of the last five economic downturns'). We would not seek to extend the technique to smaller company shares and special situations. The main pitfall is the risk of being premature.

By way of illustration let us look at the UK equity market. In Chart 2.49 is the familiar picture of the All Share Index for a period of five years. From day to day it is volatile but there exists a medium-term trend, embodied in the six-month rolling average shown in the same space. It is evident that at times when the market climbs too far above its trend line, it becomes overbought and prices are unsustainable; sooner or later profit-taking sets in, and the bubble is pricked (or, at the least, a long period of consolidation becomes necessary). Likewise an oversold market is apt to experience recovery. And now to the lower display in Chart 2.49. This comprises an arithmetical indicator of the extent of **overbought/oversold** conditions. Take, for example, January 1994, when the market was very heavily overbought; the indicator showed a reading of 80. By July, the market had fallen below trend; hence a reading on the lower chart of only 30. (The software package we have used is a fairly basic one, namely Meridian Software's 'Chart Analyst'. However, a similar indicator is available on Reuter Graphics using the 'RSI' study. Alternatively ADP/Quotron in the UK, supplies **overbought/oversold** as a standard item, derived from the former Dogfox package).

At its best and simplest, the approach we favour is to recommend purchase of long-term fundamental favourites when they happen to be oversold, and sales of weaker long-term propositions when they are overbought.

The **overbought/oversold** indicator is at its best when dealing with entities where investors are moved by a broad swathe of sentiment factors. The Nikkei faces a particularly wide mixture of prospects (see Chart 2.50). On the one hand many observers had been bullish for most of 1994 on the grounds of imminent economic recovery. On the other hand, even factoring in putative benefits of this, value in the market appears somewhat restricted. None of this should pose a problem, however, for the student of **overbought/oversold** conditions. He ought to have anticipated the blandishments of the bulls by buying

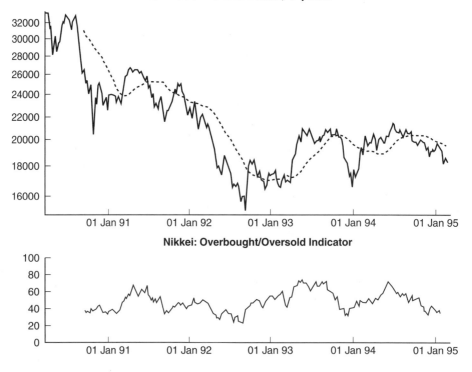

Chart 2.50 Nikkei Index, 5 years

stock late in 1993, with the Nikkei not much over 16,000. He could then have taken his profits the following summer at over 21,000 (with a useful currency gain into the bargain).

Finally, bringing the matter back to individual stocks, a good example is BAT Industries. Throughout its history this has been very much a 'sentiment' stock. During the days of exchange controls it seemed almost never to be bought or sold other than on exchange rate factors; more recently it has been prone to scares on the tobacco litigation front, interspersed with confidence surrounding the growth of cigarette sales in developing markets. We regard it as a pre-eminent trading stock.

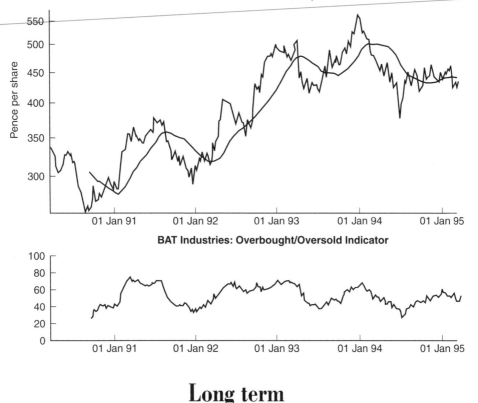

Chart 2.51 BAT Industries, 5 years

Long term

When stock recommendations go adrift, frequently the cause is nothing to do with errors in company analysis; it is the hostile influence of external business trends, often of a long-term nature. For example during 1992–3 the consumer- branded product and pharmaceutical sectors – bastions of the US and UK markets for the preceding decade – experienced severe underperformance because of the climate of deflation. This could have come as a shock

Chart 2.52 Average Annual Short-Term Interest Rates: 300 years (1694 to 1994)

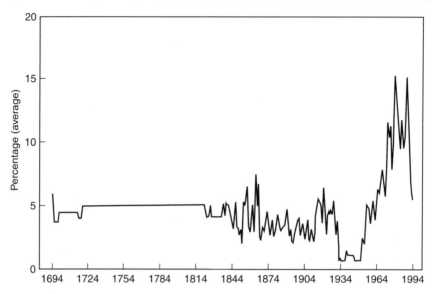

to anyone habituated solely to five -or ten-year charts of economic variables. Nonetheless looking at the long-term context it is clear that the inflationary 1970s and 1980s were a very unusual period. This is conspicuously reflected in UK interest rates over the past three centuries, as shown in Charts 2.52 and 2.53.

Chart 2.53 Average Annual $2\frac{1}{2}\%$ Consols Yield (1694 to 1994)

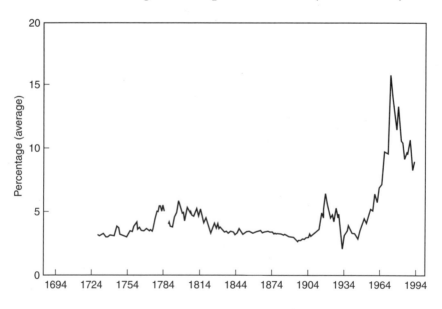

Chart 2.54 US Consumer Goods relative to S & P 500, 20 years

— S&PCNSG/S&PCOMP

Source: Datastream

Chart 2.55 US Capital Goods relative to S&P500, 20 years

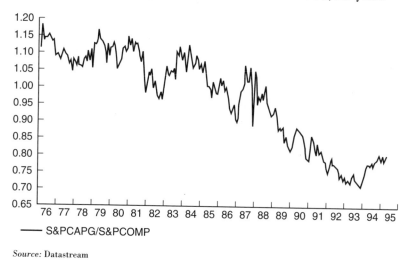

— S&PCAPG/S&PCOMP

Source: Datastream

None of this constitutes proof that any return of deflation will be long lived; but it makes one wary of assuming that it will be purely temporary. On this basis we favour a lower long-term weighting in the aforementioned consumer and branded product areas than was appropriate during the 1980s. Charts 2.54 and 2.55 shows just how far, on Wall Street, the consumer goods sector outperformed during that decade: and the mirror image is the underperformance of capital goods. Now, however, the humbly valued dollar is bringing renewed prosperity to the mid-West and the capital goods industries.

By further extrapolation, one tends to a certain scepticism on the subject of gold, where the upsurge in bullion at the end of the 1970s was remarkable in the long-term context.

Gold carries no dividend income. Technology threatens perpetually to cut the cost of new production. Almost all the gold ever mined is still in existence. We feel a basic lack of enthusiasm for 'the barbarous relic'. The charts are remarkably similar when one looks at oil. For conservative portfolios, heavy exposure to the Exploration & Production sector would seem unappealing. Of course for both commodities, especially oil, there is the compensating possibility of supply disruption in unstable producing regions.

Chart 2.56 Gold, US$ per ounce, 100 years

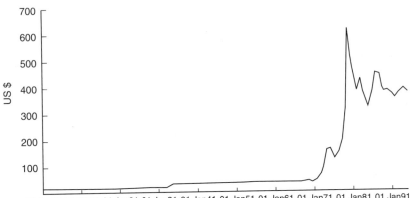

Chart 2.57 Gold, re-based, in real terms, 100 years

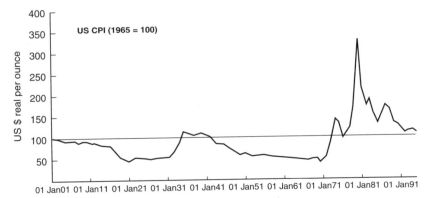

Chart 2.58 Crude Oil, rebased, in real terms, 100 years

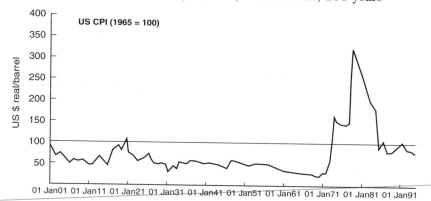

Finally, we come to the long-term view of international equity markets, and below one may see an interesting comparison between London and Wall Street.

Apart from the fact that capital growth has been faster on Wall Street (though to nothing like the extent of the faster population and GDP growth – emerging market investors take note!), these charts have made us suspicious of the overwhelmingly bearish view of Wall Street taken by professional investors. The fact is that earnings on the London market became somewhat bloated in the latter 1980s; a phenomenon some have referred to as 'the

Chart 2.59 UK Equities, in real terms, 100 years

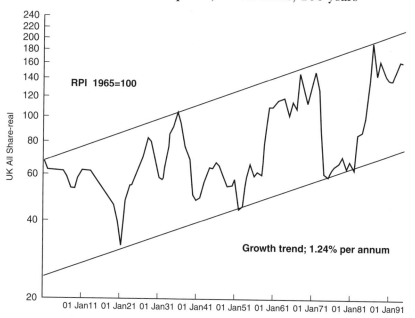

Chart 2.60 US Equities, in real terms, 100 years.

CPI (1965=100)

US S & P–real

Growth trend; 1.90% per annum

01 Jan11 01 Jan21 01 Jan31 01 Jan41 01 Jan51 01 Jan61 01 Jan71 01 Jan81 01 Jan91

Chart 2.61 US versus UK Earnings Per Share, 30 years

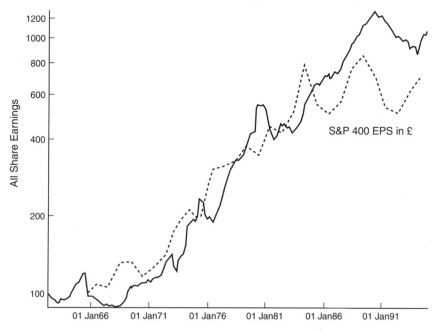

All Share Earnings

S&P 400 EPS in £

01 Jan66   01 Jan71   01 Jan76   01 Jan81   01 Jan86   01 Jan91

Chart 2.62 UK Reverse Yield Ratio; 100 years*

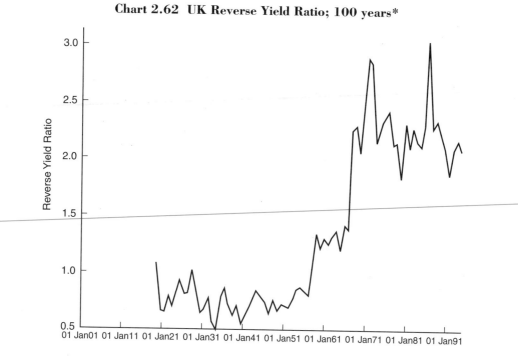

Maggie Thatcher Effect', while in the US they are only now beginning to recover from a long depression, originally initiated by dollar overvaluation in the period 1984/5. Added to resurgent US technological leadership and stringent accounting practices, this has made us incline to a contrary, and somewhat more positive, view of US markets.

Incidentally, it is our suspicion that the UK investor – whether pension fund or private individual – is overcommitted to equities, and underinvested in bonds. If we are genuinely embarking on an era of low inflation, then the chart above suggests that the reverse yield ratio is way out of kilter. Time alone will tell.

*Unless otherwise stated, charts in this article are compiled by Matheson Securities. ♀

FOLLOW THE LEADER

Vivien MacDonald

*The author has worked for **Edinburgh Financial Publishing** for almost five years. Previously she was an analyst with **Credit Lyonnais** and trained as a* *stock broker with **Bell Lawrie White**. She currently manages **Directus**, which is a specialized service monitoring directors' share transactions in their own companies. She is also the managing editor for* The Inside Track *and* The Value Investor *monthly newsletters. In addition she writes a regular column for* The Financial Times.

People-watching is always interesting and in the world of investment the people are all the more exciting because their actions equate to money! Certain individuals take centre stage in the financial pages because of their immense personalities and derring-do. But not every businessman is an Alan Sugar or a Robert Maxwell. The majority are less well known, less high profile but, to the companies they work for, equally important. The group of people that give most companies their direction and momentum are the directors. Directors of quoted companies are in a unique position to set an example to investors. They have the best insight into the real potential or problems facing their company. They alone are in the position to evaluate what is happening. No amount of press releases or analyst visits can compare.

Directors of UK quoted companies are obliged by law to make public their dealing (or the dealings of their spouses and children under the age of 18) no matter how small or insignificant. The requirements of other markets are not so stringent. In Germany there are currently few disclosure requirements, allowing many individuals to hide behind the anonymity of large banks. In Australia directors are not required to announce their dealings. However in both the US and Hong Kong it is mandatory to make public these transactions and consequently information on directors can be collected and analysed. In the near future the European Commission is committed to moving other European markets into line with the UK.

Relevant transactions are announced by the company to the Stock Exchange. In both the US and the UK specialist information companies collect this data and then analyse and disseminate it, giving investors the most pertinent details. Transaction information is also carried by some broad sheet newspapers, including *The Financial Times*, and some weekly journals.

Directors buy when they believe that the market price for their stock does not reflect the true potential for the company. They may know of specifics, such as a new plant coming on stream or a new director or a new product that has not been fully appreciated by the market. Before they can deal, the information, if significant, must be made available to the investing public. While they are known in the United States especially, as 'insiders', directors are constrained by the restrictions preventing insider dealing just like any other investor.

It is not hard to come across instances of successful director buying. The most spectacular offer the clearest reason why it is worth following 'insiders':

The share prices of both Shandwick (Chart 2.63) and Danka (Chart 2.64), had been in the doldrums for some time. In Shandwick, new management and a new sense of direction gave the shares a much needed boost and directors were well positioned to take advantage of the moment. In Danka the directors

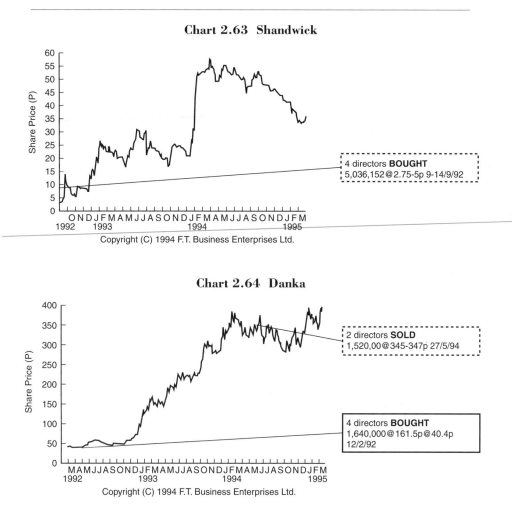

Chart 2.63 Shandwick

4 directors **BOUGHT**
5,036,152 @ 2.75-5p 9-14/9/92

Copyright (C) 1994 F.T. Business Enterprises Ltd.

Chart 2.64 Danka

2 directors **SOLD**
1,520,00 @ 345-347p 27/5/94

4 directors **BOUGHT**
1,640,000 @ 161.5p @ 40.4p
12/2/92

Copyright (C) 1994 F.T. Business Enterprises Ltd.

could see how the company had built up much better momentum than its competitors and that the stock was spectacularly undervalued, relative to industry multiples in the US.

The usual time lag between a director anticipating a price rise and the price rise happening is judged to be about three months. However, directors are not generally dealing for the short term, so whatever was good news when they dealt should continue to have a beneficial impact for more than three months. The reasons for buying stock are clear: the share price is expected to rise.

The usual time lag between a director anticipating a price rise and the price rise happening is judged to be about three months.

261

In certain circumstances, companies require that all their executive directors hold a nominal quantity of stock so it is common to see new directors buy as soon as they are appointed. While most transactions measured by the number of directors' dealings are on the buy side, the bulk of volume measured by value are, in fact, sales. There are many more reasons for selling. A share holding can make up a large part of a director's personal wealth. Many deals involve some form of 'house keeping', for example releasing cash to pay taxes; covering liabilities such as losses sustained by Lloyd's. Other deals give a window to the private lives of directors. For example divorce settlements; school fees; transfer of stock when a child reaches majority or bequeathed in a will. Directors may also sell to invest in another project, such as a different company or a yacht or a new conservatory.

Given so many reasons for selling it is necessary to go back to the directors or the company to find out why. In most cases, particularly in the UK, directors are keen to keep the market informed if the reason for the transaction is prosaic. There are also examples of uncannily good timing, where on the sell side Directors reduce their holdings shortly before the price slides.

To establish the importance of a sale or a buy signal, there are a couple of rules of thumb. Broadly a proportion of 10 per cent is deemed to be significant. Therefore if a holder of 40 per cent of a company capitalized at £200m sells £5m worth of stock it is not necessarily as significant as if a director doubles his holding from a value of £40,000 to £80,000. A second key indicator is the number of directors dealing together, or within a short time of each other. In the UK the specific times during which a director or his family may deal is strictly regulated. Apart from being prohibited from dealing when they are 'insiders' in the Financial Services Act's sense of the term, they may not deal during the two-month period prior to either interim or final results. This period is referred to as the 'closed period'. An indicator of good results is buying just before the company goes into its closed period. The size of the company is not a deciding factor. Directors of blue chips may not hold as large a proportion of stock but their deals can be as significant as directors of newly arrived companies.

Despite the rigorous code structure, there are instances where the rules are bent or ignored altogether. A director may deal during the closed period; or with 'insider knowledge'; or he may simply not report the transaction as fast as the system demands. Blatant flaunting of the rules is rare, but penalties for doing so are not strongly enforced and this is not an area that the City would appear to have as a priority.

Directors may also try to support their share price by buying shares in the market knowing that people will be aware of the purchases. There are cases where directors have bought stock knowing that there would be a thunderstorm on the horizon but hoping to put off the first drops of rain.

Confusing signals are sent out when directors deal in their options. Options were originally intended as a way of giving directors a personal incentive to make their company perform better on the market. They give the right to buy during a period three years from the date of grant at a predetermined price, and extend for a fixed time period. A board may allocate up to 2 per cent of its equity as options each year. In terms of watching directors, what they do with options can be hard to establish. Firstly, directors may simply exercise their option and keep the equity. Secondly, they may exercise the option and then sell some stock at the current market price, use the money to cover their cost and keep the rest. Finally, they may purchase and then immediately sell all the stock. In none of these scenarios is it clear whether their actions are positive or negative. The first case is the most positive, since they are having to fund the purchase from their own wallets. However, the last case may simply mean the director is realizing a bonus to which he or she is entitled. Furthermore, at any time a director may have multiple options running.

Much investment advice can appear to be based on such complicated scientific formulae as to be akin to astrology. Yet, however much finely tuned analysis is put into stock selection, the company's profitability is ultimately dependent on the people who run it. The human factor is not just important on a company by company basis, but also because directors as a whole are part of the market. The direction they give as a group can be a good lead indicator for the direction the market will take. In the UK there is broadly a ratio of two buys for every sell month by month. Where this dips or rises there is often a corresponding move in the market a short time after.

The Inside Track monitors this activity and tracks the Buy/Sell ratio. The Buy/Sell ratio is based upon all directors' transactions notified to the Stock Exchange in any given month, and is plotted against the FT-SE 100. It is based on the number of directors' dealing and not the value of the deals. No transactions which involve company share schemes, bonuses, options, scrip dividends or non-beneficial holdings are included. The chart below shows the ratio from January 1992 to April 1995. The concentration of highs was in late 1992 and the recent lows in early 1994. That is consistent with hindsight, which shows late 1992 was a good time to purchase UK stocks and early 1994 marked a high in the market.

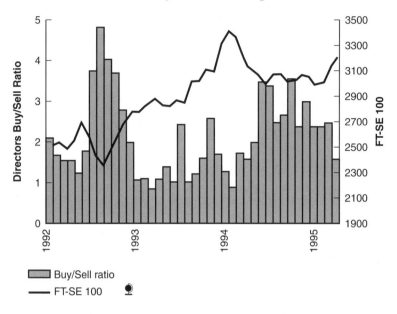

Chart 2.65 Directors Buy/Sell Ratio compared to FT-SE 100

THE SHORT SIDE

Michael Murphy,

*Michael Murphy founded **The Overpriced Stock Service** in 1983. The OSS is the premier short-selling Investment advisory newsletter in the world. He is the President and Chief Investment Officer of **Negative Beta Associates**, a registered investment advisory firm specializing in short-selling for tax-free funds. He manages the GEM Short Fund, a limited partnership, and the Monitrend Technology Fund, an open-end mutual fund that can sell short up to 25 per cent of its portfolio. His article on performance measurement in the* Financial Analysts' Journal *won a Benjamin Graham Award.*

Short selling

All it means is borrowing stock, selling in the open market, waiting for the stock price to go down, then buying back at a lower price and returning them to the person that lent them to you. Your profit is the difference between your sales price and your purchase price. That doesn't sound like very much, but those two little words arouse more emotion and elicit more misinformation than any other pair of words related to the stock market.

Short selling is a technique used by a few sophisticated money managers and knowledgeable individual investors. Selling a stock before you buy it is counter intuitive to most investors and stockbrokers when they first think about it. Shorting is also regarded in some quarters as vaguely disreputable. (It is usually regarded that way by people who have never tried it and do not know very much about it.) In point of fact short selling helps capital markets work by adding liquidity and driving overpriced stocks down to fair levels.

A plot of stock price moves, past or anticipated, usually looks like a perfectly normal bell curve in the middle with two 'fat tails'; too many badly under-priced and badly overpriced stocks. The whole function of the capital markets is to shove the under-priced ones up and the overpriced ones down, bringing the expected returns into a normal relationship. Half of this never-ending process cannot work efficiently without shorting.

Making some investments on the short side is a practical, profitable thing to do, and because few investors sell short it offers interesting profit and hedging opportunities. In bull or bear markets, short selling can make money, hedge your portfolio, and give you added peace of mind. In a bad bear market, understanding how to sell short could be the skill that keeps you from financial disaster. Short selling is a way to stay rich as well as get rich.

Even if you only sell short shares of one stock one time, you'll have done something 99.9 per cent of stockholders in the world never will do. And, like many parts of the stock market that are relatively uncrowded, you'll probably find short-selling a lot more profitable than simply buying stocks and hoping they go up.

Even if you only sell short shares of one stock one time, you'll have done something 99.9 per cent of stockholders in the world never will do.

There are strict rules surrounding short-selling to make sure investors don't go too far astray, hurting themselves, a brokerage firm or the whole capital market system. But all you need to start short selling is a margin account at a brokerage firm. Unlike many other lesser-known investment techniques the mechanics of selling short are simple. Pick your victim and resolve to start small in order to keep the risks low. Deposit collateral with your broker – long stocks, bonds, Treasury bills or cash. Get a clear understanding with your broker as to how much 'shorting power' your collateral gives you.

Just as in going long, you can put up 100 per cent of the value of the short sale in collateral or you can go on margin as high as 50 per cent. We strongly suggest that you do not leverage your short sale portfolio, unless you are a very sophisticated investor. If a short sales goes against you it can deplete required collateral very rapidly. Calculate how many shares you can afford to short. Tell your broker this is an opening short sale order. Set the minimum price at which you will sell, and say 'or better', which in this case means you (gladly) will accept any higher price.

Suppose you decide that Intergalactic Widgets is badly overpriced and due for a tumble. You tell your broker to open a short position of 100 shares at $50 or better. Before entering your order, your broker will check with their firm's stock loan department to be sure the stock can be borrowed. If you can't borrow a stock, you can't short it. Your broker may borrow 100 shares from another account at the same firm, or he may go to another brokerage firm or even a fund. You don't care where he borrows it.

He then sells Intergalactic Widgets in the open market for $50 a share. For all listed stocks and most over-the-counter issues he must wait for an uptick – a price higher than the previous trade. This rule is designed to block short sellers from mercilessly pounding a stock down. He also expects you to put up collateral – cash or other securities – as account equity against the short. Suppose you put up $5,000 in cash.

Then bad news comes out. Intergalactic Widgets promptly declines from $50 to $30. You tell your broker to 'cover my short at $30 or less.' Your broker goes into the open market and buys 100 shares of Intergalactic Widgets for $30. He then delivers those shares back to the original lender. The lender, who may be a long-term holder of Intergalactic Widgets and couldn't care less if the price temporarily falls or rises, is made whole.

The broker credits your account for the difference between the $5,000 he took in when he shorted the stock and the $3,000 he had to pay out to buy the stock back. That's your profit – $2,000 (less commissions on both transactions, of course). The $5,000 in equity you put up is still in the account, so your account value has grown to $7,000 and you're ready to do it again.

There are so many reasons to sell short. In our view, the most important reasons are:

● to make money from the decline of an overpriced stock

● to make money from the decline of an overpriced industry

● to make money from the decline of the entire market

● to 'hedge' or protect your long positions from a market decline with offsetting short positions.

● to provide very efficient diversification

● to earn a high return on your cash collateral.

Overpriced stocks Generally, whatever criteria you use to pick long investments can be turned on their head to pick short sale opportunities. High valuation, heavy insider selling, weakening stock price momentum, deteriorating balance sheets, falling cash levels – all can be used to identify opportunities.

If you track the most heavily shorted stocks you'll find that most of them go down and sometimes even go out of business. There are reasons why people short those stocks, having to do with deteriorating businesses, bad accounting, over-hyped prices and even dishonest management. When a fraud is exposed the company often goes bankrupt, which means you never have to cover your short position. In many jurisdictions if there is no closing transaction there is no taxable event, so profits on these ultimate shorts can be withdrawn from your account tax free. Consult your tax adviser.

Here are a couple of cautionary tales which made good money for the shorts.

Cascade International was a chain of women's clothing stores that told Wall Street they were undergoing rapid growth from perfume and cosmetics departments. The company reported a steady expansion in the number of stores with increasing revenues and earnings. However, management often gave different figures for the number of stores open, so we called every store in California to find out what other stores they knew about, and quickly learned the actual number of stores open was less than half of management's claim. After checking two other states with the same result, we recommended selling short. The company's auditor was a sole practitioner, not a major firm. Virtually every borrowable share was sold short when the president left the country and disappeared, leaving the company in shambles. It turned out the president had been selling unregistered stock and booking the proceeds as income in order to show sales.

Flight International was the 'Rent A Russian Air Force' company that bought Lear jets and then contracted with the US Armed Services to run 'readiness drills' – mock attacks on bases, airports and ships. Their financial gimmick was to depreciate the jets over the normal 18-year life, even though they were flying in high-G turns about ten times as many hours per day as the average jet. In addition to reporting 'earnings' due to under-depreciation, they persuaded the US government to front-end load the contract payments by paying about 150 per cent of the hourly rate in the first year of the three-year contract, 100 per cent in the second year and 50 per cent in the third. About halfway through the second year the company ran out of cash and went into bankruptcy.

Overpriced industries One of the key tip-offs to a promising area for short selling is a large inflow of fresh capital to an industry. The companies in that industry will take advantage of the availability of funds at attractive rates and substantially increase capacity. Of course, increased supply causes price to fall 'unexpectedly', and what might have made sense for one company to do turns out to make no sense at all for the entire industry. Commercial office space, airline fleet capacity, paper manufacturing and computer disk drive assembly come to mind as industries recently exhibiting this problem.

Market declines Since 1951 the stock market has declined about one-third of the time. The average drop in declining months was larger than the average gain in rising months. That confirms most people's intuitive understanding that the market drops at a more rapid rate than it rises. Profiting from declining markets is a compelling reason to sell short.

Hedging Hedge funds can be long or short stocks, and often can use options to enhance returns. The classic hedge fund tries to maintain a close balance of the total positions. A key concept for hedgers is the 'net long' exposure. A portfolio invested 50 per cent in stocks with risk, or beta about equal to the overall market, and 50 per cent in cash has a 'net long' position of 50 per cent exposure to market fluctuations.

Suppose the owner of this portfolio wanted to keep more money in stocks in order to participate in their higher long-term return, but was unwilling to take on more market-related risk. In that case, the portfolio stock position could be taken up to 60 per cent, cash reduced to 40 per cent, and a 10 per cent short position initiated. The 'net long' position of the portfolio is 60 per cent stocks minus 10 per cent short, or the same 50 per cent as in the original portfolio.

If there is a sharp market drop, these two portfolios should behave about the same. Over time, the additional 10 per cent in stocks should earn a better return than keeping that money in cash. At the same time, there is no reason a carefully chosen 10 per cent short position should not also beat the return on cash.

Efficient diversification Investors diversify to find investments that are not correlated with stock market returns or with each other, in order to reduce the risk that one bad trend can wipe out a whole portfolio. Rather than a loose correlation to market moves, the short sale portfolio has a high but negative correlation to market moves. If the market takes the long equities down, the short sales will rise, and vice versa. A portfolio of short sales provides almost ideal diversification that is easy to predict, control and measure.

High return on cash In order to sell short, you must put up collateral, which can be short-term government securities, bonds, or cash. You continue to collect interest on fixed income securities, and the broker will pay interest on your cash. When your broker opens your short sale position, stock is borrowed and sold in the market. Cash comes into your account, although you cannot withdraw it. The broker uses this cash to fund their business, instead of having to borrow from the bank. If you have a short sale account of $250,000 or more, you should ask your broker to share this interest saving. It is quite common for brokers to pay 75 per cent of the broker call loan rate on the total short proceeds, in the form of a 'short market credit'. In addition to the trading profits on your short sales, your collateral is earning interest at about 1.5 times the short-term rate. If your short sales only break even (after commissions), you'll get a far better total return on your cash collateral than you would in bills!

What are the risks? If you buy a stock for $10, the worst it can do is go to $0, causing you a 100 per cent loss. If you short a stock at $10, it could double against you to $20, causing you a 100 per cent loss. Or double again, causing you a 400 per cent loss. Or again and again . . . It is mathematically true that you can lose an infinite amount on a short sale. It also is mathematically true that bumble-bees can't fly. However, in the real world bumblebees fly, and short sellers don't lose more than 100 per cent of their money unless they are very stubborn.

Your odds of getting caught in a true short squeeze, where stock cannot be borrowed and the broker 'buys you in', are minimal. There have been only a few real short squeezes in recent years, such as Resorts International, Viratek and Home Shopping Network. If you look at the charts of these companies, you'll see that, if the short seller had 'staying power' (meaning cash to meet margin calls), the positions always ultimately made money.

However, there's a much easier way to limit your loses. Decide in advance how much you're willing to lose on a short, just as you would with a stock that you're long. The broker will ask you to meet your margin calls when they come due, and will liquidate your assets to meet those calls if you can't. So short selling is analogous to buying stocks on margin. Don't ever meet a margin call – you're just being stubborn. Cover, take your loss, and live to fight another day. In general, use a 25 per cent loss as a limit. If a position goes against you to the extent of 25 per cent, you probably either analysed the situation incorrectly, or missed some important factor in the situation, or your timing is off. Cover the position and reshort the stock later – at higher or even lower levels.

We suggest you beware of selling short companies with under $50 million in market value, under one million shares in float, or less than five brokers making a market in the stock. If you're determined to short such a stock, put a very small percentage of your money into it. The problem is that it's easy for brokerage firms to manipulate the price of small stocks that meet two or more of the above criteria, and that can mean they'll run the stock up against you.

A final reason to sell short You'll be a better long investor. When you can only make money on the long side, there is a natural tendency to hope things turn out well, to be optimistic in your expectations, and to overstay a bull market. These are especially acute problems for professional money managers in a quarterly performance derby who have to squeeze every last nickel out of a situation when it's going up. If they don't, they are afraid someone else will. That someone else then may have better performance and get all the clients.

In addition, due to the way most brokerage firms pay and reward their analysts, right now there is a bias in the system towards figuring out what could go right. It makes a saleable story. That's why analysts' earnings estimates are almost always high and, as you get closer and closer to the actual earnings, they tend to reduce their estimates.

For the ultimate perpetual bulls, look at the mutual fund managers. Most mutual fund investors don't realize managers are legally prevented from protecting the funds by short selling. Individual investors can short sell, but those highly paid money managers, who are supposed to be the experts, for the most part cannot.

Investors who are uncomfortable shorting individual stocks have only a few options.

1 Private partnerships: Our GEM Short Fund has a minimum of $50,000, which is about as low as private partnerships ever get. After a one-year commitment, investors can add or withdraw funds monthly. Two leading consultants on placing money in private short selling partnerships are Michael Gayner and Harold Strunk.

2 Mutual funds: In addition to our Monitrend Technology Fund, which goes long technology stocks and short a wide range of stocks, a few other mutual funds can sell short up to 25 per cent of their portfolio value.

   (a) The Robertson Stephens Contrarian Fund holds out of favour technology stocks and a large position in junior golds, then shorts over-valued growth stocks.

   (b) The Rydex Ursa Fund stays short the Standard & Poor's 500 Index at all times.

   (c) The Lindner Bulwark Fund holds low P/E value stocks and, from time-to-time, shorts high flyers.

Short selling will give you a more balanced view of the market and of individual stocks. After you get used to making money when stocks go down as well as up, you will develop a certain detachment from what you hear and read about businesses. You'll no longer have to hope that everything works out right, or hope a company can come through on bullish projections, or hope other investors are willing to pay higher and higher prices for your stock. ♀

> After you get used to making money when stocks go down as well as up, you will develop a certain detachment from what you hear and read about businesses.

OPTIMIZING A BALANCED PORTFOLIO WITH SHORTS

Michael Long

*Michael R. Long is the General Partner of Charlotte, NC-based **Rockbridge Partners**. He does consulting work and also conducts manager searches. He has written articles about short selling for Barrons. **The Rockbridge Short Sellers Index** is regularly used by* The Wall Street Journal *to report the performance of short selling money managers.*

While one should always be careful not to draw faulty conclusions from optimized solutions (especially in the world of investing!), it may serve a useful purpose to examine these 'perfect answers', anyway. I have frequently been asked what percentage of a stock portfolio should be hedged with a short selling strategy. My candid response, 'that it should probably all be hedged and stay that way', may be a bit too radical for most people. So Ranier Partners' Kelley Price and I worked on 'the answer' by examining the past ten years to come up with a more objective response to this question.

The research consisted of simply back-testing the entire range of long/short combinations to find the one which yielded the greatest returns with the least risk. The S&P 500 with dividends was used to represent the returns possible from the long side of the portfolio. The Rockbridge Short Sellers Index, which averages the net returns of 20 leading short selling managers each quarter, was used as a proxy for the returns available from short selling. We then calculated the annualized rate of return resulting from each combination of longs and shorts. To measure risk, we used the standard deviation of the returns, which tells you how much variation or volatility is hidden in those returns. A weighting of 62 per cent long/38 per cent short ended up yielding both the highest return, 16.6 per cent, and the least risk, a standard deviation of 3.3 per cent, for the ten-year period ending June, 1994. Interestingly enough, this combination actually yielded a higher rate of return than either being long or short. In addition to producing higher returns, the combined strategies were 57 per cent less volatile than the S&P. The actual results appear in the accompanying Chart 2.66.

Chart 2.66 Hedged Portfolios vs Long or Short only

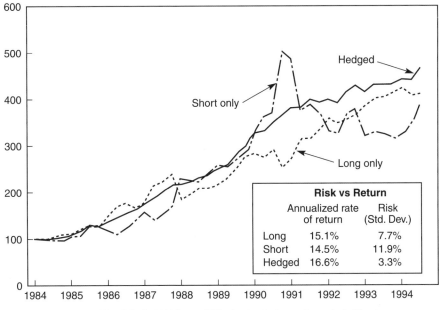

The Hedged Portfolio is 62% long, 38% short, rebalanced quarterly. The Long Portfolio uses the S&P 500 with dividends included. The Short Portfolio uses the Rockbridge Short Sellers Index.

How do you get better returns from combining two strategies than is available from either separately? It comes from a quarterly rebalancing of two strategies that each produce positive returns independently but do so at alternating periods. While it looks like two plus two equals five, the added profitability is not some modern math trick, but rather the result of the benefits of dollar cost averaging. There is an implicit assumption that returns regress to the mean, an assumption that is impossible to quarrel with.

The point of all this is not to suggest that investors rush out and put 62 per cent of their assets into stocks, 38 per cent into short sales, rebalance it quarterly, and then go fishing. It is unrealistic to think that the future will mirror the past with any such precision. For that matter the direction of the stock market may not even be up over the next ten years, and could even possibly be down. In that case our error will be that we didn't hedge enough. In any event, the 62/38 mix will probably continue to produce superior returns with below average risk compared to an unhedged portfolio, and this is probably the critical issue for most people since over 99 per cent of all equities appear to be unhedged. So, it should be obvious that introducing short selling can reduce risk without penalizing returns. And should we ever see another bear market, it may very well save the portfolio (and the portfolio manager as well).

Short selling is often characterized as high risk, and there is no question that an individual short sale can be a very high risk proposition. But a collection of them can greatly decrease this risk to acceptable proportions, and a collection of professional managers can further decrease risk. Short sales used in combination with long positions should actually reduce the volatility of the portfolio, and this hedge should help to increase the total return, as well. In my opinion, anyone suggesting that a portfolio of longs is either superior or more conservative than a hedged approach probably hasn't studied the issue sufficiently or, worse, isn't in a position to benefit from such findings. ♀

> **Short selling is often characterized as high risk, and there is no question that an individual short sale can be a very high risk proposition. But a collection of them can greatly decrease this risk to acceptable proportions,**

Specific Focus

Buy a Company – Nothing Down
Using Dividends to Divine Value
Merger Arbitrage
Beating Blue Chip Indices with the HY 5 System
Relative Performance

BUY A COMPANY – NOTHING DOWN

Michael Metz

*Michael Metz is Chief Investment Strategist of **Oppenheimer & Co Inc**, which is a privately owned securities brokerage and investment banking firm. Mr Metz began his career as an analyst with **Standard & Poor's**, then **Nuveen & Co** and started at **Oppenheimer** in 1969. He and an associate, Norman Weinger, were pioneers in the use of computer technology to assist in identifying undervalued equities. Today, as Chief Investment Strategist, he is primarily responsible for advising retail and institutional investors and brokers on investment strategy and portfolio selection. He also actively manages investment partnerships for some of the firm's high net-worth clients. When asked about the stress involved in making predictions about anything as unpredictable as the stock market, Mr Metz is reported to have stated, 'The most important talent a strategist can possess is the ability to forget what he said three minutes ago'.*

Among the more dramatic features of the American entrepreneurial scene in the mid-1980s was the acceptance of the use of leverage to buy entire publicly owned companies. The leveraged buyouts (LBOs) of the 1980s were based on the concept that public businesses were sufficiently under-priced that virtually their entire purchase price could be financed simply by using the assets acquired as collateral for borrowings.

The basic approach of the individual entrepreneur is profoundly different from that employed by the traditional, passive stockholder. The latter appraises companies by the criterion of a dividend discount model that assigns a value based on a projected future stream of earnings and dividends, within the context of specific interest rate assumptions. During a decade of inflation, the modest valuation of companies reflected their extremely low projected real rates of return on assets. In contrast, for the entrepreneurial investor, companies became extremely under-priced relative to their collateral value. The entrepreneur appraises public businesses quite differently. He examines the leveragability of an asset base – aiming to determine whether he can borrow sufficient amounts by pledging the assets acquired to finance their purchase.

In computing the leveragability of a business, the most conservative creditors will lend only against the collateral value of current assets, such as inventories and receivables (and, of course, cash), since these can normally be liquidated with expedition and ease. However, even for these relatively liquid assets, some discount to carrying values is necessary to provide a margin of safety for the lender.

At Oppenheimer we have used our computer to screen for those companies that, on the basis of balance sheet entries, would be particularly attractive to an acquirer, since their assets, theoretically, could provide collateral values sufficient to permit borrowing the entire purchase price. **In essence, a buyer conceivably could use the borrowing power of the acquired company to finance its purchase completely.**

Our screen structure is set up as follows, with the financials for Acme Metals as of December 1994 provided by way of illustration (see Table 2.8). Column I shows the reporting date for all the subsequent balance sheet entries. Column II is the company's market capitalization in millions of dollars, based on the current market price of the common shares.

The remaining columns are all per share numbers. Column III is the cash. Of course, cash is valued at 100 per cent in terms of its value as collateral. Column IV is receivables net of the allowance for doubtful accounts, discounted by 25 per cent. We assume that a lender, for example, would lend 75 per cent of face value. Column V is inventory; we have discounted the carrying value of inventories by 50 per cent. Column VI is gross plant: here we have arbitrarily discounted this value by 80 per cent to arrive at its valuation as collateral, more conservative than the 60 per cent discount that we have used in prior screens. This change reflects the probability that lending institutions are, themselves, tightening standards of lending on relatively illiquid assets, such as fixed plant and equipment, particularly in view of the deflation in commercial and industrial real estate values in some areas. Column VII is what we characterize as total borrowing power per share, calculated by adding the collateral values in Columns III through VI.

Column VIII represents total existing liabilities (debt included in current liabilities and long-term debt) against the corporation, which, presumably, would have to be paid off before new encumbrances could be placed on the assets. Current accounts payable and other current liabilities, however, need not be deducted from the asset base since they normally contain no prior claim on collateral and would not have a preferential claim in the event of a change in control to a leveraged buyer. In essence, a company's customers are providing working capital.

Next, total debt (Column VIII) is deducted from total borrowing power, as computed in Column VII, to arrive at net borrowing power per share (Column

Table 2.8 Per Share Information

Net Borrowing Power> Market Price	I	II	III	IV	V	VI	VII	VIII	IX	X	XI	XII	XIII
	Quarter Date	Market Value $m	Cash	REC 75%	INV 50%	GR PLT 20%	Total Borrow Power	Total Debt	Net Borrow Power	Price 1994 13th Dec	Excess	Book value per/sh	Price/ Sales
ACME Metals Inc	6/94	90.3	13.25	8.41	3.69	14.71	40.06	10.07	29.98	16.25	13.73	17.31	0.2

IX). To fit the parameters of this screen, this figure must exceed the current market price (Column X). The excess (Column XI) is, theoretically, the amount of borrowing power still available to the purchaser of the target company after having alrady borrowed enough to pay the market price for all outstanding shares. In essence, the buyer has leveraged out completely, using the acquired company's assets as collateral, and still has excess funds. Column XII is the reported book value.

Various caveats should be noted. All balance sheet figures must be examined more closely. In the case of receivables (Column IV), we believe a 25 per cent discount for collateral purposes is generally reasonable. However, with some businesses, particularly those dealing with numerous small, poorly financed customers (such as sole proprietor retailers), a larger discount might be more reasonable. Conversely, where the government or a 'blue chip' corporation is the major customer, a smaller discount would be in order.

For inventories, in the case of fungible items such as those used in the metal-fabricating or food processing industries, the 50 per cent discount may be too large. In other instances, e.g. where finished consumer fashion items are sizeable, a much larger discount would be appropriate. Regarding gross plant (Column VI), some obsolete or poorly located facilities would not command a collateral value much above salvage value. In many instances, however, the 80 per cent discount would prove overly conservative.

The liability side also merits scrutiny. In certain cases, some of the debt may take the form of mortgages on specific plants or pieces of real estate. The company may be in a position to incur general obligation debt without having to re-finance such existing obligations. Moreover, debt carrying a fixed coupon below prevailing market rates often can be retired at a discount to face value. A critical consideration is whether trade relationships would be hurt by the injection of additional leverage. For example, suppliers might be wary of the leveraging and insist on earlier, or even simultaneous, payment. Thus, the subject company might have greater working capital requirements than under its present, less leveraged financial structure.

In many cases, borrowing power may prove materially larger than it appears on the surface. A substantial LIFO reserve could considerably enhance the collateral value of inventories. The plant account might be dramatically understated and include unencumbered assets that would support large new secured borrowing. On the other hand, off-balance-sheet liabilities, such as pension obligations or pending litigation, conceivably could constitute prior liens and reduce borrowing power. Pension plans, however, may also be over funded.

Ultimately, of course, the critical consideration is whether a leveraged purchase of a company makes sound business sense. That determination, in turn, is largely a matter of whether projected pre-tax undedicated cash flow would be sufficient to service the new debt and generate adequate funds for maintaining the profitability of the company.

An increasingly significant variable in determining the attraction of a business to an entrepreneurial buyer – either financial or strategic – is the price-to-sales ratio (PSR). This is the ratio of the total market capitalization of a company, including its debt, to gross sales. A low price relative to sales, compared, of course, with the industry norm, is a critical consideration.

The buyer often projects that, through the elimination of duplicative research and development, marketing and distribution costs, the return on sales can be increased dramatically. The buyer, in essence, adds value through his ability to carry more of the 'top line', down to the 'bottom line'. This consideration has been a major element behind the merger trend in the health care and pharmaceutical industries and the consolidation wave in the banking sector.

In a period of more moderate inflation, as is considered probable over coming years, under valuation is more likely to be found in intangible assets, such as competitive standing, franchises, marketing organizations and distribution networks, which normally do not show up on balance sheets. Moreover, in an atmosphere of fiscal drag for an extended period because of the high public sector borrowing requirements of most industrialized nations, sales growth will be more difficult to develop internally. Consequently, acquirers are expected to continue to emphasize buying sales, and low PSRs.

Perhaps the most intriguing opportunities will eventually surface in the emerging markets. Assuming the valuations in these markets become more reasonable, there could be attractive opportunities for entrepreneurs and for corporate buyers seeking strategic entries to these areas.

USING DIVIDENDS TO DIVINE VALUE

Geraldine Weiss and Gregory Weiss

*Geraldine Weiss co-founded **Investment Quality Trends** in 1966. She became Editor and Publisher in 1968 and has served in that capacity ever since. She was the first woman to publish a stock market advisory service. Today, **IQT** is consistently ranked as a top performer by **Hulbert Financial Digest**. Geraldine co-authored an investment best seller, Dividends Don't Lie. As a television per-*

sonality, she has appeared on Wall Street Week, The Changing World of Business, Moneytalk, Marketwrap *and* Moneyline. *Dubbed 'The Grande Dame of Dividends' by the* Los Angeles Times *and 'The Dividend Detective' by* Personal Investor *magazine, Geraldine has been featured in virtually every financial publication nationwide.*

Gregory Weiss is an Investment Analyst and Associate Editor for **IQT**. *He has appeared as a featured guest on* KWHY – The Business Channel *and* KNSD-TV News, *and is frequently quoted in investment publications such as* Money Magazine, Forbes, *and* Personal Investing.

How Do Dividends Connect With Stock Prices?

The oldest cliche in the stock market is Baron Rothschild's advice to investors, 'Buy low and sell high'. Sure, that's easy for him to say; but how do we know when a stock is low priced or high priced? What determines the relative measures of 'high' and 'low' in the stock market?

In fact, Rothschild did not tell investors to buy low and sell high. What he said was, 'Buy cheap and sell dear,' advice which has been misquoted for many years. While the words 'low' and 'high' by themselves have little meaning in the stock market, the words 'cheap' and 'dear' are relative terms which refer to value. Investors who follow Rothschild's advice to buy cheap and sell dear understand the meaning of the market.

Dividends connect with stock prices in very specific ways. In addition to providing income, they are the most reliable tool by which value is measured. By dividing the current price of a stock into the annual dividend, we can determine the dividend yield. And, by relating the dividend yield to the high and low yields which repeatedly have occurred at peaks and valleys in the price cycle of that stock, we can determine whether the current price is cheap or dear.

For example, let us suppose that a stock which is priced at $30 per share pays a dividend of $1.50 per share. By dividing 30 into 1.50, we see that the current dividend yield is 5.0 per cent. If that 5.0 per cent yield repeatedly has marked a low point in the price trend of the stock in question, we know it is cheap and historically good value is available. When that dividend is increased, the value of that stock rises.

Using this same example, if research shows that a 2.5 per cent yield repeatedly has occurred at the top of a rising price trend after which the stock has declined, we can assume that a 2.5 per cent dividend yield identifies an Overvalued area in which a sale should be considered. If the dividend is increased, thus raising the prices at Undervalue and Overvalue, the stock will be given more headroom and a decline can be averted.

The strong dividend connection to stock prices also is evidenced in other ways. We know that when a dividend is increased, the value of the stock often rises. A rising price trend is supported and in fact inspired by frequent dividend increases. However, when a dividend is cut, the price of a stock generally falls as the value of the holding is reduced. Even the suggestion that a dividend may be lowered can result in a declining price, as investors anticipate a loss of value.

> **When the dividend yield is historically high, the price will be 'low', the stock will be 'cheap' and a purchase can be made.**

When the dividend yield is historically high, the price will be 'low', the stock will be 'cheap' and a purchase can be made. But, when the dividend yield is historically low, the price will be 'high', the stock will be 'dear', and a sale should be made. Just as Baron Rothschild advised: 'Buy cheap and sell dear'.

What is the Dividend Yield/Total Return Approach?

Dividends provide a springboard to value in the stock market; and dividend yield is the tool we use to identify attractive buying and selling areas. The term 'total return' refers to the combination of dividends and capital gain.

The stock market offers current income, plus growth of dividend income, plus capital gains. The combination of good value, plus attractive long-term investment growth potential is the object of the dividend yield/total return approach.

After many years of witnessing the apparently irrational behaviour of the stock market, we have observed some truths to be absolute. One of those truths was best said by Charles Dow, founder of *The Wall Street Journal* and creator of the popular Dow Jones Averages: 'To know values is to know the meaning of the market.'

No one will disagree with that. But, just how does one identify value in the stock market? How does an investor know when a stock is Undervalued where it can be bought, or Overvalued where it should be sold? After all, one investor's idea of good value to another person may be mere speculation. For the answer to that question, we look again to the unique barometer of dividend yield.

We have observed that when all other factors which rate analytical consideration have been digested, the underlying value of dividends, which determines yield, will in the long run also determine price. The key to value, therefore, lies in yield as reflected by the dividend trend. History shows that individual stock prices fluctuate between repetitive extremes of high dividend yield and low dividend yield. These reoccurring extremes of yield establish what is identified as Undervalued and Overvalued price levels. When a dividend is raised, the prices at Undervalue and Overvalue are raised automatically to continue reflecting the historically established yield extremes. Most importantly, each stock has its own distinctive high and low profile of yield and must be evaluated individually.

Babcock & Wilcox/McDermott/United Technologies-merger chronology (all information is from prospectus and joint proxy statement issued 22 February, 1978):

28.3.77	United Technologies Corp ('United') proposal of $42/share for any and all
4.4.77	B&W rejects United proposal
6.4 to 13.5.77	McDermott purchases 1,205,600 B&W shares in open market transactions at ($39.75 to $45.125/share)
5.8.77	United amends offer to $48/share
10.8.77	McDermott proposes $55/share for 4,300,000 shares
14.8.77	B&W recommends McDermott offer to stockholders
18.8.77	United amends offer to $55/share
19.8.77	McDermott increases offer to $60/share
23.8.77	United increases offer to $58.50
	McDermott increases offer to $62.50
25.8.77	McDermott amends offer to provide $2.50 special dividend/share declared by B&W to be payable to tendering stockholders and increases number of shares it will purchase to 4,800,000
25.8.77	United terminates its offer
16.9.77	McDermott owns 49 per cent of B&W outstanding stock
2.12.77	McDermott issues press release concerning United's interest in acquiring McDermott
8.12.77	Terms of B&W – McDermott merger announced
30.3.78	Stockholders approve merger effective 31.3.78.

A. Parity Calculation

Terms: 1 Babcock & Wilcox ($34.50) = $62.50 for 4,800,000 common B&W shares (39 per cent) and 1 $2.20 convertible preferred stock plus 1 $2.60 preferred stock for remainder

Gross Spread:

On tender:	(0.52)	(62.5 – 34.5)
On sale:	(0.48)	(56.0 – 34.5)

$24.88

B. Practical Application

1 Position taken: 100 B&W long at $34\frac{1}{2}
2 Date position taken: 29 March 1977
3 Tender shares purchased: 16 September 1977
4 Cash received for 52 shares: 26 September 1977
5 48 shares sold: 16 September 1977
6 Net spread:

$2,488 Gross spread
   (95) Interest cost (5.9 per cent interest on 3,450 for 171 days)
    (2) Interest cost (6.5 per cent interest on 1,176 for 10 days)

   325 Dividends on long position $0.375 ex date: 6/6

$2,716 Net spread   0.375   9/6
                                  2.5   9/6

7 **Annualized return on capital**

(a) Average statement of Financial Condition
29 March 1977 – 16 September 1977

    Assets
    100 B&W long $3,450

    Liabilities and Capital
    Bank borrowings $3,083
    15 per cent 'Haircut'   367
                                   $3,450

(b) Average statement of Financial Condition
16 September 1977 – 26 September 1977

    Assets

    52 B&W tendered $1,794

    Liabilities and Capital
    Bank borrowings $1,794

Average capital employed

$$\frac{(171 \text{ days})}{(356 \text{ days})}(\$3,083) = \frac{(10)}{(366)}(\$1,794) = \$1,493$$

$$\text{Return on Capital} = \frac{\$2,716}{\$1,493}$$

= 182 per cent per annum pre-tax

As far as getting involved in merger arbitrage as an investment strategy, 'for many are called, but few are chosen.' There are private investment funds that take individual investors, but the minimum amounts are often quite onerous. In the alternative, with particular insight into a transaction, one can often invest direct, but a one-target strategy can prove to be very expensive. A diversified portfolio of arbitrage investments is required in order to proceed in the long run. ♀

BEATING BLUE CHIP INDICES WITH THE HY 5 SYSTEM

Charles Fry

*Charles Fry is the Chief Executive of **Johnson Fry**, a company which he started 25 years ago, and which is now a London listed company involved in the financial services industry.*

The basis of all equity investment is the fundamental emotions of fear and greed. Fear of loss but expectation of profit. Any equity investment system to be successful must, therefore, address this fact.

Equities, of course, rise and fall in value. Some fall to zero. It is important to avoid these. One way of doing so is to invest only in blue chip shares and to define this category within a narrow base (i.e. the Dow Jones Industrial Average in the US and the FT-SE-30 in the UK). No stock in the FT-SE-30 Index has ever gone bust. In addition, the FT-SE-30 gives a broad spread of British industry (as does the Dow in the US), including only one bank and no property companies. So stick to Index stocks and the risk (or fear) is reduced.

But aren't blue chip portfolios boring and modest performers? The answer is 'yes', unless the best performing elements of the Indices are chosen. So how do you do that?

Any share has a value in the market that is the collective opinion of all those who buy and sell it. Opinions, of course, vary and shares go in and out of fashion. They move in a cycle. Buy at the bottom of the cycle and sell at the top and you will be rich. So let's look at how you can do this in a very simple fashion.

The idea was originated by the American fund manager Michael O'Higgins and discussed in detail in his book *Beating the Dow*. It has been developed and marketed in the UK using the FT-SE-30 Index by Johnson Fry. It works like this. Identify the ten highest yielding shares in the Index and invest in the five lowest priced. Rebase your portfolio once a year, making any changes using the same criteria. Johnson Fry calls this the Hy5 system. Many investment managers scoff at the simplicity of such a system ('Using only yield as a criteria is a nonsense'). That would be fine if the performance of investment managers matched the performance of the Hy5 system. It doesn't.

Chart 2.68 shows the 25-year performance of a £10,000 investment in 1969 in the Hy5 system compared to investing in the All Share Index (which generally outperforms the more narrow FT-SE-30) and to a Building Society deposit. Costs are ignored and gross income reinvested. What this graph shows is that Hy5 outperformed the FT-SE All Share by an average of 8 per cent per annum over 25 years. A quite staggering performance, achieved by investing in large, stable, blue chip companies. Remember roughly 75 per cent of unit trusts and mutual funds do not beat the main market indices.

Chart 2.68 Performance History Dec 1969 to Dec 1994

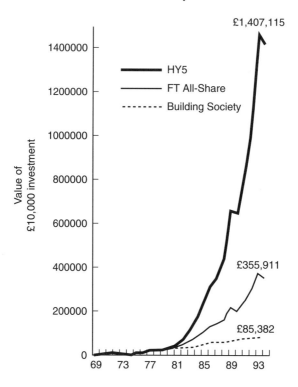

Building Society deposit rate is average rate on ordinary shares (Source: BZW). Illustrated returns relate to the simulated peformance of the HY5 system and take no account of share transaction charges.

Does it always work? No system always works, but Table 2.9 shows how it has worked for the past 25 years. It has outperformed the FT All Share for the last 14 years, every year.

What shares would the system have held? A selection of the portfolios is shown in Table 2.10. The quality is self-evident.

The most interesting question is why does the Hy5 system work. Investing in high yielding shares will tend to indicate they are out of fashion and probably having a rough time. They are, therefore, recovery candidates either through a cyclical change in their fortunes, management shake-ups or take-over (or sometimes a combination). But why the 'lowest priced' share of the ten highest yielders? This is more difficult. Michael O'Higgins sites the wide divergence in price between shares in the Dow (say, $120 to $10) and the fact that movement in a lower priced share is likely to be more than in a 'heavy'

Table 2.9

Y/E 31 Dec	HY 5 (%)	FT-SE All-Share (%)	HY5 Annual performance relative to FT-SE All-Share (%)
1970	0.7	−3.4	4.1
1971	51.3	47.4	3.9
1972	1.3	16.4	−15.1
1973	−18.0	−28.7	10.7
1974	−53.1	−51.8	−1.3
1975	212.8	152.1	60.7
1976	−2.9	2.2	−5.1
1977	71.0	49.2	21.8
1978	1.9	8.5	−6.6
1979	−0.7	10.5	−11.2
1980	33.6	35.4	−1.8
1981	15.6	13.8	1.8
1982	49.5	29.2	20.3
1983	62.2	29.2	33.0
1984	45.3	32.0	13.3
1985	44.3	20.1	24.2
1986	28.9	27.5	1.4
1987	14.2	8.0	6.2
1988	20.6	11.5	9.1
1989	52.8	36.1	16.7
1990	−2.1	−9.7	7.6
1991	24.5	20.7	3.8
1992	25.7	20.5	5.2
1993	43.3	28.4	14.9
1994	−3.5	−5.9	2.4
AVERAGE **RETURN**	28.8	20.0	8.8

priced one. In the UK, the divergence in price is not as large but, on analysing 25 years (and various interim periods), it is quite clear that the five **lowest** priced outperform the five **highest** priced consistently and by a margin. This looks like a case of don't knock the system, look at the facts.

The beauty of the Hy5 system is that it doesn't rely on people. People are emotional, people are ambitious, people always think they know best (or better than the next fund manager), and people generally like to move with the herd. Hy5 doesn't use people – it uses facts (unemotional, boring facts). Fund managers come and go, change jobs or retire. The Hy5 system does none of these. It just works.

Table 2.10

1970	
1 BOC	
2 LONDON BRICK (HANSON)	
3 SPILLERS (DALGETY)	
4 TATE & LYLE	
5 WOOLWORTH (KINGFISHER)	
Yield at start of year (%)	6.3
Performance over year (%)	
Hy5 System	0.7
FT-SE All-Share	−3.4

1975	
1 BOC	
2 DUNLOP (BTR)	
3 GRAND METROPOLITAN	
4 LONDON BRICK (HANSON)	
5 SPILLERS (DALGETY)	
Yield at start of year (%)	18.7
Performance over year (%)	
Hy5 System	212.8
FT-SE All-Share	152.1

1980	
1 BOC	
2 COURTAULDS	
3 DUNLOP (BTR)	
4 IMPERIAL TOBACCO (HANSON)	
5 UDS (HANSON)	
Yield at start of year (%)	13.5
Performance over year (%)	
Hy5 System	33.6
FT-SE All-Share	35.4

1985	
1 ALLIED-LYONS (ALLIED- DOMECQ)	
2 BICC	
3 GKN	
4 IMPERIAL TOBACCO (HANSON)	
5 VICKERS	
Yield at start of year (%)	6.3
Performance over year (%)	
Hy5 System	44.3
FT-SE All-Share	20.1

1990	
1 ASDA	
2 BLUECIRCLE	
3 BP	
4 BRITISH GAS	
5 NATWEST BANK	
Yield at start of year (%)	5.6
Performance over year (%)	
Hy5 System	−2.1
FT-SE All-Share	−9.7

1994	
1 BICC	
2 BLUE CIRCLE	
3 BRITISH GAS	
4 HANSON	
5 LUCAS	
Yield at start of year (%)	5.0
Performance over year (%)	
Hy5 System	−3.5
FT-SE All-Share	−5.9

Does the Hy5 System work anywhere? The answer is that it is difficult to obtain the necessary statistics to find out, except in well-developed markets. In the US, Michael O'Higgins has published statistics from 1973 to 1991 which show an outperformance of the Dow by the basic Hy5 system of an average 9 per cent per annum (Source: *Beating The Dow*).

Johnson Fry have recently compiled statistics from the French and German equity markets. The Hy5 System works in these markets (as you might expect it to) and would have produced gains of 583 per cent and 503 per cent in France and Germany compared to Index rises of 443 per cent and 290 per cent respectively over 10 years. ♎

RELATIVE PERFORMANCE

Carlton G. Lutts

*Carlton G. Lutts is president of **The Heritage Corporation**, which publishes* The Cabot Market Letter, *a stock market advisory newsletter, and* Cabot's Mutual Fund Navigator, *a mutual fund letter. He has developed a unique variant of Momentum Analysis, which combines both fundamental and technical approaches to investing. Mr Lutts has held engineering, marketing and management positions with **General Electric**, **Raytheon** and **United Shoe Machinery Corporation**. He has been issued six patents on automatic machinery.*

Over the past 25 years, we have developed an approach to stock selection called Momentum Analysis. It's based on our philosophy of investing in the advancing stocks of successful, fast-growing companies, not in the stocks of problem companies. It's an approach you can understand, because you've observed momentum in action yourself, either in your company or companies you've worked for.

A Company is Either Gaining or Losing Momentum

Some companies are on the road to success due to factors such as excellent management, a unique new product or service, or simply by being in the right place at the right time. Other companies drift towards failure because of poor management, lack of new products or increased competition. The stock market is measuring, day by day, all of the thousand pieces of information it receives in the form of buy or sell orders for a given company. These bits of information are reflected in the price of the stock . . . faster than most investors realize. As this information is pieced together, day after day, it starts to form a momentum trend that gives us the first indications of a change in the fortunes of the company. The study of these changes in company fortunes (and hence stock trends) is what we call Momentum Analysis.

Why Momentum Analysis Works

Momentum Analysis works because you can't hide a company's recent problems (or its new successes) under a bushel basket! As soon as a significant change (for the better or the worse) takes place, it is bound to be reflected in the price of the stock.

With a major, well-known company, a negative change in momentum may take weeks to develop. And at first you may not even see it reflected in lower stock prices but only in a loss of positive momentum. Eventually, however, the price of the stock will suffer as the change in momentum grabs hold. More often than not a change in momentum is the forerunner of a significant change in stock prices.

How We Measure Momentum Using Relative Performance

Relative performance (RP) is simply a measurement of how a stock is acting relative to the market as a whole.

We like to chart a stock's relative performance on a weekly basis to get a visual representation. We do this by dividing the weekly closing price of the

Relative performance (RP) is simply a measurement of how a stock is acting relative to the market as a whole.

Chart 2.69 Minnesota Mining & MFG. Co. (MMM)

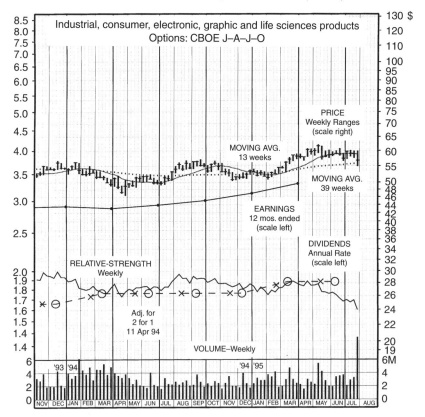

Source: Securities Research Company

Chart 2.70 International Game Technology (IGT)

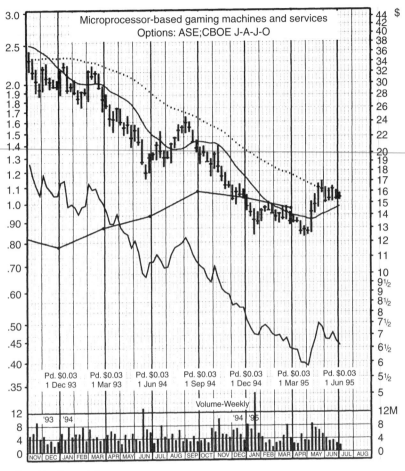

Microprocessor-based gaming machines and services
Options: ASE;CBOE J-A-J-O

Pd. $0.03   Pd. $0.03   Pd. $0.03   Pd. $0.03   Pd. $0.03   Pd. $0.03   Pd. $0.03
1 Dec 93   1 Mar 93   1 Jun 94   1 Sep 94   1 Dec 94   1 Mar 95   1 Jun 95

Volume-Weekly

Source: Securities Research Company

stock by the weekly closing price of the Dow Jones Industrial Average. This
value, plotted week after week, generates what we call the stock's relative performance (RP) line. When a stock's RP line is moving upward, it shows the
stock to be performing better than the general market. When it drifts downward, worse. And when the RP line is virtually level, it tells you the stock is
performing about the same as the averages.

We believe a stock's price at any moment reflects all that is known about the stock; all the facts, rumours, company earnings (real and anticipated), hopes, expectations and even failures. Since these bits of information are all factored into the present stock price, it becomes exceedingly important to note the general trend of the stock over a matter of weeks, to observe the relative performance of the stock and how it may be changing.

Three Types of Relative Performance Lines

Most stocks, like most businesses, are mediocre in their performance. They do no better or no worse than the averages. These stocks do not interest us. Stay away from them! Their relative performance is essentially flat and their price advances are slow (or non-existent). Minnesota Mining & Manufacturing is a good example. On Chart 2.69, the relative performance (RP) line is the solid continuous line located directly below the weekly price ranges.

Then there are stocks that consistently perform worse than the averages. They just seem to go from bad to worse, month after month. To many investors, these stocks appear to be 'great buys' as their prices go down and down. But in reality these stocks are reflecting the tremendous number of growing problems the companies must contend with. Stay away from these too! Let someone else guess where the bottom is. Notice in the chart of International Game Technology (Chart 2.70) how the RP line was on a down-trend throughout 1994, with the stock dropping from 34 to 16.

The stocks we are interested in have relative performance lines that are continually and persistently moving ahead on a positive, steep slope, with very brief corrections or consolidations. The shorter the RP correction, timewise, the stronger the situation. Stocks with corrections lasting only two, three or four weeks before the RP line advances again are much stronger than stocks that have more typical corrections of eight or ten weeks. Look at Chart 2.71 of Printronix and you'll see what we mean. Note the shallow and brief pull-backs in the RP line. This is a classic example of spectacular momentum. It's a clear sign that intense investor accumulation of the stock is taking place, month after month.

Chart 2.71 Printronix, Inc. (PTNX)

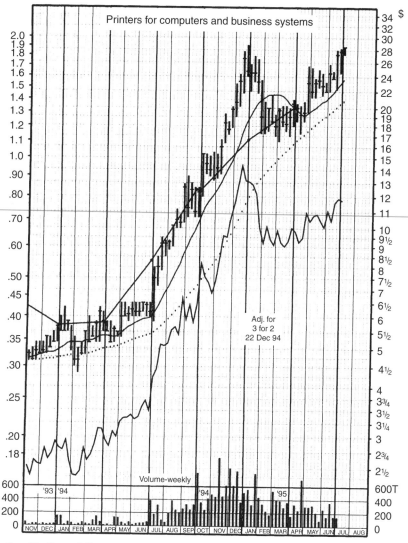

Printers for computers and business systems

Adj. for
3 for 2
22 Dec 94

Volume-weekly

Source: Securities Research Company

So, the large majority of stocks are not for us. Some are in well-established downtrends, while most are drifting along in a state of mediocrity. The principal objective of our Momentum Analysis approach is to keep our money invested at all times in the best performing stocks. That's the key to profitable investing! ☻

Trading Strategies

Pockets of Predictability
The Impact of Elections

POCKETS OF PREDICTABILITY

David Schwartz

*David Schwartz is Editor of the **Schwartz Stock Market Handbook**, an annual guide to investors on the best and worst times to buy and sell shares. He also writes the widely read 'The Month Ahead' column for Investors Chronicle magazine and is a frequent contributor to the weekend financial press.*

According to conventional wisdom, the stock market fluctuates in a random and unpredictable manner. No one knows where share prices are heading, not even the pros.

Conventional wisdom is wrong. The stock market is anything but random and unpredictable. Price shifts often repeat the patterns of the past. Better still, historical price trends frequently signal where prices are heading in the days and months ahead. If you find this hard to believe, look at the wide differences in profitability associated with various months of the year. If share prices fluctuate as randomly as some suggest, each month would generate a similar level of profit over the long run. There might be differences in any single year of course, but over the very long run, say 50 years, these differences would wash out. January price increases would be the same as June increases. But in the real world, some months are very profitable and have been for most of this century. Others are consistent money-losers. A hypothetical UK investor, who started with £1,000 just after the First World War and invested only in January, would have run up his portfolio to over £5,000 by 1994. In contrast, a June investor, during this same period, would now be worth a little over £500.

The lack of randomness occurs in other stock markets as well. A hypothetical US investor starting with $1,000 in 1926 and investing only in July, would now be worth over $3,000. But the same-sized investment in shares during September would have shrunk to just $365. Trends like these are not isolated events. There are many of them that operate throughout the year.

Short-Term Trends

Some trends run for just a few days. Take the last week of December for example. It is the most profitable week of the entire year for UK investors.

Prices rise 81 per cent of the time during this fabulous week. By way of contrast, the third week of May is profitable just 40 per cent of the time. Don't dismiss either trend as a short-term fluke. Both have been running since before the Second World War.

Some short-term trends are calendar-related. Others are associated with a specific event like the UK's Budget Day, when the government announces tax changes and spending plans for the year ahead. Over the years, Budget Day has been shifted around a great deal. At the beginning of the century, it was usually scheduled in May. After moves to April and then to March, it is now presented in late November. Despite the shifts, one element remained constant, Britain's pre-Budget media coverage. No Budget Day would be complete without speculation about tax increases and loophole closures. With news like this, it is not surprising that prices rise just 28 per cent of the time in the week preceding Budget Day. In most years, it pays to stand aside during this money-losing stretch.

Historic trends can often help investors to forecast where prices are heading in the months ahead. Take September, a bellwether month for UK investors. It is not commonly known but September price drops are usually followed with increases in the final three months of the year. Since 1959, there were 16 years when September prices fell by at least 0.67 per cent. Shares rose in the next three months in 15 of those years. The sole exception occurred in 1974 at the tail end of a vicious bear market. In years when September prices rise, the odds of further price rises in the last three months of the year are roughly 50:50. For US investors, the June Signal provides a useful preview of where shares are heading in the three months ahead. Since 1950, June prices fell 1.74 per cent or more in 14 different years. Prices rose in the next three months in 13 of those years. In all other years since 1950, Wall Street's third quarter record was 14 up and 17 down.

It is not commonly known but September price drops are usually followed with increases in the final three months of the year.

Annual Trends

The June price trend also provides useful information about the year ahead on both sides of the Atlantic. In the UK, there were 23 occasions since the First World War when June prices shifted within a relatively narrow range of −3.14 per cent to +0.63 per cent. In 20 of those 23 years, share prices were sharply higher 12 months later. The US version of the June signal is slightly different, but just as useful. Since 1926, American share prices shifted within a small range on 40 occasions, no more than −2.03 per cent on the down-side and no more than +4.43 per cent on the up-side. Prices rose still further in the next 11 months in 33 of those years (83 per cent). In the remaining 28 years with bigger price shifts, Wall Street's record for the next 11 months is simply horrid, 11 up and 17 down.

Some forecasts about the future are triggered by broad stock market cycles, not by monthly or quarterly price shifts. One example is the stock market's occasional tendency to drift within a tight trading range for many months and then break out in a major, double digit price shift. Knowing, in advance, the direction of this breakout is critically important to investors and historical price trends can be of assistance. Since the First World War, there have been 38 occasions when shares fluctuated in a tight trading range for nine months or longer (double counting eliminated), with prices ending no more than 2 per cent higher or lower than their starting point. Nine of those occasions turned out to be bull market peaks or were influenced by atypical events like the Second World War and its aftermath. If we ignore these occasions, we are left with 29 long-term plateaux. Amazingly, the stock market rose 26 times in the following 12 months, once these plateaux ran their course.

The circumstances surrounding each of the three exceptions to the rule are also revealing. After the plateau of 1956, shares rallied sharply until mid-1957 when interest rates were suddenly raised to their highest level in 37 years. Investors were caught by surprise and share prices fell. The plateau of 1965 was also followed by rising prices for more than half a year until the infamous July measures of 1966 (wage and price controls and higher taxes), again caught investors by surprise. The third plateau occurred in 1970, an era of 5 per cent inflation. Shares suddenly dropped as inflation skyrocketed and newspapers began carrying reports of 20 per cent wage increases. In other words, stock market prospects were good all three times until a surprise event broke the bubble.

Information like this can be of tremendous value. Obviously, no investment action is tipped by this trend if shares have plateaued after a long-term up-move since it might be a bull market peak. But if prices fell sharply a year or so ago, and then began to drift sideways for nine months or more, history is signalling good odds that prices will rise when they ultimately break out of their tight trading range.

if prices fell sharply a year or so ago, and then began to drift sideways for nine months or more, history is signalling good odds that prices will rise when they ultimately break out of their tight trading range.

Bear markets

Historic price trends can also help investors to navigate the treacherous waters of a bear market. It is a valuable benefit since bear markets are quite frightening to experience. Share prices drop, often violently. Portfolio values evaporate. Most investors feel trapped, not knowing what action to take.

A good starting point is to tally every large stock market drop in history, 15 per cent or more, regardless of whether the experts officially classify it as a bear market or not. In the UK, there are 20 members of this special club since 1919, when proper records first began. This tally leads us to an important observation. Big falls occur quite frequently, once every four years or so. To investors conditioned to lengthy up-turns, be warned: history is signalling that the 1980s was a rare event. This point has very serious implications for followers of the Buy-And-Hold theory of investing which became so popular in recent years.

Another striking point about these big falls is that 16 are in excess of 20 per cent. Ten exceed 25 per cent. In other words, once prices fall by 15 per cent, the odds are high they will fall much more.

The chart below proves what most of us already believe, that stock markets move much faster than in the old days. In the first half of this century, expansions typically ran for five years and doubled on average. When a bear market arrived, it was usually long and painful – 35 months and a typical decline of 49 per cent. The pattern changed in the second half of the century. The average up-turn shrank to just two years in the 1950s to mid 1970s. Since then, it shortened even further, a fact distorted by the 1980s. In the last 20 years, the typical up-turn (excluding the 70-month up-swing that ended in 1987) ran its course in 17 months. But the typical increase remains about the same as a half century ago. In other words, prices now rise the same amount in about one-quarter the time.

Today's down-turns are also more frequent and shorter. In the past 20 years, a bear phase arrived every 2.5 years, and ran for six months on average. The pre-war norm was every 7 years and a typical run of 35 months. The more recent falls are milder as well, possibly because they occur more often. However, their relative mildness also explains why share prices have risen so high in recent years. There are no guarantees for the future of course. No one knows how the next bear market will unfold. But an historical trend analysis like this helps investors to anticipate the likeliest alternative.

There are hundreds of correlations like these that tip off the direction of prices in the weeks and months ahead. Many signals have been flashing their message for decades. Clearly, the stock market is not as random as many investors think. A good trading strategy to follow is to treat these historical trends as guides, not inviolate rules. Trends change. Take April for example. Starting with 1940, UK prices rose 44 out of 50 Aprils, helped in part by the spring budget which has now been shifted to November. Will April prices continue to rise with the same frequency as in the past? Possibly not.

THE BEAR GETS SHORTER
The 20 Biggest Falls Since 1918 & Their Duration

	Start of Fall	Size of Fall (per cent)	Duration (months)	Average Decline (per cent)	Average Duration (months)
Phase I	Feb-20	47%	20	49%	35
	Apr-28	60%	49		
	Dec-36	55%	42		
	May-47	32%	29		
Phase II	Oct-51	26%	8	30%	14
	Jun-55	26%	17		
	Jul-57	21%	7		
	Apr-61	22%	15		
	Aug-64	16%	11		
	Jul-66	21%	3		
	Jan-69	37%	16		
	May-72	73%	31		
Phase III	May-76	32%	6	23%	6
	Oct-77	16%	3		
	May-79	23%	6		
	May-81	20%	5		
	Jul-87	37%	4		
	Sep-89	22%	13		
	May-92	18%	3		
	Feb-94	18%	5		

Source: Datastream

Another problem to consider are sudden economic or political events that make a hash of these guidelines. Witness the stock market's reaction to the threat of interest rate rises. Still, a thorough knowledge of history goes a long way to increasing the odds of a profitable investment in the days and weeks ahead. ♀

THE IMPACT OF ELECTIONS

Yale Hirsch

*Yale Hirsch is the President of the **Hirsch Organization** based in Old Tappan, New Jersey, which Publishes the annual* Stock Trader's Almanac, *now in its twenty-eighth annual edition, and five investment newsletters* Smart Money, Ground Floor, Beating the Dow, Higher Returns, *and* Turov on Timing. *He is a stock market historian and analyst and could probably tell you, within reason,* *what the stock market is likely to do any hour, on any day, in any future year. His best known indicator is the very accurate January Barometer, which states, as January goes, so goes the entire market year. Other innovations have included the Santa Claus Rally, the quadrennial political/stock market cycle, and investing in the Best Six Consecutive Months of the Year.*

On Wall Street Week in December 1981 with the Dow at 900, he predicted a 500 per cent move by 1990 from the 1974 bottom. This was achieved on 16 July 1990. Mr Hirsch appears often on Cable News Network, CNBC and other business news networks, and is widely quoted in newspapers and financial publications.

One aspect of activity that has an influence on financial markets, and which rolls around with unfailing regularity, is the election cycle. The US remains the longest standing and most complex democratic country, so records of how political behaviour affects US markets have most longevity. While no two electoral systems are the same, politicians the world over share one common goal: to stay in office. This means that, while the material that follows relates only to the US, local analysts can translate some of the lessons into their own political calculus and apply similar reasoning on how their politicians in power will try to use the markets to assist in the re-election process.

How the Government Manipulates the Economy to Stay in Power

Most investors know that bull markets tend to occur in the third and fourth years of presidential terms, while markets tend to decline in the first and second years.

The 'making of presidents' is invariably accompanied by an unsubtle manipulation of the economy. Incumbent administrations are duty-bound to retain the reins of power. Subsequently, the 'piper must be paid', producing what I have coined the 'Post-Presidential Year Syndrome'. Most big, bad bear markets began in such years – 1929, 1937, 1957, 1969, 1973, 1977 and 1981. Note, also, that our major wars begin in years following elections – Civil War (1865), First World War (1917), Second World War (1941) and Vietnam (1965).

Some cold, hard facts to prove economic manipulation appeared in a book by Edward R Tufte, *Political Control of the Economy*. The author investigated the timing of stimulative fiscal measures designed to increase per capita disposable income – which would have provided a sense of well-being to the voting public. Measures included: increases in federal budget deficits, government spending and social security benefits; interest rate reductions on government loans; and speed-ups of projected funding. Some of the findings were:

Federal Spending During 1962–73, the average increase was 29 per cent higher in election years than in non-election years.

Social Security There were nine increases during the 1952–74 period. Half of the six election year increases became effective in September, perfectly timed to remain fresh in voters' minds as they went to the polls eight weeks later. The average increase was 100 per cent higher in presidential than in mid-term election years.

Real Disposable Income Accelerated in all but one election year between 1947 and 1973 (excluding the Eisenhower years). Only one of the remaining odd-numbered years (1973) showed a marked acceleration.

These moves were obviously not coincidences and explain why we tend to have a political (four-year) stock market cycle. To paraphrase Gilbert and Sullivan, we're not the very model of a modern free economy.

The Reagan administration was no different from others. We paid the piper in 1981 and 1982 and then came the longest peacetime expansion in history – eight straight years. The US temporarily repealed the four-year cycle and avoided any recessions. However, we ran up more deficits than the total deficits of the previous 200 years of our national existence.

Alan Greenspan took over the Fed from Paul Volker in 1989 and was able to keep the economy rolling until an exogenous event in the Persian Gulf pushed us into a real recession in August 1990 which lasted long enough to choke off the Bush re-election effort in 1992. Three other incumbents in this century failed to retain power: Taft in 1912, when the Republican Party split in two; Hoover in 1932 in the depths of the Great Depression; and Carter in 1980 during the Iran hostage crisis.

It's difficult to imagine what rabbits the Democrats can pull out of their hats to manipulate the economy to stay in power after the 1996 election, having lost both the Senate and the House in 1994, and lacking an incumbent candidate with perceived presidential stature. Nonetheless, one can assume they will do their best, which is why a second dictum is extremely important.

No Losses in Last Seven Months of Election Years

Since 1940, when the fall of France jolted the market, investors have barely been bruised during election years, except for a brief span. In the table below, a very positive picture can be seen for May and June, and especially the last seven or eight months of the election year.

- January through April losses occurred in five of eleven previous election years. Incumbent parties were ousted on four of these five losses.

- Only three of the last eleven presidential Mays were down, in 1956, 1976, and 1984. During two of these years, the market was in the process of topping out.

- Only June 1972 and June 1992 in the presidential series were losers. The market moved higher in the others.

Table 2.11 Last Eight Months of Election Years Bullish (S&P 500)

Election Year	Change First Four Months	April	May	June	Dec	April to Dec % change	May to Dec % change
1952	−1.9	23.32	23.83	24.96	26.57	13.9	11.4
1956	6.4	48.38	**45.20**	46.97	46.67	−3.5	3.3
1960	−9.2	54.37	55.38	56.92	58.11	6.9	4.1
1964	5.9	79.46	80.97	81.69	84.75	6.7	4.7
1968	1.2	97.59	98.68	99.58	103.86	6.4	5.2
1972	5.3	107.67	109.53	**107.14**	118.05	9.6	7.8
1976	12.7	101.64	**100.18**	104.28	107.46	5.7	7.3
1980	−0.9	106.29	111.24	114.24	135.76	27.7	22.0
1984	−3.0	160.05	**150.55**	153.18	167.24	4.5	11.1
1988	5.8	261.33	262.16	273.50	277.72	6.3	5.9
1992	−0.5	414.95	415.35	**408.14**	435.71	5.0	4.9

Down months are bold

- Comparing month end June with month end April shows losses only in 1956, 1972 and 1984, for the 60-day period.

- For a longer perspective, we've extended the table out to December and see only one losing eight-month period in an election year between April and December: 3.5 per cent in 1956. There were no losers in the last seven months of these years.

It may be even more interesting to reverse this process. Instead of asking what electoral cycles can tell us about the market, let us explore what the market can tell us about the likely results of these elections.

Predict 1996 Winner One Year in Advance

Knowing AAA corporate bond yields would have enabled you to foretell the outcome of each presidential election between 1920 and 1988 – one year in advance. Dick A. Stoken* discovered that, when the level of long-term interest rates was relatively high one year prior to the election, the party in power was ousted one year later. This phenomenon was at work in the elections of Harding (1920), Roosevelt (1932), Eisenhower (1952), Kennedy (1960), Nixon (1968), Carter (1976) and Reagan (1980). (*See* Table 2.12 overleaf).

Table 2.12 Interest Rates One Year Prior to Presidential Elections

Election Year	Interest Rates November 15 1 year earlier	Incumbent Party	Popular Vote %	Challenging Party	Popular Vote %	Plurality Vote %
1920	High	Cox (D)	34.1	*Harding (R)*	60.4	26.3
1924	Low	*Coolidge (R)*	54.0	Davis (D)	28.2a	25.8
1928	Low	*Hoover (R)*	58.1	Smith (D)	40.8	17.3
1932	High	Hoover (R)	39.7	*Roosevelt (D)*	57.4	17.7
1936	Low	*Roosevelt (D)*	60.8	Landon (R)	36.5	24.3
1940	Low	*Roosevelt (D)*	54.7	Wilkie (R)	44.8	9.9
1944	Low	*Roosevelt (D)*	53.4	Dewey (R)	45.9	7.5
1948	Low	*Truman (D)*	49.6	Dewey (R)	45.1b	4.5
1952	High	Stevenson (D)	44.4	*Eisenhower (R)*	55.1	10.7
1956	Low	*Eisenhower (R)*	57.4	Stevenson (D)	42.0	15.4
1960	High	Nixon (R)	49.5	*Kennedy (D)*	49.7	0.2
1964	Low	*Johnson (D)*	61.1	Goldwater (R)	38.5	22.6
1968	High	Humphrey (D)	42.7	*Nixon (R)*	43.4c	0.7
1972	Low	*Nixon (R)*	60.7	McGovern (D)	37.5	23.2
1976	High	Ford (R)	48.3	*Carter (D)*	50.4	2.1
1980	High	Carter (D)	41.9	*Reagan (R)*	51.8	9.9
1984	Low	*Reagan (R)*	59.1	Mondale (D)	40.9	18.2
1988	High	*Bush (R)*	53.9	Dukakis (D)	46.1	7.8
1992	Low	Bush (R)	37.4	*Clinton (D)*	43.0d	5.6

a) La Follette (Progressive) 16%;
b) Thurmond and Henry Wallace combined 5%;
c) George Wallace 13%;
d) Perot 18.9%.

Winners in italics

*Strategic Investment Timing, Probus

Source: The Hirsch Organization – 1996 Stock Trader's Almanac

Rates on AAAs rose swiftly during the spring of 1987 reaching 9.10 per cent by May. This should have translated into a loss of the White House by the Republicans in 1988, but the Democrats blew it when their candidate turned out to be inept.

Third party candidate Ross Perot may have cost Bush his re-election in 1992, despite low interest rates in the prior year.

The stock market acts as a supplement to the predictive power of the   bond market. Though not infallible, the Dow Jones Industrial Average (with just seven exceptions) has foretold the outcome of the presidential elections in this century. When the venerable average gains ground between New Year's Day and Election Day, the incumbent party will usually win the election. A loss in the average during the period will usually result in the 'ins' being ousted.

Chart 2.72 designed by the late Ralph A. Rotnem of Smith Barney, Harris Upham tells the story. The Dow tends to move up and gain 15.1 per cent on average, based on the 15 elections when the incumbent party retained the presidency. An average loss of 1.5 per cent can be seen in the run up to the election when the incumbents lost (eight times).

There is one other indicator of who the next president is likely to be.

Market Acts as a Barometer between the Last Convention and Election Day

The direction of the Dow between the close of the last presidential convention and Election Day reflects voter sentiment.

Of the 15 presidential elections since 1900 where the incumbent parties were victorious, 13 were foretold by rising stock prices. The two exceptions were minor (–0.5 per cent in 1948 and –2.3 per cent in 1956). Gains for the period averaged 7.8 per cent. Conversely, dissatisfaction with an incumbent party is, most times, reflected by a decline between the last convention and election day. Here, six out of nine election years produced declines.

With this information, perhaps political parties could dispense with a great deal of money spent on polling and just focus on buying large numbers of Dow futures! Note that all these predictions are apolitical. The only issue is whether the party in power is going to win or lose.

Chart 2.72 Stock Price Trend in Election Years, 1900–1988

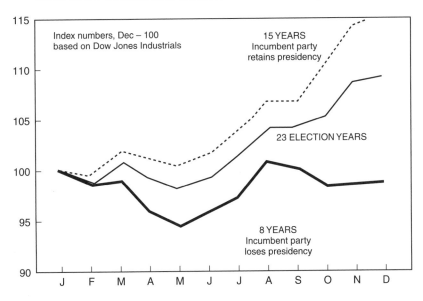

Table 2.13 Post Convention to Election Markets

Year Incumbent Party Won	% change based on Dow Jones Industrial Average % Change	Year Incumbent Party Lost	% Change
1900	8.3	1912	−1.8
1904	22.6	1920	−9.1
1908	9.6	1932	48.6
1916	15.9	1952	−2.8
1924	6.7	1960	−3.1
1928	22.4	1968	5.6
1936	11.5	1976	−0.8
1940	9.9	1980	1.4
1944	0.8	1992	−1.3
1948	−0.5		
1956	−2.3	Average	4.1
1964	4.8	Excluding 1932	−1.5
1972	1.5		
1984	1.0		
1988	5.4		
Average	7.8		

PEOPLE YOU KNOW AND TRUST

James Morton

James Morton is the Editor of The Global Guide to Investing *and as Director of Chelverton Investment Management runs the global micro cap Chelverton Fund. In his 20 years advising on investments, he has tried every analytical approach known, and found only the one which does not need a computer comes closest to being infallible.*

It has been said by many people, including a number of writers in this book, that the one infallible way to do well in investing is to stick to things you know and people you trust. If you are one of the world's great biochemists involved in research into swine disease, and you can identify the company closest to bringing out the next magic bullet, you are obviously well placed to buy shares in that business.

The majority, with rather more mundane qualifications, may have to focus on the Peter Lynch shopping mall approach. Common sense is a pretty good investment indicator of last resort. For those who do not have complete confidence in their own ability to spot the next Dustbuster, if it feels good, smells good and tastes good, by golly it probably is good. But does that mean it will be a good investment?

I believe that it is a lot easier to make money following people you trust and who have demonstrated a track record. The problem with the shopping mall syndrome is that you never get more than a snapshot of a market place. There is no guarantee that your particular taste is shared by sufficient people to ensure that your favourite video game will be the latest and greatest since Donkey Kong. Consumer attitudes have become remarkably fickle and the buying public has never been more fragmented.

Specialized knowledge in a technical sense can still provide the investor with an edge, but generalized common sense, while it may steer you away from obvious catastrophes, can only work well on very rare occasions. Someone who walked into one of the first Body Shops could perhaps have seen the potential and bought shares early, but the reality is that many of the best businesses do not come to the public market until they are at a point where they are relatively fully valued.

When most individuals are presented with the opportunity of a lifetime to back Uncle Fred in his latest retail concept, or cousin Peter, who is setting up a sub-contracting machine shop, it is a good idea to remember that, in the vast majority of cases, you have just been invited to throw your money away. But, if not good old Fred or bright young Peter, then who?

Anyone with a little money set aside cannot be too careful. Dishonesty is no more rampant in the investment business than in your average topless bar, but that may not be entirely reassuring if you are about to part with your life savings. What I continue to find surprising, even after 20 years in financial services, is to what depths people will sink when they are desperate. I have invested in no less than three businesses where fraud ultimately brought the company crashing down. One of these was introduced to me by someone I had known for several years who wilfully misrepresented the income statement and balance sheet, while claiming to be doing me a favour as 'a good friend'. Interestingly, the level of misrepresentation seems inversely related to the level of academic achievement. My own experience is that I have had the best results co-investing with people I went to school with, less good results co-investing with people I was at university with, and the worst results of all investing along with people who were with me at business school.

The most productive and successful approach of all is to invest in people who have been very successful, whether I know them personally or not. There is nothing more trustworthy than an unambiguous investment record. The investor in question has publicly put his or her reputation on the line by risking a large sum of money themselves. Any one of our ten Global Gurus would make a good guide. If you see them materialize as holders of a large stake in a public company, you can make a reasonable assumption

The most productive and successful approach of all is to invest in people who have been very successful, whether I know them personally or not.

that that business is an attractive value. Of course, investing is not a passive activity and circumstances can change quite rapidly, so one must pay particular attention to share dealings by significant holders of a stock. The same lessons can apply as discussed earlier in section on Directors' Dealings (p.259).

In addition to our Global Gurus, if certain names crop up on the share register, that can be a good indicator. Bill Simon has a phenomenal record, not just with private investments, but also in the public markets in the US. When the name Warren Buffet appears as a major shareholder, the market capitalization of a company can easily jump by 10 per cent. In the UK, Bob Morton (no relation) made money for a lot of investors over the last ten years. Luke Johnson has taken several shells and turned them into successful companies with commensurate returns for the people who got in with him at the ground floor. Other individuals who seem to be able to work their own brand of magic, particularly in the small company sector, include Christopher Stainforth, who operates out of Guinness Mahon and made shareholders of Regal Hotels and Coal Investments into happy campers, and Colin Keith, who hangs his hat at Hambro New York and numbers among his successes EHP and North American Mortgage.

Remember that blindly following successful individuals into a situation is not a good strategy. The recipe can go sour. Even the best get it wrong sometimes, and their involvement should not be a substitute for your own research or analysis. What has Buffet done lately? His last good deal was his investment in Wells Fargo in 1991. The problem, when you get to the size of Buffet, is that your choices are fairly limited. Salomon Brothers has not been a home run, US Air may yet have to be bailed out by British Airways, and he got into American Express after other investors, including Michael Price, bought at lower prices.

Consider the case of Alan Baldwin. His stint at Securiguard made a lot of shareholders smile. Those who followed him into Business Technology Group have been left with a sour taste in the mouth. A name change to Berkeley Business Group has only seen the share price slide further, losing, as of June 1995, two thirds of the investment in the initial rights issue.

The bottom line is that your own investment is your own responsibility. That aside, the average investor cannot begin to have the time, nor let's face it, the ability of the great investors, who devote their lives and talents to making a science out of what is probably one of the most arcane arts. Following the greatest investors around the world into specific markets and specific companies is about as good a strategy as you will ever find; and it is more likely to produce returns which gets close to their superior results than any other single strategy that I am aware of. ♀

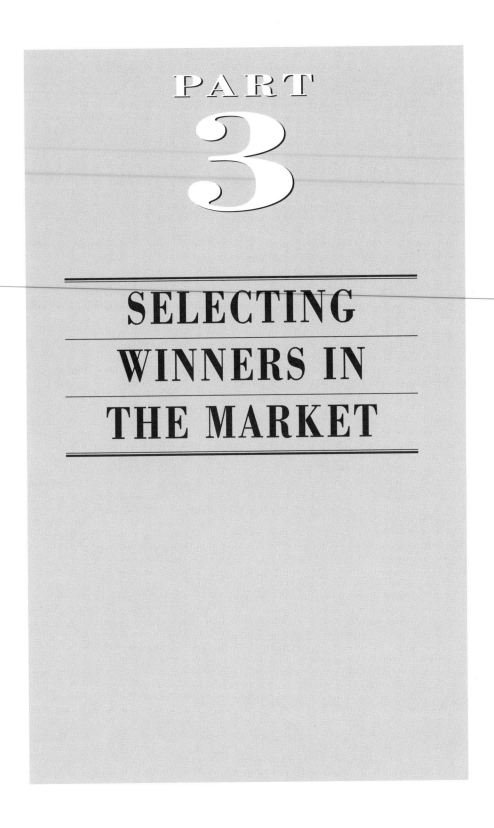

PART

3

SELECTING
WINNERS IN
THE MARKET

The UK

The UK

Equities

The Blue Chip Sector
Stock beyond the FT-SE 100
The Unquoted Markets

Fixed Income

THE BLUE CHIP SECTOR

Richard Koch

Richard Koch is an entrepreneur, strategic consultant, writer and investor. Currently Chairman of Odyssey, he was a founder of the **LEK Partnership** *and* **Strategy Ventures plc** *and has been a Partner of* **Bain & Co**. *He has provided start-up finance for several successful ventures, including* **Belgo**, *the acclaimed mussels-and-frites restaurant group, and* **MSI**, *the rapidly growing hotel group, where he is Chairman. In 1990 he originated the rescue of* **Filofax**. *Since his involvement,* **Filofax** *shares have gone from 30p to over 250p.*

Richard Koch's books published by Pitman comprise: Wake Up and Shake Up Your Company *(with Andrew Campbell)*; The Successful Boss's First 100 Days; The Investor's Guide to Selecting Shares That Perform; The Financial Times Guide to Management & Finance; *and* The Financial Times Guide to Strategy.

Why Buy Blue Chips?

One reason to buy blue chips is supplied by the definition. Blue chip shares are those in large companies with solid balance sheets and credit ratings. The first reason to buy blue chips, therefore, is their relative **security**. Curiously enough, the term 'blue chip' derives from the casino, where the largest denomination chips used to be blue.

Despite the derivation, blue chip shares companies are unlikely to go bust. It can and does happen: in the UK, companies like Maxwell Communications and British & Commonwealth were at times included in many 'blue chip' lists. But if blue chips are selected carefully, the risk should be extremely low.

311

A second reason to buy blue chips is that they generally offer a satisfactory **income**. Since 1919, UK dividend yields have averaged 5 per cent and dividends have grown, in real terms, at nearly 2 per cent per annum. The yield has generally been lower than putting the money on deposit, but often not by a huge margin.

The third, and most important, reason for buying blue chip shares is the combination of reasonable security and income with **capital appreciation**. It is almost universally true, everywhere around the world, that the long-term investor has done better out of blue chip shares, with relatively low risk, than out of any other major conventional investment medium, with the sole possible exception of shares in smaller companies.

In the UK, for example, data from brokers BZW show that in the 74 years after 1918, blue chips showed an average annual compounded total return of 11.9 per cent, or 7.3 per cent in real terms. The comparable returns from UK government bonds were only 5.7 per cent and 1.2 per cent respectively, and for money market deposits 5.4 per cent and 1.0 per cent. For someone who invested for 14 years or longer, whatever the period taken since 1918, the probability of bonds or cash performing better was less than one in thirty.

These apparently small annual percentage differences make a huge difference over the long haul. For instance, a UK investor putting £100 into a building society savings account in 1950 would have been able to withdraw £813 in 1992, but the same £100 put into blue chips would have returned £14,198 – over 17 times as much!

There are learned disputes about whether small company shares perform better than blue chips, or vice versa. This debate will run and run: it can never be settled definitively because it depends on the period. It should probably be conceded that the return on smaller companies runs ahead of that on blue chips for a greater proportion of the time, but the difference is generally not pronounced. For an individual investor who wants reasonable security without sacrificing too much return, blue chips offer a very attractive cocktail.

Which blue chip market?

For investors in OECD countries, their home stock market should normally be given priority, for three reasons. First, there will be no currency risk. Second, transaction costs will be lower. And third, and most significantly, it will be easier to know the investee companies and to track developments.

There is an argument for diversifying amongst a number of primary country markets, which could include the US, UK, Japan, France and Germany. For those who are content to track the stock market index, this might not be a bad solution. It is relatively more attractive to do so if you are a long-term investor based in a country that has a long history of depreciation against other leading currencies, as is the case with the UK, Italy and Spain.

Investors who want to be active in stocks, however, may be wise to concentrate entirely on their home market. In the UK, for example, blue chips have been such a good investment partly because UK companies have built up business overseas providing an element of built-in international diversification.

> **Investors who want to be active in stocks, however, may be wise to concentrate entirely on their home market.**

They have thus been able to benefit both from more robust overseas economies and from exchange translation profits as the pound weakened.

Index-tracking versus share selection

For investors who are not confident about their ability to select shares, the best solution is to 'track the index'. The most 'blue chip' way to do this is to select the narrowest index available – in the UK, for example, the FT-SE 30. That way you will only invest in the largest and safest companies. The easiest way is to invest in a Tracker Fund (after ensuring that it is tracking the index you want). The fund will almost certainly slightly under-perform the index because of marketing and administration costs, though these are usually much lower than with conventional funds.

The slightly more difficult way is to construct a Do-It-Yourself fund. This involves constructing a portfolio that exactly matches your market index. You will then have to watch for additions to and deletions from the index and buy and sell accordingly. The DIY method will normally be cheaper and has the advantage that you can select an index to suit your own risk profile and the amount you wish to invest.

If you decide to do it yourself, it is probably best to choose at least 10 shares (to reduce risk) but not buy too many, as this will increase the transaction costs. If you plan to hold the shares for a very long time, this latter constraint becomes less important. Indeed, if you are a long term investor and have the time to monitor changes to the index, the DIY solution will almost certainly enhance your returns.

Index-tracking of either the managed or DIY species is highly likely to produce good long term returns. It is, however, more fun, and often more profitable, to select between blue chips and construct your own discretionary portfolio.

How to pick blue chip winners

How should you select your own blue chip portfolio? The key is to select 'good companies'.

Good companies share four attributes:

- attractive financial characteristics
- market power/competitive advantage
- good, alert management
- a winning culture.

They will normally also have an impressive long-run stock market pedigree.

A majority of blue chips are not 'good companies' in the sense that they have all four of these attributes. Many are 'good in parts'. Avoid these, even if they are said to be 'on the up'. There are enough good companies. It is both safer and more rewarding to confine your investments to them. Let's elaborate somewhat on the four attributes.

Attractive financial characteristics include strong cash generation, a high return on capital, and a stable/rising trend of profits and cash flow without violent fluctuations.

Market power/competitive advantage. A good business must have some business franchise, and, frankly, some degree of monopolistic power. It must have something that other firms want, do not have, and cannot easily obtain. This may be a brand, a location advantage, customer appeal, market leadership, a low cost position, superior technology, or some other definable advantage that can be defended against competition.

Good, alert management is a must. Avoid the arrogant or complacent, and those who proffer excuses for failure to deliver. Search for the hard workers who are genuinely interested in their employees and above all their customers.

A winning culture. A can-do mentality throughout the firm is essential. It goes along with high levels of energy and commitment amongst employees. When you call the company, visit it or run across employees, see if they are alive or bored. Do they move fast? This is one of the simplest, most effective, and least used tests of investment.

One example of a good company is Shell. It has high market shares in its most important businesses. For generations it has been financially strong and generated huge amounts of cash. It has a cult of technical competence; although somewhat bureaucratic, it is redeemed by its professionalism. It has used its market power wisely and unobtrusively. It has a great brand and loyal customers. It has cultivated governments adroitly. Over the long haul, if you can be sure of any company, you can be sure of Shell.

Other good blue chips from the UK include Cadbury Schweppes – with its high market shares in confectionery and niche soft drinks, strong brands, excellent marketing, impressive cash generation and sensitive management – and Marks & Spencer, with its legendary customer trust and loyalty, its thinly-layered, hands-on management, and its tremendously strong internal culture.

We cannot guarantee that these firms will continue to out-perform the market, but, given a choice, wouldn't you rather invest in firms that have such winning attributes?

Another way of selecting companies

If you lack confidence in your ability to select 'good companies', there is another, even simpler way. This is to back stock market winners. You could, for example, choose to select the ten best performing blue chips over the past 10 years. This method is likely to lead you to 'good companies' that have a virtuous circle of attributes causing the good long-term performance.

One caveat: future performance may not follow past performance. A structural discontinuity may occur, upsetting the driving forces behind good performance. You are unlikely to observe this discontinuity early enough to protect yourself. But you can spot a rapid consequence of the discontinuity, and take corrective action.

Very simply, look for a drop in the share price. If any of your shares start going down, this may be the first stage of a long-run decline. (It may not, of course, but it is better to be safe.) A good rule to use is that if any share falls by 15 per cent from your purchase price, sell. Additionally, if any share drops by 10 per cent relative to the market, you should also sell. Only buy back in if the price stabilizes and starts to rise again.

A good rule to use is if any share drops by 10 per cent relative to the market, you should also sell.

Just as important as knowing what to buy, is knowing when.

When to buy

A terrific strategy is to buy blue chips whenever the market is at a cyclical low. This is not easy, but the four rules below will help.

One way is simply to wait for a serious market setback: when shares decline by at least 10 per cent from their previous nominal high. This may involve waiting for a few years. Since 1978, there have been five such chances in the UK, (1981, 1984, 1987, 1990 and 1992) one roughly every three or four years.

A second, similar way is to buy when the index falls at least 7 per cent below its nine-month moving average.

A third is to wait until the market Price Earnings Ratio (P/E) is low. Market average P/Es fluctuate amazingly. In the UK, the market P/E since 1965 has oscillated between 4.0 and 22.5! An analysis of the London market conducted in 1993 divided the P/Es each year into four batches and looked at the average returns from investing in each batch. The quartile containing the 25 per cent of years with the lowest P/Es yielded a compound annual return of over 32 per cent! Whatever market you are in, it is a good idea to invest only when the blue chip average P/E is in its lowest quartile. As a rough guide, this should mean a P/E of under 12, and preferably in single figures.

A fourth way (often leading to similar results to the third), is to look at the dividend yield. Buy when dividend yields are in their highest quartile. In the UK, dividend yields have a long history of tending to move between 4 per cent and 6 per cent, and a good guide is to buy when the yield is above 5 per cent, preferably above 5.5 per cent.

For all these measures, it is often wise to wait until they have stopped improving (from the point of view of the value-seeking investor) and started to move into reverse (with shares beginning to become more expensive) before investing heavily.

Few people have the patience to pursue these timing strategies, despite the fact that these have always worked in the past. On no account start investing when the market is near a cyclical high.

When to sell

The rules are the reverse of the 'buy' ones. As an illustration, UK rules that have worked well in the past are to sell when any two of the following apply:

1 when the market is more than 15 per cent above its recent cyclical high
2 when the market is more than 10 per cent above its moving nine-month average
3 when the historic P/E is over 17 (adapt this to other markets by selling when the P/E is within 25 per cent of its peak)
4 if the dividend yield drops below 4 per cent.

You could, of course, decide to hold for a generation or more. Provided you bought when the market was low, there is merit to locking up your portfolio and losing the key. With a long enough timescale, even the disasters of 1929–32, 1974 and 1987 look like blips on an ever-upward chart. Selecting safe, 'good' companies, buying at a cyclical low, and holding for a very long time may sound like a boring strategy. Quite possibly, however, it could make you rather rich. 🌑

STOCKS BEYOND THE FT-SE 100

Anthony Bolton

*Anthony Bolton has worked in **Fidelity's** London office since the inception of its UK unit trust business in December 1979. He runs the group's two largest unit trusts: Fidelity Special Situations Trust, which mainly invests in British small and medium sized companies, and Fidelity European Trust, which invests in Continental European shares. Each trust has achieved an average annual return for investors of about 23 per cent per annum over the life of the trusts 15 and 9 years respectively. Both rank in the top decile in their respective fund universes.*

316

Fidelity is the world's largest investment management organization with total assets exceeding £190 billion for 8 million investors worldwide.

Undoubtedly the real winners in investment terms are to be found outside the leaders. One big advantage that the private investor has over the large institutions is that he or she can invest a major portion of their wealth in secondary stocks. Big institutions are forced to invest the majority of their portfolios in the FT-SE 100 type companies which have the liquidity that can accept the large institutional cash flows. However, smaller stocks will generally grow faster, are less well researched and are more likely to be taken over than their bigger brethren. So how does a private investor select winners in these stocks and, as important, avoid the disasters?

Know What you Own

My first piece of advice is that it is essential to know the companies in which you invest and choose only companies that have businesses that you can understand. By reading company reports, press comments and, if you have access, stockbroker reports, you should attempt to know your prospective share purchases as well as if you were investing money in 100 per cent of a private business rather than a small percentage of a public one. Avoid tips and do some research. Concentrate your portfolio in a few stocks that you can follow closely. Avoid areas such as high technology (unless you have a special knowledge of the area). It will be very difficult if nearly impossible to spot when the environment for complex companies changes and therefore when you should be selling them.

You should be able to sum up in a few sentences why you own a particular company.

In managing my portfolios, I see personally over 300 companies per annum and have the back up of our in-house European Research team of 40 people who see over 1,500 companies. In addition, we have access to the research of all the main stockbrokers. Normally our meetings with companies are conducted at the highest level and at most meetings either the managing director or finance director is present. An average meeting lasts from an hour to an hour and a half.

I like to meet every company I own at least once personally and we will try to have contact with our main holdings at least quarterly. I will go to the follow-up meetings (or take part in telephone calls) with many of my major holdings but at times I will let one of my colleagues do this and report back to me.

Obviously this level of contact with one's investments is impossible for the private individual but it does emphasize how important we believe the individual company analysis to be. However, the private investor has an advantage over me. Because of the size of portfolios I run (in total about £1.5 billion) I own shares in about 300 companies. Keeping on top of these investments is a major exercise in addition to seeking out new candidates to own in my portfolios. A private investor with 6-10 holdings and some spare time should be able to get to know their holdings relatively well. In America, many companies are prepared to talk directly to private investors. In the UK, management may often be less accessible and more reserved, but it is worth trying, since no one else is in a better position to answer the most pertinent questions.

Information Advantage

If you do have special knowledge of a particular industry or area of business (such as an industry in which you work) you should try to use this to your advantage. You should be able to follow a specific company in the industry better than the average investor. You may even be able to talk to customers, competitors etc. who can give you a better insight into the company, its activities and its success. You may have access to trade press and other sources not available to other investors.

The stockmarket deals in perceptions; if you know the reality is different, then you may be able to use this to your advantage.

What Type of Company to Buy

Having established that the company's business should be easy to understand, probably the best type of companies to own are those in long-term growth businesses. I like to invest in companies with a particular business advantage such as a niche area, a product that can't be substituted, high margins and an area without regulation. Ideally they should have some sort of unique franchise and be businesses that can generate cash. Earnings, dividends, assets and cashflow all have their attractions but in the long term free cash flow (cash flow less maintenance capital expenditure and working capital) is the most attractive attribute. You want businesses that generate free cash over and above their business needs. Maintenance capital expenditure is that essential to maintain the fabric of business and would exclude acquisitions and only a proportion of major new plant or property investments. It would include upgrading or maintenance type capital expenditure and investment in rental assets in a rental type business.

Analysing the business dynamics is the key to successful stock selection. Try to find companies which could grow significantly over the long run. Avoid businesses whose success is only due to temporary circumstances that could change. Ask yourself can this growth reasonably continue for some time. Once you own the shares, then monitoring for any changes is important. If you understand the business well, you should be able to spot if things are changing. However, the most important thing is to understand how a business

318

makes money and what are the most important internal and external variables which affect its fortunes.

Of course earnings, dividends, assets and gross cash flow are all important. In some companies, a significant discount to assets may be the key attraction. However, a business that can grow significantly in the long term, and does not need extra capital, is uniquely valuable. Hence the focus on analysis of free cash flow.

The key to good investment is to buy companies at reasonable valuations. A great company bought expensively can take a very long time to turn into a good investment and the downside is greater if things start to go wrong.

In the funds I manage, I also buy a lot of turnaround candidates. These are fine for professional investors but can be more risky for private investors. I particularly like businesses that are out of favour with investors today, but which I believe investors could become much more interested in in the future. Often these can involve changes of management or refinancing. I seek out companies that investors have forgotten about or given up on, where I believe things are changing and sentiment could improve on a one to two year view.

Another factor I will look for is areas where there is a greater chance of corporate activity and where the investor is not paying extra for this. I believe that although the stockmarket often bids up take-over stories in the short term, throughout much of their life companies with an above average chance of being taken over sell at no extra premium.

Management

Everyone wants to own companies with good management. The trouble is that it's ultimately only a good long-term record that is the proof of above average management and you will only know this after the event. Often the management who impresses in meetings are not equally endowed with business expertise. I look particularly for management who demonstrably have the shareholders' interests as first priority and who are honest with investors about their successes and failures.

Running European portfolios as well as British I come across a lot of management who seem to have outside shareholders' interests very low on their lists of priorities. I am much more careful of investing in these companies. In the long term I agree with Warren Buffet's view that he would rather invest in a good business with average management than a poor business with excellent management.

When to Buy or Sell

Ideally your activity should be low. You want to find a good company and stick with it for several years. You should have a time horizon of at least three to five years to invest in stocks so that hopefully you don't have to sell out at an inopportune time.

Try to buy when the market's depressed or when a stock is going through a temporary hiccup. I normally sell when either the company's shares become distinctly overvalued, or when I find something better or when the business or environment in which the company operates changes for the worse so negating the original reasons for owning it. Don't sell a share just because its gone up. If you do this you will miss owning any spectacular winners. An overvaluation which would concern me is when a company sells at a significant premium to other similar companies on the basis of two or more important investment criteria such as P/Es, price to free cash flow etc.

Forget Trying to Predict the Market Overall

A huge amount of time is spent by investors in general attempting to predict the short-term direction of the stockmarket and the economy. Very, very few investors can do this with any success and I believe almost nobody can do this consistently over time. So many individuals are either optimists or pessimists who get either the buy or the sell decision right but don't then sell at the right time or buy back at the right time. My advice to the private investor is don't waste time on this futile pastime.

Try and stand back from the herd instinct of the market. Think of setbacks as opportunities. Be pleased when there is a lot of pessimism about as there should be some excellent bargains around as well. When optimism abounds relook at each holding you own and weed out any one where you think things might be changing for the worse.

The best private investors have a temperament that allows them to step back from the herd.

The Downside

First remember investing is a game of odds; you won't get everything right; there will always be adverse surprises. You will be doing well if your successes outnumber your failures by more than 2 to 1. Therefore it is very important to protect the downside from failures. One way is to stick to what you understand and avoid fads and fashions. Try to question conventional thinking and institutional glamour stocks.

Remember companies with no debt can not go bust. Undoubtedly my biggest mistakes over the years have been with endebted companies. In these cases when things go wrong, the downside is 100 per cent and until one's lost 100 per cent, there is always the possibility of further downside. In general, I would recommend the private investor to stick to well financed smaller companies.

The Double Checks

Two double checks I've found useful are technical analysis and director dealings.

When looking at stock charts, I particularly follow relative strength. When this deteriorates I won't automatically sell a stock but I will re-examine the fundamentals and look extra hard to see if there is a factor I've missed. I also find charts useful for identifying turnaround candidates.

Also ignore director deals at your peril, particularly if two or more directors are acting the same way and in reasonable size. Again I won't necessarily sell when the director sells but it is often a factor when added to others that causes me to act. Also purchases can be useful in getting me to have a second look at a company I don't own or to increase my weighting in one I do own.

Also ignore director deals at your peril, particularly if two or more directors are acting the same way and in reasonable size.

I hope in these few words I've been able to share with you some tips I have learnt during my investment career. There is little original thought in investment and much of this advice has been distilled from recommendations over the years from colleagues and competitors adapted to my own personal experience.

Happy hunting. ♆

THE UNQUOTED MARKETS

John Jenkins and Emma Jenkins

John Jenkins is Chairman of **S. J. & S. Holdings Ltd** *which is parent to the market making firm* **J. P. Jenkins Ltd** *and the independent news service* **Newstrack Ltd**. *He began work with his father's firm* **S. Jenkins & Son** *in the 1960s, becoming independent again in 1991, after being taken over just prior to Big Bang by* **Guinness Mahon**. *Emma Jenkins joined the family business in 1993 to assist in setting up and running* Newstrack.

J. P. Jenkins *is the leading market maker in the unquoted sector registered to trade in over 800 stocks of those actively making markets in the shares of approximately 200 companies.*

Introduction

The market for unquoted companies in the UK (not to be confused with the Unlisted Securities Market) is a fascinating area for the private investor, but also a very high-risk one.

Up until June 1995, the unofficial market for shares in unquoted companies has been a dealing facility under Rule 4.2 (previously Rule 535(2)) of the London Stock Exchange. Although originally included in the rule book for allowing member firms to trade in suspended securities from the official list to close positions, it evolved in the 1980s to become a market in its own right. This was facilitated by the Exchange through an amendment of the rule, allowing member firms to take positions in such stocks, where previously the dealing facility only allowed matching of bargains to take place.

As well as the amendment in the rule, two market making firms in particular sought to specialize in trading in these unquoted shares, namely J. P. Jenkins Ltd and Winterflood Securities. Since J. P. Jenkins was set up to specialize in Rule 4.2 stocks in February 1991, and other market makers and brokers joined in, the volume of trade in Rule 4.2 stocks has increased dramatically. Until very recently, the Stock Exchange has never acknowledged publicly the existence nor the success of this 'unofficial' market. The level of activity has forced them to recognize a need for a new junior market for unquoted companies. Between January 1994 and December 1994, approximately £104.6 million was raised by a combination of established Rule 4.2 companies and start-up businesses with no trading record. In the 12-month period to 30 June 1994, the Stock Exchange noted that 264 companies had had their securities traded under Rule 4.2 accounting for a total volume of £482.4 million. These numbers are increasing monthly.

This section will cover the old Rule 4.2 Stock Exchange dealing facility (which ceased in September 1995), the Alternative Investment Market (AIM) (its successor), and OFEX, an off-exchange dealing facility for companies not eligible to join the AIM.

Tax Advantages for Investors

The Finance Act 1994 introduced some important incentives for investors to assist unquoted trading companies to raise finance. These tax advantages relate to investments in qualifying unquoted companies and are discussed in *Finance for Unquoted Companies – Tax Advantages for Investors* from Baker Tilly. Companies with a trading facility under the Stock Exchange Rule 4.2 or listed on the Alternative Investment Market (AIM) are not quoted for this purpose. Investors should seek professional advice

Type of Companies Traded

So who were these Rule 4.2 companies? J. P. Jenkins in conjunction with *Newstrack*, has sought to provide statistical information. A point to note is that any shareholder of an unquoted company could, without the permission of the company in question, submit the report and accounts of that company to the Exchange, via a member firm, in order for the company to be granted a dealing facility. We believe that some companies previously traded on the Rule 4.2 market, were not there at their own behest, namely one well-known breakfast cereal company.

Until its demise the Rule 4.2 market had been a popular exit route for ex-Business Expansion Scheme (BES) companies, so there were a relatively large number of residential and commercial property companies. The market contained brewers, public houses, hotels and restaurants, transport services, computer technology, multimedia, football clubs, property development and investment, building and construction, telecommunications, gold mining, exploration, recruitment consultants, food, retailing, toys and insurance. The list goes on – every bit as diverse as the official list.

The size of the companies in terms of market capitalization, also varied very greatly, ranging from £570.7 million to £0.5 million. Table 3.1 below shows the top five companies and their basic statistics as at February 1995.

Table 3.1

Company	Sector	Price as at 8 February 1995[1]	Market Cap[2]	P/E Ratio	Yield %	Net Asset Value[1]	Div[1]
National Parking Corporation Ltd	Business Services	485	570.7	17.03	3.35	203	13
Weetabix Ltd (Non Vtg 'A' Ord)	Food	2050	242.1	12.34	1.75	876	28.75
Gan Life and Pensions (formerly General Portfolio)	Financial Services	185	201.4	7.46	0.00	234	nil
Mid-Southern Water Co	Utilities	3300	115.9	13.60	5.15	708	136
Southern Newspapers plc	Media	440	103.8	11.2	3.84	221	13.5

[1] pence
[2] £ million

Liquidity

For the more progressive Rule 4.2 companies, liquidity depended on the number of shares in issue, the ability of the sponsoring and/or shop broker to promote the stock with his own clientele, and whether the type of business the company was involved in, caught the imagination of the private investor. For example, Memory Corporation plc was placed at 45p per share on the Rule 4.2 market in December 1994 and, by May 1995, the shares were trading at

225p. The company recycles, designs and develops computer chips. For the more established Rule 4.2 companies however and those subsequently traded off exchange after June 1995, liquidity has and can be a problem. In the case of some of the companies, trades were matched occasionally. This is particularly true of the majority of the shares of football clubs.

The AIM

The 'unofficial' success of Rule 4.2 (which as a market was virtually unregulated) prompted the Stock Exchange to take a decision to provide a more regulated but still 'unquoted' market for small, growing, new companies which would to an extent avoid the need for these companies to go to venture capitalists.

A long consultative period produced the Alternative Investment Market (AIM) effective on 19 June 1995. The AIM will replace the USM which closes on 31 December 1996, and also effectively replaces the Rule 4.2 dealing facility. The 'unquoted' status of the AIM companies for tax purposes also means that venture capital trusts may invest in those which also qualify under the VCT legislation. Accordingly it is likely that there will be an increasing number of tax efficient investment opportunities.

Unfortunately, the Exchange is requiring that AIM companies retain a nominated advisor and nominated broker at all times, and pay a listing fee (none was payable under Rule 4.2). Many companies will not feel that they can justify to their shareholders the expense of AIM. On the other hand, the Stock Exchange has received many thousands of enquiries from other unquoted companies who are eligible to join the AIM during 1995.

The scope of the existing Rule 4.2 will be reduced to its original purpose in June, although there is a transitionary period until 29 September 1995 for all companies who were granted a Rule 4.2 dealing facility before 1 May 1995.

OFEX

There has been outcry from those existing Rule 4.2 companies who cannot or will not join the AIM. In response, the Stock Exchange has stated that member firms can deal 'off-market' in the shares of companies who do not have a listing on any exchange, or who have not been refused a listing at any time. John Jenkins at J. P. Jenkins has taken up the gauntlet, and has said that, as well as making a market in all AIM stocks at the launch, he will also make markets in unquoted companies on his own dealing facility 'OFEX' which will be run as Rule 4.2 was run. There will be price visibility through, *Newstrack*'s unquoted news and information service, currently available on Bloomberg, ICV, QST and Reuters worldwide. The *Newstrack* service will also carry other information on the companies as well as covering comprehensively the AIM.

It must be stated that OFEX is not to be considered as a market in competition with the AIM. It is only a dealing facility, and is highly risky. No investor protection will be available from the Stock Exchange or any other body, nor from S. J. & S. Holdings, the parent company of both J. P. Jenkins Ltd and Newstrack Ltd. ♨

UK FIXED INCOME

Tim Knowles

*Tim Knowles joined **Flemings** as Director of **FIPG** in August 1994. Formerly he spent 12 years working in fixed income investment for **Saudi International Bank, Morgan Stanley and Goldman Sachs.***

*__Flemings__ is unique amongst UK investment banks in that investment management has been its original and single most important business since the firm's inception in 1873. The Group has always been private and, today, approximately half the share capital is owned by the Fleming family and employees. **Flemings** manages funds totalling approximately £48.5 billion.*

Introduction

Bonds can and should play an important role in investors' portfolios - as generators of income, as a means of reflecting an opinion on changes in interest rates, and as a diversification from equity, property and other asset classes. The UK fixed income markets provide a wide range of opportunities for investors seeking to achieve these objectives.

UK Government Bonds

Analysis of the fixed income opportunities available to sterling-based investors begins with UK government bonds, known as the 'gilt-edged' market, supposedly from the practice, in the market's early days, of issuing government bond certificates with gold edges. This is the oldest government bond market in the world. The origins of the UK's public debt can be traced back to the late seventeenth century, while the 3% Consolidated Annuities, issued in 1751, are still traded (in their converted form) today. Based on recent measures of bonds outstanding, the UK currently has the sixth largest government bond market in the world, with a total outstanding issuance approaching £200 billion. Government bond yields form the base from which other medium to longer term interest rates are set. Gilts therefore provide a lower yield than other sterling fixed income investments, but investors are compensated by the main attractions of the market, namely:

Credit Quality: All gilts are fully guaranteed by the government of the United Kingdom. No distinction in credit terms is drawn between those issued in the name of the 'Treasury', the 'Exchequer', or any other nomenclature to designate a specific purpose to which funds were applied (e.g. 'War', 'Gas'). The UK Government enjoys the highest credit standing, rated AAA by the leading rating agencies.

Liquidity: Total customer-related turnover in the gilt market in 1994 was £825 billion. Gilts are very liquid, easily traded instruments, with deal denominations ranging from many millions of pounds to £0.01!

Wide Choice of Maturities: Maturities range from a few months to more than 20 years, for dated issues; while a small portion of the market (approx £3 billion) is comprised of 'irredeemables'; bonds which will only be redeemed at the government's option. Investors can select securities which match their particular requirements for cash flow and price volatility.

Wide Choice of Coupons: Gilt rates range from $2\frac{1}{2}$ per cent for some irredeemable stocks to the $15\frac{1}{2}$ per cent bond due September 1998. This gives investors the opportunity to invest for their particular income requirements and/or tax considerations.

Special Features: Further choice is given by gilts with particular characteristics. The Floating Rate Gilt due 1999 resets the rate payable every three months. The 7% Treasury due 1997 is an example of a conversion stock which can be converted, at the holder's option, and on specific terms, into the 9% Treasury due 2012.

Index-linked gilts provide a further range of opportunities, rare in the mainstream international bond markets. First issued in 1981, these bonds have their interest and redemption proceeds linked to the principal measure of UK inflation, the Retail Price Index. With a guaranteed real rate of return (if the bond is held to maturity) index-linked bonds can be viewed as an independent asset class, with something of the inflation-hedge characteristics more normally associated with an equity combined with the income and redemption features of a bond.

The story has been told that at a meeting of the European Bond Commission in 1991 the UK market was described by one member as one of the most 'primi-

The story has been told that at a meeting of the European Bond Commission in 1991 the UK market was described by one member as one of the most 'primitive' government markets in Europe.

tive' government markets in Europe. Aspects of the UK market are less developed than European counterparts – principally because, as other markets underwent deregulation and reform in the late 1980s, the UK market contracted in size and importance under the government's Public Sector Debt Repayment programme. Consequently, the gilt market has lacked features such as:

- an established repo market;
- payment of interest without deduction of withholding tax;
- recognized stripping procedures (dividing a bond into separate coupon and principle cash flows to create a series of zero-coupon securities);
- settlement through international clearing operations (Cedel/Euroclear);
- futures contract based on a notional 10 year bond.

Some of these inefficiencies (notably the development of repo and strips markets) are being addressed and indications are that the gilt market will become a more efficient investment medium.

Non-Government Bonds

The gilt market comprises approximately 60 per cent of the outstanding pool of sterling-denominated bonds. Other fixed income investments fall into two categories: those issued, like gilts, under the regime of the domestic market; and offshore, or 'Euro', issues, structured to attract foreign investors. It is not feasible to draw up an exhaustive list, but non-government securities include the following:

Eurosterling Market
- Bonds

- Floating Rate Notes
- Mortgage-backed Securities
- Convertibles
- Medium-Term Notes (MTNs)

Domestic Market
- Corporate Bonds (secured, like debentures, or unsecured)
- Convertibles
- Bulldogs (issued by foreign entities)
- Municipals/Local Authorities
- Preference Shares/Zero Dividend Preference Shares
- Permanent Interest-bearing Shares (PIBS)

Each security class has its own particular characteristics. Their main advantage is a higher yield than a similar maturity gilt, because they do not provide the same credit quality, or the accessibility. Most non-government issues are targeted at institutional investors – indeed the minimum denominations of some would preclude all but the very largest private investors. However, preference shares and PIBS are often directed towards private investors; and debentures share a characteristic of gilts, in that they can be purchased in nominal amounts to the nearest £0.01.

The UK markets in corporate, municipal, local authority and mortgage-backed securities are more developed than those of many continental countries

– but are significantly less sophisticated than in the USA. High long-term interest rates in the 1970s and early 1980s, and the existence of a sophisticated domestic banking system as an alternative source of finance, have deterred corporate debt issuance. A few local authorities have issued long-dated bonds, but most derived their finance in recent years from the Public Works Loan Board, at terms more favourable than in an open market. The mortgage backed sector began in 1987, with the first issue for The Mortgage Corporation, and grew rapidly in the late 1980s housing boom: but the flow of new issues has declined as rising interest rates and recession in property reduced demand for mortgage finance. In all these sectors, inefficiencies can provide opportunities for successful investment, but on the whole investors would be recommended to secure professional advice on individual securities.

How to Invest in UK Bonds

One of the most attractive features of gilts is their accessibility. Existing issues can be purchased through a wide range of financial intermediaries, principally banks, investment managers or stockbrokers. They can also be purchased, in amounts up to £25,000 per day per stock, by application at a post office. New issues can be purchased at auction, again through the agency of a financial intermediary; or by postal applications using forms published in the national press. (This latter technique, incidentally, avoids commission or dealing expenses.) Stock certificates are deliverable directly to the investor or to a nominated custody agent.

Investment in non-government bonds is best undertaken through a specialist in the sector. One of the best sources of advice on the relative merits of such fixed income securities are the Independent Financial Advisers (IFAs).

Collective investment schemes, or unit trusts, are arguably of only limited value for government bonds. Accessibility and the absence of credit considerations imply that the serious private investor has limited need for a gilt unit trust. However, fixed income unit trusts that invest in non-government securities can provide a means of investing efficiently in a range of securities which may otherwise be inaccessible. The announcement in the autumn 1994 Budget that some fixed income unit trusts investing in convertibles, corporates and Eurosterling bonds (but not gilts), would be PEP-able, should encourage investors to this sector.

Taxation Treatment of UK Bonds

The UK domestic bond market is unusual amongst the world's markets in that coupon (or dividend) payments are made to registered holders net of tax. Tax is withheld at the prevailing basic rate of income tax (currently 25 per cent). Any adjustment to the investor's tax liability is made by subsequent assessment: a non-taxpayer would be entitled to an eventual refund, while a higher-rate taxpayer is liable to incremental tax.

This system has acted as a deterrent to private investment in gilts. In addition, although many investors are institutions entitled to receive coupons gross of tax (e.g. charities, pension funds) the existence of withholding tax has caused significant pricing differences, with high coupon (large tax liability) bonds trading at a higher yield than securities with low coupons. Non-UK investors have also, it is thought, been deterred by the taxation treatment. In recognition, the authorities have issued 'FOTRA' gilts ('free of tax to residents abroad'), the coupons of which are paid gross of tax to registered foreign holders. There are, though, no 'FOTRA' corporate bonds, which explains the virtual absence of non-UK investors from this sector of the market.

As of 1995, the UK authorities may be taking the first steps in recognizing that a complicated tax structure dissuades investors from participating in the domestic market. A repo market in gilts will commence from early 1996, accompanied by the payment of gross coupons to institutional (but not to private) investors. It remains to be seen whether gross coupon payment will become the order of the day for the whole market. The experience of countries which have removed withholding tax as part of a wider process of deregulation (e.g. France in the late 1980s) demonstrates the benefits in terms of market efficiency and wider investor involvement.

Coupons on Eurosterling securities are paid gross of tax to the bearer of the bond. If, however, a UK bank is appointed to collect the coupon, it may be required by law to deduct withholding tax. Investors should seek specific advice.

Development of a strips market in gilts necessitates the equal tax treatment of income and capital gains. Accordingly from 1996 the exemption from capital gains tax which has applied to gilts will be superseded by a new regime treating capital profits as income for tax purposes – though private investors with medium-sized holdings may continue to enjoy capital gains free of tax.

Investing in UK Bonds: Past Experience

Fixed income investments have historically produced lower returns than equities, but have generally proved to be less risky (where risk is defined as the volatility, or standard deviation, of returns over time). This is borne out by the most detailed analysis of the performance of UK financial assets, the 'BZW Equity: Gilt Study'. In the UK, periods of inflation, notably in the years following the Second World War and again in the 1970s, exacted a heavy toll on returns from gilts and produced successive years of negative real returns. However, in environments of stable or falling inflation, gilts have produced attractive positive real returns.

Except for two brief periods (early 1950s; late 1980s), during the twentieth century gilts have proved less risky than equities. In fact, taking the past 70 years of performance data, equities have been almost twice as volatile as gilts – but have in practice returned more, both in real and nominal terms.

Chart 3.1 UK rolling 10-year Real Return from Gilts

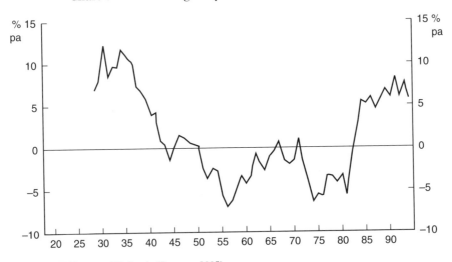

Source: BZW Equity – Gilt Study (January 1995)

Chart 3.2 UK rolling 10-year Standard Deviations of Nominal Returns

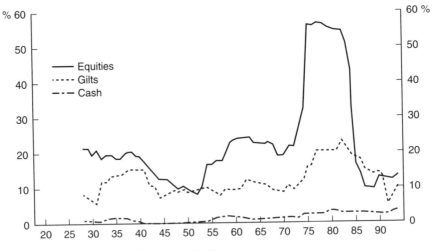

Source: BZW Equity – Gilt Study (January 1995)

The past 10 years (1985–94) have been somewhat atypical in that all finan-cial asset classes have shown good real returns. Equities, with an average annual real return of +9.6 per cent have outperformed gilts (+5.8 per cent), though at the expense of a more volatile pattern of price movement.

Table 3.2

Risk & Return Characteristics (1919–94)

Nominal Returns	Average Annualised Return	Standard Deviation
Equities	14.4	25.7
Gilts	6.5	13.3
Real Returns		
Equities	10.3	23.8
Gilts	2.8	15.1

Investing in UK Bonds: The Outlook

The total return (or yield) from a bond can be divided into three constituent parts:

- income received – which is totally predictable, equal annually to the bond's coupon (net or gross of tax);
- change in capital value – which is totally predictable if the bond is held to maturity, but much less easy to predict if the bond is to be sold prior to its maturity, as prices fluctuate in line with changes in interest rates;
- income earned on coupons received (reinvestment income) – dependent on changes in interest rates, and difficult (or impossible) to predict accurately.

There are reasons to be positive on the outlook for UK bonds. First, the yield to maturity (the market's forecast rate of return) on gilts, as of early 1995, is high by historic standards – especially when viewed in inflation adjusted terms. The average real yield on a conventional 10-year gilt over the past 20 years has been 2.3 per cent. Assuming that UK inflation remains within a 3 to 4 per cent range, the real yield is currently $4\frac{1}{2}$ to $5\frac{1}{2}$ per cent. Suppose inflation is worse than expected, rising, say to the 4.5 per cent currently discounted by index-linked gilts. Even then, the return over and above inflation is still indicated as being Close to 4 per cent per annum over the next 10 years.

Real yields are high because the UK's inflation history has not been such as to inspire confidence that inflation will not rise sharply. Additional risk premium is therefore required to persuade investors to buy bonds. But even for the investor who shares these inflation concerns, there are other, structural reasons to be positive.

The next few years are likely to see reduced government issuance, as the public sector borrowing requirement declines. Demand for gilts from pension funds is likely to increase, in the light of new minimum solvency requirements and as more fund members become beneficiaries of, rather than contributors to, their pension scheme. And with the Bank of England assuming an ever more influential role in setting UK monetary policy, the chances of an upsurge in inflation, to erode the real value of bonds, should continue to diminish. After a disappointing 1994, bond investors can view the coming years with more optimism.

Global Markets

Europe

The Benelux
France
Germany
Iberia
Italy
Scandinavia

North America

US Equities
US Fixed Income
Canada

Asia

Hong Kong
India
Japan
Asian Growth – The Five Tigers

Rest of the World

Australia
New Zealand
South Africa
Latin America
Emerging Markets

THE BENELUX

Roland Leuschel

*M Leuschel is the Manager at **Banque Bruxelles Lambert (BBL)** responsible for investment strategy. He has had a 32-year career in the bank in various capacities. Jean-Marie Louis, Senior Financial Analyst in the research department at **BBL**, assisted with this section.*

***Banque Bruxelles Lambert** is the second largest commercial and investment bank in Belgium, with around 12,000 employees.*

Introduction

Some people have perhaps forgotten that the Benelux – which is constituted by Belgium, The Netherlands and Luxembourg – was the beginning of the European Union (EU). Its foundation goes back to 1947, 11 years before the constitution of the European Community (EC). The neighbours Belgium and The Netherlands, which were unified by history and finally separated when Belgium got its independence in 1830, have simultaneously a lot of similarities and several differences in their financial markets.

Common points are. . .

- Both countries are relatively small though with a difference in the concentration of population: 14.5 million residents in The Netherlands compared with 10 million people in Belgium, where the surface area is almost identical.

  The market share of Belgium measured in terms of the capitalization of the world stock markets is about 0.7 per cent (US dollar 78 billion) compared to 1.6 per cent in The Netherlands (US dollar 183 billion). The capitalization in Belgium and Holland represents respectively 37 per cent and 58 per cent of the GDP, in comparison to 110 per cent in the United Kingdom.

  In Belgium and in Holland only a small part of the population are shareholders: as few as 6 per cent Netherlands and 10 per cent in Belgium in comparison to 22 per cent in the United Kingdom and almost 25 per cent in the United States. In Belgium this percentage is higher than in Holland, in spite of the country's reputation to prefer 'no risk placements' and bonds (conservative attitude stems from the 'good family father' of the Belgian investor). The main reasons are legal and fiscal measures taken at the beginning of the 1980s to encourage risk-capital investment.
- In The Netherlands and Belgium there is a predominance of the oil sector (Royal Dutch represents 30 per cent of the total market capitalization in Holland, Petrofina 10 per cent in Belgium), 'banks', insurance (ABN. AMRO,

336

ING, Aegon on the Dutch side, Générale de Banque, BBL, Kredietbank, Forties AG, Royal Belge on the Belgian side), consumer goods (for The Netherlands, Unilever and Heineken) and, in Belgium, the three most important retailers (Delhaize, GIB and Colruyt).

- The interest rates in Belgium and Holland are often close together, not directly but indirectly because of their link to the Deutschmark. This explains the strength of the Dutch guilder and the Belgium franc moving in a band. Both currencies have risen by more than 100 per cent against the US$ during the last decade.

- The markets in Belgium and Holland are very 'US dollar sensitive'. For Brussels the correlation between movement in the US dollar and the Belgian stockmarket has reached an average of 70 per cent over the last five years. This means that, if the US$ rises, there is a probability of 70 per cent that the Belgian Bourse will advance.

Chart 3.3 Movement of Dutch and Belgian Currencies

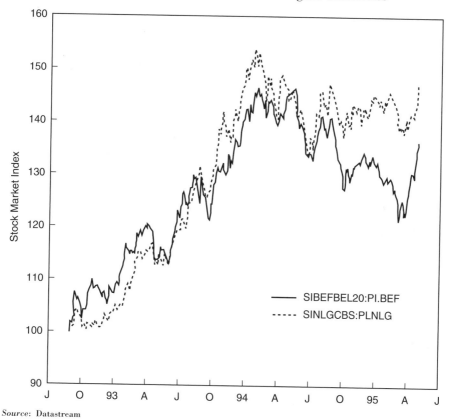

Source: Datastream

- Finally since September 1992, the beginning of the boom of the European stock markets, Amsterdam and Brussels developed in the same direction, with a small delay of the Belgian stockmarket which lagged the move of the Dutch market. Both are up about 40 per cent in the last two and a half years.

Based on the estimated earnings for 1995, the two stockmarkets have more or less identical P/E ratios: 11 for Amsterdam (based on the CBS index) and 12 for Brussels (BEL 20 index). Both are reasonable and within the range of the European P/E average. It should be noted that accounting practice is conservative in Holland. Dutch banks and insurance companies often have substantial hidden reserves, like in Germany.

- However the yield from the market in Brussels has always been much higher: 4.8 per cent gross on the basis of the estimated 1995 dividends, compared to 3.1 per cent in Amsterdam. The reason for this is the important role of the financial sector in Belgium, where banks, insurers, utilities and holding companies represent 60 per cent of the total market capitalization; and the Belgian investor has always been yield-minded.

. . . but the points of view, which are divergent, are dominant

- Belgian mentality is closer to the 'Latin way of life', whereas the Dutch mentality is very Anglo-Saxon. After all, the Dutch are more business-minded.
- The long tradition of entrepreneurship in Holland explains the number of industrial companies with international vocation and extensive overseas operations. The best examples are Royal Dutch, the main shareholder of the English oil group Royal Dutch/Shell, which is the fourth most important company in the world based on turnover, the consumer goods manufacturers, Unilever (21st in the world), and the electronics giant, Philips (32nd). For comparison, the most important Belgian companies are less substantial. Petrofina, the sixth largest oil company in Europe, ranks only 130th. Even if Belgium is characterized by a smaller number of international companies, some have adopted aggressive strategies to build up abroad, mainly in the United States. The best example is the retailer, Delhaize, which realizes 56 per cent of its profits with its American subsidiary Food Lion. Petrofina, too, realized 30 per cent of its profits in the US via its subsidiary Fina.

Belgian mentality is closer to the 'Latin way of life', whereas the Dutch mentality is very Anglo-Saxon. After all, the Dutch are more business-minded.

- The industrial shares, however, are less represented in Brussels. They aggregate to one-third of the market capitalization, compared to 57 per cent in The Netherlands. This difference is caused by a characteristic of the Belgian market, where holding companies play an important role in the market (23 per cent). One of the largest is the Group Bruxelles Lambert, with interests in oil (Petrofina); electric utilities (Tractebel, Electrabel); radio and TV (Audiofine) and financial services (BBL, Royal Belge).

- On the other hand, in contrast to Belgium, most of the big Dutch companies are listed on international exchanges like London and New York. That's not so surprising because 35 per cent of Dutch stocks are held by foreign investors compared to 23 per cent in Belgium.

- Contrary to The Netherlands, the Belgian stock market is characterized by a smaller liquidity, more than 60 per cent of the Belgian stocks are held in fixed hands, which can sometimes be a big handicap for international investors. International investors also don't appreciate very much that the Dutch stocks are often issued without voting rights.

- Another factor of differentiation is the absence of important pension money on the Brussels stock market. Contrary to what we observe in The Netherlands, where the pension funds reach an impressive sum of US$330 billion, there is a mere US$8 for Belgium. Only the ABP (Algemeen Burgelijk Pensionfonds), which centralize the pensions of all Dutch officials, manage the total sum of US$100 billion. An important part of the Dutch debt is held by the pension funds.

- The Amsterdam stock market is one of the first financial markets which followed Chicago by opening an option market (EOE) in 1977, which has established itself as the most important option market outside America. In Brussels the creation of an option market is far more recent, as it was set up in 1992, and, so far, only about ten shares take part.

- Finally, a subject which is always discussed, especially abroad, is the importance of the Belgian public debt, which amounts to almost 300 billion US dollars and is 120 per cent of GDP. The Netherlands, though significant at 250 billion US dollars is lower at 80 per cent of GDP. In Belgium the government is obliged to reduce sensitively public debt in the future.

- As far as the fixed income market is concerned, there are only public bonds: the traditional issues for private investors and the Obligation Lineaire Obligaties (linear bonds). As long as the holder is not a Belgian private investor, the OLOs are wholly exempt from withholding tax. In order to reduce the number of separate issues while, at the same time, increasing the total amount outstanding (which improves liquidity), each new issue is assimilated to an existing 'line' with identical characteristics, hence the name 'linear bond'. Accrued interest must, in this case, be added. OLO is an investment instrument which is book entry only, with no physical certificate, and more appropriate to professional investors.

We cannot conclude this comparison of the two main Benelux markets without mentioning that Brussels is becoming more and more the decision centre of Europe, having a trump card with a cosmopolitan character and so much of the EU machinery of government. ●

FRANCE

Julian Sturdy-Morton

*Julian Sturdy-Morton is a Director of the London based International Corporate finance team of **Credit Lyonnais Securities (CLS)**. Julian Sturdy-Morton has 20 years' experience working in the international markets, formerly with **Morgan Grenfell** and **Orion Bank**.*

***CLS** is among the top ten most active banks in the international equity markets and has been very active in the equity new issue and privatization programmes of many countries, especially France (where **Credit Lyonnais** is the leading equity new issue house).*

The French Stock Market, unified under the Paris Bourse in 1991, is the second largest in Continental Europe, ranking marginally behind the Frankfurt Stock Exchange. It is also the most technically advanced as a result of extensive intervention by central government during the 1980s. The trading activities of the Bourse are complemented by MONEP, the options market, and MATIF, the futures market. Since 1991, member firms throughout France have been able to trade in all listed securities through the most advanced computerized dealing and settlement system in the world without paper certificates as a result of the rather inelegantly named policy of *dématérialisation*.

A high proportion of the market is held by private investors (31 per cent in 1994), following various measures to encourage private share ownership. Furthermore, France has one of the highest proportions of foreign stocks listed, in large measure due to regulations previously in force that compelled certain categories of investor to hold only Paris listed stock. As a result, there are 748 domestic and 215 foreign companies listed on the official market of the Paris Bourse.

> **A high proportion of the market is held by private investors (31 per cent in 1994), following various measures to encourage private share ownership.**

Government intervention has played an important part in the market's evolution. There were three discernible motives for a series of measures which can be regarded as part of a cohesive policy to increase the size of the market and strengthen the trend towards wider share ownership in France: the need to create a market that is large enough to fund a privatization programme that will, when concluded, have accounted for 8–10 per cent of GDP (equivalent to over 25 per cent of the float at the current capitalization of the Paris Bourse), a desire to create a market which will compete in terms of size and international importance with London and the need to create a savings medium to meet the pension requirements of the French population into the next century in the virtual absence of comprehensively organized non-state pension provision. In many respects, the policy, although never advanced in exactly these terms, has been remarkably effective in achieving these goals.

France now has a stock market that rivals Germany's in size (in spite of Germany being a country whose GDP exceeds France's by almost 40 per cent); it has one of the highest levels of private savings (and, in particular, private equity investment) in Europe, with French mutual funds accounting for almost half of all mutual funds in the European Union and a stock market almost one-third of which is owned by retail investors; and it has made successful progress in placing shares in privatized industries, including the massive Elf Aquitaine privatization in 1994 (estimated to have been the largest privatization in the world relative to GDP).

The Current Situation and Outlook of the French Economy

The French economy is growing strongly, after suffering a deep recession in 1992–3 which continued into 1994. Forecasts for growth indicate that GDP will advance by 3.1 per cent or more in 1995, while inflation remains well controlled (at approximately 1.7 per cent). Two major problems remain, and both played a large part in the 1995 presidential elections that saw Jacques Chirac elected as president of the Republic at his third attempt: unemployment is high (at 3.3 million, it is the highest, proportional to population, of any of the major economies in Europe); and excessive centralized expenditure has yet to be addressed comprehensively: both the government's massive budget deficit – Ffr 301 billion in 1994 (over 4 per cent of GDP), and expected to exceed Ffr 275 billion in 1995 – and the chronic shortfall in the social security system, which is unable to meet demands for benefits and pensions without a level of radical overhaul which has, to date, been politically unacceptable. Measures to reduce payments, cut the minimum wage rates paid to graduate apprentices or shift the burden of pension provision from public to private sector have not yet been successfully implemented.

A major pillar of French economic policy has been the coupling of French fortunes with those of the Germans, France's most important trading partner. In addition to measures to encourage an increasing closeness between the two economies, the government has, in recent years, sought to shadow the German currency through its *franc fort* policy, retaining an artificially high international rate of exchange through the imposition of high interest rates. The advantages of this policy are well appreciated; the disadvantages are that France's fundamental problems have not been addressed and that the French economy was greatly affected by the unexpected severity of the German recession in the early 1990s.

The following chart compares the ten-year OAT (Obligations Assimilables du Trésor, the equivalent of a UK Government tap stock), with the French consumer price index (CPI) showing the determination with which interest rates have been used to control inflation and sustain the *franc fort* policy.

Chart 3.4 Comparison of French Consumer Price Index with OAT

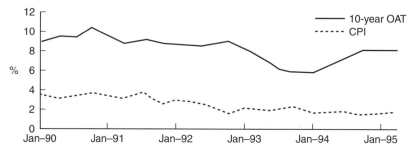

Source: Credit Lyonnais Securities

At heart France remains a *dirigiste* economy managed by a highly qualified élite taking decisions at the centre and intervening for reasons of national prestige or with political intent, often in the face of opposition from France's trading partners and from the European Union authorities in Brussels.

The bright star in the French economic firmament is the growth in investment which is forecast for 1995 (+4.9 per cent) and 1996 (+4.6 per cent), following a dearth of capital expenditure in the 1980s. This trend, which is comfortably above the EU average, is strongly encouraged by the government and is expected to result in a strong equity market during the balance of the year. There are, however, two negative factors to set against this: unemployment (at 12.5 per cent) is considerably higher than in any other major EU economy and falling more slowly than elsewhere, and the PSBR of 4.4 per cent of GDP (1995 forecast) is higher than the EU average or the EMU convergence rates and is being reduced only slowly. These are the two main concerns that face the government of Jacques Chirac.

The French Privatization Programme and Changes in the French Capital Markets

By 1982, at the very time when the UK government embarked on a programme of privatization, the French had amassed the largest concentration of state-controlled businesses of any country in Europe: 24 per cent of all employment, 50 per cent of investment, 33 per cent of turnover and 23 per cent of exports in France were controlled by the government. This was the result of three stages of development – state-founded companies (like Elf Aquitaine, a vertically integrated oil explorer, refiner and retailer of petroleum products), companies seized or nationalized after 1945 (like Renault, the French market leader in cars, in the first instance, the large banks in the second), and entities nationalized in 1981 (46 companies in all – some for ideological reasons, but most because they needed state assistance to restore balance sheets that had suffered during the preceding recession). At that time, the French capital markets were small in capacity, antiquated in procedure and domestic in orientation. Even market making in French shares was conducted in London, not in Paris.

The change of government in 1986 marked the first moves to restore a large portion of the state sector to private ownership. This process followed a long period of modernization and preparation.

Encouragement of private investment   The Loi Monory, introduced in 1978, the Compte d'Epargne en Actions, in 1983, and the Plan d'Epargne en Actions, in 1988, and still in force, are all fiscal measures to increase private ownership of shares. The policy has been successful. Today there are 11.2 million private equity investors in France: over a quarter of the adult population.

The main Paris Bourse index is the CAC 40 list of 40 leading companies accounting for almost 80 per cent of market capitalization, by which the performance of the market is generally measured. Within this index, one category (banking and insurance) stands out above the rest. Eight banks and two insurers account for 22 per cent of the CAC 40 capitalization (16 per cent for the banks and 6 per cent for the insurers). The tendency among banking and finance groups (such as Groupe Suez and Paribas) to hold shares in other companies means that this effectively under-represents the degree to which the market is a vehicle for the financial groups to control capital movements and, eventually, industry and commerce in France in alliance with the state. However, few of these financial groups rank among the world leaders.

In the oil sector, by contrast, where two companies (Elf and Total) together account for 12 per cent of the CAC, France has two major international companies with wide-ranging overseas activities and a strong foreign shareholder base: Elf, for example, was one of few foreign companies listed in the US after privatization to attract strong after market demand from US investors, exceeding the original placement.

Food and beverage (incorporating luxury goods) accounts for 11 per cent of the market. Companies such as the cognac, champagne and fashion group LVMH (the second largest member of the CAC 40 after Elf) are world leaders in the peculiarly French industry of luxury goods. Most of LVMH's sales are generated outside France, although the company remains firmly controlled by French shareholders (notably the Arnault Group).

Attraction of smaller companies to the market   The Second Marché was introduced along the lines of the USM in the UK as a means of attracting companies that wished to release only as little as 10 per cent of their capital, or had too short a track record to qualify for the *côte officiel*. There are about 100 participants and a fairly high migration rate to the full quotation, with the result that the number of companies listed is fairly static.

Internationalization of traded instruments MATIF, now the third largest futures market in the world after Chicago and Osaka, was launched in 1986 and MONEP, now the largest equity derivative trading exchange in Europe, was launched in 1987. Together these two markets have helped to attract foreign investors and have helped the French market to gain the experience needed to handle equity market making, which was first permitted in France at the same time.

Modernization of the Stock Exchange's structure In 1988 more capital was introduced to the market through the liberalization of the rules on the ownership of brokers. Banks, in particular, have since acquired substantial holdings in member firms increasing the scope of their activities and enabling them to develop internationally. Finally, the authorities tackled the market's procedures with the introduction of paper free trading (in 1984) and electronic settlement through the highly sophisticated RELIT system, which came on stream in 1992.

In 1986–7 the French government privatized 12 companies and raised over Ffr 70 billion. This programme was stopped by the crash of October 1987, but it had provided an excellent basis for future privatizations. Over ten million private investors participated in the offers and over 30 per cent of the shares were placed with institutions outside France.

In 1993 legislation was introduced to allow the sale of a further 21 companies (including 12 banks, the insurance and manufacturing companies that had been listed for sale in the 1980s and nine new names, such as Renault and Air France). The programme amounts to the sale of some Ffr 300 billion of assets over three years, almost a quarter of all proposed privatizations in Europe during the period. Major companies that have been privatized to date (including BNP, one of the largest commercial banks; Elf Aquitaine; Renault; Rhône Poulenc, a major chemical and pharmaceuticals group; and UAP, the leading insurance group in France) now account for almost half the CAC 40 by number.

The privatized companies have been extensively restructured and recapitalized while still in the state sector, prior to privatization. Fresh capital was attracted by the sale of a variety of debt and quasi-equity instruments, which served both to bring new investors to the markets and to strengthen the companies without loss of state control, maximizing the state's eventual revenues. Non-voting shares, TSDIs (a self-funding form of perpetual floating rate note) and preference shares are gradually being redeemed in the course of privatization but have resulted in France being one of the most sophisticated capital markets worldwide.

In preparation for the 1993 privatization programme, the French government launched the Balladur bonds (more prosaically called the 6% government bonds due 1997) as the central instrument for the attraction of retail demand and to secure a high proportion of the proceeds of privatization in advance of flotation. This issue was destined to raise Ffr 50 billion. After being offered through 43,000 banks and post office branches throughout

France, the issue closed at a record size, Ffr 110 billion. The bonds offer fiscal advantages and priority subscription rights in privatization issues (over Ffr 10 billion have been surrendered in this fashion to date) and a guarantee of capital security or gain upon exercise or redemption. They should cover approximately one-third of the expected proceeds of the current programme and serve further to broaden the retail shareholder base in France.

The Structure of the Paris Market

Four categories of investor can be said to dominate the Paris stock market: strategic investors (*noyaux durs*); private investors; mutual funds and foreign investors. Insurance companies, whether as members of *noyaux durs* or as direct shareholders, are also important.

The breakdown of holders, as of September 1994, is illustrated in Chart 3.5:

Chart 3.5 Breakdown of French shareholders by category (September 1994)

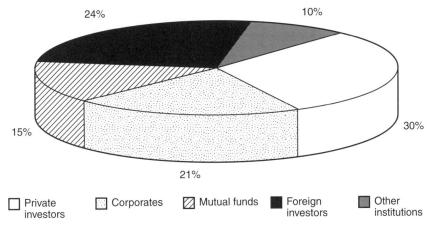

24%   10%

15%   30%

21%

☐ Private   ☐ Corporates   ▨ Mutual funds   ■ Foreign   ▨ Other
   investors   investors   institutions

Source: Bourse de Paris

Noyaux durs have a significant role to play in a market where the pension fund industry scarcely exists, although strenuous efforts are being made to encourage private pension provision as the state system comes under increasing pressure.

This role can be illustrated by looking at the situation at Elf. Even fairly small stakes can be held by *noyaux durs*. UAP, BNP and Société Générale de Belgique (a Belgian financial holding company controlled by Groupe Suez) each holds 1.4 per cent of Elf. Sofexi (an investment subsidiary of Renault), Paribas (the banking and investment group) and AXA (an insurance company) each holds between 1 per cent and $\frac{1}{2}$ per cent. Stakes are held by Crédit Agricole (the agricultural mutual savings bank), Caisse Nationale de Portefeuilles (an investment group controlled by the Albert Frère group) and UBS (the Swiss bank).

These investors are tied into the company by means of a shareholders' agreement. Taking Elf as a starting point, it is also worth noting that:

(a) Elf owns 3 per cent of Suez
(b) Elf owns 5 per cent of Petrofina
(c) Suez owns 5 per cent of UAP
(d) UAP owns 6.9 per cent of Suez
(e) BNP owns 19 per cent of UAP

One can also see that:

(f) Albert Frère controls CNP and Petrofina
(g) SGB owns 10.8 per cent of Petrofina
(h) CNP owns 4.3 per cent of Paribas

Turning to Albert Frère, in addition to other stakes, it

(i) owns 7.6 per cent of SGB
(j) owns 2.2 per cent of UAP
(k) and UAP owns 1.4 per cent of Elf, and so the web of interconnection goes on.

Understanding these relationships can be a critical component of assessing value in the French stock market.

Fixed Income Market

At the end of 1994, public sector debt outstanding in France stood at Ffr 2,479.6 billion and borrowing by the state was expected to increase that by more than 10 per cent per annum. Government debt in France has been greatly simplified since 1980 and Treasury issues now fall into three categories.

OATs 5-30 years
(Obligations Assimilables du Trésor – a small series of Treasury issues to which fully fungible bonds can later be added).

BTANs 2-5 years
(Bons du Trésor à Taux Fixe et à Intérêt Annuel – short dated bonds with annual coupons).

BTFs 1 year or less
(Bons du Trésor à Taux Fixe et à Intérêt Précompté – short dated fixed rate Treasury bills issued at a discount and redeemable at par).

The trend towards fungible tap stock issues began in 1986 and has created a pool of large (Ffr 50-100 billion) and highly liquid issues, which has served to attract foreign as well as domestic investment funds. Transparency, achieved through the introduction of open competitive tenders for all but a small proportion of state funding, has also served to increase liquidity and attract investors.

Retail demand accounts for more than 10 per cent of sales of government debt through the network of domestic bank branches. Application procedures were greatly simplified in 1993 and this route was most gainfully employed in the launch of the Balladur bonds. ♒

GERMANY

Professor Dr. Norbert Walter

*Norbert Walter is the Managing Director of **Deutsche Bank Research**, **Deutsche Bank's** think tank, covering a wide spectrum of issues ranging from country rating to company analysis. During his years at the renowned **Kiel Institute for World Economics**, where he became Professor and Director, he was a consultant for German economic policy makers. He is a regular commentator in printed and electronic media at home and abroad. His determined market-economy orientation is best reflected in his books,* What Would Erhard do Today, More Market – Less Intervention *and* On the New Wealth of the Nation.

Reunified Germany

The early 1990s mark a historical break in Germany's economic development. After decades of central planning in the GDR they brought a fundamental change of the entire economic system as well as the reintegration of the new federal states into the world economy. For the old Länder it meant an extreme endurance test for society's established institutions. This test has not yet been passed. Over the short term, the fall of the Iron Curtain gave rise to a deep transformation crisis for the old East German economy, and with the unification boom and the following recession the former West Germany experienced an economic roller-coaster. It must be expected, however, that the consequences of unification will not be restricted to short-term adjustment shocks but will imply that after the transitional phase existing structures will be changed considerably in both the new and the old federal states.

The concept for German reunification was the integration of the new federal states into the west German economic system as quickly and comprehensively as possible without fundamental reform to the western system itself. This concept allowed high speed from the start. No new institutions, systems, regulation had to be discussed, decided and implemented: The privatization of formerly state-owned enterprises has been by and large completed, gaps in the infrastructure are increasingly being closed, the western legal system and regulatory framework has been established in eastern Germany, regional and sectoral economic support measures and labour market policies only differ in terms of quantity but not quality from those pursued in western Germany. Industry associations and trade unions are striving to install west Germany's system of collectively negotiated wages in the east. Given the immense pressure to take immediate action at the time of German unification, there were few realistic alternatives to the way things were handled in many areas even though some mistakes, e.g. as regards property rights (restitution instead of compensation) and wage policy (fast adjustment of east German wages to west German levels), could surely have been avoided.

West Germany's banking sector pioneering the new federal states

Among the structural issues that have been dealt with head on is the East German banking system. Laying the foundation for a modern financial system is an important building bloc for a thriving market economy. Without stable money and a credible financial system savings are not attracted and investments cannot be properly financed.

Only a good four years after reunification it can be said that private banking has lived up to this task. Before 1990 investment by east German enterprises was financed through the GDR's state bank at their discretion. A western-style, fully-fledged banking system did not exist. Credit was granted not based on profitability and efficiency but rather according to plan, i.e. political and ideological goals. As deposits, interest rates and clearing procedures were standardized and laid down centrally, the required technical infrastructure was either non-existing or unsuitable for a system based on market principles. When the DEM was introduced to East Germany in the middle of 1990 this meant complete reconstruction of the country's financial system.

Even before German-German Monetary, Economic and Social Union took effect on 1 July 1990, numerous west German banks opened up representative offices in the former GDR and thus created the preconditions for the establishment of a comprehensive branch network. With great determination, investment capital of several billions, and a temporary transfer of more than 5,000 West German managers, a modern and well-functioning two-tier banking system was established over a short period. Shortly after the middle of 1990 private banks in East Germany were able to provide the same complete coverage of banking products as in the west.

The establishment, modernization and equipment of the large number of branches required billions of invested capital. By the end of 1994 just under DEM 6 billion were spent on the purchase of real estate and branch equipment, especially state-of-the-art technology. This is an extraordinarily high amount for a personnel-intensive sector like banking. Today, technical standards in East German banks outstrip those in West Germany. It is not only the enormous amount of fixed investment, however, that is remarkable. Mention must also be made of the transfer of know-how. To give an idea of the magnitude of the effort it should be mentioned that Deutsche Bank opened some 380 branches in the new *Länder* (compared to 1,500 in West Germany). Between 1990 and 1994 more than 700 East German staff received training in West Germany.

The German Stock Market

Market Structure

The stock market still plays a less significant role in the economy than in other countries. Only 666 listed companies exist. Market capitalization at the end of 1994 totalled DEM 774 billion, or 23 per cent of GDP, not only far below the level in the US or Japan, but even below ratios in some developing countries.

This arises from a number of structural factors. The first is the highly developed system of public pensions. The state pension insurance scheme runs on a pay-as-you-go basis, with the result that there is no capital accumulation. A second reason is the tax system. In Germany, like in many other countries, debt financing is more advantageous, tax-wise, than equity funding. Interest on loans and bonds reduces taxable profit for the assessment of corporate tax. A third complex of problems concerns the backlog in deregulation and innovation. Until the 1980s, the German capital market was relatively strictly regulated, and many well-established financing methods regularly employed abroad, were not permitted. Only since the mid-1980s have the authorities been pursuing a policy of step-by-step deregulation (authorization of floating rate notes, zero bonds, and ECU bonds, for example).

Until the 1980s, the German capital market was relatively strictly regulated, and many well-established financing methods regularly employed abroad, were not permitted.

Currently, securities trading in Germany is still decentralized. German stocks and bonds are traded on eight different regional exchanges but the Frankfurt Stock Exchange leads with roughly 70 per cent of trading volume. For reasons of efficiency there are long-term plans to bring together the regional stock exchanges in Frankfurt. Abolishing floor trading is also being considered.

The main indicator for the German equity market is the DAX, the 30 stocks best fulfilling the criteria of trading volume, market capitalization and early opening prices. The DAX is automatically adjusted for ex-dividend mark-downs, changes in the capital structure and other price changes not caused by

Chart 3.6 The DAX Performance Index from Dec 1980 to 20 May 1995

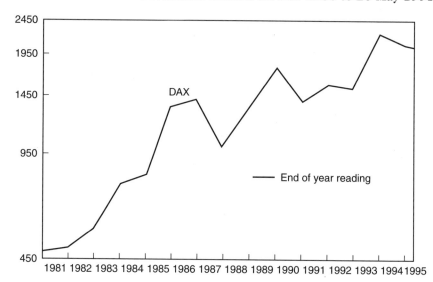

Source: Deutsche Bank Research

the market. It is not only regarded as a yardstick for performance but also as the basis for options and futures traded on the DTB (Deutsche Terminbörse).

The performance of the DAX in the period from December 1980 to 20 May 1995 is shown in Chart 3.6. The index design takes into account the importance of the DAX companies. Chart 3.7 contains the list of the seven largest DAX stocks whose respective weighting factors each exceeds 5 per cent. These are all well-known international companies.

Chart 3.7 Seven largest DAX stocks

Name	Capital 1994 (DEM million)	DAX weighting in %
Allianz	1,040.0	11.22
Daimler-Benz	2,562.6	9.32
Siemens	2,753.5	8.26
Deutsche Bank	2,381.2	7.40
VEBA	2,430.0	5.89
Bayer	3,416.9	5.54
RWE	2,650.8	5.47

Chart 3.8 reflects the shares of the various sectors as of May 1995 with financial services, chemical/pharmaceutical, and automobiles making up over 50 per cent of the total.

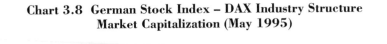

Chart 3.8 German Stock Index – DAX Industry Structure Market Capitalization (May 1995)

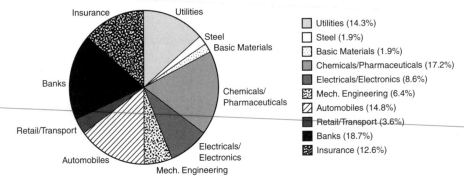

Source: Deutsche Bank Research

Market Perspectives

The German equity market stands to benefit in the coming years from the Second Financial Markets Promotion Act and the privatization of Deutsche Telekom.

The Second Financial Markets Promotion Act contains a whole raft of provisions that will win greater recognition for the German market. These include insider rules, compulsory publication of news likely to affect share prices, wider disclosure of shareholdings (from 5 per cent) and, reduction of the nominal value of shares to as low as DEM 5 (currently DEM 50). Furthermore, the act paves the way for the takeover code planned from 1995 as well as the possibility of carrying out capital increases at market prices.

The privatization of Deutsche Telekom will have a considerable influence on the DAX. Assuming the company is valued at around DEM 60-80 billion, after privatization the stock will probably have a weighting of around 15 per cent. The DAX will also become less volatile since Telekom will reduce the compound weighting of the heavily represented cyclicals.

The Power of the Banks

There is a growing public perception that banks have (too much) power and that they abuse this power. However, opinions held about banks frequently do not reflect the facts. The influence that banks exert through their shareholdings and representation on supervisory boards as well as the significance of their proxy votes at annual meetings have been greatly overestimated. The size of the banks' shareholdings, pegged at 0.5 per cent by the German Bank Association in its latest survey, (October 1993) stood at 1.3 per cent in 1976, which means the banks have been reducing their holdings considerably. The banks were prepared to make even broader and faster reductions were not tax considerations standing in the way. Capital gains, are, according to current law, subject to taxation as earnings even when they are immediately reinvested in new shares. As a result any large divestiture could lead to serious financial losses.

The acquisition of some new holdings will continue to be necessary, especially in companies in need of capital reorganization. Banks have been repeatedly asked by various companies to step in as 'crisis managers'. Similarly, banks are also pressured by public opinion to take a stake in failing companies in order to maintain jobs.

There are also misconceptions about the market shares held by individual banks in Germany. The three large private banks have a total market share of a little over 9 per cent (measured by business volume). If one adds their holdings in other financial institutions (such as their subsidiary mortgage banks) the figure rises to 13 per cent. This is a very low level of concentration by European standards.

Chart 3.9 Degree of concentration of selected bank markets at end of 1993

	Market share* 3 largest institutes	in % of the 5 largest institutes
Germany	13	20
France	25	36
Spain	26	38
Italy	23	37
Great Britain	21	30
Netherlands	59	69
Switzerland	46	51
* in relation to domestic business		

Source: Deutsche Bank Research calculations

The German Bond Market

Market Structure

Currently the volume of bonds outstanding in the DEM market (excluding Schuldscheine – non negotiable borrower's notes – but including DEM Eurobonds) is DEM 2.8 billion. This puts the German bond market third in the world, and first in Europe. From 1989, the year when the Berlin Wall came down - to 1994 the total volume of DEM bonds outstanding has nearly doubled. This is primarily due to the sharply increased financing needs of public authorities in the context of reunification.

Market Sectors

The domestic bond market can be grouped into public authorities, banks, and corporates. The corporate bond market is nearly non-existent, with only three issues currently outstanding. Only high-quality issues like public sector bonds and bank bonds are traded in the domestic market. This is also reflected by the fact that not one domestic bond has been declared non-performing in Germany's postwar history.

Bank bonds can be divided into four: Kommunalobligationen (municipal bonds), Pfandbriefe (mortgage bonds), issues of special credit institutions and other bank bonds. The first three categories should be regarded as comparable to AAA issues because they are either secured by a first-class pool of assets and additionally by the issuing bank's assets or are government-guaranteed (special credit institutions). The other bank bonds are only secured by the issuing banks' assets.

DEM Eurobonds (DEM-denominated bonds issued by foreign borrowers) are another group of growing importance. This segment has grown considerably since several liberalization steps of the Bundesbank. Recent credit ratings play a more important role in this market which is predominantly composed of sovereign and supranational issuers.

Most public sector bonds are straight bullet. New issuance is concentrated in the long-term (10-year) and the medium-term (4-5 year) segment, which provide the underlying paper for the Bund and Bobl futures contracts. In the bank sector straight bullet bonds dominate but registered bonds are also common, meeting the needs of institutional investors (unrealized losses on registered bonds do not have to be shown). Bank bonds are predominantly in book-entry form while only a minor part is physically deliverable. The range of products in the DEM Euromarket is highly diverse ranging from straight bullet bonds over floaters to all other types of structured bonds. DEM Eurobonds are usually physically deliverable. Due to less lengthy and less costly issuing procedures on the highly deregulated Euromarket, corporate issuers prefer it to the domestic market.

Chart 3.10 tracks changes over the last 15 years in two key rates which can influence interest movements acros the whole bond market.

Despite their outstanding importance to international investors, public sector bonds make up only 46 per cent of the market, as compared to 54 per cent for bank bonds. However, the share of the public sector has been rising. The percentage of Deutschmark Eurobonds in the overall Deutschmark market has remained relatively constant at 11 per cent.

Chart 3.10 Key rates in Germany

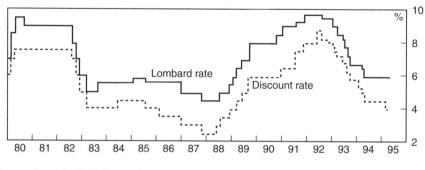

Source: Deutsche Bank Research

Investors

The domestic banking sector is not only the most prominent borrower but also an important investor in the German bond market. At the end of 1993 banks held 36 per cent of all domestic bonds outstanding. Domestic non-banks are another important group of investors. At the end of 1993 private individuals held an 11 per cent of share of domestic bearer bonds. The combined share of insurance companies and investment funds accounted for another 14 per cent. Foreign investors play an increasingly important role. At the end of 1993 foreigners held as much as 28 per cent of all domestic bonds outstanding. Since 1991 foreign purchases of German bonds have increased markedly climbing to reach 58 per cent in 1993. Since the beginning of 1994 foreigners have been net sellers.

Market Perspectives

The growth of the German bond market looks set to continue. The overwhelming importance of currency performance for international bond transactions at times of rising market volatility will further increase the interest of issuers and investors in Deutschmark bonds. The German government bond market has all the attributes of a highly mature and efficient market, with derivative instruments available in all segments. The one major shortfall, the lack of a liquid market for short-term government paper, will probably persist as the Bundesbank shows no signs of changing its stance regarding 'short-termism' in government financing. However, the widely discussed introduction of a Pfandbrief futures contract would help vitalize the mostly domestic Pfandbrief sector. ♀

IBERIA

Brian Williams

*Brian Williams is the Research Director for **Lloyds Investment Managers Ltd.** He started with **Bank of London** and **South America** as an analyst and subsequently became Research Manager of **Lloyds Bank International**. Following the integration of LBI investment operations, he was appointed Research Manager for the combined group. He retains responsibility for international research and investment strategy.*

***Lloyds Investment Managers Ltd**, a wholly owned subsidiary of **Lloyds Bank plc**, is one of the largest institutional fund managers in the UK, with over £10 billion under management. The business focus is on the management of assets for domestic pension funds, unit trusts, investment trusts, country funds, international property, fixed interest and treasury portfolios. LIM manages the First Spanish Investment Trust and the Portugal Property Fund, and are advisors to the Portugal Fund.*

In several senses, both Spain and Portugal are economies in transition. With populations of 39 million and 10 million respectively and having GDP per capita well below the average of the EU, both countries are emerging from the shelter of high regulation and government influence, and are laying the foundations to meet the challenges of an increasingly open and broadening European Union. Indeed, membership of the EU (since 1986 in both cases) has been the spur for change. Deregulation, reform and privatization are key components in the drive to achieve economic convergence with other EU economies and ultimately, by reaching the Maastricht thresholds, to be founder members of the Economic and Monetary Union (EMU). Despite the renewed ERM turmoil in early 1995, and the probability that full EMU is unlikely in the foreseeable future, the political resolve is likely to remain intact. Having pinned their colours to the EU mast, neither country finds it acceptable to be in the slow lane of a multi-speed Europe.

Spain

After eleven years of economic growth (1982–92), averaging 3 per cent per annum, the Spanish economy dipped into recession in 1992–3, with GDP falling by 1.6 per cent from economic peak to trough. The subsequent recovery was led by exports initially, not least because the peseta suffered a series of devaluations as the Exchange Rate Mechanism fell into disrepute and disrepair. However, by 1994 there were signs that economic growth was becoming more broadly based and hopes of sustained growth improved markedly.

Chart 3.11 Spain – GDP past growth and future forecast

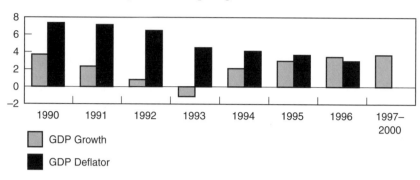

GDP Growth

GDP Deflator

Source: OECD

The OECD forecasts that GDP growth will be 3.0 per cent and 3.2 per cent in 1995 and 1996 respectively, and has a medium-term forecast of average growth of 3.4 per cent through the year 2000. This pace of economic activity would be above that expected for the EU as a whole and illustrates the potential attractions of Spain as an investment area. However, it is important to survey some of the factors that will influence the future and will determine whether hopes are turned into reality:

1 The closer link with the EU that is the policy of both the government and the main opposition parties is already being seen in the growing proportion of trade with EU member countries, up from 58 per cent in 1987 to some 65 per cent now. Aided by the competitive level of the peseta after its devaluations and by the maturing of the Single Market, it would not be surprising to see over 70 per cent of Spanish trade, and perhaps even 75 per cent, being with the EU by the early years of the next decade.

2 There is a need to make sure that the peseta's advantage is not eroded away by a rise in inflation. In this respect the newly acquired independence of the Bank of Spain should provide a bolster against the vagaries of party politics. The Bank of Spain has set a long-term inflation target of 3 per cent, which it hopes to attain by 1997. Flexing its muscles, the Bank has already criticized the government's fiscal policy and in January 1995 raised official interest rates. Subsequently, facing renewed peseta pressure, the government opted for further devaluation rather than yet higher interest rates, but ended up getting both! Then, in June, responding to disappointing inflation data, the Bank of Spain pushed interest rates higher again. The next year or so is expected to test the resolve of the monetary authorities as cyclical pressures and the legacy of a weak peseta threaten to push inflation higher.

3 A continuing process of deregulation, reform, privatization and infrastructural improvement is expected to contribute to maintaining, if not enhancing Spain's competitive position. A major challenge is the emergence of low wage cost economies in the east of Europe, but there is a series of recent and prospective moves to assist in countering this threat:

356

(a) Labour market reform in 1994 made some significant revisions to the Workers Statute. These revisions, *inter alia*, provided for an easier dismissal process, increased geographical mobility of employees, greater functional mobility, flexibility of working hours and more emphasis on local collective bargaining.
(b) The process of overhauling Spain's archaic property rental laws is underway, although change is not expected to be quick.
(c) The government has been engaged in the process of totally or partially selling off state-owned companies. Privatization is expected to be a continuing theme.
(d) There will be growing involvement by the private sector in areas previously dominated by the government, such as infrastructure, health care and pensions. Private sector mobile phone operators can already challenge Telefonica, with the latter body losing its monopoly of basic telephone services in 1998.

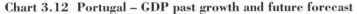

Portugal

After a fairly shallow recession in 1993 (-1.1 per cent), Portugal is now set on a recovery path. The OECD estimates 1994 GDP growth to have been 2.0 per cent and forecasts 1995 and 1996 growth to be 2.9 per cent and 3.2 per cent respectively. In its initial stages economic recovery was dominated by exports and that is expected to continue to be a key element of growth although, as the business cycle matures, a recovery in fixed investment and, to a lesser extent, personal consumption, should be evident. Fixed investment, including construction, should be a prime beneficiary of major foreign investment (Portuguese wage costs are much lower than those of Spain) and of EU transfers that are planned to be almost double the level of the previous six-year period. The OECD forecasts medium-term GDP growth of 3.0 per cent for 1997 through to 2000.

Chart 3.12 Portugal – GDP past growth and future forecast

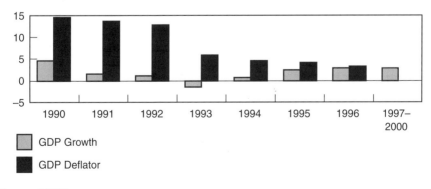

Source: OECD

357

Portugal's commitment to the principles of EMU has resulted in measures to improve the budget deficit and inflation. The former has benefited recently from better tax receipts and a lower interest cost (due to lower rates), whereas the latter has recently fallen to a 25-year low. There are attempts to reduce the burden of regulation and direct government influence in the economy, with the privatization programme being a key element of those policies. The weight of state enterprises in the economy fell from 21 per cent of GDP in 1988 to 14 per cent in 1993, even with privatization plans behind schedule.

Politics

Both Spain and Portugal have had a turbulent past, but recent years have seen democracy firmly established. Felipe Gonzalez' PSOE party has been in power in Spain since 1982 but, faced with the prospect of withdrawal of minority party support (specifically the CiU, the Catalan regional party) and a succession of scandals, may not survive until the next scheduled general election in 1997. Recent municipal and regional elections on 28 May 1995 highlight the problems facing the Socialists, the Popular Party overtaking them in share of the vote, and municipal elections in Catalonia saw the CiU lose support. The opposition hopes to wrest power from the Socialists and may not have to wait its opportunity for much longer if the Catalans consider there is more to be gained from separation from the Government.

In Portugal, elections are much closer – parliamentary in October 1995 and presidential in January 1996. Prime Minister Cavaco Silva has said that he will not stand again in his current role, perhaps setting the scene for a presidential bid next year.

Financial Markets

Investment in Spain and Portugal has provided a roller-coaster ride. In the five years to the end of 1994 the equity markets fell by a net 2.6 per cent and 11.8 per cent respectively in local currency terms, with both markets weakening erratically through to late 1992, rallying into early 1994 and then suffering renewed weakness. A combination of recession and currency uncertainty took its toll.

The bond markets have also shown pronounced volatility, particularly around periods of currency uncertainty. This volatility has also found expression in changing yield differentials with the 'benchmark' for Europe, German government bonds. It is worth noting, however, that, despite variation in yield relationships, Portugal's premium over Deutsche Mark bonds has fallen from over 10 per cent in 1991 to circa 4 per cent now, while Spain's premium, although much higher than in early 1994, has yet to reach 1992 levels. With both countries showing sizeable budget deficits, albeit with some reductions in fiscal imbalances compared with the past, debt issuance is a continuing problem.

With non-resident investors' appetite constrained by the currency factor, it is not surprising that resident investors have been increasingly important contributors to the bond markets in recent years. In Spain, for instance, residents currently hold some 87 per cent of debt, up from 72 per cent in 1993. Most newly issued debt is fixed rate, with annual coupons, although Portugal announced the reintroduction of floating rate debt in late 1994.

As the table below illustrates, both stock markets are dominated by financial and utility companies, a situation not unusual for countries moving from an environment where regulation and government involvement have been high. Progressive deregulation and privatization should see greater industrial diversification of the indices in years to come.

Stock Market Breakdown by Sector per cent*

Spain (FT World Spain Index)		Portugal (BVL Index)	
Banks	32.9	Banks	49.9
Insurance	1.1	Real Estate & Other Financial	11.5
Real Estate	1.4	Telecommunications	4.8
Oil	12.3	Consumer Goods & Services	18.6
Utilities	27.8	Construction	5.1
Telecommunications	11.8	Paper & Packaging	7.4
Consumer Goods	2.5	Steel & Engineering	2.5
Construction	3.8	Other	0.2
Basic Materials	2.1		
Other	4.3	* End April 1995	

Both countries have moved to improve the efficiency of their stock markets. For instance, Spain introduced a new computerized and centralized settlement and registration system in 1992. This is essential, not only to increase the appeal of Spain and Portugal to international investors, but also to assist the developing domestic funds management industry.

Funds under management are growing much faster than nominal GDP. In Spain, the mutual fund industry has grown from 1.2 trillion pesetas in assets at the end of 1990 to 11.0 trillion in March 1995. This nine-fold increase compares with a stock market that rose by 20.4 per cent over the same period. The pension fund sector is much less developed, valued at only 1.55 trillion pesetas at the end of March 1995, but is also growing rapidly. Asset values are 21 per cent up on the year and membership is up 16.5 per cent. Not surprisingly, there has been a demand for a wider range of investment vehicles which, *inter alia*, has seen the rapid development and use of derivatives in Spain, with Portugal following suit this year.

Key financial indicators for both countries are contained in the following table:

Financial Market Data

	1990	1991	1992	1993	1994
Spain					
Equity Market (per cent Change on year)	–24.9	+12.8	–11.7	+49.1	–12.8
End Year PER	8.3	9.1	9.0	14.7	12.3
End Year Div. Yield	5.0	4.7	5.4	3.4	4.0
End Year Govt. Bond Yield	14.8	11.9	13.0	7.9	11.6
Portugal					
Equity Market (per cent Change on Year)	–35.1	–7.7	–17.2	+59.6	+11.5
End Year PER	17.2	22.3	14.2	22.3	15.6
End Year Div. Yield	2.9	4.0	5.3	3.0	4.0
Currency					
Peseta/DM (End Year)	63.7	63.7	70.5	82.3	84.9
Escudo/DM (End Year)	88.5	88.5	90.6	101.8	102.7

Source: Datastream

Equity market valuation in both Spain and Portugal is broadly similar to the European Union average, based on price earnings ratios and dividend yields. The Portuguese price earnings ratio has lost its emerging markets premium, Portugal being increasingly viewed as an industrial economy within Europe, while the Spanish price earnings ratio is slightly above its five-year average,

Chart 3.13 PER relative to the Average for the European Union

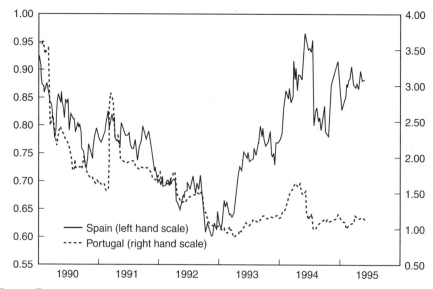

Source: Datastream

Chart 3.14 Dividend Yield Relative to the European Union Average

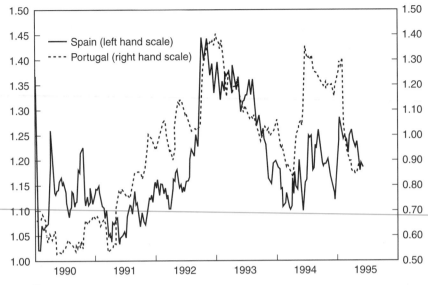

Source: Datastream

reflecting progress in deregulation and institutional change that has seen greater acceptance of the country by international investors. ♀

The information and data in this report are from sources we consider to be reliable but are furnished without responsibility on our part. Any views expressed are those of the author and are not necessarily those of the Lloyds Bank Group. Lloyds Investment Managers is regulated by IMRO.

ITALY

Giovanni Grimaldi

*Giovanni Grimaldi entered the fund management business in 1985, at the inception of the industry in Italy, responsible for the international investment department at **PRIME**. He currently manages approximately US$ 1 billion for three main funds. He is also Managing Director of a joint venture launched in 1988 between **PRIME** and **Merrill Lynch Asset Management** of the US.*

*   **PRIME**, one of the leading money management firms in Italy with about US$ 5 billion in assets, offers a wide range of mutual funds and life insurance products. **PRIME** is owned 95 per cent by **FIDIS** (the **FIAT** sub-holding for financial services) and 5 per cent by **Sumitomo Life Insurance** of Japan.

About Equities

The Italian market is very small compared to its economy, which is the fifth largest in the world. In fact, the equity market capitalization relative to Italian GDP is only 18.6 per cent. As of 15 February 1995, there were less than 200 companies listed on the Milan stock exchange with a market capitalization of US$192 billion.

Table 3.3 Profile of the Italian Equity Market

Year	Companies listed	Market cap (billion lire)	Annual Volume Traded	Comit Index (1972=100)
1987	205	140.7	41.6	488
1988	211	175.8	41.3	590
1989	220	220.9	53.2	688
1990	223	176.1	50.6	515
1991	225	179.5	31.0	508
1992	228	154.6	33.1	446
1993	216	246.5	103.9	619
1994	205	267.8	186.4	583
1995	196	310.2	25.3	673

Source: Banca Fideuram

The main reasons for the underdevelopment of the Italian equity market are both cultural and structural. Most Italian businesses are family-owned and very often the owners are also the founders of the companies. As such, they are very reluctant to share control with and be accountable to others. In addition, until recently, Italy has been lacking the institutional investors which have helped the development of the most advanced equity markets. There is only one kind of institutional investor in Italy: the mutual funds industry which started as recently as the second half of 1984. Total assets managed by the 354 mutual funds stood at 130 billion lire (about $80 billion) at the end of 1994, of which a mere 21 billion lire (about $13 billion) are invested in Italian equities. The pension funds industry has not taken off yet for a number of reasons, paramount is the very unfavourable tax treatment. Life insurance schemes tend to be invested almost entirely in fixed income securi-

The main reasons for the underdevelopment of the Italian equity market are both cultural and structural. Most Italian businesses are family-owned

ties. Therefore, the main actors on the Italian equity market are currently limited to: individuals, mutual funds / private asset management schemes and foreign investors.

Perhaps the biggest impediment to the development of the Italian equity market has been the competition coming from the Italian debt market, which is the third largest in the world and which has afforded over the years a 'risk-free' rate often in excess of 10 per cent.

Another historical factor limiting the appeal of the Italian stock market – at least to the more conservative investors – has been the considerable level of risk associated with it. Chart 3.15 covers equity performance over the most recent 20-year period. The Comit Index (a proxy for the Italian market) has outperformed both the German FAZ and the US S&P 500. However, most of the overall performance was due to three years: 1980, 1985, 1993. Put another way, the average volatility of the Comit Index over the last 20 years has been equal to 25 per cent, which is much higher than the 15 per cent experienced by the S&P 500 and the 17 per cent of the German FAZ. This means that relative to the US, market timing in Italy is much more important to overall performance than stock selection.

However, in spite of this note of caution, a number of interesting developments are taking place which will make the Italian equity market more attractive, more liquid and less risky in the future.

Chart 3.15 Comit, S&P 500 and FAZ indexes (log scale)

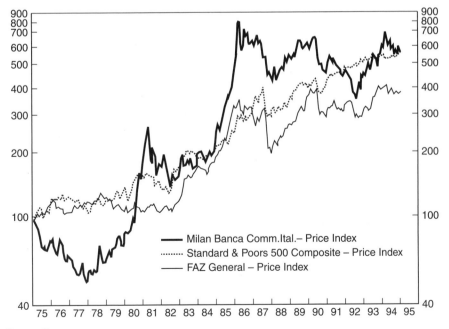

Source: Datastream

Italy is experiencing its big bang. The traditional individual broker (*agente di cambio*) has been replaced by companies, called SIM, which are much stronger financially: and are also under closer scrutiny by both the CONSOB (the Italian SEC) and by the Italian Central Bank. The old stock exchange where prices were formed once a day with the outcry system in a physical location has been replaced by a computerized network similar to the British SEAQ, allowing continuous dealing. The traditional monthly accounting period is going to be replaced by a cash settlement system during 1995.

The process of privatization of state-owned companies which started on a significant scale in 1994 is set to continue for several years. This is going to provide major benefits: it will foster a better management of those enterprises, it will help reduce the budget deficit and it will also broaden the stock market. Commercial banks have become universal banks (as in the German system) and can now take stakes in industrial companies.

Even more importantly, the government has finally decided to remove the penalizing tax treatment for the private pensions funds thus allowing them to become in a few years a significant market player with important stabilization effects.

Key Sectors

In Italy there are three types of shares listed: ordinary shares, preference shares (limited voting right in exchange for more protection in case of bankruptcy), and savings shares (no voting right in exchange for protection in case of bankruptcy plus higher dividend relative to the ordinaries). Both the preference shares and the savings shares trade at discounts to their ordinaries which can vary between 10 per cent and 60 per cent.

The Italian equity market is very highly concentrated. The 10 largest stocks account for over 50 per cent of the total capitalization. The structure of the market is contained in Table 3.4.

Table 3.4 The Italian Equity Market: Sector Weights and Multiples

Sector	Neutral Weight (as of March 1995)		1994	1995
Industrials	29%	P/E	24.2	18.6
Insurance	24%	P/CE	3.7	3.3
Telecommunications	19%	P/BV	1.3	1.2
Banks	16%	Div Yield %	2.3	2.6
Financials	9%	EPS growth %	48.6	41.7
Utilities (non phone)	3%			

There are four main sectors:

(a) **Industrial** is based on the four large traditional blue chips: Fiat, Montedison, Pirelli, and Olivetti. We favour the first two because they hold a significant market share at European or world level in a number of business segments. However, all four companies have undergone dramatic restructuring and streamlining in recent years. In addition, they should benefit greatly from the severe devaluation of the Italian lira.

(b) **Insurance** is dominated by Generali, a world-class public company, which derives about 50 per cent of its premiums internationally, and which has always sold at a premium relative to the sector.

(c) **Telecommunications** is principally made up of Telecom Italia (the service provider) and STET, its holding company, with manufacturing and international activities. At current prices they are both attractive, especially in light of two additional benefits: the spin-off of cellular phones by Telecom and the privatization of STET (both to take place in 1995).

(d) **Banking**, in 1994, suffered one of the worst years in recent memory. Mergers and acquisitions have made San Paolo and Banco di Roma the two largest listed banks. However, the greatest appreciation potential may come from some regional banks that may be subject to takeover (as has happened to Credito Romagnolo).

The two main utilities are Italgas and Edison, which offer good and growing cash flow and represent solid long-term holdings.

Among medium-size companies we currently find attractive Burgo in the paper sector and La Rinascente in the distribution sector.

About the Fixed Income Market

The Italian fixed income market is composed almost exclusively of government (and government-backed) securities. The corporate sector is practically non-existent. The size of the market is quite large because the Italian government debt at the end of 1994 had reached about 122 per cent of the GDP. Total debt outstanding amounts to 1.7 trillion lire (about $1 billion).

However, it should be noted that, unlike many other countries, Italy – because of its very high savings rate (about 20 per cent) – is able to finance domestically, without the need for foreign capital.

There are currently four main types of government securities:

1 BOT, Italian treasuries with short-term maturities of 3, 6, and 12 months

2 BTP, fixed rate government bonds with maturities of 3, 5, 10, 30 years

3 CCT, floating-rate government bonds with maturities of 5, 7, 10 years

4 CTE, government bonds linked to the ECU, with 5-year maturity.

The size of each type and segment is shown in Table 3.5. There is a 12.5 per cent withholding tax on all government securities levied on both the coupon and the difference between the issuing price and the redemption price. Foreign holders are allowed to claim back such amounts.

Table 3.5 Structure of Fixed Income Market (as of February 1995)
(figures in billion lire)

Maturing in	BOT	BTP	CCT	CTE	Other	TOTAL
up to 1 year	415.5	12.0	146.5	12.0	6.0	592.0
1-3 years	=	207.0	112.0	13.3	42.7	375.0
3-5 years	=	161.0	170.0	28.3	14.5	373.8
5-10 years	=	157.0	134.0	=	=	291.0
more than 10 years	=	26.6	=	=	=	26.6
TOTAL	415.5	563.6	562.5	53.6	63.2	1,658.4

Chart 3.16 Key Italian Interest Rates (1985–95)

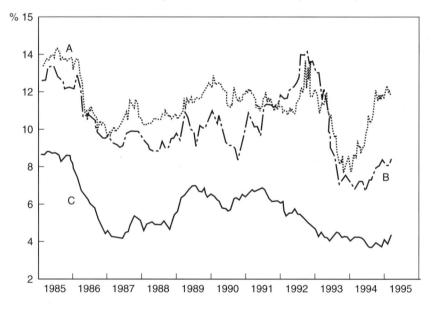

A Italy bond yield govt. long term – middle rate
B Italy three month Treasury bill rate (end period)
C Italy Consumer Price Index (fam. of w'kers & off. emp) ann. inflation
   High 14.32–29/7/85, Low 7.67–11/10/93, Last 11.82–20/2/95
   High 14.10–30/9/92, Low 6.60–31/5/94, Last 8.46–4/2/95
   High 8.78–15/5/85, Low 3.63–15/7/94, Last 4.30–15/2/95

Source: Datastream

As of March 1995, Italian Treasuries yield (gross) around 10 per cent, and 10-year bonds yield around 12 per cent. Chart 3.16 contains historical rates for comparison. In the context of a 4.0 per cent inflation rate, the real gross yields of approximately 6 per cent at the short end and over 8 per cent at the long end appear attractive.

The spread between the Italian long bond and the German bund in the last five years has been moving in a wide range (170 to 600 basis points) depending on the differential in the perceived political and financial risk in the two countries. Due to deep political and social changes taking place in Italy, the 1995 spread is close to the top of the range. Given the scenario of inflation under control, progress in attacking the deficit and a currency which has already devalued well in excess of 40 per cent versus the Deutsche Mark since 1992, such a premium provides an interesting opportunity. ◗

SCANDINAVIA

Stefan Dahlbo and Raana Farooqi-Lind

Hagströmer & Qviberg and its subsidiaries provide financial services mainly on the Swedish stock market. Hagströmer & Qviberg Fondkommission AB is one of the leading independent brokerage firms and a market maker in Sweden. Operations include trading in shares and options, asset management, corporate finance, individual retirement savings and premium bonds. The group includes United Securities, specializing in the fixed income market, and two fund management companies.

Stefan Dahlbo is the Managing Director of Hagströmer & Qviberg. Previously he was at Alfred Berg, where he set up the international equity department.

Raana Farooqi-Lind works within institutional sales at Hagströmer & Qviberg Fondkommission. She was previously employed by Morgan Stanley & Co Inc, New York.

Stock Markets

The Nordic markets offer broad international exposure due to the global nature of the larger quoted companies. These exchanges have experienced spectacular performance and increases in liquidity and efficiency during the last two years. This as well as removal of restrictions on foreign ownership and tax reductions in the early 1990s, has generated increased investment. Compared to the rest of Europe, Nordic P/E ratios in early 1995 are low, with Denmark being the most expensive, but still low compared to the core markets of Germany and France. Corporate profitability is high and peak earnings for a number of early cyclicals are expected in 1996, while the business cycle is expected to continue in high gear until 1998.

Economic recovery in Sweden and Finland is being driven by the export sector. Both countries can be classified as classic two-tiered economies with a booming export sector and lagging domestic sector. This has not changed since the currencies of both countries were devalued in 1992. Sweden's greatest challenge is coming to grips with its ballooning national debt, concern for which resulted in Moody's downgrading of Sweden's long-term debt rating, while Finland must deal with one of the highest unemployment rates in Western Europe. Unemployment has started to decline, however about one-third of this unemployment is structural. In both countries, real disposable income of households is expected to continue to fall in the future and household consumption to rise only slowly. The boom in the export sector is expected to continue as demand recovers in the EU countries as well as the newer Asia-Pacific markets.

Norway, thanks to its strong oil and gas sector, did not go through a similar recession. The economy is dependent on oil revenues, and thus future oil prices, although the mainland economic development should soon be the focus of government policy. Norway, unlike Sweden and Finland chose not to join the EU which, thanks to its strong economic recovery, is not expected to have negative economic results. Consumer demand and confidence is increasing as are consumer imports. This is in contrast to Sweden and Finland, where the rise in imports has been for manufacturing inputs.

Denmark is also experiencing growth, led by the domestic sector, after a period of fiscal loosening aimed at stimulating the economy. Denmark's main challenge is its long-term structural unemployment of approximately 12 per cent.

The Nordic stock exchanges had spectacular performances during 1993, with Helsinki increasing 92 per cent, Oslo increasing 65 per cent, Sweden up by 52 per cent and Denmark rising 40 per cent. The increases in 1994 were lower, given the effect of the turbulent interest rates worldwide. Denmark lost value.

Turnover, efficiency, number of shares and foreign ownership have increased on all exchanges. This has been helped in large part by the liberalization of the exchanges, with restrictions on foreign ownership removed and taxes on turnover abolished. In Sweden and Finland, foreign ownership increased sharply during the last two years, with currency devaluation making stocks on these exchanges attractive. Foreign ownership of the listed securities in Norway and Sweden is approximately 30 per cent, in Finland approximately 20 per cent and in Denmark approximately 11 per cent.

New issue offerings on all exchanges were very high in 1994, due in part to the government privatization programmes, and is expected to continue to be high in the future although not as high as in 1994.

Sweden

The Stockholm stock exchange has seen turnover double over the last two years. It has three listings; the A-List, the OTC-List and the O-List. The General Index is the most quoted and increased in value by 4.6 per cent in 1994. A total of 299 companies are listed. The OMX Index is the options market index and the SX-16 Index (comprised of the most traded shares) is also commonly quoted.

During 1993, the top 28 firms stood for 80 per cent of the turnover, and within the index Astra and Ericsson shares make up nearly a quarter of the total value.

Many of the most actively traded stocks are companies which are world leaders in their product categories. These include: Astra and Pharmacia (Pharmaceuticals), Ericsson (telecommunications), Volvo (automobiles), Asea (engineering), Electrolux (white goods/consumer durables), SKF (engineering/ball bearings), Stora Kopparberg and SCA (forestry products), Trelleborg (mining and industrial products), Atlas Copco (industrial equipment), Sandvik (tools), and AGA (industrial gases). Ericsson (see page ?) and Astra are probably the best known companies.

The economic recovery is expected to continue in the near future as is the profitability of the listed companies. The forestry products companies are expected to outperform during the next two years, especially AssiDomän, given the increases in pulp prices and the company's large forestry assets. Other stock likely to outperform include: Stadshypotek (banking), Synetics (medical instruments), Investor, and Hennes & Mauritz (retail).

Industrial companies comprise 41 per cent of the exchange market capitalization, chemical and pharmaceutical companies 20 per cent, while forest and forestry product companies comprise 8 per cent and bank and insurance companies 7 per cent.

Norway

The Oslo exchange has two listings, Bourse 1 and Bourse 2 (equivalent to the OTC). Turnover and efficiency has increased sharply during the last two years. There were a total of 146 listed companies at the end of 1994. The General Index, which is the most commonly quoted index increased in value by 7.4 per cent during 1994.

Domestic institutional ownership is high. The largest 20 companies accounted for 75 per cent of turnover during 1994. The 15 largest domestic companies based on market value account for approximately 71 per cent of the total market value. A feature which is common for the quoted companies is their strong asset backing.

New issue offerings were at a record high last year and are expected to remain high during the next few years when oil companies are likely to require to raise additional capital. The most actively traded shares include those of: Hafslund Nycomed (pharmaceuticals and hydro power), Norsk Hydro (fertilizers, oil, gas, light metals), Saga Petroleum (oil and gas), Kvaerner (shipbuilding, offshore), Orkla (foods and chemicals), Norsk Skogsindustrier (wood processing), Aker (cement, building materials, offshore), Elkem (ferroalloys, aluminium), Unitor (maritime equipment and services), DNL (aviation), Uni Storebrand (insurance), Vital (insurance), and Wilrig (offshore).

Norsk Hydro is by far the dominant company on the stock exchange. Shipping companies comprise the largest single industry sector, with 15 per cent of the exchange market capitalization and include, among others, Leif Hoegh & Co, Bergesen and Vard. Banks comprise 10 per cent of the market capitalization.

Finland

During 1993, the Helsinki Stock Exchange was one of the best performing exchanges in the world, with the All Share Index increasing by 92 per cent. Turnover, efficiency and liquidity have increased while restrictions on foreign ownership and stamp duties have been abolished. Foreign ownership of listed companies averaged approximately 20 per cent but is concentrated on Nokia, which represents more than 20 per cent of turnover and is owned about 60 per cent by foreigners. This could imply that approximately 45 per cent of all foreign investment is held in one company.

The most important index is Unitas Generalindex, which includes all shares traded on the exchange. Another commonly quoted index is the HEX-20 Index. Due to the smaller number of listed companies, the exchange is very concentrated. The five largest shares represent approximately 40 per cent of the total public listed value. The major market players are institutions, banks and insurance companies, funds and trusts.

The OTC market, which is operated by the brokerage houses, was established in 1985. The third market is called the Mäklaristan. There are two option markets, Finland's Optionsmäklare and Finland's Optionsbörs. The secondary bond market is still not fully developed and does not have a high degree of liquidity.

The most traded stocks include: Huhtamäki (food and pharmaceuticals), Kone (lift and handling equipment), Nokia (telecommunications), Metra (construction), Kansallis-Osake-Pankki (banking), Instrumentarium (health care) and Unitas (banking).

Nokia is probably the best known and is the world's second largest portable phone producer. Forestry companies represent almost 25 per cent of the stock market capitalization and include Kymmene, United Paper Mill, Enso-Gutzeit and Metsä-Serla. Industrial companies represent over 40 per cent of the stock market capitalization and include Masa Yards (ship building), Rauma-Repola (conglomerate), Valmet and Outokumpu (both in metals and engineering).

Denmark

The capital markets in Denmark started to take off in 1983 and during 1988 the share price increase was one of the highest in the world. The bond market in Denmark is and has been much more popular than the stock exchange. The stock exchange has 415 listed companies. The ten largest companies comprise approximately 30 per cent of the value. The commonest index is the KFX Index, compilation of which started in 1989. Another commonly quoted index and an older one, is the Total Index. There are three different listings, Aktiemarknad I, Aktiemarknad II and Aktiemarknad III.

The exchange is one of the most computerized in the world. The major players are insurance companies, mutual funds and pension funds. The most quoted index is the total index. In Denmark the attraction has been the relative strength of the domestic economy.

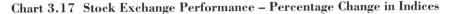

The most traded shares include: Novo Nordisk (bio-technology), Sophus Berendsen (environmental services, engineering), Den Danske Bank, Danisco EM (foods, packaging), Unidanmark (banking), ISS International Service System (cleaning services, catering), Baltica (insurance, banking), D/S Svendborg (shipping), Carlsberg (brewing), FLS Industries (machinery and engineering), Hafslund Nycomed (health and personal care), J Lauritzen (shipbuilding), and Danske Luftfartselskab (aviation).

Novo Nordisk has been the most actively traded company during the last five years. The industry sector represents 32 per cent of the market capitalization on the exchange, while the shipping and banking sectors represented 19 per cent and 13 per cent respectively at the end of 1993.

The Nordic stock markets should continue to present attractive alternatives to the global investor. However, unlike 1993, when the markets as a

Chart 3.17 Stock Exchange Performance – Percentage Change in Indices

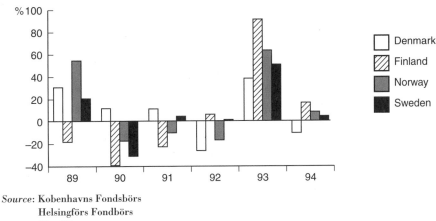

Source: Kobenhavns Fondsbörs
Helsingförs Fondbörs
Olso Börs
Stockholms Fondbörs

whole outperformed, in the future stock selection will be increasingly important. Price performance potential exists for the lesser known shares of the
smaller companies.

Fixed Income Markets

Denmark has been, and is still, the dominant Scandinavian market and activity
is high. (In 1993, the average daily turnover on the equity market amounted to
Dkr 612 million, while that in the bond market was Dkr 44.7 billion.) In
Sweden, the bond market, which is called SOX-market, had a turnover of SEk
29 billion during 1994. In Finland, bond trading is mainly conducted over the
telephone by banks and brokers. In both Finland and Sweden, the largest borrowers on the domestic markets are the governments. In Norway, the turnover
in bonds and certificates during 1993 amounted to NOk 3.6 billion.

The key interest rates in Denmark include the CD Rate, the Repo Rate, and
the Discount Rate. In Finland, the interest rate system comprises long- and
short-term market rates and an administratively regulated base rate, which
plays an indicative role. The Helibor (Helsinki Interbank Offered Rate) is
quoted daily, and Helibor rates are calculated for 1, 3, 6, 9 and 12 months.
The key rates include the Tender Rate and the Discount Rate. The key interest
rates in Norway include the Central Bank Overnight Lending Rate, the two
Week Interbank Rate and the Deposit Rate, while those in Sweden include the
Lending Rate, the Repo Rate (replaced the Marginal Lending Rate on 1 June
1994 and fluctuates between the Lending Rate and the Deposit Rate) and the
Deposit Rate.

Table 3.6 presents some of the benchmark interest rates in Sweden since
1990 as at year end.

Table 3.6 Benchmark Interest Rates in Sweden

	6 month T-bill %	5 year Bonds %	10 year Bonds %
1990	14.43	12.73	12.30
1991	13.11	10.54	10.00
1992	10.14	9.60	9.70
1993	6.77	6.39	7.27
1994	8.46	10.33	10.84

Interest rates in Sweden have been high due to the higher risk premium
attached to lending to the country. Chart 3.18 is a presentation of the benchmark ten year bond over the last ten-years.

Chart 3.18 Swedish Interest Rates (Jan. 1985 – May 1995)

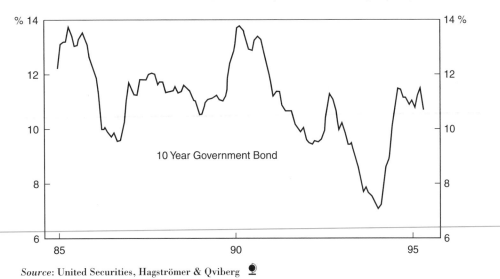

Source: United Securities, Hagströmer & Qviberg

US EQUITIES

Vincent Bajakian

*Vin joined **Wellington Management Company** in 1961 as a security analyst following ten years in New York in the investment department at **American Express** and with two prominent investment banking and brokerage firms. In 1972 he was named portfolio manager of the **Wellington Fund** (now the $10 billion **Vanguard/Wellington Fund**) and later formed the Equity Income Group, which manages $1 billion of corporate and public pension funds.*

Marvel at the investor in US equities. Even as he seeks simplicity in his investment activities, he is faced with more alternatives and more voices vying to serve him than he can hope to comprehend, and a marketplace so liquid that he is free and able to change his mind like a spinning weathervane, if he is so inclined.

For the US equities market is the world's largest, accounting for approximately 40 per cent of the market value of all stocks, even after dramatic growth outside the US. Although down from 70 per cent as recently as 1970, the US share still amounts to a staggering $6 trillion in market capitalization, spread over 8,300 equities trading on three main venues: the New York Stock Exchange, the NASDAQ and the American Stock Exchange. In addition, a few thousand stocks of small companies trade on regional exchanges or 'over-the-counter' through a telephone and computer network connecting dealers.

373

And most of these stocks trade freely. On an average day, some 600 million shares worth an aggregate $16 billion, change hands on the exchanges and over-the-counter, easily ranking Wall Street the most liquid of the globe's markets. This is impressive and on the whole desirable. Whether such a level of liquidity contributes favourably to investment performance is another matter.

On an average day, some 600 million shares worth an aggregate $16 billion, change hands on the exchanges and over-the-counter,

One would think that the ease with which stock ownership is transferred would foster smoother changes in the general level of stock prices, more in line with the undulations in the economy and corporate profits. Not so. Like all financial markets, the stock market in America is volatile. Since 1926, the Standard & Poor's 500 Composite Stock Price Index, a widely used benchmark, has produced annual total returns (price change plus dividend income) ranging from a loss of 43 per cent in the Great Depression year of 1931, to a gain of 54 per cent only two years later. More recently, in a highly unusual display of volatility, the index rose 40 per cent and fell 35 per cent in a single year, 1987. Looked at over a long period of time, 1926 to 1994, the annual return averaged 10.2 per cent, well ahead of the 3.1 per cent rate of inflation over the same span. For the shorter period since the Second World War, results are not much different: an average annual return of 11.9 per cent versus inflation at 4.4 per cent, a worst-year loss of 26 per cent (1974), and a gain of 53 per cent in the best year (1954).

These gyrations are largely responses to changes in economic conditions and to swings in the psychology of expectations. A useful measure of this psychology is the ratio of the share price to current earnings, or P/E (Chart 3.19 facing). The long-term average for this ratio is about 15, but it has ranged as low as 5 during times of great scepticism, to as high as 28 when earnings were thought to be growing to the sky.

Similarly, the price paid for $1 of dividends has fluctuated, averaging 24 since 1926, equivalent to a yield of 4.2 per cent

Believe it or not, there are more than 600 investment-related publications, 25,000 securities analysts and portfolio managers, 22,000 registered investment advisors and 5,000 mutual funds sorting through this and other kinds of investment information, all with an eye to helping the US investor. The reasons for such massive activity are many and include a growing propensity among individuals and corporations in the US to invest in common stocks as a means of long-term saving.

Interim fluctuations aside, my view of the US stock market for the balance of the 1990s is highly optimistic. Among the reasons for this optimism are:

● The end of communism. The failure of state ownership and control of economies in the former Soviet Union and elsewhere to keep up with the free and market-driven societies of the world is deeply bullish for the United

Chart 3.19 S&P 500 P/E Ratio

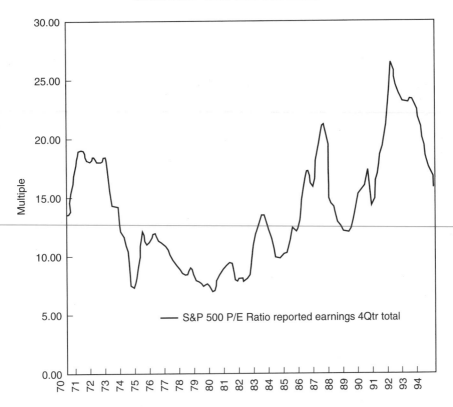

States. Not every country is going to make the transition to a market economy successfully. In the process, though, companies providing the necessary raw materials and equipment will benefit. Great corporations the world over will be competing as economies open up, and the preponderance of these contenders, I believe, will be American.

- The world-wide need for capital, already large just to modernize and replace existing infrastructure in developed countries, will only climb as emerging nations seek to install new communications, transportation, energy and other systems. High returns have to be in prospect if the required capital is to come forth.

- The bulk of the costs and economic disruptions caused by the end of the Cold War is now behind the United States. The economy of the early 1990s bore the burden of heavy cutbacks in defence spending and the associated ripple effects on many companies and industries. Further cuts of comparable magnitude are not likely. Another problem for Western economies was the release of huge amounts of certain raw materials, including aluminium, nickel and chrome from the former Soviet Union, which wrecked those markets for a time. A growing world economy has absorbed most of these new supplies and no comparable excesses are visible from any source for at least the next few years.

- A rise in productivity is under way in the United States. American corporations have rarely been as competitive in world markets as they are today. We are still in the early stages of feeling the effects of the micro-processor, as applications continue to multiply in business and industry and accelerate in consumer markets. Smaller and faster computers and easier-to-use software are freeing up countless hours for designers, engineers, clerks, writers, musicians, and production and service workers. Overall productivity is also getting a boost from the virtual revolution that is taking place in the way the work process is managed.

Few industries will fail to participate in the favourable trends that I expect. Probably the safest bet is oil and gas. The first requirement of an expanding world economy is conventional energy and since energy is a depleting resource, prices and profits must be adequate to encourage the investment needed to replace and increase reserves. Today's surpluses are not that large and will be erased well before the 1990s are gone. Several major oil companies have been producing satisfactory earnings despite currently low prices for oil and natural gas, thanks mostly to vigorous cost cutting. I expect these companies to benefit importantly from the higher prices for energy that lie ahead.

Similarly, well-managed companies producing raw materials and capital goods – aluminium, copper, chemicals, paper, machinery – will thrive because of the aforementioned expansion in global business activity. These companies are typically regarded as cyclical investments that flourish for a couple of years before they overexpand and then suffer price declines and plunging profits. But if we're right about faster and more persistent growth ahead, foreseeable capacity in these areas is barely sufficient and profits will stay higher for longer than many analysts now expect. Even if decisions were made today to expand capacity meaningfully, it would take several years to plan, build and bring into production the new facilities.

I cite only these two sectors because they are so fundamental to world expansion. It is hard to list other sectors that would not also derive at least some benefit from these trends. One might ask why technology is not listed as a third sector. Of course it has an important role to play, but the biggest beneficiaries of technology are the users who get the benefits of these rapid advances at ever decreasing prices. The innovators in technology face stiff competition in a roller-coaster business. For those companies that can establish and, importantly, hold leading positions, it is a very profitable business, as Microsoft and Intel have shown. But their position is fully recognized in the market. To find the next leader in technology means that you are going to have to speculate on a company's ability to innovate and hold on to their lead. This is a sector that is very titillating to the investors, but which is fraught with risk.

Chart 3.20 The US Equities Market 1994, by Sector

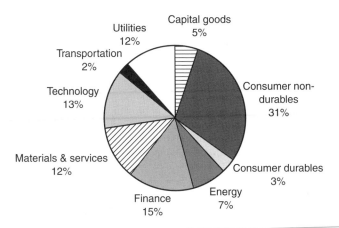

Source: Wilshire Associates Incorporated

When it comes to choosing individual stocks, the investor has available to him a vast array of techniques and complex methodologies. I prefer to use only a few, simple guidelines to help identify the one or two essential 'hooks' or 'critical variables' that drive a stock towards its potential. The more elaborate the argument for a particular investment, the less likely there is a case at all. This emphatically is not to say that careful analysis is not required; it is, but only as a means toward building the analyst's conviction about the 'hook', if there is one.

I rely on just two requirements. First, there must be present, or in store, some dynamic, something changing, that will be favourable to the company's earnings or asset values. Second, that good dynamic must be available at a relatively low price, or at least a price that doesn't already reflect that dynamic.

The first requirement might take a number of forms: a change in management, a change in business strategy, a new product, a new factory, a sensible acquisition or getting rid of a money-losing operation, a rapidly growing part of a company achieving enough size to have a more noticeable effect on overall earnings, a large mineral discovery, and so on. Or, the changing dynamic may be external to the company: supply-demand factors for its products may be shifting; there may be new legislation or changed regulatory policies; or a key competitor is weakened. These changes may be perceived in advance because the investor is especially alert, or they may be more generally recognized but with differing opinions as to their significance.

Price is the second crucial criterion, so often ignored. Obviously we want to pay a low price. But low relative to what? Low could be relative to a number of things: earnings, dividends, cash flow, or the value of underlying assets, as compared with historical ratios. The advantages of a low entry price are obvious. The risk of loss is reduced and the potential reward is enhanced.

Although insistence on a low price may cause the investor to miss opportunities here and there, it protects him from joining the bandwagon crowd. The surest prescription for loss is, 'The prospects for plastic rail cars are boundless, the stocks are getting away from me and I must participate at any price. Some (greater) fool will bail me out.' Maybe.

This low-price, or 'value', approach often means taking a stand that is contrary to a prevailing view in the marketplace, since by definition a much-loved security will not carry a bargain price. But, contrary investing should not be confused with ornery investing which is the mindless and arbitrary opposition to current thinking, whatever it is.

Let's consider some actual cases we've experienced at Vanguard/Wellington Fund. We are always on the lookout for good companies whose shares, for one reason or another, come under extraordinary pressure. Such an opportunity appeared in 1993-early 1994, when the initial healthcare proposals of the Clinton Administration contained provisions to regulate the prices of pharmaceutical products. This caused a near-panic among investors in drug stocks, who feared that price controls on top of increasing pressure from private insurers and employers would end the industry's long record of superior earnings growth. Shares of the best companies, such as Abbott Laboratories, Johnson & Johnson and Pfizer Inc., were driven 30 per cent to 35 per cent below previous highs to multiples as low as 12 times upcoming earnings. The Fund easily acquired large positions in each of these companies in a fear-driven marketplace that seemed oblivious to some simple logic.

In the first place, drugs made up only a small percentage of the nation's health bill yet they made people well, kept them at work and out of costly hospitals. And the companies were constantly developing new and improved products. To choke off the industry's incentives would have been counterproductive to say the least. We believed that the issue was too clear and too important to be allowed to end with an illogical decision to control drug prices. Besides, the companies we had singled out had impressive arrays of new products the prices of which would be even less likely to be controlled. The shares have since appreciated 50 per cent to 60 per cent.

Another instance when it paid to investigate a stock whose price had collapsed was Northrop Corporation (now Northrop Grumman). When the Soviet Union broke apart, it was clear that America's military spending would decline. Stocks of most defence contractors fell but none more sharply than Northrop's. The company's huge B-2 stealth bomber program was threatened with cancellation, debt was large and its recent past was chequered under a previous CEO. But with shares selling at 5 times earnings and yielding 8 per cent on a secure dividend, investors appeared to be overlooking the fact that Northrop had significant business and earnings apart from the B-2.

More important, the cancellation or curtailment of a defence programme actually creates extraordinary cash flows in the near term as programme

R&D ceases, and equipment and inventories are liquidated. There could even be sizeable penalty payments by the Government. Ultimately, the B-2 programme was radically reduced and the cash freed up was used not only to reduce debt, but to buy in stock, raise the dividend, and to acquire Grumman Corp., another aerospace concern of comparable size. Earnings have increased and as a result of the savings from the combination, they will grow solidly over the next several years. The shares have more than tripled from their low of 14 in 1990.

Along with buying at a low price, another crucial element for successful equity investing is patience. Everyone agrees that it is a virtue and can be richly rewarding, yet it appears to be in short supply even among professional investors. For example, the average institutional investor managing mutual funds, pension funds and other large pools of money in the US turns over 70 per cent of the equities in these portfolios each year. And the same the next year and the year after that. A more patient approach, like that of Vanguard/Wellington whose equities have turned over at less that 25 per cent per annum, allows time for good stock selections to bear fruit and at the same time minimizes transaction costs borne by the portfolio. Even when the research and reasoning are correct, it may be many months before one's views are embraced in the marketplace. But that's where the best gains reside – just over most people's time horizon.

Unfortunately, no bell rings when patience melts into procrastination. All that can be said is, we try to be awake to evolving changes in our investment assumptions. It has been useful to set up well thought out trigger points in advance. I keep guidelines for selling simple. If the positive change we have been expecting doesn't come about, it may be time to sell. The trigger may be falling short of a certain earnings level by a certain time, or it may be a deadline for an expected important event. We give ourselves some room, though, so that if the miss is by a small margin, we don't necessarily give up and sell the stock. But if the expected action or trend keeps receding into the distance, we probably have misjudged the situation and action is required.

The other key reason to sell a stock is because its price has risen beyond the range of established value criteria. Assume an investor bought a stock near the lower end of its historical valuation relative to earnings, cash flow, dividends or asset value. That band of value slopes upward and the stock after a couple of years now sells at the top of it. There is a nice gain, but at this level of valuation it is clear that the clever investor is no longer alone in his affection for this stock. He may be well-advised to sell and reinvest the proceeds in a more undervalued situation.

In the end, successful investing in the US, like anywhere else, requires ordinary portions of an inquiring mind, common sense, knowledge of self, humility and a fascination with the process. A little luck doesn't hurt either. ♣

US FIXED INCOME

Arthur J. MacBride

*Arthur MacBride is a Co-Director of Fixed Income at the **Boston Company Asset Management Inc** in Boston, Massachusetts. He oversees approximately $6 billion of fixed income assets invested for corporate and public pension plans, endowments, foundations and unions, as well as several mutual funds distributed through the **Dreyfus Family of Funds**.*

Overview and Introduction

The US bond market is the largest, and most liquid, fixed income market in the world. The growth and diversification that has taken place since the early 1980s is nothing short of astounding. The market value of the Lehman Brothers Aggregate Bond Index, one of the broadest measures of the market, was $650 billion at the end of 1980. As of 31 December 1994, it stood close to $4 trillion. This differential was caused primarily by a substantial increase in borrowing by the US Treasury and the development of the US mortgage and asset-backed market. Chart 3.21 tracks the major market sector growth.

Chart 3.21 Growth in US Fixed Income Market

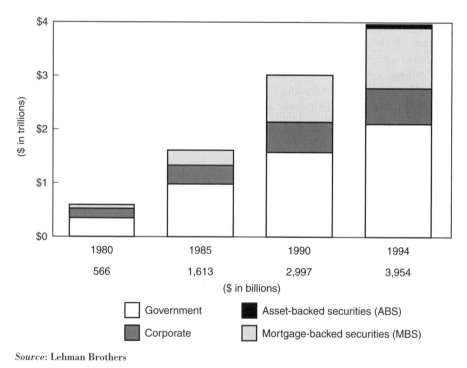

Source: Lehman Brothers

380

The focus of the chapter is a review of the major sectors of the US bond market, as well as the major risks of investing in these areas. We also will briefly discuss different investment management approaches, performance measurements which are used to evaluate investment managers, and some pitfalls an investor might encounter. All this with NO maths, honest.

US Governments

The starting place must be US Treasury securities. With a market value of $1.8 trillion, this is the largest sector. These securities are backed by the full faith and credit of the United States government and, therefore, are considered risk free. The enormous size of the market, the continuous issuance of securities, and the lack of credit on prepayment risk contribute to making this sector one of the most liquid markets in the world. Treasuries are issued at auctions which take place throughout the year on a regular schedule, with maturities ranging from three months to thirty years.

Over the last ten years, the average yield on the one-year US Treasury Bill and the 30-Year US Treasury Bond were 6.3 per cent and 8.19 per cent respectively. As of 31 March 1995, the T-Bill yielded 6.48 per cent and the Treasury Bond yielded 7.43 per cent.

The important point to notice is that interest rates have historically followed a cycle in which they tend to rise as the growth in the economy increases, and fall as the economy slows. Short rates, such as the 1-Year

Chart 3.22 US Interest Rates

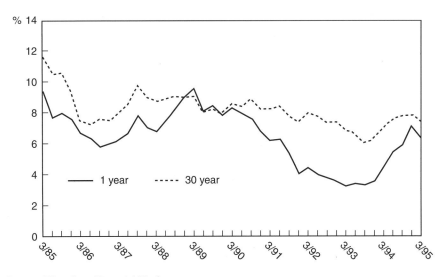

Source: Bloomberg Financial Markets

Treasury Bill rate, are highly correlated with the actions of the Federal Reserve, whereas longer rates are influenced more by the market's expectation of future inflation.

At any time the yields available on all outstanding Treasuries constitute the Treasury yield curve off which US fixed income securities are priced. 1994 provides a somewhat unique study in the yield curve. As you can see in Chart 3.23, interest rates rose dramatically and the curve flattened in shape.

Investors must not only be conscious of the level and direction of interest rates, but also the shape of the yield curve. Movements in the yield curve tend to follow a cyclical pattern that anticipates turns in general business activity. Rising interest rates traditionally have been associated with periods of rising credit demand and higher inflationary expectations. A tight monetary policy drives up short rates and produces a flat curve, as in 1994. In the post-war era, flat or inverted curves have been a precursor to economic slow downs. A steep yield curve, as pictured by year-end 1993, is caused by monetary easing in periods of economic sluggishness. This stirs expectations of a revival in economic activity and credit demand.

	3 mths	6 mths	1 year	2 years	3 years	5 years	10 years	30 years
31 Dec 93	3.08	3.29	3.58	4.23	4.51	5.20	5.79	6.35
31 Dec 94	5.68	6.50	7.16	7.70	7.78	7.83	7.83	7.88
Change	2.60	3.21	3.58	3.47	3.27	2.63	2.04	1.53

Chart 3.23 US Treasury Yield Curve

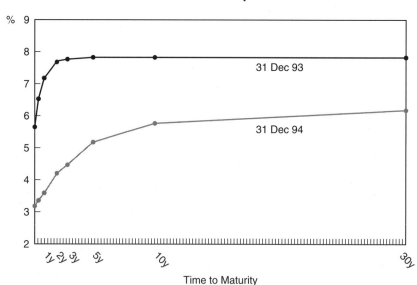

Time to Maturity

Source: Bloomberg Financial Markets

US Agency Sector

The term 'governments' encompasses both Treasuries and what are commonly called Agencies. This group is next in line in the borrowing chain. There are some 17 Agencies or Government Sponsored Enterprises, 'GSEs', but the top five represent the lion's share of borrowings. The five major GSEs all share AAA ratings from both major rating agencies, due to their status as federally chartered institutions with strong implicit support from the government, although none of these has its debt guaranteed. The major GSEs are:

● Federal Farm Credit Banks (FFCB).

● Federal Home Loan Banks (FHLB).

● Federal Home Loan Mortgage Corporation (Freddie Mac).

● Federal National Mortgage Association (Fannie Mae).

● Student Loan Marketing Association (Sallie Mae).

Although the GSEs are sponsored by the Federal Government, there is no direct government ownership. Fannie Mae, Freddie Mac and Sallie Mae are all public companies, and FHLB and FFCB are owned by member institutions. These issues currently offer very little spread over US Treasuries. Over the past year, the general level of Agency spreads – measured as the spread of a ten-year Fannie Mae security over ten-year Treasury yields – has averaged 35 basis points.

Mortgages

Since its inception in the early 1970s, this market has blossomed into the second largest part of the US fixed income markets. The growth in mortgage credit has been driven by several sectors, but principally single family residences (75 per cent) and commercial (18 per cent). Total mortgage debt in the US exceeds $4 trillion, of which $1+ trillion has been securitized. There are two basic types of mortgage related investments: mortgage pass-through securities, which allow investors to share proportionally in all the cash flows of a group of 'pool' of mortgages; and collateralized mortgage obligations (CMOs). There are three principal GSEs.

Freddie Mac (FHLMC) is a stockholder corporation established in 1970 to increase the supply of money available to home buyers and multi-family investors. It accomplishes these goals by purchasing residential loans from lenders such as commercial banks and savings and loans. Freddie Mac then either resells the loans in the form of mortgage participation certificates (PCs), or retains them in its own portfolio.

Fannie Mae (FNMA) was established in 1938 to provide liquidity. Fannie Mae supports the secondary market for home loans by purchasing home loans and issuing mortgage backed securities. Originally owned by the government,

Fannie Mae was converted into a private corporation in 1954. FNMA has total assets well in excess of $200 billion (as a reference point, IBM's total assets are approximately $80 billion).

Ginnie Mae (GNMA) was split out of the original Fannie Mae in 1968 and was established within the Department of Housing and Urban Development. GNMA securities are actually guaranteed by the full faith and credit of the US Government, whereas FNMA and FHLMC are not. GNMA securities are backed by pools of mortgages insured by the Federal Housing Authority and the Veterans Administration.

The pass-through securities issued by these entities all contain prepayment risk. Simply defined, prepayment risk is how fast home owners pay back their mortgages. These prepayments are driven by declining interest rates and, therefore, investors are forced to reinvest at lower yields. Historically, the spread over Treasuries has averaged approximately 1 per cent for regular 30-year mortgage securities.

Collateralized Mortgage Obligations, or CMOs, are bonds created by the redirection of the cash flows of mortgage pass-through securities so as to mitigate prepayment risk. This does not eliminate prepayment risk, but transfers it, in differing amounts, to the various CMO bonds or 'classes'. This restructuring or re-engineering of the principal and interest cash flows from various mortgage pass-through securities can produce a broad array of securities to meet differing requirements of various fixed income investors. The restructuring can produce classes with 'regular' fixed income characteristics (Planned Amortisation Classes, for instance) or classes with more volatile characteristics (inverse floating rate notes, interest-only notes, or principal-only notes as examples). CMO new issuance in 1994 was $119 billion, which brought total outstandings to over $800 billion – not a small market.

Asset Backed Securities (ABS)

This market is expanding dramatically. 1994 saw record breaking issuance of $74 billion and 1995's volume will likely exceed $80 billion. The principal products include credit cards, auto loans and home equity loans. In 1994, credit cards dominated, with 41 per cent. These securities are similar to mortgage securities in that they represent an interest in the payments of principal and interest on the underlying loans. These securities generally have very strong credit characteristics due to the nature of the underlying loans, their geographic and economic dispersion, and the structural characteristics in the securities. They also tend to be a short duration security, which makes them a likely choice in a defensive environment. Given their high credit quality and limited interest rate risk, they trade tight to Treasuries. ABS securities, in the two-year area of the yield curve, are currently trading at approximately 50 basis points over Treasuries. These securities can be a good alternative to short corporates.

Corporates

The investment grade corporate bond market (rating categories AAA through BBB) also has experienced exceptional growth. Corporates can be issued with different embedded features such as call options, put options, sinking funds, refunding provisions, or extendible maturities.

In examining investment grade corporate bonds, it is helpful to use the Lehman Brothers Investment Grade Corporate Index, which includes all publicly traded issues that are rated BBB or higher. Using this as our guide, the value of the corporate bond markets at the end of 1994 was $634 billion. New issuance of investment grade corporate securities was $80 billion in 1994, down 61 per cent from 1993 predominantly due to rising interest rates.

The corporate market can be analysed by industry classification, maturity, and credit quality rating. The industry classifications are four primary divisions comprising industrials, utilities, finance and Yankees (foreign companies issuing debt in the US). Industrials represent the largest portion at 35 per cent. In terms of maturity, approximately 63 per cent of the investment grade corporate market is intermediate, or less than ten years. The decision of what maturity to issue depends on the financial objectives of the issuer and the demand for debt in the market. The yield spread should compensate the investor for the risks.

The market can also be analysed by rating. Approximately 53 per cent of the investment grade market is rated A. Credit ratings are provided by independent rating agencies such as Moody's Investor Services and S&P Corporation. Many corporate investors rely on an independent rating agency to determine credit quality. The major change in the credit quality of the market has occurred in the BBB rated component, which represented less than 10 per cent of investment grade corporates in the early 1970s while, today, they represent 25 per cent of the market, including household names such as General Motors, Sears and Paine Webber.

Corporate investors monitor the credit quality of the corporate market by watching the relationship of rating downgrades/upgrades. These trends can illustrate developing industry trends as well as macro-economic cycles.

Typically, the higher the credit rating, the less the spread over a comparable Treasury security. At year-end 1994, the average spread between the investment grade corporate market and a comparable duration Treasury security was 84 'basis points'.

The performance of the investment grade corporate market was -3.9 per cent in 1994. Corporates have provided average annual returns of 8.2 per cent over the last five years, and 10.6 per cent over the last ten years. Corporate securities outperformed comparable duration Treasuries by 71 basis points over five years and 106 basis points over ten years. Over the last ten years, performance has been inversely related to credit quality. For example, the BBB corporate market had average annual returns of 11.06 per cent over ten years, compared to 10.47 per cent for the AAA corporate market. It appears that the additional 0.59 per cent annual return from investing in BBB versus AAA securities compensated investors for assuming greater credit risk.

Below-Investment-Grade Corporates (High Yield or 'Junk' Bonds)

The below-investment-grade market includes all securities that are rated less than BBB and, according to Lehman Brothers, is $137 billion. The average yield was 11.28 per cent as at the end of 1994 and duration was 4.7 years. The greatest use of below-investment-grade new issuance in 1994 was to refinance bank debt, which accounted for 30 per cent. The greatest change in the use of new issuance over the last ten years was the decline of leveraged buyout financing, which accounted for 33 per cent of new issuance in 1989 versus 0 per cent in 1994.

The largest component by rating category is the B rated sector. Several changes have occurred since 1990, when high yields suffered from the triple threat of regulations limiting investment by financial institutions, economic recession, and the collapse of Drexel Burnham Lambert, the market's leading underwriter. Since the dramatic decline of the high yield market in 1990, buyers of these securities have required improved financial structures and stronger convenant packages. The percentage of debt issued below B has declined from 65 per cent in 1988 to 18 per cent in 1994. In addition, the percentage of debt issued as senior in the capital structure has increased from 19 per cent to 78 per cent in 1994. The below-investment-grade market serves as an alternative means of financing from bank debt and private placements. Some high yield issuers start out as a high yield new issue, others are downgraded. Securities that enter the high yield market due to a downgrade are called 'fallen angels'.

The typical buyers of high yield bonds are mutual funds, insurance companies and total return investment managers. The growth of the market over the last ten years has resulted from the growth of high yield mutual funds, which saw positive fund flows in 9 of the last 11 years. The average spread historically in the high yield market is 300-500 basis points over comparable Treasuries. The lower the rating, the higher the spread that investors demand, and the higher chance the issuer will default.

The high yield market fell 1 per cent in 1994. The annual returns from the high yield market over the last five years was 12.63 per cent. This outperformed comparable duration Treasuries over the same period by 510 basis points.

Municipal Bonds

Municipal Bonds are issued by states, local governments and a variety of municipal agencies to finance a wide array of public facilities. Projects for which municipal governments issue tax exempt debt are diverse, including school construction, highways, water and sewer, public power, airports, ports, housing and healthcare facilities. The tax exempt bond market is very large but fragmented. There is currently in excess of $1.2 trillion of municipal debt outstanding. During recent years, annual issuance of new municipal debt has ranged from $150-300 billion, with the size of a new issue averaging approximately $20 million. A distinguishing feature of most municipal debt is that bond interest is exempt from federal taxes and, in some cases, state and local taxes as well. Consequently, investors are willing to accept lower returns.

Municipalities finance the debt service on their bonds through either the imposition of general taxes (general obligation bonds) or the collection of fees generated by the financed project (revenue bonds). In addition to offering fundamentally high credit quality, many municipal bonds are further enhanced with private insurance, which guarantees timely payment.

Investment Risks

Investors expect to earn premium or 'spread' over Treasuries for any investment with risk. Below are a few key determinants to keep in mind.

Risks that apply generally to all fixed income securities:

Interest rate risk:	Generally, the longer the maturity of a bond, the more its price fluctuates for a given change in interest rates. A frequently used measure of this risk is duration, which quantifies the percentage change in price of a fixed income security for a change in interest rates of 1 per cent.
Economic or political risks	Such as the Gulf War and German reunification.
Yield curve risk	This goes hand in hand with interest rate risk. The wrong position on the curve can undermine excellent security selection or the correct interest rate call.
Structure risk	Are the bonds callable, or putable? Do they contain a sinking fund, or prepayment risk?
Supply risk	Scarcity may generate added value in fixed income.
Liquidity risk	Illiquid securities generally trade cheaper.

Risks that apply principally to corporate bonds:

Default risk	The number one risk investors think about; the inability of the corporation to repay its debt.
Event risk	Take-overs, LBOs and restructurings are usually unforeseen.
Rating risk	Ratings provide generic credit measurement and can move up or down, affecting value.

Risk that applies principally to mortgages:

Prepayment risk   Mortgages that repay early can dramatically affect the expected cash flow.

Indices

Several US investment banks produce fixed income indices. Merrill Lynch, Lehman Brothers and Salomon Brothers provide well-known indices. The Lehman Brothers Aggregate Index is one of the most widely used and can be considered a likely benchmark when tracking your investment performance.

Management Styles and Pitfalls

There are three principal types of fixed income style: interest rate anticipation, sector rotation and security selection. They are relatively self-explanatory and each has its virtues. Investors should choose a style that fits long-term goals and risk tolerance.

The two major pitfalls are lack of understanding and not enough diversification. A thorough understanding of fixed income securities is imperative. The importance of diversification and the controls to ensure it cannot be overstated. ♣

CANADA

Patti Croft, Avery Shenfeld and Ken Bowen

Patti Croft is a Senior Economist and Vice President at **CIBC Wood Gundy**. *Independent surveys of institutional bond and equity clients rank Ms Croft amongst the top economists in Canada. Avery Shenfeld is a Senior Economist and Assistant Vice-President. Dr Shenfeld joined* **Wood Gundy** *after seven years as an economics consultant with* **Ernst & Young**. *Previously, he served on the economics faculty at the* **University of Toronto**. *Ken Bowen is a London-based institutional equity salesman with* **Wood Gundy**.

Established over 125 years ago, the **Canadian Imperial Bank of Commerce** *(***CIBC***) has grown to become Canada's second largest financial institution.* **CIBC** *currently has 41,000 employees in 1,400 branches worldwide, and had an asset base of C$151 billion at October 1994.* **CIBC** *purchased* **Wood Gundy** *in 1988, acquiring the full service capability of one of Canada's leading investment dealers. In 1993–4, the US-based* **Greenwich** *survey ranked* **Wood Gundy** *economists number one in Canadian economic research among international fixed income institutional investors.*

Economic Overview

Canada has a well-diversified economic base whose structure is affected by its proximity to major US markets, as well as by its large geographic expanse. At purchasing power parity, its per capita GDP (C$25,645 in 1994) is among the highest in the OECD.

As in other high-income countries, the service sector accounts for the majority of economic output, representing two-thirds of GDP. Within the goods industries, the extraction and processing of mineral and forest resources plays a key role, as does the automotive industry, which is closely integrated with that of the United States. Other major industries include food processing, electrical products (especially communications equipment) and machinery, as well as electric utilities. Exports accounted for 35 per cent of real GDP in 1994, with over 80 per cent destined for the US market.

Following a deep recession in 1990–91, Canada has been in an export-led expansion which gradually accelerated to a 4.6 per cent real growth rate in 1994. Exports were boosted by a depreciating currency, a booming US market, and recovering world commodity markets. Domestic demand growth has been held back by fiscal restraint and rising interest rates. A lull in export demand and a sharp spike in short-term interest rates saw Canada's economy stall in the first half of 1995, but a US rebound in the latter half of the year should enable the economy to grow by close to 2.5 per cent in 1995, and 3 per cent in 1996.

The Bank of Canada has a 1 to 3 per cent target band for inflation. Although the price impacts of a depreciating currency, sales tax increases and strong global commodity markets have pushed the CPI to the upper end of this range, the longer-term outlook for inflation remains favourable. Labour markets still show ample slack, with the unemployment rate at 9.5 per cent in May 1995 (vs an average 7.5 per cent in 1989) and March 1995 average hourly earnings up a mere 1 per cent from a year earlier.

Fiscal policy is currently geared towards unwinding a sizeable debt and deficit burden at both the federal and provincial levels of governments. Rising taxes initially bore the brunt of fiscal restraint, but spending at both levels of governments is now also sharply in decline in real terms.

The Canadian dollar, valued as of June 1995 at roughly US$0.73, is closely tied to the US currency, but has shown a longer-term trend to depreciate against the US$, with periods of appreciation linked to commodity price gains or monetary policy tightening in Canada. Although already well below purchasing power parity, the C$ is expected to see a modest further depreciation against the US$ over the next few years, owing to its heavy external indebtedness (roughly 40 per cent of GDP) and the resulting outflows of interest payments.

The Canadian Equity Market

As of the end of 1994, the equity market in Canada was the seventh largest in the world in terms of market capitalization, with a market share of 2.2 per cent. In US dollar terms, the market value of shares traded on Canadian exchanges amounted to $317 billion, roughly one-twentieth the size of the US equity market.

Equities, or common stock, have been traded on organized stock exchanges in Canada since the 1870s. Trading nowadays is conducted on four main exchanges in Toronto, Montreal, Vancouver and Calgary.

> **the market value of shares traded on Canadian exchanges amounted to $317 billion, roughly one-twentieth the size of the US equity market.**

The Toronto Stock Exchange (TSE)

The TSE is by far the largest exchange and accounts for about 80 per cent of the total dollar value of equity trades on the Canadian exchanges. About 1,300 companies are listed on the TSE, which is the principal exchange for trading Canada's largest and better known companies. The ten largest Canadian stocks account for about 26 per cent of TSE market value, and movements in the share prices of these companies have a significant influence on the market as a whole.

Overall movements in TSE stock prices are measured by a number of indices. The most widely used is the TSE 300 Composite Index, which is regarded as the benchmark for the Canadian market, in much the same way that the Dow Jones Industrial Average is used as the indicator of US market activity, or the FT-SE-100 for the UK equity market. The TSE 300 measures changes in the prices of 300 stocks, representing 14 industry sectors, and whose relative weighting in the index is calculated according to their market float. The base year chosen for the TSE 300 was 1975, when the index was established at a level of 1,000. The TSE also introduced a TSE 35 Index in 1987 which forms the basis for stock index futures and option contracts on the underlying index. For instance, investors can replicate a portfolio of stocks in the TSE 35 Index through a single purchase of Toronto 35 Index Participating units (TIPS).

Trading of TSE stocks is carried out either by the Modified Floor Trading System or by the Computer Assisted Trading System (CATS). The Modified Floor Trading System is linked to an electronic central order book and enables TSE issues to be transacted on the floor of the Toronto Exchange. This system accounts for about 75 per cent of total trading volume. The CATS system is fully automated. Orders may be entered on terminals in brokers' offices or on terminals on the exchange floor itself. Plans are afoot for transacting all TSE equity trades on an electronic trading system which is likely to be a modified version of the existing CATS system. The exchange floor will be closed down completely and this system is expected to be implemented in late 1996.

The Montreal Exchange (ME)

The Montreal Exchange is the second largest in Canada and accounts for about 16 per cent of the Canadian stock exchanges' total market value.

Around 900 equity issues are traded on Montreal, many of which are dual-listed on the Toronto exchange. Trading is effected through a combination of open-floor trading and formal trading posts.

Vancouver Stock Exchange (VSE)

The Vancouver market accounts for just 3 per cent of total Canadian equity trading by market value, but lists over 2,000 securities. Stocks traded in Vancouver tend to be companies with a relatively small market capitalization, many of which are small, speculative junior mining companies. Liquidity, or the ability of a stock to be bought easily or sold at reasonable prices can sometimes be a problem compared with the larger Toronto exchange, and wide price fluctuations can be expected with some issues. Vancouver uses a fully automated, computerized trading system for all equity trading.

Alberta Stock Exchange (ASE)

Alberta has a market share of Canadian share activity of just 1 per cent and trades about 800 issues, two-thirds of which are resource based. Because of its geographical location in the oil drilling region of Western Canada, the Alberta Exchange has had a long and established history of trading junior oil and gas companies. Approximately 30 per cent of all Alberta issues are traded electronically.

Many investors perceive the Canadian economy to be predominantly resource based, highly sensitive to cyclical influences and therefore regard the Canadian stock market as being more of a play on commodity prices – worth having a look at when the global economy is expanding, but to be avoided like the plague when growth falters. Canada is, indeed, abundant in natural resources, principally forest products, base metals, precious metals and oil and gas, and these sectors are a highly significant contributor to Canada's export growth. However, an investor should not overlook the fact that the Canadian stock market provides considerable exposure to some of the largest industrial and consumer product companies in the world. A breakdown of the TSE 300 Index shows that the resources sector has approximately a 37 per cent weighting; consumer products has a 15 per cent weighting; industrials 22 per cent, and interest sensitives 26 per cent.

The four largest quoted Canadian companies also reflect this sectoral mix, and themselves provide exposure to different cyclical influences.

BCE Inc The largest company in Canada, with a market float of C$13.1 billion. BCE provides telecommunications services and equipment both in Canada and overseas. Once considered a utility because of its defensive qualities, BCE now provides broad exposure to more growth oriented businesses such as cellular/wireless, long-distance telecom and telco equipment manufacturing.

American Barrick The third largest gold company in the world, with a market capitalization of C$11 billion. Gold companies are sensitive to movements in the underlying commodity price which responds to inflationary expectations and movements in interest rates.

Seagrams Consumer products. Market capitalization C$7.4 billion. Traditionally one of the world's largest distillers, with an impressive brand portfolio including Chivas Regal, Glenlivet and Martell. Recently the company has divested its holdings in the DuPont chemical company and is expanding its reach as a global media and entertainment company with its acquisition of MCA Inc.

Royal Bank of Canada Market capitalization C$9.5 billion. Canadian chartered bank with 1,700 branches in Canada offering a wide range of banking services, including commercial, corporate and investment banking. Banks are sensitive to the interest rate cycle and are generally held by investors in anticipation of declining interest rates.

Fixed Income Market

Canada is the world's ninth largest sovereign bond market, accounting for 3 per cent of global bonds outstanding according to a leading index. Net public debt outstanding of the federal government amounted to C$546 billion as of 31 March 1995, equal to 73 per cent of national GDP. Canada's federal finances have deteriorated markedly in the past decade as the ratio of debt to GDP has almost doubled. The federal deficit peaked at C$42 billion in 1993 (5.9 per cent of GDP) but is on track to hit the federal government's target of C$39.7 billion in the current fiscal year (4.1 per cent of GDP). Nonetheless, in April, Moody's downgraded Canada's foreign currency rating to Aa2 and its domestic rating to Aa1.

Over the past five years, Canada's ten provinces have significantly increased their role in global capital markets. The onset of recession saw aggregate provincial deficits balloon from C$10 billion in 1990 to a peak of CS$25 billion in 1992. The province of Ontario (accounting for 40 per cent of national output) is the world's largest non-sovereign borrower. Provincial marketable direct and guaranteed debt outstanding stood at approximately $280 billion as of May 1995, equal to 38 per cent of GDP. The other major players in the domestic capital markets are the municipalities (with CS$36 billion in outstanding debt) and corporations ($141 billion debt outstanding).

Foreign investors have played a greater role in financing federal and provincial deficits. Foreign holdings of Canadian bonds and bills have soared from $116 billion to almost $400 billion over the last decade. Foreign investors own 23 per cent of federal debt outstanding, and 40 per cent of provincial debt. The bulk of the debt of the federal government is C$ denominated (95 per cent), in contrast to 54 per cent for the provinces.

Canadian federal government bond yields closely track those of US Treasuries. In 1990, 10-year Government of Canada bonds yielded 11.5 per cent. The yield trended down to a cyclical low of 6.4 per cent in early 1994.

As the US Federal Reserve moved to tighten monetary policy, yields backed up to a peak of 9.4 per cent, but have rallied since January 1995 to 7.9 per cent, as of June.

Over the past five years, the spread between Canadian and US 10-year government bonds has ranged from a low of 60 basis points in late 1992 to a high of almost 300 basis points in the fall of 1990. The Canada/US spread is driven by the C$/US$ exchange rate, political risk and fiscal risk. The peak in the spread in 1990 coincided with heightened political uncertainty during the Quebec constitutional talks at the time of the Meech Lake Accord. Fiscal risk has risen during the first half of 1995 in conjunction with the sharp slowdown in the economy, while political risk has also moved higher, owing to a possible fall referendum on Quebec sovereignty. Ten-year Canada/US spreads stand at 180 basis points as of June 1995.

Our outlook calls for 10-year government of Canada bond yields to rise over 9 per cent in the next twelve months to mid-year 1996. This is based on our view that the pace of the US recovery will pick up, once again, in the second half of 1995, driving Treasury yields higher. Canadian bonds should underperform in the short-term, as wider spreads reflect negative investor sentiment on the C$, Canadian politics and the fiscal position. ●

HONG KONG

Archie Hart

*Archie Hart has been involved in the investment business for eight years, the last five being in Hong Kong with **Crosby**. He is the Deputy Managing Director at **Crosby Securities (HK)** and currently manages **Crosby's** Hong Kong company research operation.*

***Crosby Securities** is one of the largest institutional stockbroking businesses in the Asian region. Headquartered in Hong Kong, the company has 13 offices in 11 countries throughout Asia, with global distribution capabilities from five major financial centres throughout the world.*

Introduction

It is probably fair to say that 'the outlook for the economy and stockmarket of Hong Kong is extremely uncertain' as of March 1995. But then again it has probably been fair to say that for the last 129 years in which stocks have been traded in Hong Kong. Uncertainty in the Territory is the rule rather than the exception, and the success of Hong Kong is primarily due to its marvellous ability to adapt to the tremendous volatility in its circumstances.

No discussion of Hong Kong is complete without the mention of the dreaded word '1997'. That date has established a significance in the west as heralding a turning point in the history of Hong Kong. However, in many respects it is merely a 'mile-post' in a journey that started 17 years ago with Deng Xiao Ping's opening up of China to the outside world.

Deng Xiao Ping's radical 'open door' policy has led to Hong Kong becoming much more integrated into China than is generally realized. Since 1978 there has been a more than ten-fold increase in travel between the two countries. Hong Kong manufacturing industry employs at least five times the number of workers in China than it does in Hong Kong. Bilateral trade has increased 50-fold in the last 15 years to over US$50 billion. Hong Kong companies are also the single largest providers of foreign investment into the Chinese economy, while China is almost certainly the largest 'foreign' investor in Hong Kong.

Hong Kong used to be an international city with a strong Chinese flavour. It is now a Chinese city with a strong international flavour. This close relationship has led to the Hong Kong stockmarket being considered as the ultimate China play.

The 50 Years after 1997

In the early 1980s the British government decided to initiate discussions on the future of Hong Kong. These discussions led to the signing of the 'Joint Declaration' by the governments of the PRC and the United Kingdom in September 1984.

The Joint Declaration provided for the UK to restore Hong Kong to the PRC, with the provision that the PRC would then set up a 'Hong Kong Special Administrative Region' (SAR). This SAR would then govern Hong Kong with a high degree of autonomy (except in defence and foreign affairs) for 50 years after the hand-over. Hong Kong's legal system, founded on British principles, would remain intact. Its social and economic systems would also remain unchanged, with rights such as freedom of speech ensured. Deng Xiao Ping defined this policy as 'one country, two systems'.

The above has now been stipulated in the 'Basic Law of the Hong Kong Special Administrative Region of the People's Republic of China'. Unfortunately, by its nature, no such document could hope to be all encompassing and various ambiguities within it continue to excite fierce debate. This has eroded public confidence in the post-1997 constitutional arrangements, although perhaps this obscures a broader issue. For better or for worse Hong Kong's prospects are now irrevocably tied to that of China.

The Hong Kong Dollar Peg

The central and overriding economic policy of the Hong Kong government is the maintenance of the 'Peg'. The peg – or linked exchange-rate mechanism –

was established on 17 October 1983 after a massive depreciation in the Hong Kong dollar and pegs the Hong Kong dollar to the US$ at a rate of HK$7.80 to US$1.00. Backing the peg are the US$ certificates of indebtedness which the three note-issuing banks are required to hold as cover for the issue of Hong Kong dollars. Thus each HK$7.80 is directly backed by US$1.00 in the Exchange Fund.

Underpinning the Hong Kong dollar are huge foreign currency reserves in the Exchange Fund, Hong Kong's extremely strong fiscal reserve situation and a battery of 'anti-speculation' rules. There is much debate over the long-term future of the peg, but in the short term the maintenance of it is not in question given the government's over-riding objective of maintaining confidence in Hong Kong in the run-up to 1997.

Hong Kong's Stockmarket

Hong Kong's earliest stock exchange was established in 1891, but records of stock trading date back to 1866. By the early 1980s there were four stock exchanges which were eventually merged into one in April 1986. This unified computerized exchange was the scene for a wild speculative run up to the inevitable crash in October 1987. The subsequent closure of the exchange for a week and the uncovering of various corrupt practices devastated international confidence. This resulted in a largely successful clean up of Hong Kong's stockmarket. Since 1987 an increasingly greater say has been given to large international brokers in the exchange's affairs, the Securities and Futures Commision (SFC) has been established as a new statutory regulatory body, and the Hong Kong Securities Clearing Company has been established to enable electronic central clearing. Lately the exchange has introduced an 'Automatic Order Matching and Execution System'.

The benchmark index used to measure the Hong Kong stockmarket is the Hang Seng Index. This was first published by the Hang Seng Bank (a subsidiary of HSBC Holdings and one of the largest local banks) in 1969, but in fact the base day for the index was originally 31 July 1964. This value-weighted index has as its constituents 33 of the largest and most liquid stocks. It is currently undergoing the most significant restructuring in years as the Jardine group companies delist from Hong Kong and are replaced. The overwhelming characteristic of the index is its concentration on property and property related companies. Direct property companies account for a quarter of the index alone, banking and finance companies (which probably generate over half their profit from property related lending) for a quarter and the commercial and industrial sector (where a significant proportion of earnings are derived from property activities) for at least another quarter. Property related activities almost certainly account for at least 60 per cent of the Hang Seng Index's market capitalization.

For someone outside Hong Kong this emphasis might seem a little strange but, in Hong Kong, scarcity of land has resulted in some of the most expensive property prices in the world. (See Chart 3.24.) For this reason there is a strong argument that it is not the health of Hong Kong's (or even China's) economy that is the key determinant in driving Hong Kong's stockmarket, but rather the health of its property markets.

Chart 3.24 Residential Property Prices in Hong Kong (1984–1995)

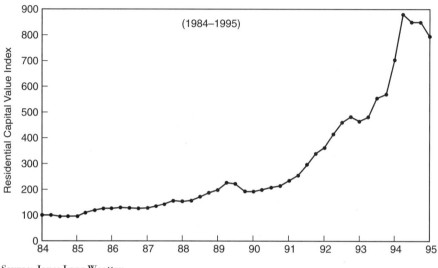

Source: Jones Lang Wootton

Several statistics indicate the importance of Hong Kong's property markets to its economy. One study has estimated that Hong Kong's property is collectively worth US$420 billion. Property activities provide around one-third of government revenues and, also account for one-third of expenditures. Annually, investment in property accounts for 60 per cent of all capital investment in Hong Kong. Property and construction companies employ one-twelfth of the labour force. Finally another indication of the close relationship between Hong Kong and China, is that, by one estimate, companies from the People's Republic of China are estimated to have invested US$10 billion in Hong Kong's property markets.

The Major Sectors

Hong Kong's property companies are strongly represented in the Hang Seng Index, with many of Hong Kong's largest companies being primarily involved in real estate. Essentially they can loosely be put into two categories; developers and investors. Developers primarily build residential property (which in Hong Kong generally means high-rise flats) for sale, while investors generally lease office property to tenants. It is important to note that rental is perhaps not as secure an activity as in the UK, given that the standard lease term is generally only three years.

The commercial and industrial sector is dominated by several major groups with long histories, diverse business interests and generally strong balance sheets. Hutchison Whampoa is the trading arm of Cheung Kong, with interests in property, container terminals, energy, telecommunications, retailing and trading. Wharf and Wheelock are primarily engaged in real estate. Swire Pacific has huge property and industrial interests but is perhaps best known for its ownership of Cathay Pacific, Hong Kong's airline. The newest major entrant to the HSI in the conglomerate sector is the Chinese conglomerate CITIC Pacific, beneficially owned by the PRC government but in fact a company that has leveraged its impeccable connections in Beijing to build a significant presence in both the Hong Kong and PRC economies.

The banking and finance sector is dominated by HSBC Holdings. After its acquisition of Midland this stock is now one of the largest ten banks in the world, and is by far the largest stock by market capitalization in the market. It has recovered from its problems in the late 1980s and now looks better placed than it has for some years. The local banking sector remains extremely well capitalized, with a capital adequacy ratio of 17 per cent at the end of 1993.

However, the banking environment is changing in many ways, which seems likely to lead to a gradual concentration in the banking industry. Banking disclosure is now rivalling that of most western markets. For 30 years, competition for small retail deposits has been controlled by the 'interest rate rules' of the Hong Kong Association of Banks which set maximum rates payable on various types of small deposit accounts. These rules are now being gradually relaxed which seems likely to bring greater competition in the banking market. Finally the possibility of China becoming a major market for Hong Kong's banks is edging closer.

The utility sector of the Hang Seng Index consists of four companies. Hong Kong Telecom, a listed subsidiary of Cable & Wireless, provides both domestic and international telephone services in the Territory. While competition is growing, and regulation gradually tightening, its prospects remain good with opportunities beginning to open up in China. Hong Kong's two electricity generating companies, China Light & Power and Hongkong Electric, offer tremendous stability, given regulatory regimes largely unchanged in 30 years and locked in until 2008. Finally Hong Kong & China Gas is Hong Kong's monopoly supplier of piped gas.

Fixed Income

Hong Kong's bond markets are still in their infancy. The Hong Kong Monetary Authority only created a domestic bond market in 1990, through its 'Exchange Fund Bills and Notes Programme'. 1994 was something of a watershed for this market, with the July 1994 issues of three-year Exchange fund notes, the first to mature after 1 July 1997. In September 1994, the Monetary

Authority issued its first five year notes, which were issued at only a 37 basis points premium to US Treasuries (due to the currency peg, Hong Kong interest rates tend to trade in tandem with US rates). By the end of 1994 the total outstandings of Exchange Fund Bills and Notes was HK$ 52.3 billion.

The private sector debt market has also grown rapidly, as well, with 1994 seeing a 2.6 times increase in outstandings to HK$ 60.1 billion. The government is focusing on further expanding Hong Kong's debt markets in the future, partly in an attempt to compete aggressively with Singapore, which has ambitious plans in this area.

The Outlook

The Exchange's ambition 'is to become a gateway to China for the world'. In 1993 a 'Memorandum of Regulatory Cooperation' was signed by the Exchange, the SFC, the China Securities Exchange and the Shenzhen Stock Exchange. The first tangible result was the listing of Tsingtao Brewery in July 1993, the first PRC incorporated enterprise to obtain a listing in Hong Kong. Nearly two dozen more such enterprises have followed. These listings add a new depth and diversity to the Exchange.

There is much discussion of the risks of investment in Hong Kong's stockmarket, and they undoubtedly do exist. In a 21-month bear market up to the

Chart 3.25 Hang Seng – 1 January 1980 to 10 March 1995 monthly

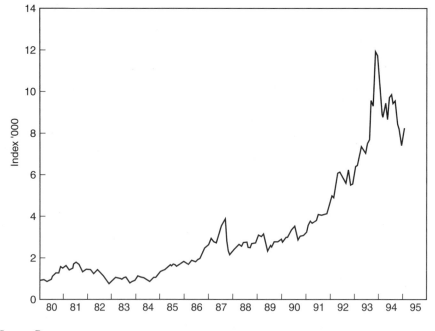

Source: Datastream

end of 1974 the Hang Seng Index (HSI) fell 91.1 per cent from its peak, while in a 27-month bear market up to October 1983 the HSI fell by 61.2 per cent. The recent one year 42.9 per cent fall to 23 January 1995 is mild in contrast. However the rewards appear not be emphasized enough. Chart 3.25 shows that the HSI is up nearly 25-fold in the past 20 years. In this time it has returned (capital growth only) 18.6 per cent per annum in local currency terms and 13.5 per cent in US$ terms.

As long as China continues its economic success, and Hong Kong retains its entrepreneurial flair, the Hong Kong stockmarket appears set to continue its wild ride. Investors who have the required strong nerves should hang on for one of the world's last true 'white-knuckle' rides. ♌

INDIA

John Moore

*Based in Bombay, John Moore is the Country Head of **Barings Investment Bank**, which employs 30 professionals in two subsidiaries: a merchant bank, **Barings India Limited** and **Barings Securities (India) Limited**, a member of the local stock exchange. **Barings Securities** employs more than 12 analysts in Bombay producing a full range of research products. **Baring Asset Management** is registered with the Securities & Exchange Board of India as a Foreign Institutional Investor. **Barings'** specialist offshore funds have over $200 million invested in India. In each of the past five years, all independent polls have ranked **Barings** as the top investment bank for the quality of its Asian research.*

*John Moore worked previously for **Sanpaolo Bank of Turin**, where he ran their capital markets department in London and for **Banque Indosuez** in Bahrain and then Hong Kong, where he ran their Asian investment banking business.*

General Overview of India

India is one of the many countries which, after 45 years of self-imposed isolation and the discrediting of socialism, has re-joined the liberal, trade-based world economy. It is difficult to understand either the country's potential or the problems it has to resolve without putting these in their historical context.

In the eighteenth century India was the richest country in the world and, until the middle of the nineteenth century, India and China between them produced more of the world's GDP than all other countries combined. The industrial revolution, the exploitation of the Indian economy by its imperial masters and the well-intentioned but disastrous policies of its post-independence governments all stifled the inborn talent for trade and industry among Indian entrepreneurs and left the economy distorted and unproductive.

By 1991, India was bankrupt. The disintegration of the USSR, India's major trading partner, and the effects of the Gulf War had emptied the treasury but was a blessing in disguise. India had exchange reserves sufficient to cover only two weeks' imports and the IMF, as a condition for aid, required the Congress party government to liberalize and reform the economy.

Despite political constraints, the government's reform programme has successfully produced a sea-change in the country's economic performance and prospects: foreign exchange reserves now stand at more than US$ 20 billion or nine months' imports; industrial growth is running at 10 per cent per annum; corporate profits rose by 70 to 80 per cent in 1993–4 and are expected to rise by a further 30 to 50 per cent in 1995–6; and *The Economist*'s Economic Intelligence Unit has recently and for the first time rated India as a better investment risk than China.

India's strengths are:

- A relatively stable, tolerant and open society, with a democratic parliamentary government operating through a secular constitution which guarantees a separation of powers.

- Good macroeconomic management: inflation is a reasonable 8 to 12 per cent per annum, the trade and capital accounts are satisfactory and the budget deficit is large but controllable.

- An 'institutional infrastructure' familiar to international businessmen and investors: a functioning legal system with an independent judiciary; international accounting standards; and developed banking and financial markets.

- Good resources: rich mineral resources and fertile land; a well educated work force, where the use of English is widespread; and world class management and entrepreneurial talent.

- A growing and increasingly wealthy middle class of about 250 million consumers.

The country's weak points are:

- Population growth, compounded by female illiteracy, which at 2.5 per cent per annum on a base of 950 million people absorbs a large part of the increase in the country's wealth.

- Inadequate infrastructure, particularly in power, telecommunications and transport, which limits the potential for economic growth.

- An incomplete reform programme, which has not yet started to tackle the huge, labour dominated and uncompetitive government owned sectors of the economy.

- An inefficient, time-consuming bureaucracy, linked to low productivity.
- Democratic government, which slows down reform and makes it difficult to implement.

Political Outlook

The governing Congress party, responsible for implementing India's economic liberalization programme since 1991, is riven by internal disputes between reformers and left-wing traditionalists. Judging by its failure in recent state elections, Congress will lose its absolute majority after the next general election, due some time before June, 1996 but may manage to cobble together and lead a left-of-centre coalition government. Alternatively, the next government may well be formed by the right-wing BJP party, probably in coalition with other nationalist parties. Despite a mainly cosmetic antipathy to high profile foreign consumerism and a more worrying tendency to encourage Hindu sectarianism, the BJP and its allies are natural economic liberals.

Therefore, whichever party wins, Indian and international businessmen and foreign investors are confident that the reform process may be slowed down or re-prioritized but will not be reversed. Too many voters have started to enjoy the benefits of an expanding economy. In addition, US$ 40–50 billion required over the next five years for vital infrastructure and industrial development will ensure continuation of reasonable and open economic policies.

India's Financial Markets

India is a modernizing rather than an emerging investment market: the country's principal equities market, the Bombay Stock Exchange (BSE), was founded in 1875 and is the oldest in Asia. Its market capitalization is about US$130 billion. There are some 7,000 quoted companies, of which 300–350 are regularly traded. Indian companies raised $15 billion of new equity in 1994–5. A retail equity culture is well established; mutual funds, in basic form, flourish; and the 21 per cent personal savings rate is high.

The equity market is dominated by industrial stocks, representing more than 75 per cent of market capitalization, followed by the services sector with 16 per cent and agriculture with 8 per cent. It is well diversified: no industrial sector accounts for more than 10 per cent of the market, shares of public sector companies represent less than 25 per cent and the top 35 companies cover less than one-third of total capitalization. Investors are offered a wide choice of large, medium and small sized companies: 21 companies have a market capitalization of over US$1 billion and more than 500 companies are in the US$20–500 million range.

Despite its inefficiencies, the Indian market is normally reasonably liquid: average turnover has increased dramatically from about US$940 million per month in 1990–1 to more than US$2.2 billion per month in 1993–4.

More than 450 stockbroking members of the BSE offer investors an inadequate but improving service and some, in response to demand from their foreign institutional clients, have started producing research which is comparable with international standards. Four foreign stockbroking firms are members of the BSE or the NSE: Barings Securities, Jardine Fleming, Morgan Stanley and Peregrine Capital; and three have joint ventures with local members: James Capel, Merrill Lynch and Smith New Court.

Like the US market before 'Mayday' in 1975, the UK before 'Big Bang' in 1986 and European financial markets before the early 1990s, India's financial market is developed but in need of radical reform. Since 1991, the government has introduced many reforms: the Capital Issues (Control) Act, 1947 was repealed, the office of the Comptroller of Capital Issues abolished and the Securities & Exchange Board of India was established with statutory powers to supervise and regulate the primary and secondary markets. Recently introduced legislation will, in time, provide 'paperless settlement' and a modern system for securities registration and custody.

However, much remains to be done: for example, settlement and custodian inefficiencies continue to inhibit liquidity and cause problems for equity investors. Corporate issuers are squeezed out of the government dominated bond market, which is large, with outstanding issues totalling about US$ 40 billion.

Although maturities go out to 20–30 years, the market has normally been illiquid, except in short-term paper. The reasons for this are a hang-over from a controlled interest rate environment resulting in a flat yield curve and from the previous practice of practically obligatory placement, for reserve requirement purposes, with state-owned commercial banks, which hold the bonds to maturity and do not trade them. The authorities are currently taking steps to modernize the market with, for example, the introduction of primary market dealers.

The table below gives the yields available over the 14-month period to May, 1995 on the more actively traded 91- and 364-day government paper:

Month 1994–5	364-day Treasury bill Yield (per cent)	91-day Treasury bill Yield (per cent)
April	9.87–9.94	7.25–7.33
May	9.77–9.82	7.21–7.75
June	9.82–9.99	7.75–8.75
July	9.82–10.02	8.58–9.08
August	9.51–9.71	8.00–8.25
September	9.42–9.92	8.08–9.08
October	9.42–9.47	8.33–9.21
November	9.49–9.54	8.25–8.75
December	9.83–9.91	9.00–10.26
January	10.56–10.86	10.51–11.10
February	11.23–11.48	11.10–11.48
March	11.73–11.94	11.40–11.99
1995–6		
April	12.08–12.21	11.99–12.03
May	12.50–12.52	11.95–12.07

In addition to the 20 traditional 'open outcry' exchanges dominated by the BSE, two new Bombay-based exchanges have been established:

- the Over The Counter Exchange of India (OTCEI) started operating in 1992, with the objective of helping to promote small companies with less than US$1 million of net worth;

- the National Stock Exchange (NSE) started trading debt securities in July and equity securities in November, 1994. Impatient with the BSE's reluctance to introduce much-needed reforms, several government-owned financial institutions set up the NSE, which offers transparency, increasing liquidity, efficient management of the unwieldy settlement process and has the potential to become a leading Asian institutional market.

Foreign Investors in Indian Securities

Foreign investors may not deal directly in Indian equities but may invest indirectly, either through London-traded Global Depository Receipts (GDRs) or through offshore funds registered with the Securities & Exchange Board of India (SEBI) as Foreign Institutional Investors (FIIs).

Since access to the international market was opened to them in mid-1992, about 50 Indian companies from the main industrial and commercial sectors have issued GDRs. They include large, professionally managed industrial companies such as Larsen & Tubro, as well as companies from the dominant family groups such as the Tatas, Birlas, Mahindras, Singhanias, Murrugappas and Goenkas.

GDRs are US$-denominated securities, listed in London or Luxembourg, which avoid the inconveniences of local settlement. Barings and other specialist emerging market investment banks are active lead managers, market makers and traders in Indian GDR issues, which are traded either over-the-counter or through SEAQ International on the London Stock Exchange.

A short summary report is set out below on three companies, all of which have issued GDRs and which Barings' research believes have particularly attractive growth prospects.

Indian Petrochemicals Corporation Ltd (IPCL)

- India's only fully integrated petrochemical company, with a gas and naptha cracker at the core, making IPCL a low cost producer of ethylene, the basic petrochemical building block.

- IPCL is the market leader in plastic resins and also has a strong presence in fibres and fibre intermediates, which are likely to maintain medium-term growth of 10-15 per cent per annum.

- Strong earnings growth will be sustained in FY3/96 on the back of further improvements in margins and a marginal rise (7 per cent) in sales volumes.

The improvement in margins will come mainly from the ongoing rise in global prices of petrochemical products, particularly in fibres and fibre intermediates and polypropylene.

Tata Engineering & Locomotive Company Ltd (TELCO)

- Has a strong brand name and a dominant market share of 72 per cent in medium/heavy commercial vehicles (M/HCVs) and 51 per cent in light commercial vehicles (LCVs). The industry is on the uptrend with growth of 32 per cent in commercial vehicles in FY3/95.

- TELCO launched Sumo, their utility vehicle, in December 1994. Sumo received an overwhelming response, with over 90,000 bookings. For FY3/96, TELCO plans to sell 15,000 Sumo vehicles.

- The company plans to triple its combined LCV and passenger vehicle capacity by 1998. In addition, the company plans to modernize and expand its M/HCV facilities and to introduce a range of new higher performance commercial vehicles using Cummins engines.

- TELCO also plans to launch a small family car by mid-1996 with an initial capacity of 100,000 vehicles a year at a cost of Rs 10 billion. Benz is a possible collaborator.

Indian Aluminium Company Ltd (INDAL)

- India's largest aluminium refiner, with a dominant market share in the higher value-added market segments and substantial backward integration.

- The near complete vertical integration means that INDAL is well placed to benefit from bullish aluminium prospects, while cushioning earnings from any decline in prices.

- Strong earnings growth should be sustained through FY3/97 on the back of higher output of value-added products and improved margins. Margin improvements will come from cost savings through higher in-house metal production.

- Earnings growth in FY3/96 and FY3/97 could be even better, thanks to restarting of part of the shut down metal capacity at Belgaum by relocating it to Hirakud and Alupuram, where power costs are also significantly lower than at the other locations.

More than 300 offshore funds are registered as FIIs, of which some 50 are active investors. The following table lists a selection of the more active offshore funds which invest in India:

Selected Closed-end Offshore India Equity Funds

Fund Name	Size ($m)	*1995 Performance (%)	Manager
Baring Peacock Fund Ltd	63	-2.90	Barings
Himalayan Fund Ltd	269	-18.43	Indosuez
India Fund A Shares	76	-25.42	Unit Trust of India
Fleming India Ltd	63	-14.65	Flemings
India Magnum Fund	396	-15.30	Morgan Stanley

Source: Micropal Emerging Market Fund Monitor
* In US$ terms with gross income reinvested from 31 December 1994 to 31 May 1995

As with equities, foreign investors may only invest in the domestic Indian bond market indirectly, through FII registered funds, which may hold up to 20 per cent of their assets in debt securities.

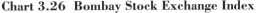

Outlook for the Indian Stock Market

The BSE-Sensex Index of the 30 leading stocks broke through to new highs in late August, 1994 but, despite strong fundamentals, the market has been in decline since then, as shown in Chart 3.26:

Both domestic and international factors have caused this decline. Domestic factors include a tightening in monetary policy by the Reserve Bank of India,

Chart 3.26 Bombay Stock Exchange Index

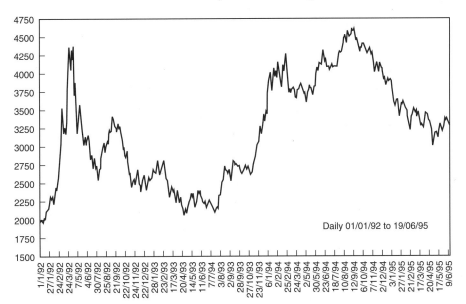

Daily 01/01/92 to 19/06/95

Source: Barings Securities (India) Ltd.

continued heavy selling by Unit Trust of India, the country's largest institutional investor and domestic political uncertainties. Foreign investors are concerned by these uncertainties but have been more influenced by the general move away from emerging markets in the wake of the Mexico crisis in January and by the expectation, in early 1995, that US$ interest rates would continue to harden.

International investors have begun to differentiate between emerging markets. They recognize that India will not be another Mexico: its macroeconomic management is sound and it is less vulnerable to down-turns in world trade than other emerging markets. The strong earnings growth expected from Indian companies over at least the coming 18–24 months means that many international investors are now active buyers of Indian shares at the cheap multiples of June 1995 and, following their lead, the market will probably rally moderately.

> **The long-term prospects for the Indian stock market, discounting any blips for election uncertainties, are strongly positive.**

The long-term prospects for the Indian stock market, discounting any blips for election uncertainties, are strongly positive. Foreign investors would be well-advised to buy on weakness over the next 6–12 months. ♀

JAPAN

Rod Birkett and Antony Gifford

*Rod Birkett joined **Flemings** after eight years in Japanese stockbroking. He was appointed a Director of **Fleming Investment Management Ltd** in 1993. He manages **Save & Prosper Japan Growth Fund** and **Fleming Japanese Investment Trust**. Antony Gifford joined **Flemings** in 1994 as an Investment Analyst assisting the Japanese fund managers, following two years with **Nikko Securities**.*

*At 31 March 1995, the **Flemings** group had £8.4 billion under management invested in Japanese equities. **Fleming Japanese Investment Trust** has a market capitalization of approximately £440 million, and is the largest and top performing Japanese investment trust. **Save & Prosper Japan Growth Fund** is an authorized unit trust of £260 million, and has top decile performance over three years.*

It is well known that investing in Japan is very different from investing in the other major markets of the world. For those who have never followed Japan closely it is perhaps the multitude of differences between the Japanese financial and economic models and those of the Anglo-Saxon markets that intimidates and discourages Western investors.

Cultural Differences

The first difference between the Japanese and Western models is cultural, and concerns the attitudes and approaches of the Japanese people. In all aspects of Japanese society there has historically been an emphasis on the importance of long-term relationships. Within industry the results of these cultural differences are dramatic. The Japanese worker has historically shown greater loyalty to a single employer, usually throughout a career. A strongly unionized labour force has been less confrontational, although they had their disruptive periods in the 1960s, in its relations with employers than in, for example, the UK or France. The unions have been rewarded by greater influence over management as well as with security of employment for the work force.

The Japanese savings rate is currently about 18 per cent compared with only 4 per cent in the USA. This has played a significant part in providing cheap financing.

The second significant difference is that Japanese people are historically a nation of savers. There are a number of reasons for this, in particular the low level of employer funding of pension schemes. The Japanese savings rate is currently about 18 per cent compared with only 4 per cent in the USA. This has played a significant part in providing cheap financing.

Politics and Bureaucracy

The Liberal Democratic Party began a period of continuous government in 1955 which lasted until 1993. In practice, the government was less stable than this might infer, with the LDP comprising a number of powerful factions participating in a constant battle for influence and control. The LDP was, throughout this extended period, a mainstay of a relationship of mutual self-interest with the bureaucracy and the big industrial *keiretsu*. This relationship has recently been described as the Iron Triangle. The recession of the first years of the 1990s, coinciding as it did with further scandals reaching to the upper echelons of the LDP, led to the unimaginable – loss of power – and then, in 1993, a coalition government of reformists took power. Nineteen ninety-three is seen as the year that the Iron Triangle ended. It had been in existence for a long period and had historically exerted huge influence over all threads of the Japanese system.

The bureaucracy in Japan has always had massive influence over Japanese society and the economy. Coupled with an independent central bank, the civil service was, and is, an immensely powerful force. Japanese industry has always operated under heavy regulatory controls imposed by powerful

407

ministries, in particular the Ministry of International Trade and Industry (MITI). MITI has traditionally had a responsibility for long-term economic planning in which industries regarded as 'necessary' for Japan's economic growth were encouraged and protected until they were established.

The exceptional and enormously long periods of economic growth enjoyed by Japan can be attributed to the merits of the financial and economic system. It is, however, necessary to recognize that the differences in the culture and politics of Japan and the stability they provided are an essential part of the picture.

The Economy

The manufacturing economy that expanded so dramatically benefited from access to cheap, long-term finance and was thus able to make long-term investments in order to achieve technological innovation and advanced production techniques. The economy thrived on the production of steel, ships, automobiles and electrical goods, and on the ability to sell worldwide. The ability to generate such a powerful economy from the debris of the war and without the benefit of large stocks of natural resources had led observers to dub this growth a 'miracle'. It was, as I shall try to explain, the result of an economic and financial system unlike those prevalent in the West, although with similarities to West Germany. This system supported an economy that grew at an average rate of approximately 5.75 per cent from 1965 to 1990. It was not all rapid growth. The energy price shock of the mid-1970s was a worrying time for the Japanese, but the impression of an economy experiencing growth with controlled, and usually modest, inflationary pressure is, in a general sense, correct. The Bank of Japan has earned an enviable record of inflation control and the economy has shown a resilient ability to grow, fuelled by exports, despite a currency with a relentless record of strength.

The Financial System

The financial system accepted lower income returns in order to support the growing manufacturing sector. The major domestic institutions were investing for the very long-term, hence their greater interest in growth ahead of income. Banks expected to have a long and fruitful relationship with corporate clients and cemented this relationship by being more involved in management and by holding the shares of relationship companies. In this respect, the Japanese system shares characteristics with the German model, in which the relationship bank has historically held a major stake in important clients and has often had representation on the supervisory board.

The equity and bond markets were as accommodating as the banking system as providers of corporate financing. This was cheap and sometimes at almost no cost to the borrower. Huge domestic savings institutions were accommodative of the wishes of the management to a degree that would seem astonishing to a Western management. Fund managers in Japan met their absolute targets relatively easily without the short-term pursuit of dividend income for which the Anglo-Saxon stock market investors are criticized by industry.

In the speculative, and ultimately disastrous, bubble economy of the late 1980s, the Japanese banks moved into a period of reckless lending at rates still indicating low credit risk. As an alternative to dividend income, the Japanese investors became astute at turning capital growth into income without the need for high dividend pay-outs.

Financing tools such as low coupon bonds with equity warrants attached were developed to reduce further the borrowing costs of corporate Japan. In the case of this tool, the two parts were separated, with the bonds bought by domestic institutions and the warrants traded as geared equity similar to a call option. On simultaneous expiry the exercise of the warrant funded the cost of redeeming the bond and, because of the warrant attachment, the bonds were attractive to investors despite very low coupons. In fact, in the late 1980s, companies were able to issue dollar warrant bonds that, when swapped into yen, meant that they were actually borrowing at negative interest rates!

The economic growth being fuelled by manufacturing made Japan a net exporter of both goods and, more latterly, of capital. As the trade surplus mushroomed, the country became the biggest global net saver and the yen has strengthened from a rate of over ¥350=$1 in 1975 to the rate of about ¥80=$1 as of April 1995. Japan is now the world's largest creditor nation, with overseas financial assets of ¥171 trillion providing annual investment income of some $41 billion, about 30 per cent of the current account.

The Japanese stock market has differed from international comparables to at least the same extent as other areas of the Japanese model. With a heavily regulated economic system and the cross holdings between corporates and their relationship banks, the management of Japanese corporations has never required incentives to maximize return to shareholders in the way that is common in most Western markets. In the absence of demands for higher dividend pay-outs or the threat of take-over, management was able to invest heavily not only in productive assets and developments, but also in investment portfolios. Consequently, investment in Japanese equities has historically been an investment in assets rather than an investment in an earnings stream.

Valuation methods such as price/earnings ratios and yields fail to provide meaningful comparison with other stock markets. Alternatives such as price to book ratios and net asset valuations are more meaningful but, due to the difference in accounting policies, are still difficult for an overseas investor to use for comparative purposes. An example of arcane accounting policy is the system by which corporate investment portfolios remain valued at cost in the accounts until they are sold, often for a huge bookable profit. An extreme current example of a company with huge, unrealized gains on equity holdings is the cotton spinning company, Nisshinbo Industries. At 31 March 1995, Nisshinbo had unrealized gains of ¥218.8 billion, compared to a total market capitalization of only ¥188.7 billion!

Ratio Comparison

While the Japanese stock market looks expensive on an international comparison of price/earnings or on a yield basis, it can be shown to be reasonable value in other comparisons. It is also worth pointing out that ratio comparisons do help with investment decisions within Japan. As at June 1995, 52 per cent of the Tokyo Stock Exchange first section companies were on a price/book ratio of less than 1.5 while, in the US, only 17 per cent of the S&P 500 companies were trading below 1.5. Similarly, on a price/cash flow basis, the Japanese market is now no more than 10 per cent more expensive than the US, despite the Japanese market being near the bottom and the US market near the top of their respective earnings ranges. The reason for these differences is that the return on assets is poor in corporate Japan and, as previously mentioned the stock market remains an investment in assets. P/E ratios will continue to fall as Japanese companies pursue cost-cutting to boost returns.

Many of the more interesting Japanese equities are global leaders offering the investor participation in well managed companies generating profits in multiple geographic markets. Toyota is the prime example of a Japanese corporation that has maintained world class competitiveness over the long term. Toyota has consistently led the way in new, more efficient production methods, in close relationships with parts suppliers and in quality control in the mass production of automobiles. The company is now one of the top three automobile manufacturers in the world, and has coped with the strengthening of the yen on every occasion. The management of Toyota is held up as an example to automobile manufacturers worldwide and to other Japanese manufacturers.

A less well known, but equally impressive, example of a Japanese company successful in world markets is Kyocera. The company is the world's leading manufacturer of ceramic packaging for use in the semi-conductor industry and a leading manufacturer of artificial limbs. A third example of a suitable Japanese company is Fanuc, a world leader in factory automation equipment and robots.

The 'Bubble'

Japan is now in a state of flux as a consequence of the speculative asset price bubble of the late 1980s that burst in such dramatic style. As with all such bubbles, the valuations of assets and equities, lost touch with reality and, when this confidence was questioned at the end of 1989, the bubble burst with dire consequences for the real estate, construction and financial sectors. The resulting hangover continues to be a drag on the economy as the banks are overwhelmed by bad debts and property collateral which is now worth considerably less than book value. Bank bad debts are currently estimated to be over ¥40 trillion. This is equivalent to about 10 per cent of GDP, and works out at approximately 60 per cent of the market capitalization for the entire banking sector as of May 1995!

Chart 3.27 of the real estate market shows the severity of the bubble and the sharp falls in the value of land which hurt so many investors, and had a knock-on effect in equities.

The scale of the real estate price bubble can be illustrated by the startling statistic that, in the late 1980s, there was a period when the value of the grounds of the Imperial Palace in Tokyo exceeded the value of the land of the whole of the state of California.

Chart 3.27 Japanese Commercial Land Prices

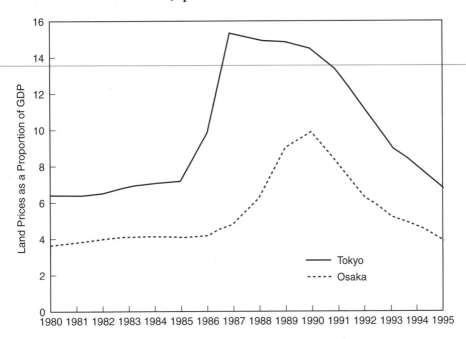

Source: National Land Agency

Fixed Income

Japan is a country dependent on imports of raw materials and was subjected to the oil shocks of the 1970s, following which the Japanese government became increasingly risk and inflation averse. A successful low inflation monetary policy has meant that Japan has been able to maintain low interest rates through the 1980s and 1990s and brought bond yields lower.

Chart 3.29 of JGB new issuance shows the dramatic deterioration in the government balance sheet through the most recent recession and in the aftermath of the bursting of the asset price bubble.

411

Chart 3.28 Yield on Government Benchmark Bond (8 to 10 years)

Source: Datastream

Chart 3.29 Japanese Government Bond New Issuance

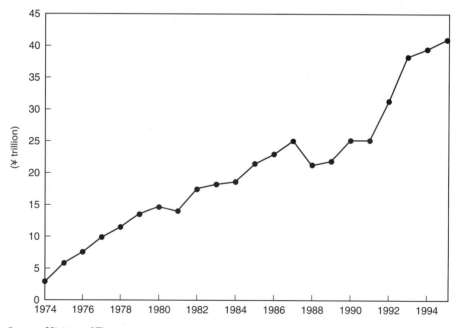

Source: Ministry of Finance

The demographic problem of an ageing population that Japan will soon have to face means that the fiscal position is unlikely to improve dramatically, even when economic growth returns.

The Changing Face of Japan

Changes in Japanese society are already evident. The younger members of the work force are very critical of the older generation of the growth economy. Younger Japanese have a more Western outlook, being less able to depend on lifetime employment and more motivated by the maximization of their own quality of life. They are looking to work shorter hours with less company loyalty and therefore a greater willingness to move in order to further their careers.

The political system is now beginning to represent a two-party democratic system. The LDP is no longer the single dominant force in Japanese politics, but will continue to be influential for the foreseeable future. Although the two-party system has yet to emerge, the recent changes to the electoral system will, over time, push Japanese politics down this route.

The stock market in 1994 initially reflected a slow recovery before the structural problems and political impotence took a toll. 1995 and 1996 will provide investors with opportunities as the economy recovers and the government is finally forced to accept the painful structural remedies that are necessary. The continuing strength of the currency will test the ability of Japanese industry to respond, although companies continue to adapt by increasingly moving production or input sources overseas to become more currency neutral.

Japanese equities will become more recognizable to the Western investor, as the underlying assets have now fallen in value or are being sold to realize funds for restructuring or to cover investment losses. Given time, I believe that we can expect to see gradual increases in dividends and changes to accounting procedures. Concepts such as return on equity, previously ignored, are being studied with interest by both management and domestic institutional investors. Banks that previously lent recklessly at rates becoming of the most conservative credit risk will begin to appreciate the finer points of credit analysis and will understand that collateral other than property can provide the same, if not greater, comfort to a lender.

The Japanese will be forced to converge with Western practices, a process that has already begun. None of the restructuring that is necessary will happen overnight. As the model and the stock market become more familiar to Western observers, the greatest investment opportunities will fall to the investor who correctly judges the timing of the various transitions to be made. 🌐

ASIAN GROWTH – THE FIVE TIGERS

Kathryn Langridge

*Kathryn Langridge is the Head of Asian investment at **Perpetual** in the UK. She manages $600 million, including Perpetual Asian Smaller Markets Fund, and the Perpetual International Emerging Companies Fund, both Triple A rated by Fund Research. She lived in Asia throughout the 1980s, working for **Jardine Fleming** in Hong Kong, Singapore and Malaysia.*

*Founded in 1973, **Perpetual** currently has £4 billion under management on behalf of private and institutional investors. Its unit trust range covers all the major equity markets of the world. Over the last three years, **Perpetual** has won more than 40 awards, and has been named as The Sunday Times International Unit Trust Manager of the Year in four out of the last six years.*

' Asia's time has come,' – Goh Chok Tong, Singapore's PM

'The Pacific Century', 'The Asian Growth Miracle', 'The greatest economic power on earth': the clichéd descriptions of the trajectory of Asian growth are well known, but difficult to refute. Excluding China, GDP expanded by an average of 6.6 per cent in 1994, compared with an equivalent growth rate in the OECD countries of 2.5 per cent. The Asian Development Bank expects that, 'Asian economies are still likely to grow at least two to three times as fast as economies in other regions', for the rest of the century. These numbers tell their own story.

Table 3.7

Average GDP growth rate	1975-1993 %	1987-1996 %
NICS		
Hong Kong	16.2	5.9
Korea	8.1	8.1
Singapore	15.1	8.6
Sri Lanka	17.7	8.0
Taiwan	20.4	7.4
South East Asia		
Indonesia	11.3	6.6
Malaysia	13.4	8.3
Philippines	3.4	3.8
Thailand	11.4	9.7
Indian Sub Continent		
India	6.2	5.0
Pakistan	8.3	5.2
Sri Lanka	4.0	4.5

Sources: ADB, Jardine Fleming

A few statistics and forecasts capture what this growth represents and where business opportunities are greatest. By the year 2000, Asia will comprise roughly two-thirds of the world's population. China will be 40 per cent of this, India 33 per cent; both now at the earliest stages of economic liberalization and market opening which is unleashing the buying power of millions of consumers. In 1991, 70 per cent of urban Chinese households had colour TVs against only 1 per cent ten years earlier; 80 per cent had washing machines, against 6 per cent in 1981. China which has grown by 9 per cent per annum since 1978, will be the largest economy in the world early in the twenty-first century if current trends persist, and India could conceivably be not far behind.

Infrastructure spending, excluding China, will total almost $600 billion by the year 2000, and China alone could spend as much as a further $500 billion. Asia is power deficient: even the most developed Asian countries have less than half the *per capita* installed power base of the US – China has less than 5 per cent. Over $550 billion is expected to be spent by the turn of the century on electricity generation in the region. By comparison, total investment in the Channel Tunnel was $8.7 billion.

A mere catalogue of statistics fails to describe adequately the vigorous, interactive processes at work, which make the Asian growth phenomenon sustainable. Catalysed by foreign direct investment from Japanese, and later, European companies, the process of export and investment led growth began first in Hong Kong and Singapore, to be followed in the seventies in Malaysia, Thailand, Taiwan and South Korea. As the competitive advantages of investing in Asian manufacturing became widely known, so the region became increasingly a magnet for foreign investment.

The essence of this process is free but intense competition. As ever, lower cost manufacturing bases develop (now even Burma and Cambodia are opening up), the availability of cheap unskilled labour and an absence of tariff barriers has become no longer sufficient to ensure competitive advantage. As a result, the region has been pulled from the front by the higher technological needs and capabilities of its markets, and pushed from behind by producers of ever cheaper basic, manufactured commodities in successively, for example, Vietnam. The maturing economies (such as Singapore, Taiwan and Korea) have been progressively forced up the value-added scale. No longer manufacturers of cracker trinkets, these economies are now among the world's most efficient suppliers of complex electronic components and specialize in filling commercial niches which may be too small for larger nations.

No longer manufacturers of cracker trinkets, these economies are now among the world's most efficient suppliers of complex electronic components and specialize in filling commercial niches which may be too small for larger nations.

At the same time, intra-regional trade and capital flows have become increasingly important, reducing dependence on the mature economies. This has given the region considerable resilience during periods of slow global growth and has lessened the impact of the Japanese recession since 1991. Over 40 per cent of Asian trade is now with other Asian countries. Asia understands and increasingly supplies its own needs and rapid growth has become self feeding. In addition, the strength of the yen since 1985 has created further impetus to the migration of manufacturing to the lowest cost, most efficient sources to be found throughout Asia.

Chart 3.30 Asian Exports by Destination (excluding China and India)

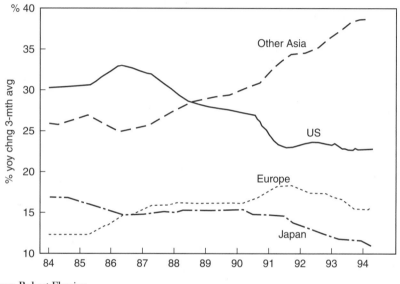

Source: Robert Fleming

The perception that Asia is merely dependent on foreign direct investment is, however, misplaced. Encouraged by low tax structures, Asia's propensity to save stands in marked contrast to that of America. Asian savings rates are among the highest in the world, averaging almost 32 per cent of GDP : the four main ASEAN economies of Singapore, Thailand, Malaysia and Indonesia average almost 40 per cent. Capital investment levels are also exceptionally high, equivalent to 31 per cent of GDP in 1993, suggesting healthy trends in domestic investment in education and infrastructure, so vital for sustained growth.

This accounts for the remarkable achievement of high growth with generally low inflation and suggests an essentially stable picture of long-term economic health. Asian economies are structurally sound, and are essentially characterized by prudent public finances (there are budget surpluses in Singapore, Thailand and Malaysia), high savings rates, steadily climbing foreign reserves and a broadly stable history of careful currency management. Current account deficits exist but are driven by imports of capital goods which

416

Chart 3.31 Asian Savings and Investment (1992)

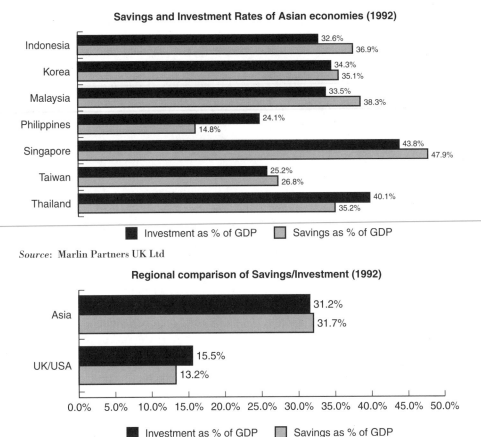

Savings and Investment Rates of Asian economies (1992)

Indonesia — 32.6% / 36.9%
Korea — 34.3% / 35.1%
Malaysia — 33.5% / 38.3%
Philippines — 24.1% / 14.8%
Singapore — 43.8% / 47.9%
Taiwan — 25.2% / 26.8%
Thailand — 40.1% / 35.2%

■ Investment as % of GDP   ▧ Savings as % of GDP

Source: Marlin Partners UK Ltd

Regional comparison of Savings/Investment (1992)

Asia — 31.2% / 31.7%
UK/USA — 15.5% / 13.2%

0.0% 5.0% 10.0% 15.0% 20.0% 25.0% 30.0% 35.0% 40.0% 45.0% 50.0%

■ Investment as % of GDP   ▧ Savings as % of GDP

Source: Marlin Partners UK Ltd

are in turn building the productive base of the economy, and are largely funded by long-term capital flows.

While it may be clear that Asia will achieve rapid compound growth, this does not, however, come risk-free to the investor who has to juggle a complex series of factors. This is not a homogeneous region: there are relative successes and failures, pockets of excess and areas where reform has been slow or even non-existent. Infrastructure constraints are apparent in places, labour short-ages are pushing up costs. Political risk is high; Indo-China is only just recovering from two decades of conflict; there are political succession prob-lems in Indonesia; both the Philippines and Thailand have suffered coups in recent years.

Growth and liberalization of the region's economics have been accompanied by the rapid development of the financial industry as capital has chased the high returns implicit in the region's growth rates. In 1993 alone, the stockmarkets of

417

Indonesia and the Philippines rose in excess of 100 per cent as portfolio investors became attracted to the same characteristics of growth and stability which had encouraged direct investment. In the decade 1983 to 1993, the market capitalization of the region rose more than 1700 per cent, representing a compounded annual growth rate of 30 per cent. By 1994, total Asian market capitalization (excluding China, India and Japan) totalled $1 trillion, having almost tripled as a percentage of global market value between 1987 and 1993, to 12.5 per cent.

Indonesia presents a useful illustration of the development of one stockmarket. In 1988 there were 24 listed companies which rarely traded; annual turnover as a percentage of market capitalization was 2 per cent; market capitalization was $2 billion. After five years of accelerating GDP and earnings growth, of deregulation and reform, there are now over 200 listed companies, annual turnover rose to 30 per cent in 1993 and market capitalization to $49 billion by the end of 1994. Chart 3.32 lays out comparable statistics for the major stock markets in Asia, excluding India and Japan.

There are, however, a number of practical problems in relation to investing in Asia. Developing political structures imply a high degree of political risk. Portfolio investors must be prepared for volatility and unpredictable short-term shifts both in the markets and their underlying currency. The dangers are typical of any emerging market. Volumes are often erratic and thin, disclosure may be weak, accounting procedures inconsistent, floods of new paper may erode earnings growth, and so on. Some markets remain all but closed to foreign investors: Korea, Taiwan and India, for example, are best accessed via the medium of a closed-end country fund.

In general, however, characteristics of sound investments in the developed markets are very much the feasible target of the investor in Asia. Good focused management, a proven ability to adapt to change, strong balance

Chart 3.32 Asian Capital Markets 1995

	Market cap US$Bn	No. of listed shares	PE 1995E	EPS growth %
Hong Kong	294	528	11.7	16.1
Indonesia	57	225	16.3	32.2
Malaysia	225	504	23.0	13.7
Pakistan	10	650	12.5	22.0
Philippines	51	195	18.5	29.5
Singapore	155	248	21.0	16.7
South Korea	195	701	13.7	30.2
Taiwan	190	329	18.2	24.0
Thailand	156	496	19.3	19.4

Source: Barings Securities International Limited

sheet, a history of not compromising minority shareholders, and a sound record of earnings and dividend growth should all be necessary criteria for investment. In thematic terms, companies focusing on the growth of the domestic economy are likely to perform well. The consumer is fast emerging: this will benefit retailers, distributors, manufacturers of basic products, and financial services companies. The infrastructure boom will produce construction, power and telecommunications giants, and benefit ancillary local industries and suppliers; cable producers, steel and cement companies, road builders and so on.

Examples are easy to find. In Malaysia, Renong Berhad is a holding company with 13 publicly listed and over 100 private subsidiaries and associates, making it the most comprehensive and largest proxy on Malaysian infrastructure development. The group's activities include engineering, expressways, toll collection, telecommunications, power, property development, hotels, oil and gas, transportation and financial services.

Development Bank of Singapore Ltd is a good proxy for the domestic economy in Singapore, with exposure through its expanding loan book to the buoyant manufacturing and housing sectors. Singapore banks in general offer strong capital ratios, high asset quality, strong balance sheets, operate under a strict regulatory environment, and have diversified earnings. DBS Bank is the largest in terms of assets in Singapore.

With demand for electricity in Thailand growing 14 per cent between 1987–1991 and forecast 8 per cent per annum up to 2006, Banpu Coal, as the dominant player in the power generation industry, is well placed to benefit. Banpu is involved in power generation, coal mining and trading, engineering, and power-related infrastructure. The company is in a rapid expansion phase, and will generate high quality, rapidly growing earnings from new power plant projects in Thailand and Indonesia.

Telephone penetration in the Philippines remains among the lowest in the world at 1.5 lines per 100 population. A possible five-fold increase in the market between 1993–2000 will leave the dominant provider, Philippine Long Distance Telephone, with earnings growth in excess of 20 per cent, even as new competitors enter the industry. PLDT has come through a far-reaching, and successful, rationalization programme, and can expect rapid line growth, higher call volumes, higher international traffic, and high quality earnings.

Semen Gresik is the holding company for the Government of Indonesia's cement interests, and will control 40 per cent of industry capacity by 1998. Cement demand grew 20 per cent in 1994, and demand will exceed supply until 1997, when new plants will increase capacity by 50 per cent. Following a number of attractively priced recent cement plant acquisitions, Semen Gresik is set to become the largest, and purest, cement producer in Indonesia, in an environment where it can sell all it produces.

The region is complex and fascinating, each country at a different stage of development and maturity, and at a different point of its economic, political and business cycle. The likelihood that its broad-based growth profile will be reversed is low. Economic reform and liberalization are entrenched, rapid economic growth rates are highly sustainable. There can be little doubt that an economic revolution is taking place in Asia, which will transform the global economy, and holds out among the world's most exciting long-term prospects for investors. ♀

AUSTRALASIA

McIntosh Securities Ltd

McIntosh Securities Ltd is a leading Australasian-based group specialising in institutional and private client broking, and corporate finance. It is the only stockbroker listed on the Sydney Stock Exchange. McIntosh is 19.1 per cent owned by the ING Group. The research team consistently ranks in the top five in broker rating surveys in Australia and New Zealand. The group's activities are undertaken through offices in Melbourne, Sydney, Brisbane, Perth, Port Moresby, Auckland, Wellington, Hong Kong, Tokyo, New York and London.

Executive Summary

The Australian and New Zealand equity markets have performed strongly in the past decade on the back of a number of economic reforms: most notably the introduction of economic policies that have reduced inflation to below OECD levels, deregulation of labour markets, and lower tariffs that have encouraged more import competition and have led to an acceleration in manufactured exports. While the Australasian equity markets are now firmly entrenched in Asia, accounting standards are more similar to the UK than they are to Japan, Korea or Taiwan. Australia is unique in that more than one third of market capitalization is in resource companies (with strong exposure to gold, coal, oil, iron ore, alumina, natural gas, aluminium and copper). The New Zealand market has large privatized utilities (NZ Telecom is the largest) and strong exposure to forestry (Fletcher Challenge, Carter Holt Harvey). ♀

AUSTRALIA

John Banos

John Banos is a Director (and Head of Asset Allocation and Portfolio Strategy) at stockbrokers McIntosh & Company. John is a CFA and an affiliate member and lecturer to the Securities Institute of Australia.

Brief History

The national stock market, located in Sydney, came into existence in 1987, at which time the six state stock exchanges amalgamated to form what is now referred to as the 'Australian Stock Exchange' (ASX).

Size

The ASX is capitalized at A$ 301 billion (excluding overseas companies), or A$ 489 billion including overseas companies. Of those equity markets that are totally open to foreign investors, Australia is the third largest market in Asia after Japan and Hong Kong. Australia comprises a little under 2 per cent of the Morgan Stanley Capital International index and the FTA-World index. There are currently 1184 companies listed on the ASX, of which the largest 317 comprise the All Ordinaries index.

Trading

Trades are now conducted through a single computer-based trading system referred to as SEATS (Stock Exchange Automated Trading System). Previously, trading floors existed in all six state stock exchanges. The system operates on a priority system based on both price and the time at which the bid or offer was lodged. SEATS automatically executes a trade once the buying and selling side are matched.

Settlement

Settlement now occurs five business days after trade. However, the ASX is now phasing in a fully automated settlement system known as CHESS (Clearing House Electronic Sub-Register System). The advantages of such a system are: (a) future trades will be scripless; (b) registration is immediate; (c) settlement time will eventually be reduced to three days.

Sectors

Resources

The unique feature of the ASX that distinguishes it from other developed markets is the large weighting of resource companies, which together amounts to a little over one-third of the All Ordinaries index. The resource sector comprises the following sub-sectors: gold, other metals, solid fuels, oil & gas and diversified.

The three largest Australian resource companies are:

1 **BHP** is Australia's largest company. Group annual sales now approach A$ 17 billion from activities that are largely in steel, petroleum and minerals. BHP Steel is the world's thirteenth largest producer. BHP Petroleum ranks fourteenth in the world on the basis of the size of its reserves. BHP Minerals is a major global producer of copper, iron ore, coal and manganese. The holding company also has substantial service businesses: transport, engineering and insurance, and a 37 per cent interest in Foster's Brewing. About one-third of BHP's assets are now located outside Australia, and two-thirds of sales are priced in US dollars.

2 **CRA** – an Australian mining conglomerate controlled by RTZ in the UK. CRA is one of the world's largest iron ore producers with annual output in the vicinity of 48-50 million tons per annum. CRA is also becoming a major producer of thermal coal. Total production in 1995 will be approximately 29 million tons, of which a significant component comes from Coal & Allied (a listed subsidiary) and the newly commissioned Kaltim Prima mine in Indonesia. CRA operates the Argyle diamond mine (60 per cent ownership), producing, on an equity basis, in excess of 26 million carats per annum.

3 **Western Mining (WMC)** – established nickel mining, smelting and refining operations based on the Kambalda deposits in Western Australia. WMC discovered the major copper-uranium ore body at Olympic Dam in South Australia. In the 1980s, the company diversified into oil and gas interests in Australia and America with varying degrees of success. The Mt Keith nickel deposit was acquired in 1991 through a joint take-over with Normandy Poseidon, which will take WMC's total nickel output to around 96,000 tons per annum by 1996. WMC announced, in July 1994, the acquisition of 40 per cent of the Alcoa US aluminium assets.

Industrials

Important sub-sectors within the industrial market include banks; media (dominated by News Corporation) and diversified industrials – the latter incorporates BTR Nylex (a subsidiary of BTR plc) and Pacific Dunlop (one of the world's largest producers of tyres, batteries and condoms).

Three of the largest Australian industrial companies are:

1 **News Corporation** Under Rupert Murdoch, News Corporation has become one of the world's largest, and most diversified, media empires. The extraordinary pace of growth can be gauged by the increased in News Corporation's asset base by almost 35 times since 1983, from A$ 800 million to almost A$28 billion. Growth has been achieved via major acquisitions (of Fox Film, Metromedia, Triangle, STAR TV etc) and the organic growth of businesses such as newspapers, Fox Broadcasting and BSkyB. The group is now aggressively pursuing its global media strategy.

Strategies are focused more on growing existing assets – especially Fox Television and STAR TV – and through minor acquisitions that enhance vertical integration.

2 **National Australia Bank (NAB)** Australia's largest bank (in terms of shareholders' funds), with a market capitalization of around A$ 17 billion. NAB has strong regional banking franchises in Australia and New Zealand. In addition, NAB acquired Northern Bank, Clydesdale Bank and National Irish Bank in the UK in 1987. February 1990 saw Yorkshire added to the group, and 1995 saw the acquisition of Michigan Bank in the US.

3 **BTR Nylex** A subsidiary of BTR plc and Australia's largest manufacturing company. The company has operations spanning industrial products (packaging and polymers), building materials and componentry for rail, road and air transport. The company is significantly diversified overseas. Foreign earnings (from the US, UK, Taiwan, Malaysia and China) represented almost 50 per cent of operating profits in 1994 and should increase in future years.

Valuations

The price to net tangible assets (NTA) of the All Industrials index has averaged 1.4x in the past two decades. Share prices have risen to over 2x NTA during speculative booms, but have tended to fall to NTA or lower during economic 'hard' recessions – as occurred during 1974, 1982–3 and 1990. P/NTA has historically been an excellent guide to absolute value in the Australian share market.

The All Industrials prospective price earnings ratio (P/E) has averaged 8.8x in the past three decades and 10.3x during the lower inflation 1960s. P/E ratios have been substantially lower during the high inflation era of the 1970s, and above average during the speculative 1980s.

Chart 3.33 Price/Asset Backing for all industrials

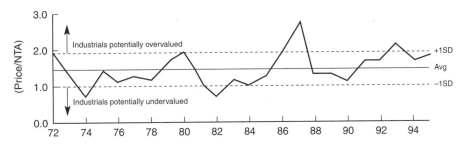

Sources: ASX, McIntosh

423

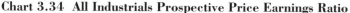

Chart 3.34 All Industrials Prospective Price Earnings Ratio

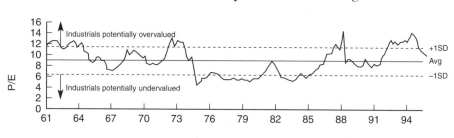

Sources: Knight-Ridder Financial, McIntosh

The Australian resource sector has consistently traded on higher P/E ratios than the industrial sectors. Resource P/E ratios have tended to increase to very high levels at the bottom of the earnings cycle (and ahead of commodity price booms) and have fallen to similar levels to the industrial market when resource earnings are near their peak.

Chart 3.35 All Resources Prospective Price Earnings Ratio

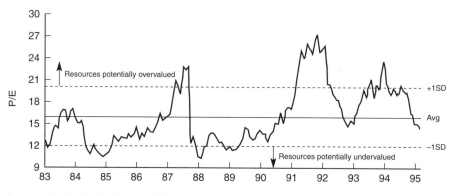

Sources: Knight-Ridder Financial, McIntosh

Table 3.8 Equity Market Statistics

All Ordinaries Index @ 2042

| | Years to June | | | |
	1994	1995	1996	1997
EPS growth (%)	13.0	16.4	14.1	10.7
Price earnings ratio (x)	15.7	13.4	11.8	10.7
Dividend yield (%)	3.8	4.3	4.8	5.2

Source: McIntosh

Fixed Interest Market

The debt market has an average daily turnover of A$5.8 billion, and is dominated by Commonwealth and semi-government securities. The corporate debt market is small, with only a handful of Australia's largest companies issuing paper.

Within the short-term securities market (i.e. cash, Treasury notes, promissory notes, bills, CDs), total reported turnover for FY 94 was A$1,024 billion. For the corresponding period, total reported market turnover in the long-term securities market (i.e. Commonwealth, semi-government and corporate bonds, mortgage backed securities, FRNS) was A$1,963 billion.

Liquidity has increased through the futures market. The Sydney Futures Exchange ('SFE') is the tenth largest in the world and was the first to implement an after-hours screen dealing system (SYCOM). SFE traded interest rate products include 90-day bank bill futures and three- and ten-year Treasury bond futures. In FY 94, turnover at the SFE was a record 21.4 million contracts. ●

Table 3.9 Interest Rates – Actuals and Forecasts

Year (end June)	90 day Bank bill (%)	10 year bond (%)
1991	10.50	11.15
1992	6.40	8.90
1993	5.25	7.35
1994	5.45	9.65
1995 (f)	7.50	8.80
1996 (f)	9.50	9.25
1997 (f)	8.50	8.50

Sources: RBA, McIntosh

NEW ZEALAND

Sean Allison

*Sean Allison is the Investment Strategist for **Hendry Hay McIntosh** in New Zealand. Sean has worked as a financial analyst and economist in New Zealand over most of the ten-year economic reform period. He is a member of the New Zealand Association of Economists and Society of Investment Analysts. He is also a member of the New Zealand Stock Exchange.*

Heading into the second half of the 1990s, the New Zealand economy is yielding all of the long awaited benefits of the massive structural reform

425

programme of the previous ten years. Government is running a large fiscal surplus and debt repayment at the national level is accelerating. Inflationary pressures remain subdued, despite strong real growth, thanks mainly to the 0–2 per cent target range for inflation which the central bank is required to police.

Real economic growth, in recent years, has been dominated by a surge in new private sector investment mainly aligned to manufacturing and tourism. Reflecting the growth in capital expenditure and recovery in income, import growth moved up sharply over 1994–5 eclipsing robust export growth. Looking forward into 1995–6 and 1996–7, we see a more balanced performance. Export growth is concentrated in the fast-growing Asian markets, where New Zealand's competitiveness as a food supplier and processor has allowed for a rapid development of product range. Forestry remains a fast-growing export oriented industry once again aimed primarily at the Asian region. We expect real growth to average around 3 per cent through 1997, and this should be sufficient to support underlying profit growth for the listed corporate sector of around 10 per cent. We favour investment in telecommunications, where new technology absorption is high, and tourism, where strong demand from new, untapped Asian markets will bolster the overall growth through to the turn of the century.

Table 3.10 Economic Statistical Summary

March year-end	1994 A	1995 E	1996 F	1997 F
Investment (yr%)	18.9	23.1	8.5	5.3
Exports (yr%)	8.5	6.4	6.0	6.6
Imports (yr%)	12.0	17.0	6.5	6.3
GDP(yr%)	5.5	6.4	3.4	2.9
Government Balance (% of GDP)	0.9	3.2	3.7	5.1
Inflation (yr%)	1.3	4.0	2.0	0.1

Source: Reserve Bank of New Zealand

Table 3.11 Equity Market Statistics

March years	1994 A	1995 E	1996 F	1997 F
Earnings Growth (%)	17.0	14.5	18.0	11.0
Price Earnings Ratio	14.3	12.5	10.5	9.4
Dividend Yield (%)	4.5	4.9	5.4	6.0

Source: Hendry Hay McIntosh

Major stocks in New Zealand with international recognition are:

Telecom Corporation of NZ

Shares of Telecom are listed on the New Zealand and Australian Stock Exchanges. The New York Stock Exchange lists the shares in the form of ADRs (1 ADR = 20 ordinary shares). TEL is a full service telecommunications company. Operations embrace local service (1.6 million lines), national and international tolls (480 million and 80 million calls per annum respectively), directory, cellular (297,000 subscribers), mobile, radio and equipment rental and sales. Over the past five years, the telecommunications market has deregulated. Competition has emerged in tolls (Clear Communications 20 per cent market share), cellular (Bell South) and equipment sales. Prices for services have fallen dramatically. Against a background of deregulation, TEL has dramatically improved its operating efficiencies, service and profits.

Carter Holt Harvey

Carter Holt Harvey's (CAH) history dates back more than 100 years to three family businesses. The most recent name to be added stemmed from the 1985 takeover of Alex Harvey Industries. In early 1986, CAH – in joint venture with Chilean interests – announced it had taken a 30 per cent interest in Chile's largest company, forest products giant OOPEC. In 1990 CAH merged with New Zealand's largest forest owner, Eldere Resources. CAH's core operations involve plantation forestry, log and chip exporting, lumber and plywood, medium density fibreboard, pulp and paper production, building products manufacture and packaging. International Paper has recently taken a controlling interest in CAH.

Fletcher Challenge

Fletcher Challenge was formed in 1980 through the merger of three NZ companies: Fletcher Holdings, Challenge Corporation and Tasman Pulp & Paper Company. During the 1980s, FLC expanded internationally, buying Crown Forest Industries in British Columbia and Columbia Forest products. Further pulp/paper related acquisitions followed in Australia, Brazil, Chile and the UK. In December 1993, each ordinary share was split into two targeted shares: the Ordinary Division and the Forests Division. Although the company remains as one legal entity, earnings for the Ordinary Division share are derived from all of the original assets, excluding the company's solid wood plantation forests in New Zealand and Chile. ♀

427

SOUTH AFRICA

Richard Stuart

*Richard Stuart is a Director of **Martin & Co Inc**, which is the leading stock-broker in South Africa. Its research has been voted number one for the past 17 years in a poll of South African institutional investors by the* Financial Mail, *the country's leading financial weekly. It has established sales offices in London and New York with its international joint venture partner **Robert Fleming & Co Limited**. **Martin & Co** provides research and equity brokerage services, and also dealing and research in bonds and derivatives, as well as corporate finance and discretionary fund management.*

South Africa is increasingly coming onto the radar screens of international investors,. From March 1995, South Africa went into both the IFC's and MSCI's emerging market indices in a big way, with a weighting of between 8 per cent and 12 per cent for the MSCI indices and 13 per cent to 21 per cent of the IFC's global and investable indices. No longer can South Africa be consigned to the 'too hard' basket, nor can investors pretend it doesn't exist. Quite simply, international investors will have to take a view on South Africa. Most have very little exposure to South Africa. The message is clear. Foreign investors have to become net buyers of South African equities and will increasingly become the price setters at the margin.

As a mix of developed and undeveloped economies, South Africa has many of the features that investors are familiar with in first world situations. In particular, it has a very well-developed contractual savings industry. Understanding the savings flows is essential to understanding asset pricing. In an environment where inflation has averaged close to 15 per cent per anum for the past 15 years and where there has been no capital gains tax, by far the most effective savings medium has been provided by the life assurance and pension/provident fund industries. The industry has ballooned to the point where its annual cash flows have risen from the equivalent of 5 per cent of GDP in 1980 to the current level of near 10 per cent. These annual cash flows are pursuing long-term growth assets to match the long-term nature of their liabilities. With exchange controls bottling up cash within the domestic economy, it is little wonder that, throughout the sanctions years, the contractual savings industry proved a ready receptacle for the steady stream of equities being ditched by foreign investors and multi nationals withdrawing.

Now the game has changed. The world is rediscovering South Africa. In 1993, for the first time in a decade, foreigners turned net buyers of equities. But the interesting point about the R2.8 billion (+/- $600 million) committed in 1993 is that the vast bulk was invested in gold shares, diamond share De Beers, and other commodity shares. Only when Nelson Mandela visited the United States and called for the removal of sanctions, did demand broaden out into financials and industrials. Predictably, the first to arrive were the cavalry, in the form of hedge funds.

In the eight months to August 1995, the net inflow has been a substantial R3.9 billion. This is the result of a growing accumulation of industrial and financial shares in firm offshore hands, a huge increase on the R160 million net inflow in 1994. Through a period of labour unrest characterized by new union leaders flexing their muscles (the old leaders had gone to parliament), to the current remarkable consensus and commitment to a market-driven economy, international fund managers have flooded through the system, getting up to speed with the corporates and economic prospects. The main body of the army has arrived and sufficient believe the story of the new South Africa to impact equity prices.

The story is based on legitimacy. Rarely in history has any nation undergone such a profound change of direction. Not only South Africa, but the whole sub-continent had been quarantined by the isolation brought on by apartheid. Re-integration into the mainstream of international trade and renewed access to world capital markets has transformed the growth prospects of South Africa and its neighbours. The infrastructure that is in place is now set to support South Africa in playing its natural role as the engine for growth of the whole region.

The infrastructure base is impressive and under-utilized. Eskom, the power utility, produces more than half the entire electricity in Africa. Massive modern power generating sets sit atop coal fields in the Eastern Transvaal churning out the second cheapest power in the world. And having planned for much more rapid economic growth, one-third of its generating capacity lies idle. Telkom, the telephone utility, has more than half of the installed telephone lines in Africa, with over 80 per cent already digital. The harbour and road system could carry much more traffic. Cement companies are running at 80 per cent capacity. The banking system is in great shape, strongly capitalized and overprovisioned. The stock exchange, the tenth largest in the world in terms of market capitalization, is well developed. Western style accounting and regulatory systems prevail. Corporates have very strong balance sheets. The property sector, which is largely owned by the institutions, is virtually ungeared. An entrepreneurial ethos flourishes. In short, South Africa has the delivery systems in place in order to absorb and distribute the international capital flows that are necessary to fuel the growth phase that lies ahead.

What finally brought the economy to a halt and precipitated political change was financial sanctions. After P.W. Bothe's infamous 'Rubicon' speech of 1985, South Africa was cut off from world capital flows and was forced to become a capital exporter. A large current account surplus had to be sustained in order to fund debt repayments. In the nine years through to 1993, South Africa repaid foreign debt at an average rate of 3 per cent of GDP per annum. In addition, capital flight of large proportions took place on an unrecorded basis. The legacy of this debt repayment programme is that the country finds itself very underborrowed by international standards. Over this period the foreign debt to GDP ratio fell from 45 per cent to 15 per cent.

That the South African economy was able to withstand such a haemorrhaging for so long was thanks to mineral exports. Despite the terms of trade turning against the country, in that minerals failed to maintain prices in real terms, South Africa still exports nearly a quarter of its GDP on an annual basis. Approximately 70 per cent are resources led by gold, platinum group metals, steamcoal, ferroalloys and diamonds. While the manufacturing export base suffered badly from sanctions, the core export base, being irreplaceable, remained intact.

Even before the new government of national unity (GNU) took office, economic prospects were beginning to look up. With the help of tax concessions, a new generation of major export projects was under construction, and the commodity cycle had started to turn. What was needed was for the GNU wholeheartedly to embrace a free market approach to the economy and to act decisively in bringing the violence under control.

In South Africa, we live in remarkable times. The responsibilities of government and the need to deliver a better life to the electorate have concentrated politicians' minds on the art of the possible. The GNU has already committed itself to a policy of cutting back the size of the bloated civil service reducing government's overall claim on GDP, moving to zero-based budgeting, embarking on a process of privatization, dismantling protective tariff structures and subsidies that led to distortions and inefficiencies within the economy and a hands-off approach to wage negotiations. A somewhat sceptical international investment community still needs to be convinced.

The first impediment was the dual currency system, which was originally designed as a means of preventing money from leaving the system but later acted as a barrier to money entering the economy. This has already been abolished, but there is further to go. The ultimate end play is the complete abolition of capital controls. For until these go, the exchange rate will continue to be viewed with suspicion and financial markets, in particular equity markets, will not become sufficiently liquid for prices to be truly tested.

South Africa is about to embark on a phase of massive spend on the upgrading of the social infrastructure. South Africa has one of the highest GINI co-efficients of any economy in the world. The first world infrastructure has to be extended further down the pyramid. Housing, electrical distribution, water reticulation, roads, telecoms, clinics and schooling are where the money will be spent. These objectives are embodied in the Reconstruction and Development Programme (RDP), which has become the Holy Grail of economic policy initiatives.

Even though we have yet to move into the reconstuctional phase, the infrastructural stocks have already made strong moves. Conglomerates with operations linked to gross domestic fixed investment, such as Murray & Roberts and Barlows, are anticipating better times. Cement producers Anglo Alpha and PPC are likely to be prime beneficiaries of renewed growth. Construction companies such as LTA and Group Five are looking forward to a boom.

So far, the consumer-based industrials are lagging, but their day will come. As economic recovery takes hold, the rate of urbanization will accelerate. Only just over half the labour force is employed in the formal sector, with probably another 20 per cent or so involved in the so-called informal sector. Current estimates are that, out of a total 40 million population, only 7 million can be described as consumers in the Western sense of the word, but this figure is set to double over the next decade. Beer-based consumer group, SA Breweries, is a world class business and the largest industrial by market cap. Powerful food groups such as Tiger Oats, Premier and Foodcorp should flourish. Packaging groups Nampak and Consol dominate their sectors, while consumer-based industrials, Anglovaal Industrials and Melbak, embrace quality operations. The retail sector is efficient and unassailable, but already highly rated. Generally the market is characterized by top-class business, strongly funded, with dominant market shares.

Current estimates are that, out of a total 40 million population, only 7 million can be described as consumers in the Western sense of the word, but this figure is set to double over the next decade.

The resource cycle has a life of its own. The mining houses have traditionally been the easy way to play the broad commodity cycle, with Anglo American and Gencor the leading lights. More focused investors will zero in on the platinum counters such as Rustenburg and Impala, or ferroalloys producer Samancor.

Access to foreign finance is crucial. Government has regained access to international debt markets, now that an investment grade rating has been achieved. IMF facilities are in place, which has acted as a seal of approval for credit lines from commercial banks, and corporates are being allowed to access international equity markets by the Central Bank.

The debt market is around R260 billion as of June 1995. The real returns to investors are currently the best ever on record (and records go back to 1937). The 10-year bond gives a real return of 6 per cent, high by any standard. This has to be put into the context of the movement over the last 10 years.

Annual Average Interest Rate (1985–1995)

	High	Low	Average
10-year rate %	16.9	13.9	15.8
3-month rate %	18.1	8.9	13.5

The growth phase of the economy is likely to be longer, stronger and more sustainable than anything the current generation of businessmen has seen. There is still a remarkable reluctance to believe that the economy can produce the 5 per cent plus growth rates that are necessary, not only to better the living standards of all South Africans, but also to make South Africa a competitive investment destination with Asian alternatives. So far, the policy stance of the GNU is encouraging, as is the rapid improvement in business confidence.

The stock market has already done a good job of anticipating better times. Historically, South African institutions have dominated pricing and have been reluctant to push the ratings above a 15 P/E. International investors seem to have a more bullish perspective. The trailing P/E for the market as a whole, as of August 1995, is 16 times, and the industrial sector is on a similar multiple. Coming off a depressed base, strong earnings growth is likely to unwind this multiple rapidly over the next two or three years. The question about the sustainability of growth can only be answered by the way economic policies evolve. The strength of the contractual savings industry ensures foreigners that investing in South Africa is not a game of musical chairs. Backing the whole pricing system is one of the most developed long-term savings industries in the world, with a vested interest in maintaining asset values. ♥

LATIN AMERICA

Richard Watkins

Richard Watkins is Chief Executive of the **Latinvest Group**, *a London and New York based investment bank specializing in Latin America. He joined the City in 1972, subsequently spending four years in Venezuela, two years in Australia and five years in New York – before returning to London as Chief Executive of* **Schroder Securities**. *In 1992, Watkins, with three colleagues and two Latin American Investment Banks,* **InverMexico** *and* **Bozano Simonsen**, *set up* **LatInvest**.

The **LatInvest Group** *offers research-based brokerage, capital markets and corporate finance services with respect to the Latin American markets. The Group has offices in London, New York, Geneva, Mexico City, Rio de Janeiro and Caracas.*

Latin America

Latin America comprises seven principal markets listed below; 1994 has seen Ecuador become the eighth emerging market in the continent, albeit that its present market capitalization amounts to only $2.1 billion. Of the seven established markets, Argentina, Brazil, Chile and Mexico are the major protagonists, representing more than 90 per cent of Latin America's total market capitalization.

Table 3.12

Mkt Cap US$bn	'92	% tot	% GDP	'93	% tot	% GDP	'94	% tot	% GDP	'95E	% tot	% GDP
Argentina	18.6	7.3%	8.2%	43.9	10.6%	17.2%	34.8	8.5%	12.9%	34.9	8.4%	12.7%
Brazil	45.3	17.8%	11.1%	99.4	24.0%	22.2%	155.0	37.7%	23.8%	173.0	41.6%	29.0%
Chile	29.7	11.7%	72.1%	44.9	10.8%	103.0%	68.3	16.6%	130.9%	83.2	20.0%	151.2%
Colombia	8.7	3.4%	16.6%	12.3	3.0%	21.5%	17.9	4.4%	25.1%	16.5	4.0%	20.1%
Mexico	138.7	54.5%	41.5%	200.6	48.5%	55.6%	122.0	29.7%	33.7%	95.0	22.8%	38.1%
Peru	2.6	1.0%	6.6%	5.0	1.2%	12.3%	8.2	2.0%	16.5%	8.5	2.0%	16.1%
Venezuela	10.8	4.2%	17.9%	7.9	1.9%	13.2%	4.9	1.2%	8.6%	4.7	1.1%	8.3%
Total	254.4	100%	21.9%	414.0	100%	32.5%	411.1	100%	27.2%	415.8	100%	30.4%

Table 3.13

	Mkt.Cap March 1995 US$ bn	No of stocks	12-month perfmnce	Index	5-year High	5-year Low
Argentina	30.0	152	−40.8%	367	882	80
Brazil	133.0	545	−20.4%	33723	65614	3693
Chile	57,2	278	34.8%	5305	5699	867
Colombia	17.1	205	−202%	830	1052	399
Mexico	70.0	206	−66.2%	1822	2781	522
Peru	6.3	60	−9.3%	1139	1526	*100
Venezuela	4.8	95	−2.7%	1210	1497	**1000

*commenced 12.91 at 100

**commenced 12.93 at 100

The 1980s, The Brady Plan and Economic Regeneration

The 1980s witnessed a period of economic turmoil in Latin America. This turmoil had its origins in the misinformed concept during the 1970s that countries were incapable of becoming insolvent. International banking institutions were overzealous in channelling money into Latin America. The subsequent world recession witnessed the debtor countries declaring that they were unable to service their debts, beginning with Mexico in 1982. Mexico's debt of $87 billion was equivalent to 46 per cent of GDP, Brazil's $93 billion 40 per cent. These ratios worsened throughout the decade.

The restructuring policies of the debtors produced very few positive results in the 1980s, which saw the failure of the Plan Austral in Argentina and the Plan Cruzado in Brazil. The 1985 Baker Plan which was designed to increase the flow of credit to the region to enable the economies to grow, also ended in failure.

In March 1989 US Treasury Secretary Nicholas Brady announced the Brady Plan. This represented a watershed in Latin American regeneration. The broad aims were to reduce commercial bank debt and to rekindle economic growth. Essentially the plan allowed a certain amount of the debt to be converted into 10 – 30 year bonds, named Brady Bonds. In some circumstances a portion was written off completely. The Brady Plan was endorsed by the IMF and the World Bank and became the catalyst for a move toward stabilization, restructuring and free market reforms.

Of primary importance was the need to address budget deficits. The marked imbalance in public finances during the 1980s was one of the most important components of the economic crisis that affected the region. This was caused by low tax receipts and poor controls in government spending, exacerbated by the sharp drop in external financing and the debt burden. Most Latin American nations have now managed to balance their budgets. This has been achieved primarily through cuts in spending both in consumption and investment, and through the sale of fixed assets including privatization, which has provided the capital inflows to balance the public accounts. Tax revenues have also increased, both as a result of reforms and due to a widening of the tax base in reaction to economic growth.

The crisis years had given rise to a lack of credibility to the region's currencies and central to the stabilization process was a strong currency. Most countries used an anchored exchange rate, with slight readjustments (Chile) or a band with a fixed floor but with an adjustable ceiling (Mexico). A back-up of foreign reserves was established. Argentina went further in 1991 by establishing an exchange rate at a fixed parity to the dollar. Inflation was brought under control, falling from 4925 per cent in 1989 to 4 per cent in 1994 in Argentina, and from 2775 per cent to 15.4 per cent during the same period in Peru.

Alongside tighter monetary programmes came the move to open up the region's economies to imports to improve local competitiveness and encourage exports. Tariffs were lowered, and foreign investment legislation updated. Trade within the region has also been encouraged with the Andean Pact and MERCOSUR. Mexico recently joined NAFTA, while Chile looks set to become a member. Agreements with other blocks such as the European Community are also being considered.

This search for overall efficiency, fiscal equilibrium, control of inflation and promotion of competitive markets has seen the region become an attractive emerging market over the last five years. Local businessmen have repatriated capital, and the international financial community has ploughed money into the region after the drought of the 1980s. However, the collapse of the Mexican peso in December 1994 has made many people think again.

Mexico

Table 3.14

Mexico	1989	1990	1991	1992	1993	1994	1995E
GDP $bn	205.3	244.5	287.7	334.4	361.0	362.5	320.0
Inflation	20.0%	30.0%	19.0%	12.0%	8.0%	7.0%	20.0%
Public Sctor Balance % GDP	−5.6%	3.9%	−1.5%	1.6%	0.7%	−0.5%	0.4%
External Debt US$bn	89.9	93.2	109.7	115.5	125.3	137.3	148.1
Trade Balance US$bn	1.2	−0.9	−7.3	−15..9	−13.5	−17.0	−3.4
Current Account US$ bn	−6.1	−7.1	−14.8	−24.8	−23.3	−27.9	−14.9
Current Account % GDP	2.9%	2.9%	5.1%	7.4%	6.5%	7.7%	4.7%
Foreign Reserves US$bn	6.9	10.3	17.7	18.5	24.0	6.5	15.0
Market Capitalization US$bn	22.6	32.7	98.2	138.7	200.6	122.0	95.0
P/B	0.9	1.4	2.5	2.3	2.9	2.0	1.3
P/E	8.4	11.9	14.5	13.5	19.0	80.0	30.0

Mexico's recent political and economical history epitomizes the volatility that can be found in the world's emerging markets. Thirty years of steady growth came to a grinding halt with the 1980s debt crisis which gave rise to Mexico being set up as the pilot of the Brady Plan. The subsequent successful turn-around saw record foreign inflows, steady growth and very good market performance. Then in 1994 uncertainty started to rock the boat. Social unrest in Chiapas was followed by the assassination of the PRI presidential candidate Collosio, and later on of the PRI Secretary General. Finally 1994 ended with the most disastrous devaluation of the peso which was intended to drop 15 per cent, but which ended the year 60 per cent down.

The timing of the devaluation caught the world unawares since the September Pacto for continuity had committed itself to the continued pegging of the peso. The theory behind devaluing the peso was sound enough. The peso was overvalued, resulting in a substantial current account deficit of close to $30 billion. However, when devaluation was instigated without warning, the government had insufficient funds to support the currency. This led to the floating of the peso which created panic because of the size of the current account deficit and also because of the lack of confidence in the government's ability to pay around $20 billion in dollar-denominated short-term debt owed in the first six months of 1995. Finally, President Clinton announced a package worth $50 billion which is an actual line of credit as opposed to a provisional guarantee.

Immediately following the crisis Mexico's reaction in trying to contain the situation was deemed very lethargic. On 9 March the long awaited economic programme was announced. It is closely modelled on the 1982 post-devaluation Chilean plan which proved very successful. The plan has stabilized the peso. It currently stands at 6.35 pesos/US$ 7 April 1995 having fallen as low as 7.85 from a pre-devaluation level of 3.45. It should settle close to its present level. The devalued peso will instigate a trade balance turnaround. From an $18 billion deficit in 1994, the government expects a trade surplus of $5 billion for 1995, and it may well be higher.

The $50 billion loan agreement dictates that expansion of the monetary base must be kept below inflation and cannot exceed 10 billion new pesos ($1.57 billion). This will ensure that the currency is not undermined by being printed excessively which would instigate inflation. An index has also been introduced (UDI) initially for deposits and loans whereby inflation will be accounted for so that a real return can be guaranteed. This allows borrowers to renew loans which they had previously defaulted on, or not renewed as interest rates soared. The concept of the UDI is similar to the UF used in Chile after 1982 and the URV used in Brazil in the recent Real Plan.

One area for concern is the debt position of both the public and private sectors. Total public debt by the year-end 1995 will total about $135 billion or 54 per cent of GDP. Comparisons to the 1980s crisis are extreme as, in that period, Mexico's debt reached 87 per cent of GDP. The Brady Plan has also established a system that has made servicing this debt manageable with a substantial proportion not due until 2019. In the private sector there is a fear for companies with a high foreign debt uncovered by foreign income. At the end of the third quarter 1994 Mexican quoted companies had $30 billion of debt which was denominated in foreign currency. Some $10 to $20 billion matures in 1995. Companies that need to roll over may encounter difficulties.

The stability and recovery that Mexico will hopefully witness as a result of its harsh economic programme will inevitably result in a recession. The economy will contract by around 4 per cent with wage, price and credit restraints topped by redundancies. The private sector is being choked by high interest rates and borrowers crippled by their debt burdens while inflation is eroding purchasing power.

All sectors will be affected by the harsh economic measures. Manufacturing will be hurt by weak consumer demand and construction by high borrowing rates. The banking sector will also face difficulties with non-performing loans increasing and high interest rates taking their toll. The government has avoided a potentially critical situation by outlining, in addition to the UDI a number of steps to recapitalize banks as a number have fallen below the 8 per cent capital requirement. Of a total of eighteen banks, six have asked for help to recapitalize and more will need funds. Despite these factors some stocks at current levels have become bargains and this may be the case for some time.

Mexican companies of note include Telmex, Cemex, Cifra and Grupo Modelo. Telmex is Mexico's principal telecommunications company and the country's largest firm with a market capitalization of $17 billion. In 1991 Telmex was

Chart 3.36 Mexico: BMW

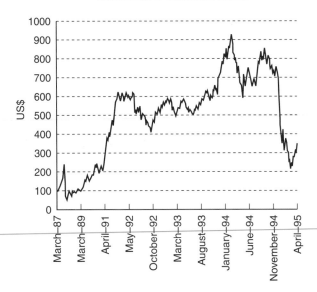

quoted at $3 billion and reached a peak of $30 billion before the devaluation. It is part owned by the US company South Western Bell (10 per cent) and has a strategic alliance with Sprint Corporation (US) Market opportunities abound as Mexico still has only eight lines per 100 inhabitants compared to 55 in the US. Telmex has invested heavily recently and generates a sizeable free - cash flow leaving it poised to combat competition, although competition is likely to be fierce.

Cemex is the third largest cement company in the world after Holderbank and Lafarge. It has a 60 per cent share of the cement market in Mexico and has been on an acquisition trail in the last two years in Spain, Venezuela, the Caribbean and the US This has left it heavily indebted in US$ but it has an asset base of $5 billion; 44 per cent (17 million tonnes) of the company's capacity is abroad and 50 per cent of its assets are foreign.

Cifra is Mexico's largest retailer with sales of $2.95 billion (post devaluation) and a market capitalization of $4.7 billion. Cifra sits on a sizeable cash position which, invested at currently high interest rates, should generate handsome profits compensating for the decline in operating profits in the weak economic environment. The joint-venture relationship that it has with Wal-Mart of the US has helped Cifra to approach operating efficiencies of similar standards.

Modelo is the leading brewer in Mexico (55 per cent market share) and is ranked twelfth in the world. It exports to 72 countries, and brands include Corona. Modelo's Initial Public Offer in early 1994 left it free of debt and with a comfortable cash position.

Argentina

Table 3.15

Argentina	1989	1990	1991	1992	1993	1994	1995E
GDP $bn	69.7	141.8	180.9	226.0	255.3	269.9	273.0
Inflation	4924.0%	1344.0%	84.0%	18.0%	7.0%	4.0%	4.5%
Public Sector Balance % GDP	−21.7%	−2.3%	−1.7%	0.4%	2.0%	0.0%	0.4%
External Debt US$bn	56.9	54.0	55.3	63.5	65.2	66.7	72.4
Trade Balance US$ bn	5.4	8.3	3.7	−2.6	−3.7	−5.8	−3.0
Current Account US$bn	−1.3	1.9	−2.8	−8.4	−7.8	−10.5	−8.7
Current Account % GDP	−2.0%	2.8%	−1.5%	−3.7%	−2.9%	−3.9%	−3.2%
Foreign Reserves US$bn	2.9	6.0	8.9	12.5	17.0	15.6	11.5
Market Capitalization US$bn	4.2	3.3	18.5	18.6	44.0	34.8	34.9
P/B	1.1	0.3	1.7	1.2	2.1	1.4	1.2
P/E	22.1	3.1	38.9	30.7	23.3	15.8	11.4

Over the last few years Argentina has managed to produce some impressive economic results. Since 1990 the economy has grown by more than 30 per cent, third in the world only to China and Thailand; manufacturing productivity has risen by 56 per cent. This has been achieved primarily by the stability brought about by a new monetary policy introduced in July 1991 and by the privatization of state enterprises. The monetary policy fixed the new peso to the US$, and disallowed money in circulation to exceed the level of hard currency reserves. However, this fixed parity has lead to an over valuation of the peso which in turn has given rise to an increasing trade deficit.

After the Mexican devaluation there were fears that Argentina would be next. However, the government stood firm protecting the peso, and remains committed to the convertibility plan. This attitude stems from the belief that devaluing might mean a return to inflation which is currently at 4 per cent. It would also increase the burden on 60 per cent of the largest Argentinean companies which have dollar-denominated debt.

Despite this, capital flight totalled $7.4 billion or 16 per cent of the banking system in two and a half months of 1995. The resulting crisis saw the Interbank rate soaring above 60 per cent in an attempt to stop the outflows. In mid-March Cavallo, the Finance Minister, announced an $11.4 billion rescue package. This stabilized the situation and quelled the liquidity squeeze. Interest rates have fallen to below 10 per cent and enough confidence has been instilled for some capital to have returned.

But a similar financing problem could resurface. Annual amortizations for the years 1996 to 2000 amount to $4.8 billion, $6.9 billion, $7.1 billion, $8.6 billion and $7.8 billion respectively. The availability of funds to cover these payments depends upon disciplined fiscal controls and the return of confidence in the banking system.

The outlook for the Argentinian market is therefore one of caution. The smaller banks were and are particularly vulnerable. If liquidity again becomes a problem and interest rates rise substantially bad loans will increase The consumption sector and heavily geared companies should also be avoided.

Interesting companies include YPF, the main oil and gas company with approximately a 60 per cent share of the market. There is no clear competitor as the other 40 per cent is split. YPF was privatized in 1991 and, since then, has increased production and improved its operating margins from 6 per cent to 17 per cent. The company has invested heavily and just completed the acquisition of Maxus, a US based oil company with operations in Indonesia (60 per cent), Latin America and the US.

The bottler Baesa is also aggressive in terms of foreign business. In 1994 it purchased the franchise of Pepsi in Brazil. As a result of this investment of $400 million the company's gearing has risen to from 50 per cent to 70 per cent. However, in the short term, it should outperform the market as a result of its Brazilian operation. The Argentinian market will experience a decrease in volumes due to a general consumer slowdown.

Siderca manufactures seamless steel tubes and has the highest ratio of export sales to total revenues, at 80 per cent. Domestically it has 90 per cent of the market and it is looking strong in 1995 due to the weak dollar and the earthquake in Kobe. The earthquake will mean that the Japanese steel industry will be more involved nationally, and less internationally.

Irsa is a real estate company with a market capitalization of $220 million. Irsa specializes in buying dilapidated buildings from the government, and reselling them once they have been renovated. Irsa is not heavily geared and has capital which, in the present climate, it can use to buy property cheaply.

Chart 3.37 Argentina Merval

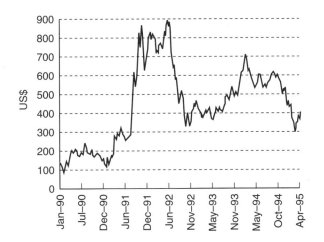

Brazil

Table 3.16

Brazil	1989	1990	1991	1992	1993	1994	1995E
GDP $bn	447.6	476.2	402.4	408.9	447.7	653.0	592.0
Inflation	1636%	1639%	459%	1129%	2491%	892%	35%
Public Sector Balance % GDP	−6.9%	1.2%	1.4%	−2.1%	0.4%	0.0%	0.2%
External Debt US$bn	111.4	116.2	116.3	125.5	133.0	125.7	129.5
Trade Balance US$bn	16.1	10.7	10.6	15.5	13.0	10.5	5.0
Current Account US$ bn	1.0	−3.8	−1.0	6.5	−0.6%	−4.2	−10.0
Current Account % GDP	0.2%	−0.8%	−0.3%	1.6%	−0.1%	−0.6%	−1.7%
Foreign Reserves US$bn	9.7	10.0	9.4	23.7	29.1	38.0	25.0
Market Capitalization US$bn	44.4	16.4	42.8	45.3	99.4	155.0	173.0
P/B	0.67	0.34	0.75	0.41	0.79	1.30	N/A
P/E	12.0	N/A	32.7	24.1	36.9	21.2	16.3

Brazil has been late in joining the stabilization party. Until the 1994 Cardoso Plan it was not able to curb inflation (2,491 per cent in 1993). The previous two attempts instigated by President Fernando Collor were based respectively on a financial asset freeze and a price wage freeze. They both failed because the withdrawn liquidity found its way back into the system.

The Collor administration, however, did create the platform for the Cardoso Plan. Public finance, trade policy and privatization were addressed. The 1989 public sector deficit of 6.9 per cent of GDP was turned into a surplus; import tariffs were lowered and outright prohibitions on over 1,800 items lifted; privatization and deregulation of government companies and industries began in earnest, resulting in a marked improvement in performance, most notably at the steel company, Usiminas.

The Cardoso plan was introduced on 1 March 1994, when he was finance minister. It introduced the Unidade Real de Valor (URV) as a new index in which contracts, salaries and prices could be quoted. This index, now extinguished, was the average of the other three indexes (CPI-FIPE, CPI-IBGE, General Price Index-FGV). Once confidence was established, the index itself became the currency meaning that it was no longer a tool to simply reflect price increases, but became the price itself. The new currency, the Brazilian real was created in July, whereby 2,750 cruzeiros became one real which equalled one URV. One real was valued at one US$.

Cardoso was swept to presidential victory in October 1994 on the back of his plan. Inflation is still under control. Since its introduction the currency has appreciated against the US$, and the country has been experiencing a massive consumption boom despite real interest rates of over 50 per cent but the result has been a trade deficit for the first time in many years. Recent steps to rectify this include devaluation and targeted import tariffs. This will see some rise in inflation as domestic capacity falls short of demand.

The consumption boom will slow down with a pick up in inflation. There are also credit restrictions being imposed on banks and retailers such as high compulsory reserve requirements and restrictions on the period over which the purchase of goods may be financed. Extended pay-back periods have contributed considerably to the consumption boom. Banks are also likely to begin to compete aggressively for deposits thus encouraging saving.

Medium-term prospects are bright for well-run private banks, such as Bradesco, Itaubanco, Unibanco and Banco Nacional, as they shift from the Treasury management strategies which offer huge profits in a hyper-inflationary environment, towards the medium-term lending which renewed economic stability should facilitate. It will be a much longer haul for the state banks, which are overstaffed, debt laden and susceptible to political influence. At the same time, the extreme discounts that their stock prices command in the market make them attractive as speculative investments.

The first line stocks, such as Telebras, Petrobras and Eletrobras are interesting simply on account of their high liquidity, which makes them attractive as index proxies. In addition, privatization is a likely prospect at least for the electrical and telecommunications sectors. Especially interesting at this stage are construction and cement firms such as Cimento Itau,which should be a prime beneficiary of a long-term upturn in construction activity particularly in the public sector .

Chart 3.38 Brazil IBOVESPA

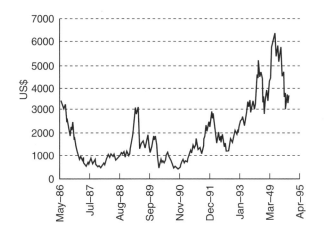

Chile

Table 3.17

Chile	1989	1990	1991	1992	1993	1994	1995E
GDP $bn	28.1	30.2	34.0	41.2	43.6	52.2	55.0
Inflation	21.4%	27.3%	18.7%	12.7%	12.2%	8.9%	7.5%
Public Sector Balance % GDP	na	na	1.4%	0.8%	1.9%	1.7%	1.5%
External Debt US$bn	16.3	17.4	16.4	18.2	19.2	21.6	22.0
Trade BalanceUS$bn	1.6	1.3	1.6	0.7	–1.0	0.7	1.4
Current Account US$ bn	0.7	–0.6	0.0	–0.7	–2.1	–0.6	–0.5
Current Account % GDP	–2.5%	–2.0%	0.0%	–1.7%	–4.8%	–1.0%	–0.8%
Foreign Reserves US$bn	2.9	5.4	6.6	9.0	9.8	13.5	14.0
Market Capitalization US$bn	9.6	13.6	28.0	29.7	44.9	68.3	83.2
P/B	0.67	0.34	0.75	0.41	0.79	1.30	N/A
P/E	12.0	N/A	32.7	24.1	36.9	21.2	16.3

The Chilean economy is the most dynamic and well-run of the region. It has produced GDP growth and fiscal surpluses since the mid 1980s and, in 1994, inflation stood at 8.9 per cent. In addition its social programmes are an example to other Latin American countries: it is currently undertaking a $1.2 billion poverty alleviation programme.

Despite the criticism that could be aimed at General Pinochet's dictatorship, it was he who established the economy as it is today. Soon after the bankruptcy of the Chilean banks and larger corporations in 1982 Pinochet oversaw the introduction of free-market policies. Chile was a number of years ahead of its Latin American counterparts. Chile today is reaping the benefits from having had a dictator who was able to push through policies that at the time may not have been very popular. The forced pension contributions deducted from salaries are a case in point. Not only are these beneficial for the individuals concerned, but it means that Chile now has a considerable amount of capital in pension funds that it can invest in its own market.

Chile uses an exchange rate pegging system which is adjusted when deemed necessary. The currency is not at risk, but in the aftermath of the Mexican devaluation it is worth mentioning that the current account stands at -1 per cent of GDP ($0.6 billion), while foreign reserves amount to $13.5 billion. Unlike Mexico, capital inflows to Chile are mostly long-term direct investment. The economy is indexed, and although de-indexation is unlikely to occur in the short term, the low levels of inflation offer a good opportunity to tackle this issue.

The privatization programme began in 1986 and has been virtually completed, although there are still some smaller companies in the electricity sector such as Edelnor and Colbuln which are in the process of being wholly sold off.

There are also concessions given to the private sector in public works such as toll roads and bridges. The copper mining concern CODELCO however is to remain in public ownership.

Chile recently joined the Asia-Pacific Economic Council (APEC) and is seeking to extend its trade agreements. Towards the end of 1994 it was invited to join NAFTA, with negotiations expected to begin in May 1995 and membership anticipated for mid 1996. Membership of MERCOSUR also seems likely as Argentina and Brazil are Chile's two largest trading partners

Economic growth should average almost 6 per cent over the next five years, driven by investment. World copper demand promises to be high and the combination of rising prices and production will ensure that copper export revenues will almost double by 1999. Long distance telecommunications are cheap due to the recent introduction of a multicarrier system, and fierce competition should ensure they remain so. Chilean prospects are very positive on the whole, and exporters should perform particularly well once the currency begins to weaken, which it should do by mid 1995.

Companies of interest include Endesa, the largest listed company with a market capitalization of US$ 5.9 billion and the country's major power and energy generator (2,513Mw capacity). It also operates 18 per cent of the Argentine generating system. Energy demand is expected to grow at 6 to 10 per cent annually through to 2003.

As an exporter, Soquimich will benefit from weakening in the currency. Soquimich produces fertilizers, industrial chemicals and iodine. In 1994 it invested US$60 million, and plans to invest US$75 million in the Minsal mine which produces potash.

Viña Concha y Toro is the largest Chilean wine producer. It is also the only wine producer to trade on the New York Stock Exchange having sold ADRs at the end of 1994. Prospects are good. Concha Y Toro has already made its name internationally. It now owns 2,000 hectares compared to 593

Chart 3.39 Chile IGPA

in 1989. Many of the new vineyards will start to produce high quality grapes in 1996, allowing the company to increase productivity from its own grapes 3.3 times by 1999.

Fixed Income Securities

Mexico

The Mexican Market is the most open to foreigners, who hold around 60 per cent of local government debt. There is no tax on governments, and a very low tax on corporates. Holding bonds for only 24 hours is possible. There is a wide variety of bonds in both dollar and peso denominations, ranging from 28-day to 10-year maturities.

Chart 3.40 Mexico: Real Rates

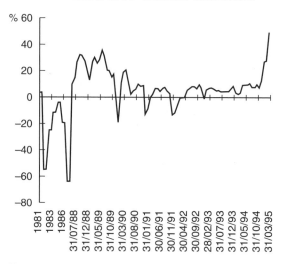

Source: Grupo Financiero Invermexico

Argentina

The minimum period of time that fixed income securities can be held in Argentina is 1 month. They are primarily longer term bonds of 1, 5, and 10 years, with a present yield rate of 17 per cent (February 15, 1995). Recently Letras de Tesoro, which have a 91 day maturity date have been issued. All bonds are issued in both dollars and pesos. Around 30 per cent of the longer term bonds are held by foreigners.

Chart 3.41 Argentina: Interbank Rate

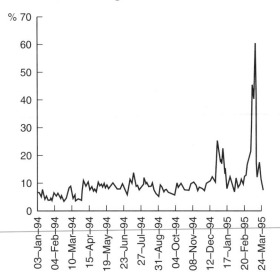

Brazil

Recently the Brazilian government has created a tax for foreigners entering the fixed income market. It was introduced some five months before the new real at 5 per cent, reached 9 per cent at year end 1994 and is currently back at 5 per cent. This is to discourage foreigners from jumping in and out of the market, and has led to a decrease in foreign players. They currently hold

Chart 3.42 Brazil: Annualized Real Interest Rates –
(monthly CDi deflated by IGP-M)

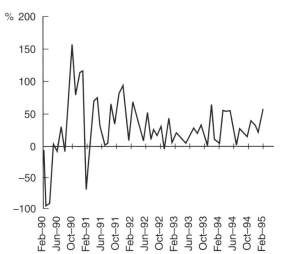

around 8 per cent. Corporate bonds have a three-year maturity. Government bonds range from 35 days to one-year.

Chile

Fixed income securities are virtually closed to foreigners. The rates offered are very low and foreigners can only partake via a fund based within the country which has to have been established for a year before it can purchase bonds.

Chart 3.43 Chile: Monthly Real Rates

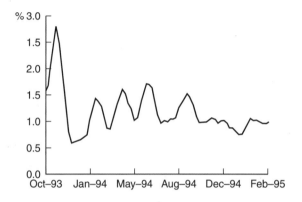

Overseas Listing

Many larger Latin American companies have sought to have themselves listed in New York and Europe as ADRs (American Depository Receipts) and GDRs (Global Depository Receipts.) Being listed abroad gives them access to more

Table 3.18

Most traded stocks Jan – 21st April 1995 Local vs ADR traded. (US$m)	Volume of local shares	Volume of NYSE ADR's
Telefonos de Mexico	2,372	17,390
Telefonica Argentina	2,361	1,412
YPF (Argentina)	1,774	3,117
Telecom (Argentina)	631	582
Endesa (Chile)	339	98
Telefonos de Chile	256	2,092
Enersis (Chile)	202	158
Maseca (Mexico)	184	77
Televisa (Mexico)	170	2,725
ICA (Mexico)	156	580

capital. In many cases ADR/GDR trading exceeds the volumes in the local markets. Below are the ten most traded Latin American companies in the first three and a half months of 1995, which are traded both locally and as ADRs. Five of these trade more in New York than in their own markets.

Large companies can make up a considerable percentage of the total market capitalization of their countries.. For instance in Argentina YPF, Telefonos and Telecom constitute 55 per cent of Argentina's total market capitalization, and in Peru, CPT and Southern make up 46 per cent of the market. ◑

EMERGING MARKETS

Dr. Mark Mobius

Mark Mobius is Managing Director of Templeton Investment Management (Hong Kong) Ltd. He manages US$7 billion in emerging markets' assets for Templeton funds. Known as the 'Indiana Jones' of the investment world, Dr Mobius won the closed-end Manager of the Year Award from Morningstar in 1993 with a stunning 97 per cent gain in his Emerging Markets Fund and 74.5 per cent in Templeton Developing Markets Trust. He wrote The Investor's Guide to Emerging Markets published by FT Pitman. More recently, Dr Mobius won the CNBC award as the 1994 First in Business Money Manager of the Year.

What are Emerging Markets?

The step from international investing to the creation of a specific emerging markets category has evolved over a long period. The 100th anniversary report of the Alliance Trust of the United Kingdom, established in 1888, relates how that trust was invested in, what was then, a primitive emerging market: America. An international portfolio was quite limited in the early days of global investing, so that when foreigners started investing in Japan in the 1960s, it was considered to be risky and pioneering.

The actual birth of the 'emerging market' category had to wait until 1986, when the International Finance Corporation, the World Bank subsidiary, started to promote capital market development in less-developed countries. Eleven institutional investors put US$ 50 million into a fund. At that time, the manager was reported to have told investors that it might take one year to invest that money. By 1993, funds totalled more than US$1 billion, and the managers were quoted as saying that if given US$ 50 million now, it would take a month to invest. In 1987, when Templeton started Templeton Emerging Markets Fund, it was the world's first fund listed on a stock exchange with investments in emerging markets as its specific objective.

We now have a list of 124 countries we would consider to be 'emerging', either because they (1) have low or middle per capita incomes; (2) have undeveloped capital markets with the market capitalization representing a small portion of their gross national product; or (3) are not industrialized. Nonetheless, the range of suitable countries, although expanding, is quite limited. Many emerging countries do not have stock markets or even any kind of formal capital market. Many still restrict foreign investment or impose foreign exchange restrictions which make it impossible to transfer money into or, more importantly, out of the country. Some still impose harsh taxation which makes investment unrealistic. Therefore, out of the 124 emerging countries, as of January 1995, only 32 have functioning stock markers in which foreigners could realistically invest.

Argentina	Hungary	Philippines
Bangladesh	India	Poland
Botswana	Indonesia	Portugal
Brazil	Israel	Singapore
Chile	Jordan	Slovakia
China	Korea	South Africa
Colombia	Malaysia	Sri Lanka
Czech Republic	Mexico	Taiwan
Greece	Morocco	Thailand
Hong Kong	Pakistan	Turkey
	Peru	Venezuela

Many countries have stock markets where ten companies account for over half the total capitalization. The concentration of trading value is even more noticeable, due to the tendency of many emerging markets companies to be closely held by families or governments with the 'free float' limited. Often, ten stocks account for over 50 per cent of trading in emerging markets versus less than 10 per cent in the US and the UK.

Trends in Emerging Markets

A number of global demographic trends have had, and will continue to have, a dramatic impact on economic growth and the development of emerging markets. With a longer life, people have more time to learn how to read and write. Studies have found that a one-year increase in schooling can augment wages by more than 10 per cent and raises GDP significantly. In Peru, for example, it was found that if farmers had an additional year of schooling, it increased

Education promotes entrepreneurship. Entrepreneurs see new opportunities, are willing to take risks and change methods. They make the connection from innovation to actual production.

448

their probability of adopting modern farm technology by 45 per cent. In Thailand, farmers with four years of schooling were three times more likely to use new fertilizers and chemicals than farmers with one to three years of schooling. Education promotes entrepreneurship. Entrepreneurs see new opportunities, are willing to take risks and change methods. They make the connection from innovation to actual production.

The impact of new technologies on the ability of the people of emerging countries to learn is great. Probably the biggest impact that technology has made is the growth in communications. Recent strides in the ability to communicate around the world more cheaply and more effectively have enabled emerging nations to obtain information and technology more rapidly.

The combination of better education, higher capital inputs, and the impact of new technology, is having a dramatic and accelerating impact on productivity growth in the emerging nations. According to the World Bank, the United Kingdom took over 50 years, between 1780 and 1838, to double output per person. The United States did it in about 47 years, whereas Japan was able to double output per person in about 34 years. However, the emerging nations of Turkey and Brazil did it in less than 21 years and Korea and China have been able to do it in 11 years.

Those trends which have been most positive in converting emerging markets into attractive and respectable destinations for investment funds can be summarized as:

- greater freedom of political expression;

- increased flow of information;

- shift from state ownership to privatization;

- growth in global trade along with liberalization;

- fiscal reform, particularly a less repressive tax regime;

- creation of new capital markets.

China is the prototype, and also, of course, the most important emerging country. In China, as in other parts of the world, particularly in the former socialist or communist societies, there is a great deal of pent-up demand. This demand has not been fulfilled by the low quality production offered by state-owned companies. This, combined with significant pent-up savings, results in a potent brew. China and other emerging markets are moving towards manufacturing and away from agriculture.

The Case for Investment

Investors in developed countries have looked to emerging markets for higher returns and lower risk or lower volatility through diversification. Performance of emerging markets can vary greatly. Over the seven years ending 31 December

1994, some emerging markets yielded startling returns. Argentina showed a rise of 750 per cent in dollar terms, Mexico a rise of 613 per cent, and Chile a rise of 561 per cent. Over the same period, investors in the London equity market saw an increase only of 95 per cent.

When US investors move from only domestic investments, they diversify. Diversification intensifies when they move to emerging markets. The correlation co-efficient of the Canadian stock market indices and US indices has been found to be as high as 0.8, out of a maximum of 1.0. The correlation co-efficient of the aggregated emerging markets against the US is as low as 0.4. It is likely that, as the world gets smaller, and with more global investment, the correlations between developed and emerging markets will increase.

Perhaps just as important is the wide range of variation and characteristics found in emerging markets which tend to be more extreme than across developed markets. For example, as of December 1993, the average P/E in emerging markets ranged from 8.5 in Bangladesh to 44.0 in Peru. This compared to a range of 20.7 to 67.8 for developed markets. Price to book values in emerging markets during that same year ranged between 0.6 for Brazil and 7.2 for Turkey, whereas the range for Japan, the US and the UK was 2.0 to 2.6.

Emerging markets constitute a small part of the current total global market capitalization. As at 1993, the total capitalization of the world's three major stock markets (the United States, the United Kingdom and Japan) was about US$ 9.4 billion. By comparison, the emerging markets constituted US$ 1.9 billion.

However, the potential for growth in emerging equity markets is great. The developed markets' ratio of market capitalization to GDP averaged 93.8 per cent in 1990. In emerging markets it was below 75 per cent, with many capitalizations representing less than 10 per cent of GDP. These numbers indicated that emerging markets have a long way to go. Between 1980 and 1993, emerging markets capitalization grew by 1,219 per cent, whereas that of developed markets' grew by about 361 per cent.

Current indications are that the number of companies listed on emerging stock markets is growing faster than in the developed markets. In addition, there has been a significant shift in emphasis in economic policy from providing debt for industrial growth to equity.

Opportunities in Emerging Markets

Probably the most exciting aspect of emerging market development in the world today is the creation of new equity markets. In eastern Europe, the requirements of privatization have generated great interest in capital markets. Even in Romania, a securities law has been formulated and a stock exchange opened. Over 200,000 small private businesses are operating with 8,000 joint stock companies registered. Stock exchanges are now being run or established in Poland, the Czech and Slovak republics, Moldova, and other former Soviet republics. In India, with a population of 897 million and a savings rate of over 20 per cent of GDP, the stock market has grown rapidly. In the Muslim countries, the religious prohibition against interest creates a particularly fertile ground for the development of stock markets.

Emerging market investment may be made in four major ways:

1 Direct investment in stocks of emerging markets.

2 Indirect investments by purchases of emerging market companies listed in developed markets.

3 Open or closed-end mutual funds, investment trusts or investment companies.

4 Depository receipts of emerging market companies.

According to Lipper Analytical Services – International Corporation, of over 745 funds in existence at the end of 1994, there were 98 global funds, 221 regional Asia funds, 65 regional Latin America funds, 23 regional European funds, and over 338 individual single country funds.

Investors need to remain aware of risks which can trap the unwary. These relate both to the mechanisms which govern the capital markets, and to the environment in which these markets operate:

● inefficient and insufficient custodial, and settlement structure

● limited or non-existent investor protection

● uneven fairness and transparency

● currency fluctuations and convertibility

● capricious government interference and even manipulation

● civil unrest.

Other risks are due to the lack of good information. In emerging markets we are constantly reminded of the need for independent research and careful checking of what company officials and underwriters tell us. To paraphrase that great film pioneer, Samuel Goldwyn: 'A verbal promise isn't worth the paper it is written on'.

This presents many problems, since each country has different accounting standards. One sign of the need for better accounts was recognized when a major international accounting firm won a US$ 2.6 million contract to develop accounting standards for China. In Brazil, the complications of inflation accounting and rapid changes in tax applications create substantial problems. In countries where inflation is very high, monetary restatement of financial statements in line with inflation has become mandatory.

One example of the degree to which revisions can affect accounts for emerging market companies, particularly those in countries emerging from socialist economies, can be seen in work required to revise and assess the accounts of one Chinese company listed on the New York Stock Exchange at

451

the end of 1992. According to the underwriters, accounting work took 11,000 man- hours for the three years restated in line with American standards.

Care must be taken when interpreting accounting terms. The words may be English, but the meanings could differ substantially. One set of Sri Lankan accounts uses the term 'fictitious assets' to describe prepayments. One firm in China used a term which was translated by the Hong Kong Chinese as 'pension fund liabilities'. In fact, the Chinese characters used by the mainland Chinese had a different meaning. The right translation was 'development reserves'.

Differences in accounting practices are great and too numerous. Some of the more common ones include the following:

- off-balance sheet items
- revenue recognition
- treatment of intangibles
- consolidation of subsidiaries
- reserves
- multiple classes of shares
- currency exchange
- vauation of assets or inventory
- depreciation

As we adopt a value oriented, bottom-up investment philosophy, we do not base our buy and sell decisions on economic, political or social indicators, although these macroeconomic variables play a key role in our decisions to invest in that country. Some of the more critical macro variables that we consider include average annual growth rate of GNP per capita, real GDP growth, inflation rate, life expectancy at birth, adult literacy rate and historical performance of the specific stock markets.

We emphasize that the stock must meet the following two requirements:

1 It must be a bargain in terms of its ability to generate earnings over the next five years so that it will be cheap relative to:
(a) its own history;
(b) other stocks in its market; and
(c) other stocks in its industry internationally.
2 It must have good growth prospects, with a high growth rate over the next five years.

We sell on the basis of whether we can find something that's cheaper than what we already have. The idea is to search for something that's roughly 50 per cent cheaper. Otherwise there's no justification for selling.

The Future

The development of emerging capital markets offers the future promise of outstanding benefits for developing nations' economic growth. They will provide the means whereby these nations may distribute ownership of privatized companies, allow market forces to allocate financial assets and provide a stimulus for attracting new equity capital for growing companies. There are numerous problems in the emerging world and high risks but, in emerging markets investment, it is necessary to be optimistic. 'The world belongs to optimists; the pessimists are only spectators.'

With better communications, improved travel, more international commerce and generally better relations between nations, the opportunities for mankind and for emerging markets' investors are better than they have ever been before. In Asia we are entering a golden era with opportunities for travel and leisure never before dreamed of by millions of Asians. New hotels, new resorts, lower cost and faster air travel, and a host of developments are opening the world to more people. With the demise of communism and the shift in China and India towards free enterprise, the opportunities for the creation of wealth are unparalleled. Taking a long view will yield excellent results for the investor prepared to be patient.

It is not good use of an investor's time to try to determine which market will perform better and when, since it is impossible to tell. However, by choosing the best investment bargains, the investor will naturally be in the best performing markets at the right time. Over the next five years, I feel that there are good opportunities in Argentina, Brazil, China, Greece, Hong Kong, India, Indonesia, Mexico, the Philippines, Portugal, Russia, Thailand, Turkey and South Africa. ♀

PART 4

INVESTING

IN SPECIAL

INDUSTRIES

BIOTECH

Dr. Keith G. McCullagh and Dr. Nick R. Scott-Ram

*Dr McCullagh has served as **British Biotech's** Chief Executive Officer since the Company's formation and in 1993 became Chairman of the BioIndustry Association. Prior to this he was Director of Research for **G.D. Searle & Co.**, an international pharmaceutical company.*

*Dr Scott-Ram has a BA in zoology and a PhD in the philosophy of science. Before joining **British Biotech**, he was involved in establishing **Oxford Virology** plc, a start-up vaccine company where he was Managing Director. At **British Biotech** has held various positions involved in research and business development, and is currently Manager, Corporate Administration.*

*__British Biotech plc__ is an international, development-stage pharmaceutical company based in Oxford. **British Biotech** has used medicinal chemistry and genetic engineering to pursue research in cancer, inflammatory, vascular and viral diseases. The main product focus is in cancer, where three products are in development, including BB-10010, a genetically engineered bone marrow protector.*

Introduction

Biotechnology has a meaning and significance beyond its original use as a term describing the industrial applications of biology. Today, biotechnology spans a wide diversity of advanced sciences including genomics, medicine, microbiology, biophysics and agriculture. In addition, biotechnology has become an exciting area of financial investment. Biotechnology companies, focused on the applications of one or more of these advanced technologies, have been perceived by investors as capable of achieving breakthrough products and businesses. The biotech industry sector is still relatively young, being less than 20 years old, but it has grown extremely rapidly both in terms of its technology and in the number and variety of its companies. Consequently, it has not yet settled into familiar patterns or an instantly recognizable language which investors can understand. Despite this, biotechnology can offer substantial returns to investors who take the time to differentiate these companies which combine real opportunity with solid business fundamentals.

A Brief History

The foundations of biotechnology were laid in the 1950s after Watson and Crick elucidated the genetic code with the discovery of the chemical structure of DNA. However, it was in the early 1970s with the discovery by Cohen and

Boyer of a method of cutting and splicing pieces of DNA, that biotechnology came of age as an industrial science. Molecular biology was transformed from a dry descriptive science into the tools of genetic engineering. It became possible to isolate genes, to instruct cells outside the body to make large quantities of human proteins, to engineer novel drugs, to identify genetic defects with precision and to understand the mechanics of human, animal and plant life.

A new industry rapidly emerged in the USA, led at first by Cetus, then Genentech and a few years later by Amgen, Biogen, Chiron, Immunex and others. By the middle of the 1980s a broad range of new bioscience companies poured each year into the US capital markets. With these companies came a myriad of new products,: medicines, diagnostics, plants and processes. In addition, these companies spawned a new breed of manager – intelligent, highly skilled entrepreneurs who were as good at pioneering new financing methods as they were at conceiving and producing new bioscience products. According to the report *Biotech 94* by Ernst & Young, the US industry numbers in excess of 1,270 companies, over 250 public, with combined revenues of $10 billion in 1993. In the USA, biotechnology stands for the science of molecular and cell biology. It now describes a new industry which is increasingly recognized as likely to make major contributions to the quality of life and the US economy.

For a variety of cultural and economic reasons the growth of biotechnology in the United Kingdom and Europe has lagged some 10 years or more behind. This situation is rapidly changing. In the European Union's White Paper on Growth Competitiveness and Employment and the Commissions September 1994 Communication *An Industrial Competitiveness Policy for the EU*, biotechnology was singled out as one of the fields offering the greatest potential. There are now over 500 companies in Europe, with the lion's share in the United Kingdom.

Chart 4.1 The European Biotech Industry: Year of Company Foundation

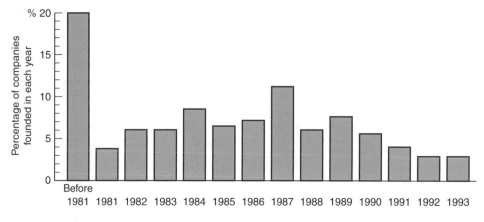

Source: Ernst & Young

458

The European market for products which are in some way dependent upon biotechnology is estimated at £30 billion by Arthur Andersen in their report *UK Biotech '94*. Projections for the future growth compiled by the Senior Advisory Group on Biotechnology in their paper *Community Policy for Biotechnology: Economic Benefit and European Competitiveness* indicate biotechnology-based revenues of around £70 billion by the end of the decade. Investment research and development is also increasing. Last year over £30 billion was invested in biotechnology R&D in the United States alone. European research and development expenditure is significantly lower, but growing rapidly.

The London Stock Exchange

In the United Kingdom the main reason for the emergence of the bioscience sector has been the relaxation of listing requirements for scientific research and development companies on the Stock Exchange. In 1992 British Biotech was the first company to achieve a quotation in London, with a simultaneous quotation on NASDAQ in the United States. In 1993, seven more companies came to the market, raising nearly £125 million. At the end of 1993 the UK bioscience industry had raised a total of £879 million.

At the beginning of 1995, revisions were made to the Listing Rules for scientific research based companies. The changes, following widespread consultation, allow a wider range of research based companies access to the public equity market while still maintaining investor protection. In particular, companies involved in agriculture and food technology, in addition to pharmaceutical and diagnostic companies, were encouraged to seek a listing. For biopharmaceutical companies, the criteria include at least two medicines in clinical trials under internationally accepted regulatory scrutiny. Additionally, a company must have incurred expenditure amounting to not less than £20 million in research and development over a period of not less than three years which has demonstrably resulted in the creation of intellectual property of significant worth.

Investment Opportunities

In the United States the biotechnology industry has been through a number of apparently cyclical phases since the euphoria created by Genentech's public offering in 1980. The initial excitement appeared justified when Genentech received Food and Drug Administration (FDA) approval for the first genetically engineered product, recombinant human insulin ('Humulin'), used for the treatment of type I diabetes. However, although a stream of product approvals followed, there were lean years when biotech company fortunes appeared to lag. It was not until 1990–91 that the first biotech product 'block-

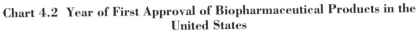

Chart 4.2 Year of First Approval of Biopharmaceutical Products in the United States

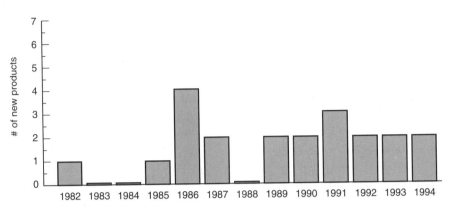

Source: Ernst & Young

busters' arrived on the scene in the form of Amgen's 'Epogen' (recombinant erythropeoetin used to stimulate new blood cell production in anaemia) and 'Neupogen' (a recombinant white blood cell growth factor used in cancer treatment). Sales of Neupogen in 1994 alone were $829 million.

On the back of the successful launch of these products, a biotech bull market emerged in 1991 with the number of quoted biotech companies almost doubling. However, by 1992 this rapid rise was cut-short by a number of product failures and a shift in investment to other sectors. Since then, the US biotech market has undergone an overall downward correction, fuelled in part by the spectre of health care reform legislation, cost containment fears and continuing product failures and disappointments.

Despite these fluctuations, the fundamentals of investing in biotechnology remain the same. In biopharmaceuticals, over 20 products have been approved by the US FDA and a further 74 are in Phase III clinical trials in Europe and North America. Last year the first genetically engineered food, the 'Flavr Savr' tomato was launched by Calgene and approvals have now been received for a number of other genetically modified crops.

Biotechnology is also beginning to flourish in other parts of the world. Japan has always maintained a strong interest through its large multi-national businesses. Australia has also been active. Within the last five years, at least seven Asian governments have designated biotechology to be a promoted industry. In particular, Indonesia, Malaysia, the People's Republic of China, Singapore, South Korea, Taiwan, and Thailand are investing in biotechnology. In other parts of the world, activity is more sporadic.

Investment in the biotechnology industry, as in any other industry, should be based on the fundamentals of a given company. However, unlike other advanced technology sectors, the development time scales for biotechnology products can be anything up to 12 years, and the resultant cash negative period can be quite lengthy. Consequently the normal parameters by which a company can be judged, for example P/E ratios, EPS, and so on, cannot be applied to many biotechnology companies since most of them do not, as yet, have marketed products generating revenues and earnings.

In some cases, an indication of cash burn may be used. Cash burn represents a simple reduction in cash from one year to the next, and includes capital expenditure as well as profit and loss, although external financings are excluded. Market capitalization may also be based on a multiple of research and development spend. The size of loss incurred by any biotechnology company is not directly correlated to its overall performance since this loss is a reflection of the investment in research and development, rather than trading activity. Paradoxically, the more rapidly a product proceeds through development the more rapidly will research and development expenditure escalate.

This means that a biotech company has to be evaluated primarily in terms of the quality of its research and development. The decision on which company to invest in should be based on the judgement of a company's technology platform, the ability of the company's management, both scientific and business, to convert this platform into a profitable enterprise, including the ability to raise the financial resources necessary, and the appropriate stock market valuation given the probabilities of success and the company's likely future worth.

Assessing the technology platform may be difficult for the non-technical investor. It is vital to rely on the information contained in expert research reports. Always compile the assessment from more than one analyst's opinion. What is important is that the technology is new, provides broad product and commercial opportunities and is proprietary. The latter is very important to understand. A highly innovative company which has failed to build a strong portfolio of international patents protecting its inventions is unlikely to be commercially competitive. This is much more true in biotechnology than in computing or telecommunications.

The key to success will ultimately lie with two major factors: the research base and how this is translated into a project development pipeline, and the management expertise. Irrespective of how innovative or exciting a new technology is, it must be converted into a product which can generate significant revenues. Companies which develop innovative new products for markets which are either poorly served by existing products or for which there are no equivalent products, are much more likely to succeed than those which develop 'me-too's'. In biopharmaceuticals, diseases such as arthritis, osteoporosis, cancer and neurological diseases (e.g. multiple sclerosis and Alzheimer's) represent real unmet medical needs where significant opportunities and demand for new products exist. By contrast, new treatments for high blood pressure or bacterial infections are not so obviously required.

A company should also be assessed on the basis of management experience, since this is the key to transforming an exciting technology base into an innovative new product. Companies which have experienced, high quality management are more likely to succeed. It should be recognized that biotech managers need an entrepreneurial quality to find creative ways of developing the business, combined with a strong vision of where the company is going. Leadership, entrepreneurialism and experience are prerequisites for building a successful biotechnology business.

All development stage biotech companies are faced with a number of challenges. The first concerns financing and how a company should finance the late stages of development, international product registrations and commercial launch. The second turns on how a company successfully commercializes its products. Third, how does a company deliver return on its investment? While there is no one 'correct answer' to these questions, management must be able to demonstrate a coherent and sensible strategy in addressing these issues.

While the development of innovative, patented drugs which are breakthroughs in clinical medicine, and which address large markets with high margins are a sine qua non, the manner in which this is done will vary. Companies have to be able to demonstrate effective risk management and this can be done in a variety of ways, such as investment spread across a portfolio of projects or sharing risk through partnering agreements with larger established companies. Potential investors should look carefully at these factors.

The Future

In the United States a number of companies have been extremely successful in delivering substantial returns to investors. Included amongst these are Amgen, Biogen, Chiron, Genentech, Genzyme and Immunex. In the United Kingdom, there are now a number of established biopharmaceutical companies, such as British Biotech, Celltech and Scotia Pharmaceuticals, which are listed and which have already provided early stage investors with a substantial return on their original investment. However, existing valuations are only a fraction of what they will be if research and development programmes come to fruition.

Partnerships with large, established companies have been an important component in the development of many biotechnology companies. Partnerships may be an additional source of revenue, resources and expertise while, for the major company, they provide access to new technologies and products. A number of biotechnology companies have major equity partners, such as Genentech and Hoffman La Roche, Genetics Institute and American Home Products, and Chiron and Ciba-Geigy. Smaller research boutique companies may be fully acquired for their technology base, e.g. Glaxo and Affymax. Corporate partnerships of one form or another will always be a key part of the industry, since many biotechnology companies help bridge the gap between early stage research and late stage development.

Although the industry is still relatively young, it has an exciting future ahead as new technologies and products are developed. The visible fruits of the industry today are the result, for the most part, of applying the tools of genetic engineering to the manufacture of human proteins that were already proven or known to be highly likely to be therapeutically useful as injectable drugs. During the twenty-year period when these protein medicines were being developed, the tools of biotechnology, enhanced and supplemented along the way with computer and chemistry technologies, have been focused on discovering the molecular origins and mechanisms of human diseases and ill-health. Today there are hundreds of new drugs under development which when combined with the fruits of the human genome mapping are likely to provide substantial commercial opportunities in biotechnology.

Biotech companies will be at the forefront of this revolution, not only because they are generally more creative and innovative than larger, more established companies, but also because they have an entrepreneurial attitude to achievement. In a very tangible way, most biotech company managements are strongly aligned with shareholder interests. There will always be risks involved in investing in biotech, and there will always be risks in managing a business based primarily on products still at the research and development stage. However, if successful, the rewards can be substantial for manager and shareholder alike. ♔

BREWING

Sir Charles Tidbury

*Sir Charles Tidbury has enjoyed a career of 42 years in the brewing industry rising to become Managing Director and then Chairman of **Whitbread plc** from 1974 to 1984. He has been a Director of a number of leading regional brewers, including **Boddington, Marstons, Morland** and **Vaux**. He is currently on the Board of **George Gale**, a leading Hampshire based regional brewery and is Deputy Chairman of **Inspec plc**, a specialty chemicals company. He was Chairman of the **Brewers' Society**, President of the **Institute of Brewing** and President of the **British Institute of Innkeeping**. He is President of **Brewing Research Foundation International**.*

On considering the brewing sector as a home for funds, uncertainty – anathema to all city institutions – seems to predominate.

Poor Market Backdrop

First, demand hardly excites relative to some other business areas. After at least two decades of steady annual growth, UK beer consumption peaked in 1979 and has fallen at varying rates since, by a full 16 per cent. Though the customer has gone on drinking 'less but better' (ie more lager and premium brands generally), various factors have conspired to erode what was very much a beer culture.

Changing life-styles and tastes, drink-drive, the decline in manpower in heavy industries like coal and steel, and a quite harsh duty regime are certainly prominent. But they have been reinforced by the realities of recession; an ageing population more moderate in its consumption; and the dramatic growth in personal imports of beer from the near-continent on the back of excessively high tax on beer in this country.

The Pub Under Pressure

Second, if consumption overall has been poor, that element in pubs and clubs has been **particularly** so, falling by at least 27 per cent in the same period. Again, this reflects a shift in consumer habits and priorities and the growing competitive claims of other leisure pursuits. Very important, too, has been the enhanced appeal of supplies from multiple retailers like supermarkets for consumption at home at a time when often the need to economize has been compounded by the perception that beer prices in pubs and the like were 'high'.

At any rate, these and other developments have all raised large question marks over the value of the brewers' very substantial asset base in traditional pubs and over the stock of premises needed to sustain this deteriorating demand (arguably in a situation where the UK already had too many pubs).

Over-Capacity in Brewing

Third, though there are many problems of definition about what size of facilities is needed, and where in the system, to support any given level of the home beer market, there would be little dispute that production capacity was well ahead of consumption even before the roughly seven million bulk barrel contraction in beer volume experienced since 1979. This is the equivalent of three to four major breweries.

While the operators have rationalized heavily, or even given up brewing altogether, the City consensus about the degree of over-capacity, even in 1995, would not be below 20 per cent, with all its consequent adverse implications for wholesale prices and margins.

Regulatory Intervention

Fourth, these real forces for change would have been difficult enough to manage, and adapt to, even without the extra convulsions introduced by the 1989 Monopolies and Mergers Commission (MMC) Report and the subsequent enactments of the DTI Beer Orders.

Table 4.1 UK Beer Volume by Trade Channel (%)

	1989	1994E	2000F
Tied-on	44	29	19
Free-on	36	46	51
Free-off	20	25	30
All	100	100	100

Source: Brokers' estimates

The latter it would not be unfair to describe as marking an intervention by the competition authorities in an industrial sector on a scale unparalleled in peacetime UK. Besides imposing an estimated £550 million of restructuring costs on, essentially, the national brewers (and, 'incidentally', the consumer), they have enormously accelerated a process already at work whereby the major brewers' hold on the trade through their tied pubs has been sharply eroded:

So Grounds for Caution . . .

This scenario looks pretty daunting and no doubt has contributed to the weakening of investment sentiment about the domestic brewers in the last few years. It would be surprising, otherwise, when the institutions see massive structural change, often chronic price disorder, and deep-seated malaise in demand.

For some time the brewers have rather looked like 'dead money'.

. . . But Opportunity Comes with Change

While this stance may well be the right response in the shorter term to the uncertainties which have been mentioned, it is worth remembering that rewards tend to be highest to those investors able to look beyond the immediate threats to the new opportunities which they can present to the more commercially alert companies.

A new Focus for Brewing

Brewing certainly looks to be one sector in which the full rigours of competition will identify more quickly 'winners and losers'. Of course, in any real sense the companies have always been in contention, but there can be little doubt that a high degree of vertical integration between the producer and the owner of tied outlets has tended to inhibit the scale of incursion possible into the beer market.

This commercial inertia is being greatly eroded by the sharply enhanced focus being applied to wholesale brewing and distribution as effectively stand-alone activities based on more realistic transfer prices and on the ability to source new business in the open market. To this, the brewing cost-base is proving quite critical, as is the reach of distribution and service and the possession of **genuinely** 'must have' brands.

Whether this leads to really appreciable changes between companies in terms of operational scale remains to be seen, but there are **some** signs that market shares are shifting more appreciably, even if there remains no realistic prospect of any single UK concern 'doing an Anheuser-Busch', as in the USA, to achieve a predominant position with comfortably over 44 per cent of its domestic market.

How quickly these developments tone down the often cut-throat pricing policies which have accompanied the drive to 'detach' volume from deregulated houses must also be a moot point. So far, the major companies have (more or less) managed to maintain operating profits in cash terms. A step change in profitability, however, is probably going to be contingent on further realignment of the industry among three or four national players, against five currently and, possibly, six when the MMC began its enquiry.

Meanwhile, however, it is worth noting that, among the quoted major companies – Bass, Allied-Domecq, Whitbread and Scottish & Newcastle – profit dependence on 'brewing' as such now scarcely ranges above 30 per cent of group. When account is taken of the large other/international interests of Allied Domecq and Bass, the average would be little more than 20 per cent. These are not large numbers.

The Retail Challenge

The move from a process-driven management culture based on brewing has gone hand-in-hand with the recognition of the growing commercial opportunities in the pub and beyond. It is fair to say that, for the nationals, the days have long since gone when the pub was regarded as little more than a 'tap' for the brewery product.

Any simple description like 'food in pubs' would do the grossest disservice to the quite enormous extensions seen in the brewers' retail offering to the public, ranging through:

- segmentation of the pubs themselves to target the customer base much more precisely;
- a whole raft of eating concepts/brands designed to meet the needs of every age group, lifestyle and depth of pocket;
- the extension of leisure services, e.g., hotels and golf;

466

- new products in the take-away area based on existing restaurants and off-licences;

- overseas expansion in chosen field.

All this has had huge implications for the depth of management resources called for by what is, in any case, a more **discriminating** and value-for-money conscious clientele (skills in catering, branding and marketing, site search and development, financial control and staff recruitment and training, among others). The potential is already greater than expenditure on beer.

Chart 4.3 The UK Eating Out Market in Context

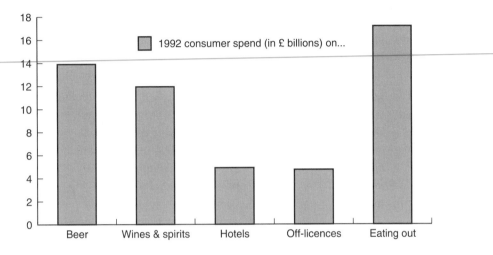

Source: Trade and Brokers' estimates

So it should not surprise that Whitbread now bids fair to being the biggest operator in the UK eating out market, or that Bass is a leader in international hotels.

'Small Is (or can be) Beautiful'

Nor, certainly, should the investment appraisal ignore the claims of the many regional and local brewers which, in the UK, unlike Belgium or Germany, provide a long tail of companies with either full or partial access to equity investors.

They have had the advantage of effectively being ring-fenced from the provisions of the Beer Orders, while being offered the new commercial opportunities that go with 'guest beers' and with the scope to extend their tied estates via the forced disposals of the majors.

That said, they cannot be immune from the wider influences working on the wholesale beer market generally, and it is significant that several of the largest concerns, like Greenalls, Boddington and Devenish, decided, at quite an early stage, that it was not worth maintaining a brewing operation when it was actually cheaper to source from outside.

To the extent that the most credible names in traditional ales such as those of Marston's, Greene King, Gales, Ruddles and Boddington itself are, in fact, very much fewer in number than is commonly supposed, it is possible that more will follow the 'retailing route'. but it need not be a point of demerit if – as has been seen – it enhances value to shareholders and releases resources which (sometimes) do deference to no more than a family history in brewing.

Final Thoughts

Broadly speaking, then, we are talking about companies which:

- are, in terms of reported profits, in the world senior league and usually much bigger than the dedicated, branded beer companies like Carlsberg and Heineken;

- are well-endowed with assets (including brands);

- are showing strong, and improving, cash flow trends;

- have been able to invest heavily in re-balancing their businesses to exploit areas of stronger growth offering better returns than the core activities; and

- do not carry high intrinsic risks (i.e. by and large 'brewery', or brewery-based, companies do not hit financial brick walls).

From the investor standpoint, there are two caveats. One is the **strategic grasp**. If the old style groups were not exactly simple themselves, their widening complexity of business puts a high premium on depth of management and planning resource. This must be a critical part of the investing equation; so is the ability of management to adopt and practise the new marketing skills needed for successful consumer retailing.

The other is the **interventionist** threat. There is a 'visibility' about brewing and pubs which has attracted a degree of attention from the UK competition authorities which the lowly producer of widgets is unlikely to generate. The latest probings by the Office of Fair Trading into the extent of differential beer pricing between the free market and brewers' own tied pubs are a pointed reminder that the industry's 'behaviour' remains under close scrutiny. Brewers also need to co-operate with the Treasury; Customs and Excise; the Home

Office; Transport; Trade & Industry; Agriculture and Heath and Social Services. That's one reason why a career in brewing has been so fascinating and rewarding for over 40 years, with all the changes it entails. ♀

BRANDED CONSUMER PRODUCTS

Robin Field

Robin Field has been Chief Executive of Filofax Group plc since October 1990. Filofax was floated on the USM in April 1987 at 120p valuing it at £17 million. The shares reached 207p but, by the spring of 1990, the company was losing money at a rate of over £2 million per annum, liabilities exceeded the market value of assets, and the shares touched 20p. Following a change of management the company has recovered to strong and growing profitability and the shares have passed previous highs. Mr Field is also a Director of Sunleigh, which owns the brands of 'Maclaren' (infant products, particularly pushchairs), 'Laser' and 'Dart' (sailing dinghies and catamarans) and 'Powa Kaddy' (electric golf trollies).

The Oxford English Dictionary defines a brand as a trade mark but, when we speak of branded goods, we mean something more precise and more valuable than simply this. It is not difficult to register a trade mark; it is very difficult and can be very expensive to establish a brand. Brands have a mystique. My daughters want to wear Doc Martens boots not for any quality or even any design style about the boots themselves but because they are Doc Martens.

Herein lies the first danger for the investor. If I go to the City and say I have a boot company to bring to the market, investors will be sceptical and will want to see a lot of data about financial performance, market share, competitive position and prospects. If I go to the same investors and say that I represent Doc Martens boots, investors may ask the same questions, or at least some of them, but they will not listen properly to the answers. All that I say will be filtered through a warm glow in response to the brand name. 'We know this is a good one, our children never stop asking us for the product.'

And, of course, the investors will often be right to feel a warm glow. Strong brands can command super-normal returns. But they do not have to do so. The very advantages that a strong brand offers can lead management to complacency and extravagance.

The story of Filofax provides a useful illustration of both the value and the pitfalls to management and investors alike of a well-known consumer brand.

From 1981, when the product first gained retail exposure, to 1987 the turnover of Filofax doubled every year. Because, especially in the early years, this growth exceeded management's expectations the expansion of infrastruc-

ture and fixed costs to handle increased business only followed sales and profits more than doubled every year.

Much of the growth in sales came from very rapid rises in unit prices
assisted, and disguised to some degree, by the inflationary climate of the 1980s
in which the public perception of relative retail values became confused.

No one was so confused, however, that a variant of the simple diary (retail
price in 1987 perhaps £5) retailing at between £65 and £500 failed to attract
attention. Herein lay both an advantage to the brand and a danger to management.

It is said that advice is perceived to be worth what you pay for it. Similarly,
a tool that claims to organize your life at a price of £65 **must have** something
special about it. 'If it's that good we had better buy one.' Demand grew; prices
rose ever higher.

Journalists spotting the trend wrote, 'What is this product that offers so
much?' 'What is this company that can grow so fast?' 'Who are these managers that can walk on water?'

And of course, while the publicity was good for sales in the short-term, it
was disastrous for management ego: 'We must be able to walk on water,
everyone says we can.'

It was also disastrous for investors. If you had looked at Filofax's flotation
financials for December 1986, a number of very worrying features screamed at
you. A company with no manufacturing capacity and a highly seasonal product had been absorbing, and not generating, cash. Inventory had risen and
now appeared to account for five months' cost of sales; four months of sales
were outstanding as debtors.

Did investors query these phenomenon? Apparently not. They had heard of
Filofax; some of their wives had bought Filofaxes. They had read the press
hype. The offer was over-subscribed and the shares reached a 70 per cent premium to flotation price before any more information was announced.

Meanwhile, the management was suffering from similar delusions.
Although sales growth was beginning to slow they had been told that they had
an unstoppable phenomenon. The only problem many of them had known for
six years was how to meet demand. They assumed that growth must continue,
that competitors didn't exist and that any slow down was a useful respite in
which to build stocks and invest in further warehouse capacity.

As sales started to fall, more management – particularly expensive marketing management – had been hired, extra products were launched to join an
already bloated product line and a growing inventory; and £4 million was
spent in the UK alone on advertising to persuade the public to buy products
that had become uncompetitive.

When I first got to know the company in the summer of 1990 a number of
issues were obvious. Of these the most significant was that, while Filofax sales
were falling, competitors' sales of organizers were rising fast. Looking back it
was evident that in the very years when Filofax turnover (boosted by unit
price rises) was growing fastest, competitors' unit sales of vastly cheaper orga-

nizers were overtaking them and Filofax was losing market share. Cushioned by the adulation given to their brand, Filofax management had never observed this competition. Investors, who had failed to ask about competition in April 1987, assumed that because Filofax sales were going south the organizer boom was over and the market was disappearing. Nothing was further from the truth.

The second relevant issue was that retailers, when questioned, were convinced of the value of the Filofax name. Despite an extraordinary lack of service, despite an arrogance that bordered on megalomania, retailers still would be eager to stock the product if only the price were right. Retailers' judgement was that while end users were reluctant to pay a 100 per cent price premium they would be willing to pay a 15 per cent premium to have the named brand.

Third, it was evident that not only were Filofax's prices far higher than competitors', but also were their costs. Filofax was not a manufacturer, and given its volume and prestige, in theory, should have been able to buy in at little over manufacturers' marginal cost of production. A lot of the inherently superior margin of a branded product lies in leveraging leadership to keep costs down. Other suppliers, however, were sourcing far cheaper products. Some were retailing organizers at less than Filofax was buying them. With hindsight it was clear that in the years when demand far exceeded supply Filofax buyers had been willing to offer any price incentive in order to accelerate deliveries. As demand drifted down, manufacturers had not, of course, volunteered to bring their prices back down.

> **A lot of the inherently superior margin of a branded product lies in leveraging leadership to keep costs down.**

This offered an opportunity, but even more enticing was the discovery that Filofax's principal UK competitor, who had gained most from the former brand leader's loss of share, had its own UK manufacturing plant with a cost floor based on UK wages. If a cheaper source of supply than the UK could be found the competitor would be faced with an uncomfortable choice between closing a factory and seeing Filofax costs drop below theirs.

Finally, while Filofax product design and features had remained static, and had been overtaken by several competitors, the product line width had expanded beyond all control. The same basic (and it was very basic) binder was available in a bewildering variety of sizes and a huge assortment of (mainly exotic) skins. Name a creature and Filofax would have ordered several thousand binders made of its hide and proudly placed them in its catalogue and in stock. I don't know what a Karung is, but I inherited an awful lot of its skin in 1990. Similarly, name a subject: bridge, chess, photography, bird watching, wind surfing, and Filofax would have commissioned several specialist inserts, had tens of thousands printed and put them in inventory oblivious to the fact that, given a user base of no more than, optimistically, eight per

471

cent of the population, eleven out of twelve exponents of any particular subject would never be in a position to use the product. Product line expansion has its place, but only if it is driven by providing differentiation which is valued by consumers. This sort of segmentation was artificial and did not enhance the underlying value of the Filofax product.

> **Product line expansion has its place, but only if it is driven by providing differentiation which is valued by consumers.**

The result was of course, not only a huge overhang of worthless stock, not only an administrative burden of vast complexity, but total confusion among retailers as to what among this array they should stock, and among end users as to what a Filofax retail display might contain.

Once these issues had been uncovered, correcting them and exploiting the huge remaining appetite for the brand within a fast growing organizer market would be simple. The opportunity was enormous.

Here, again, investors lost out. Just as in April 1987, through failing to ask the right questions and being instead mesmerized by the brand myth, they bought when they should have sold; in April 1990, blinded by the myth operating in the other direction, they sold when they should have bought.

Once a rescue rights issue in the summer of 1990 had paid down the overdraft, the company was very quickly brought under control. Head count was reduced from over 200 to 75, product cost was reduced and a complete new range of cheaper organizers was introduced so that, by 1991, 85 per cent of the organizers sold were completely new models introduced since October 1990.

If Filofax had been Anonymous Plc with a product that no investor had any opinion on, no doubt the dangers would have been obvious. But not for Filofax; it was a brand; investors knew all about it and didn't need to look at the data, 'We know Filofax; it was the yuppie product whose sales stopped in 1987'.

What are the lessons in the Filofax story for investors and managers looking at consumer brand companies? I can think of five:

1 Ignore the hype. Don't be distracted by the noise surrounding a brand and, in particular, remain sceptical about the congratulations that you yourself and your product receive.

2 Prune your product line. Examine the individual profitability of each stock-keeping unit and throw it out if it doesn't justify its existence.

3 Renew your product line. Successful brands will be copied; only by continual innovation will you stay one step ahead of the competition.

4 Consistently review prices. The worst reason for adopting a particular price is yesterday's price list. Some prices can go up, some must come down, but never should they stay the same – the market doesn't.

5 Focus on those activities that add most value. If you own a key brand, you must earn superior margins. Don't turn yourself into a manufacturing company and satisfy yourself with manufacturing margins; don't allow yourself to become a warehousing company with warehousing margins; don't become a transport company with transport margins. Only carry out those activities which are essential to adding most value to your brand. Let someone else do the rest.

But those are the negative lessons. The positive one is that the right brand name can be so strong that, like Filofax, even after years of abuse it can bounce back with a rapidity that can astound all observers. ♀

MEDIA

Robert Devereux

*Robert Devereux has been a partner and shareholder with Richard Branson in **Virgin** since 1980. During that time, he has been responsible for the development of the Group's media and entertainment activities.*

*He ran one of Europe's biggest film production and distribution companies, **Virgin Vision**, responsible for bringing to the UK such films as 1984 and Another Country.*

*He created the largest European interactive entertainment company, **Virgin Interactive Entertainment**, and launched **Music Box**, Europe's first music channel. He oversaw the launch of **Virgin 1215**, the UK's second national radio service, which is now the most listened to commercial radio station in the UK. Mr Devereux is also Chairman of **Virgin Publishing**, the UK's leading publisher of entertainment books.*

Introduction

As in any industry, success in media depends on an ability to predict and satisfy the demands of a market place in a profitable manner. In the case of the media world, the market place is driven by audience demand for 'content'; – information, education and entertainment. Whatever the format, newspaper, television show or a CD ROM, the principles remain the same. The content presented has to satisfy the demands of an audience if it is to succeed.

In the media industry, content is king

It is important to remember that it is the appeal of content that will secure subscriptions to a magazine or attract audiences and advertisers to a television channel, not the medium itself. This has never been more clearly demonstrated than during the 'video format wars' at the start of the 1980s. Sony's Betamax format was technically superior to VHS, but failed to win broad mass market acceptance owing to the paucity of Hollywood films released on that format. VHS had a lock on the most popular content and that drove the purchase decision of the hardware. Similarly, television research shows that, despite heavy branding, viewers' loyalty is to individual shows rather than the channels themselves.

Following the 'video format wars', electronics manufacturers realized the need to ensure that different content providers were prepared to publish on a new format before the format was launched. When competing against rival formats, the manufacturers also realized the value of securing content on an exclusive basis in order to boost sales of their new product. This thinking has driven many of the alliances between manufacturers and electronics companies over the last decade. Sony, for example, has been able to use its purchase of Columbia records to ensure that CBS/Sony Music titles were available at retail for its Mini Disc format.

Strong content will appeal to the consumer across all different media. The *Star Wars* property, for example, has performed well as a film, book, video and computer game. The ability to exploit a single group of rights across a variety of media is one of the core skills in most media organizations. This is because it is one of the main ways of reducing risk when investing in content – rights can be pre-sold to cover the costs of production. The more versatile the product, the more valuable, because more types of rights can be sold, and into more markets.

While a strong property might perform well across different media, the actual process of choosing which core rights to invest in is the most difficult management challenge. A television company, for example, will receive thousands of programme proposals each year. Some will be unsolicited, some will come with key talent in place. While any one of the titles might turn out to be a hit of the year, most will be just standard performers. Picking winners is one of the key skills required for success in the media industry. Few people have this skill, which is why those who do are so very valuable.

The appeal of content is difficult to predict – 'no one knows anything'

Dependence on content is why investing in entertainment companies has traditionally been seen as a risky business. It is essentially a creative activity, with a fashion element thrown in for good measure. Although risk can be managed, there is no clear relationship between the

Dependence on content is why investing in entertainment companies has traditionally been seen as a risky business.

level of finance involved and the reward. Putting £10 million into a new project will not, of itself, lead to a movie that is twice as appealing as one costing £5 million. There may even be a law of diminishing return. The most expensive movies have been more notable as financial flops.

The fundamental problem is that it is impossible to predict what will succeed. Every title is a different product with its own characteristics and brand positioning, quite unlike anything that has gone before or anything that will come after. The conditions during which the film is released are also unique - an action film might perform better than expected if the only other films released that month are romances. All sorts of extraneous factors not predictable when a film goes into production can affect the climate when it is released and its reception.

The appeal of a new film, book or TV series cannot be easily researched as there are no clear benefits to test. Market research will not help a publisher know how many copies of the new Martin Amis title he is going to sell. Few focus groups would have predicted that *Absolutely Fabulous*, a BBC show about a dipsomaniac fashion PR, would become one of the most successful British comedies of the last decade.

Conversely, as Sony found out with *The Last Action Hero*, having a heavily researched, high concept movie with a known star such as Arnold Schwarzenegger does not guarantee box office success. The difficulty of predicting performance is one of the reasons behind the popularity in Hollywood for remakes of successful films leading to almost annual releases of another version of *Friday 13th*. This spills over into TV, resulting in shows the audience already knows or for the creation of branded series such as *Indiana Jones*. Why else the sudden spate of made-for-movie TV shows headed by Tom Cruise in Paramount's *Mission Impossible*? That's the thinking behind Polygram's $156 million purchase of Lew Grade's ITC, which is chock full of rights from the 1960s and 1970s – hits such as *Thunderbirds* and *The Prisoner*. Follow the rights and you will find the key to the core values.

Follow the rights and you will find the key to the core values.

Equally, while putting an expensive marketing campaign behind a known property might guarantee a strong opening weekend, good word of mouth is by far the most important factor in the success of a film, book or video game. For example, the films *The Flintstones* and *The Jetsons*, released in the same year, were both based on an old TV cartoon and were both less than critically acclaimed. Their performance at the box office, however, was completely different. The reason for the relative success or failure of each title lay with the word of mouth generated by the first audiences. This is why the opening weekend of any film is considered so important.

Multiple choice for multiple audiences

The vagaries of consumer taste and the difficulties in researching the appeal of new titles lead most media companies to publish across a wide range of projects in the belief that the highs will more than counteract the flops. There is a level of security that comes with volume – the sensible investor will focus on companies who are large enough to present a broad catalogue of rights, rather than those who depend on a single group of properties.

The need for a broad catalogue grows with increasing fragmentation of audience taste. Fragmentation happens as mass media audiences are picked off by services or products that fit more closely to their requirements. This process is illustrated by the success US cable networks had in gradually eroding the share of viewing taken by the major terrestrial broadcasters, ABC, NBC and CBS. From a commanding position in the mid 1970s, the three major networks have seen their share of the audience fall to below 50 per cent.

The key management skill in media business is, therefore, the ability to manage creative risk, to get the hit titles in place and minimize the downside from the inevitable failures. There are few people with such editorial judgement. The investor should look first and foremost at the editorial track record of the team he or she is investing in.

The investor should look first and foremost at the editorial track record of the team he or she is investing in.

Getting closer to the market through distribution

Content and distribution go together in larger media organizations. As a publisher and distributor you can leverage your position in both content creation and distribution – owning the distribution vehicle means that you are more likely to achieve shelf-space for all your titles. A good example is the distribution of films to TV stations. Broadcasters can buy the hit titles, but only if they take them in a studio package that has been fleshed out with relatively poor performers.

Owning distribution networks also brings the content provider closer to the market place – the content feeds the distribution system, the distribution system funds the development of the content. There is an issue about how far down the distribution chain a media company should go – should a publisher also be a retailer for example?

Time-Warner owns and operates a large number of cable franchises in the States. The company decided to set up cable networks itself rather than leave distribution and subscription management to the specialist cable operators and telecommunications companies. Time-Warner argues that, by being the subscription manager and gateway keeper, it remains closer to public taste than its competitors.

However, Time-Warner also acknowledges that, as the provider of the pipe into consumers' homes, it is in direct competition with traditional telecommunications companies. The company has had to move into the provision of telecommunications in order to preserve the strategic position it created for itself. The Time-Warner strategy flies in the face of the approach taken by Disney, which focuses entirely on the development of content with a strong audience appeal, leaving the actual broadcasting or exhibition of its films to third parties.

There is a second danger that owning content, distribution and retail outlets leads to user end product that offers too narrow a range of propositions. Viewers don't want to see 'Time-Warner' movies, but rather hit titles from all the different studios. The interests of Time-Warner as a publisher, distributor and retailer are likely to pull in different directions. The need for a clear focus becomes all the more critical, given the changes now going on in the media industry worldwide.

The investor should therefore play close attention to the relationship between the media company and the distribution channels in the market place. How easily can a film production company secure exhibition? Does the publisher own a direct marketing operation through which retail can be supplemented or bypassed? Doe' the publisher have a brand which can be leveraged through an owned and operated distribution network?

The digital revolution

The media industry is currently undergoing a major structural change. The next decade is going to see a revolution in communications, entertainment, information and leisure. The revolution is going to be the result of choice, diversity and consumer control. It is going to be driven by the consumer's ability to interact with, and control, the media and entertainment that they purchase.

The revolution is driven by the convergence of three industries; computing, telecommunications and the entertainment industry itself. The culmination of this process of change will be network publishing. Over the next decade, developed media markets will see a series of new products and services come on-line. The services will be based on an ability to store ever increasing amounts of data in ever decreasing amounts of space and to transmit that information at ever increasing speeds to an almost infinite number of locations. This is the 'superhighway'.

It is not going to be built by the publishers, but by the cable companies and telecommunication companies, currently the most active players in this revolution. The cable companies and telecommunication companies will provide a gateway to the publishers content – they will collect revenue and distribute content on behalf of the publishing community. It is uncertain how much content the gateway companies will create themselves.

The future home will contain at least three access points to a superhighway interactive service. There will be a family-entertainment point based on the television and located in the family room. There will be an adult/work station based on the PC located in the home office and there will be a kids/entertainment device based on a game platform located in the bedroom.

These stations will be used for entertainment, information and education. They will enable the consumer to choose what they want, when they want it and where they want it. The fact that this superhighway is a two-way network rather than a one-way channel inviting passive viewing means that there will be a range of new creative opportunities open to new and existing publishers.

The impact of the superhighway on current media businesses cannot be exaggerated. There is simply not enough leisure time for these developments to occur without existing media losing significant market share. As pool halls and pubs lost share of leisure time to the cinema, cinema lost to TV and TV to computer games. The evolution is inevitable. However, just as cinema creates the value of the on-demand film library, so broadcast television will continue to create the value of the on-demand television library. In addition, for those broadcasters who are also programme producers, there will be an opportunity to replace existing revenue streams. It is likely that the safest media investments over the next couple of years will be found in those companies who are focusing on their core competencies in the creation of content. This strategy will provide the most secure route into the superhighway of the future. ☽

MINING

Algy Cluff

*J. G. Cluff is the Chairman and Chief Executive of **Cluff Resources plc**, a British based company with all of its mineral activities in Africa, principally in Zimbabwe, Tanzania and Ghana. The company has an annual production capacity of 130,000 ounces of gold and a wide spread of exploration interests. The company is listed on the London Stock Exchange and **Cluff Resources Zimbabwe Ltd** (85 per cent owned) is listed on the Harare Stock Exchange.*

There are three categories of mining company. First, the 'Majors'; those with production of one million ounces of gold per year. There are perhaps fifteen of these, American, South African, British, Australian and one African (Ghanaian), Ashanti. Secondly, the 'Independents'; those with production of 100,000 ounces per year upwards. There are possibly fifty such companies. Then there are the 'Juniors'; those companies with little or no production but a determination to discover some. Clearly the same valuation parameters cannot be applied to a company with production/profits as would be applied to one without production but possibly with a high potential to securing production. However, the rough criteria for valuing mining companies are as follows: production; reserves; political risk; exploration; management.

Production

This is the key to achieve relative security of investment although high levels of production can be misleading if they are also high cost. There are manifold methods of valuing mining companies and some analysts have their own methodology. However as a quick guide to a company's value a price is put on ounces of annual production and/or ounces of reserves in the ground. A range of $1,000 to $100 per ounce of projected annual production is used to calculate a gold mining company depending on where the company operates and, to an extent, the quality of management. North American production would command the highest premium – around $1,000 per ounce although North American-based stocks are increasingly beset with environmentally based difficulties. These can and increasingly do, raise questions over whether or not a mine will ever be developed, and more recently, and seriously, the level of abandonment costs a company will be committed to as the price for a new mine approval. Some potential costs are now so enormous that many companies are reviewing whether they should be operating in North America at all.

These requirements have recently spread to South Africa where presently it is understood that there are mines which cannot afford to close and are therefore limping along at a loss in order to protect the group which owns them from that financial exposure. In the case of single mine operations, it is likely that bankruptcy will be the only method available to such operations.

In North America even if approval for mine production is obtained and with abandonment arrangements which can be absorbed, the time taken to receive such approval can extend to ten years as the various levels of permitting are sought. No wonder one North American mining executive opined at last year's Denver Gold Conference that there is now a greater political risk to conducting business in America than almost anywhere else. Nevertheless those existing producers in North America with the benefit of large reserves still command a substantially higher production premium than their South American, Australian and African counterparts, – thirty times earnings being the average in North America as compared to twenty-five in Australia, twenty in South America and fifteen in Africa.

Reserves

The size and quality of a company's gold reserve base plays a major part in its share valuation. Until recently, the standardization and classification of this reserve varied in the major gold producing nations of South Africa, Australia, USA and Canada. There is now a convergence in generally accepted standard international definitions with the terms 'ore reserve' and 'mineral resource' outlining the main classifications. An 'ore reserve' (further subdivided into proved and probable) can be defined as that portion of a mineral resource on which technical and economic studies have been carried out to demonstrate that it can justify extraction at the time of determination and under specific economic conditions. A 'mineral resource' (further divided into measured, indicated and inferred) can be defined as an identified in situ mineral occurrence from which valuable minerals may be recovered.

From an investor's standpoint it is wise to confine his attention to the 'ore reserve' figure which must be separately identified in a company's report and accounts. Broadly speaking a value of $100 per ounce of gold in the ground is widely used as a means of valuation of reserves in North America and $50 elsewhere, although in certain countries, Zaire, for example, it would be as low as $10. A popular valuation comparison between gold mining companies relates the 'ore reserve' base to market capitalization.

From an investor's standpoint it is wise to confine his attention to the 'ore reserve' figure which must be separately identified in a company's report and accounts.

Political Risk

No country is isolated from political risk, even the Western democracies. Britain's last Labour government imposed so many tax increases on North Sea oil producers that eventually they were paying tax on income as well as their profits. In addition Tony Benn established the British National Oil Corporation (only to be correctly dissolved by Mrs Thatcher) which achieved nothing other than representing probably the most conspicuous waste of executives' time since the last war.

On the face of it dictatorships represent the greatest political risk but in the event they often contrive to provide a more constant and benevolent basis for partnership with the private sector than do democracies.

North American investors prefer their investments to be either in Canada or the USA. Second on the list would be Central, South America and Australia. Definitely third would be Russia, the CIS and all African countries including South Africa. European investors would accord a higher rating to Africa and a lower one to South America but are increasingly wary of Russia and Eastern Europe. China does not feature in a mining context as to date virtually no contracts have been signed with Western companies. Those that have concern refracting ore and prospects with grades of less than grammes/tonne. India is only now beginning negotiations with mining companies in particular with diamond companies in Orissa.

Within Africa, as in South America, listing the good and bad countries from an investment standpoint is a somewhat haphazard procedure. Often the country which has a commendable leadership lacks any mineral potential or vice versa. However, of these sub-Saharan countries, the most favoured, from a geologist's perspective, and which also have a good to tolerable attitude to foreign investment, I would rate the following (in no order of preference): Botswana, Burkina-Fasso, Ethiopia, Ghana, Guinea, Mali, Namibia, South Africa, Tanzania, Uganda, Zambia and Zimbabwe. I would also keep a close eye on Angola and Zaire, the latter containing some of the world's richest deposits of minerals, particularly copper. Zaire is exhibiting signs of wishing to revive its economy, and of welcoming foreign investment. That country could, once again, become one of the most sought after mining addresses in Africa.

Assuming no company is mad enough to deliberately invest in a country from which it is unable to remit dividends, the most important criterion – other than the geology – is the law. Where Africa is increasingly scoring is that not only does there exist an abundance of prospects but also virtually all African countries have a legal system based on a European model be it Spanish, British, Portuguese or French. This is in sharp contrast to Russia and the CIS where legally speaking there really is no system.

Exploration

Where you are valuing a company with earnings based on diminishing reserves it is essential for the survival of that company that it maintains a vigorous exploration programme. You must therefore endeavour to value that exploration. The quality of exploration acreage is vital. It is often astonishing what high values markets do place on pure exploration. There is no satisfactory means of valuing exploration acreage other than the 'closology' principle which is as good as any other. It is a perfectly simple procedure to acquire a geological map of a prospective country and to identify which companies are well entrenched on known gold belts. The same, of course, applies to copper, platinum and so on.

The important point for the investor with regard to exploration companies is to pick management which only acquire good acreage and then know what to do with it. It is a cardinal error for management to reduce its stocks in prime acreage too early – ideally not until a drilling campaign has occurred which will hopefully serve to add value to that licence. On the other hand management which constantly resorts to rights issues to fund unsuccessful exploration programmes should be avoided.

The important point for the investor with regard to exploration companies is to pick management which only acquire good acreage and then know what to do with it.

Management

The management of large mining companies is often impenetrable and constantly changing, but such large companies often develop a culture of their own and behave in a fairly consistent manner. The management of small companies is usually all too frequently the reflection of one strong personality which is sometimes but generally more often is not a recipe for success.

Perhaps the most reliable and easily valued companies are the independents where the strong personality necessary to create and drive a company operates but within the context of a strong team and disciplined by an equally strong team of non-executive directors.

Operations and Structure

Other aspects of particular importance about which management should be consulted if no mention is made in a mining company's published information are in my view the following:

(a) Water

Is the mine a 'dry' mine, ie. is the intrusion of water not a concern to management? If so well and good but is there enough water to sustain the mine's operations? In countries subject to drought it is important to establish that a mine may or may not have to close owing to water shortages.

(b) Safety

What is the safety record of the company in which you are investing? If it is lax the possibility of inexcusable fatalities arise with the quite proper risk that the countries' mining authorities may force closure of the mine.

(c) Labour relations

Management's record in this area is crucial. A company with low margins and high gearing could be put out of business by a prolonged labour stoppage. If you are able to visit a mining operation pay particular attention to the quality of the housing and the general attention to the welfare of the staff whether it be children's education, health care or community centre activities.

(d) Gearing

Pay particularly careful attention to a company's gearing. Management often has no alternative but to assume high levels of borrowing in order to develop new discoveries into mines. But the mining business is subject to vagaries which are manifold and are to a large extent beyond the ability of management to control – the gold price itself, shortage of foreign exchange reducing or curtailing dividend remittances in Third World countries, environmental requirements in North America for example are some of the factors which can turn a heavily borrowed company into a bankrupt one in a short time.

The mining investment scene is, of course, dominated by giant organizations such as RTZ, BHP and Anglo-American, but there is ample scope for the entrepreneur. Curiously, virtually every international independent (or entrepreneurial) mining company seems to have English speaking origins. They are almost all American, Canadian, British, South African or Australian. There are scarcely any Japanese, Italian, German, French, Dutch or Spanish junior mining companies. Investors must, therefore, look to the Stock Exchanges of those Anglo-Saxon countries to identify the mining company they prefer. The exchanges most closely connected with mining are those of Toronto, Johannesburg and Perth. Providing due regard is paid to at least some of the criteria highlighted in this article, the scope for reward in mining investments remains as attractive as ever before. ♀

PROPERTY

Sir Nigel Mobbs

Slough Estates plc, founded in 1920, owns properties with a portfolio value of £1.8 billion, situated in the United Kingdom, Canada, the USA, Australia, Belgium, France and Germany. The Group is one of the largest owners and developers of industrial estates in Europe and, together with its substantial portfolio of office and retail developments, manages 31 million square feet of space occupied by some 2,400 tenants.

Sir Nigel Mobbs has been Chairman and Chief Executive of the company since 1976, having joined the company in 1960. He is a former President of the British Property Federation. In addition, Sir Nigel Mobbs is Chairman of Kingfisher, and a non-executive Director of Barclays and Howard de Walden Estates.

Property development and investment is a cyclical activity that both anticipates and responds to user demand and investor sentiment. The provision of shelter for a comprehensive variety of activities from homes to factories calls for a range of compatible management and technical skills. A successful property enterprise has to combine creative vision with the prudent deployment of funds which in turn produce a commensurate investment return for the risk incurred.

Experience of the past seven years demonstrates clearly the pitfalls of undertaking property ventures that did not measure adequately the strengths and weaknesses in a market which was moving into over-supply. Anticipated values evaporated and such cash-flow that was generated after leasing concessions and lower rental rates was inadequate to service external debt. This experience was not confined to the UK, but was reported in most mature economies.

Despite these short-term set-backs, the property sector has for the past 50 years fulfilled a generally useful community service despite political intervention, economic stop-go and inflation. The sector has modernized Britain's towns and suburbs; it has created direct and indirect employment; it has improved the built environment; it has produced better working conditions; and it has provided a relatively secure investment media for individual savings.

What, then, are the ingredients to determine the success of an active property development and investment company in what is a very competitive and fragmented sector?

A successful property company must have entrepreneurial management who have the vision and experience to identify an opportunity and then through their skill and commitment manage the long process of design, funding, construction and marketing to see the project through to a satisfactory conclusion to the satisfaction of the ultimate user and investor. An experienced property team will comprise a range of complementary skills including finance, building, surveying and legal disciplines. Experience will be gained by professional qualifications and by 'on the job' knowledge.

The developer has to be far-sighted and patient as projects can take years. By his vision, the developer must be able to anticipate both the project user's needs and those of the investor. He needs to be sensitive to the interests of the community and others affected by his proposals. He may need to negotiate site assembly and mediate between conflicting opinions.

Property development and investment is a very political activity. At all stages a project is subject to legislative constraints, public opinion and the whims – often capricious – of elected authority. Local authorities will seek to gain advantage from allowing development to proceed and there is a fine balance between what is acceptable infrastructure gain which is directly related to the project and municipal extortion to extract peripheral community benefits out of a project's limited profitability.

The regulatory maze and the creeping intervention of ever-increasing environmental law enmeshes all aspects of the development process. The project team has to be sensitive, resilient and at times obdurate to advance the progress of a project. They must respect adopted policies but they should also resist and challenge ill-conceived and reactionary ideas.

We live in times of rapid change in technology, working patterns and lifestyles. The most important include a greater use of automation, information technology and the merging of office and industrial skills. These factors influence the accommodation needs of a wide range of businesses. The skilled property entrepreneur must be capable of understanding and anticipating such changes. He must be able from his experience to influence the location, design and specification of buildings to prevent environmental harm, to economize on energy usage and provide accommodation that is durable, efficient and economic to use and occupy.

In all property decisions the choice and identification of the correct location is critical to the ultimate success of a project. A good location is greatly influenced by accessibility to transport and the availability of a range of employment skills. The professional property team should have the experience and judgement to make these decisions. Qualitative and quantitative analysis is an important factor in decision-making but such methods can only be an aid to personal judgement honed by experience and market knowledge.

> **A good location is greatly influenced by accessibility to transport and the availability of a range of employment skills. The professional property team should have the experience and judgement to make these decisions.**

The users of buildings expect the owner and developer to produce a product which enhances their individual needs whereas the investor is seeking investments that suit a range of alternative uses. The developer's skills lie in reaching a compromise between these separate but complementary interests. He needs to lead and influence the team of architects, engineers and cost consultants; he needs to obtain the permits and approvals by negotiation; and he needs to rationalize and mediate the conflicts. But above all he needs to transmit to the team a sense of enterprise and pride in the design of the project. Consequently the developer must possess all the qualities of leadership, persuasion and decisiveness.

No project will succeed without adequate funding. There are many differing ways of financing projects. The successful entrepreneur will explore and negotiate the arrangements that best suit the individual characteristics of the scheme and its eventual use and ownership. Leverage is a critical element. Loan to value ratios are the most common benchmark, with ratios of 75 per cent to 80 per cent. However, in recent years, with property values declining, lower ratios are deemed to be more prudent. Cash flow to debt service ratios are often more critical when rental income is the only source of cover for interest payments. A cover of 1.2 times is a prudent measure. The key element to successful funding is to tailor the package to the project and to allow some provision for adverse project results by subscribing real risk equity.

In recent years too many projects were conceived for investment reasons rather than user needs. Too many schemes were financed on short-term arrangements with no pre-committed permanent funding and too many promoters had inadequate cash flow to subscribe real risk equity or to support debt service shortfalls. Consequently too many good projects were blighted by the wrong funding package and by weak patronage.

485

At the conclusion of a project, the long-term investor, who may happen to be the developer, will wish to own a project which will satisfy the user and a project which will improve in value as rental income increases in real terms which will in turn enhance value.

The owner or investor will wish to receive a total return on his investment which exceeds the risk free return of investing in government bonds but also compensates him for having risked his own money in the conception of the project and the various risks inherent in owning buildings leased to third-parties. Consequently the building owner must have an interest in who occupies his property. The owner must focus his attention on customer satisfaction and the proper maintenance of his investment. It is in the owner's interest to ensure that his properties remain fully occupied and income producing. Empty property destroys value.

The choice and stability of the tenant is important to the security of a property investment. The quality of the lease terms, the definition of rent review clauses and repair covenants, are important. A high grade corporate covenant secured for a minimum of 15 years may provide the best valuation, but might also offer a rental return too slender to reward the equity owner. Conversely, a lesser credit might offer a better revenue return, but a lower valuation.

These are all the ingredients that I believe a successful property company should mobilize in achieving its goals.

Slough Estates was founded 75 years ago this year, not as a property company but as a company renovating and selling war surplus transport after the First World War. Included in the original transaction was a site of 600 acres together with 1 million. of factory space at Slough, west of London. As the sales of trucks declined, so my predecessors, who included my grandfather, leased vacant buildings to other businesses including many household names such as Mars, Johnson & Johnson and Westons Biscuits. Hence was born the concept of the managed industrial estate and the creation of the Slough Trading Estate.

Today we still own and manage the same estate, which now comprises some 7.6-million square feet. The Estate remains the largest single investment. It has benefited from its proximity to London, Heathrow Airport, the excellent road and rail network to the west of London and the quality of living in the Thames Valley, underlining the value of a good location.

Over the years we have expanded our UK portfolio to some 17.1 million square feet. in 42 locations to include retail centres and offices as well as our core industrial property interests. Overseas we have developed and own 13.7 million square feet. in Canada, Belgium, Australia, USA, France and Germany. The Group believes in owning a portfolio which is diversified by sector and geography. Property sectors and locations do not always progress in a synchronized manner and diversification provides for cyclical protection. Geographic diversity also provides for political, economic and financial hedging. Slough Estates is a predominantly industrial property company but, as locations evolve, so higher and better value opportunities arise. Specialist investment may have its attractions, but the wrong choice can, at times, be an embarrassment. Hence the need for some spread of portfolio interest.

Slough Estates has enshrined a set of principles and a management approach which we feel embody the essential elements of a successful property company. Investors should look to see whether these attributes listed below are present as one part of the analysis to determine whether an investment is likely to work out favourably.

- Be involved in the whole development and property management process.

- Complement in-house skills by carefully selected external expertise – architects, engineers, builders and other consultancy.

- Build simple, flexible buildings for a wide range of business needs in prime locations.

- Maintain a strong balance-sheet with an endowed revenue stream from a long-standing property portfolio. This is the essential resource to provide flexibility and choice in how to fund new projects.

- Actively manage the portfolio to improve values. Promote the enhancement of the portfolio infrastructure and protect it against environment risks. Nurture the portfolio to maximize occupancy income.

- Work with customers to improve their business opportunities by providing good accommodation in the best locations.

These are all factors that are crucial to ensuring continuity of objectives and in providing for enhancement of shareholder value which is, in the final analysis, the primary measure of long-term success for a publicly-listed property company. ♇

RETAIL: DEPARTMENT STORES

Andrew Jennings

*Andrew Jennings is Managing Director of **House of Fraser plc**, which was re-floated in the London Stock Exchange for £410 million in April 1994, after almost a decade in private ownership. Mr Jenning's entire working life has been spent in retail store management, initially in South Africa with **Greaterman's Organisation**, **StuttaFords** and **Garlicks Store Group**. He returned to the UK in 1991 as General Manager of **Harrods**, becoming Managing Director of **House of Fraser** in 1992.*

The foundation of department stores lies in the late eighteenth and early nineteenth centuries, in Western Europe and, above all, in Great Britain. During the French revolutionary wars, Napoleon contemptuously dismissed Britain as 'a nation of shopkeepers'.

Britain was swiftly becoming a nation of shopkeepers. The merchant, commercial and professional classes expanded rapidly as the Industrial Revolution took root, demanding the same clothing and homewares which had previously been the prerogative of the landed classes. With revolution, Britain's great urban centres – Manchester, Liverpool, Glasgow and Birmingham – were growing with blossoming town centres which provided the base for new generations of shopkeepers whose names and stores were to be key elements in British retailing two centuries later. Jollys in Bath, Kendals in Manchester, Cavendish House in Cheltenham, Binns in the north east, had all been established by the time Britain's shopkeepers escorted Bonaparte to exile on St Helena following the Battle of Waterloo in 1815.

Throughout the nineteenth century, department stores grew and grew, selling men's and women's fashions, curtains and carpets, furniture and cooking utensils, clothes, yarns and foodstuffs to the expanding urban population. Sales were fuelled by the growing middle class with rising disposable incomes. It was not just in the UK. Department stores flourished and have continued to prosper in Continental Europe, North America, South Africa, Japan and Australia.

Of course, social and economic conditions do not stand still – and nor can any commercial enterprise, if it is to continue to survive and prosper. These shifted rapidly after the Second World War in the UK and elsewhere. Growth in disposable income reached unprecedented levels, providing the funding for competitive retailers to develop. Education and awareness continued to grow, producing a consumer interest in specialist areas of business (whereas department stores were seen as generalist). Transportation methods improved with the explosion of car ownership, allowing consumers greater freedom in choosing where they wanted to shop.

In these circumstances, department stores found they had more competition; a situation exacerbated in the final quarter of the century with the development of out of town centres and shopping malls, and the appearance of 'Category Killer' specialists with unbeatable range and prices over a limited area of merchandise. The US leads the way, the UK was first to follow, and other parts of the world are playing catch-up, as focused chains like Toys 'R Us break new ground in Japan and continental Europe. Fragmentation evolved to slice and dice the retail market all the way from Blockbuster Video to PetsMart. Against this background, it is valid to ask, 'How can department stores survive?'

In fairness, many stores lost their way for a period. They were complacent about their prosperity, failing to acknowledge that evolution was essential if the potential of their historic strengths was to be maintained and fulfilled. Consumers, not least in Britain, retain an affection for the department store concept. The long-standing history and reiteration of an established store encourages customers through the doors.

It is often overlooked in the rush to get on board new trends just how powerful these brand names can be in their local community. In the 1920s, the Harrods regional division purchased Kendals in Manchester and changed the name to Harrods. But even the mighty name of Harrods had to be changed back to Kendals within six months as there was a major hue and cry and the matter was raised in the House of Lords. Similarly, during the 1980s, the then management of the business decided to change one or two of the store names to House of Fraser. Here again, there was great resistance and the names were changed back. Not least, London taxi drivers could not cope. Names, for retailers, can be assets every bit as important as brands in consumer products, even if they do not appear on the balance sheet.

Based on our observation at House of Fraser, we believe the way forward for department stores is as a collection of specialist businesses under one roof, each appealing to a defined segment of the population and providing consistency of product to match defined needs. If a proportion of the business is aimed at the contemporary customer, then the ladies' fashion, men's fashion, fashion accessories and fashionable housewares must consistently be contemporary.

All out of town shopping centres have bent over backwards to attract a department store tenant to anchor the site. 'More than 70 per cent of all mall traffic comes through department store doors', is the American experience. The move from the high street to out of town proves the department store concept can flourish in a new environment. House of Fraser stores at Meadowhall and Lakeside lead the group in sales growth. Securing these premier high traffic locations is one essential element for the strategy of any retailer who expects to succeed in the competitive climate of the 1990s.

So what is it that the consumer still likes about department stores? Having conducted research, the answer is quite simply:

● The convenience of authoritative ranges of fashionable merchandise under one roof.

● Branded merchandise well presented and effectively co-ordinated in an up-market environment.

● Good customer service, either at the point-of-sale or in the many facilities that are available to the consumer:

 – home delivery
 – personal shopping services
 – gold card lounges
 – hair and beauty salons
 – restaurants.

These are the traditional strengths of department stores. So, against this background, let us look at the myth of the death of the department store.

Since the beginning of the 1990s, it is the multiples which have come under pressure, while department stores have begun to increase sales again and claw back market share. Specifically, the top five department store groups in the UK have gained against the 20 leading multiples.

The customer base for department stores is growing in numbers and in spending power. The baby boomers of the Second World War are now customers. At House of Fraser, the core customer is the 35-54-year-old, categories ABC1. Understanding the quality of the core customer is a good leading indicator of likely profitability in this sector. Demographics are on the side of the department store. An increase of approximately 2.5 million people in this age category is anticipated over the next decade in the UK. Simultaneously the growth of the economic middle class in the UK is an advantage, as are social class changes. The rich may not be getting richer, but they are certainly becoming more numerous.

Similar trends can be observed across all mature economies. The rise of the middle class in many developing countries is likely to lead to the same sort of retail evolution. Within this environment of constant change it is critical that a retailer finds a focus, defines its role and articulates a clear strategy. Those that do will succeed, while those who cannot will wither. The House of Fraser has a simple objective: to establish itself as a focused, up-market department store group based on a clear vision of its customer, supported by the consolidation of a merchandise policy designed to capture, retain and grow that customer base. There are lessons in its strategy for all department stores, reflecting that retailing has, again, become a leisure interest, not a simple necessity with convenience dominating.

This merchandise focus will be supported by the development of stores to ensure they are in the right location and possess the appropriate structure by:

- refurbishing the store environment to lead with a competitive edge. Investors can tell a lot about a retailer by visiting its outlets;

- establishing the most efficient information systems to ensure an excellent control on inventory. Return on capital employed is a critical measure for investor and management alike;

- developing a centralized distribution centre to gain substantial margin and stock turn enhancement and considerable cost savings. Leveraging economies of scale is essential to retail profitability;

- developing a strong charge card base to develop future loyalties. A repeat customer is a retailer's most valuable asset;

- building the highest standard of customer service at every level. This is the cornerstone of our business. Retailers have to provide more than just product, and those who understand how to supplement value delivered through superior service will prosper;

- developing human resources within the organization. This will require constant training and upgrading of personnel.

Investors looking to select shares which will be rewarding should examine how the retailer is addressing these issues. The House of Fraser has developed a strategy based upon a well-defined merchandise policy, upon high quality, well-located selling space, upon an efficient information and distribution system and upon exceptional customer services.

A key element underlying its refurbishment programme is the conversion of selling space from stocking low margin items to a greater emphasis on top quality design labels. This involves the conversion of individual stores, dependent on size and location, from historic full range to speciality or limited assortment stores and by the development of non-productive space.

This is just part of the equation. The other part is to satisfy the needs of differing customer populations. Retailers of all stripes have to get close to their customers to differentiate themselves from the crowd. The customer who lives and shops in Glasgow has different requirements form the customer who lives and shops in Darlington. Therefore, the policy the House of Fraser has adopted is that of lifestyling of the merchandise into four key areas: high fashion, contemporary, classic and essential.

The customer expects a consistent merchandise appreciation to ensure a successful shopping experience. Historically, the House of Fraser stocked a wide assortment of merchandise in little depth. Excess proliferation leads to lost sales due to stock outs in the best sellers and margin erosion due to mark downs on slow moving items. Today, House of Fraser is reducing the number of line options stocked across all stores to enable a clear focus in the assortments offered to the identified customer base.

Part of the merchandise strategy is to continue to reduce the supplier base, which not only assists in clarity of offer, but also brings efficiency in stock turn, distribution and, more importantly, better trading terms. Retailers who constantly strive to improve in all these areas will be the companies whose customers come back and whose shareholders enjoy increasing returns.

Central to this positioning is more efficient stock control through an efficient, technology-driven buying chain. House of Fraser has committed some £20 million to installing a single, integrated buying system which will stretch from electronic point of sale (EPOS) technology in-store to a full third party centralized distribution system, involving a single warehouse supplying all the group's stores. The impact will be manifold: greater stock turn; more efficient stock controls; increased ability to respond to customer demand on a store-by-store basis; and greater ability to convert in-store stock holding into selling space.

House of Fraser's store programme has three primary objectives, driven by those factors which are essential elements of every successful retailer:

- locations which are in the centre of large catchment areas for the customer base – not just existing, but potential;

- the creation of an internal shopping environment which customers enjoy and will return to, and which enables the product offering to be clearly and attractively displayed;

- the conversion and upgrading of the store environments to support and accommodate the changing product mix.

These programmes are supported by drives to develop a customer base with a strong loyalty to a store and, concurrently, to encourage greater spend by individual customers. The pivot of this drive is the charge card. By 1995, House of Fraser had 685,000 active holders whose spending, through the FraserCard, represented 30 per cent of total group sales. Significantly, the price of a transaction through the FraserCard is some 28 per cent higher than the average value of all other transactions.

In common with the ordinary charge card, holders are offered special promotions during the year. Additional benefits are conferred on Gold Card holders, including access to Gold Card lounges in many stores, a concept borrowed unashamedly from the international airlines. The lounges allow customers to leave shopping, watch television, read newspapers or generally relax, with free refreshments provided.

The existence of a wide charge card customer base creates other benefits. The company is provided with structured and very precise marketing lists, even down to a database of the particular merchandise categories most utilized by individual card holders. Developing loyalty schemes and intelligent cross-marketing using proprietary information will be one visible hallmark of a progressive retailer in the 1990s.

In conclusion, to grow and prosper, retailers should be able to present investors with a very clearly defined strategy which builds on documented strengths:

- specific stores, their history and their positioning;

- an identified customer base, with its demographic and spending growth;

- a merchandise mix in optimum balance with the identified customer base;

- a policy of quality space in the best locations;

- a culture of superior service.

The strategy that the House of Fraser will be implementing will ensure prosperity for this department store group well into the twenty-first century. Retailing leadership will accrue to those who espouse these policies. ♀

SHIPPING

Atle Kigen

*Atle Kigen is Senior Vice President in the Kværner Group. He is a member of the board of **Kvaerner Warnow Werft** in Germany and **Kværner Rosenberg** in Norway. He was formerly Business Editor in Aftenposten, the biggest morning paper in Norway, and Editor-in-Chief of Økonomisk Rapport, a weekly business magazine.*

492

Kværner is one of the world's leading companies involved in all aspects of the shipping industry. Forty-seven per cent of 1994 revenues of NOK 26 billion were from ship building and shipping.

Shipping has always been more important to Norway than any other nation during the last millennium. The story of Norwegian shipping is, in many respects, a proxy for the global market. Norway's lengthy coast means it has always been a nation of seafarers. Its first golden age as an international shipping nation extended from 700 AD to the end of the thirteenth century. Substantial population growth in this period stimulated Norwegians to cross the sea in search of wealth and trading opportunities. The wanderlust of the Vikings has left its mark in several parts of the world.

The more recent history of the maritime industry begins with the repeal of the British Navigation Acts in 1849. This sparked a period of powerful growth, based on national trading needs as well as extensive traffic between third countries. Wooden-hulled sailing ships dominated this era. The growth in the fleet from 1850–80 can be attributed largely to relatively cheap production factors, Norwegian seafaring skills and plentiful supplies of cheap labour for the country's shipyards.

From Sail to Steam

The introduction of steam-driven ships and the transition from pure tramp operations to liner traffic created a completely new situation, requiring owners to address technology and increased capital demands. Market segmentation became more important. After 1918, Norwegian owners initiated a major commitment to tankers for shipping crude oil. They were among the first to see the need for such tonnage, which launched a new period of growth.

The Great Depression at the end of the 1920s put an effective halt to progress. Norwegian shipowners were rescued by the Shearwater Plan in 1932, which basically brought all independent tanker operators into a major pool that shared profits. Markets gradually recovered, and the pool ceased to operate, but the concept did not die, as the structure was an economically rational way to manage these assets. When it revived in 1939 it was extended to new classes of vessel and embraced ownership from other countries, notably Sweden, Germany and Holland.

The inter-war years witnessed a gradual transition from tramping based on relatively low-cost second-hand tonnage to more durable relations with customers through long-term contracts. This period was also marked by great new-building activity and high level of technological innovation. Norwegians built the first dedicated fruit carriers with refrigerated holds, and the first ships for carrying heavy loads like railway wagons. The market was quick to adapt to the specialized requirements of new cargoes. This was also an opportunity to improve profitability over more standard fare. Such advances were the first signs of what was later to become the trademark of Norwegian shipping; a

Table 4.2 World Fleet by Ship Type as of 1 January 1995 (vessels over 300 gt)

	Mill dwt
Oil tankers	270.9
Gas tankers	13.9
Chemical tankers	8.0
Combined carriers	26.9
Bulk carriers	218.9
Container ships	38.9
Other	104.3
Total	681.8

Source: ISL Bremen

commitment to technologically advanced and specialized ships. The development of different categories is laid out in Table 4.2.

Norwegian ships played a very central role during the Second World War in freighting supplies to the Allied forces. A British maritime journal concluded that the contribution by Norway's merchant fleet during the first years of the war was worth more than a million soldiers. But this carried a high price – about half the fleet was sunk and more than 3,000 seamen lost their lives.

The war was naturally followed by a huge need for new tonnage to ship essential raw materials for reconstruction. Norwegian owners wanted to buy or build about 2.5 million gross tons, but the authorities felt this would absorb too much of Norway's currency reserves and introduced a licensing system. After currency restrictions were relaxed in the early 1950s, the country's tonnage again expanded rapidly. A sharp increase in international trade fuelled a new boom.

All fleets were badly hit by the long slump that persisted from 1973 to 1987. A combination of weak freight markets and high domestic pay levels put pressure on owners to transfer their ships to flags of convenience in order to cut wage costs by hiring foreign crews. Since wages are virtually the only element in operating costs that vary between countries, it is understandable that owners wanted to minimize them in order to compete. Towards the end of the 1980s, ship owners were also given the opportunity to register ships under foreign flags. The result was that the fleet under Norwegian flag was greatly reduced, while the fleet of Norwegian-owned and managed vessels under foreign flags increased significantly.

These moves immediately unleashed another investment boom in Norwegian shipping. This was an important factor in the recovery, combined with a marked improvement in second-hand tonnage values that prompted substantial purchase and sale of vessels during 1988–90. Norwegian owners played a very active role in such 'asset plays', and were involved in more than 50 per cent of all second-hand transactions worldwide.

494

Specialization as a Survival Strategy

Conscious specialization, preferably in segments that require advanced technological capabilities, has run like a red thread through the long and turbulent history of shipping. Combined with technical innovation, these two aspects marked out the long-term survivors in the industry.

Norway's maritime community forms a highly compact 'cluster' of companies, with the interaction of internationally competitive players in Norwegian shipping success. New technology and new operation methods were employed to

Conscious specialization, preferably in segments that require advanced technological capabilities, has run like a red thread through the long and turbulent history of shipping.

reduce costs; ship owners searched for new markets or segments of markets where superior expertise and know-how could secure market share. The strong involvement in the offshore oil industry, the ever-increasing number of shipping companies managing ships owned by others and the sale of shipping know-how through the establishing of consulting companies are examples of this new trend.

Norway has remained in the forefront of this industry for a very long time. While the former maritime powers, Britain and the USA, have seen their capacity decline by 50 and 17 per cent respectively in 1850 to one and four per cent today, Norwegian capacity has risen from 3 to 6 per cent overall, and still ranks fourth, measured by dead-weight tonnage. Table 4.3 includes flags of convenience.

Table 4.3 World Fleet by Major Flag as of 1 January 1995 (vessels over 300 gt)

	No	Mill dwt	% share dwt
Panama	4,177	95.7	14.0
Liberia	1,525	93.7	13.7
Greece	1,448	52.4	7.7
Cyprus	1,522	38.3	5.6
Bahamas	1,000	33.9	5.0
Norway	1,147	32.0	4.7
Japan	3,635	30.5	4.5
Malta	979	25.3	3.7
China	1,847	22.6	3.3
Singapore	699	18.1	2.6
Other countries	18,271	239.3	35.2

Source: ISL Bremen

Strategic Choices

In order to study the strategic choices facing shipowners, it could be appropriate to segment the market with a somewhat simplified matrix that focuses attention on two main dimensions.

One concerns the extent that economies of scale exist in the operation of the tonnage. The other relates to the extent of the specialization that is possible for either ship or transport service. This matrix yields four 'strategic' choices:

1 Contract shipping: many economies of scale, little specialization

2 Tramping: few economies of scale, little specialization

3 Industrial shipping: many economies of scale, high specialization

4 Specialized shipping: few economies of scale, high specialization

Shipowners can be said to focus on nine international sectors:

- dry cargo,
- crude oil,
- refined oil products,
- car carrying,
- cruising.

- chemicals,
- gas,
- liner traffic,
- 'open hatch' bulk carriers (conventional tonnage fitted with specialized equipment),

The matrix in Chart 4.4 illustrates the strategic choices made by Norwegian owners.

Chart 4.4 Strategic Choices of Norwegian Shipowners

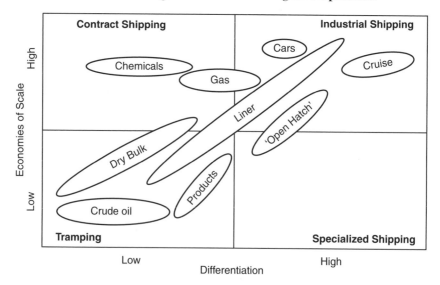

This illustration is not intended to place the individual sectors exactly in the simplified matrix, but to show the diversity of the strategies available in shipping and the forces that make it possible for owners to differentiate their product away from the extreme position of almost perfect competition.

Sources of Norway's Success

Classic macroeconomic theory on comparative advantages explains the success of nations with certain industries in terms of production factors, such as land, labour, capital and natural resources. The theory states that a nation has a comparative advantage in sectors that make intensive use of production factors amply available to that country. Supplementary theories suggest that countries trade with each other in relatively similar product categories. This is explained by economies of scale in production, different preferences between consumers and differences of a more cultural character.

The well-known US economics professor, Michael E. Porter, has proposed a methodology for understanding competitiveness on the basis of five key factors and on chance. Professor Porter places particular emphasis on the interaction between these factors. His basic hypothesis is that an industry will tend to be very dynamic when all these factors function closely together. All the indications are that this is a typical feature of the Norwegian shipping industry.

1 Factor conditions. Norway's long coastline means that the sea has alway been an important transport route. The country's coast can accordingly be seen as a substantial advantage. Virtually the entire population has a relationship with the sea and seafaring. Historically, Norway has had access to a large supply of qualified mariners. But international shipping has liberated itself from national factors of production. Most of the factors required for shipping can be acquired in international markets at level prices. Some exceptions apply. One of the most important is that Norway's shipping industry has attracted a very large share of national investment, not least because of favourable tax rules and a lack of alternatives.

2 Demand conditions. It is a long time since Norwegian shipping could base its operations on the domestic market, which has increasingly been replaced by a global market. This has given the industry a professionalism needed to survive tough international competition.

3 Related and supporting industries. A unique feature of Norway's maritime sector is its scope and completeness embracing shipyards, ship's, gear, broking, insurance agency operations, classification, financing, research and education – to name merely the most important elements. This dynamism and interaction plays a crucial role in securing the industry's technological leadership.

497

4 Competitive arena. Norwegian shipowners are showing a clear tendency to prefer both specialization and sectors characterized by entry and exit barriers, so that they can exercise some market power.

5 Government. The authorities have played an active part on several occasions, influencing – positively and negatively – the terms governing the country's shipping sector. Establishing the NIS and historically favourable tax terms have been two important examples of positive action.

Good Basis

Norway's very complete maritime community has unquestionably played an active role in developing the shipping industry. The result has been a picture which highlights most elements essential for a company to succeed in the shipping sector and also raises a couple of red flags.

- Consistently sought out the sectors where technology plays a relatively heavy role.

- Taken the lead in many sectors in developing new transport solutions in both technical and commercial terms.

- Built up a solid and to some extent dominant market share position in a number of markets.

- Benefited from favourable tax terms, plentiful access to qualified mariners and a good supply of risk capital.

- Opted for a more capital-intensive form of operation than their counterparts in most other countries. This has raised barriers to entry but also led to a high level of debt in periods when capital is in short supply, making owners more vulnerable to depressed markets.

- By making a commitment to specialist sectors, shipping loses some of its flexibility because selling second-hand tonnage is more difficult.

- Experience indicates that shipping can be hard hit by international events and the vagaries of chance. Successful companies are often those who bought and sold at the right points in the cycle.

The price variations can be very significant, as illustrated in Chart 4.5.

Chart 4.5 Historical Vessel Prices (in constant 1994 US $)

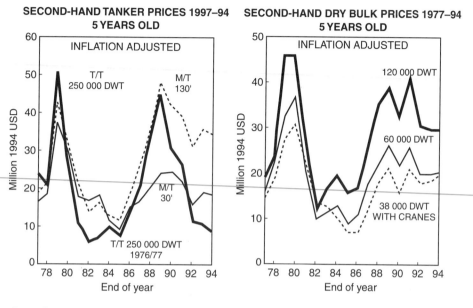

**SECOND-HAND TANKER PRICES 1997–94
5 YEARS OLD**

INFLATION ADJUSTED

T/T
250 000 DWT

M/T
130'

M/T
30'

T/T 250 000 DWT
1976/77

Million 1994 USD

78 80 82 84 86 88 90 92 94
End of year

Source: Fearnleys

**SECOND-HAND DRY BULK PRICES 1977–94
5 YEARS OLD**

INFLATION ADJUSTED

120 000 DWT

60 000 DWT

38 000 DWT
WITH CRANES

Million 1994 USD

78 80 82 84 86 88 90 92 94
End of year

Source: Fearnleys

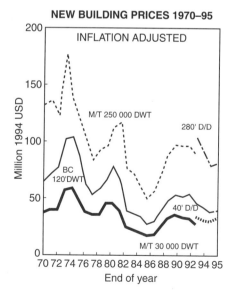

NEW BUILDING PRICES 1970–95

INFLATION ADJUSTED

M/T 250 000 DWT

280' D/D

BC
120'DWT

40' D/D

M/T 30 000 DWT

Million 1994 USD

70 72 74 76 78 80 82 84 86 88 90 92 94 95
End of year

Source: Fearnleys

Bright Future

Shipping is currently in the middle of a slump, with relatively depressed market conditions in most sectors. However, the position has brightened somewhat over the past couple of years and cautious optimism can once again be justified. Coming decades will also be increasingly characterized by greater environmental awareness and growing requirements for new logistical solutions. The links between owners and research institutes, ship's equipment suppliers and shipyards, accordingly represent an important source of new competitive advances.

Kværner – a Maritime Cluster

The Kværner group is, to a large extent, a complete maritime cluster on its own. It has a substantial stake in shipowning, even after an agreement to merge its gas carrier fleet to Norway's Havtor group in exchange for shares. In addition, Kværner ranks as one of the world's three largest shipbuilders – and the biggest in the Europe – and is a leading supplier of ship's gear.

The group launched its own 'Ships for the Future' research and development programme in 1994, involving expenditure of more than NOk 500 million (ECU 60 million) over a three-year period on ships, equipment and maritime transport systems. Kværner has brought together its front-end shipping expertise, and is also co-operating with leading research and education institutions.

Substantial maritime know-how in several group companies explains why the former Moss Værft subsidiary could build its first liquefied petroleum gas carrier in 1965. Another company, Kværner Brug (now Kværner Energy) became a part-owner of the vessel, which initiated the group's involvement in gas shipping in 1977. This reflected a desire to take advantage of vertical integration from design and construction to ownership, management and sale of tonnage.

Strategically, the goal was to develop an industrially-anchored shipping business in medium-sized gas carrier tonnage. 'Industrial' shipping offered a number of benefits to the group:

● Increased market know-how and broad contacts.

● Improved opportunities for shipbuilding through better harmonization with the market and ideas for developing new solutions.

● Shipbuilding expertise also yielded advantages for technical operation of the ships.

These are all elements investors should look for in trying to assess whether a shipowner's stock will make a good investment.

Kværner became involved in refrigerated carriers (reefers) in 1988. It also acquired interests in two listed shipping companies, Western Bulk Shipping and Den norske Amerikalinje. These two investments reflected in part a desire to maintain centrally placed 'listening posts' in the market, not least with an eye to the group's shipbuilding role. A balanced portfolio avoids excess dependence on one sector and too much exposure to the cycle of a single industry.

The Kværner fleet of gas carriers has been marketed through two pools; Kværner Havtor Pool in co-operation with Havtor, and Igloo Pool together with Neste of Finland. Both organizations are market leaders for their type of tonnage. Co-operation with other gas ship operators has optimized management and operation as well as ensuring a high level of service. The strong market position also provides better access to long-term contracts of affreightment and flexibility in developing new markets for the pool participants. Four of Kværner's current reefers are marketed through the Lauritzen Reefer pool, while the other four are fixed on time charters. A strong pool position is another key factor which drives profitability and should be an area of analysis for potential investors. ♟

TELECOMMUNICATIONS

Lars Ramqvist

*Dr Lars Ramqvist is President of **Telefonaktiebolag LM** Ericsson and Chief Executive Officer of **Ericsson**, the Swedish-based telecom supplier and systems house. Dr Ramqvist joined **Ericsson** in 1980 and served in a number of leading positions before being elected President and CEO in May, 1990. He holds a PhD in solid state physics and chemistry and is a member of the Royal Swedish Academies of Sciences and of Engineering Sciences. Dr Ramqvist is also a member of the European Round Table of Industrialists.*

***Ericsson** has 76,000 employees worldwide. Net sales in 1994 exceeded US$11 billion.*

The once stodgy telecommunications industry is undergoing a period of explosive growth, and at the same time the rules of the game are being changed almost daily. New and complex technology, like Asynchronous Transfer Mode (ATM) is being developed at an unprecedented pace. New players, some with no formal telecom background, are entering the arena with a mandate to run a network. Regulatory agencies can make or break an operator by allocating or revoking transmission frequencies.

Since I know how difficult this makes running a telecom supplier I can appreciate the problems faced by the institutional investor, not to mention the private player. Two facts stand out amid the turmoil. First, change is the only constant we can count on; second, any company that doesn't invest heavily in the continuous development of new systems and products isn't a safe investment.

any company that doesn't invest heavily in the continuous development of new systems and products isn't a safe investment.

The Demand

Have you ever heard someone say: 'There are just too many telephones in the world'? I doubt it. Just the contrary. You can usually find a phone close at hand in the industrialized world, but close at hand is still too far away unless you have one in your pocket. The explosion of mobile telephony in the last decade is an unmatched success story for the suppliers, for the operators and, we contend, for the users.

In Sweden we have 16 or 17 mobile phones per hundred people (this is May, 1995), but in Japan only 3.5 per cent of the population has a mobile phone. Telia, the largest mobile operator in Sweden expects 90 per cent penetration by the end of the century. Do you think the Japanese market is going to be far behind?

Mobile telephony is glamorous, but consider – only 15 per cent of the world's population has access to <u>any</u> telephone services. Sweden has a long tradition as a leader in telecommunications. This is reflected in the country's telephone density, which is the highest in the world, with 70 subscribers per 100 inhabitants. It is followed by a number of countries in Western Europe and North America that have between 40 and 65 telephones per hundred inhabitants. There are very great opportunities for global telecommunications to expand in the heavily populated countries in Eastern Asia. China, with 1.2 billion inhabitants, has only 1.5 telephones per 100 inhabitants, for example, but has very ambitious plans to increase the number of subscribers in coming years. There is a comparable situation in parts of Eastern Europe, where demand for telephone services far exceeds supply. When the economies in

Chart 4.6 Subscriber Lines per 100 Inhabitants

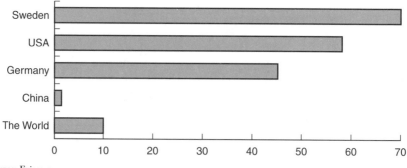

Source: Ericsson

these countries improve, conditions will be ripe for the large investments in telecommunications that the countries recognize are necessary.

It took from 1876, when the telephone was invented, to the beginning of this decade to enlist the first half billion subscribers. In the ten years from 1990 to the end of the century we will see that number double, and ten years from today we expect to see a doubling of the current 700 million subscribers.

The demand for POTS, plain old telephone service, will continue to increase throughout our lifetimes. When that demand has been satisfied it will be followed by a desire for mobility that the suppliers and operators must meet. In many advanced countries, data traffic is growing faster than voice traffic in the same telecom infrastructure, and in a few years I assume there will be demands we can't even imagine today.

As I write this, Ericsson has just posted increased sales for the fourteenth consecutive quarter. There is a legitimate international demand for increased telecommunications - if there are problems facing the industry, demand is not one of them.

Technical Development

The pace of development is increasing. Five years ago everyone was talking about ISDN, Integrated Services Digital networks. We don't hear much about it today, but we know that ISDN has entered the mainstream, and services are available in an increasing number of countries.

The hot topic today is ATM, which can be described as super-ISDN with exceptional capacity and switching speeds. We haven't seen many installations yet and we aren't even sure what will drive ATM sales, the interconnection of office LANs (the European scenario) or the domestic market's desire for video on demand (the American scenario). By the end of the decade I assume that ATM will have an established role in the public network, and we'll be talking about radio-based interactive multimedia, or some other fantastic new concept.

The components that filled a circuit board ten years ago (and kilometres of cabinets ten years before that) are etched today on a chip the size of a fingernail, a three-million-transistor chip that can handle all the telephone traffic generated in Stockholm. But despite the development of microelectronics, telecom can't be called a manufacturing industry any longer. Eighty per cent of the value of our products relates to the intelligence programmed into them. Adapting our systems to different markets means reprogramming them.

> But despite the development of microelectronics, telecom can't be called a manufacturing industry any longer. Eighty per cent of the value of our products relates to the intelligence programmed

AXE, our primary switching platform, is 20 years old and selling better than ever, but last year it absorbed an additional five thousand man years of new development. Our original switch and the current version share only their modular concept, and their name.

Sixty-two per cent of our sales last year came from products that didn't exist three years earlier. The industry has to live with technical challenge; it has to thrive on change. This means the risks are substantial even for established suppliers, just as the potential rewards are enormous. One smart idea can establish a company as a niche supplier, and one missed opportunity can demote an established supplier it to a secondary position. An example from Ericsson: ten years ago only 6 per cent of net sales related to mobile communications, last year it was 50 per cent.

There is only one conclusion I can see. We have to invest – and invest heavily – in new technology, both hardware and software. As a supplier, our job is to determine which standards to support and what technology to develop. The investor's problem is to evaluate our selections and back the companies that have made the best choices, without being misled by marketing hype, irrational arguments, or wishful thinking.

Operators face the same dilemma. Where a variety of technologies are available the operator has to make the right choice the first time. He is literally risking a fortune on his selection. A mobile network operator is concerned with installation speed, the number of calls that can be handled within a cell, voice quality and hand-off, the cost of expanding the system, interworking with other systems, how easily additional services can be added to his platform and the quality of service his supplier can provide. His success may also depend on the cost and availability of handsets for his system.

Market Development

There used to be a joke that we had only two customers in every country, the Minister of Communications and the Director of the PTT. Even if that was never true, the deregulation of the telecom markets has changed the way we do business. Once there were monopoly PTTs, government authorized or government run. Now you can buy, or even win, the mandate to set up and run a public communication network.

The old PTTs could invest in the long term. The new players are interested in quick return on investment. The old PTTs could set their charges to match their investment needs; the new operators face tough price competition from the first day. The old PTTs had established competence in the field of telecommunications; the new crowd are often financially astute, but need to buy the technical support they can't provide in-house.

When we dealt with the old PTTs we were expected to master the technology. Now in addition we have to meet market-oriented trends. Mobility, flexibility, speed to market, increased transmission efficiency, operation and maintenance tools – these are requirements the operators emphasize in dealing with the suppliers. The operators who master these requirements improve their competitive position. You want to invest in the most competitive operators. The competitive supplier is the one that can improve the competitive position (and investment value) of his operators.

This is where the 'one smart idea' company falters. As we've seen, the pace of development means that a lot of good ideas will meet in open market competition. The successful supplier acknowledges the precarious market position of operators, and invests in providing the necessary support.

Long term success, i.e. a sure investment, depends on the willingness of supplier and operator alike to reinvest profits in continuously developing new systems, products and services in order to maintain a competitive position. ♔

THE ASIAN TRADER

Dr Victor K. Fung

*Victor Fung began his career at **Citibank** in New York and, after serving as an Assistant Professor at the **Harvard Business School**, he joined **Li & Fung** in 1977 as Managing Director and is now its Chairman. He is concurrently Chairman of **Prudential Asia**, the Asian investment and merchant banking arm of **Prudential Insurance**, and Chairman of the **Hong Kong Trade Development Council**. He was made a Commander of the Order of the British Empire in 1993.*

__Li & Fung__ was established in Guangshou (Canton) in 1906 by Fung Pak-liu, Victor Fung's grandfather, and the Hong Kong office was set up in 1937 by Fung Hon-chu, his father. Dr Fung and his younger brother, William, who is currently the Group Managing Director, are the third generation to manage the company. From its beginnings as a China trader, __Li & Fung__ has evolved into the premier Chinese multinational trading company, with a network of 17 sourcing offices in 11 countries. Turnover in 1994 was HK$ 6 billion, and market capitalization at end-1994 was HK$ 2.8 billion.

Introduction

Hong Kong came into being in 1842 as a trading post for merchants in the Pearl River Delta to sell their wares to the rest of the world. It has thrived against a background of turbulent economic and political events in China and East Asia to become the world's fifth largest trading territory. Li & Fung has been very much a part of Hong Kong's history, and we have kept alive, in our organization, the dynamism and entrepreneurship that are behind Hong Kong's remarkable success. Our story illustrates the key themes of change and adaptability which are fundamental in trading, since only the fleet of foot survive and prosper.

505

The principal business of Li & Fung is the sourcing of time-sensitive consumer products with mass market appeal from Asia for export to retailers in the developed markets of USA, Western Europe and Japan. We are organised around six product groups; garments, fashion accessories, plastics, handicrafts, sporting goods and household products, and work with over 2,000 manufacturers within Asia to source these products.

To provide valued added to our customers who have multiple alternative vendors from which to choose, we have developed in-depth knowledge of products which goes beyond simple sourcing. We act as specialist consultants to the parties in a transaction. Our services include the provision of manufacturing information to customers, working capital to manufacturers and trade financing, sourcing raw materials and components, planning and managing the production process, designing of products and packaging, and shipping consolidation. The competitive advantage lies in being able to blend elements of this expertise to match the weaknesses and gaps in a customer's capability. The traders of the 1990s are not shippers, they are very effective, multi-faceted service organizations.

The Evolving Nature of Business

Although Li & Fung has been in trading since 1906, the way it carries on this business has evolved over time. Until 15 years ago, there was little product specialization; sourcing was handled for any product on an 'as required' basis. It was a straightforward broking operation with little value added to the sourcing process. Our success has been due to our ability to anticipate and respond to change, and to evolve our business in tandem with major shifts, particularly in the operating environment and the nature of the retail business.

Until the 1960s we operated out of just the Hong Kong office, sourcing primarily from Hong Kong-based factories. We started to diversify geographically with a regional office in Taiwan in 1968, in Singapore in 1973, and in Korea in 1987. We now have, in addition, a network of sourcing offices located in Thailand, Malaysia, Philippines, Indonesia, Sri Lanka, Vietnam and seven cities in China. The expansion of our network reflects the growth of business as well as the product shift within Asia. We had to stay one step ahead of our competitors and two steps ahead of our customers.

The development success of the east Asian economies has been phenomenal. However, production costs have increased in line with prosperity, and factories in these economies have had to seek continually to move to lower cost countries. In particular, the economic liberalization of China, which began in 1978, has caused the majority of Hong Kong manufacturers to move their production facilities across the border. Factories in Taiwan and Korea have also moved to China, as well as to other South-east Asian countries.

Li & Fung has made a conscious policy not to own any production facilities and remain flexible. This encourages continual searches on behalf of our customers for lower cost producers who can deliver the required quality to deadline. The end result is far higher efficiency as we extend our sources of supply to new and more cost-effective producers. Investors looking to understand successful trading companies should be less concerned with ownership of physical assets and more with the sourcing capability and record.

> **Investors looking to understand successful trading companies should be less concerned with ownership of physical assets and more with the sourcing capability and record.**

Recently, retailers have been faced with a need to sustain profitability when consumers are more value conscious. This means that more retailers are concentrating on volume growth, keeping control on costs within the supply chain. The inevitable consequence is the increasing reliance upon more efficient or lower cost suppliers, particularly in Asia. Traders like Li & Fung provide a vital role in this process.

Generational Change

In addition to these external changes, like many other Asian trading concerns, our company has had to manage generational changes. It started life as a Chinese family business and, by 1973, had the necessary track record and structure to be listed on the then Hong Kong Stock Exchange. The public offering was 113 times over-subscribed, a historic record which was not surpassed for another 14 years. Notwithstanding the listing, shares in Li & Fung continued to be held by various family members, most of whom subsequently became less involved in the management of the business. In 1989, my brother, William, and I arranged a management buy-out. We also took the opportunity to restructure the company into two core businesses – one for export trading and the other for retailing. The trading business was re-listed on the Stock Exchange of Hong Kong in 1992.

Management Practices

Over the years, we have developed management practices that are unique to our business and corporate culture and which have served us well. Two examples of these practices are our entrepreneurial style and our proprietary co-ordinated regional network (CRN) system.

Our entrepreneurial style is to motivate individual employees, and to create responsibility and accountability at all levels. Elements include a flat organization structure and incentives based on performance measurable on clear criteria. Employees are organized into product-based business units, each of

507

which is run as a profit centre. Within each business unit there are specialized teams dedicated to specific customers. The units buy from the centralized support group such services as finance, accounting, human resources management, and technology at prices which are market competitive. These are the keys to a successful Asian trader in the 1990s, and in the next century. Investors should not expect a good return from companies which cannot be innovative internally, as that entrepreneurial culture is a vital sign they can succeed and change in a competitive environment.

> **Investors should not expect a good return from companies which cannot be innovative internally, as that entrepreneurial culture is a vital sign they can succeed and change in a competitive environment.**

The CRN system is a centralized communication network designed to manage the complex matrix of products, countries and profit centres and obviate unproductive inter-unit competition within the company. It enables our major customers whose requirements range across several sourcing countries working with any of our business units to enjoy competitive pricing, efficient delivery and consistent service. Scale and investment in technology will become more and more critical to future growth for Asian traders.

Financial Performance

Operating margins tend to be slim for service companies operating an agency business with little risk. The net profit margin for Li & Fung has remained stable at about 3 per cent, which is the highest among the large Hong Kong export trading companies.

A measure of the financial health of a trading company is its cash flow. Li & Fung has always maintained a positive cash flow and a strong and liquid balance sheet. As at 1994 year-end, the company had a net cash balance of HK$ 325 million. This gives a trader fiscal flexibility to move quickly, and take advantage of opportunities.

Forward Integration

While we, at Li & Fung, have avoided backward integration into production, we have actively sought forward integration into distribution companies in our major markets. This has generally been in the form of a minority investment into companies with strong growth potential which could benefit from our sourcing capabilities. There are currently eight such investments. Good traders use these to consolidate competitive positions and provide critical market intelligence.

We have set up, in San Francisco and Brussels, two teams dedicated to seeking out such investment opportunities. Although the purpose of the investments is to enhance the core service business, in some instances substantial financial benefit has resulted from the investment itself. For example, in 1992 we invested US$ 400,000 in equity and loans for a 50 per cent interest in Cyrk Incorporated, which designs, develops, sources and distributes high quality products for promotion programmes and custom-designed sports apparel and accessories in the USA. Following Cyrk's listing on Nasdaq in July 1993, Li & Fung sold its investment in stages, raising a total US$ 65 million.

The Future

As more factories continue to proliferate in newly industrialising countries, notably China and India, retailers' need for sophisticated sourcing intermediaries who know Asia will increase. This need will further deepen as consumers become even more demanding in relation to value for money. There have never been more opportunities for growth and the potential for investors in the sector is immense, though not without risk. Li & Fung is well positioned to benefit from this opportunity. Other traders who can provide investors with a good return will show similar characteristics in operating structure and performance. ♀

UTILITIES

James E. Rogers

James E. Rogers is Vice Chairman, President and Chief Operating Officer of **CINergy Corp.** *Previously, as Chairman, President and Chief Executive Officer of* **PSI Energy**, *Mr Rogers led PSI through its merger with* **The Cincinnati Gas & Electric Company** *to create* **CINergy Corp.** *The merger was completed in October 1994. Prior to joining* **PSI** *in 1988, Mr Rogers was Executive Vice President, Interstate Pipelines, for the* **Enron Gas Pipeline Group.**

CINergy Corp, headquartered in Cincinnati, Ohio, serves approxiamtely 1.3 million electric customers and 400,000 gas customers in a 25,000 square mile area of Indiana, Ohio and Kentucky. Based on owned generating cability of over 11,000 megawatts, **CINergy** *is the thirteenth largest investor-owned electric utility in the United States.*

Equity in the nearly 200 investor-owned electric power companies in the United States was once commonly referred to as 'widow-and-orphan' stock because of its stability and steady, if unexciting, yields. But the American electric power industry is in the midst of a transformation, and investors' view of electric power stocks will never be the same. Its role in an investor's portfolio has to reflect these changes.

As public utilities, US electric power companies have been heavily regulated but largely protected from competition. An investment in an electric utility was seen as only slightly more risky than money in the bank. Utility stocks were an alternative for income investors, with yields of two to three times those of the industrial group. Utility stocks traded at prices that moved consistently in an inverse relationship to interest rates.

If managing an electric utility was no great challenge in this environment, neither was picking electric utility stocks. Investors' main concern was the regulatory environment in a utility's service area. The first state public utility commissions were created in the first decade of this century, and today America's retail electric service is regulated by 50 different regulatory bodies in 50 states. Utilities that appeared to enjoy constructive regulation, evidenced by timely recovery of costs and a healthy return on investment, were viewed as attractive investments. Utilities whose requests for rate increases typically faced hostile scrutiny, delay, and reduction were viewed less favourably. This kind of information was readily available to investors.

Today, the world of electric utility stocks is much more difficult and risky for investors. While there are still sound income investments – and some new growth opportunities – analysts are cautioning investors to be much more selective. But the fact is that even professionals are struggling with how to evaluate electric utilities in the midst of rapid change.

The challenge for investors is that the electric industry in the United States is undergoing a fundamental shift from a regulated to a competitive environment. As global competition drives US companies to cut their energy costs, the demand for low-cost energy is spawning new enterprises and technologies to compete with electric utilities. That demand is also getting a response from public policy makers. They are breaking down regulatory barriers that have perpetuated huge disparities in prices charged by different utilities, with industrial rates ranging from more than 10 cents per kilowatt hour in the north-east to 3 cents or less in some other areas.

Competition will spread inexorably, each time someone figures out how to provide energy services better and cheaper than the local utility, or the utility figures it out first. The relevant market will no longer be the service territory, where the utility enjoyed a protected monopoly, but the entire region, where customers will have access to all the suppliers on the transmission grid. That region will be defined by the technological and economic constraints on the long-distance transmission of power – overcoming those constraints would allow for a truly national market.

The history of other regulated industries – natural gas, telecommunications, transportation – is a warning that some electric utilities face sharply declining earnings as competition expands. This increased business risk is reflected in actions by credit ratings agencies. For example, in late 1993 Standard & Poor's revised its outlook on about one-third of the US electric utility industry from stable to negative.

Utilities face the limits inherent in any mature market. But there are other changes imposing further limits on some utilities' future growth: the loss of utilities' monopoly over generation and transmission and the erosion of their distribution franchise. As a result, many utilities are facing the prospect of flat or declining earnings and increased business risk.

Not so long ago, electric utilities could build value for shareholders simply by adding new facilities to the 'rate base'; the investment in facilities to serve customers, on which the utility was allowed to earn a return through rates. Customers were willing to pay, both because the cost of electricity was going down and because new facilities were required for growing demand. Today, with rising costs, slower demand growth, and more options, customers resist or avoid paying for additions to the rate base.

The prospect of flat or declining earnings casts doubt on utilities' ability to provide dividend growth. Just to maintain current levels, many utilities already have high payout ratios, with 90 per cent or more of after-tax earnings going to pay dividends. In recent years, a growing number of US utilities have cut their dividends. Possibly the most unnerving dividend news for utility investors was a 33 per cent cut by the parent company of Florida Power and Light, a financially healthy utility with a rapidly growing service area.

The lesson is that investors cannot judge utilities simply on the basis of current yield. They need to assess the company's ability and commitment to sustain and increase the dividend. In general, the factors that are critical to sustaining the dividend are the same factors that affect credit quality, such as cash flow and debt coverage, and investors should pay attention to the credit ratings of potential utility investments. But investors also need to assess a

> **The lesson is that investors cannot judge utilities simply on the basis of current yield.**

company's prospects in an increasingly competitive environment. While electric utility stocks, as a group, continue to trade at prices inversely related to interest rates, prices of some individual stocks clearly have been affected by investors' concern about the impact of competition on the utility.

The absolute prerequisite for success is low costs. Utilities with high-cost generating capacity face the imminent loss of large customers, particularly in regions where substantial excess capacity is available. That's why a number of utilities have been discounting prices to their largest, most vulnerable customers. Despite the efforts of regulators to allocate the costs of 'stranded investment' in the transition to a competitive market, shareholders will surely face write-offs of high-cost assets – generating plants, long-term contracts, and regulatory deferrals – as customers obtain the ability to seek out low-cost power.

In particular, investors are wary of utilities with nuclear plants. While nuclear plants have low marginal costs, utilities will not be able to recover their massive investment if they must sell power at market prices. Then there are millions of dollars in decommissioning costs when the plant reaches the end of its useful life, and that's often years before a plant was originally scheduled to close.

Having recited this litany of horribles, however, I should emphasize that the dangers for investors in electric utility stocks are also potential opportunities. Devastating as it may be for current holders, a write-off of uneconomic assets or a cut in the dividend, with a related drop in the share price, can create an investment opportunity for new investors who may get a good buy on a utility with lower costs and/or greater ability to pursue dividend growth – a company that has faced up to its competitive situation.

More importantly, restructuring can create new assets of greater value to investors. We will continue to see more consolidations like the merger that created CINergy Corp., a combination of two low-cost, financially healthy utilities. Bringing together The Cincinnati Gas & Electric Company and PSI Energy fundamentally changed the companies' cost structure and 'critical mass' in a competitive market, increasing the value of shareholders' investment. The merger is projected to create $1.5 billion in cost savings in the first ten years of CINergy's operations, including an estimated $485 million in capacity deferrals and $313 million in labour cost savings, with other cost savings in the areas of financing, power production and materials management. Our experience to date bears out these projections.

Not all utility mergers have created shareholder value, and some have gained notoriety for increasing costs. But survival in a more competitive environment will require many more companies to pursue consolidation and then capture every possible benefit. And this will spell opportunity for investors.

There is no magic formula for identifying merger opportunities. PSI's selection of CG&E as a merger partner was the result of a long, complex analytical process. Having said that, let me offer two suggestions. **Don't** limit potential mergers to companies that are directly interconnected: with the advent of mandatory open-access transmission, geographically separate partners can still create an integrated system using the transmission of a third party. **Do** go beyond the numbers to assess the 'doability' of a merger, the likelihood that the two managements can come to terms – including the willingness of one CEO to step aside for a time.

Another kind of restructuring is the de-integration of the traditional utility into its component parts. Generation, transmission, and distribution are fundamentally different businesses. As the industry moves towards competition, electric power is becoming a commodity, and generation is an increasingly volatile business – no place for 'widows and orphans' to invest. But the local distribution franchise can still provide a secure source of dividend income, a purer investment made available by breaking up vertically integrated utilities or creating different classes of stock for different parts of the company.

Investors seeking growth might look to electric businesses operating outside the United States. Newly industrializing countries are facing explosive growth in demand for power - between 5 and 7 per cent per year in parts of Asia and

Latin America, compared with approximately 2 per cent in the US. And privatization of state-run electric systems around the world offers the opportunity to capture significant efficiency gains. Because these countries are leapfrogging past the privately owned but heavily regulated US industry to create market-based systems, there is greater business risk than in traditional utility investments. Then there is the political risk of countries in transition. At the same time, the growing number of market entrants is driving down margins. Still, demand growth is so strong that there continue to be favourable risk/reward opportunities.

What all of this suggests is that the quality of management will become increasingly critical to the value of electric utility stocks. A legacy of low-cost power plants cannot guarantee continued success. With the commoditization of electric power, financial skills are becoming more important than engineering skills in our ability to deliver low-cost power to customers. And as 'ratepayers' become 'customers', the value of the local distribution franchise will depend more and more on developing new services around kilowatt-hours of electricity.

At CINergy, we're using our cost leadership and knowledge of energy markets to protect and expand our customer base. To compete with aggressive new non-utility competitors who market and broker power, we're combining our physical assets and our market experience to provide a bundle of services – delivered power, risk management, and merchant services – to meet customers' specific needs. And we recognize that, as the regulated sphere becomes smaller, we must become **more** attuned to the regulatory process at the state and federal levels, to shape a competitive environment in which we have the opportunity to win.

For management and for investors the transformation of the US electric utility industry presents a whole new level of challenge. But opportunities remain for those who can sort out the changes and develop a strategy for success. ♀

VENTURE CAPITAL
From Seed Capital to Superstock
William R. Hambrecht and William D. Easterbrook

*William R. Hambrecht is the founder and Chairman of **Hambrecht & Quist**, which is a venture capital, investment banking and securities brokerage firm, specializing in emerging growth companies in chosen industries, including technology, life science and branded consumer products. William D. Easterbrook is an Advisory Director of **Hambrecht & Quist** and manages portfolios of public securities in the firm's venture capital funds.*

*The authors wish to acknowledge the significant contributions of colleagues at **Hambrecht & Quist** including Daniel H. Case III, Chief Executive Officer, Standish H. O'Grady, Managing Director, and Kate M. Geldens, Venture Associate, in the production of this section.*

During the last half-century several major equity asset sectors have produced unusually high returns, especially relative to the performance of alternative investments such as real estate, commodities, and fixed income (shown in Table 4.4). United States venture capital (VC) has been one of the more successful asset performers, registering a 14.0 per cent annual return

Table 4.4 Asset Returns by Sector
(Annual Rates of Return Through 1994)

	Modern Times (a)		Last Ten Years	
	Annualized Return	Standard Deviation	Annualized Return	Standard Deviation
Venture Capital	14.0%	33.6%	9.0%	10.0%
US Equities				
S&P 500	11.9%	16.5%	14.4%	13.0%
Small Capitalization	14.4%	26.5%	11.1%	19.0%
Non-U.S. Equities				
EAFE (c)	11.7%	26.8%	17.6%	28.3%
Emerging Market Equities	16.9%	26.3%	18.7%	30.6%
Fixed Income				
T-bills	4.7%	3.2%	5.8%	1.9%
U.S. Long Treasury Bond	5.0%	9.9%	11.9%	12.1%
Corporate Bonds	5.3%	9.6%	11.6%	10.4%
Real Estate				
U.S. Farmland	9.9%	7.4%	6.2%	4.8%
Residential Housing	7.2%	4.1%	4.3%	1.5%
Real Assets				
Commodities (b)	3.9%	28.1%	2.9%	16.1%
Gold	9.9%	36.6%	2.2%	13.3%
Art	10.5%	27.9%	11.5%	35.7%
Inflation	4.4%	3.8%	3.6%	1.4%

Sources: Morgan Stanley, MSCI, Frank Russell Co., Salomon Brothers, Lehman Brothers, National Association of Realtors, Art Market Research, T. Rowe Price, Brinson Partners, IFC, Ibbotson Associates

(a) Modern Times (for most of the asset classes listed) is the period from 1945 to 1994, with the exception of Gold (1972–1994); Art (1977–1994); EAFE (1950–1994); and Emerging Market Equities (1945–1994 and consists of various markets over time according to their stages of development up until 1975, after which the IFC Composite Index is used).

(b) Commodities are represented by an equally weighted basket consisting of crude oil, copper, grains, precious metals, livestock, and softs (i.e. coffee, sugar, corn).

(c) An index for equities of Europe, Australasia and Far East markets.

from 1945, comparable to the returns for the US S&P 500 market index, US small capitalization stocks, and emerging growth stocks, whose returns ranged from 11.4 per cent to 14.4 per cent. These returns are in contrast to the 4 per cent to 7 per cent range of returns typical for fixed income securities, residential housing, commodities, and most metals. However, during the last ten years the VC industry has under performed other equity sectors, turning in a 9.0 per cent annual return, compared with gains of 14.4 per cent for the S&P 500 and 12.5 per cent for emerging growth stocks.

With these performance data in mind, we will try to: (1) analyse the reasons for the recent performance of VC assets; (2) present our reasons for believing that venture returns could be in the 15 to 25 per cent range during the next ten years; and (3) advance our thesis that for improved returns venture capitalists should consider the management of company securities for a period well beyond the traditional exit period (usually after the initial public offering (IPO) of the company takes place).

The Start of a New Venture Cycle?

To help explain the single digit VC returns of the last ten years we should recall the extremely attractive profits made in the late 1970s, which attracted increasingly large amounts of capital. In 1983 a then record $3.4 billion was committed in the US to private VC funds, and after flat to down commitments for three years a new record of $4.2 billion in commitments was achieved in 1987. By 1991 commitments had declined significantly to $1.3 billion but have recently improved to $2.5 billion in 1992 and 1993.

The high returns on VC in the 1970s were fostered by several factors:

1 The initially unrecognized need for capital to finance rapidly growing companies especially those in the technology sector,

2 Reductions in the US capital gains tax rates,

3 Relaxed regulations permitting large pension funds to allocate money to higher risk (and higher return) investments such as VC and emerging public growth stocks,

4 Active sponsorship of small companies initially by investment banking firms specializing in rapid growth sectors such as semiconductors, computers, communications and software,

5 An IPO market which peaked in 1983 at a level which would not be seen again until 1991.

These high VC returns (often in the 25 to 40 per cent range for the 1976–83 period) led to the development of a classic cycle – frequently referred to as 'start-up fratricide' – in which too much capital and too many people were chasing too few quality investment deals. This led to inferior single digit

515

percentage (or negative) returns for VC in many of the last ten years, exacerbated by the crash in 1987.

During the past seven years (from 1988) total capital under management has stabilized in the $31 – $35 billion range, contrasting with about $5 billion in 1980 and under $100 million in 1970. This stagnation bodes well for future returns. We believe there is a reasonably good chance that venture returns could improve in the next decade for the following reasons:

- In VC the 'lemons ripen before the plums'; most funds in their early stages have poor (or sometimes negative) returns as the inferior investments ('lemons') take their toll, but after several years the 'plums' begin to improve returns. After the high level of activity in the late nineteen eighties many of the plums have yet to fully ripen.

- The broadening of the VC industry should reduce risk and lessen dependence upon the more limited focus from 1960 through the mid 1980s, which was primarily based on computer hardware in the corporate environment. In the past ten years VC investments have expanded into:

  - New industries such as life sciences, healthcare services, environmental technology and services, and branded consumer goods.

  - Computer-related sectors which have matured and broadened with more investments in software, multimedia, networking, wireless, and personal computing devices as the industry has taken on more of a consumer focus; some semiconductor companies now generate one-third to one-half of their business with consumer products, contrasted with a negligible amount twenty years ago.

  - New geographic sectors, particularly the 'tiger' countries of South East Asia.

  - Turn around and restructuring situations, including the rescue of troubled or over leveraged companies.

- Valuations for higher growth technology stocks are still relatively cheap by historical standards. The price/earnings valuation of these stocks has varied between 1.0 and 2.0 times the broader market indices (such as the S&P 500), and currently (March, 1995) this relative measure stands at approximately 1.35.

- The net exit of money and people from the venture arena in the late 1980s and early 1990s should be positive for VC returns.

- Venture cycles typically last ten to fifteen years, and returns are estimated to have only re-entered the double digit percentage range in the last two years. Periods of relative strength for small capitalization stocks also appear to be cyclical, lasting from seven to fourteen years; after a period of under performance from 1983 to 1990, the small stock cycle became strong in 1991 through early 1995.

Based on the thinking presented above we would expect future returns to be better than the single digit 1983–93 decade, but probably lower than the heydays of 1973–83 when returns of 20 per cent to 40 per cent were common. Our guess is that VC returns could be in the 15 to 25 per cent range in the 1995–2005 period.

Managing the Complete Venture Cycle – Beyond the IPO

The venture capital industry has progressed from its infancy thirty years ago, to its current position with over $30 billion of capital under management. It is an industry which, by some estimates, has added more than $500 billion in capital stock value from an original investment of less than $20 billion.

One of the legendary early venture successes was the investment made by American Research and Development in Digital Equipment (the mini computer company), which provided spectacular returns. The initial 1957 AR&D investment of $70,000 purchased approximately 77 per cent of Digital, whose market capitalization thirty years later was close to $20 billion. Similar successes were enjoyed by Kleiner Perkins in Genentech (life science) and Tandem Computers (fault tolerant computers). The initial investment of $200,000 in 1976 in Genentech was valued at over $30 million in 1982; the $1.45 million Tandem Computers investment in 1975 was worth nearly $150 million seven years later. More recently, software companies such as Adobe Systems (document software) and Sybase (database software), which were initially funded, and later brought public, by Hambrecht & Quist, have produced superb returns both as private and as public companies. The initial investment in Adobe was at $0.15 per share and in Sybase at $0.38 per share; adjusted for splits the stocks went public at $1 3/8 and $6 3/4, respectively, and have recently traded as high as $52 and $57, respectively.

These highly visible successes, and many others, have fostered our feeling that venture investments managed through and beyond the IPO will give improved results. A recent study of the post-IPO stock performance period done by Hambrecht & Quist covering the 1988–94 period does indicate that venture capital returns are improved if venture investors take a longer-term orientation to the management of the portfolio of successful investments that become public.

It is natural for a venture capitalist, who has nursed a young company through many tribulations perhaps over

Our study of recent IPOs suggests strongly, however, that patience, through a period of at least eighteen months following the IPO, may be rewarded with significant extra returns in the technology sector.

a period of several years to heave a sigh of relief and sell out soon after the IPO when highly profitable liquidity is tempting. Such selling has been strengthened by the often violent stock market changes, and by the poor performance of small company equities from 1983 to 1990. Our study of recent IPOs suggests strongly, however, that patience, through a period of at least eighteen months following the IPO, may be rewarded with significant extra returns in the **technology** sector.

Technology IPOs Outperform

The post IPO stock price performance study evaluated more than 1,200 IPOs in the US from the beginning of 1988 to the end of 1994. This covers a period (1988–90) when small capitalization stocks under-performed versus the market, and a period (1991–94) when they outperformed; the time frame therefore balances poor and good times. The IPOs were classified into three groups, according to business sector; technology, life science and all other.

Chart 4.7 IPO Price Relative to Market

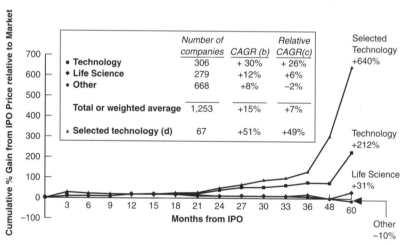

	Number of companies	CAGR (b)	Relative CAGR(c)
■ Technology	306	+ 30%	+ 26%
◆ Life Science	279	+12%	+6%
● Other	668	+8%	–2%
Total or weighted average	1,253	+15%	+7%
▲ Selected technology (d)	67	+51%	+49%

Selected Technology +640%

Technology +212%

Life Science +31%

Other –10%

(a) The study considered IPO's made by the top 25 underwriters during the period 1988-1994 in the United States. The three sectors analyzed were:
  • Technology: Electronic related technology including computers, semiconductors, communications, software and networking products.
  • Life Science: Biotechnology, medical products and instrumentation, healthcare and medical services.
  • Other: All IPO's excluding those in Technology and Life Science.
  The stock price for each IPO was examined from the data of the IPO for a period of up to five years. The price performance relative to the market was obtained by subtracting the performance of the S&P 500 Index from that of the stock for the periods shown in the chart above, measured from the date of the stock's IPO. Each stock was equally weighted for the aggregate data.

(b) Compound annual growth rate of equally weighted, aggregated stock prices for companies with five years of history following IPO.

(c) Compound annual growth rate of equally weighted, aggregated stock prices relative to the market companies with five years of history following IPO.

(d) Technology companies for IPO's underwritten by Hambrecht & Quist in 1988-1994 period.

The stock price performance of each IPO was examined from the date of the IPO for up to seven years, and the results were aggregated giving equal weight to each stock. The data was then assembled using the time from the IPO as the base line so that stock performance could be measured using the IPO date as a reference point. From these data the stock price performance relative to the S&P 500 was plotted, shown in Chart 4.7; in this chart the performance of the S&P 500 is subtracted from the stock price performance for the precise period measured (i.e. three calendar months from the IPO date for the first period, six calendar months for the second period, and similarly for the times shown up to the maximum seven-year period covered in the study).

The study shows that technology IPOs significantly outperformed IPOs in both the life science and other sectors. For technology stocks with four and five years of history since IPO, the **absolute gains** averaged 214 per cent and 279 per cent, respectively (representing compound annual growth rates of 33 per cent and 30 per cent), contrasted with 40 per cent and 79 per cent for life science stocks, and 41 per cent and 44 per cent for all others.

The study indicates a pattern of performance relative to the market; three periods were identified:

- a strong initial short-term (3-month) gain relative to the market from the initial offer price (25 per cent for technology, 15 per cent for life sciences and 13 per cent for other IPOs)

- flattish performance for the next 12 to 18 months

- improving returns for technology stocks from a period starting about 18 to 24 months from the IPO date; the life science and other IPOs do not show such a period of improving returns.

We believe that this three-period pattern for technology stocks is explained by the sector's extremely high visibility and historic higher-than-average-returns. The initial period of strength following the IPO can be attributable to the excitement which develops in anticipation of the IPO, as the company tells its story in detail for the first time to a broad audience, and as securities analysts write about and 'talk up' the company's prospects.

A period of desultory performance typically follows the strong period after the IPO and is due to the selling of the stock by early investors in the company making sure of significant profits. This redistribution often constitutes a significant percentage of the ownership of the stock and can take several calendar quarters before it is exhausted.

Selectivity Pays Off

The strong relative returns realized by the technology sector were registered without any selectivity applied and represent an average for all technology

IPOs. As an example of what might be obtained with selection of investments we have also shown in Chart 4.7, the relative performance of the 67 technology companies included in the study and underwritten by Hambrecht & Quist. We believe that the superior returns of this segment are primarily attributable to the knowledge base residing in an underwriter which focuses on the technology sector, and which helps to breed classic big winners such as Synoptics, Solectron, Parametric Technology, Sybase and Adobe Systems.

Often a common thread between such winners is the original source of the ideas and people from which successful young companies are born. For example, Xerox's Research Park in Palo Alto, California, was the source of many highly successful companies in the past 20 years, such as VLSI Technology, Synoptics and Adobe Systems.

The selection for investment of such companies early in their history is still something of an art. Venture capitalists have often relied upon good rules of thumb, such as selecting companies which have a few good people (if there are questions about management, solve them **before** investing) or which have 'killer' applications for their potential products; in addition, markets can be selected which have huge potential size, or where there is some early confusion. But it is hard to deny the importance of the source of an idea; if first class managers from Intel, Hewlett-Packard or Xerox's Research Park have researched, and carefully thought out, a product, upon which they are willing to bet their careers, it is often good enough for the first early investment to be made.

> **But it is hard to deny the importance of the source of an idea; if first class managers from Intel, Hewlett-Packard or Xerox's Research Park have researched, and carefully thought out, a product, upon which they are willing to bet their careers, it is often good enough for the first early investment to be made.**

The concept of selecting investments on the basis of how good the business is has long been espoused by successful investors. Warren Buffett is perhaps most famous for this idea and, as he says, 'A good business is not always a good purchase, although it is a good place to look for one'. The best business, and the companies in them, usually exemplify the advice given to entrepreneurs by the late Robert Noyce, a founder of Intel (the development and growth of which has been the paradigm of success in the semi-conductor industry). 'Start with a growing market. Swim in a stream that becomes a river and ultimately an ocean. Be a leader in that market, not a follower, and constantly build the best products possible.

Summary

We expect investments in venture capital to yield excellent returns into the beginning of the next century. The incredible pace of technology and its rapidly expanding applications, especially into new consumer and geographic markets, should foster improved venture returns. Potentially the best returns, on the order of 20 to 30 per cent, could be achieved by venture capitalists who chose to manage their investments well into the public lives of the companies they nurture.

PART
5

INVESTING
FOR THE NEXT
DECADE

LONG WAVE CYCLES

Robert R. Prechter, Jr

*Robert R. Prechter, Jr is President of **Elliott Wave International**, one of the world's largest providers of technical analysis. **EWI** offers institutional and private investors round-the-clock market commentary via electronic delivery on Reuters, Bloomberg, Knight-Ridder, Telerate and UniLink. **EWI** also provides investors with educational services that include monthly publications, conferences, workshops, video tapes, special reports, and books by Robert Prechter, R.N. Elliott, and others.*

The Wave Principle

The Elliott Wave Principle is a detailed description of how markets behave. The description reveals that mass investor psychology swings from pessimism to optimism and back in a natural sequence, creating specific patterns in price movement. Each pattern has implications regarding the position of the market within its overall progression, past, present and future. The number of waves at successively lower degrees reproduces the Fibonacci sequence.

A Major Sea Change

Perhaps the most useful aspect of the Wave Principle is that it provides an excellent long term perspective that allows the investor to anticipate major trend changes. For example, the completion of a bear market pattern in the Dow Jones Industrial Average in 1974 set the stage for the record-breaking advance, which A.J. Frost and I forecast in our 1978 book, *Elliott Wave Principle*. In 1982, *The Elliott Wave Theorist* projected that the Dow Jones Industrial Average would climb all the way to 3,700, more than a decade before that level was achieved.

Today, another financial sea change is taking place, one even more important than that of the early 1980s. Although the Dow Jones Industrial Average and the World Stock Index are at all-time highs and global economic forecasts are uniformly optimistic, long-term wave patterns indicate that 1995 will witness the start of a decline of historic proportion in world stock prices. This analysis will focus on US markets.

The Wave Pattern

The *Elliott Wave Principle* argued that the bear market low of 1974 had dramatic implications. Specifically, that low marked the end of wave IV of the

Chart 5.1 The Elliott Wave: 1920–1977

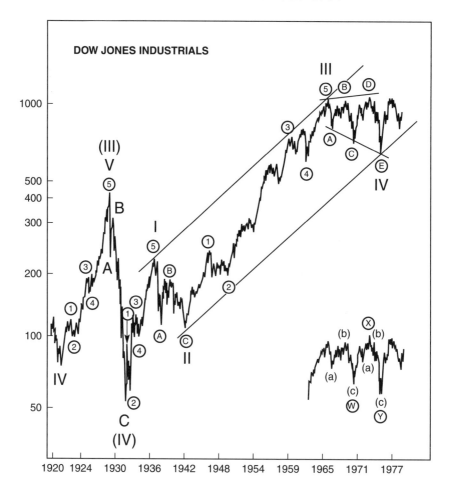

ongoing 'five-wave' bull market of 'Supercycle' degree (labeled I-II-III-IV-V) from the 1932 low, implying a great bull market ahead for wave V. Chart 5.1 shows the complete labelling up until that time.

Chart 5.2 shows the same labelling updated. Not only has our 1970s labelling proved correct, but those familiar with the Wave Principle will now see a completed textbook five-wave formation from 1932 to 1995.

Chart 5.4 shows that the structure in Chart 5.2 is a component of a larger five-wave pattern dating from the year 1784. This larger structure is of 'Grand Supercycle' degree.

Chart 5.2 The Elliott Wave: 1932–1995

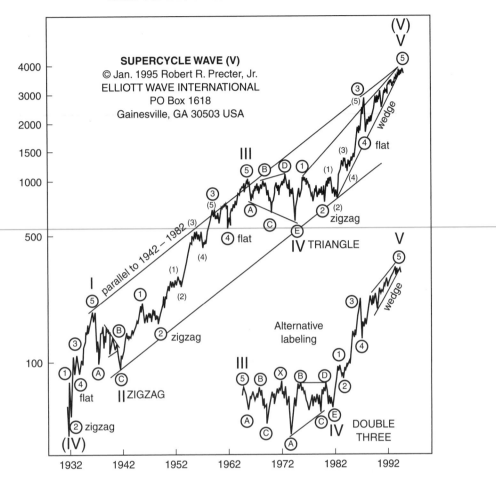

Price Length Relationships in the Supercycle

Chart 5.3 shows a study of relevant price multiples in the advance from 1932. Let's examine the relationships among the three rising waves: I, III and V. Those unfamiliar with Fibonacci mathematics should refer to the summary on page 533.

The percentage gains for the first two advances in the Supercycle are as follows:

Wave I, from the 1932 low at 41.22 to the 1937 high at 194.40, produces a gain of 371.62 per cent.
Wave III, from the 1942 low at 92.92 to the 1966 peak at 995.15, produces a gain of 970.98 per cent.

Chart 5.3 Price Relationships in Supercycle (V)

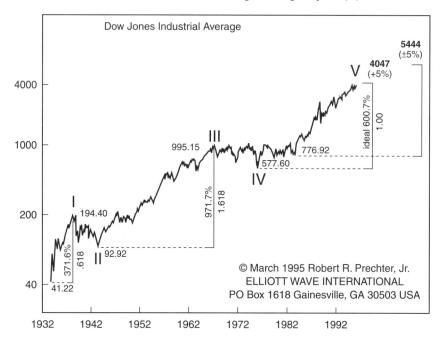

Dow Jones Industrial Average

5444 (±5%)

V 4047 (+5%)

III 995.15

776.92

577.60

IV

I 194.40

971.7% 1.618

ideal 600.7% 1.00

II 92.92

371.6% .618

41.22

© March 1995 Robert R. Prechter, Jr.
ELLIOTT WAVE INTERNATIONAL
PO Box 1618 Gainesville, GA 30503 USA

1932   1942   1952   1962   1972   1982   1992

Thus, the gain of wave I is a Fibonacci .382 times the gain of wave III. In fact, 371.6/971.7 = .3824, which is perfect to three decimal places. Therefore, the following conclusion is suggested:

> Wave V, from the 1974 hourly low at 572.20 (or closing low at 577.60), should produce a gain of 600.67 per cent.

Why 600.67 per cent? An advance of that amount would make wave V's percentage gain a 1.618 multiple of wave I's gain and simultaneously a .618 multiple of wave III's gain. In other words, the percentage gains may be completing a Golden Section, so that **I is .618 of V, which is .618 of III, which by definition equals I + V.** Thus, as shown in Chart 5.3, the following formulas would hold:

I/V = V/III = φ, and I + V = III.

A 600.75 per cent advance from the 1974 low of 577.60 projects <u>4047</u>. The same advance from the 1982 low, the alternative labelling for the end of wave IV shown in Chart 5.3 projects <u>5444</u>. Before discussing how either of these might pertain to the actual high, let's explore one other set of relationships that has been useful in pinpointing highs in the past.

Fibonacci Multiples Of Peak Values

The same method of calculation that pinpointed the all-time high to date in the Dow Jones Transportation Average on 2 February, 1994 and the high in gold in January may pertain to the Dow Jones Industrial Average. First observe that the high of wave III at 995.15 is less than three points shy of **2.618**, or ϕ^2 (where $\phi^2 = 1.618$), times the high of wave (III) at 381.17. Within the Supercycle, if wave V ends at a level that is **4.236**, or ϕ^3, times the high of wave III at 995.15, and wave (V) ends at a level that is **11.0896**, or ϕ^5, times the high of wave (III) at 381.17, it will top at <u>4215–4227</u>.

Chart 5.4 Price Multiples of Peak Values

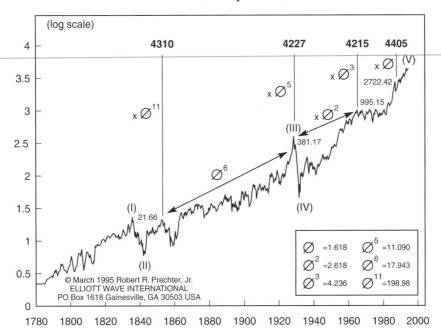

These two adjacent degrees of trend will generate multiples between their third and fifth wave peaks that are the third and fifth powers of ϕ **if** the DJIA ends its rise in the 4115–4127 range. The result, moreover, will be to create three peaks that are related by three powers of phi that are adjacent terms in the Fibonacci progression, i.e. 2, 3 and 5.

Supporting Computations

These are not the only turning points in the stock market that project this target area. The peak of wave ① at 1004.65 times **4.236**, or ϕ^3, projects <u>4256</u>. The 1853 high of 21.66 times **198.98**, or ϕ^{11}, projects <u>4310</u>. Finally, the 1987 high of 2722.42 times **1.618**, or φ, projects <u>**4405**</u>. Given the years and distances involved, these are slight differences from 4215.

Summarizing the Price Targets

Combining all relationships presented above, if the Dow follows the ideal script, it will top in the **4047–4405 range,** which can also be expressed as <u>**4226** + **or –4 per cent**</u>.

If the Dow stages a 'blowoff,' it is likely to carry to near **5444**. Despite the high 'feel' of the latter figure, it is important to realize that it is only 30 per cent above the ideal target just above 4200. Thirty per cent is less than 5 per cent of the 627 per cent gain that wave V is targeted to achieve at the lower number. For all practical purposes, the big potential that lay ahead 21 years ago and 12 years ago has been realized.

Fibonacci Time Intervals

Nineteen-ninety-five is the most probable year for a top because as shown in Chart 5.5, it is tied by a Fibonacci number of years to every important turn of Cycle wave V. It is **21** years from 1974, the starting date of wave ①, **13** years from 1982, a starting date for wave ③, **8** years from 1987, the starting date of wave ⑤, and **5** years from 1990, the starting date of wave ⑤ by other measures, such as the Value Line index. A peak in 1995 would also complete two overlapping bull markets of equal Fibonacci time length; 1974–87 took **13** years, and 1982–95 will have taken **13** years.

Chart 5.5 DJIA Time Counts

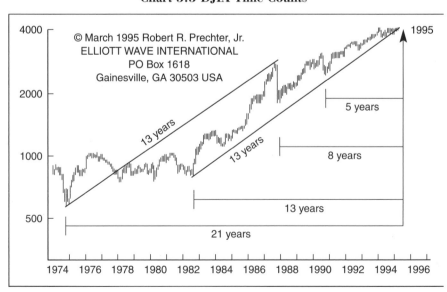

Probability of Occurrence

It is necessary to keep in mind that with price changes of hundreds and thousands of per cent involving durations lasting up to 153 years, this many long term relationships form a remarkably tight target cluster. The cluster is so tight, in fact, that the slight differences in calculated target levels can be attributed entirely to minute variations in the method of data maintenance in the past century and a half.

How likely is it that the social psychology of the United States since its founding will actually prove to reflect these Fibonacci mathematics, which are at the highest degrees of trend? After all, only one of the price relationships has been registered for certain, the .382 ratio between the gains of waves I and III. A final bull market high in the 3,980–4,100 range and a historic downside reversal are required to bring the entire interlocking web of relationships into being. To expect the Dow Jones Industrial Average to be that precise, to terminate its uptrend in a specific year after rising 600 per cent from 1974, 9,500 per cent from 1932, 64,000 per cent from 1842 and an estimated 700,000 per cent from the start of the Grand Supercycle in 1784, and then effect a reversal of historic proportion, is a tall order.

Bonds

Chart 5.6 is a chart of the US bond market from its peak in 1946. This wave structure is a textbook example of five waves down followed by three waves up, which terminate right at the peak of the preceding fourth wave. The time element reflects Fibonacci mathematics, as the orthodox low in 30-year Treasury bonds occurred in 1980, 34 years after the peak, and the high in 1993 was registered 13 years after that low. Needless to say, few investors were concerned about risk at the 1993 top, as bond mutual funds were enjoying their biggest year of capital inflow in history. In other words, the public aggressively bought the top.

Despite today's widespread opinion that bonds offer an unprecedented buying opportunity as a result of the decline of 1994, the Elliott Wave pattern requires a decline in bond prices to well below the 1981 low, probably ending in the early years of the next decade. Such a development strongly suggests that a debt crisis (based upon fear of default), and perhaps ultimately a currency crisis, will be among the financial problems that the US and the world will face near the end of this bear market.

Chart 5.6 Bond Buyer 20-Bond Index

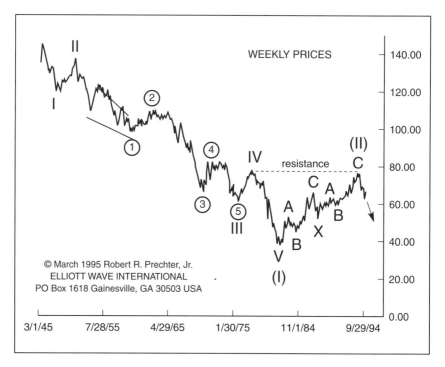

© March 1995 Robert R. Prechter, Jr.
ELLIOTT WAVE INTERNATIONAL
PO Box 1618 Gainesville, GA 30503 USA

The Economy

Despite today's favourable reports and the attendant bullish outlook by economists, the patterns shown here emphatically indicate that the US economy, and by extension the world economy, is about to begin a multi-year contraction. Ultimately, it will experience not simply a recession, but a depression.

What To Do

The magnitude of the financial calamity that will accompany the bear markets in stocks, bonds and the economy will dwarf any previous such difficulty many countries have experienced. It is imperative that you have your house in order before the new trend begins. For

Despite today's favourable reports and the attendant bullish outlook by economists, the patterns shown here emphatically indicate that the US economy, and by extension the world economy, is about to begin a multi-year contraction. Ultimately, it will experience not simply a recession, but a depression.

starters, have no long-term funds in stocks or bonds. Be wary of owning real estate for investment purposes. Certain events will signal that gold and silver should be owned, but unless and until those events occur, explore stable currencies and stay in the safest cash equivalents. Put your energy into choosing the right currency at the right time. Avoid the now too popular exercise of picking stocks and 'high yield' debt instruments in an attempt to 'outperform' the market averages. Outperforming the traditional investment markets is no longer an acceptable goal, as these markets will be falling, and outperforming will simply mean losing less money. Your proper focus now should be preserving your assets in what, over the next several years, will almost certainly prove to be one of the most challenging investment environments in the history of the world. If you are successful, you will be able to scoop up bargains of historic proportion at the ultimate bottom.

The Fibonacci Ratio

The Fibonacci ratio is .618 or ϕ (phi), the only number which when divided into 1 equals itself plus 1, i.e. 1.618. ϕ is the ratio between adjacent terms (after the first few) in any additive sequence that derives from adding two successive terms to get the next, which is why nature employs it so ubiquitously in its growth patterns. Alternate terms in such sequences are related by ϕ^2, or .382, whose inverse is 2.618. A Golden Section is a length divided into two parts so that one part is .618 of the whole and the other is .382 of the whole, and therefore .618 of the first part. The most common additive sequence found in nature is the Fibonacci sequence, which derives from the number 1 and proceeds by adding the previous term to each current term to generate the next, producing the sequence 1, 1, 2, 3, 5, 8, 13, 21, 34, 55, 89, 144, etc. For a more complete discussion of this ratio and its properties, see Chapter 3 of *Elliott Wave Principle*. ♀

THE TWELVE CHORUSES
OF A MARKET CYCLE

John Train

John Train is the Chairman of **Montrose Advisors**, *in New York, which manages diversified strategies in investing. His books include* The Money Masters, The New Money Masters, *and, most recently,* The Craft of Investing. *He writes columns in* The Financial Times, The Wall Street Journal, *and other publications.*

Market cycles have a life of their own, like the ups and downs of a manic-depressive patient.

The choruses sung at each stage, from 'Excelsior' on the way up to 'De Profundis' in the cellar, are not based on objective data; they are just rationalizations for the herd instinct, which is all but irresistible.

1 The Washout: 'Stocks Are Going Way Down.'

At the bottom of a market crash, business news is usually terrible, and many authorities declare that things will probably get worse. The public dumps stocks, without regard to value.

Eventually, though, a point is reached where everybody who can be scared into selling has sold. Usually the final battle occurs in a few days of extremely high volume – a 'selling climax'.

At this point the ordinary investor, who has gone over the waterfall, is groggy, bruised, and sick, his ears ringing. He does not want to hear about stocks ever again. The few professionals and institutions have the field pretty much to themselves. What they buy goes up, since there are almost no sellers left.

Then, some weeks later, the old lows are quietly tested on modest volume, but it doesn't attract much attention. Experienced investors are confident that better weather lies ahead. It's odd, but major bottoms are almost never a spike. They have two roots, like a tooth.

2 The Early Surge: 'Things Look Better, But It's Too Early to Buy. Wait For a Pullback.'

The government, shocked by the decline, and as always beset by the clamour to 'do something', announces public works and other stimuli, which of course will only take effect many months later. So the pundits declare that this time the stimulus isn't working: 'It's like pushing on a rope.' In fact, however, the government will get what it wants, and as soon as its intentions are clear it's time to act.

Months go by, and prices rise. A few mutual funds will have been started during the bottom area. You read that the Hercules Fund has risen 75 per cent in six months.

When 'everybody' is waiting for a buying opportunity, there will ordinarily be no buying opportunity.

> When 'everybody' is waiting for a buying opportunity, there will ordinarily be no buying opportunity.

3 The Surge Continues: 'Prices Seem High. It's Too Late to Buy.'

More months pass, and the market establishes an upward channel. Higher prices pull in buying from the institutions waiting on the sidelines; this additional buying pushes prices still higher.

The general public moves from feeling that it's too early to buy to feeling that it may be too late. On the way up in a bull market, stocks seem expensive, since one is comparing the current prices with those of the recent past.

4 The Second Stage of the Rocket: 'Maybe It's OK To Buy.'

A year or so after the bottom, and with prices much higher, the public, watching from the sidelines, becomes interested. There are a number of downward bounces, or tests, against the bottom of the market's rising channel. Each time the recovery starts from a higher level than before. The longer the channel remains intact, the more it seems invulnerable.

5 Not a Cloud in the Sky: 'Buy!'

More months go by, the market is way up, and the public is hooked. Business news is excellent. The 'standard forecast' is optimistic. Jazzy new funds proliferate. Market volume soars.

Some particular market area – 'one-decision' growth stocks, Japan, gold, emerging markets – becomes a market darling, if not a mania, and is bid up to irrational levels.

Also, we see the latest variation of the margin account: the leveraged trusts of the 1920s, the 'Chinese paper' of the conglomerate era, the LBO bank loans, or, this last time, the use of derivatives – puts, calls and the like – on a vast scale.

6 The Blowoff: 'Stocks Can Only Go Up.'

Hot managers become famous. Young, glib, impatient of conventional wisdom, they collect huge sums from trustful and greedy investors hoping for miracles. They chase new themes as a pack. It then becomes profitable to jump aboard a trend – in the early 1970s, the newest growth stock; in the 1980s the next takeover candidate, in the early 1990s, the latest emerging country – instantly, before the less hot managers get hold of it and run it up.

7 Coasting: 'The Market Is High, But This Time Is Different.'

As the months wear on, stocks hesitate; their upward pace slows, with only a few favourites making new highs. The market analyst detects this by the loss of 'breadth', a falling ratio of advances to declines.

Business starts to peak, but enthusiasts rationalize that the government has mastered the business cycle, or that there is an absolute shortage of stocks because of an insatiable appetite for them, or that equities are the only refuge from inflation, or that emerging markets are a new world, or that hedge funds can make 20 per cent a year in any market, or just that it's a 'new era'.

However, in a bull market enough stock is 'manufactured' to satisfy everyone. 'When the ducks quack, feed 'em.'

8 The Top: 'Hold.'

The government, concerned about speculation and economic overheating, starts leaning against the wind. The Federal Reserve raises the discount rate a notch, and then another. Here again, the government gets what it wants, and in time will wrestle down a runaway bull market. So after the Federal Reserve Bank has made its intentions clear it's time for the prudent investor to move toward the sidelines.

Another few months pass, and we see a series of vicious reactions, or chops. The arrival of belated 'second chance' buyers halts each decline and puts the list up to new highs. Those who sold feel foolish, while the buyers are jubilant.

> Here again, the government gets what it wants, and in time will wrestle down a runaway bull market. So after the Federal Reserve Bank has made its intentions clear it's time for the prudent investor to move toward the sidelines.

9 Over the Hump: 'It's Too Soon to Sell.'

The public remains heavily in the market, but the professional investors are edging out. A downward channel is established. It is like the ogre's dinner party, at which the last guests to leave are eaten themselves. When chairs begin to be pushed back and napkins placed on the table, the wise diner prepares to dash for the exit as soon as there is any excuse to do it. This crush at the door is why the market goes down much faster than it goes up. The lower-quality stocks start declining significantly.

10 The Slide: 'Prices Are Cheap, But It's Too Late to Sell.'

After a few more months pass, a number of issues have fallen appreciably from their highs, perhaps 15 per cent, but the public is reluctant to sell, because on the way down in a bear market, stocks seem cheap. The market, like a tired horse that no longer feels the whip, sinks on bad news but fails to respond to bullish company announcements.

11 'It's OK to Sell.'

Often some extrinsic event punctures the balloon, such as a stunning major bankruptcy. After a while we may see a severe decline, with perhaps 25 per cent marked off the prices of the more volatile issues. There is often a powerful deceptive recovery, which one might call the 'trap rally'.

12 The Cascade: 'Sell!'

Now the river sweeps over the brink, carrying everything with it. A cardinal point of market strategy, if one is a trader at all, is to get out before this cascade, even if one has already lost 15 or 20 per cent.

Business news is bad, and the standard forecast is for stormy weather ahead. The hot fund managers have to meet redemptions but find out that illiquid securities can't be sold and depart in disgrace. As for the margin operators and leveraged funds, their borrowings turn out only to have hurried them to disaster. (Aggressive managers as a class lose more money than they make, because you can only raise money for aggressive vehicles when the pot is bubbling and the lessons of the last collapse have been forgotten. This kind of money comes in most readily when the cycle is nearer its end than its beginning. Relatively little money is thus in the aggressive pools of capital on the way up, and a lot on the way down.)

13 (or back to 1 again) The Selling Climax: 'The Market's Going Way Down.'

The torrent crashes down the falls. In the final plunge some stocks give up in a day their gains of a year, and drop 30 percent in a week. It is so sudden and so awful that for a while many investors can't quite believe it. Volume dries up.

So here we are again, four years or so after we started out, half drowned, bones broken, washed out.

But if you've kept some reserves intact, and know enough to recognize real value when it's being dumped by panicky, uninformed sellers, and have the guts to act, then at these moments you can make the buys of a lifetime. We've had eight economic storms since World War II. Each time investors became convinced that the skies would never clear or the sun shine again. But it always does. ♀

537

The Impact of Politics

Labour's Approach to the Dynamic Market Economy
Government Policy and the Investor

LABOUR'S APPROACH TO THE DYNAMIC MARKET ECONOMY

Gordon Brown, MP

Gordon Brown was elected to the Executive Committee of the Labour Party in Scotland in 1977 and became Chair in 1983. He entered Parliament for Dunfermline East in 1983 and was elected to the Shadow Cabinet in 1987, holding the position of Shadow Chief Secretary to the Treasury from 1987–9. He then became Shadow Trade and Industry Secretary from 1989–92. He became the Shadow Chancellor in 1992. Prior to entering Parliament, Dr Brown was a lecturer at **Edinburgh University** *and* **Glasgow College of Technology** *before joining* **Scottish TV** *in 1980 as a journalist and then Current Affairs Editor.*

To prepare and equip our country to meet the challenges of today and the needs of tomorrow, Britain requires a new economic approach which breaks with the failed dogmas of the past and gives our country a new beginning.

Britain cannot tax, spend and borrow – or devalue – its way to economic success. Wholesale nationalization is not the way to ensure an economy run in the public interest.

That is why Labour's new statement of aims and values commits our party to 'a dynamic economy, serving the public interest, in which the enterprise of the market and the rigour of competition are joined with the forces of partnership and co-operation to produce the wealth the nation needs and the opportunity for all to work and prosper'.

But just as old left solutions cannot answer Britain's economic problems, nor can those of the new right. The Conservatives are disqualified by their dogma from tackling Britain's fundamental economic problems. Crude laissez faire economics, an obsession with privatization, an undervaluing of skills and investment, an unwillingness to construct a partnership between employers and employees – and public and private sectors – mean that the Conservatives have become the party of stop-go, wasteful expenditure, neglected investment and unfairness.

538

There are three pillars to Labour's economic approach which will help transform the British economy from a sluggish into a dynamic economy.

First, a dynamic economy requires a stable and consistent approach to the overall management of the economy. Labour seeks a stable low inflation environment, a platform of stability from which we can build our industrial strength, enhance the skills of our workforce and help businesses to flourish in the new world markets.

The Government has made a number of changes to the structure of monetary policy-making since Britain left the ERM: the publication of the inflation report, monthly monetary meetings and granting of power to the Bank of England over the timing of interest rate changes. But these have not been accompanied by the greater stability, openness, accountability, or transparency in decision-making that we seek. Moreover, decision making has not been placed in an explicitly medium-term framework.

Labour's Medium-Term Growth Strategy will be underpinned by making the process more open and transparent and we would also reform the structure of the Bank of England in order for it to fulfil its current advisory role on a more objective basis. Only if the Bank can demonstrate a successful track record of advice will we consider moving any further towards greater operational responsibility over interest rate decisions.

On fiscal policy, Labour would maintain a firm commitment to prudence and take an explicitly long-term view. We are committed to meeting the golden rule of borrowing. Over the economic cycle, government will only borrow to finance public investment and not to fund public consumption. Second, alongside this golden rule commitment, we will keep the ratio of Government debt to GDP stable on average over the economic cycle and at a prudent and sensible level.

The second element of our approach to ensuring a dynamic economy is based on the belief that to prepare for a new century, Britain needs effective and fair competition and a government that is a champion of consumers.

The divide is not, as the Tories say, between the Tories who will allow business to flourish and Labour which will second-guess the decisions of business. It is between Labour that believes competition and the setting of the highest standards go hand in hand and the right whose laissez faire policy of competition without regulation has produced monopoly and inefficiency.

If we look closely at Tory attitudes to competition, the difference between rhetoric and reality becomes obvious. They have replaced public monopolies by private monopolies, serving no competitive goal and in many important areas our economy is monopolistic rather than competitive, overly dominated by cosy cartels.

The mistake the right make is assuming that markets will automatically work in the public interest. Their strong presumption against making the public interest count – objecting to any public 'interference' in the working of the market – and their suggestion that the only acceptable form of regulation is self-regulation allows the abuse of market power by big firms and cartels and sharp practices on the part of unscrupulous firms to the detriment of the consumer.

New Labour has a vision of competition far more suited to a complex modern economy, and one which will, I believe, ensure a more efficient and dynamic economy and a better deal for the consumer. Markets can operate efficiently and be characterized by fair dealing only if there are rules which protect the interests of consumers from unscrupulous firms through proper information and protect firms from the anti-competitive actions of others.

That is why Labour is considering a Competition and Consumer Standards Office that replaces two quangoes, the Monopolies and Mergers Commission and the Office of Fair Trading and brings together the investigative functions of both to root out restrictive practices, such as price-fixing and rigged tenders, and anti-competitive practices such as abuses of monopoly power. In contrast to the current exclusive reliance on an administrative approach, a Labour government will actively seek out and adopt a 'prohibitive' approach to anti-competitive practices and abuses of monopoly power, outlawing certain forms of anti-competitive practice.

The Competition and Consumer Standards Office would be charged with rooting out restrictive practices with a new presumption in favour of competition and powers to impose financial penalties where restrictive practices are proven, bringing the UK finally into line with the best European and international practice. There would of course be an appeals mechanism for companies who feel they have been harshly treated.

The third essential ingredient for a dynamic economy is a culture for long-term investment on the part of companies and owning institutions and a commitment to the highest possible levels of investment in people and infrastructure -and a rejection of the short termism that has plagued the Tory years.

The divide is not between privatization and nationalism in retaliation, or public fighting private. It is between Labour which would ensure a partnership to encourage the investment we need and the Tories who would minimize any potential role for government.

A future Labour government will not attempt to substitute our judgement for the commercial judgement of investors and manager. But government must address the recognized problems of short-termism.

The challenge is to encourage long-term commitment from institutional investors so that they can properly exercise their responsibilities as owners of British public companies, in short to build a new culture of partnership and long-term relations. We need more openness and transparency in corporate governance, building on the work of Sir Adrian Cadbury's committee.

Institutional investors should actively participate and vote at annual general meetings on the composition of boards and appointment of non-executive directors. This approach is now established practice in the United States.

I would also like to see all pension fund trustees draw up a clear code of conduct for their voting policy and the activities of their fund managers.

Indeed, I know that, encouraged by the national association of pension funds, many pension funds are already establishing codes of conduct and voting policies which they are making public.

As well as these reforms of corporate governance, we need to encourage long-term investment in other ways. I believe we need to look at the ways in which the corporate tax and financial system can encourage long-term investment, and how we can offer positive incentives for long-term investment. I am particularly interested in the CBI's proposal to reward long-term investment through the capital gains tax system and this option is being actively considered in our corporate tax review.

We will also now broaden the consultation on another possible reform, canvassed by Sir David Walker while he was at the SIB, to encourage non-acceptance agreements between shareholders and companies. These involve shareholders committing not to sell their shares over a fixed period in return for greater sharing of information.

> **We will also now broaden the consultation on another possible reform, canvassed by Sir David Walker while he was at the SIB, to encourage non-acceptance agreements between shareholders and companies.**

While I recognize the role take-over and mergers can play as a spur to efficiency, I want to see reform of the rules which govern take-over bids. There is a strong case for shifting the burden of proof in take-overs so that the bidding company must show that the take-over would increase efficiency and serve the public interest.

Labour's vision is of a dynamic economy where industry is able to and is given the incentive to plan for the long-term; the public sector works in partnership with the private sector to secure the investment Britain needs; and there is an effective partnership between competition and regulation for the benefit of the consumer. That is our plan to modernize Britain and that will be our programme in government. ♀

GOVERNMENT POLICY AND THE INVESTOR

Anthony Nelson, MP

*Mr Anthony Nelson, MP, was appointed Minister of State, Treasury, on 20 July 1994. Mr Nelson became Member of Parliament for Chichester in October 1974. He had previously been with **N.M. Rothchild and Sons Ltd**. Mr Nelson* *was a member of the Select Committee on Science and Technology, 1975–9; Parliamentary Private Secretary to the Minister for Housing and Construction, 1979–83; Parliamentary Private Secretary to the Minister for the Armed Forces, 1983–5, and a member of the Select Committee on Broadcasting, 1988–92. From April 1992 to July 1994 he was Economic Secretary to the Treasury.*

The Government wants to see a competitive and versatile investment industry underpinned by adequate protection of investors and depositors. The Government contributes to the health of the investment industry through its conduct of economic policy and regulation of financial services.

The Economic Framework

The objective of the Government's economic policy is to secure sustainable economic growth and rising prosperity. Macroeconomic policy is set to achieve permanently low inflation and sound public finances. This is essential if businesses and investors are to plan with confidence for the future. The Government's microeconomic policy aims to improve the efficiency of markets.

The Role of Regulation

Financial services regulation plays a key role in securing market efficiency. In setting the framework of regulatory rules the Government must leave firms free to innovate and to compete in an increasingly international market, while at the same time ensuring adequate investor protection.

The Government does not see these objectives as conflicting. Regulation need not be red tape, provided it is appropriate and responsive to market developments. Investor confidence requires open, free and fair markets in which all participants adhere to best practice. This confidence is essential for the continuing success of the UK financial services industry.

Responsibilities of Investors

Of course regulation has its limitations. It cannot and should not be a substitute for the common sense and responsibility of investors. However determined the Government is to encourage high standards of regulation and investor protection, unless investors observe these rules they may be vulnerable to pressure selling of inappropriate products.

The Government and the industry should therefore take every opportunity to remind people of the five golden rules of sensible investment:

- the buyer should always beware;

- investors should spread their investments;

- seek good advice;

- read the small print; and

- recognize that authorization is not a guarantee.

The Government and the regulatory authorities are keen to encourage investors to observe these golden rules by providing for full disclosure of all relevant material and by developing conduct of business rules for those who offer advice and other services to investors.

The regulatory bodies

The SIB

The Securities and Investments Board (SIB) and the various regulators it recognizes, including the Self Regulatory Organizations (SROs), regulate all those involved in investment business. They do so by authorization, monitoring, supervision and enforcement. They require high standards of honesty and competence from those who participate in the various investment markets.

Regulation is kept continually under review to ensure the authorities are able to respond to market developments quickly and effectively without impinging on market freedoms. That way investors can be confident that the regulators understand a rapidly changing market and institutions can be sure that their conduct of business will not be hampered by outdated and cumbersome rules.

An example of this is the review of the UK equity market the SIB initiated in 1994. The purpose of this review is to examine the implications of market changes such as globalization, increased competition between exchanges and the development of new technology. The Government has asked the SIB to take into account, in its review, the Director General of Fair Trading's report on the trade publication rules of the London Stock Exchange and its rules relating to market makers.

The Bank of England

The Bank of England has general responsibilities to protect the stability of the financial system and to be the lender of last resort in the event of a liquidity crisis. The Bank has also a specific role as supervisor of the UK banking sector. It has powers to regulate banks, protect depositors and keep under review developments which may affect these duties.

The Building Societies Commission

The Building Societies Commission, established under the Building Societies Act 1986, is responsible for the prudential supervision of the building society sector. As well as oversight of the financial stability of these institutions, the BSC regulates building societies to ensure the savings of their customers are adequately protected.

Insurance

The Department of Trade and Industry's (DTI) Insurance Division is responsible for authorizing and supervising insurance and re-insurance companies writing business in the UK through powers conferred on the Secretary of State by the Insurance Companies Act 1982. The legislation and the DTI's supervising operations are designed to provide protection for life and non-life insurance policyholders against the risk of insurance company failure. The Act requires companies to comply with criteria of sound and prudent management. The legislation and the financial requirements were comprehensively overhauled in 1994 as a result of the implementation of the various single market Directives.

The Single Market

The Single Market in financial services requires common access and minimum standards throughout the European Union. This is achieved by vesting in home states responsibility for authorization (for example, 'fit and proper' and minimum initial capital) and for continuing prudential supervision (for example, capital adequacy). Financial service providers are entitled to do business across the European Union (EU) solely on the basis of their home state authorization.

The requirement to have a system of authorization and the clear assignment of supervisory responsibilities should strengthen investor protection. Making it easier and cheaper for firms to do business across the EU should improve competitiveness and increase the range of services and financial products available to investors.

Non EU Countries

The Government continues to encourage countries outside the EU to remove discriminatory restrictions against portfolio and direct investment by institutions and individuals. We believe strongly that the liberalization of international capital markets has benefits for both the receiving and importing countries. That is why we play a lead role in encouraging OECD countries to remove their remaining reservations to the Codes of Liberalisation of Capital Movements and Current Invisible Transactions and to remove restrictions on national treatment.

We are also continuing to work for a comprehensive Multilateral Investment Agreement. This would provide a framework for encouraging the growth of international direct investment and would be open to participation by non-OECD countries.

On the financial services side, the General Agreement on Trade in Services (GATS) should provide the first global framework of rules governing trade in services. The Government, with the help of the industry, is playing a major part in encouraging countries within the EU and elsewhere to adopt an open and unrestrictive agreement.

Developing new investment products

As well as being responsible for economic policy and regulation, the Government has a duty to facilitate the development of new markets and products. I should like to outline some recent and prospective developments which I hope will prove attractive to investors deploying their funds and businesses seeking to raise capital.

The Industrial Finance Initiative

Last year the Treasury conducted a wide-ranging investigation into the provision of finance to businesses. We consulted business people working across the spectrum of British industry and providers of industrial finance. We identified a clear need to make it easier for small and medium-sized firms with potential to grow. Key to achieving this is increasing the pool of capital on which firms can draw to fund investment. The Government announced recently several measures to achieve this.

Venture Capital Trusts

Venture Capital Trusts are designed to attract the funds of smaller, more cautious investors into dynamic, potentially high return businesses. It is hoped that Venture Capital Trusts will generate risk capital in the unquoted company sector while at the same time giving investors the security of a quoted pooled vehicle. In this way risk capital should become more widely available for new businesses and more manageable for investors.

PEPs and Corporate Bonds

Bond finance has been little used in the UK compared with many of our competitors. The PEPability of corporate bonds should encourage their greater use by both firms and investors.

545

Changes to the Enterprise Investment Scheme

An important source of finance for small growing firms is the 'business angel' who can invest expertise as well as money. The expanded Enterprise Investment Scheme will appeal particularly to this group of investors.

Open Ended Investment Companies

Finally we plan this year to introduce legislation to allow the formation of onshore open-ended investment companies, a form of collective investment scheme already familiar elsewhere in Europe. The industry can look forward to a new and flexible product which will fill a gap in the market, enabling the UK to compete more effectively at home and abroad. The Treasury published draft regulations on 2 May 1995. Following a period for consultation, they will be laid before Parliament for approval. ♀

PRIVATIZATION

Mark Phelps

*Mark Phelps is the senior fund manager in **Kleinwort Benson Investment Management**'s global investment team. **Kleinwort Benson Investment Management** was responsible for the launch of the* KB European Privatisation Trust *at the beginning of 1994, which attracted the largest ever subscription for any investment trust ever launched. **The Kleinwort Benson Group** is also one of the world's leading advisors to governments on privatization and the sale of state assets.*

Given that privatization did not exist in any meaningful sense prior to 1980 it is hard to comprehend just how far it has come in the past two decades, and how far it is likely to go in the next. In the UK alone, the Government has sold off $90 billion worth of assets in the past sixteen years. Globally in 1994 $60 billion worth of assets were sold and the pace is likely to continue at a similar level for at least the next three years. Privatizations are now being undertaken in all parts of the world by governments of all political persuasions, with a variety of motives, and many of the sales will be marketed to investors as the 'opportunity of a lifetime'.

So, are investors likely to make money from these opportunities? Well, if the history of the UK privatization programme is anything to go by, the answer is clearly yes. Out of the 49 privatization issues over the past 16 years only one is showing a loss on its sale price to investors as of March 1995. That is Rolls-Royce. Even BP's November 1987 share sale, which proved a disaster in the middle of the crash of that year, is now showing a respectable profit. Out of all the privatizations since 1979, only five have gone to a discount in early dealings, Enterprise, Britoil, Cable & Wireless (twice) and BP,

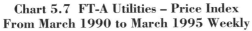

**Chart 5.7 FT-A Utilities – Price Index
From March 1990 to March 1995 Weekly**

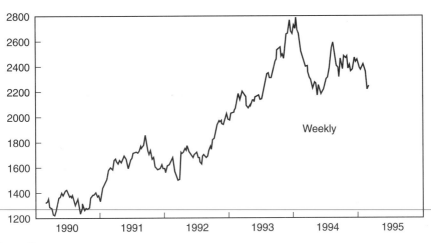

Source: Datastream

and only six have failed to beat the Footsie Index during the periods they have been quoted on the stock market.

It is worth noting, though, that secondary issues in companies already on the market have faired nothing like as well as the initial wholesale offerings, even prior to the recent sale of the power generators. Nevertheless, investors who backed all or most of the governments offerings in the past have a portfolio of shares that have handsomely outperformed the stock market. High- lighted in Chart 5.7 is the performance of the utilities sector, which includes the privatized water, gas, electricity and telecom companies. This index has outperformed the All Share Index by 17.5% over the most recent five year period.

The experience of privatization in other markets has been mixed with offerings in the rapidly growing Asian market such as Singapore Telecom doing very well compared to the poor performance of the Japanese flotations such as NTT and JR East. So what makes for a successful privatization from an investor's standpoint? The key would appear to be the attitude and motives of the government toward selling state assets. These can be to:

- reduce the size of the governments debt;

- develop a capital market;

- increase competition;

- encourage wider share ownership;

- improve services;

- increase efficiency.

From an investor's standpoint, a number of these motives are not necessarily compatible or likely to encourage a good return. Indeed, if a government's sole aim is to achieve the best possible price, what's in it for the investor? Countries that have put wider share ownership and development of a capital market as their top priority have usually provided a better background for investments than those purely looking to reduce their budget deficits.

From an investor's standpoint, a number of these motives are not necessarily compatible or likely to encourage a good return. Indeed, if a government's sole aim is to achieve the best possible price, what's in it for the investor?

A good example of this is the contrast between the British Telecom privatization and the sales of Pakistan Telecom and NTT in Japan. The initial BT offer focused heavily on promoting wider share ownership, typified by the 'Tell Sid' advertising campaign. The issue was priced 'to go', and left all parties very satisfied with the outcome. The prime focus of the NTT and Pakistan Telecom sales was to achieve the highest possible price. The subsequent poor stock performance damaged the prospects for both privatization programmes and generally left all parties unhappy.

With this in mind investors should focus on the possible attractions of privatization in two ways, one geographic and the other by sector.

Certain regions of the world are more predisposed to a capitalist model than others and have a market framework within which shareholders can invest. However, the real bargains may yet come in the less developed markets and probably early in the process, when prices are often at their lowest. Certain sectors are also more likely to be privatization targets, notably:

- telecoms
- electricity
- oil and gas
- financial services
- transport.

Telecoms have so far proved the most popular of all, as investors understand the product, can identify significant growth opportunities and are often investing in private monopolies. However, recent changes in technology have seen competitive pressures increase dramatically to the detriment of privatized companies such as Telmex in Mexico, where deregulation is only two years away. Electricity and oil and gas have many attractions, particularly an asset base that is easily valued and unlikely to be subject to significant technological change. Financial services are probably the area of greatest risk as values can be more difficult to determine, the companies often have few assets and a lack of controls can result in significant losses. Transport should also provide significant opportunities for investors but 'state pride' in subsidising the national airline or rail service appears to continually get in the way of successful privatizations.

Looking at the privatizations undertaken so far, the opportunity for investors to achieve a return has generally come in two parts. First, the asset is priced cheaply to encourage a successful sale and a 'staging' opportunity presents itself. Second, the company, often with new management freed from the bureaucracy of state control, is able to achieve greater efficiencies, open up new markets and generally increase profitability. Dividends have often increased considerably in excess of the market and share prices have risen accordingly. This is a relatively easy process where a state monopoly has been transferred to the private sector, albeit regulated, but even in areas of significant competition productivity has increased. According to 'Privatisation and Recession', published by the Centre for the Study of Regulated Industries, 'total factor productivity' at British Telecom has grown by an average of 7.2x between 1984 and 1994, well in excess of improvements in industry as a whole.

Given that the greatest returns may come from good company performance post-privatization, rather than just at the initial stage, investors focusing on future issues should identify whether significant changes in the companies' culture are likely to benefit shareholders. One of the problems with Eastern Europe, particularly Russia, is that privatization has been achieved for huge swathes of industry but little has changed. The first stage began in Russia in 1992 with the disposal of small businesses such as shops and restaurants. The next stage saw the auctioning off, in exchange for vouchers, of 15,000 medium and large state enterprises, which between them employ 86 per cent of Russia's industrial workforce. In most cases, the voucher auctions gave workers and managers a controlling stake in firms. The hitch? Soviet managers have proved to be ineffective owners. Often they have neither the capital nor the knowledge needed to survive in the market economy. Many of these shares are now worthless because the issuer is bankrupt or unwilling to make a price in them. Only the 50 largest companies have achieved a relatively liquid market in their shares.

If this market is to develop from a casino, with shares rising and falling by as much as 50 per cent in a week, into a means of raising capital for Russian companies and a home for long-term investment, Russia's stock market needs a few basic rules enforced by a credible regulator. These include establishing shareholders rights, clarifying who owns the land on which private enterprises are sitting, and establishing a central depository and a custodian for shares to make the secondary market more liquid. Since the state has a residual stake of around 30 per cent in nearly all of the privatized companies, and stage three involves selling these stakes to finance government spending, it is greatly in the government's interest to get these things right. These existing companies, together with the likely flotation of Gazprom, the oil and gas company valued at $25 billion, the electricity company UES and Aeroflot, may all be offered within the next two years.

Elsewhere in Eastern Europe it is also unclear which governments consider which privatization goals to be the most important. One approach, typified by the Czechs, was to push companies into the private sector as quickly as possible, gambling that private owners could reorganize firms more effectively than the state. Poland and Hungary prefer to reorganize first and sell later. The Czechs gave out vouchers that entitled citizens to bid for about 60 per cent of the shares on offer. Most Czechs entrusted their vouchers to one or more of about 600 investment funds. These funds act as surrogate owners but since most of them are owned by banks there are doubts about what sort of owner they will be and whether entrepreneurship will be encouraged. In Hungary and Poland about 40 per cent and 30 per cent respectively of the state-owned enterprises for sale have been privatized, and the pace is likely to continue to enable governments to meet budgetary targets.

In Poland a programme of mass privatization (MPP) has been designed to transfer about 400 mostly medium-sized companies into the private sector. The MPP is a clever answer to a problem that bedevils all privatizers in Eastern Europe; how to unload hundreds of firms at once without giving them away to small shareholders who can neither invest new money nor guide their managers. Those tasks will fall to 15 funds in which all adult Poles will receive a proportion. Fund managers will be paid according to the rise in the asset value of those companies and will be encouraged to raise additional cash. How quickly this plan can be enacted is, however, open to debate and it may yet be some time before outside investors can participate.

In Latin America the privatization programme is well under way and may only have a further 18 months to run for the major sell-offs. Here again, telecoms, oil and gas assets and electricity utilities have led the way with Chile in the vanguard. Notable laggards, however, are Brazil, Columbia and Bolivia. With the exception of Chile, the Latin American privatization programme has mainly seen state monopolies become public companies with little competition in the early years. This has offered rapidly rising profits for companies such as Telmex and very good stock market returns. Longer term, the ability of such monopolies to become competitive before deregulation must be questioned, and accordingly, the best returns may be seen in the early years. Looking ahead, Latin America continues to offer attractive investment opportunities, particularly in the utilities areas, assuming the currency turmoil can be resolved.

Asia may yet prove to be the area with the greatest investment opportunities for privatization in the latter half of the 1990s. Greater political stability, although sometimes totalitarian, sounder public finances and a rapidly growing individual shareholder base, even in previously communist states, all offer encouraging prospects. The problem? The demand for capital is so great that the sheer quantity of issues envisaged may hold back the market. The good news is that for an issue to succeed in this environment it may need to offer shareholders a higher return. This is the situation seen in China last year when a cap of 12 per cent was put on the annual rate of return offered to foreign investors wanting to build and operate power plants. Not surprisingly investors switched their attention to other power hungry, Asian countries, and now China is having to raise the rate of return in order to encourage capital to return.

In telecoms, China may face a similar problem. At present it only allows foreign firms to provide advice and to supply and manufacture telecom equipment, but bans foreigners from the potentially more lucrative business of owning and operating services. Given that an estimated $90 billion of investment will be needed to match telecom demand in Asia, currently growing at 17 per cent per annum, and that elsewhere in the region more liberal regimes operate, China may be forced to change its policy.

As recently as five years ago, most telecom operators in the Asia Pacific region were state run. Now around 30 telecom firms are listed on local exchanges. They range from privatized giants such as Singapore Telecom and Pakistan Telecom to new competitors such as Thailand's Telecom Asia and Globe Telecom in the Philippines. Several countries have pushed telecoms to the top of their agenda, because they fear that without an efficient telephone system their overall economic growth could stall. Privatization and competition are the only way to attract the necessary foreign investment and know how. This brings us back to the question of government motive for privatization. A desire to see rapid rates of economic growth enhanced by privatized telecoms companies should provide a very profitable background for investors. However, beware issues from governments with large budget deficits demanding top prices and make sure the regulatory environment is clearly defined.

The resulting cross-border comparison, as of April 1995, shows surprising variety.

Company	Price/ Earnings	Yield%	Price/ Book Value	Price/ Cash Flow
British Telecom	14.0x	5.5	1.8x	6.3x
NTT	139.0x	0.7	2.3x	6.4x
Singapore Telecom	33.0x	0.8	12.6x	26.2x
Telebras	16.4x	0.8	0.5x	3.0x
Telecom Italia	25.0x	2.4	1.7x	3.3x

Looking at this data, it is apparent that each issue is priced relative to its own market rather than as companies that are directly comparable on a global basis.

So what of the UK in this rapidly privatizing world? Having decided the Post Office is not for sale, the last great privatization may well be the railways. Railtrack, the network operator will probably be the first to go, but a number of key questions are still unresolved. The government's real focus of attention is the Private Finance Initiative (PFI) designed to attract private sector capital to finance and service public sector contracts which involve capital assets. The initiative has gained momentum recently with the chancellor announcing measures to force government departments to seek private sector funding for all capital spending. Recognized PFI projects are valued at £16 billion with many more still under consideration. PFI is a major opportunity for investment in UK infrastructure such as the Channel Tunnel Rail Link (CTRL).

For all these projects, which will also include smaller developments, such as hospitals and water treatment plants, a suitable level of return will be identified to attract the necessary type of finance, whether debt or equity. These projects will offer quasi-utility income streams and wide diversity. Investment opportunities are likely to emerge through a number of specialist funds being set up currently, as well as direct investment in companies that bid for specific projects.

PFI Projects envisaged in the next 5 years

So where will privatization lead investors over the next decade? Telecoms and utilities will continue to lead the way in almost all parts of the globe, although for politically correct reasons the term 'privatization' may not figure very

Chart 5.8 PFI projects envisaged in the next five years

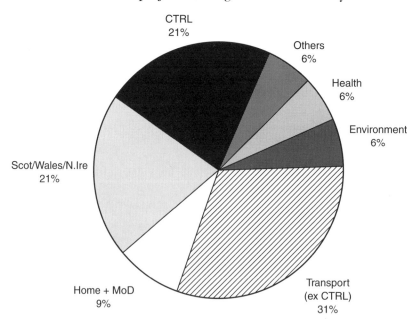

Source: Morgan Stanley Capital International Perspective

552

highly. Are there any lessons from the past investors we can use to help them? Yes, focus on new wholesale offerings where possible in preference to secondary sales, identify the governments' motives for sale and keep an eye on regulation. Bargains are often best at the beginning of a programme but the risks are also higher. Diversify your investments by region and sector to obtain a sensible spread and consider using privatization funds wherever possible to avoid specific risk. ♀

THE ECONOMICS OF FREEDOM

Dr. Kim R. Holmes

*Dr. Holmes is Vice President and Director of foreign policy studies at **The Heritage Foundation** in Washington DC.*

*Founded in 1973, **The Heritage Foundation** is a research and educational institute whose mission is to formulate and promote conservative public policies based on the principles of free enterprise, limited government, individual freedom, traditional American values, and a strong national defence.*

A free market renaissance of sorts has preceded the East Bloc's fall and a worldwide discrediting of socialism. Countries around the globe are shedding their socialist legacies. This progress has been spotty, however. While some countries have made great strides in liberalizing their economies, many others have not. This is a conclusion of The Heritage Foundation's *Index of Economic Freedom*, a quantitative measurement of economic freedom in 101 countries, and a worthwhile stop for any investor wishing to evaluate the investment climate worldwide.

Authored by Bryan T. Johnson and Thomas P. Sheehy, the *Index*, which is updated annually, gauges economic freedom in each country by focusing upon 10 key factors: trade policy; taxation policy; government consumption of economic output; monetary policy; capital flows and foreign investment policy; banking policy; wage and price control policy; property rights protection; regulations; and the black market. Each country's performance in these areas is given a numerical 'score'. For example, in the area of corporate taxes, a nation earns a '1' if it has limited or no taxes imposed on corporate profits. A flat corporate tax of less than 25 per cent earns a '2'; a top rate between 26 per cent and 35 per cent earns it a '3'; a top rate between 36 per cent and 45 per cent earns a '4'; and top rates above 46 per cent earn a '5'. A lower score reflects fewer restrictions on economic freedom.

Some of the 10 factors weighed equally by the *Index* are complementary. The size of a country's black market, for example, is a function of its wage and price control laws and the extent of its regulation. While additional factors could be considered, together these 10 provide a comprehensive snapshot

Table 5.1 The Thirty Most Economically Free Countries (1994)

FACTOR COUNTRY	Trade	Taxation	Gov. Consump.	Monetary Policy	For. Invest.	Banking	Wage/Prices	Property Rights	Regulation	Black Market	Ave.
1 Hong Kong	1	1.5	1	2	1	2	1	1	1	1	1.25
2 Singapore	1	2.5	1	1	1	2	1	1	1	1	1.25
3 Bahrain	2	1	3	1	2	2	2	1	1	1	1.60
4 U.S.	2	4	2	1	2	2	2	1	2	1	1.90
5 Japan (a)	2	4.5	1	1	3	3	2	1	2	1	1.95
6 Taiwan (a)	2	2.5	2	1	3	2	2	1	2	1	1.95
7 U.K.	2	4.5	3	1	2	2	2	1	1	1	1.95
8 Canada	2	4	2	1	3	1	2	1	2	1	2.00
9 Germany	2	5	2	1	2	2	2	1	2	1	2.00
10 Austria	2	4.5	3	1	2	1	2	1	3	1	2.05
11 Bahamas	5	1	2	1	4	2	2	1	1	2	2.10
12 Czech Rep.	1	4	2	3	2	2	2	2	1	3	2.10
13 So. Korea	3	3.5	1	1	3	3	2	1	3	2	2.15
14 Malaysia	3	2.5	2	1	2	1	2	2	2	2	2.15
15 Australia	2	4	3	2	2	2	2	1	3	3	2.20
16 Ireland	2	5	2	1	2	2	2	1	2	3	2.20
17 Estonia	1	3.5	2	4	1	3	2	2	2	1	2.25
18 France	2	4	2	1	3	3	3	2	2	2	2.30
19 Thailand	3	3	1	1	3	3	3	1	3	3	2.30
20 Chile	4	3	1	3	2	3	3	1	2	2	2.50
21 Italy	2	5	3	2	2	2	2	2	2	3	2.50
22 Spain	2	5	2	2	2	2	3	2	3	2	2.60
23 El Salvador	2	2.5	2	3	2	2	2	3	3	2	2.65
24 Oman	3	3.5	5	1	3	2	3	2	2	1	2.65
25 Sweden	2	4.5	5	2	2	3	2	2	3	3	2.65
26 Belize	5	4	2	1	2	3	2	2	3	3	2.70
27 Panama	4	3	2	4	2	1	2	3	3	3	2.70
28 Paraguay	3	2.5	1	4	1	2	3	3	3	5	2.75
29 Slovakia	2	4.5	3	3	2	3	3	2	2	3	2.75
30 Greece	2	3	3	3	2	4	3	2	3	3	2.80

(a) In case of a tie, the countries were ranked alphabetically.

Source: The Heritage Foundation

of each economy and allow for an accurate comparative assessment of economic freedom.

Economic freedom is not as prevalent as one might expect. Of the 101 countries examined by the *Index*, just 43 were found to possess 'free' or 'mostly free' economies while 50 possess economies that are 'mostly unfree' and eight possess 'repressive' economies.

That so many of the world's economies are not free is unfortunate. As 'The Curve of Economic Freedom' demonstrates, countries with the highest levels of economic freedom (a lower *Index* score) enjoy the highest levels of development. Likewise, countries with the lowest levels of economic freedom (a higher *Index* score) suffer the lowest development levels. Roughly translated, this means that countries which protect private property and the value of their **countries which protect private property and the value of their currency, impose a low tax burden, welcome international trade and foreign investment, and minimize government intervention into their economies enjoy greater prosperity.**

Chart 5.9 The Curve of Economic Freedom

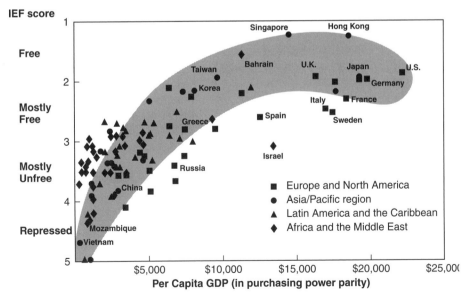

Source: The Heritage Foundation

555

currency, impose a low tax burden, welcome international trade and foreign investment, and minimize government intervention into their economies enjoy greater prosperity.

Investment Tool

While a non-free and unprosperous economy may offer profitable business and investment opportunities, these opportunities are select and usually entail working through host governments, cutting deals to obtain mineral concessions, government contracts or exclusive retail distribution rights. Some investments, precious minerals for example, often do better when producing countries are politically and economically deteriorating. Many other investments are based on an economy's anticipated improvement. As such, economic fundamentals and economic freedom should be considered.

The *Index* provides a look at fundamentals and is a valuable initial stop for an investor wishing to explore investment opportunities in a given country or region. The *Index* can also be useful in discerning nascent and potentially profitable economic trends. *Index* findings for South Africa, Uganda, Mexico, the Czech Republic, and China provide contrasting stories and food for thought for international investors.

South Africa is blessed with extraordinary resources and economic potential. It is the sole African country with significant elements of a developed economy. It is also poised to be the engine of economic growth in a region which may be on the verge of overcoming years of war and socialism.

The democratic transition in South Africa has gone as well as can be expected. The potential for great instability remains however, particularly after Nelson Mandela departs the presidency. Political stability will depend in large part upon South Africa's economic performance. Although improved slightly, the South African economy has been sluggish, with economic growth pegged at some 3 per cent for 1995. One reason for this is that the much anticipated post-sanctions flood of foreign investment has not materialized. These economic ills can be blamed largely on South Africa's statist economic policies.

The apartheid-era economic system has been carried over into the new South Africa. It is characterized by state intervention into most aspects of the economy. The South African economy was judged by the *Index* as 'mostly not free,' scoring a 3.00. While some economic liberalization has occurred, a long road remains to be travelled. High corporate taxes and tariffs and burdensome labour regulations are particularly harmful to the economy. Liberalization is desperately needed. However, there is a continual temptation to increase spending on social programmes and undertake other government interventions to improve quickly the lives of previously disenfranchised black South Africans. The key is whether the new coalition government can continue to resist this formula for economic stagnation.

Africa, apart from South Africa, is treacherous ground for investors, being replete with imploding states and fraught with risk. But there are a few countries experiencing significant economic growth. Once war-torn Uganda, has a dynamic economy by any standard, having grown 8 per cent in 1994. Not surprisingly, Uganda scored a 2.94 on the *Index*, placing it behind only Swaziland among sub-Saharan countries.

Uganda has undertaken fairly dramatic economic liberalization. Indian businessmen who were banished in the early 1970s by Idi Amin are now welcome and are returning in droves. Government marketing boards for coffee, cotton and other produce have been disbanded. With such reforms, foreign investment is arriving in Uganda: some $200 million in the two years since 1992. The establishment of a stock market is in the works. Several banks in Uganda, including Barclays and Nile Bank, pay close to 20 per cent on deposits. The Ugandan shilling is fully convertible.

Nearly $9 billion in foreign investment flowed into Mexico between August 1993 and August 1994. In early 1995, the Mexican peso collapsed and it became clear that many investors had given Mexico a better bill of health than economic conditions warranted. While the United States and the international financial institutions will prop up the Mexican economy in the short run, the *Index*, which rates Mexico as 'mostly not free', identifies many fundamental problems in the Mexican economy, including a regulatory environment that is corrupt and burdensome to business. It is unlikely that these shortcomings will be addressed, particularly as long as Mexico is leaning on the crutch of a foreign bailout.

With the fall of the Iron Curtain, many analysts looked to Poland and Hungary to be in the vanguard of economic liberalization. These countries instead have been backsliding with their economic transitions, while the Czech Republic has advanced the furthest among the former East Bloc states. In fact, over 80 per cent of the Czech economy is now in private hands. The Czech economy is also prospering. Predictably, the Czech Republic's Index score betters those of Poland and Hungary, reflecting its superior economic conditions.

China is also rated 'mostly not free' by the *Index*. While many international investors continue to view China as a good destination for capital, China's *Index* score reflects the tight government control that remains. It is no coincidence that the bulk of China's foreign investment is concentrated in experimental 'pockets' of economic freedom, primarily in Guandong and Fujian Provinces. Expanded foreign investment throughout China and general economic prosperity remain unlikely until China embraces economic freedom on a national level.

Political Freedom Trap

It should be noted that among those countries with the top 10 *Index* scores, four are rated as possessing 'Partially Free' or 'Not Free' political systems by

New York-based Freedom House. These include Hong Kong, Singapore, Bahrain and Taiwan. Of course, the hope is that these and other countries undergoing economic liberalization will gradually develop political systems respectful of individual liberties. This is happening in Taiwan, as it happened in South Korea.

Some countries are attempting to move forward with substantial economic and political liberalizations simultaneously. Boris Yeltsin is waging this struggle in Russia. Unfortunately, economic liberalization in Russia has been less than impressive. Zambia is another country struggling with this task. Assuming power in 1991 as Zambia's first democratically elected president, President Frederick Chiluba has not had much success liberalizing Zambia's statist economy. As with Yeltsin, Chiluba's efforts have threatened his government and the cause of democracy in Zambia. In both cases, economic liberalization would probably be easier to accomplish under a less democratic regime. Be wary of a country attempting to move on democratic and economic reforms at once.

Beware of the World Bank and IMF

World Bank and International Monetary Fund orthodoxy is now considerably more market-oriented than it was in the 1960s and 1970s, when parastatals, import substitution, price controls, and other government interventions were championed. But even with their greater market emphasis, World Bank and IMF structural adjustment reform should not be confused with promoting economic freedom.

Whereas the *Index* 'rewards' a lean government (one consuming a minimal percentage of gross domestic product) and low taxation levels, the new orthodoxy often encourages governments to enlarge themselves by collecting greater tax revenues. Moreover, other *Index* factors such as regulation largely escape the attention of the World Bank and the IMF.

Czech Prime Minister Vaclav Klaus has complained about the statist orientation of the international financial institutions. This insight has encouraged Klaus to speed through economic liberalizations which enhance economic freedom in the Czech Republic. Klaus has also complained about development aid prolonging the day of reckoning when needed reforms are made. If you can identify a country with an improving Index score which is not instituting its economic reforms at the barrel of the gun – an IMF and World Bank structural adjustment agreement/aid package – but rather because it recognizes that doing so is in its best interest, you may have found the next Chile.

The *Index of Economic Freedom* demonstrates that there is a real lack of economic freedom in the world. Today, only a handful of countries are blessed with free economies. There is a bright side to this. Plenty of diamonds are lying in the rough for the international investor to seize. ♀

EMERGING WORLD IMPACT ON GLOBAL ASSET PRICES

Richard M. Young and Peter Sullivan

*R. M. 'Mike' Young is Director of European Investment Strategy for **Merrill Lynch**. Based in London he is responsible for advising clients on portfolio and investment issues with particular focus on the Europe. Dr. Young has a PhD in economics. During the past 25 years has been active in the academic, public and private sectors in the areas of economics and finance. Peter Sullivan is a European Investment Strategist for **Merrill Lynch**, analysing European asset markets. Previously, Mr Sullivan worked in the **Government Economic Service**.*

Merrill Lynch is one of the world's largest financial services firms with more than 500 offices in 32 countries. The firm is unique by virtue of having a leading private client business serving the financial needs of individual investors as well as being a top tier investment banking firm.

We believe that the single most important **secular trend** affecting the global economy and global asset markets during the 1990s is the ongoing process of integrating the emerging markets into the global marketplace. While the attractions, and the risks, of investing in the emerging markets have been aggressively marketed to investors, we believe that a proper understanding of some of the major implications for the developed world is still evolving. In particular we believe that two of the implications are: (1) that real long-term bond yields are likely to remain high for some time on a global basis; and (2) that real wage growth will remain weak in the industrialized world. If we are correct there are likely to be dramatic implications for asset prices and investors in the industrialized world.

Relative Factor Supplies Have Shifted

The fundamental reason for our expectations is the ongoing adjustment of prices to the shift in relative supplies of the basic factors of production in the global economy. The 'emergence' of the emerging economies means that for the time being labour is the relatively abundant factor of production, and capital the relatively scarce factor.

The visible manifestation of this is the difference in relative wages and relative productivity of labour between the developed and the developing world. A survey of the literature on technology transfer indicates that, while there are dramatic differences across industries and among countries, a rough rule of thumb would suggest that labour costs in the emerging markets are likely to be 20 per cent, or less, of their developed market equivalents while productivity is generally 40 to 60 per cent. Our calculations suggest that, on not unreasonable assumptions regarding the ratio of sales to capital and labour costs to total costs, moving an enterprise from the developed world to the developing world can increase return on equity by a factor of two to four times.

With the return on equity of the S&P 500 near 15 per cent, this suggests that the return on equity for equivalent investments in these markets could range from 30 to 60 per cent. This seems to us to more than reflect risk and offers the potential for companies to collect a 'rent'

Our calculations suggest that, on not unreasonable assumptions regarding the ratio of sales to capital and labour costs to total costs, moving an enterprise from the developed world to the developing world can increase return on equity by a factor of two to four times.

by relocating. This 'rent' reflects the stickiness in the adjustment of relative wages to the shift in the global supply of accessible labour.

An Historical Analogy

This view of relative factor supply changes needs some explanation. Clearly we have not had a dramatic change in the number of people at any recent point in time or a dramatic fall in the supply of capital. We believe that evolutionary change in the regulatory and technological environment has raised the risk adjusted marginal return on physical investment in the emerging markets, and by extension in the global economy, quite dramatically.

The basic regulatory change has been the elimination of a variety of restrictions on for profit enterprises having access to the labour in the emerging markets. These included both the nationalistic and communist restrictions on control, repatriation of profits and investment in Latin America, eastern Europe and the ex Soviet Union. Their demise or diminution has increased access and reduced risk premia. The technological innovations we would point to would include communications and the shift of production capabilities to an electronic from an electro/mechanical base. This former has lowered the costs of command and control and the latter appears to have reduced the skill demands of technology transfer.

A useful analogy can be found in the development of British agriculture and the British economy during the second half of the nineteenth century. The similarity to recent events lies in the effect of regulatory change, in this case the repeal of the Corn Laws in 1846 which created market access for agricultural products from outside of Great Britain, and technological change in the form of the steamship and the railroad. In combination these events allowed the exploitation of cheap land available in the then emerging economies and effectively shifted the relative supply of land, capital and labour on a global basis.

The impact was dramatic both in terms of the shift in the patterns of trade and on relative prices. Ashworth's *An Economic History of England 1870 to 1939* cites a general price index for agricultural products. During the closing decades of the nineteenth century the price of agricultural commodities in Great Britain appears to have fallen by about 30 per cent and the returns to agricultural land plummeted. Ashworth noted that imports of wheat rose to 77 per cent of British consumption in 1893–5 from 50 per cent twenty years earlier. The price of the output most directly associated with the factor of production in excess supply and the returns of the factor itself fell dramatically.

At the same time, the factors of production in relative scarcity, capital and labour, saw their returns rise rapidly. Capital appears to have earned a higher return than at any time during the past 125 years. A study by Michael Edelstein *Realized Rates of Return on UK Home and Overseas Portfolio Investment in the Age of High Imperialism*, indicates that the real return on domestic debentures in the decade to 1885 averaged just under 5 per cent. This appears to have been the highest decade average over the period since 1870. Work by A. L. Bowley, *Wages and Income in the United Kingdom since 1860*, provides a picture of the other element in the equation. For labour the real wage appears to have risen by near 40 per cent between 1860 and 1880 and a further 50 per cent over the period from 1880 to 1900, a compound rate of increase of about 1.9 per cent per year.

The high returns to capital and labour during this period cannot, of course, be separated from the ongoing industrial revolution and the rising importance of industry relative to agriculture. This may well have increased the demand for capital and labour, and hence their returns, even if the increased ability to exploit the agricultural lands had not occurred; but we believe that the shift in the effective relative supplies of factors was a major influence in factor returns and indicates the potential influence on returns to capital and labour of the emerging markets.

Implications for the 1990s

The implications for the developed world are potentially dramatic. Real wage growth is likely to be modest in the developed economies. The dynamic of this will look like, and in fact be, the impact of competitive pressures on wages in the traded goods sector, particularly in those most directly competitive with products produced with relatively low skilled labour. In a recent study on Trade and Jobs in US Manufacturing for the Brookings Institutions' Jeffrey Sachs and Howard Shatz point out that the greatest impact of the increased competition should be on the jobs and wages in the low skilled area of the economy which they presume will bear the brunt of the competitive pressure. Their research suggests that this pressure is already visible in the US.

It is also likely that companies will be attempting to match the potential risk adjusted returns on capital in the third world. This process is already underway. What has been termed 'restructuring', 'downsizing', 'productivity enhancing' activities by the corporate world in the developed economies could just as easily, but perhaps less politically acceptably, be termed 'capital return enhancing'. The key point is that if enterprises in the developed world are to maintain competitive returns with opportunities in the emerging low cost economies, managers will have to continue to 'sweat' assets/capital aggressively.

In addition to the implications for wages and job creation in the low skill end of the market, we believe that the high marginal returns to investment will keep real bond yields higher on average through this cycle as they appear to have done during the 1875–85 period. This high level will reflect the increased returns available on physical capital as a result of access to emerging market cheap labour and the need for real returns on financial assets to match this after adjusting for risk and liquidity. Chart 5.10 traces the evolution of real bond yields in the US, UK, Germany and France over the past five years.

Chart 5.10 Real 10-Year Bond Yields

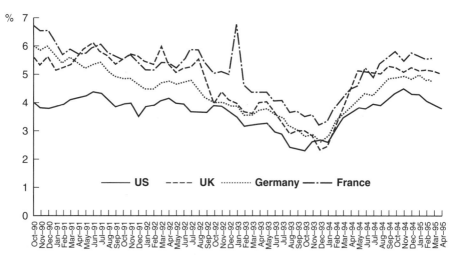

Sources: Datastream, Consensus Economics Inc; London.

These rates are calculated using 10-year nominal yields corrected for the 10-year inflation expectations taken from Consensus Economics biannual surveys. Real yields are presently in a range of 4 to 6 per cent. In many of the peripheral markets real interest rates appear to be even higher. The tendency of yields to decline during 1991–3 and to rise since reflects the pace of the global business cycle and the first falling and then rising demand for capital over the course of that cycle. Our expectation would be that real rates might very well average near present levels in the core economies over the course of the cycle, but that they could rise from present levels if, and as, the current global expansion continues.

Investment Implications

If we are correct in our presumptions regarding real interest rates and wages, the investment implications are likely to be profound. We believe that in general the high real interest rates are likely to imply that price/earnings ratios (PER) in the major industrial markets will fall to lower levels at the peak earnings year than generally anticipated. The key factor is that the inverse of the PER bears a close resemblance to a real interest rate. It can be demonstrated that the PER can be written as a relationship between expected real dividend growth, the payout ratio, the equity risk premium and the real bond yield. Our conclusion regarding the effect of higher real yields at the peak assumes that the other variables which go into the determination of the PER behave approximately as they have in past cycles.

If real interest rates are higher throughout the cycle then PERs are likely to be lower. If we are correct, then it is possible that PERs in the major industrial markets could well fall to single digits near the peak earnings year. What should be emphasized in this view is that it is very positive for investors. As the owners of the scarce resource investors can expect to get more for their money. In particular, one view of lower PERs is that investors should be able to purchase any given earnings stream at a lower price than had previously been required.

The implications for equity market prospects depends on the rate of increase of earnings between now and the peak earnings year. It will be increasingly important for investors to match long-term growth prospects with valuations. Even if multiples are falling, equity prices can rise if earnings growth is fast enough. Broadly speaking if the global business cycle peaks during the 1997–9 period, we believe that the underlying trend in equity prices for the major economies could be sideways for the next few years. Within this context companies with visible stable earnings above the market average are likely to see stock prices outperform.

Aside from the broad market implications we believe that adjustment to these pressures may have implications for the sectors of the markets in which investors will find long-term value. Any business that has a heavy dependence on low skilled labour and produces goods that can flow through world trade is likely to find itself at a competitive disadvantage if current production is not largely in the emerging markets. Competitive pressures will keep margins under pressure until, and unless, it makes the shift to a cheaper cost base. Generally speaking we would expect that a developed world labour cost could protect margins best in industries that require a high proportion of skilled labour or in industries outside of the traded goods sector. The sectors under pressure in the developed world will, in many cases, be those that have already seen some relative decline: textiles, steel and chemicals. Those that will benefit will include pharmaceuticals, information technology and others that have a high research and development component.

Finally we note that businesses that rely heavily on debt financing, for example housing and cars, may find demand growth in the developed world modest. High real interest rates, coupled with weak wage growth and slow population growth suggest that the low price, entry level segments of these markets are particularly likely to experience sluggish growth. ♀

FREE TRADE: WINNERS AND LOSERS
John Peet

John Peet is Executive Editor of **The Economist**. *Before that, he worked successively in the Britain department, as Washington correspondent and as finance writer. Prior to joining the newspaper, he worked for some years in the* **Treasury**, *including a stint in Brussels, dealing with the European budget.*

An awkward paradox lies at the heart of any published investment advice. If the advice (sell ICI, say) is obvious, the markets will have already taken it on board. If it is not obvious, but still correct, the markets will react to it instantaneously, so that most sensible advisers will have already acted. The best sort of investment advice, therefore, is often general, not specific; and it is about spotting trends rather than discrete events. So what are the key macro-economic trends that investors would be considering as the century draws to a close? Many are, perhaps, decidedly favourable. But there are also several wild cards to look out for.

Start with the favourable. The prospects for world economic growth are as good now as they have been for 30 years. Most of the rich industrial countries have put recession behind them; few are threatened by a strong revival of inflation. Meanwhile, many developing countries are on a roll; not just the East Asian miracle economies, but much of Latin America, Eastern Europe, India and Southern Africa. Recent World Bank forecasts suggest that rich countries will grown by nearly 3 per cent a year over the next decade; and that developing countries will grow by nearly 5 per cent. That gap may seem small. Yet if current growth rates persist for, say, the next 25 years, they will lead to some huge changes.

Today's 'developing' countries may, by the end of this period account for over 60 per cent of gross world product, up from 45 per cent now; while the share of 'rich industrial' countries could fall from about 55 per cent to below 40 per cent. China is likely to become the world's biggest economy; India, Indonesia, Thailand and a possibly unified Korea will be close behind. Of today's rich countries, only the United States, Japan and Germany will rank in the world's top eight.

In almost all countries, free trade and free markets are winning increasing support. The collapse of Soviet communism has played a big role in converting

Chart 5.11 Relative Size of Largest Economies

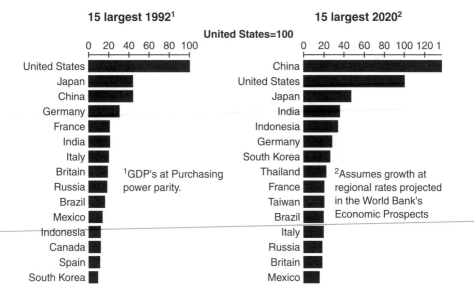

15 largest 1992¹   15 largest 2020²

United States=100

¹GDP's at Purchasing power parity.

²Assumes growth at regional rates projected in the World Bank's Economic Prospects

Source: World Bank

poor countries to a belief in market forces. The passage of the GATT Uruguay round, the establishment of the World Trade Organization and the example set by such fast growers as South Korea and Hong Kong have all helped to push policy-making in a sensible, non-interventionist direction. So has the spread of privatization, as more countries realize that even utilities can benefit from being subjected to market disciplines.

Trade is clearly a key factor in all this. After a hiccup in the mid-1970s, the past decade has once more seen the volume of trade growing faster than national output. During the past decade, the growth in trade averaged over 4 per cent and exceeded 8 per cent in three years. Even when national production declined due to the recession global trade continued to grow.

The birth of the World Trade Organization, which will provide a broader framework of trade rules than the GATT by taking in whole new areas such as services and agriculture, should speed it up still more. Companies and sectors geared to exports will flourish. And as more countries discover that the classical economic case for free trade applies to services as much as to traditional goods, trade in services will boom. Finance, legal services, information technology, media and entertainment are examples of businesses that in future seem likely to weigh more heavily than, say, cars and consumer electronics in world trade. Protected domestic markets in such services will be dismantled. The same goes for many public utilities such as telecoms, electricity and gas distribution, all of them businesses that are now learning fast about competition and trade.

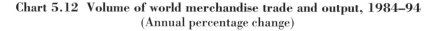

Chart 5.12 Volume of world merchandise trade and output, 1984–94
(Annual percentage change)

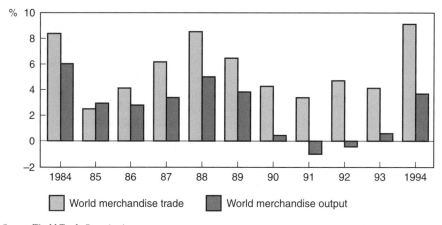

Source: World Trade Organization

There are big sectoral implications from such a change in trade patterns. Knowledge-based industries, in particular, will surely outperform more traditional ones. That points to design companies rather than manufacturers; to software houses rather than computer makers; or to media and entertainment groups rather than electronic firms. Even within sectors there will be changes: for instance, the health-care business may be less dominated by old-fashioned pill-makers, with more exciting opportunities in, say, computerized medical care, a business that could boom, thanks to the growing ranks of the elderly.

> There are big sectoral implications from such a change in trade patterns. Knowledge-based industries, in particular, will surely outperform more traditional ones.

It all sounds exciting for investors. Yet there are also dangers. Consider one historical parallel for British investors. A century ago, there was a period both of rapid growth in trade and of huge outward British investment as capital-holders sought to maximize returns. At times, as much as 5 per cent of British national income was being invested abroad, much of it in such developing economies as Russia, Argentina and South Africa. Investors soon discovered, however, that high returns meant high risks. Several Latin American countries, and later, Russia, defaulted. In an even eerier coincidence, Barings almost went under; but in 1890, unlike 1995, it was rescued by the Bank of England.

Those who piled into Mexican and Argentinian bonds during 1994, only to register huge losses in early 1995, may be worried by this historical parallel. They should certainly be cautious, as they no doubt will be after recent experience. But they are probably wrong to be too worried. Overall, British foreign investors did extremely well in the late nineteenth and early twentieth centuries. Had it not been for the two world wars, a substantial rentier class, living on the proceeds of foreign investment, would have been established. A similar pattern is at work now: British GNP, which includes overseas investment earnings, is growing faster than British GDP which does not.

As for the spread of trade to services and knowledge-based industries, here too there are risks. A sinister development is that some countries are still displaying an atavistic fondness for protection: think of France's efforts to limit the showing of Hollywood movies on European television, or America's troubles persuading China to pay some respect to software copyright. As competition from so-called poor countries spreads from traditional sectors like basic manufacturing into higher-skilled services, the pressure to put up barriers to imports will intensify. In the service sector, barriers can be more complex, more creative, less easy to quantify and much harder to monitor. Governments must resist the temptation to resort to the nationalist card if they are to sustain the growth in prosperity that trade has brought.

There are a few more general risks to watch for. One is the general market cycle, which shows no signs of going away. The cycle may increase pressure on governments to slow down the advance of world trade by erecting tariff, or more likely, non-tariff barriers. Even such a free-trading nation as the United States continually threatens to impose tariffs against Japan. A further danger will come from the environmental movement, which is increasingly hostile to trade on the grounds that it increases growth (and so produces more pollution) and encourages countries to overexploit natural resources. If governments were to fall for talk of resource constraints or global warming, they could easily be persuaded to impose taxes and regulations that might be fatal for world prosperity. So far, fortunately, they seem not to be: pressure to 'do something' about global warming has, if anything, diminished.

This positive picture of an enlarged world trading activity embracing all sectors of the economy argues strongly for carefully selected spreading of assets into knowledge-based business, service industries and emerging markets. That leads to the biggest question of all: where to go, and what financial instruments to choose? One word to reassure the most cautious investors first. It is possible to benefit significantly from growth in developing countries and in gee-whizz services while still investing largely in traditional domestic companies. The ones to go for are those that are investing substantially abroad – trading companies, oil majors and consumer-goods multinationals say – and those on the frontier of high technology business such as telecoms and electronics groups. The ones to avoid could be those tied too firmly to rich-country markets or low-margin activities: retailers, for instance, or traditional chemicals groups.

But a more exciting strategy is to invest directly in emerging markets and in high technology. Here the best guide is to go for the prospects for greatest growth. Geographically, that means South-East Asia, perhaps Brazil, South

Africa and maybe India. (China needs careful thought, for it poses substantial political risks; many foreign investors have found it easier to put money in than to get it out again.) Those with more taste for a gamble could do worse than take a punt on Russia, for instance in a top-flight national resource company such as Lukoil. As for which business to choose, multimedia start-ups, biotechnology and software firms all promise fabulous returns – so long as you pick the right ones. In general, service industries look likely to offer better returns to investors than traditional manufacturing over the next decade.

A portfolio, of course, should always be balanced; but in general, the sectors to go for are those that will benefit from trade. In low-wage economies, that will sometimes mean manufacturing; in higher-wage economies, which now include places like Korea and Taiwan, services, including financial services and anything to do with information.

Thanks to favourable macroeconomic developments, the next decade should be an excellent one for investors, provided they are willing to take a few risks and provided they keep on top of economic changes. That will at least make a nice change from the dismal early 1990s, even if the heady days of the mid-1980s never quite return. ♀

THE DEMOGRAPHICS OF GLOBAL INVESTING

Richard F. Hokenson and Michael S. Rome

*Richard F Hokenson is Chief Economist and Demographer at **Donaldson, Lufkin & Jenrette Securities Corp (DLJ)**. Mr Hokenson has written extensively over the years in the field of demographic economics. Prior to joining **DLJ**, Mr Hokenson was a Senior Economist at **Merrill Lynch Economics** and a Senior Economist at **Data Resources Inc**. Michael Rome is Research Associate at **DLJ**, where he concentrates on economic forecasting and demographics. Prior to joining **DLJ**, he worked at **National Economic Research Associates**.*

__Donaldson, Lufkin & Jenrette Securities Corp__ was founded in 1959 as an equities research boutique. It has grown into a multi-billion dollar full service investment bank with nearly 5,000 employees and 24 offices worldwide.

Successful investment strategies will increasingly be those where the investment horizon moves beyond the already industrialized world (developed Europe, North America and Japan). The basic genesis for this evolving investment environment is the imposition of a demographic super-cycle of ageing populations that are not replacing themselves. For various reasons, it is unlikely that the already-developed world will ever import enough people to make a material difference to that outcome. **The new dynamic, therefore, is that ageing populations will increasingly generate surplus capital, which will be reflected in low domestic interest rates and the persistence of low nominal growth.** That process is most clearly visible in Japan, which is the most rapidly ageing country on planet Earth. But the ageing process is not unique to Japan. The principal difference between Japan, developed Europe and North America is only one of timing, with North America being the 'youngest' old country and Europe in between.

An increased global orientation is not restricted to direct investments in emerging economies, but also involves identifying companies, many of whom are based in developed countries, which are making forays into emerging economies. This will be particularly important for companies that are involved in the production or distribution of consumer goods. Lower-priced consumer goods, particularly household products, cosmetics, beverages or clothing, will have an advantage over higher-priced goods, because the majority of consumers in emerging regions lack the purchasing power of individuals in developed countries. The average person living in China is more likely to purchase a can of soda or a T shirt than a personal computer or automobile, at least in the near term until incomes rise.

Ageing populations result in a dramatic compositional shift in consumption towards services (e.g. health care, financial services or leisure services) and away from goods. For example, because the majority of savings are accumulated in the ten years prior to retirement, the need for financial products and advice swells in conjunction with an ageing population. The demand for consumer goods, on the other hand, is shifting from developed to emerging

Chart 5.13 Developed Countries Population Change by Age Group: (1990–2000)

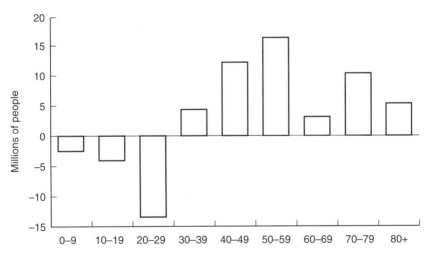

Sources: Bureau of the Census, DLJ

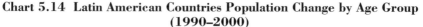

Chart 5.14 Latin American Countries Population Change by Age Group (1990–2000)

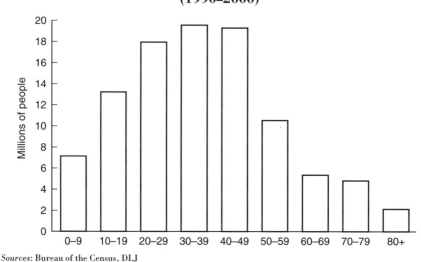

Sources: Bureau of the Census, DLJ

economies. It is with this in mind that we turn our attention to the principal emerging economic regions of Latin America and Asia.

Charts 5.13, 5.14 and 5.15 are the basic road maps for understanding the shift in international investment opportunities. All three charts display the same concept of examining how populations are changing on an age basis in the already developed world, Latin America and emerging Asia during the 1990s.

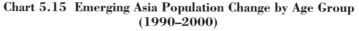

Chart 5.15 Emerging Asia Population Change by Age Group (1990–2000)

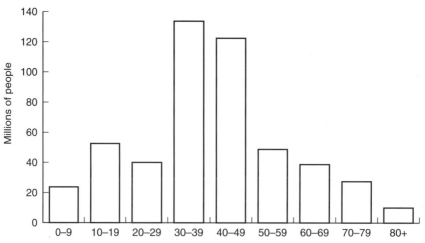

Sources: Bureau of the Census, DLJ

570

The already developed world is defined as encompassing northern, western and southern Europe, North America, Japan, Australia and New Zealand (about 800 million persons, or about 15 per cent of the world's population). While there are some differences between Latin America and emerging Asia, they are still more similar to one another and both are quite different from the picture painted in already developed countries.

Chart 5.13 is unique in the sense that the 1990s represents the very first time that this picture has ever appeared, i.e. it is the first time that the already industrialized world is experiencing a contraction in the number of young adults and teenagers. The important point to note is that this observation is a fact not a forecast; it simply represents the impact of the passage of time. The ongoing decline in the number of young adults and teenagers represents the onset and persistence of below-replacement fertility in nearly every industrialized country. The additional and more important observation is that what is occurring in developed countries in the 1990s is not unique to this decade. The dawn of the new millennium will not see developed countries with more young adults or more teenagers. Thus, this represents a structural break from the past, a structural break that will tend to limit returns on **domestic** investments.

The dawn of the new millennium will not see developed countries with more young adults or more teenagers. Thus, this represents a structural break from the past, a structural break that will tend to limit returns on domestic investments.

That will be particularly true for real assets, e.g. office buildings or residential real estate. Below-replacement fertility means that populations and labour forces in already developed countries will reach a maximum and then begin to contract. That will result in long-run excess supply of real assets and negative real rates of return. Real returns on domestically based financial assets will be positive but low. That will be particularly true for interest rates. It will be increasingly important for investors to distinguish between countries and companies. Companies whose principal business is the domestic production or distribution of consumer goods in already industrialized countries will see very little growth in their market. Resultant market share fights are much less appealing than the opportunities presented by emerging economies.

Considering the different profiles displayed there will be very significant and divergent trends in the age distribution of populations. Developed countries will experience substantial growth in the population that is old and a shrinkage in the proportion of the population that is between the ages of 15 and 64. By the year 2025, only 61.8 per cent of the US population will be neither very young nor very old versus 65.6 per cent in 1991. Within Latin America, that percentage increases from 58.5 per cent in 1991 to 66.3 per cent by the year 2025. Within emerging Asia, that percentage increases from 60.3 per cent in 1991 to 65.4 per cent in 2025.

Chart 5.16 Emerging Asia Age Breakdown in 1991

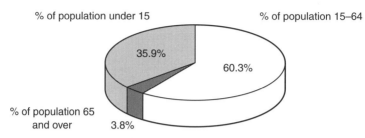

% of population under 15

% of population 15–64

35.9%

60.3%

% of population 65 and over

3.8%

Chart 5.17 United States Age Breakdown in 1991

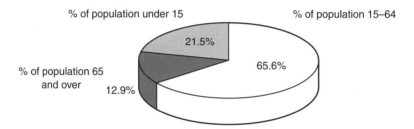

% of population under 15

% of population 15–64

21.5%

65.6%

% of population 65 and over

12.9%

Chart 5.18 Latin America Age Breakdown in 1991

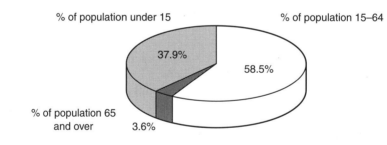

% of population under 15

% of population 15–64

37.9%

58.5%

% of population 65 and over

3.6%

Chart 5.19 Emerging Asia Projected Age Breakdown in 2025

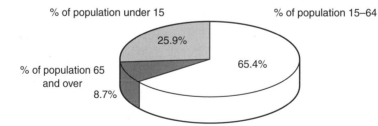

% of population under 15

% of population 15–64

25.9%

65.4%

% of population 65 and over

8.7%

Sources: World Development Report 1993, Census Bureau, DLJ

572

Chart 5.20 United States Projected Age Breakdown in 2025

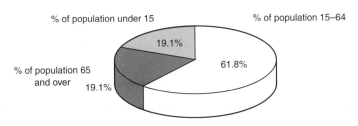

% of population under 15   % of population 15–64

% of population 65
and over   19.1%   19.1%   61.8%

Chart 5.21 Latin America Projected Age Breakdown in 2025

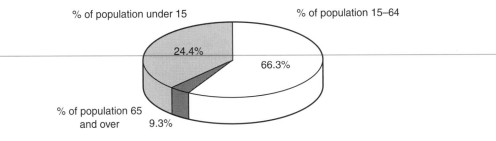

% of population under 15   % of population 15–64

24.4%   66.3%

% of population 65
and over   9.3%

Sources: World Development Report 1993, Census Bureau, DLJ

While it is true that the age profiles of both Latin America and emerging Asia are impressive, it is important to note that there are differences between the size and growth rates. In terms of total size, Asia has a substantial advantage. In 1990, there were nearly 3 billion persons living in Asia versus only about 409 million persons in Latin America. Two countries, China and India, dominate the Asian population (two out of every three Asian residents is either Chinese or Indian). In terms of growth, however, the advantage goes to Latin America because Asia has a longer history of a lower birth rate reflected in a more pronounced decline in the number of youngest residents as compared to Latin America.

Although the differences in population growth by age are compelling, the fundamental cornerstone behind our optimism on emerging economies is the re-establishment of the trend towards convergence in per capita nominal GNP denominated in dollars versus that of the United States. The rationale for this position is not hard to understand because the principal investment appeal of any emerging economy is its ability to grow faster than the already developed US economy. It should be noted that Charts 5.22 and 5.23 decompose that faster growth by displaying the underlying trend in per capita nominal GNP as well as total GNP. Growth is bolstered by more rapid population growth.

Chart 5.22 Latin American relative to the United States Total Nominal GNP (solid line) and Nominal GNP per capita (dotted Line)

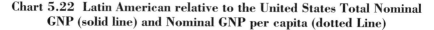
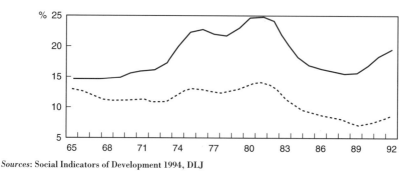

Sources: Social Indicators of Development 1994, DLJ

Between 1990 and 1992, per capita nominal GNP increased by 23.0 per cent in Latin America and 24.8 per cent in emerging Asia. Both figures are well above the United States, which posted an increase of only 5.8 per cent. In terms of total GNP, note that faster population growth adds substantially to the acceleration in per capita income relative to the United States. Although per capita income for Latin America as a whole is less than 10 per cent of the United States, total GNP is nearly 20 per cent as large. Similarly, although per capita income for emerging Asia is less than 13 per cent of the United States, total GNP is 28.3 per cent of US GNP.

Chart 5.23 Emerging Asia relative to the United States Total Nominal GNP (solid line) and Nominal GNP per capita (dotted line)

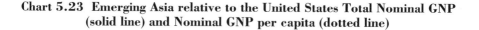
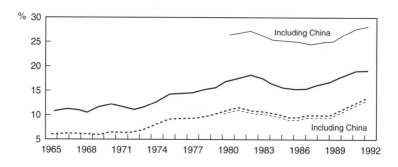

Sources: Social Indicators of Development 1994, DLJ

An important point to emphasize, however, is that trends that are apparent for a region as a whole are not necessarily replicated in each individual country. Within Latin America, Honduras, Nicaragua and Peru have yet to show any definitive signs that their downward trend in relative per capita nominal GNP has been reversed. In Colombia, Ecuador, Guatemala and Venezuela, relative per capita nominal GNP has certainly stopped falling, but a definitive upturn has yet to be established. On a more positive note, the strong re-establishment of convergence is clearly underway in Argentina, Chile, Mexico, Panama, Paraguay and Uruguay. The results are also encouraging for Brazil and Bolivia.

Within Asia, India, Nepal and Bangladesh have yet to show any definitive signs that their downward trend in per capita nominal GNP has been reversed. For Bhutan and Laos, there does not appear to be a consistent trend one way or another. In Pakistan, the Philippines, and Sri Lanka, however, there appears to be solid evidence that the prior deterioration has been arrested and may have already begun to turn up. The evidence of a sustained reversal is much stronger for Malaysia and Indonesia. Of the 21 major countries in emerging Asia, there are four which have staged relatively consistent improvements in per capita nominal GNP since 1965. These are Hong Kong, South Korea, Singapore and Thailand. In Papua New Guinea, however, things have gotten worse after having initially improved.

An important issue underlying faster economic growth in emerging economies is more rapid growth in the labour force. In 1990, there were only slightly more people employed or looking for work in Latin America than in North America. That differential will expand dramatically as Latin America will need to create more new jobs between 1990 and 2020 than there are jobs today in the United States (in excess of 121 million). In contrast, the US labour force is expected to increase by only about 20 million.

The comparison with Asia's much larger population is even more daunting. In 1990, for every 100 persons employed or looking for work in the United States, there were 1,128 Asians who were working or seeking employment. That differential will continue to expand as Asian population growth translates into a further 550 million people of employable age between 1990 and 2020. China, India, Pakistan, the Philippines and Vietnam are the primary drivers of labour force growth within Asia. And although China will still have a larger population in the year 2020, India will create more new jobs between 1990 and 2020 (169 million) than will China (144 million). This reflects the much sharper declines in fertility that have occurred in China. Partially as a consequence of this, by the year 2000, there will be more people in China who are over the age of 60 than there will be persons in Japan.

Another labour force related issue is the difference between per capita income and family or household income. Although data on family income (household purchasing power) is unavailable, we can infer that it is likely to be higher or advance faster than per capita income if there are more family members employed. There is a very interesting contrast between Asia and Latin America. Asia has a higher percentage of women in the paid labour force but there has been almost no change in that percentage in the last 22 years. Latin America, on the other hand, has a somewhat smaller percentage of the labour force comprised by women, but nearly every country has seen fairly strong growth in that ratio. We can infer that family or household income is higher in Asia (relative to per capita income) but growing faster in Latin America.

In the US during the 1970s and 1980s, the increase in female participation and consequent increase in household purchasing power was a major factor contributing to the success of brand name pricing and also the outlook for women's apparel. It would not be surprising to see similar trends in other regions where females are entering the labour force in larger numbers. Within Latin America, this would be particularly true for Mexico which has seen the largest increase.

Another important feature of rapid economic growth in emerging economies – Japan in the 1950s and 1960s and the Newly Industrialized Countries (NICs) in the 1970s and 1980s – is the ability to pull workers from low productivity farming into higher productivity manufacturing and services. The edge here goes to Asia which has a much higher proportion of its work force employed in agriculture (51 per cent) than does Latin America (34 per cent). Within Asia, the greatest potential exists in Nepal, Bhutan, Laos and Cambodia which all have more than 70 per cent of their work force still on the farm. The relocation of the work force in these countries will accelerate the demand for equipment, machinery and other capital goods. Within Latin America, the greatest potential exists in Guatemala and Nicaragua, which have rates in the upper 40s.

Although we are optimistic about the future of emerging economies, it should also be pointed out that strong inequalities in the distribution of income are a major factor that inhibits growth potential. Even though there has been some improvement, a large share of Latin America's wealth is still concentrated in a small fraction of the region's population. On average, 54 per cent of the income in Latin America is held by just 20 per cent of the population. Brazil reveals the most inequitable distribution with 67.5 per cent of that country's income in the top 20 per cent of the population and only 7 per cent of the income in the bottom 40 per cent. Unlike Latin America, Asia has a relatively equitable distribution of wealth. On average, 20 per cent of the population holds 44 per cent of the income in Asia and the bottom 40 per cent of the population holds 19 per cent of the income compared to 13 per cent for Latin America. Malaysia has the least favourable distribution by a wide margin. The distribution of wealth also has implications for the types of goods consumed. Economies with relatively uneven distributions of income are more focused on luxury items, which are not necessarily the types of goods that drive an economy over the long run.

The last point is that optimism regarding emerging economies is often tempered by fears of a 'global capital shortage'. Infrastructure and social capital needs are large and seemingly boundless in scope, encompassing such diverse and basic requirements as access to safe water, electricity, roads, airports and communication. In 1990, for example, only 61 per cent of Asian residents and 71 per cent of Latin American residents had access to safe water, a fundamental need for crops and sanitation. Until that reaches 100 per cent, infrastructure demands will remain high. These are just a few examples which should set investors thinking about the impact of inevitable demographic forces on the allocation of their portfolios. ◐

RESOURCE CONSTRAINTS: FACT OR FICTION?

Steven A. Pfeifer

*Steven A. Pfeifer is an Oil Analyst at **C. J. Lawrence/Deutsche Bank Securities Corp.** Formerly associated with **Amoco Corporation** and **Atlantic Richfield Co**, he is a member of the National Association of Petroleum Investment Analysts and the Society of Petroleum Engineers.*

***C. J. Lawrence**, founded in 1864, is a New York based securities firm. It maintains an active energy research team dedicated to identifying the emerging trends that will impact the oil industry.*

When considering an investment strategy for the next decade, a key factor influencing one's investment style is the expected availability and demand for basic resources. The availability or shortage of basic commodity resources can profoundly impact the general macroeconomic environment. A period of limited resources contributes to upward pricing pressures and calls for an investment strategy designed to preserve capital during a period of higher inflation. Conversely, a period of surplus resources contributes to downward pricing pressures and calls for an investment strategy designed to grow capital in a lower inflation environment.

Oil is the most important commodity affecting global economies. A period of abundant oil supplies and low prices in the 1960s contributed to low inflation and strong worldwide economic growth. Constrained production by OPEC in the 1970s led to a fourfold increase in real oil prices from 1973 to

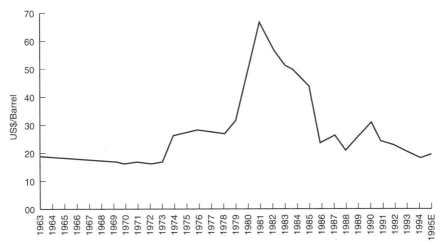

Chart 5.24 Oil Prices in 1995 Dollars

Sources: DRI/McGraw-Hill, C.J. Lawrence/Deutsche Bank Securities Corp estimates

577

1981. The 1970s were characterized by high inflation, stagnant growth, and major economic upheaval as the world economies absorbed the impact of significantly higher oil prices. Major industries such as automobile manufacturers, airlines, and steel companies were forced to adjust to the dramatically changed operating environment. Since 1981, world economies have benefited from the reversal of the oil price shocks of the 1970s. From 1981 to 1994, oil prices declined by over 70 per cent in real terms, contributing to the modest inflation rates enjoyed by most developed OECD economies during the early 1990s.

So much for the past. What does the future hold for oil availability and prices? To answer these questions, we consider two factors:

1 Worldwide oil reserves, and

2 Future oil demand and supplies throughout the world.

Worldwide oil reserves are adequate, but. . .

The world has adequate proven oil reserves through the next decade. Currently discovered oil reserves are nearly one trillion barrels, equal to about 40 years of supply at current demand levels. These numbers, however, fail to tell the whole story, as a few countries control the access to much of the world's oil reserves. Approximately 77 per cent of the world's oil reserves are controlled by OPEC and 65 per cent are controlled by five key Middle Eastern members. Going into the next decade, the question is not whether adequate oil reserves exist, but whether the nations controlling these reserves will develop them rapidly enough. Also factoring into future supplies is the price at which these nations will be willing to increase production to meet rising demand.

Historically, the amount of proven reserves has not been the determining factor influencing oil prices. During the 1970s, oil prices rose dramatically even though the world had 32 years of proven reserves. During the 1980s, prices fell dramatically with roughly the same 32-year supply. Therefore, oil prices must be influenced by other factors.

. . .the excess capacity cushion is shrinking

The balance between world demand and available production capacity is the most critical factor influencing oil prices. Although adequate proven reserves exist, only one-third of these reserves have been brought into production. To meet future world demand, several hundred billion dollars of capital investment will be required over the next ten years to bring new capacity on line. The long two- to three-year lead time required to convert proven reserves into producing oil fields can result in supply/demand imbalances. The reserves may be available, but the capacity may not.

Chart 5.25 Worldwide Excess Oil Capacity as a % of Total Capacity

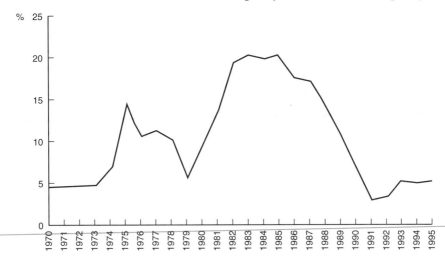

Sources: International Energy Agency, Robert J. Beck's *Oil Industry Outlook, Ninth Edition, 1993–97,* copyright PennWell Books, 1992, C.J. Lawrence/Deutsche Bank Securities Corp estimates

Over the past ten years, world oil demand has been gradually approaching capacity limits. In 1995, world oil production increased to 95 per cent of capacity from 80 per cent in 1985. In examining the tightening oil capacity utilization rate, we divide oil supplies into two sources: OPEC and non-OPEC. Governments and oil companies generally produce non-OPEC oil supplies at their full available capacity (equal to about 98 to 99 per cent of total capacity due to maintenance downtime). OPEC, on the other hand, historically produces at rates below available capacity. In the past, this excess capacity acted as a supply cushion against unanticipated supply outages or demand surges. This capacity cushion has decreased significantly. In 1985, OPEC production equalled only 54 per cent of its available capacity, providing a cushion of 14 million barrels per day. In 1995, OPEC production equals 90 per cent of its available capacity (excluding Iraq), providing a cushion of only 2.9 million barrels per day of excess emergency capacity. (Including Iraq, OPEC production equals 85 per cent of available capacity, providing a supply cushion of 4.4 million barrels per day.)

Most OPEC countries cannot produce significant incremental barrels above current levels. Approximately 85 per cent of OPEC's excess capacity is controlled by only three key Middle Eastern countries: Saudi Arabia, Kuwait, and the United Arab Emirates. The tightening worldwide capacity utilization rate leaves the world more vulnerable to either unexpected supply outages or stronger-than-expected growth in demand.

World oil demand – watch the emerging economies

The components of world oil demand are undergoing a significant shift from the mature to the developing economies. The mature economies drove demand during the 1960s and early 1970s. Abundant oil supplies, low prices, and the population's desire for increased mobility all contributed to the insatiable thirst for oil. From 1960 to 1973, demand in the mature OECD countries grew at an average annual rate of 7.6 per cent. The two oil price shocks of 1973 and 1979 forced the mature OECD countries to restructure their economies and implement conservation programmes to control consumption. As a result of these actions, worldwide consumption remained relatively flat from 1973 to 1985. Following the oil price crash of 1985, demand growth resumed in the OECD economies, but only at an annual rate of 1.5 per cent, or one-fifth of the rate experienced during the 1960s and early 1970s.

During the next ten years, oil demand will be increasingly influenced by the emerging economies. OECD oil demand is expected to continue growing at about 1.0 to 1.5 per cent per year. Demand in the non-OECD economies outside of the former Soviet Union, however, is expected to be more robust. Over the past five years, oil demand in these countries has grown 4 to 5 per cent per year. Rapid growth is expected to continue as the developing countries continue to modernize and industrialize.

China provides an example of the potential impact that the developing economies may have. In 1994, Chinese oil demand per capita equalled only 0.9 barrels per person, well below the annual per capita consumption levels of 23 barrels per person in the US, 16 barrels per person in Japan, and 14 barrels per person in South Korea. If China were to follow the South Korean model and embark on a rapid industrialization programme, the potential impact on oil demand is daunting. China would require an additional 7 million barrels of oil per day at an annual per capita consumption level of only 3 barrels per person. By comparison, OECD Europe consumed 13.6 million barrels per day in 1994. Other developing economies such as India, Indonesia, and Brazil also have low per capita oil consumption levels. The impact of future population growth implies an even greater increase.

Going forward, the share of total world oil demand accounted for by the OECD countries is expected to drop from 58 per cent today to 50 per cent by 2005. In contrast, the share accounted for by the developing countries is forecast to increase from 35 per cent today to 42 per cent in 2005. Total world oil demand growth will accelerate as the rapidly growing economies account for a greater portion of world oil demand. After stagnant demand growth for the past 15 years, the world is entering a period of accelerating demand. Given increasing worldwide demand and a lim-

Total world oil demand growth will accelerate as the rapidly growing economies account for a greater portion of world oil demand.

Chart 5.26 World Oil Demand

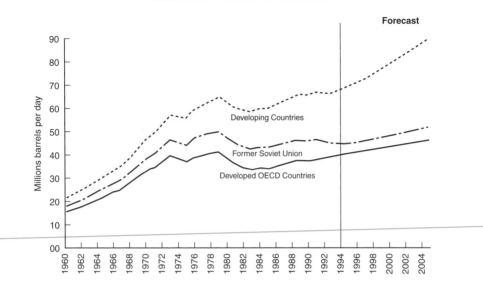

Sources: Energy Information Administration, C.J. Lawrence/Deutsche Bank Securities Corp estimates

ited excess capacity cushion, future oil prices will be determined by whether or not new capacity expansions occur rapidly enough to satisfy rising demand.

Non-OPEC supplies

During the last 20 years, non-OPEC production grew at an average annual rate of 1.9 per cent, increasing from 29 million barrels per day in 1975 to 42 million barrels per day in 1995. Non-OPEC growth was driven by the discovery of major new petroleum provinces in Alaska and the North Sea, which together accounted for over 50 per cent of the increase in non-OPEC production from 1975 to 1995.

Technological advances over the past five years also played an important role in non-OPEC production growth. New subsea well-completion techniques and advanced seismic technology have allowed oil companies to develop smaller oil accumulations that were previously not large enough to economically bring onto production. These new technologies have enabled non-OPEC countries to continue to grow production in mature petroleum provinces.

Going forward, we expect non-OPEC supplies to grow at about 1.5 per cent a year, adding 6 million barrels per day to supply by 2005. Development of new fields in Columbia, Brazil, and Vietnam will contribute. Although new technology will allow the development of smaller oil fields, capacity in the mature provinces is expected to decline. (North American production is already declining, and North Sea production should peak around the year 2000.) Increases in non-OPEC capacity will not be sufficient to meet increasing demand. From 1995 to 2005, non-OPEC capacity growth will only meet approximately one-third of the 19 million barrels per day of anticipated total incremental world oil demand.

OPEC supplies

With 77 per cent of the world's known oil reserves, OPEC countries are expected to provide two-thirds, or 13 million barrels per day, of the incremental world oil supply that will be required by 2005. Growing demand should allow OPEC to increase its share of world production from 40 per cent in 1995 to 47 per cent by 2005. An expanding market share will increase OPEC's influence over pricing.

If OPEC is the key to world oil supplies, then the Middle Eastern members are the key to OPEC. Saudi Arabia, Iraq, Iran, Kuwait, and the United Arab Emirates control 65 per cent of the world's known oil reserves. As the world's lowest cost producers, these countries will dominate future capacity expansions.

The ability and willingness of these five Middle Eastern OPEC members to expand their productive capacities will be an important factor impacting future oil prices. During the next ten years, these countries will have to invest over $5 billion a year to add the incremental capacity required. At the same time, weak oil prices in 1995 are increasing the competition within these countries for the declining oil revenues. Several countries have reduced domestic spending programmes. The Saudis, for example, were forced to cut domestic spending by 20 per cent in 1994 and an additional 6 per cent in 1995. Faced with declining oil revenues, there can be no guarantee that these countries will expand production capacities rapidly enough to meet accelerating world demand.

Conclusions

After falling in real terms for the past 13 years, oil prices are poised to bottom and begin moving higher over the next ten. The world will no longer enjoy the deflationary benefits of a falling real oil price. Accelerating demand, a shrinking excess capacity cushion, and the need for future capacity additions place the world in a delicate supply/demand balance. In a perfect world, with correctly predicted demand growth and reliable supplies, such a delicate balance would not be a cause for concern. In the real world, however, demand cannot be perfectly predicted, and supply outages are all too common given the unstable political regimes in many oil-producing countries. Accelerating demand, and a shrinking capacity cushion, may well lead to increased volatility and upward pressure on oil prices over the next decade.

While a return of the major supply shocks of the 1970s seems unlikely, the world may well experience mini 'price spikes' during the next decade. These spikes may be caused by political instability in producing countries, demand surges as the emerging economies increase oil demand, or insufficient capacity additions by OPEC. Investors should closely follow these developing trends over the next decade for signs of the beginning of these mini 'price spikes'.

Energy companies should benefit from a more hospitable oil price environment. During the past 13 years, these companies have taken aggressive steps to adjust to falling prices. Past cost-cutting efforts, however, were offset by the 70 per cent decline in real oil prices. Future earnings should benefit from the double impact of both rising prices and lower costs. We recommend that investors focus on companies that have attractive growth prospects and are aggressively reducing internal cost structures. Our top picks among the major oil shares are Mobil and Phillips Petroleum. Future earnings at Mobil should benefit from ongoing restructuring and the company's strong position in the rapidly growing Pacific Rim, where it has the greatest refining leverage of the major oils. Phillips will benefit from ongoing cost reduction efforts, as well as a 10 per cent increase in oil production in 1995 and 1996. ♀

GREEN INVESTING

Simon Baker

Jupiter Tyndall Group plc is an international investment management group active in all the main sectors of fund management business including private clients, investment trusts, unit trusts, pension funds and charities. The company is seen as a market leader in the sector of 'green' investment. Its two principal products in this area are the Jupiter International Green Investment Trust plc and the Jupiter Ecology Fund.

Simon Baker is Head of the Green Department, which comprises the pro-active Jupiter Environmental Research Unit, a dedicated team of researchers.

In 1988 the first green unit trust in Europe was launched by Jupiter Tyndall, at the time largely ignored by the investing community and being seen as a fad. It has since been joined by other funds as the subsector has grown, surprising the sceptics by their performance, on average low second quartile. Green and ethical investments are very much in vogue at the moment due to the growing public concern over environmental, health and fair trade/welfare issues; however these concerns may wax and wane as they have done in the past.

The argument against 'green investing' – simply investing in companies that are good for the environment and are addressing various ethical issues – is that the universe of companies is relatively small, thereby making good financial performance more difficult to achieve. While there is an element of truth in this, the restricted universe of companies, which results from the negative and positive criteria adopted by a fund, can actually enhance financial performance. Indeed, ethical unit trusts out-performed both equity growth and equity income funds in the five-year period to August 1994.

The negative criteria mean that investment areas of potentially damaging stocks are avoided. A green fund will not invest in industries such as tobacco, or in companies that do not comply with health and safety regulations, or operate in oppressive regimes. During 1994 alone this meant that green funds avoided shocks delivered to tobacco stocks following US judicial rulings, the ongoing shocks to Turner & Newall from escalating asbestosis provisions and the volatility of the more esoteric emerging markets.

The development of positive criteria has shown that companies which show good environmental performance are generally well managed and proactive, being aware of environmental trends and keeping abreast of the legislation and change. Ecological concern can open up new markets, lead to savings in resource costs and enhance a company's image. The profits record of many of the companies within the green universe are often the envy of their peers.

Other forces in driving green investment forward are legislation, litigation and education. Education from primary schooling upwards is increasingly concentrating on the environment and will enlarge the market place for environmental products or for products produced in a green way. There is a growing number of young people who are environmentally aware, which is reflected in their investment decisions. Investment products will be subjected to similar pressures, both personal investments such as unit trusts and group schemes such as pension funds. Some local authorities are looking to have a proportion of their funds managed in an ethical/environmental manner following representations from employees and pensioners.

Legislation and litigation are linked, the latter often being the implementation of the former. Environmental legislation is a worldwide phenomenon;

> **The development of positive criteria has shown that companies which show good environmental performance are generally well managed and proactive, being aware of environmental trends and keeping abreast of the legislation and change. Ecological concern can open up new markets, lead to savings in resource costs and enhance a company's image. The profits record of many of the companies within the green universe are often the envy of their peers.**

584

emanating in the 1970s and early 1980s in the US and then spreading to other developed countries. For the proactive company this can provide the opportunity of developing largely recession-proof businesses in new areas of operation. For example legislation on vehicle emissions was first passed in the US in 1975, and in Japan in 1976, while in Europe the fitting of catalysts to petrol engines became mandatory in January 1993. Johnson Matthey, the platinum refining group manufactured the first autocatalyst in 1974 and is now the world's largest supplier with capacity to produce 30 million systems, around a third of the world demand. This growth will be repeated as technology, only now in its infancy, becomes essential to comply with future legislation.

An example of litigation affecting an industry was court action taken by environmental groups to safeguard the North American spotted owl, which was threatened with extinction. A protection order was put in place covering 500,000 square miles of forest where tree felling was no longer permitted. As well as, hopefully, ensuring the survival of the species, the order had the effect of rendering two paper and pulp mills uneconomic due to the distance their raw material, trees, would have to be transported. This in turn raised US and European pulp and paper prices helping to make the use of waste paper economic again, and so giving a cost advantage to manufacturers of recycled paper such as David S. Smith, which operates its own waste-paper collection schemes. Future environmental litigation could well have a dramatic impact on the way industries operate.

Since the mid 1980s the EEC has increasingly been at the forefront of environmental legislation, taking up the running from the USA, which, when the Republican party holds the balance of power, as they do again now, tends to put less emphasis on environmental matters. A new EC environmental commissioner has recently been appointed, Ms Bjerregaard from Denmark, who is likely to be more hard-line than the previous commissioner. As far as the UK and Europe are concerned, there are a number of developments of which the following three are potentially very important to the future of environmental investment: the European Environment Agency, the implementation of recommendations made by the UK Royal Commission on Environmental Pollution in their report on *Transport and the Environment* and the probability of the Labour party coming to power in the UK at the next election.

The European Environment Agency (EEA) is the environmental monitoring, verification and compliance arm of the European Commission. In October 1994 it formally opened its office, and is now working on its first programme. The EEA's practical impact will be felt when it starts verifying compliance figures, in particular bathing water and drinking water standards. Currently these are carried out by member states without cross checking.

That the Agency is now up and running, with teeth, should alone increase levels of compliance. This is beginning to be seen in another area – recycling. Most of Europe meets the current target of recycling 15 per cent of the post-use plastic waste as laid down by the EU packaging directive, but not the UK.

The Government has moved to close this gap with clauses in the Environment Agency Bill on producer responsibility and a National Waste Strategy. British Polythene, a major polythene recycler, is the only company in the UK that has the machinery to clean and recycle dirty post-consumer waste, old refuse and silage sacks etc, and will be well placed to benefit from an increase in recycling.

The Royal Commission on Environmental Pollution (RCEP) published its report on transport and the Environment in October 1994, and came up with 110 recommendations the most pertinent of which are as follows:

- to introduce stricter control and increased monitoring of emissions;

- to discourage freight haulage by road;

- to halve the £19 billion road building programme ;

- to encourage the further use of public transport and promote fuel efficiency by increasing petrol costs by 9 per cent per annum;

- to increase resource recovery and recycling of vehicles;

- to encourage the use of urban public transport through methods such as route priority.

It is likely that these suggestions will be implemented in some form over the next few years and examples of companies that would gain include Neotronics and Halma (monitoring devices), Greenway (recycled oil), Casket and Atag (bicycle manufacturers) and the urban bus companies such as GRT, Go-Ahead and Badgerline. There would also be companies that may suffer a loss of business, most notably NFC (road freight) and road constructors such as Tarmac.

One of the main planks of the Labour party's environmental policy is a coordinated transport initiative. Should Labour return to power then the implementation of the RCEP proposals may be given higher priority. Other areas that the Labour party's environmental document In Trust for Tomorrow stresses include:

- renewable energy sources and energy efficiency;

- a clean bill of rights (legally enforceable environmental rights of the individual);

- a commitment to reduce UK carbon dioxide emissions by 20 per cent by 2010 and to phase out ozone depleters by 2000;

- to put protection of the environment at the heart of every government department.

It is likely that a Labour government would more actively support international environmental treaties and EU directives, generally making it tougher for the polluter and opening up new opportunities for best practice and pollution-solving companies.

Finally the significance of technological advances cannot be ignored in terms of rendering one industry obsolete by creating another. The Holy Grail of energy from renewable sources such as wind, bio-fuel 'energy crops', the sun, and hot rocks has moved substantially. Current costs per kwh for these types of energy are roughly 4.3p for wind, 8.7p for crops, 6p for solar and 12p for hot rocks. Traditional fossil-fuel power generation costs around 3.0p/kwh, but this does not include any environmental externalities. Hot rocks are still some way from being commercial, solar is more viable, while wind power in countries with the space and the favourable climatic conditions presents a genuine alternative, sometimes a cheaper one. Mexico, India, Pakistan and parts of the US and the UK are ideal for wind turbines.

The US is often at the forefront of technological improvements and there are two quoted US companies which are involved in the design of turbines and operate wind farms, Kenetech and New World Power. The beauty of the system is that the times of peak demand winter (heating) and summer (air conditioning) can be, for instance in California, the time when the wind blows the strongest. Worldwide the use of wind power is in its infancy and the potential market is enormous.

Worldwide the use of wind power is in its infancy and the potential market is enormous.

Other areas where technological advances are making radical alternatives feasible include the development of the lithium battery, which has reduced battery weight by a third – crucial to the development of the electric car. Video telecommunication and the global information superhighway have the potential to change the way business and personal communication is carried out.

These significant trends can only become more influential over the next decade, having a positive effect on companies operating in relevant areas. Investors looking ahead to the next millenium would be foolish not to pay heed to the growing impact of green investing.

PART

6

MANAGING
YOUR OWN
PORTFOLIO

Where to Find Useful and Usable Information

What the Papers Say
Investment Newsletters: An Objective View
Investment Newsletters: A Personal View
Databases

WHAT THE PAPERS SAY

James Morton

James is the Editor of The Global Guide to Investing *and as Director of* **Chelverton Investment Management** *manages the* **Chelverton Fund**, *a specialist investment fund, which invests in the micro cap sector of the stock market. He constantly trawls national and local newspapers in the UK and US as well as the financial press from around the world in pursuit of an information edge.*

The maxim 'you get what you pay for' does not necessarily apply to investment advice. A lot of the very best investment information is free or, at least, extremely cheap. Newspapers are a classic case in point. Most investors read a number of newspapers. Skip over the sections on political, economic and social change, all of which are essential ingredients to sound management of an investment portfolio. The intelligent investor will require two skills to avoid being overwhelmed by the deluge of data available:

- An ability to select the best sources.

- A filter to focus on relevant information only.

The best sources will vary, depending on the investor's area of interest. Two publications which every serious investor should read regularly, wherever they are:

- *The Financial Times*. I hardly need say that the **FT**, without a shadow of a doubt, maintains its position as the best business publication in the world today. The weekend edition is required reading, even for people who only dabble in investing.

- *The Wall Street Journal*. Try to get the US edition. Both the European and Asian editions mix more local news with a US hard core and end up falling between two stools.

591

After that, each country differs in the quantity and quality of business coverage. To some extent that variance is a statement about their relative cultural priorities. Needless to say, there is more complete reporting, and most variety, in the US and, within the US, in New York. *The New York Times* has an excellent business section. *The Investor's Business Daily* could only exist in the US, and is rather data-heavy. It has the virtue of an element of unique presentation in profiling accumulation/distribution and relative strength ranking on stocks which is not available anywhere else. Once outside New York, the quality of coverage deteriorates. By the time you reach Memphis, you wonder whether anyone cares.

The British seem to feel that business reading is best left for weekends. The daily newspapers report the main events during the week, if without much enthusiasm, but on Sunday no serious paper is without one, if not two, sections on business and finance. The average investor will find a wealth of information, but beware!

The propensity of these papers to give tips is somewhat suspect and subject to interesting coincidences. What should the reader conclude, when no less than three of the top papers all recommended the same relatively unknown stock on one Sunday in November 1994? Is this company the hottest thing since Nintendo, or should one hold fast to the contrarian strategy and avoid it like the plague? Or how to reconcile, on the same Sunday, the urgings of one columnist to buy a certain stock which is being trashed in the columns of a competing paper as a strong sell?

how to reconcile, on the same Sunday, the urgings of one columnist to buy a certain stock which is being trashed in the columns of a competing paper as a strong sell?

I have the greatest respect for Quentin Lumsden, in the *Independent on Sunday*. His recommendations reflect sound fundamental research. He has a real eye for finding undervalued stocks. A good review from him can move a stock price. So, too, can comment from Kevin Goldstein-Jackson; but perhaps the best advice is to treat all tips with caution and concentrate on applying the analytical approaches recommended in the *The Global Guide to Investing*.

Interestingly, *The Mail on Sunday* profiled the 1994 tipsters' progress. Only three publications beat shares picked by the Random Walk Method. *The Independent* came top, with *The Mail* second and *The Investor's Chronicle* third.

Which leads nicely to the next topic – magazines. There are two publications which are more or less required reading: The *Investor's Chronicle* in the UK is crisp, clean and easy to digest. Its coverage of public companies in the UK is comprehensive. If you have the slightest interest in the UK stock market, you should subscribe to *The Investor's Chronicle*. In the US, *Barron's* contains more information than anyone could ever conceivably want, but almost any financial data on US markets is likely to be there, somewhere, provided you can find it. Leaving the overload on one side for a moment, *Barron's* is worthwhile.

Don't forget, advice to buy and sell specific companies is intended to provoke ideas for evaluation, not generate instant action. When a fund manager recommends a stock in the press, it is often because he or she already has a large position. That said, these two publications offer sound, practical investment advice and a wealth of important information.

Elsewhere in the world the availability and quality of business coverage is patchy. A list, by no means comprehensive, of selected sources for global investors follows above.

Leading Business Newspapers and Periodicals of the World (excluding USA & UK)

Publication	Country	Publication	Country
Affarsvarlden	Sweden	The Financial Mail	South Africa
The Age	Australia	The Financial Post	Canada
L'Agefi	Switzerland	Gazeta Mercantil	Brazil
Asian Age	India	German Brief	Germany
Asian Business	Japan	Handelsblatt	Germany
Australian Financial Review	Australia	The Herald	New Zealand
Bangkok Post	Thailand	The Indonesian Times	Indonesia
Börsen Kurier	Austria	The Japan Economic Journal	Japan
Börsenzeitung	Germany	Jeune Afrique Economie	Cameroon
Blick durch die Wirtschaft	Germany	Kauppalehti	Finland
Business Day	The Philippines	Korea News Review	South Korea
Business Line	India	Luxemburger Wort	Luxemburg
Business Standard	India	Made in Turkey	Turkey
The Business Times	Singapore	Malaysian Business	Malaysia
O Comercio do Porto	Portugal	Milano Finanza	Italy
China Post	Taiwan	Mondo Economico	Italy
Corriere della Sera	Italy	National Business Review	New Zealand
Dagens Naeringsliv	Norway	Neue Zürcher Zeitung	Switzerland
Dagens Industri	Sweden	La Nouvelle Marche	Togo
Diario Economico	Portugal	Nikkei Financial Daily	Japan
The Dominion	New Zealand	Die Presse	Austria
Far Eastern Economic Review	Hong Kong	Il Sole 24 Ore	Italy
L'Echo de la Bourse	Belgium	South China Morning Post	Hong Kong
Les Echos	France	The Straits Times	Singapore
Economische Dagblad	The Netherlands	Sydney Morning Herald	Australia
Ephimeris Diakirixeon	Greece	Ticaret	Turkey
Erhverus-Bladet	Denmark	Toronto Stock Exchange Daily Record	Canada
De Financieele Ekonomische Tijd	Belgium	Trends - Tendances	Belgium
Het Financieele Dagblad	The Netherlands	Weiner Zeitung	Austria
El Financiero	Mexico	Wirtschaftswoche	Germany

INVESTMENT NEWSLETTERS: AN OBJECTIVE VIEW

Mark Hulbert

Mark Hulbert is Editor of the Alexandria, Virginia, based **Hulbert Financial Digest (HFD)**, *the only objective source for the performance of investment advisory newsletters. Mr. Hulbert has been tracking newsletter performance since 1980. As of 1995, about 170 different newsletters (and their nearly 500 recommended portfolios) were being monitored.*

Mr Hulbert is a columnist for **Forbes** *magazine, and is on the editorial board of the* **American Association of Individual Investors.** *He is a regular commentator on* **CNBC** *television, and is frequently quoted in the* **Wall Street** Journal, **Barron's** *and* **Money magazine.**

Investment newsletters occupy a unique and valuable niche within the financial advisory industry. They often are small operations centred on one individual: their editor-advisor. Their primary distinguishing characteristic is agility in responding to market trends.

This is why investment newsletters stand out from Wall Street. The major Wall Street institutions are plagued by huge overheads, decision by committee, and a herd instinct. As legendary investor Peter Lynch put it in his best-seller *One Up On Wall Street*, 'Under the current system, a stock isn't truly attractive [to an institutional investor] until a number of large institutions have recognized its suitability and an equal number of respected Wall Street analysts have put it on the recommended list. With so many people waiting for others to make the first move, it's amazing that anything gets bought.' He concludes: 'If you invest like an institution, you are doomed to perform like one.'

Markets are quick to discount – and thus eliminate – strategies that otherwise would continue to beat market. It's rare for an investment approach to work forever. Typically, a promising strategy works for a while; until everyone hears about it, jumps on the bandwagon, and it stops working. More often than not, as investors climb off, they find that it was an investment newsletter that had been there first.

This doesn't mean that all investment newsletters beat the market. As is also true of mutual funds and professional money managers, most don't. But we all

> **Typically, a promising strategy works for a while; until everyone hears about it, jumps on the bandwagon, and it stops working. More often than not, as investors climb off, they find that it was an investment newsletter that had been there first.**

594

are far better off for their trying, since in the process we discover promising new strategies that otherwise would have gone unnoticed. 'Investment letters are the guerrilla troops of the financial world,' writes Forbes' senior editor Peter Brimelow in his classic work on the investment letter industry, *Wall Street Gurus*. 'By following them, and halting if they terminate in a smoking crater, you can see what techniques work.'

How can we know which techniques actually are working, and which terminate in a smoking crater (as opposed to what the newsletters' advertisers want us to believe)? That's the purpose of my monthly publication *The Hulbert Financial Digest (HFD)*. In it, I report how much you would have made or lost had you actually followed their recommendations. To this end, the *HFD* constructs model portfolios according to the advice contained in those letters – taking into account mail delays, commissions, transaction costs, and dividends.

More Than One Road To Riches

Only a minority of newsletters beat the market. Indeed, my data suggest that only about 20 per cent are able to do so over time. So the first step towards choosing an adviser is an appreciation of how stiff a competitor the market really is. While choosing on the basis of past performance can increase your odds of beating the market, it can't guarantee that you will do so.

The next step is to realize that there's more than one road to riches. Take a look at the accompanying table, which includes all of the investment newsletters I track that beat the Wilshire 5000 index over the five years (on both an unadjusted and a risk-adjusted basis) through 28 February, 1995. (The Wilshire 5000, which is based on every publicly traded stock within the US, and includes reinvested dividends, gained 72.2 per cent over this period). You'll notice that the theoretical foundations of these newsletters are quite contradictory.

Both the relative strength and relative value approaches have beaten the market. The relative strength approach assumes that a stock that is exhibiting above-average strength will continue to do so; therefore stocks are considered to have potential if their prices are rising faster than the market. Relative value approaches, on the other hand, focus on stocks that are significantly out of favour with other investors; stocks with potential within this category usually have prices that are relatively low. In short, relative value approaches recommend 'buying low, selling high,' while relative strength approaches advises 'buying high, selling higher.'

Stock screening services use computers to apply filter after filter to an entire universe of securities to construct a small subset that satisfies a whole host of different criteria. Mutual fund services focus their recommendations entirely on mutual funds.

The newsletters in the first three categories primarily recommend securities that trade within the US While the mutual funds recommended by the services in the final category also trade in the US, many recommended funds invest primarily in non-US securities.

Top Relative Strength Services

	Newsletter	5-Year Gain
1	OTC Insight	+218.1%
2	The Oberweis Report	+192.4%
3	MPT Review	+141.3%
4	The Chartist	+126.4%

Top Relative Value Services

	Newsletter	5-Year Gain
1	The Turnaround Letter	+179.0%
2	New Issues	+162.6%
3	BI Research	+120.8%
4	F.X.C. Investors	+83.5%
5	Value Line Convertibles	+83.3%
6	Investment Quality Trends	+74.2%

Top Stock Screening Services

	Newsletter	5-Year Gain
1	Value Line Investment Survey	+102.6%

Top Mutual Fund Services

	Newsletter	5-Year Gain
1	Timer Digest	+163.5%
2	Stockmarket Cycles	+145.9%
3	Fundline	+122.3%
4	Fidelity Monitor	+117.1%
5	The Scott Letter	+98.3%
6	Prof. Timing Service	+87.4%
7	Mutual Fund Forecaster	+85.6%
8	Chartist Mutual Fund Timer	+79.5%
9	No-Load Fund Investor	+76.1%

The initial reaction of many investors to this plurality is discouragement. They don't understand why there isn't a single answer to the question, 'What should I do with my portfolio?' In fact, however, the existence of more than one road to riches is good news. After all, if there were only one road, pretty soon everyone would be travelling on it and it would stop being a good path to follow.

Don't Follow a 'Hot Hands' Strategy

This discussion leads to yet another lesson that needs to be drawn. You probably shouldn't be jumping very frequently from one investment newsletter to another. Once you choose a letter to follow, you must be prepared to give it time in which to show its stuff.

Why not get rid of a letter as soon as it starts underperforming? Because not all market-beating approaches work equally well at each stage of the market cycle. Relative strength approaches tend to work best during the latter stages of a bull market, for example, but also can be among the biggest losers during a bear market. Relative value approaches, in contrast, tend to lag during the latter stages of a bull market.

However, and this is crucial: both approaches have more or less equal probability of making money over the long term. Thus, if you jumped back and forth between these types of services according to which currently was hot (a so-called 'hot hands' strategy), you wouldn't necessarily make more over the long term. To be sure, you might do better, if you expertly time your switches between various newsletters. By the same token, however, you also might end up doing much worse, if you get on board each newsletter just as its approach loses its hot hand.

Thus, a 'hot hands' strategy is a risky gamble: you might do better, but you may also end up doing worse. In either case, however, you most definitely can count on this strategy incurring more transaction costs and brokerage commissions along the way.

When are you justified in jumping ship to another newsletter? Only in the event you wouldn't choose your original letter if you were starting out all over again. You shouldn't drop a newsletter even in the unfortunate event it underperforms the market over the next three months or even a year. Only if its trailing five-year performance drops below the market's would you be justified in doing so.

You need to be prepared to follow a letter for several years. If picking an investment newsletter is not exactly the same as a marriage for life, it's closer to that than it is to the one-night stand which is how many investors treat their relationship with an adviser. That is why you need to choose an investment newsletter with such care. ♀

Source of Ratings: Hulbert Financial Digest, Alexandria, Virginia

You need to be prepared to follow a letter for several years. If picking an investment newsletter is not exactly the same as a marriage for life, it's closer to that than it is to the one-night stand

INVESTMENT NEWSLETTERS:
A PERSONAL VIEW

James Morton

James is the Editor of The Global Guide to Investing, *also manages the* **Chelverton Fund** *a specialist investment fund. which invests in the micro cap sector of the stock market. He makes extensive use of newsletters to find unusual and interesting ideas for further analysis. Over the last ten years he has read and subscribed to well over 100 newsletters in the US, UK and Asia.*

There is a newsletter for every occasion and every investment style. No-one has ever tabulated precisely how many are out there. In the US, estimates range upward from about 800 to several thousand. In the UK, the number is significantly smaller with, pehaps, only 20 of substance. In part, that is due to the Sunday newspapers and, in part, to a regulatory environment which assumes anyone who wants to start a financial newsletter is a criminal.

The quality of these letters is extremely varied. They range from tip sheets of the most pernicious variety, where speculators use literary licence to ramp their own investments and push worthless stock onto gullible punters, to extremely well written, carefully researched and insightful publications.

In the US annual subscription rates can vary from as little as $24 up to a serious chunk of change, $300–400, and even more for professional publications. A good place to start would be T*he Hulbert Financial Digest.* Hulbert has the virtue of highlighting which newsletters have made money for subsribers. Ignore carefully scripted claims and examine the performance data. Critics claim the calculations have not always been directly comparable across publications. Don't let that put you off. Nobody else produces anything else as useful for determining how to spend money allocated to purchasing investment advice.

Remember the great attraction of newsletters is that you should be buying ideas, data, analysis and a point of view which is not going to duplicate regular sources. If you can find similar stories in *The Wall Street Journal*, look elswhere. The whole point is to find information which others may not have, and learn about opportunities both to sell and buy stocks before the mainstream investment community. There are three main types of newsletter which can be useful.

Company Specific/Tip Sheet

These letters provide recommendations on specific stocks. Most have a fairly bad record. Dick Davis is a long time survivor in an industry notorious for high turnover. His *Digest* is a synthesis of the best of the rest and a good value. Geraldine Weiss has a letter which will appeal to the conservative investor seeking superior income. Carlton Lutts writes for investors who like momentum. If you have a big budget, buy the *Outstanding Investor Digest* and the *Red Chip Review*.

In the category of specialized newsletter, The Thomas Herzfeld letter on closed-end funds is the most comprehensive publication covering that sector, and provides essential reading for anyone who wishes to invest in countries around the world where dealing in single stocks can be difficult for the individual.

I have personally purchased and reviewed over 100 newsletters during the last ten years. Very few actually made me money. The one I would point to unreservedly as having a consistently superior track record is the *Fledging Newsletter*. Bob Scheuermann is a stock picker par excellence who ferrets out companies that are not easy to find and nobody else has heard of. And he understands the businesses he writes about. But isn't that exactly what you are paying for? Most of our global gurus make this point. You should be buying stocks before the thundering herd spots them.

Market Related

These newsletters cover the markets themselves and often involve sophisticated technical analysis. Hulbert does not have a lot of kind words for the record of market timers, but there are exceptions. Several of the writers featured in *The Global Guide to Investing* have demonstrated an ability to understand markets and market movements over a prolonged period of time – which is why I invited them to contribute.

Marty Zweig features on any short list at the pinnacle of this group. James Stack of InvesTech is one of the most respected analysts in the financial community, even though he has opted out of Wall Street and writes from the less frenetic locale of Montana. Robert Prechter, at the *Elliott Wave Theorist*, is widely considered to have unique insights into long-term trends, and Dan Sullivan of *The Chartist* has a consistently good track record.

Political/Socio-economic

In many ways, this is the most interesting category. Rather than focusing on specific investment advice, these newsletters offer alternative views and analysis of what is going on in the world and how events may shape markets. Some are plain 'wacky'; others are well informed, sometimes incredibly so. They often lead the mainstream media by a matter of months, if not years.

My favourite is the *Kent Davis Economic – Political Review*, which has a commonsensical way of looking at the world that is notably lacking in most newspapers. I also enjoy *Strategic Investments*, not for its investment advice, but for its acute political commentary and proprietary information. Now that William Colbey, ex CIA Director, has joined the staff, one wonders exactly who *SI's* sources are! Dr Marc Faber sometimes guest writes for *SI* and I highly recommend his own letter, which is a hybrid.

In the UK pickings are pretty slim. As a fund manager, I have subscribed to everything that comes my way for one year, but have only found three worthy of renewal. Overall, the quality of analysis leaves a lot to be desired. The most interesting, which has the courage to monitor its own performance, is *Techinvest*. Conor McCarthy, an electrical engineer by background, specializes in technology stocks, broadly defined. With a career including Plessey, Northern Telecom and AT&T. He has a broad understanding of the products, services and dynamics of the companies *Techinvest* follows. His record, which of late has been nothing short of spectacular, speaks for itself. The long-term survivor *Penny Share Focus* survives for good reason. Its columns contain more ideas per square inch than any of its competitors. The analysis is incisive and *PSF* features shares neglected by the main stream community. Cheap at twice the price. I also subscribe to *Sharewatch,* which occasionally spots value before the crowd.

In the specialized sector, Andrew McHattie writes the *Warrants Alert*, which provides the best coverage of that asset category. One other publication worth highlighting is *The Inside Track*. I endorse the commentary on pages 259–263. Directors' dealings are an excellent indicator of a company's prospects and of its relative future share price performance. You can find much of this information in your Saturday *Financial Times* but, for the serious investor, *The Inside Track* is an indispensable tool. Finally, one should not forget *Private Eye*. When not pre-occupied in conducting a vendetta, the *Eye* digs up dirt on companies or business personalities long before it leaks out of the City. The most unlikely revelations have a habit of turning out to be true. While not a source for making money, it can help an investor avoid pitfalls and possible losses.

Never forget: advice is no substitute for analysis. The one thing any investor should never do is rush out and act on newsletter recommendations without further research. As one component in a balanced approach to investment, the right newsletter can play a valuable role. None should be viewed as a Bible. Following with blind faith may turn into an expensive exercise. Garnished, however, with a dollop of scepticism the better letters can help you increase you investment returns. ♇

DATABASES

Jeremy Attard-Manché

*Jeremy Attard-Manché is the Managing Director of the UK and European sales desk at **Smith New Court**, New York, broking UK and European equities to US institutions. Previously he worked with **James Capel** in London and New York.*

Smith New Court is an independent equity securities house with large offices in New York, London, Tokyo, Hong Kong and Singapore, and representative offices in ten emerging market countries. Smith New Court employs around 170 equity analysts covering 2000 companies worldwide.

The purpose of this section is to identify and comment on the main electronic datafeeds that exist on the market which are helpful when covering equity markets. Clearly there are many on-line services that can be used, and we shall consider the most popular ones currently available, namely:

- ADP
- Reuters
- Bridge
- Bloomberg.

The four main uses for which we tend to rely upon these systems are:

- News service and market reports
- Price quotations
- Graphical display
- Stock price analysis.

We shall assume that all the services, except Bloomberg, support workstations that use DOS and Windows.

ADP

Automated Data Processing recently took over Quotron outside North America and they claim to be the most widely used advanced information system in the US financial community. Their UK oriented products are called Global Partner or QST, and are PC windows-based products that give access to price, news, research and graphics. QST is only available for the London Stock Exchange SEAQ (Stock Exchange Automated Quotation System) and SEAQ International. We find it particularly useful in being able to distribute Smith New Court house research to our overseas offices, and to selected clients. We find the graphics useful where the system has a five-year price history record.

The service runs under Windows. The news service comes from Extel and Agence France Presse and gives a good run-down on European companies.

Reuters

This service is very complete and is the dominant player in Europe and outside North America. It allows the user to retrieve price quotations on stocks and historic news and has good graphics and historic analysis capability. All stocks are identified by Reuter Instrument codes (RICS) and there is an on-line look-up directory for such codes.

One of the biggest advantages is that, unlike Bloomberg, the screen can be divided into smaller windows, thus enabling the user to view several pieces of information simultaneously and can be linked to an Excel spreadsheet. We often divide a screen so that one window gives a market report, another shows the biggest movers on the day by volume and by value, another gives specific stock price movements on that day, and another gives up-to-date news on all equity markets. In this way, we are able to monitor market movements without changing the screen.

Reuters uses a mouse for windows which makes it fast and efficient. If there is an asterisk next to the price or price change, you can view the recent news story by double clicking on it. Another advantage to Reuters is the ability to pop-up several window on one screen. Screen layouts created by users can be saved and retrieved by the click of the mouse.

Reuters stores news items for one year and gives historic earnings numbers on companies. This can be useful for a quick snapshot of the past earnings of the company. The Reuters Securities 2000 service provides constant up-to-date information on equities and equity derivatives and is simple to use - RIC code followed by F9. Similarly, by using the symbol E F9, all stories with any relevance to the equity market will be shown.

The graphic ability is strong and can be easily manipulated, as can the ability to create portfolios of up to 100 companies on one screen. The graphs can show a five-year trend including moving averages and volume charts. Another interesting feature is the ability to look at a stock's trade history, including price, volume, time of trade and best bid and offer at time of execution.

Reuters also gives you the ability to run software packages such as Excel. Using a spreadsheet, one can create and monitor a custom-built portfolio which is automatically updated in terms of price and news. Reuters have a cheaper, UK-only service called Equity Focus which provides all of the above with specific focus on the UK market. All of this data is available on the LAN networked Reuters terminal and over their digital data distribution platform.

Bridge

Although we do not tend to use this service heavily, those that are fans claim that it has superior charting capabilities. It does have the ability to operate up to 25 windows simultaneously. As with most of the competing services, Bridge has direct feeds to the various European exchanges. Thus obtaining price quotations is broadly similar, with a small variance in speed of delivery. Bridge also takes information from all the authorized news services, including Dow Jones News, Business Wire, Extel and Agence France Extel.

We find it useful to take advantage of some of the 100 different technical indicators, including money flow, overbought/oversold oscillators, momentum indicator; all using the database, which has a ten-year price and volume record. There is a five-year access to earnings and the ability to access brokers research from Institutional Brokers' Estimate System.

In short, as a historical database, this service is good, with its main strength being chart related. The Bridge service runs on LAN PCs under Novell.

Bloomberg

This service is becoming increasingly popular. We find that it is exceptional in providing key fundamentals, price action, news and research on over 6,000 European companies. As a research tool, Bloomberg is very strong in its ability to provide most companies we follow with a 20-page report, including EPS, P/E, beta, market cap, forecasts for profit and dividend record. and full capital structure. In many cases historical data is available for 15 years.

The news service is fast and very focused if you need specific company news. There is also an interesting Bloomberg audio feature which allows you to listen to Bloomberg news. One of the potential problems is that Bloomberg demands its own hardware and relies upon video information rather than the more common digital feed. As such, the service cannot run on a PC nor, indeed, co-exist with other Windows PC applications. Bloomberg data cannot be loaded onto an Excel spreadsheet, and they normally insist that special cabling be laid.

Nevertheless, the information is fast and concise and the ability to study a company's fundamentals in detail make this service superior, in many respects, to its competitors.

Comment from the Editor

The growing versatility of computers, with higher power, greater memory and faster modems, means that options to access information have never been greater than they are today. The difficult decision is making the trade-off between data quality and cost. Most of the databases above are essential tools of investing for professionals dealing in equities and you will find them in many financial houses in all major financial centres. The need of the individual investor, unless a very active trader with an extremely large personal portfolio, probably runs to something less complete and less expensive.

In the US, the American Association of Individual Investors, based in Chicago, has a spectacular service based on CD ROM or disk, which provides detailed five-year financial information on some 6,000 quoted companies, updated quarterly. At a price, which varies depending upon what sort of membership you have, but can be as little as $79, this is one of the great bargains of the investment age. If you do not wish to join AAII although, for the life of me, I cannot imagine why an investor would not do that, Value Line offers a more detailed database with forecasts and a respected rating system for a reasonable price; but coverage is only about 2,000 companies. This will be sufficient for someone who prefers to stay relatively in the mainstream, but will not work for more adventurous investors. MorningStar, best known for its excellent coverage of mutual funds, has a US equities service which has 200 statistics on a full 6,000 companies for $55.

For more broadly based news and information the individual investor may wish to start with CompuServe, which contains the greatest wealth of information and is cheap – an unbeatable combination. In the US, Prodigy is the in place to be if you want to see the investment frontier, which is the future - good profiles on little known companies. America Online is perhaps the most user-friendly, and has an easy interface with the Internet. S&P Xtra does the trick for prices and can be delivered over cable TV, if desired.

My personal favourite for corporate information gathering and analysis is Investex, which is often available in public libraries, although the wait in New York can sometimes run to be several hours for a half-hour slot. Disclosure remains a reliable standby. The new Wall Street Analysts 2-CD for Windows looks to be an offer hard to refuse at $49.95. Another database service deserving serious consideration is Lotus One Source.

For fixed income fans, nothing can compare with Telerate but, again, cost has to be factored in. How many individuals really can, or should, dig that deep? It is as hard to conceive that any private investor needs this quality of data as it is difficult to imagine that any professional trader would not need it. One of the most complete databases covering most sectors of the US domestic and international bond market can be accessed in a variety of media through Interactive Data Corp.

In the UK, the PC Sharewatch package, in my view the best bargain around, covers 2,000 public companies, which is the better part of the quoted universe. There is no question that Extel is a superior service and its CD ROM format extremely user friendly, but the cost differential is significant and only someone with a very large portfolio can justify the expenditure. The Extel handbook series is available on disk and is probably sufficient. The Hambro Company Guide, which comes on disk, can also be a good alternative to PC Sharewatch. Many other traditional text based services such as the Estimate Directory also offer PC format options. The most effective way to access price data is changing almost monthly. As of September 1995 the new service from Electronic Share Information should be the best bet for private investors provided the OFT can persuade the Stock Exchange to recant its recent role as King Canute in pulling the plug on this important new service. ♀

HOW TO READ THE COMPANY REPORT
Terry Smith

Terry Smith is the author of Accounting for Growth, *the best selling book on how to detect creative accounting. He is also a Partner in stockbrokers* **Collins Stewart & Co**, *a research boutique which specializes in quantitative techniques of assessing company strength and weakness and management strategies, and in valuing shares. He is a regular contributor to* Management Today, *and is currently working on his next book on* Corporate Pathology.

Using the Accounts Can Give You the Edge

For me, successful investment is about minimizing mistakes. Investing in a company whose shares underperform disastrously, or worse, which goes bust, not only depletes the investor's capital, but it also often has a psychological effect. The hapless investor is paralysed as he watches the share price descend, waiting for a rally into which to sell, and which frequently never comes, because he is not alone in wanting to sell. Even if the shares eventually recover, capital which could have been deployed into more profitable opportunities has been tied up.

But how can these losers be avoided? If you listen to some investors, you would believe that they were unavoidable, like some financial Act of God. But the main disasters of recent years – British & Commonwealth, Polly Peck, Queens Moat, Maxwell, Tiphook, Trafalgar House – could all have been avoided simply by analysing the company using its published accounts.

It is also a fallacy to believe that professional analysts have the edge over private investors in this respect. How many of them spotted the corporate disasters of the past few years? Not many. There are libraries full of bullish circulars on companies which are now bust. Full-time analysts suffer from a number of handicaps but, most importantly, their access to the companies' management, which is often seen as an advantage, can, in fact, be a handicap. They are often bamboozled by information which is supplied by the company, and ignore the more objective information which is under their nose in the published accounts.

What to Look for in a Set of Accounts

No work of this length can do full justice to this subject. All I can hope, and intend, to do is to enthuse the reader to further study by giving some hints on how to conduct an appraisal of a company from its annual report.

1 Take Little Notice of the 'Blurb'

Although you should read the Chairman's Statement and review of operations, use them only to gain a general background on what the company does and its strategy. Be careful not to get sucked into believing the purple prose on how it is performing. Very few, if any, managements announce that the company is doing badly and/or that they are to blame, although it is interesting how often the company is doing badly and their predecessors are to blame! The whole point about having accounts is that they supply a more objective numerical analysis of the situation, rather than relying upon wordy platitudes.

2 Multivariate Analysis

All that this means is there is no single number in a set of accounts which will tell you whether the company is (a) doing well or badly, and (b) can help you value the shares.

there is no single number in a set of accounts which will tell you whether the company is (a) doing well or badly, and (b) can help you value the shares.

In recent years, the London market has veered towards heavy reliance upon earnings per share (EPS) as the main measure of performance, and the Price/Earnings multiple (P/E) as the resultant measure of value, with disastrous consequences, since there has been endless scope for companies to 'fix' the earnings figure under the UK's lax accounting regime. But this was not the only problem with fixing upon this single number as a measure of corporate performance. Objective analysis of the extent to which a company's P/E can be used to predict the share value if you can forecast the EPS growth shows that this indicator has very poor predictive qualities:

Chart 6.1 Accounting Measures Fail

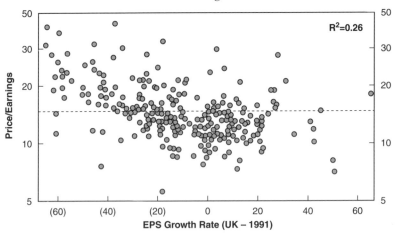

Source: Collins Stewart & Co.

The chart of EPS and P/E for the London equity market shows no meaningful correlation. Even if you could accurately predict a company's earnings growth, this is of little help in predicting the share price through the mechanism of the P/E. Another way of looking at this is to note that, on the chart, there are companies which have the same EPS growth but widely differing P/Es.

The reason for using several numbers or variables from the accounts is that it is easy for a company to improve a single number, such as EPS or gearing, if management realizes that the market is mainly judging it on that ratio, but impossible to avoid showing a true picture if a battery of numerical tests are applied. Window dressing one number will usually cause problems elsewhere.

For example, if sales are inflated and stocks are reduced by shipping goods to customers just before the company's year end, the result will be an inexorable rise in debtors, since the goods will not have been paid for. This was one of the techniques used by Fisons before its fall from grace, and could be detected by a simple calculation comparing year end debtors as a percentage of sales over the years. A continuously rising percentage would indicate that more and more of Fisons' output was not paid for at each balance sheet date. As with all of these calculations, it would have posed a question, and the astute investor would not invest until such a query had been satisfactorily resolved.

3 So Which Numbers Should I Use from the Accounts?

Unsurprisingly, there is no finite set of correct items, but some of the common items which I look at are:

Margins

What are the company's profit margins? This is commonly calculated by dividing operating profit by sales turnover. Once a number has been obtained, it can be compared with the company's peers and its own historic experience. Is the company getting better margins than its peer group and, if so, how? Is it demonstrably better in the product it makes, in cost control, or some other factor? If its margins are worse, are they capable of improvement? If the margins are looked at over time, you get a feel

If margins are as high as they have ever been, be wary of buying the shares, as earnings may be close to a cyclical peak.

for where the company is in relation to the economic cycle as it affects that industry. If margins are as high as they have ever been, be wary of buying the shares, as earnings may be close to a cyclical peak.

607

Cash Flow

Cash is king! We can argue about whether the best measure of company performance is EPS growth or return on equity for an age without reaching a conclusion. Even if we could agree which measure is best, we are still faced with many problems of comparability and the ability of companies to achieve cosmetic improvements. After all, for any measure based upon profits, it is wise to recall the words of the auditors' certificate, namely that profits represent a 'true and fair view'. When the word 'view' is used in common parlance, we are not confused about what it means: the calculation of profits incorporates a number of subjective judgements.

The same is not true of cash. Cash is a fact, and efforts to measure cash flow, in the UK, have been enhanced considerably in recent years by the introduction of cash flow statements by Financial Reporting Standard (FRS) 1. But even when we have a cash flow number provided, it is important to know what to do with it. Too often analysts say they like a company because it is 'cash generative'. But how much cash is it really generating, and relative to what?

There are several numbers for cash flow in the accounts post FRS 1. The one I like to look at is the cash flow after the company has paid for its capital expenditure, or 'fixed assets acquired', as it is usually termed. Despite the protestations of some analysts that cash flow before capital expenditure is the free cash flow which is available to the company, I take the view that very little capital expenditure is truly discretionary. The cash flow is also best looked at before the items, acquisitions, disposals and capital raising. What we are looking for is the ongoing, regular cash the company is generating from operations after allowing for the renewal of its plant and equipment.

Once a cash flow number has been obtained, it can be used in many ways. The cash cover for interest payments can be calculated in order to see how much margin for error the company has to service its borrowings. The cash flow figure can also be compared. Look at the number for retained profits. Is the company regularly making more or less, or roughly the same, as its profits in cash? This gives a feel for whether the profits are 'real'. Compare it with the amount invested in the company by shareholders, which brings us into the concept of returns.

Returns vs Growth

Another problem with the concept of EPS growth as a measure of corporate performance is that it ignores the investment which has been necessary in order to create those earnings.

As an analogy, imagine that you were about to invest some money in a building society account. In order to find the best investment, you might ask several societies for their rates. Would you invest in the one which said it would increase its rates at 20 per cent per annum for the next two years and shun the one which would not give any increase? If so, you could be making a mistake if the society with the promised 20 per cent increase has a starting rate of 1 per cent versus the market rate of 7 per cent being offered by the society with no increase. But surely you would not make such a basic error. You would ask the supplementary question about the rate of return. Perhaps so, but this is the same error which analysts and investors regularly make when they invest in the company with the lowest P/E relative to its EPS growth.

There are a number of possible measures of return which could be used. Probably the simplest is Return on Equity, or ROE. This compares the profit, net or pre-tax, with the shareholders' funds. There are more sophisticated measures. ROCE or Return on Capital Employed takes profits before interest paid and compares this with the shareholders' funds plus debt capital. This arrives at a better basis for the comparison between companies, since it eliminates the effect of gearing on shareholders' returns.

As you might expect, the most sophisticated calculations use some measure of cash flow. But here is a problem. Although FRS 1 provides cash flow numbers, it does not provide any estimate of the cash invested by the business. Comparing cash flow with shareholders' equity to get a return number is like comparing apples and pears. There are some adjustments which can be made to shareholders' funds to get closer to cash invested. Of these, by far the most important is to add back goodwill written off. This is particularly important for acquisitive companies, since the UK is virtually alone in allowing companies to write off goodwill on acquisitions to reserves. This sets up a heaven sent opportunity for managers to depress the denominator in the ROE calculation and make themselves look good.

Take the example of BET. This acquisitive services company had made a series of acquisitions by 1990 involving goodwill write offs. An investor who had passed stage one of the analytical process and calculated an ROE from stated shareholders' funds would have found a startlingly good 27 per cent and might well have bought the shares. Unfortunately for this investor, the ROE with goodwill added back was a more pedestrian 4 per cent! The market's ultimate judgement would also have disappointed the purchaser: the share price underperformed significantly for four years.

Once a good return number, preferably a cash flow return, has been calculated, what do you do with it? Again, comparison is the name of the game. Use common sense. If the company's rate of return is 4 per cent and building society deposits yield 7 per cent, why should you invest in the company? Surely it is busy destroying shareholders' investment by its very existence. What is the return like compared with a risk-free rate such as gilt yields? Why take a risk unless your return promises to be better? If the company's returns are higher than its peers in the same industry, (a) are they sustainable, and (b) is this superior performance already reflected in the price? If its shares are highly rated and its returns are likely to come under pressure, then maybe they are a sell, and vice versa.

And Finally . . . Keep It Simple!

There are many more ratios that can be calculated and questions which can be asked based upon company accounts but, above all, the message for successful reading of company accounts is to use common sense. Take the example of BTR. There are many ways in which the Hawker Siddeley acquisition in 1990 could have been queried using analysis of BTR's accounts. But perhaps the simplest would have been to compare just three numbers over a five-year period: sales, profits and short term debt:

BTR

Year's ending December	1988 £m	1989 £m	1990 £m	1991 £m	1992 £m	1993 £m
Sales	5473	6904	6742	6742	8841	9772
Profit before tax[1]	813	1045	934	788	1016	1137
Short term debt[2]	495	1498	1367	2674	2767	2365

1 Profit is less interest capitalized, and profits and losses on sale of fixed assets and termination of operations.
2 Due in less than two years.

During this period, BTR's sales had nearly doubled as a result primarily of the Hawker Siddeley acquisition, but profits had risen by less than 50 per cent. The pressure on cash flow was evident from the fact that short-term debt had risen by a factor of nearly five. An investor who had made these simple observations would have avoided the share price performance which followed the warnings about margin pressure at BTR's 1994 interims, in contrast to all the conglomerates analysts in London.

Reading the Annual Report is, in my view, a necessary condition for successful investment. Investors may get insights from their knowledge of a company's products and/or management, but this will not lead to successful investment unless the investor has a clear perspective on how these insights translate into financial results and share values: and the former can only be judged by careful reading of the accounts. ♀

HOW TO SELECT A FINANCIAL ADVISOR

David Norton

*David Norton, BSc FCA ATII FIFP, is the national Chairman of the **Institute of Financial Planning** in the United Kingdom. His firm, Tickenham-based **Norton Partners**, are chartered accountants who specialize in fee-based financial planning and tax advice for successful individuals.*

The importance of selecting the right financial advisor cannot be underestimated. Not only will you want excellent advice, but you will also wish to sleep comfortably at night without worrying about financial matters. This article sets out the key issues to consider under the following main headings:

- The personal background of the advisor.

- The firm and its services.

- The regulatory situation.

- The way in which the advisor is remunerated.

- The importance of trust in the advisor.

Personal Background

A prospective financial advisor should be able to demonstrate proper professional qualifications and a continuing commitment to professional education. Qualifications vary across countries and, in many cases, are changing rapidly, but the American Certified Financial Planner status is gaining increasing recognition, both in the United States and elsewhere in the world as a leading international qualification.

Qualified advisors will be members of one or more professional bodies. They will be required to adhere to a code of ethics. The key underlying principle in any such code is the importance of putting the client's interests first at all times. These then are the two main marks of the true professional: technical competence and professional ethics.

Establish from your prospective advisor his or her areas of expertise and experience. Can that individual advise you in all aspects of personal finance (perhaps bringing in expertise in specific areas from particular specialists), or are you evaluating a specialist, who may not be able to deal with all areas in which you require advice? If the latter, establish how you will be able to obtain advice in the areas not covered.

The Firm and its Services

The advisor you see may or may not be the proprietor of the business with which you would be dealing. Enquire as to who the proprietors are, and the status within the firm of your proposed advisor. What range of expertise is available within the firm as a whole, and how would this be applied to your personal benefit?

It is worth establishing whether the proposed advisor has close working links with other professionals, such as accountants, stockbrokers and solicitors. Good relationships are one indicator of a level of professional expertise

611

which is, at least, satisfactory. It also may well be important that your advisor is able to work well with your existing accountant and/or solicitor, to deal with personal financial planning points which require those particular areas of expertise.

Ask about the type of clientele that the firm typically deals with. Some firms specialize in particular types of professional, income, wealth or age groups. If you do not fit this profile, the firm may not be appropriate for you. If you do, their range of expertise applying to your own situation should be higher than that of a firm which has no particular specialization.

A fundamental issue with any advisor is the extent to which they are able to advise on areas where no financial product is involved. The professional financial planner should establish your personal objectives and your current situation, and build with you a plan which helps you move forward to achieve those objectives. Recommendations on products should follow from the plan. Much financial advice, particularly in the past, has been delivered with the aim of selling a financial product, rather than giving proper advice which is in the client's best interests.

> **The professional financial planner should establish your personal objectives and your current situation, and build with you a plan which helps you move forward to achieve those objectives.**

It will also be important to establish whether the advisor is entirely independent, or is tied to recommending products from only one or possibly very few sources or companies. An independent advisor, who can deal with all financial product providers in the market place, is likely to be in a better position to provide suitable advice than an individual representing only one company. Regulatory regimes vary, but in the United Kingdom all advisors have to make it clear to clients whether they are independent, or tied to one particular product provider.

A good first step would be to ask to see an example of a financial planning report produced by your prospective advisor. While a good professional will not wish to divulge any confidential information relating to another client, there will often be a specimen plan available which shows how a typical client's affairs might be dealt with. Such an example should give a fair idea of the thoroughness and professionalism of that firm.

If you are seeking to appoint an investment advisor, ask to see examples of current portfolios. Enquire as to the firm's performance record, and how this is measured. Some firms have a typical portfolio, so that performance for many clients will be similar; others will design a portfolio precisely for the individual, so there may be little correlation between different clients' investment performance.

It is always important to establish that professional advice will continue to be provided to you over the years ahead, rather than engaging in a one-off exercise which is not followed up. Establish with the advisor how ongoing services are provided, and how you will be kept informed of progress, for example on the investment performance of your portfolio. Where investment services are provided, you should receive regular valuations, perhaps every three, six or twelve months, with comments on the investment performance and suggestions from the advisor as to proposed changes. A certain amount of active management may indicate that the advisor is on his toes; too much may indicate that the temptations of receiving commission on investment switches are proving irresistible.

It is important that your advisor should confirm all advice to you in writing. This will avoid misunderstandings, and leave a clear record for the future of what was agreed.

The Regulatory Situation

Most developed countries regulate financial services, so that only authorized people are allowed by law to give investment and financial advice. In the United Kingdom, most financial advisors will now be authorized by the Personal Investment Authority (PIA), although many will be regulated by their own recognized professional body. They are required by law to advise you of their authorisation status, and the category under which they are authorized. These categories may place limits on the amount and type of investment business on which the advisor is allowed to give advice.

Many investment advisors are not permitted to handle client money as their authorization is not in that category for regulatory purposes. Some entirely reputable firms prefer not to handle client money. Many advisors operate, however, on a discretionary management basis, which means that they control your investment funds. Stockbroking services, in particular, fall into this category. You should expect to receive regular portfolio valuations and comments from the broker or advisor, and confirmation that all assets are held correctly on your behalf. The alternative to discretionary management is advisory management, whereby the financial advisor will make recommendations as to proposed investments, but the ultimate decision on whether to accept them rests with you, the client.

It is important that you enter into a client agreement, which sets out the legal and procedural relationship between client and advisor. This should cover the scope of the services to be provided, the authorization of the advisor for regulatory purposes, and the basis of the advice to be given. It should also cover the advisor's remuneration, and disclosure of any interests. The notice period, for either client or advisor to terminate the relationship, should also be specified.

You should also establish the extent to which the advisor carries professional indemnity insurance, in the unhappy event of your being dissatisfied with the advice and feeling obliged to sue for negligence. In the United Kingdom it is now a requirement for all independent advisors to carry professional indemnity insurance.

Advisor's Remuneration

You should discuss remuneration with the potential advisor. The trend is for advisors to charge on the basis of fees rather than commissions. If fees are to be charged, establish the basis. They may be costed according to the time spent by the advisor and the level of expertise involved; this may be most appropriate for a comprehensive financial planning service. For pure investment advice and management, they may be based on a percentage, for example 1 per cent per annum of the funds managed. There are a range of other possible types of fee.

If the advisor stands to receive commission from products on your behalf, you need to be clear about how this will be applied. Fee-based advisors who receive commission will normally advise you of the amount, and treat it as a part payment of fees. If the commission exceeds the fees payable, it is reasonable to expect the advisor to carry the credit balance forward against future fees, or to return the excess to you. Not all advisors operate this system and it is worth being quite clear as to where you stand.

The United Kingdom now has a regulatory requirement that most commissions arising from investment and financial business have to be disclosed to the client at the point of sale. Most other international jurisdictions have less stringent requirements.

This issue of whether your advisor is remunerated on the basis of fees or of commission is crucial for two reasons. First, you need to feel comfortable that your advisor has your own best interests at heart. But, second, the advice you need may well not involve the prescription of commission-paying products. The answer may not require a product at all.

It is quite common for advisors to offer a first interview free of charge, and this is a point worth clarifying when first arranging that interview. Thereafter, fee-based advisors will expect to charge for their advice whether or not the advice is accepted.

Trusting your Advisor

It is a fundamental point of any professional relationship that you feel comfortable with, and can trust, your advisor. Similarly, the advisor needs to feel comfortable with you. This means there must be no withholding of relevant information on either side.

Your advisor needs to understand all the facts and considerations that are relevant to advising you. You should expect to provide full details of your current financial situation, and goals both near and long term. Time involved in identifying these objectives will always be well spent. Only then will the advisor be able to formulate a plan. On matters of investment, it is also important for the advisor to understand your appreciation and tolerance of risk.

How do you find a suitable advisor? As with any professional, the best answer is to ask friends, relatives or colleague for a personal recommendation. In the United Kingdom, various registers exist, including that of IFA Promotions Ltd (0171-831 4027), although such registers are often no proof of competence. Details of qualified professional financial planners, who have passed stringent examinations and subscribe to a searching code of ethics, can be obtained from the Institute of Financial Planning (0171-930 4434).

Conclusion

There are two fundamental issues that you need to resolve when appointing a professional advisor. The first is that of professional competence – ensure that the advisor is well qualified and competent to advise in the areas you need. Second, you must have empathy with the advisor and trust him to act in your best interests at all times. If you are happy on both counts, and your trust is well founded, the relationship should be a successful one.

Checklist for Selecting a Financial Advisor

1 **Personal Background**

- Education and professional qualifications
- Professional body – see code of ethics
- Experience as financial advisor
- Expertise of advisor as financial planner and/or as specialist

2 **Firm & Services**

- Background of proprietors
- Other personnel – range of expertise
- Working closely with accountants and solicitors
- Type of clientele
- Financial planning – available with no product involvement
- Investment/insurance advice or sales – tied or independent
- Example of financial planning report
- Performance – how measured – example of current portfolio
- How kept informed – ongoing services
- All advice confirmed in writing

3 **Regulatory**

- Regulator and category – limits of authorisation
- Arrangements for client money or assets
- Discretionary or advisory – why?
- Client Agreement
- Professional indemnity insurance

4 **Remuneration**

- Fees only – any commission rebated in full (even when more than fee)
- Fees and some or all commission – how calculated
- Commission only – use of non-commission products? Advice?
- How fees calculated and billed – how often reconciled with commission (if any)
- Fees agreed in advance
- First interview free?

5 **Trust**

- Important that you feel comfortable with your advisor, and he or she with you
- Mutual trust essential
- Important that your advisor understands fully: your current financial situation, immediate and long-term objectives, and appreciation and tolerance of risk.

COMPUTER BASICS FOR INVESTING AND PORTFOLIO MANAGEMENT

John Bajkowski

John M. Bajkowski is the Editor of ***Computerized Investing*** *and the Senior Financial Analyst for the* ***American Association of Individual Investors****. He has designed and developed software for mutual fund and stock analysis. As financial analyst of the* ***AAII****, John writes two columns, one on investing in small capitalisation companies and another on analysing securities.*

Computerized Investing is considered to be the premier publication covering the use of personal computers for financial planning investment analysis and portfolio management. The American Association of Individual Investors is an independent, not-for-profit corporation formed in 1978 for the purpose of assisting individuals in becoming effective managers of their own assets through programmes of education, information and research. Current membership is 170,000.

In today's fast-paced investment world, people are increasingly turning toward computers for assistance in the investment decision process. Developments such as affordable, yet powerful computer systems, sophisticated investment software, and the growth in depth and breadth of information services have put powerful investment tools in the hands of individuals. These tools make it easier to keep investment records, plan financial goals, track portfolio performance, gather investment data, and select securities.

When selecting hardware, pick software first

Before you run out and purchase your computer, first gain a general understanding of how computer systems operate. Closely examine your needs and objectives, which will have a bearing on the best system for you. Software is the pivotal element. It will determine the type of hardware required to execute the software and the type of data that can be manipulated, along with the data source. Yet, when it comes to acquiring these components, people often take the wrong approach. They buy the hardware before finding out whether any software is available that will enable them to accomplish the tasks they have in mind.

IBM and their various clones have a significant edge over other types of computers when it comes to the quantity and quality of investment software. Does this mean that you have to buy an IBM-compatible computer? No, but be prepared to select from a smaller pool of investment software if you don't. That could mean that you have to settle for a program that may not fully meet your needs, and you may have to pay more because of a less-competitive marketplace.

When it comes to buying a computer system for personal use, it makes sense to purchase the most powerful you can comfortably afford. It is an amazing computer fact that no matter what kind of system you purchase, you will wish that it were faster and had more memory and additional storage space a few months down the line. Also be prepared to deal with the notion that soon after you purchase your hardware, it will be available at a lower price.

The software selection will also dictate the type of information service that can be used. Almost all programs allow data to be entered manually, but some of the better software will have built-in routines to access data automatically. Data retrieval routines must be written specifically for each electronic data service, so most programs will link up to a limited number of databases. Before finalizing your selection, check with the

It is an amazing computer fact that no matter what kind of system you purchase, you will wish that it were faster and had more memory and additional storage space a few months down the line.

data services supported by the software to make sure they are cost competitive and provide all the data you need.

Investment software

Hundreds of investment software programs are available that perform a wide variety of analysis on a broad range of security types.

Nearly 80 per cent of AAII members who are using a personal computer for investing look toward a personal finance and portfolio management program to assist them in the investment process. It is easy to see why this category is so popular. Keeping track of your securities, their cost basis, current value, and performance can be a time-consuming and tedious process. A computer can help you automate the process, giving you time to concentrate on your overall investment strategy and security analysis, not to mention your golf game.

Personal finance programs can be thought of as the Swiss Army knife of investment software. These programs offer modules that assist in budgeting, chequebook management, retirement planning, mortgage and loan analysis, tax planning and net worth tracking. Some programs even offer word processing and appointment management. These are mass-marketed programs, not written with investors specifically in mind. However, over the last few years, increased competition has led to general personal finance programs with portfolio management modules that satisfy the need of the average investor.

These programs are suited for the individual who wants to use the personal computer to get a grip on their financial situation. Some offer built-in chequebook management that not only allow you to print cheques via printer, but also allow you to send cheques electronically. You can establish budgets and monitor how well you meet your objectives, and track how you and your household spend money. Tracking assets is a fundamental part of these programs. However, the type of assets tracked varies greatly. Some provide flexibility in tracking both financial and real assets and liabilities, allowing you to inventory everything you own. Other programs concentrate on liquid, easily priced financial assets, while still others ignore this area totally.

Some programs now offer the built-in ability to access on-line services and update the prices of the securities in your portfolio. Like most portfolio management programs, personal finance programs can track the cost basis of each of your investments; produce year end capital gain, interest income, and dividend reports; allow you to price your current portfolio; and provide at least some basic asset class breakdowns.

If you are considering a personal finance program, keep in mind that they may not compute rates of return, and they may not be able to handle all types of securities and transactions. On the positive side, because they are geared towards the mass market, they have many users. This critical mass means that you can buy the software at a computer store or mail-order vendor instead of dealing with the manufacturer. You can also find books to assist you in using the program, and it is easier to find other computer users to help when you have a problem.

Personal finance programs are not for everyone. Some individuals find that a standard chequebook is fine and they have no need to enter and track all their assets. For these individuals, stand-alone portfolio management programs are the way to go. However, if you feel that your financial program has no focus or that you cannot keep track of where all your income is going, personal finance programs may prove useful. The key to success is determining which features will be useful and finding a program strong in those areas.

Portfolio Management Programs

Moving from the general finance program to stand alone portfolio management software is like going from your family doctor to a specialist. These programs were written specifically to help investors monitor their investment portfolios. This single-task focus allows the program to cover the subject in much more detail.

In comparison with personal finance programs, portfolio management programs will typically handle a wider variety of securities and types of transactions, allow you to track more than one portfolio, update your portfolio through an on-line service, alert you if a security's price hits some predetermined price level, provide detailed reports, and even handle multi-currency portfolios. You could expect the program to produce an accurate rate of return for both your securities and your portfolio, track security and portfolio betas and dividend yields, produce a calendar listing maturity dates of bonds, options and futures along with expected dividend amounts and payment dates, provide a breakdown of the industries and asset classes of your securities, and include a flexible cost basis determination procedure.

Of course, all of this added flexibility comes at a cost. Learning to use all the features will take time. When selecting portfolio management software, choose carefully. The start-up cost in terms of the time needed to enter the historical purchase information for all of your securities can be high. Be sure the program satisfies your current and future needs. Most manufacturers offer demonstration disks, so ask to see them before you make your final purchase. If no demo is available, ask for copies of all of the reports produced and check on the firm's return policy; some companies set time limits or charge restocking fees for returns.

If used effectively, a personal finance or portfolio management program will free you of some of the drudgery involved in keeping track of your finances.

If used effectively, a personal finance or portfolio management program will free you of some of the drudgery involved in keeping track of your finances.

Fundamental Screening

Fundamental analysis refers to the process of selecting stocks based upon underlying economic trends and long-term expectations of future company performance. The crucial variable revolves around projected growth in factors such as sales, cash flow, earnings and dividends. Software for analysis is usually broken down into two categories; screening and valuation. Screening refers to searching through a large universe of securities to locate a few that might hold promise and warrant further analysis. Valuation refers to taking one company and applying a series of models to determine if the current price can be considered fair.

Screening dictates that the search process starts with a broad universe of companies. It is not practical to enter this data by hand. Investors must either acquire the complete database and store it on their computer or dial up to another computer and have it perform the screen and return only the results.

In comparing stock screening services, critical factors include: the universe of stocks supported by the database, the depth of stock information, the flexibility of screening software, the frequency of updates, distribution methods, computer system support, and price. When contemplating a data vendor, consider the types of companies you are trying to find. If you are seeking smaller, less-followed firms, look for a service that covers a wider range of stocks.

Screening services vary in the depth of stock information they provide. Some provide a fewer number of variables and depend more on summary statistics such as growth rates when providing background data. Others provide both summary statistics and the raw year-by-year or quarterly data behind these numbers. In considering a data service, look not only at the number of variables, but also specifically at which statistics are provided. Obtain a list to determine if the program will support those screening variables you find important.

The next consideration is the flexibility of the screening software. Screening services that distribute a complete database and then allow the user to manipulate the data tend to offer more flexibility than dial-up services. This allows users to combine existing fields to create custom variables, and gives greater control in creating screening criteria.

The method of data updating may play a role in selecting a vendor. Some services allow users to receive new data either by mailed diskettes or by downloading via phone lines. Other services only offer one. The pure on-line vendors will always require a phone call to perform a screen. Screening or downloading a complete database via phone lines may add significantly to the cost. The frequency of the updates must also be considered. On-line services typically update daily or weekly. If the complete database resides on your computer, then you must select a delivery schedule, which will also determine cost. Options vary from weekly updates to annual. For investors who plan to perform screens infrequently or can limit their analysis to after-hours access, on-line services offer a good alternative to disk-based services.

Fundamental Valuation

Computers are well-suited to screening, but weak when it comes to assisting in fundamental valuation. This is because so much of the valuation rests on your personal forecasts for the economy, a company's industry, and the company itself. There are, however, a few programs that can assist investors with fundamental stock valuation. At one end of the spectrum are the macreconomic forecasting programs that make overall economic projections that, in turn, drive fundamental valuation models analysing individual companies, while at the other end of the spectrum are the programs that have compiled a series of valuation models that examine factors such as price-earnings ratios, dividend yields, earnings and sales growth rates and apply models such as the dividend discount or relative price-earnings ratio.

Entering the appropriate historical information along with your projected growth rates will enable these programs to return valuation estimates. These programs are typically spreadsheet templates originally designed to run in programs such as Lotus 1-2-3 or Excel, and some require a compatible spreadsheet. Remember that it is your judgement that drives the valuation. They can, however, provide a consistent framework in which to do analysis. Look at the valuation models supplied by the programs along with the ease of operation and data entry.

Technical Analysis

Technical analysis covers a variety of techniques that study relationships between a stock's past price and volume movements and patterns to forecast security and market price direction. Typically, these patterns are charted. Technical analysis is well-suited to computerization. It involves the manipulation of a large amount of data. Technical analysis software allows investors to quickly obtain data and plot it, applying various technical indicators such as moving averages. The better programs also allow investors to test the success of various strategies on historical data (backtesting). What once would have taken many hours, if not days, can now be accomplished in minutes.

Technical analysis programs require a great deal of price and volume data, which makes manual data entry tedious and error-prone. When selecting a program, closely examine the product to see if it supports automatic data retrieval and find out exactly which data source the program uses. If you plan to track a large number of securities, first make sure that the supported data services offer both the historical and current quotes and that the rates charges are reasonable. If you plan on building up a large database, the differences in data acquisitions costs will have an impact on the cost of operating the program. Also make sure that any data the software collects can be easily transferred for use in other software – if you should change programs or work with more than one program, your investment in the data will not be lost.

Technical analysis programs vary widely in the types of indicators they provide. They may emphasize the analysis of a particular market or security type and provide those indicators most suited for that type of analysis. Look for programs that allow you to define your own indicators and perform backtesting. In using a technical analysis program, there is still a lot of judgement involved. You must determine the appropriate indicator to apply to particular securities and investment horizons and how to correctly interpret it. Stay away from 'black box' programs that have some secret formula. It is easy to optimize a set of rules to work over a historical time period; most, however, will not work in today's market environment. If you are interested in a program that includes pre-defined rules, look for one that discloses the factors currently driving its decision process.

In using and selecting an investment program, keep in mind that the computer is only a tool to aid the user in the decision-making process. Just as buying a hammer will not make you a carpenter, buying a computer system and investment software will not make you a successful investor. It is your knowledge, aided by the information gathering and processing capabilities of a computer system, that will lead to success.

Popular Programs

Personal Finance Programs	Operating Environment
Kiplinger's CA-Simply Money	Windows
Quicken	DOS, Windows, Mac
Managing Your Money for Windows	DOS, Windows, Mac

Portfolio Management	
Captool	DOS
Investor's Accountant	DOS
Portfolio Watcher	Mac
Pulse	DOS

Fundamental Screening	
Stock Investor	DOS, Windows
US Equities OnFloppy	DOS
Value/Screen III	DOS, Mac
Strategic Investor	DOS, Windows, Mac
Telescan Prosearch	DOS, Windows

Fundamental Valuation	
AAII Fundamental Stock Analysis Disk	DOS, Windows, Mac
Fin Val/Finstock	DOS
Take Stock	Windows, Mac

Technical Analysis	
Behold!	Mac
MetaStock	DOS, Windows
Personal Hotline	Mac
SuperCharts	Windows
Telescan Analyzer	DOS, Windows
Windows on Wall Street Pro	Windows

Editorial Note: Software for the UK Investor

My personal favourite is Meridian, which offers just about every feature the serious private investor could require. There is a core portfolio management package and a charting capability. The only drawback is the transaction limitation, which is 400 per portfolio and not sufficient for heavy traders. You will need a teletext card, or something similar, for a price feed. Microtext is probably the right answer. Investors who track momentum and price movements should look at MetaStock for Windows. If you cannot live without realtime price data, PC Market-Eye fills that gap, and gives the added bonus of a news service, but the cost is high enough to deter all but the very active. Great if you can afford it, but do you need it? For historical data, the cost-effective answer is PC-Sharewatch.

Finally, of course, there is the Internet. That topic deserves a book of its own. Suffice it to say here that every serious investor needs to start now to become familiar with the medium. In only ten years from now, in all likelihood, most investing activity, including trading, will be via the Internet. Anyone alive has by now heard of Netscape. Also look out for Mosaic from Quaterdeck which should be in a software shop near you soon. Finally before buying a special purpose package check out Windows '95 and see if you can survive with that.

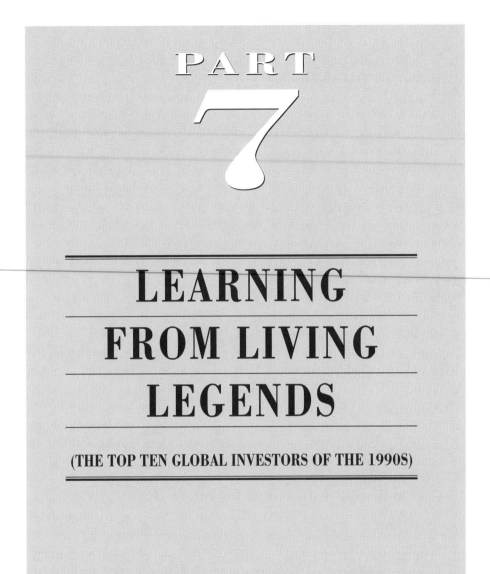

PART 7

LEARNING FROM LIVING LEGENDS

(THE TOP TEN GLOBAL INVESTORS OF THE 1990S)

MICHAEL ARONSTEIN

'Knowing What You Don't Know'

No one is more consistent in swimming against the tide when it comes to investments than Michael Aronstein. Recently elevated to the ranks of *Five Eminent Contrarians* in Steven Mintz's book, Aronstein has made more good calls about more markets more consistently than anyone else in the financial community. Not that he has won many popularity contests along the way; rather the reverse. Over the past fifteen years, Aronstein's macroeconomic analyses have led him to identify:

- the peak in energy and raw materials prices in 1980–81;
- the beginning of the secular bull market in bonds in 1981
- the ending of the bull market in real estate in 1985–8;
- the deflation of the Japanese stock market and economy in 1989;
- the strong revival of the US industrial economy in 1992.

His latest venture in physical commodity investment derives from the interplay of the most recent macroeconomic themes. The jury is still out regarding the ultimate wisdom of that undertaking but, to date, investors have been well rewarded. His new firm, West Course Capital, returned 15 per cent in 1993 and 42 per cent in 1994. For those who missed it or would prefer to forget, 1994 was the year in which hedge funds were in the ditch, the world stock index was down 2.4 per cent and the vast majority of mutual funds lost money.

Aronstein is not your run-of-the-mill investment advisor. He cannot be pigeon-holed. There is no label for his style. He's not a stock picker. He's not concerned about distinctions between different investment strategies. What he is is a cross between market psychologist and philosopher. His approach to making money is through superior asset allocation. He tries to be in the wrong place at the right time, and succeeds, to a degree, that most people only dream about.

Unlike most other managers with an extraordinary record, Aronstein had no particular affinity for the investment business and ended up in finance almost by accident as a career of last resort.

'I had been working at odd jobs since graduation. I like to say I worked for Sun Oil Company, but I was pumping gas at a Sunoco station. I worked in a medical laboratory, sold sporting goods, put out PR releases, was the instruction editor at Golf magazine, and even trained as a prize fighter.

With no clear goal, I wrote to 50 large companies headquartered in the New York vicinity. There were only two encouraging responses. Merrill Lynch offered me a training position starting out at $10,000, and IBM offered several times that. Everyone begged me to go with IBM. So, naturally, I took the job with Merrill Lynch. Wall Street in 1977–8 was a dull place, a dead end, and I thought things should get better.

Apparently I was the only person in my class at Yale they had seen exhibit interest in the traditional stock and bond business as opposed to the investment banking side. The trading side, the analysis, the nuts and bolts of the business, was not considered a promising professional path, which is why that appealed to me.'

So Aronstein started his career in bold contrarian fashion. That contra view soon became his hallmark. The contrarian investor does not just watch one market, deciding when to be invested versus when to be in cash. A truly great contrarian selects among many markets, choosing whether to go short or long, which is exactly what Aronstein has done.

'It's been my nature all along to look at situations and ideas critically to see whether or not accepted wisdom is, indeed, wisdom. I believe very strongly that asset allocation winds up being the critical judgement in any investment. It takes a certain amateurish approach not to be tied to a single class or method of operation in order to allow the distance that enables good selection among very disparate asset classes. If you become too expert in a particular approach, it tends to bind you to the one area in which that approach works. Fortunately I've never become an expert in anything. This has left me free to look from asset class to asset class without too much of an emotional tie.'

While this may sound somewhat like a butterfly browsing, Aronstein has a very disciplined and systematic approach to identifying which asset classes to buy and which to sell or short. His just happens to be a bit of a departure from the methods employed by almost anyone else, since it is rooted in behavioural science. Aronstein's analysis may seem suspect, but the way he plies his trade has the wonderful virtue, if not rarity, of employing everyday common sense.

'I look for anomalies and extremes. I try to understand the reasoning that underlies people's behaviour in relation to each asset class. Even if people are not explicit about what they are thinking, their activities tell you. Their ideas may not run any deeper than "this has gone up a lot and I think it's going to go up a lot more, so I want to be there". What I'm looking for are strongly held ideas which, at points in time, become commonplace; so commonplace that they almost become accepted as *a priori* truths – and there are none in the investment business. People believe there are, but there aren't. There have been many apparent *a priori* truths through the centuries, and a whole host in the last ten years:

- Governments don't default.
- Stocks outperform bonds over the long term.
- In a long enough time frame, stocks show positive real return.

All these are statements of conditions which have prevailed at points in the past. That does not necessarily mean they will continue in the future, but sometimes people begin to act as though they were hewn on the tablets Moses carried down – right there on line eleven. That kind of thinking gets people into trouble.'

While this challenge to conventional wisdom sounds ethereal, the simplicity with which Aronstein presents his conclusions shrouds the analytical rigour and long soul-searching process which precedes any position he espouses. Recommendations to move between asset classes evolve as the tensions in markets and values move from the sublime to the ridiculous, often beyond a point where Aronstein feels sure there must be a change in direction of prices.

'Take real estate. There was this hypothesis that values would escalate for ever at, or near, double digit rates. This was patently absurd, even accepting that it had happened for a couple of decades in some places. Running the idea out to its inevitable conclusion left you in a world where such a small proportion of the population could afford to own a house there would be no bid. Oil was the same. At $100 who would be using it?'

The trick for the individual is how to translate an insight into an opportunity to make money. Aronstein agrees that this is not always easy or obvious. 'I have had plenty of occasions in which I have been right about the environment and completely wrong about the markets which, in this business, is the same as being wrong. There are no points for great thoughts without results.' On occasion there are direct contra-relationships to play. Other conclusions require lateral thinking to find a cause and effect so the investor can segway sideways and seek capital gains elsewhere in another asset class altogether. When he lights upon the right situation, Aronstein makes big bets. Oil was the first in a series.

'People were drilling holes through the polar ice cap and melting down mountainsides to get the tar out. These are the sorts of unreasonable things which ought to happen when a price is about to change. If the behaviour of producers and end users in a market alters radically enough, then they will change the prevailing presumptions about supply and demand. A lot of people were trying to get cars to go further to a gallon and everyone was insulating their homes. I started to suspect something would give.

What can tip you off, also, is how are the people in a market doing. Are they living reasonably or like sheikhs? When people in Texas were spending $20,000 to get customized longhorn hood ornaments put on their matching Rolls-Royces, it was a good indication that the oil price had gone far enough. No trends go far beyond the point of imbecility on the part of the market participants. Oil markets had all these signs in spades.

> **When people in Texas were spending $20,000 to get customized longhorn hood ornaments put on their matching Rolls-Royces, it was a good indication that the oil price had gone far enough.**

Of course no one wanted to hear this. The one person I recall who listened very seriously to me, even though I was just a kid, was George Soros. I was very impressed just being on the phone with him. With oil I paid for our first furniture. I was short Global Marine, a very leveraged oil service company. I made about $4,000 which, at that point, was a very substantial proportion of my annual after-tax pay. I was actually long puts – the 20s. Global Marine eventually went to about 2.

Going short Japan was another decision arrived at by honing in on excesses. You had an 80 multiple market which had gone up for ever. The belief that this should continue was an article of faith. The virtual canonization of the whole nation by many of our academic economists supported the delusion. The topper seemed to be the lowering of interest rates there to the point at which corporations could almost borrow for free. With the whole Euro warrant market, they had reached a point of unlimited leverage. When you are effectively at infinite gearing, there's not much more to come after that. Again, the behaviour of the participants was a very good tip. The $3 million golf club membership, the endless corruption and tasteless extravagance.

The same thing was evident in the junk bond market in the late 1980s. There were tremendous excesses of leverage, lifestyle and conception. The great theoretical error lay in the idea that an ever more generous interest coupon could mitigate the risks of a poor balance sheet. This is one of those peculiar relationships that follows along in a linear fashion only within certain fairly narrow boundaries. Once the boundaries of risk and rates are exceeded, the process works in reverse. Beyond a certain level, the higher coupon payment simply guarantees the eventual collapse of the balance sheet.

The historical data that were drawn on to show how high bond yield could compensate for increased risk were inapplicable to original issue, high coupon junk, as the bonds under scrutiny had become high yielding through declines in their market value. They placed no additional burdens on the issuer in the form of an oppressively high coupon rate. Using these to validate the concept of intentionally distressed bonds was, at best, misguided. Beyond all of this, the 20-room ski houses and 200 m.p.h. sports cars told the tale.'

And it can work equally well the other way.

'We (at Comstock Partners) were fairly early into Latin America. By 1988 those countries had been through such a long history of failed economic adventure and so many horrible flirtations with statism, socialism and communism. They had tried so many silly approaches to economic mismanagement that we believed, finally, they had learned. There was no other path left for them to take for their next experiment but liberalization.

The forces at work seemed valid across the entire non-OECD world. It never struck me as natural that you had three-quarters of the world's population with a standard of living at such a tiny fraction of the level enjoyed in the industrialized West. It was no mystery how that had happened, but the tacit notion it would persist *ad infinitum*, that all the opportunity would remain in the highly developed nations, seemed unsound.'

Aronstein's new venture at West Course Capital was founded on more of the same sort of insight.

'The commodity story is also one of neglect. No one was interested in these markets for long-term investment. A hundred years ago people looking to make their fortune went into shipping, railroads, coal and the like. My guess is that if you examine Harvard Business School last year, not one graduate went into any of those fields, or even considered them for a career. Whereas over half the class probably considered derivatives, foreign exchange, or joining a hedge fund.

Once focused on that area, I tried to divine the ideas behind the price position of each commodity. If the market professes to know something that is unknowable and drives prices to extremes, I'll attempt to go the other way. If somebody is short citrus or soya beans or wheat because of their knowledge of the weather next winter, or if they believe that usage will be good because last year was good, I'm willing to take the other side, as long as the price seems to reflect their view.

Coffee was a fortunate example of the sort of specific analysis that I attempt. In the middle of 1993, coffee seemed to have little downside. Coffee consumption in the United States had been going down for a generation or more. From 1992 onwards, every way you turned there was a coffee shop opening up. The scattering of coffee shops in the US has probably now surpassed the level of public houses in Britain. There are three of them in the little town we live in, which has a main street three blocks long.

So if the per capita consumption trends in the US are beginning to turn even a little bit, and you had this explosion in the third world where coffee is considered to be one of the great middle-class comforts, and if the expansion of coffee production in the last few years has been minimal, you had a combination that was interesting. There was a frost in Brazil which was not predictable, but the fundamentals were compelling and the risk modest at the price point.

The same was true in 1993 of a lot of the London metals. The demand side was likely to change, if my sense of the strength of the economy was at all correct. There was this onslaught of supply as the former Soviet Union was dismantled and stripped. The whole position was anomalous in an intermediate sense. These metals were near all-time real lows. Many were selling well below production costs. Yet they were basic ingredients to the early stage of an economic recovery and some of the excess supply was a one-time phenomenon. And however well the Japanese were living in 1989 was how badly the mines and smelters and suppliers of materials were living.'

Coffee consumption in the United States had been going down for a generation or more. From 1992 onwards, every way you turned there was a coffee shop opening up. The scattering of coffee shops in the US has probably now surpassed the level of public houses in Britain.

Aronstein's performance at West Course is another triumph resulting from an ability to go against the flow. Still he remains best known, as he himself reluctantly admits, as the man who, with his colleagues at Comstock, called the peak in real estate prices.

'The only reason we went into real estate and did all that analysis was to convince people that bonds were a reasonable investment. Usually when something is cheap not only do people not like it, which is why it is cheap, but there is also some other asset which is so beguiling that people don't have time to think about the more depressed alternative. In this case the obverse of the bond story was the real estate story. To get people to look properly at bonds, you almost had to rid them of their feverish affection for real estate.

A lot of investors were really convinced all you needed to know about investing was that you buy real estate on as much margin as the banks will allow and you sit with it. And you grow rich. That was what had happened, so it was hard to argue with.

Now bonds and real estate are not only two competing asset classes. Real estate is based on borrowing, which is the exact other side of buying a bond. Real estate, along with government, was the most credit dependent enterprise on earth. The presumption that must exist for the buyer is that, ultimately, the cost of borrowing, which is the return to the lender, is less than the total return of the asset. If that is not true, then leverage works against you. In everyone's mind was the idea that the return to the lender was going to be overwhelmed by appreciation in the property. When long-term interest reached 15 per cent, to use a mortgage successfully the assumption had to be that the return would be higher, which implied an enormous escalation in rents. If that held true, after a time most firms wouldn't be able to afford to operate indoors. We'd be back to Byzantium, with commerce transacted in the open air. So the numbers just didn't make sense.

We went to the other side and recommended long bonds and electric utilities. Bonds in the US had been in a bear market from 1942 to 1981. To be talking about them as a preferred asset class from 1982 onward struck most people as ridiculous. There was no evidence to extrapolate. Of course in investing, by the time you can prove the point, it's not worth much.'

Aronstein's approach has a structure somewhat akin to Indians attacking a wagon train. He goes round and round a subject, tightening the logic in ever-decreasing circles. Then he locks onto one fundamental truth and hones in. If Aronstein cannot find the right investment in a given market consistent with his line of thought, he will pack up and move on. This marks him out from most other successful investors, who succeed by sticking to their knitting. Not Aronstein. He has made money in oil, stocks, bonds and commodities.

The 1990s have thrown up new areas which should prove fertile. This leads to fascinating, but frightening, forecasts on trends which could crystallize over the next ten years.

'The situation with government finances today is similar to where real estate was in the early 1980s. It's considered just as outrageous now to suggest that the terms under which the debts of certain of the OECD governments are going to be settled are not going to be anything like the terms which were expected. I believe there's going to be a great loss of faith in governments. Too much depends on their continuing ability to borrow money and, at some point, that will be thwarted by the markets. There are going to be reorganizations of various governments, and that implies a fairly sharp decline in the value of their securities. With the rate of change in the world, who will be a good credit in 30 years? The resources of government are not unlimited.

A tremendous number of investors are in Mexico now because of promises made by the government about their intentions to manipulate the exchange rate at some level which everyone seems to think was favourable. Any time government presumes it has the power to thwart the natural tendencies of the market, that government will wind up losing. Sooner or later. Betting against that is almost foolproof. Knowing that every time a government tries to alter the

Any time government presumes it has the power to thwart the natural tendencies of the market, that government will wind up losing.

course of markets for political purposes they are bound to fail is enormously important. I won't invest where I'm dependent on any government fighting market forces. And now they are all fighting the forces of compound interest. The idea that government securities are free from credit risk is one of the central fallacies of the present investment environment.'

Aronstein has some pointed advice for investors which flows naturally from these beliefs.

'I would try to invest in ways that are extra-governmental. This is the time for productive assets, not financial assets. Presumptions that a well-diversified portfolio of common stocks held for the long term can do no wrong is based on extrapolation in the US and only a few other countries since the Second World War. There is going to be a gradual equalization of wealth between the first and third worlds. There's so much more opportunity to move forward economically in Calcutta than in Tokyo.

I went into commodities in 1992 because of my sense of the shifting centre of gravity between the OECD and the third world. The stock markets might seem a natural way to be involved in this shift but they are too dependent upon interest rates and foreign exchange. They are vulnerable to government policy. Whereas one of the appealing things about commodities is just that: they are commodities. They are stateless for the most part. It's a big advantage. Commodities are the original concept of stores of value.

If you want 1,000 tons of Russian nickel, you can get your hands on it. You have it unloaded at Rotterdam and it sits in a warehouse. If the wrong person succeeds Yeltsin it doesn't matter. Whereas if you have a pocketful of coupons or whatever poses for a stock certificate over there, you can wake up tomorrow to find they have called time out. The next administration may say, "sorry, that's ours". It's the same in China. There are too many vagaries going into analysis of these stock markets. Commodities is a simpler approach to playing these emerging markets. Bear in mind, a couple of financial asset fortunes could, if shifted, own all of the industrial commodities supply on earth. Which suggests these prices are still too low.

When you are looking for trends, try and find things that make sense. I like non-traditional medicine. We're not using the knowledge we have. If I was buying stocks now, I'd look for companies which are in a business like that which can be part of a long-term trend. The shift away from government offers opportunities. Firms involved in certain services which replace government could be attractive. Private resolution of disputes is one example.'

At the end of the day Aronstein succeeds because he is in tune with markets which, after all, are nothing more than the sum of the behaviour of all the participants. There will always be periods when things get out of whack. That is where opportunities will present themselves.

'The market never has to do anything. Stocks can have ridiculous P/Es. Outrageous prices become the norm and can stay that way for long periods.

We look at market-related ratios like advance/decline, but it's not necessarily analysis of ratios which leads people to be on the right side of the market. Knowing what you don't and can't know becomes the key. In the end, we are attempting to analyse the ideas and behaviour of other human beings. The markets are like giant polygraph machines. Over time, they will point out self-deception and pretence with ruthless precision.

The one thing that I keep coming back to is the human factor. Economics, if it is a science at all, is a social science. The ideas driving the participants in markets and economics are ultimately the object of my analysis. If I can under-stand the sense or nonsense underlying these ideas, then I know something worth knowing.' ♀

SIR RON BRIERLEY

'*The Sage of Wellington*'

Most investment managers make their money by trading. They may identify attractive opportunities through valuation techniques that look at the total company, and they may be willing to wait several years to see the value recognized by the market, but their ultimate aim is to buy a security and sell it for a profit.

Sir Ron is the ultimate investment manager. He likes to buy the whole company or, at least, as much of it as he can get at a reasonable price, and then work at realizing the value himself. He is quite happy to own 100 per cent and to maintain that ownership position as long as the business continues to perform up to his expectations.

The results of this philosophy can be seen in the performance of Brierley Investments (BIL), his flagship vehicle until the late 1980s. Anyone fortunate enough to have invested NZ$ 1,000 in BIL in December 1961 would – assuming that all dividends and proceeds from the sale of rights had been reinvested – be sitting on all of NZ$ 3.1 million by December 1985. That translates to a record six times better than the Jarden Composite Index, which follows the performance of all frequently traded companies listed on the New Zealand Stock Exchange, and is as close to a 40 per cent compound annual rate of return over 24 years as makes no difference.

Following his retirement as Chairman of Brierley Investments in December 1989, many people made the mistake of writing off Sir Ron; but he is one of the great survivors in the investment business. While nearly all the 1980s high fliers from Australia and New Zealand have sunk without trace, Sir Ron has rebounded strongly. He is currently Chairman of Guinness Peat Group and involved in a number of other companies as an active investor. Of course the distinction between Sir Ron and others once considered his peers was that he never lost sight of what the word value actually meant, and never released his grip on a tenacious chase to analyse a business to death in the process of establishing its value. Sir Ron Brierley came into the business when he was only nineteen. Initially a writer, though always an analyst, he used that as a base to make the move into investment management.

'I had started a newsletter on the market in 1956, called the *New Zealand Stocks and Shares*, which gave me an involvement in the investment business. That ran for five years, by which time I had built up a small following, but was tired of being a commentator. That role had limited satisfaction, and I wanted to be a more active participant. Some of my subscribers seemed willing to support me and, since I had no capital of my own, making a virtue out of necessity, I set up a company and offered shares to the public. There was a very small response, but sufficient to get me started.'

That was in 1961, when Brierley Investments was formed with an initial capital of all of NZ$ 72,000 (about £36,000), of which £10,000 was made up of intangibles and esablishment costs. The goal of the new company was to invest in listed New Zealand companies. The first annual report, as at 30 June 1962, showed total investments of £22,394. As of March 1995 Brierley Investments has a market capitalization of NZ$3 billion and held interests in companies in four continents.

Brierley was always attracted by the investment world, which seemed to mesh with both his personality and his personal goals.

'I got into investing because it seemed like the easiest way to make money. Of course there was a serious interest, because investing offered an education into how all sorts of companies worked and what a business was worth. There was also a speculation involved and I have always had a bit of a gambling instinct.

My first purchase was shares in a gas company which was subject to constant rumours all around the market that it would be taken over. That was a speculative element, and it was bought out, so the investment worked well. Perhaps that was not the best of starts, because it encouraged the speculative side. It might have been better to lose money at the outset, which would have been more educational.'

Speculation is not normally the word people would choose to describe an investment made by Sir Ron Brierley. Before his name pops up on the shareholder list you can be sure he has done endless analysis on every aspect of the company, its market place and any other element he can think of which might affect the value of its business.

Where Brierley parts company with the crowd is in his willingness to go all the way. When the average manager is trying to figure out a way into an investment, he has already determined the way out, which is often that he will buy the entire business if no one else wants to pay over the odds to convince him to sell his stock.

'My philosophy is that, if you are prepared to buy one share, you should be willing to buy all the shares. There's nothing worse than being right, doing all the work, and then ending up with only 100 shares. I will have an active involvement with companies because, to me as a shareholder, I am a part owner already. However it's dressed up, one is almost always looking for ownership. It doesn't have to be a short-term aim. It could take several years to get to that point. It doesn't have to be the only aim in making an investment. An investment can end up in other ways but, before we start, we always want to be sure that we are ready to buy the entire business and we recognize that we may have to take up 100 per cent of the shares at some point.'

> **My philosophy is that, if you are prepared to buy one share, you should be willing to buy all the shares. There's nothing worse than being right, doing all the work, and then ending up with only 100 shares.**

Brierley has, indeed, ended up buying a lot of businesses outright after starting off with more modest stakes. This style continues on today. Over the last two years, the Guinness Peat Group plc, which he controls, acquired Global Funds Management Australia Ltd, Dunbar Sloane and European Art Ltd, and Brown Shipley Holdings plc, and forced Power Brewing Company to make a cash disbursement to shareholders by announcing an intention to make an offer.

This long-term quasi-proprietorial philosophy to investments is very similar to the approach adopted by Warren Buffet. One big difference is that, while Buffet sticks to the US, his home country, finding enough opportunities there, Brierley has practised his investment talents all around the world. The Sage of Wellington is the international equivalent of the Sage of Omaha. Just look at the record and you can see similarities in the investment strategy and the sorts of industries in which both men find values unrecognized by most investors. You can see shades of Buffet. An obvious example: one favourite sector for Brierley where, over the years, he has made money is the life insurance industry.

'Nobody really understood life accounts, at least there wasn't anybody around who took the trouble to look when I started out. They may seem impossibly complex, but they are like car engines. Each component is relatively simple, and they all fit together in a logical sequence. All you have to do is take the pieces apart to see the value; but most people don't do that.

We bought a stock in a number of publicly listed forestry companies early on. In the 1930s there had been a lot of entrepreneurs going around Australia and New Zealand, selling door to door, and getting people to buy quarter-acre allotments of trees. Some of these were plain fraudulent, though a few of them worked out really well. So you had these companies where shares had been sold for £1 and they had never paid a dividend, and the prices were down to two or three shillings by the 1960s. But, by then, a lot of the trees had begun to mature and inflation had made its mark, and they were valuable again. Only no one could be bothered to analyse these quaint old companies to see the value. We had very happy experiences buying these shares. Companies like Mamaku Forests and Redwood Forests were trading at a big discount from the value of their assets when we bought in.

My first major stake was in a building society, the Southern Cross Banking and Building Society. Its shares were grossly undervalued. Shareholders had been neglected at the expense of depositors, but they had a franchise that you got for free over the assets. Then we moved into a manufacturer of billiard tables with the imaginative name of Billiards Ltd. The business was being badly affected by a shift in leisure activities to other things like bowling alleys and, of course, TV was becoming an alternative; but they had cash in the bank to equal the share price and a factory which was a very valuable piece of real estate. We were interested in these ancillary assets.'

Early, Brierley had a lot of emphasis on asset value. The 1972 annual report shows holdings in many businesses with a real estate element: 47 per cent of Pinegrove Memorial Park (cemeteries), 60 per cent of New Redhead Estate and Coal Co, which operated a railway, and 100 per cent of Casey Investment and Finance, Queensland's largest Ford Motor dealer with prime sites in Brisbane, Australia.

'Property was an essential ingredient of many of the first investments. Bricks and mortar often used to be undervalued assets. I saw that assets were more important than trading. We bought into a lot of business people thought of as old-fashioned and dated – like laundries and gas companies. We have never abandoned that philosophy.'

At the same time, another critical element was already making itself felt: the franchise. That word appears a great deal in his conversation to describe an intangible asset which can be assigned true value. Vintage Brierley combines both aspects to balance an equation that equals undervalued.

'We are more sophisticated today in looking at value. You have to take into account people's perceptions of what something is worth. That can count for more than just the asset value in some industries. Packaging is an example. Packaging can create very legitimate value. We bought a Tasmanian brewery because it had such a strong franchise. When I toured the company and saw its operations you could tell the Cascade Brewery was an integral part of Tasmania, and that it had value over and above the assets.

Air New Zealand is an excellent example. It is the national airline. It has a strong market position in this part of the world and the company has become a part of the culture of the country. That means something. It's not like a lot of regional airlines in the US. There is a real value in that. There is a franchise you can't build up overnight. You have to go beyond the old, crude approach. This is an extension of trying to buy £1 for 10 shillings.'

Breweries, with their strong brands, have featured prominently in the Brierley story, as have financial service companies where assets are accompanied by names and reputation which, if used properly, have real value – in effect, strong franchises.

Sir Ron Brierley is very modest about attributing his success to any specific skill inherent to himself. Trying to pin him down is hard. Putting him in a box is impossible. Two themes, however, constantly recur as he explains why he made certain investments which worked out well: analysing a business to death and buying unfashionable businesses. No one else, even today, with more number-crunching ability at the press of a button than a room full of analysts could produce in the 1970s, analyses a business to the degree that Brierley does.

'There's a process of refinement which involves how much time to allocate to an investment. I like to go back as far as possible in time, even if it seems largely irrelevant. If the information is available I would go back all the way to the '30s and '40s and build up a chronological appreciation of how a company has evolved. You can often learn a great deal doing that.

Then there is all the conventional criterion. I don't have any faith in financial formulae. That's just an attempt to substitute for judgement, and there is no substitute for judgement. I will look at any element of the market. Almost anything or everything can be relevant to making an investment in a company. You never know what will turn out to be important: customers, operations, competitors.

I'm a glorified analyst. You should always analyse something so thoroughly you become the most knowledgeable person about that company and have something to contribute. You want to know more about it than the people on the inside: and that is possible if you set out to do it. Then you can compare and see if there's some strategy that can be implemented to achieve results that the market has not foreseen.'

> **You should always analyse something so thoroughly you become the most knowledgeable person about that company**

Brierley is not a contrarian as such, though the way he goes about buying businesses suggests the label. The only truly consistent element in his investment strategy is that of surprise. You never know what his next move will be, or when he makes it exactly why, until after he has made a lot of money for his shareholders. His current interests include several positions in companies where the financial structure is widely regarded as being very complex, if not downright dicey. Nonetheless, you know he will have done his homework and you feel sure that he will walk away with a lot more money than he put in. As of March 1995 he, or companies where he has a position of influence, have holdings where the value is not always obvious until you do detailed analyses, and where the assets often include an exclusive franchise.

- 29 per cent of the convertible cumulative redeemable preference shares of Wembley plc, a potential restructuring of the company where the main asset is the largest stadium for public events in the UK.
- 10 per cent of Australis Media Pty Ltd, which controls microwaves licences with the potential to distribute pay TV in Sydney and Melbourne.
- 8.7 per cent of Adsteam and 16.7 per cent of Tooth & Co, a restructuring of a leading Australian conglomerate.
- 30 per cent of Stanley Gibbons Holdings, the market leader in stamp dealing in the UK.

There is no question Brierley knows how to be a catalyst for shareholder value, given the positions he has taken in these companies. Brierley did suffer in the 1987 crash and that period is the one departure from an almost flawless record but, as Robert Holmes a Court noted in 1983, 'Anyone who underestimates Ron does so at their own risk'. Brierley bounced right back, taking a $25 million profit out of Bell Resources in June 1988 at the expense of the very same Holmes a Court. Which leads on to Brierley the active investor. Not that he is in a hurry but, at some point, Brierley wants to crystallize the value his painstaking analysis has unearthed and, if the market won't and management can't, he will.

'Buying unfashionable companies you have to be very patient. We go on patiently accumulating a stake for anything up to five years in the belief that we can realize that value. Our increasing influence as we build a bigger position will often help and be a catalyst for the value.

Substantial investors should be active in a positive sense. There needs to be a partnership between investors whose only role is to provide capital and management. Institutions are much more active today. When I got started, being active was frowned on. Now that type of role is more accepted. There's often an almost involuntary partnership. I usually want to have Board representation. In the end you may move from a position of influence to one of control. The degree of control should relate to the degree of ownership.

Being a lateral thinker, I am free to focus on basic comparative value, avoiding the influences of trends and fashions. Basic comparative value has always been my philosophy. Sometimes we will end up making the offer ourselves. Takeover offers create a tricky balance. You have to establish a level where you can still make an additional profit while making the bid attractive to the shareholders.

We try to anticipate what other companies might do. You always have this at the back of your mind. Sometimes you can see what a third company should do before they realize it themselves. If there is a common thread to many of our investments it's in anticipating what someone else will do. Our role is to define, seek out and expose asset undervaluation. Going in we recognize that a particular business will be attractive as an acquisition to one or more competitors in the same industry or could be a good diversification move for another company.'

If there is a common thread to many of our investments it's in anticipating what someone else will do.

Sir Ron Brierley is characteristically cautious when it comes to looking out at the future. He does not think much has changed in the investment business during the most recent decade. 'There was a huge speculative element in the 1980s and it's still here in the 1990s, though in a different shape. Now it's derivatives, currencies and complicated bonds being pushed on the personal investor, who can't possibly understand what they're buying.'

He does foresee two themes which can guide investment decisions. The first focuses on the type of stock or bond to buy, the second on where to look.

'I expect a new round of hostile takeovers. The takeover business has been pretty low key in the 1990s, but you can't stop market forces. Industry rationalization will resurrect itself. Managers will become more active in buying competitors.

Many heavy industries which were nationalized in the period of the 1940s through the 1970s are now coming back to the market. That is opening up a lot of interesting additional investment options. Then you have to invest in the Far East, because their economies are growing and are going to keep on growing. As they move from a more socialized economy to increase freedom and competition, there will be a lot of burnt fingers, but also tremendous opportunity for sound investments.'

Recommended reading: *The Way to Fortune*, Edward Westropp. 'A classic which deals with the big takeovers of the late 1950s and covers Charles Clore, Fraser and Tube Investments. A bit dated, but it still has a lot of relevance.' ●

PETER CUNDILL

'The Patient Purist'

A 20-year record of 19 per cent plus compound annual returns is so rare as to be almost unique. Canadian Peter Cundill has achieved exactly that with his Value Fund which started in 1975. These exceptional returns have been accomplished with a portfolio which has involved considerably less risk than the market as a whole. Cundill has never been less than 20 per cent in cash and has been as high as 60 per cent. The record continues. In 1994, the Cundill Security Fund was the top performing Canadian fund. Some of the private partnerships have produced a compound annual growth in excess of 20 per cent, though these are more recent additions to his investment activities.

Described by the *Sunday Times* as an 'Ace Stockpicker', Cundill is a value purist who practises the Graham and Dodd approach on a global stage. More than any other major investor Cundill holds hard to the philosophy, though the scarcity of true Graham values has lead him to extrapolate the philosophy in ways which Graham might find unorthodox. Cundill is not afraid to short markets which are overvalued when the indexes fly in the face of his basic beliefs. This role reversal gives value investing a new lease of life and provides a useful balance which enables Cundill to practise his investment approach in all manner of markets. He has also extended the concept of value beyond equities to bonds and commodities, which allows for a diversity that has enhanced core returns.

Cundill seemed fated to go into the financial services industry from birth.

'My father was a stockbroker. I think he was the longest serving trader, being on the Montreal Stock Exchange for over 40 years. My uncle, Pete Scott, was the Chairman of Wood Gundy and many of my family had been involved in and around the investment business. I suspect my father was something of a gambler. He suggested I get a chartered accountant's degree because, if I was going to gamble the way he did, I might need something to fall back on. The degree may have turned me into much more of an investor than a speculator.'

Like nearly all of the greatest investors, Cundill got a position working at the lowest level in a brokerage house as his first job and started to buy stocks early.

'I worked as an office boy for Wood Gundy in the summer of 1959 while at McGill. My first purchase was in a speculative mining stock and, within 48 hours, I had lost my complete investment of $500.

On my twenty-first birthday my godfather gave me $1,000 worth of Canadian Investment Fund, the oldest open-ended mutual fund in Canada. I held it for about 18 months and then redeemed it to go to Europe for my grand tour.'

Cundill brought to bear an unusual combination of creativity from his days of financial engineering at the Yorkshire Trust Company and the solid discipline arising from his qualification at Price Waterhouse to the challenge of starting an entrepreneurial investment practice. His approach reflects a fusion of his training with a rejection of the wilder adventures he witnessed on the trading floor.

'I'm searching for securities that trade below their seeming liquidation value. The framework is really the one set by Benjamin Graham. He took the current assets less all the liabilities, including preferred shares, at their liquidation value and divided that number by the number of shares outstanding. If the price of the security is less than that, then you examine the business. Graham allowed you to take the market value of a share portfolio or any extra assets which were not used in the business. This means you have to look at the balance sheet of a company first before you look at the statement of profit and loss. I think most professional investors tend to look at the P&L first and the balance sheet afterwards. A strong balance sheet with very little debt gives you the margin of safety. Even if the business is deteriorating, as long as it's not too badly, that allows you to fight another day.

All sorts of stocks can be value stocks, though you often have to hold them a long time. In 1974 Boeing was trading at a huge discount to book. They had expensed all the costs of the 747. By that stage, early sales and customer comment showed they were going to be successful. With development costs written off you knew you would have an easier ride.

> **A strong balance sheet with very little debt gives you the margin of safety. Even if the business is deteriorating, as long as it's not too badly, that allows you to fight another day.**

A complete contrast in industry was J. Walter Thompson, the advertising agency. JWT had gone public in the 20s in 1971 but, by the mid 1970s, the price was down to $4. The company had $10 a share in cash and marketable securities. It owned a building in Paris and in Tokyo and a long-term lease in Berkeley Square. It had a hard book value of $18 a share and no debt. There was no goodwill on the balance sheet. The company was making money and paying a dividend. We ended up with 4.9 per cent.

I was called in to meet the then President. He said, 'We have been selling stock out of the pension fund and you have been buying it. What do you know that we don't?" I said, "In theory I could end up owning this business and liquidate it at a profit, and surely someone would pay something for the name". If you look at Buffet, I think you will find he was buying Interpublic and Ogilvy and Mather at the same time.

People talk about not wanting to buy service businesses because their assets walk out the door every night at five o'clock. The reality was a lot of people had long-term employment contracts. If they left, liabilities went away and shareholders' equity increased. To an extent you want some of those people to walk.

Other service companies which can get very cheap are investment management businesses, or merchant banks. A decade ago you could buy Warburgs before they spun off Mercury Asset Management at a discount to book. You were getting Mercury for nothing and, in those days they still had some hidden reserves. More recently, Singer and Friedlander was selling at 40p. It had a liquidation value of 100p. They never lost money and were never in danger, because they had the most conservative balance sheet in the City.

One area this leads you to look at is distressed bonds. We have been actively buying these securities with a view that, when the reorganization takes place, we would end up with the equity. Banks often have large portfolios of shares and bonds. Industrial companies may own excess real estate. These are other sectors to look at. In 1993 we found computer companies were coming into our screen, even a few biotech stocks. Its not what industry or even what business so much as what value.

My accounting background has been really helpful, because 30 to 40 per cent of value investing is about looking carefully at financial statements. Ninety to ninety-five per cent of all my investing meets the Graham tests. The times I have strayed from a rigorous application of this philosophy have been the times I got myself into trouble. Sixty-five per cent of an asset allocation process is simply whether or not there are a lot of net net values around.

One of the reasons I moved into the investment business was that Graham spoke at a seminar of the Financial Analysts' Association. His speech was called "The Renaissance of Value". It was September 1974. He was able to identify a large number of candidates trading at below their net net value. Over at Oppenheimer, Michael Metz and Norman Weinger were producing a list of companies trading at below net net working capital. There were some 370 in December that year and, in addition, they did a study of companies trading below the magic sixes. That is, they were at values less than six times earnings, less than 60 per cent of book and yielding more than 6 per cent. There was any number of them and that was ignoring anything outside North America.

We now get a CD from Compustat every month for 9,000 American companies with a screen that meets our value criterion. For the last six months the list has only been between 120 and 140 total out of all that universe. Yet a large number of IPOs are down 25 to 90 per cent. Even though they have come down that far only 18 out of the most recent 150 are trading at below book value.'

Rigorous adherence to Graham's rules has caused Cundill to be extremely careful both in the way he builds the portfolio and the way he balances its composition.

'If I cannot find values, I stay mostly in cash. My first decade we were fairly fully invested. Starting in 1985 we were less. In September 1987 we were 45 per cent in cash. Simply, there were no values around. Every stock was trading at huge multiples. There was nothing to buy anywhere. More recently we are developing the concept of the antithesis of value. In some ways, new futures and options markets allow you to go short with less risk than used to be the case. We go short markets for the most part, not individual securities. That is the newest twist to our concept of value investing. In 1994 it was a useful extra weapon, particularly in Hong Kong and some of the other markets outside the US.

Valuing a market is almost like one end of a see-saw. Overvalued is when you have price earnings ratios of 25 and book to market value ratios of 2.5 or more, and when the dividend yield is below 2.5 per cent. So that tells me when I can think about shorting. Fair value is when the market has moved to a P/E of 14, book value is at 1.4 times and the yield is 4 per cent. Undervalued is when you see the P/E at six times or less, book value is 0.6 times and the yield is 6 per cent or more.

Between 1975 and 1985 there were thousands of securities in this range which were attractive to a value investor. Since 1989 most markets, especially foreign markets, have moved to being overvalued. If you look at the UK right now, you are getting closer to fair value, but my experience is that, when you are on the see-saw, you don't stop at fair value. You go through it. Conversely, when you come from being undervalued, you tend to go on up until you are overvalued. I don't think I have ever seen markets frozen for any length of time at fair value.'

> **If you look at the UK right now, you are getting closer to fair value, but my experience is that, when you are on the see-saw, you don't stop at fair value. You go through it.**

Following this approach has paid off handsomely for Cundill, but there is one drawback. He is often early, buying a stock well in advance of more broad recognition of its value or taking a position in a market long before the world wakes up and swings over to his point of view. Cundill recognizes this problem, but his philosophy copes due to another ingredient which is his hallmark and only possible when an investor possess great self-confidence.

'The other characteristic which is part of this analysis and has to kick in often is patience. We may have to wait a long time for things to go our way. We started being short the Nikkei 225 in May 1987. In October 1987 it worked briefly, but then from November 1987 to January 1990 it was a case of Mr Japan coming out from his corner every 90 days and knocking me down for the eight count. It probably cost us 7.5 per cent in performance over that period, but we made everything back and then some in the first quarter of 1990.

To get rewarded for identifying a value discrepancy you have to be patient. It's the same whether you are long a security or short a market. If the discrepancy continues, you have to have the resources to make an additional commitment.'

Cundill often will stay with the same company for many years. If the price fluctuates, he may add to or subtract from a position but, if the numbers continue to stack up, the true value investor does not get discouraged.

'We have held shares in a company called Trico Products, which is a windshield wiper manufacturer based in Buffalo. We bought it for less than net net working capital in 1982. We sold some in May 1987, sold some more in 1988, bought it back and then stopped buying in 1990. The shares were as low as $17 in February 1994 and we had paid in the 20s. Then there was a take-over which ended at $85 in December. Competitors were able to identify the value that management had built in the business, even though the financial community could not. In addition to the book of more than $37, they had a LIFO inventory which was worth $27.90 a share, and some tax loss carry forwards.'

Cundill cautions that, while Graham's approach reduces risk, nothing can eliminate the downside. There is always the potential to lose money. Graham minimizes the things that can go wrong, but there is no way to avoid bad stewardship.

'There was one oil and gas company which had $8 in cash on the books when we bought it at $5. The management managed to turn that $8 into zero in 18 months. You simply never know.'

Cundill approaches the selling decision with a similar discipline to that which he applies in buying.

'In the Value Fund we undertook a policy that we would sell half if and when the share doubled unless we could prove mitigating circumstances to our Board. If a share goes down, we have to make sure the valuation is still intact. If it is, you tend to buy more. We would only sell if the business situation was deteriorating badly or we had lost confidence in the management.

The old Graham formula was if you went down 50 per cent you sold, or if nothing had happened after two years you sold. We don't follow that.'

The scenario that Cundill sees in 1995 is more complex than in prior periods.

'Markets are beginning to go down. They may still be overvalued, but you are starting to see individual securities in almost every market which are attractive. There are nuggets appearing.

I think there will be a large number of candidates over the next decade once again. There are now at least 50,000 securities trading around the world. You can narrow the screening down to 15,000. If you never own more than 100 securities at any one time, even in high-valued markets you should find some values and you can short the overvalued markets. When the emerging markets which have been so much in fashion go bad, they will go bad for some time. They have to get boringly bad to create opportunities for the traditional value investor, but the time will come later this decade.

The biggest single difference in markets today from ten years ago is the growth in the mutual fund business. This has lead to unconscious speculation. A whole lot of people who know nothing about share markets and their risk ended up by buying unit trusts and mutual funds.

In 1994 I was travelling between Seattle and Denver next to an employee of the airline. She told me she had all her Keogh plan investments in one fund, Fidelity Emerging Markets, because it had the best record. That is one of the reasons you have extraordinary volatility in those markets because, in 1995, a lot of those people were suddenly learning and understanding about risk in rather an unpleasant way.

The degree of participation by the uninformed investor has been so large we have relatively few precedents. The American banking system is about $1.3 trillion. The growth of the American mutual fund industry at the end of 1994 was about $2.0 trillion. Five hundred billion dollars of that was in money market funds. If you take the mutual fund industry as a second banking system and view shareholder accounts as a demand deposit because anybody can get out at a day's notice, then everyone in the industry is borrowing short and lending long. There is always apparent liquidity on the way up and none at all on the way down. To a certain extent, when the unit trust business is in disarray is the best time for value investors. I've no idea whether it is about to go into disarray. We're in some pretty uncharted waters. One thing I am fairly sure is that there will be a lot more opportunities which, in the short term, means markets are likely to go down more.'

Cundill does not feel investors need to pay too close attention to changes in macroeconomic, social or political forces. Often these shifts cancel each other out. He's more on the look-out for where markets are in a cycle. He expects cycles will continue to recur with some semblance of a familiar pattern whatever else happens. For him that is the one paramount issue.

The cycle that concerns him most is liquidity.

'I'm not worried about what the rate of inflation is going to be or even the level of interest rate. You can have good markets even when there's high inflation and high interest rates. I've never seen a good stock market if it's difficult to borrow money and the banking system is tight.

If you look at the US in 1994 you can see the banks have tended to sell their government loan portfolios and lending has increased at a reasonably high rate. Then there's a number of other effects elsewhere in the world. We've had the Kobe earthquake. Does that mean the only great creditor nation will be bringing funds home? There is increasing evidence that liquidity in the global banking system is getting tighter. That's because business is better, which tends to work to the disadvantage of financial markets. In the 1980s you were going from a tough situation to an easier environment. Tight money created a lot of opportunities in the early '80s and again in 1990. It is the availability of money which is more important than the cost of money. In the second half of the '90s we may be moving the other way.'

Cundill has some relatively radical views on what this might mean.

'I was in Mexico last week, since I go anywhere which is getting beaten up. John Templeton told me about Telefonos de Mexico in 1986. The shares were trading at 60 pesos. There was a book value of 427 pesos and the earnings per share were 35 pesos. It paid a good dividend and had cash flow of 110 pesos. So it was less than one times cash flow. Here we are in early 1995. The price has now gone from a high of $78 to around half that, but it's still trading at 1.5 times book value, six times earnings and five times cash flow. It has a better debt equity ratio but, if you think there may be a nine-year cycle, we have a long way to go.

The trick is to wait through the crisis stage and into the boredom stage. Things will have settled down and values will be very cheap again. There's nothing to say that you can't see those 1986 levels again. Remember Slim, the great Mexican billionaire. He was able to buy all his influence positions in a period from 1982 to 1986. That's not long ago.

> **The trick is to wait through the crisis stage and into the boredom stage. Things will have settled down and values will be very cheap again.**

If you look at the year 1925, which was when the Ibbotson studies started in Chicago to track US markets, roughly half the time you've had markets trading with many magic sixes and half in an overvalued state. You can now find magic sixes in Hong Kong which may be an interesting area, though you have to be careful of their earnings and book value. They follow the English accounting habit of writing up or down property which tends to make a better picture in good markets, but the adjustment coming down is more painful.'

So where does a value investor go from here?

'There are very few corporate distressed securities around. On the other hand, you now have emerging market US bank debt or Brady Bonds. Last week we bought a large portfolio of Argentine, Venezuelan and Brazilian Brady Bonds, and some pre-Brady Bonds in Ecuador and Panama. These are US dollar obligations yielding 20 to 30 per cent, some with average lives as low as seven years. Many of the longer-term bonds have specific collateral in the shape of zero treasuries which are outside the host country.

We have about one million ounces of silver. We have seen four years in a row now of demand exceeding supply. There is a limited supply held in futures. The metal is trading well below the cost of production. If you were going to open up a free-standing silver mine in America, you would need a price over $6.50 over a reasonable length of time for it to make sense. Then, if you did have an inflation scare, you would get that for nothing.

In early 1993 we bought a number of Canadian gold shares which did well, not because we thought gold was due to go up, but because they were selling at net net values which were effectively below the public securities and cash on their balance sheet. If you bought Minorco at US$ 8, you got the reserves and the private holdings for nothing. It all comes down to where we can find real value. Anything which is trading below liquidation value or below the cost of production is usually a good indicator.'

Best book: John Train, *The Money Masters*. ♀

DR. MARC FABER

'Travelling a Road Alone'

The influence and impact of a small but select band of investment advisors extends way beyond the actual amount of money they manage. At the peak of this pyramid in 1995 is Hong Kong-based, Swiss born, Dr. Marc Faber, who has acquired the *nom de plume* 'Dr. Doom'. A man with extraordinary predictive powers, time and time again Faber has positioned himself and his clients in front of trends which were well nigh invisible to everyone else.

Sifting through many successes reveals a few of the most prescient:

- July 1986   Buy Thailand.
- September 1987   Buy Chile.
- January 1989   Buy oil servicing stocks.
- December 1989   Buy Nikkei puts.
- December 1991   Buy Bund call warrants.
- February 1993   Go for gold and silver.
- December 1993   Load up on cash. Short the Hang Seng.

These calls have made a great deal of money for Faber and his followers. His record as an independent manager may be short, but it could not be sweeter.

According to Micropal, over the most recent three-month, six-month and one-year period, Faber's main vehicle, the Iconoclastic International Fund, has been the top performing emerging market equity fund. He was ranked fifth over the three-year period. There are some 179 funds in the category as at the last count. His performance just keeps on getting better. The net asset value of the Fund increased by 28.3 per cent in 1994. Faber is one manager who has proved to be immune to the trials of Hong Kong and Mexico.

Dr Faber did not set out intending to enter the investment business. His interests were more broadly based.

'I studied economics at Zurich and the LSE, where I did a thesis on the financial reforms of Robert Peel. After my PhD people were saying go into advertising or the brokerage industry to learn about multinationals.

I had an introduction to Sir Sigmund Warburg. He suggested that I should join his advertising agency, as the graphology test indicated that maybe my strengths were on the creative side. However, another friend got me into White Weld. They offered me a job in New York. I had no idea what a broker did, but the salary was very generous and I would be working in the world's major financial centre.'

Dr Faber's approach to investing defies traditional definitions, but there is a clue in the name Iconoclastic International. An iconoclast derives from Greek and means a person who attacks ideas and institutions which are popular or traditional.

Another way to look at Dr Faber is to think of him as a cross between a contrarian with itchy feet and a global visionary. Just to confuse things further, Faber owns up to being an active asset allocator.

'I take an iconoclastic view of the world in the sense that, when reports are very favourable or very negative, we try to look beyond that and see if there is a mispricing of financial assets. When the news is universally in one camp you can be sure people overlook something.

We have a wealth pyramid in the world. There are a few rich people and the majority of the people are poor. So when the majority of people are bullish about something, it can't be right. If they were all right suddenly, we would have lots of rich people and only a few poor.

In general I have been travelling my road alone. I read research like everyone else, but more for the information. I don't pay attention to analysts' recommendations.'

There are some recognizable themes which emerge when Dr Faber describes his investment approach. Differences lie in interpretation and implementation and in just how widely he gets around. Faber is the investing world's early adopter. He sets trends: others follow.

'We like to buy assets which are significantly below replacement cost, or companies with high yields, and we look everywhere. We tend to be early in a market and out too early.

I travel around a lot. By travelling, I have a feel for whether a country has high or low prices, and when financial assets are in a boom period or a slump. Equally for commodities or real estate.'

This awesome ability to take a three-dimensional 360-degree look around the world means that Dr Faber invests in all different asset classes and in many different geographical markets. His greatest returns have been from investments as diverse as real estate in Northern Thailand and 3,000 Mao posters costing on average 20¢ in 1973, but now worth about $1,000 each. The one common denominator is a focus on things other people have not focused upon.

'You have to be positioned somewhere where no one else is positioned. Buy assets in markets everyone else has written off as hopeless and wait. I like it when the hotels are empty and there are no country funds. That means the risk is not so much the price as time.'

He can also look dispassionately at a company and select from a range of options for investment, of which common stock is only one.

'With companies you often have a choice. You can buy equity, or sometimes cumulative preference shares which haven't paid a dividend for years, or bonds. In a restructuring there is frequently such dilution that equity doesn't do well. If the preference shares start paying dividends again, you can have a huge windfall. The bonds now have a higher credit rating, so they also rise in value after the restructuring. Often we avoid equities but buy senior securities.'

Dr Faber is no dedicated follower of fashion in his investment analysis any more than he is in his choice of investment. If anything he values technical analysis over fundamental financial ratios, and values understanding human behaviour ahead of interpreting earnings statements.

'I watch charts closely. We like to see a base building period after an extended decline. Take commodities. I was very involved in commodities, especially during the boom periods of 1977–80 when the whole world was gambling in gold. It was really a kind of casino for well-to-do Asians. Gold, silver and platinum rose rapidly in 1980. Then they had sharp sell-offs followed by bear market rallies. On the sharp sell-offs we do not buy. I prefer to wait until an asset class has built sort of a saucer bottom – which has now happened in some commodities.

The stock market has more to do with psychology – how people feel – than with mathematical models. Modern economics neglects the psychological factor and its effect on economic life. Alone people wouldn't do certain things, but grouped together in a mass they lose touch with reality. That produces excesses of valuation.'

In the same vein Dr Faber does not adhere to any quantitative formula for selling. His decisions are driven by more qualitative assessment of market movement, analysis of macro trends and interpretation of charts.

The stock market has more to do with psychology – how people feel – than with mathematical models.

'We sell when things get to the euphoric stage. If I go to America and every institution has money in China or Mexico, it's of no interest to me any more. When we hear Citibank has private bankers running around offering a product, then you know expansion has reached a mature phase in the cycle and it's time to sell.

Or if some investment has out-performed other assets for an extensive period of time, I will sell. Take emerging markets. Not everything has gone through the roof in the last five years, but telephone stocks have. So we started shorting telephone stocks in emerging markets half-way through 1994.

Our big problem is that we are usually too early. In late 1993 we identified that the gambling industry in America was going to run into over-capacity. People were building casinos left, right and centre. Every state was opening up. Every Indian reservation had casinos, and there were riverboat casinos. Las Vegas was expanding. The stocks still went up 30 per cent from where we recommended going short before they began to go down.

The most difficult thing is to pick the absolute peak in any market. At the end there is usually a short squeeze and euphoria as dumb money rushes in. You know it's close when prices rise vertically. That is the buying climax. Look at sugar. It went to over 70¢ per lb in 1973. Experts were saying there was a genuine shortage and sugar could only go up. Then it dropped to 2.5¢ by 1985. We shorted oil in 1980, but sometimes an asset can stay over-valued for a very long period. It was 1985 before the price really collapsed.'

Although he has expertise in many types of investment, Dr Faber came to prominence because of his insights into making money out of emerging markets.

'Around 1974 I realized that, in Asia, although countries were still very poor, because of the mentality of the people and favourable fundamentals, they would get more attractive. I started to invest in Hong Kong, Japan, and even in Korea and Taiwan. People said, "You're crazy. You can't take your money out". I told these people, "I'm not interested to take money out. I believe in these countries. For the next 30 years money there will do better than money in Switzerland or the United States."'

One key to Dr Faber's success has been to place his bet, make his money, and then move on before the crowd.

'In 1985 we started with Thailand and the Philippines. By 1987 the Asian markets had had a very big run. I took a trip to Chile and saw what was essentially an Asian country which happened to be in Latin America. They were very disciplined and had a high work ethic. There was a very strong central bank. Yet the market was selling at five times earnings. After that, I invested money in Argentina in 1988 because it was similar to the Philippines in 1985. Everything had gone wrong and the valuation was unbelievably low.

Following Latin America, we looked at Hungary, Poland, Russia, India and Sri Lanka. We have also looked at Africa. At any given moment in the world there are lots of investment opportunities. The problem is how to spot them. Even if we spot them we then have the problem how to implement.

654

You and I may agree that Polish real estate is attractive, but for me to do it out of Hong Kong I still have to find a suitable local partner. You have to find someone you can trust. Especially in emerging economies, you have to do business with friends.

By friends I don't mean someone you meet over coffee in Shanghai and maybe have a few drinks and a great time. I mean a friendship which has been built up over ten or fifteen years. Your children stay in their house in the summer holidays. There has to be a strong bond, a sort of honour among thieves, because he may cheat everybody else, but not you. These people who are starting all these India and China Funds, I cannot believe they can build up those friendships in a year or two, especially as the local partners they do business with know it's not their own money.'

Dr Faber's approach to investing in countries combines a rotation not dissimilar to industry cycles in mature markets, with a bit of doing the hokey-kokey: in, out, in, out, shake it all about. Over a ten-year period in which Dr Faber caught almost every major move in every less developed country where foreign investment was feasible, he has refined a methodology which encapsulates all an investor needs to understand about emerging markets. Markets move through predictable stages with certain recognizable characteristics. To know where you are, all you have to do is look around. There is an element of inevitability. Identify the right phase and even the individual investor should be able to tell in which direction prices will move.

Chart 7.1 (pp. 656–659) is produced with the kind permission of Dr Faber from the 4 June 1992 edition of his newsletter.

Chart 7.1 The Life Cycle of Emerging Markets

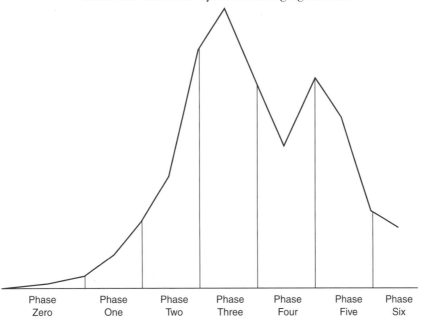

| Phase Zero | Phase One | Phase Two | Phase Three | Phase Four | Phase Five | Phase Six |

Phase Zero

Events
- Long-lasting economic stagnation or slow contraction in real terms.
- Real per capita incomes are flat or have been falling for some years.
- Little capital spending, and international competitive position is deteriorating.
- Unstable political and social conditions (strikes, high inflation, continuous devaluations, terrorism, border conflicts, etc).
- Corporate profits are de-pressed.
- No foreign direct or portfolio investments.
- Capital flight

Symptoms
- Little tourism (unsafe).
- Hotel occupancy is only 30%, and no new hotels have been built for several years. Hotels are run-down.
- Curfews at night.
- Little volume on the stock exchange.
- Stock market has been, moving sideways or moderately down for several years.
- In real terms, stocks have become ridiculously undervalued.
- No foreign fund managers visit the country.
- Headlines in the press are negative.
- No foreign brokers have established an office, no country funds are launched, and no brokerage research reports have been published for a long time.

Examples
- Argentina in the eighties.
- Middle East prior to the seventies.
- Communist countries after World War II until recently.
- Sri Lanka prior to 1990.
- Philippines between 1980 and 1985.

Phase One

Events
- The social, political, and economic conditions begin to improve (new government, new economic policies, external factors, discoveries, the rise in price of an important commodity).
- Improvement in liquidity because of an increase in exports, the repatriation of capital, and increasing foreign direct and indirect investments.
- The outlook for future profit opportunities improves significantly.
- Increase in cash balances and wealth.
- Consumption, capital spending, corporate profits and stocks begin to rise sharply.

Symptoms
- Stocks suddenly begin to pick up.
- Tourism improves.
- Foreign businessmen become interested in joint ventures and other direct investments.
- Hotel occupancy rises to 70%.
- A few foreign fund managers begin to invest.
- Curfews are lifted.
- Tax laws are changed to encourage capital formation and to attract foreign investors.

Examples
- Argentina after 1990.
- Thailand after 1985.
- Middle East after 1973.
- Mexico after 1984.
- China after 1978.
- Indonesia after 1988.

Phase Two

Events
- Unemployment falls and wages rise.
- Capital spending in order to expand capacity soars, as the improvement in economic conditions is perceived to last forever (error of optimism).
- Large inflows of foreign funds propel stocks to overvaluation.
- Credit expands rapidly, leading to a sharp rise in real and financial assets.
- Real estate prices rise several fold.
- New issues of stocks and bonds reach peak levels.
- Inflation accelerates and interest rates begin to rise.

Symptoms
- The business capital resembles an enormous construction site.
- Hotels are full of foreign businessmen and portfolio managers. Many new hotels are under construction.
- Headlines in the international press are now very positive.
- An avalanche of thick, bullish country research reports are published by foreign brokers. Foreign brokerage offices are opened up. Country funds are launched.
- The thicker the reports, the more offices that have opened up, and the more funds that are launched, the later it is within phase two.
- Countries in phase two tend to become favourite travel destinations.

Examples
- Thailand between 1987 and 1990.
- Japan between 1987 and 1990.
- Kuwait between 1978 and 1980.

Phase Three

Events
- Overinvestments lead to excess capacity in several sectors of the economy.
- Infrastructural problems and an excessive credit expansion lead, via rising wages and real estate prices, to strong inflationary pressures.
- The rate of corporate profit growth slows down, and in some industries corporate profits begin to fall.
- A shock (a sharp rise in interest rates, a massive fraud, a business failure, or some external shock) leads to a sudden and totally unexpected decline in stock prices.

Symptoms
- Many condominium and housing projects, and new hotels, office buildings, and shopping centres are completed.
- The business capital resembles a 'boom town'—lively nightlife and heavy traffic congestion.
- Frequently a new airport is inaugurated and a second one is in the planning stages.
- 'New cities' are planned and developed.
- Real estate and stock market speculators flourish, make the headlines with their rags-to-riches tales, and fill the nightclubs.
- The stock and real estate markets become a topic of discussion. There is active retail and speculative activity, much of it on borrowed money.
- The locals begin to invest actively overseas in things they have no understanding of (art, real estate, stocks, golf courses, etc).

Examples
- Thailand after 1990.
- Singapore in 1980 and 1981.
- Japan in 1990.
- Indonesia in 1990.

Phase Four

Events
- Credit growth slows down.
- Corporate profits deteriorate.
- Excess capacity becomes a problem in a few industries, but overall the economy continues to do well and the slowdown is perceived to be only temporary.
- After an initial sharp fall, stocks recover as foreign investors who missed the stock market's rise in phases one and two pour money into the market and as interest rates begin to fall.
- Stocks fail to reach a new high because a large number of new issues meet demand (the sellers are locals who either know better or are strapped for cash).

Symptoms
- Condominiums have reached prices which exceed the purchasing power of the locals. They are now advertised overseas.
- Office capital values and rentals begin to level off or fall.
- Tourist arrivals slow down and are below expectations. Hotel vacancy rates rise and discounts are offered.
- Brokers continue to publish bullish reports.
- Political and social conditions deteriorate (a coup, a strong opposition leader, strikes, social discontent, increase in crime, etc).

Examples
- Japan in the first half of 1991.
- Thailand in 1991.
- US investors in early 1930 and in the fall of 1973.

Phase Five

Events
- Credit deflation.
- Economic, but even more so social and political, conditions now deteriorate badly. Consumption slows down noticeably or falls (car sales, and housing and appliance sales are down).
- Corporate profits collapse.
- Stocks enter a prolonged and severe downtrend as foreigners begin to exit the market.
- Real estate prices fall sharply.
- A "big player" goes bankrupt (one who made the headlines in phase three).
- Companies are strapped for cash.

Symptoms
- Empty office buildings, high vacancy in hotels, discontinued and unfinished construction sites are now common.
- Stockbrokers lay off staff or close down.
- Research reports become thinner. Country funds which sold at a premium during phases two and three now sell at a discount.
- The country is no longer a favourite tourist destination.

Examples
- Thailand in 1992.
- Singapore in 1982 and 1983.
- United States in 1931 and in late 1973.
- Japan in early 1992.

Phase Six

Events
- Investors give up on stocks. Volume is down significantly from the peak levels reached in phase three.
- Capital spending falls (error of pessimism).
- Interest rates decline further.
- Foreign investors lose their appetite for any new investments.
- The currency is weakening or is devalued.

Symptoms
- Headlines turn very negative.
- Foreign brokers finally turn bearish.
- Flights, hotels, and night-clubs are empty.
- Taxi drivers, shopkeepers, and nightclub hostesses tell you how much they have lost by investing in stocks.

Examples
- United States in 1932 and at the end of 1974.
- Hong Kong in 1974.
- Japan ??
- Thailand ??
- Indonesia ??

One other macro economic insight has been fundamental to much of Faber's investment success: the paradox of inflation.

'In hyper-inflation economies you have currencies that collapse in value. Capital flight drives the exchange rate down. Frequently currency depreciation will exceed domestic price increases. In domestic terms, the stock market goes up, like in Turkey, but in dollar terms you may get extremely depressed price levels. In hyper-inflationary periods stocks can become ridiculously undervalued. The classic case was the Weimar Republic, which provided the best buying opportunities for German shares in this century. You had neckties costing less than 20 per cent in Germany compared to a similar necktie in Holland. The entire share capital of Daimler was valued at the equivalent of only 327 cars. The market capitalization of the 16 great Tietz shops equalled the price of just 16,000 suits. Stocks were down 92 per cent in dollar terms in November 1922 but, in fact, anyone who had purchased German shares after March 1919 was making money in dollar terms by November 1923. You have seen something similar in Argentina and Peru. This has interesting implications for Russia and some other countries in Eastern Europe.'

Dr Faber's view on where to invest in 1995 is a collage of contrast from the mix he would have advocated in 1985.

'In the 1990s the right asset allocation may be something totally different from the 1980s. In many cases, real estate is now relatively low. You can buy farmland in New Zealand or Australia at very depressed prices, also offices and hotels in those countries are at prices which are well below replacement cost.

You have to move from assets such as stocks selling at two or three times replacement value to another category which is selling below that cost. Take Poland. In February 1995 you could buy companies from the privatization agency at three times earnings or less. A year ago Polish stocks were selling at 40 times earnings. Today they are still at eight to twelve times. If you buy a company and the next day you can theoretically turn around and sell shares to the public for four times as much, then the spreads are very large. At the moment direct investments are much more interesting than financial assets. Recently we began to develop a hotel in Vietnam because I feel sure it's cheaper to develop property there than to buy a Vietnam fund, especially since most Vietnam funds don't have any investments yet in Vietnam.

There has been an explosion in equities with very good returns from 1990 until early 1994, especially in emerging markets. There has not been much focus on bonds. Now you can buy a five year US Treasury generating a yield of 7.5 per cent. You may get some inflation, but I doubt it will get to 7 per cent. If interest rates go up significantly, equities will be harder hit than bonds. There are cycles when bonds have outperformed equities for an extended period of time, like at the end of the last century; 1995 may be such a period. We are actually net short stocks and long fixed income. We are long five to seven-year US Treasuries. We are long debts of countries like Venezuela, Bulgaria, Brazil, the Philippines, the Cameroon, Angola, North Korea and Cuba.

Treasuries are a play on interest rates. We buy emerging market debt for very high cash flow. Cash flow over time bails us out of our mistakes. We also buy them as a play on a country improving its economic conditions. Let's say you buy Bulgarian debt and you take the view that, in five years' time, Bulgaria may do reasonably well. The yield might decline from 24 to 12 per cent, but the value of the bond has doubled. It's a warrant on economic improvement. It's similar to buying a distressed corporate bond. Conversely, if you buy an AAA they don't become quadruple A. The life cycle is such that, eventually, they become AA or A. The quality tends to go down because they have already reached the peak.

Adjusted for inflation, prices of some commodities are at the lowest level we have seen this century. Prices would have to go up significantly to trigger a huge increase in supply. In early 1994 coffee was 55¢. We took the view that the opening up of many parts of the world was favourable for coffee. In South Korea and Japan, coffee consumption has exploded over the last ten years, but they still only drink a fraction of the coffee the West drinks. When China opens up they could consume three times the world's current production. Long term, the supply/demand equation is favourable. And this low, if there is an accident, prices can shoot up dramatically. There is a similar scenario for other agricultural commodities.

In South Korea and Japan, coffee consumption has exploded over the last ten years, but they still only drink a fraction of the coffee the West drinks. When China opens up they could consume three times the world's current production. Long term, the supply/demand equation is favourable.

Commodities are not necessarily more difficult than equities. You have to be clear that, when you buy a gold contract, you have not invested $2,000. You have just purchased $38,000 of gold. If the market moves against you, you have to be prepared to back this purchase with additional margin money. The number one rule in commodities to be successful is to be very small. If you are too big you can start suffering huge losses and get scared. One of the reasons people have made so much money in real estate is that, when they buy a house, they don't watch the price every day. The problem with commodities is that people move in when they are popular. If their portfolio declines they are scared to put in more money and often exit the game. They come in at the wrong time and exit at the wrong time. In real estate, if they come in at the wrong time they usually ride it out.'

Looking around the world in 1995, Dr Faber's view of future trends is not entirely encouraging. He is unambiguously pessimistic about stocks and what he does have to say in a positive vein is more about world conditions improving than investors making money.

'In the 1980s many companies were trading below replacement value so we had bull markets with stock repurchases, LBOs and take-overs. In the 1990s most stocks are at prices above replacement cost. We may have seen major highs between 1989 and 1994.

Twenty years ago people were dealing in discrete domestic markets. In 1973 maybe US investors had a few shares in Sony or Royal Dutch. Today you can buy and sell shares anywhere in the world. Speculative excesses used to occur within markets, maybe small growth stocks or an industry sector like oil. Today speculative excesses tend to be global. People did not know much about Hong Kong, but they turned on the TV and there's some "expert" saying it's good. That bull is now over. We are in a correction, and the correction may last for quite a few years.

In the 1990s 3.5 billion people have been released from an environment of economic labour camps held there by the ideology of communism or socialism or a false view of self-reliance. Now in China, to become rich is glorious. India has begun to abandon policies which have promoted poverty. Three and a half billion people are joining our relatively small free economic system of 1.5 billion.

Look at Germany adding only 18 million people. The costs of integration have been under-estimated. There are gluts and shortages. The glut is unskilled labour. So many people are joining the labour force. One shortage, or bottleneck, is the availability of money to finance the industrialization of so many countries at the same time. The world situation has changed from generating surplus cash and liquidity to an unbelievable demand.

Whenever capital is scarce, you can have economic growth but financial assets don't perform very well because everyone wants to issue shares or bonds. Stocks may not collapse, merely move sideways for an extended period. There is also an economic recovery in the West and huge budget deficits in the OECD countries. This may translate into very high real interest rates for several years to come. Alternatively, this shortage of capital could produce the next recession in 1996.'

Whenever capital is scarce, you can have economic growth but financial assets don't perform very well because everyone wants to issue shares or bonds.

Dr Faber is cautious about making too many specific predictions, but has some recommendations.

'If you don't pay tax, the fixed interest markets are reasonably attractive. You have cash flow for reinvestment.

In Eastern Europe we should see secular improvement. These countries are bottoming out. In Asia, Japan created a domino effect in the '70s. Now we shall see the same with Poland, Hungary, Latvia and, in time, other parts of the former Soviet Union such as Byelorussia and the Ukraine. Their longer-term economic prospects are excellent. Specifically, I believe the real estate markets in Riga and Estonia are very attractive. You can still purchase a re-decorated 100 square metre apartment in a central location for around $80,000. In ten years' time, if you drive your car from Zurich to Moscow, I don't think you will see much of a difference.

I have bad news for individuals. If you look at the last century, most people who were sitting in London or Paris lost money investing in the US. They bought canals in the early 1800s, and most canals went bankrupt. Then they bought banks and many of those went bankrupt. So they moved to railroads in the last part of the nineteenth century and nearly all went bankrupt. The people who made money were the people who migrated there and started a business.

For someone in Glasgow or London who wants to make money in the emerging economies, there is only one way to do it. You have to move to Vietnam or Vladivostock or Uganda and work there.'

Some predictions are stronger than others. Dr Faber is confident Hong Kong has seen its heyday, and prices there, both real estate and stocks, are destined to go only one way – down. Faber explained his reasoning in a recent interview and in his own *The Gloom, Boom and Doom Report*.

'Free cities that become part of huge empires haven't done well. Look at the economic history of once great centres such as Goa, Tangiers, Trieste or even Venice. They all went into decline. As China opens up, the centre of gravity will move north to Tianjin and Dalian. Taiwan will start to trade directly, bypassing Hong Kong. Shanghai will surpass Hong Kong within a decade. The emergence of new centres of commercial and industrial activity in China may have negative repercussions on older centres of prosperity in Asia.

Even in China you have to be careful. The listed companies are basically badly run and many have questionable accounting. My impression is that China is in the process of gross over-building. Speculative property markets such as we find in Shanghai will experience a severe shake-out. Only when Chinese equities sell at five times earnings and at significant discount to their asset values should investors be tempted to take the plunge.'

Dr Faber believes he has got many of his best ideas from literature on the business cycle and economic history.

'A sense of history has brought me insights into a lot of things other people didn't focus on.'

He recommends reading, Dr Bresciani Turroni Constantino's, *The Economics of Inflation*, Robert Prechter on the Stock Market Cycle (see page 525) and Gustav Lebon's, *The Crowd*.

He also carefully watches commentaries from leading global strategists. Faber particularly likes Barton Biggs at Morgan Stanley and Robert Farrell at Merrill Lynch. ♀

MARIO GABELLI

'Surfing on Global Trends'

Everything down to the stationery at Gabelli and Company features a most unusual logo. The pyramid plus encapsulates the philosophy and analytical vigour which drives the direction of one of the most innovative investment firms of the 1980s and 1990s.

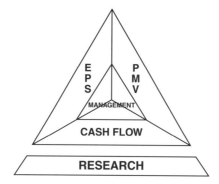

Mario Gabelli, 'Super Mario' to his friends in the media, is best known for his skill in identifying winners in that sector. His firm owns, or has owned, huge positions among most of the major media companies, including CBS,

Harcourt General, Lin Broadcasting, News Corp, Paramount and Time Warner. When Congress made noises about a looser regulatory environment for the cable industry in the mid 1980s, Gabelli loaded his portfolio with those stocks and won big, as pricing flexibility was followed by revenue increases. A recent industry dinner saw a number of notables sitting at a table; Martin Davis, Chairman of Paramount, Sumner Redstone, Chairman of Viacom and Lew Wasserman, Chairman of MCA. Herb Siegel, Chairman of Chris Craft, pointed at Gabelli and yelled across; 'This guy made money out of all of us'. A suitable epitaph one day for the man who coined, and then patented, the phrase 'interactive couch potato'. Now he runs a specialist fund bearing that legend.

In 1986, Mario Gabelli started his first mutual fund, the Gabelli Asset Fund. A $10,000 investment in the Fund at its inception would have grown to $34,040 by the end of 1994. That is equal to an average annual return of 14.9 per cent, outpacing by close to 30 per cent the 11.5 per cent per annum return of Standard & Poor's 500 Index. Gabelli Asset Fund has fared well in all climates, posting a noteworthy 16.2 per cent gain, even in 1987's volatile market. As a result, Gabelli Asset Fund has earned an overall rating of four stars from Morningstar Mutual Funds, a leading independent mutual fund research organization which ranks funds by risk-adjusted returns.

Gabelli, like so many of the very top investment professionals, started off early.

'The American entrepreneurial tradition is either to sell newspapers, shine shoes or caddy, and I guess I did all of the above. When I was 12 and already making a little money I started to hear about stocks and became interested. That carried on during my education. I traded stocks from a call box on the Columbia Graduate School of Business campus.

The course that really solidified my interest was taught by Roger Murray. He was the Graham and Dodd Professor and he wrote the fourth edition of *Security Analysis*. That, in turn, lead me to join Loeb Rhodes in 1967 and my career developed as a sell side brokerage analyst.'

The investment style at Gabelli is hard to pigeonhole. Mario Gabelli describes himself as a value investor, but that is far too simplistic. His definition of a value investor is a hybrid rather than pure Graham and Dodd and that, of course, is in part why he has managed to extract extra returns – by extending the definition and developing his unique way of looking at a company. Where he is today is the result of a migration through more traditional forms of analysis.

'You always have to do macro analysis, but you have to go on and look in depth at the company. What makes it tick and what makes it work in a competitive environment, whether the environment was inflationary or deflationary, cyclical or non-cyclical. There is a need for detailed analysis, not just the balance sheet, but the notes and also what the market thinks. You have to understand what the values appear to be as a starting point.

If you're buying a business, you should look at its Private Market Value. Some people call it intrinsic value (see Michael Price). I call it Private Market Value. My definition of value is: what if a wealthy individual wanted to own the entire company. What would they pay and why? What is the value an informed industrialist would pay to take the company off the public market as opposed to what you or I would pay to own 100 shares?

My definition of value is: what if a wealthy individual wanted to own the entire company. What would they pay and why? What is the value an informed industrialist would pay to take the company off the public market?

This approach allows us to buy stocks at a discount from value; and we also add an element to our analysis – the catalyst. This could be a management change, a stock buy-back programme, a shift in the industry structure, even a change in a government which has been hostile to a particular sector if the new administration takes a different view. Utilities, financial services or cable companies can win or suffer from this. American Express had a lot of change. Harvey Golub succeeded James Robinson. He skinned down the business. Then he spun off Lehman. Then he bought back some stock. It all helped. Another way out. Management gets old. Then they'll sell or die and get sold.

There may be a lot of take-overs in an industry. Mergers and Acquisitions may be back. When GE put a bear hug on Kemper that was the signal it's open season for hostile deals. Several years ago the cement industry in the US was taken over by a few European companies. Nearly all the leading American companies were being bought up, so we looked at the industry and owned stocks in those we thought looked like the best values prior to their take-over. Any or all of these elements can come together to add value to our holdings.'

In contrast to many managers, who focus only on their investments, Gabelli thinks about his business and how to present it to the general public in an investor-friendly format. The Gabelli group has grown to 13 separate mutual funds.

'We used to make Adam Smith's pin-maker very general in the way we specialized on US equities. Recently we have branched out, starting four global funds, each with a focus. We elected not to go country specific. Italy, Ireland, Israel and Indonesia, the 'I's of the world, are not what we've done. We have analysts who follow industries. Each analyst is now leveraging their expertise in their respective industry by expanding globally. So, if BSkyB goes public, if British Telecom is being challenged by the cable operators, if Indonesia is changing its communications industry, we will be able to identify and take advantage of opportunities. We are following those companies in those areas where we have a niche around the world. We visit the companies; we visit their competitors; we get to understand an industry really well.

So we have set up funds in telephony and one in entertainment and media. This allows us to look for values on a global basis. For example, today we have been looking at the phone companies in Canada and in Singapore, and

Telecom of New Zealand, and ended up thinking that the one in British Columbia is an absolute bargain. So we are focusing on building our position in that company and will watch the others only to see if relative values shift.'

The Gabelli approach to the market is simple and straightforward, but one cannot quarrel with success.

'We're Buy/Hold. We are bottom up. We tend not to do hedging techniques. Our 17-year record has been based on looking for bargains on a global basis. We have baked-in market timing only to the extent that if we have capital to re-deploy, to the degree that values are buoyant and the markets are lofty, we don't find bargains and it will take us a little longer to get reinvested. On balance our philosophy is to be 100 per cent invested all the time. We are not buying pieces of paper. We are buying 'businesses which will fluctuate in market price over time, but whose value over a period will have grown. For that reason we are very cash flow driven.'

The letter to shareholders in the Gabelli funds come straight to the point. 'Our focus is on free cash flow. We believe free cash flow is the best barometer of a business' value.'

'How much cash does an enterprise have after paying for capital expenditure at the end of the year? What is left to reduce debt or pay a dividend, or buy back stock or, possibly, buy other businesses? What are the cash-generating capabilities of all the businesses a company owns? What is the cash-generating ability of one type of business versus another? Then you have to decide what is the right multiple to pay for that cash flow. That is where you need to use the scalpel, not the axe, and focus your micro analysis.'

When considering how individuals should manage their own assets, Gabelli has a tested and tried philosophy which can be followed by investors.

'We are all aware of Mr Mackies' book *Delusions of Grandeur and Madness of Crowds*. It was written about 170 years ago, but it's just as applicable today, whether you are looking at companies in the media area, or cellular telephony, or biotechnology, as it was in the time of the South Sea Bubble or back in Holland in the days of tulip bulbs. There are manias which develop and common sense should enable one to avoid these excesses. You have to look at businesses which are real. A business must be fundamental to society's needs, either providing a critical convenience to the consumer or they have to come up with creative ideas to add value to necessities – things like toothpaste and soap.

I like to buy solid businesses generating good cash flow, run by good managements that really understand the shareholder and what makes the value go up. These are consistent companies. We like to hit our golf-ball straight down the middle 180 yards. We don't go 240 yards to the left or right. We want to play a nice, steady game which earns a real return of 10 per cent, that is after inflation and after tax. We believe equities are the only way to accomplish that.'

The importance of catching the wave of a global trend is one of the two critical skills which underpin the success of Gabelli. Investing with an industry that is moving in the right direction is easier and results in higher returns. What is different in the 1990s is the added emphasis on the global element of key trends Gabelli intends to ride.

'Over the last 15 years we had an inflationary bias in our thinking. We bought businesses with good franchises, good brand names and positioned our investments in front of some fairly large trends.

I like to buy solid businesses generating good cash flow, run by good managements that really understand the shareholder and what makes the value go up. These are consistent companies.

Three years ago the economy was settling down in the US. We could see a global recovery was on the way. Therefore people would travel more. So we looked for travel-related companies like American Express and we looked at hotels. We became the largest shareholder in Hilton. That was at a time no one wanted the stock. We've been to London to see Ladbrokes, which has the largest Hilton franchise around the world and so understood how their business can take advantage of this trend. At some point, Mr Hilton will succeed in selling and that will give us the catalyst for the value.'

On selling Gabelli has a disciplined approach and he adheres to it rigorously.

'We have a value at any point of time for a company. Today (January 1995) we think Hilton is worth about $100 a share. If it gets to about $85 because the market bids it up, we'll sell some off. If some brokerage house gets enthusiastic about a stock, it may get overpriced. We look for a margin of safety against our value and, if it's not there for any reason, we'll sell that specific stock. This is not static. Value increases over time as long as the company continues to perform the way we expect. We have a range of future prices. We calculate value going out five to fifteen years. This gives us the Private Market Value channel. When a stock is knocked below the channel, we're a buyer. If it goes up to, or above, then we sell.'

Gabelli feels the measurement of value has not changed and does not see any reason why the 1990s should be any different in that respect than the 1980s.

'The concept of EBITDA is one of the drivers in Private Market Value. That has become a standard for certain groups of investors. Sony talks about it in their annual report. These concepts have migrated globally. The concepts have not changed.'

The change that has occurred, and will continue to drive investment decisions over the next ten years, is all bound up in one word: 'globalization'.

'What we do differently today than we did in the 1980s and the '70s and the '60s is that, when we go out and see a company, we want to follow the company around the world. Not just one company, but all competitors who compete globally. Take beverages. We have one analyst who follows Guinness, Coors, Pepsi, Coca-Cola, and we follow their activities around the world. Telephony is another, similar industry. We need to look at relative values on a global basis. Fifteen years ago most investors used to concentrate on domestic companies. They looked at international markets primarily to understand whether competitive trends in other countries should cause them to avoid certain domestic companies and to see where opportunities in overseas markets might make a domestic stock more attractive. In the 1990s you're choosing companies based on their global performance, and it could be a US stock or a Japanese or a Germany company which offers the best value.

We are looking for solid, three to five-year trends we can ride. Travel related services should be good for the rest of the decade. Another powerful trend for the next five years is safety. We think countries around the world, in America, but also elsewhere, are concerned about safety. The American consumer is particularly concerned about automotive safety. That means air bags, anti-skid, side impact bars, four-wheel drive. There are personal concerns. Companies making and selling fire and burglar alarms should continue to do well. Three years ago I was at the New York show for burglar alarms. I was on my own. Last year three analysts showed up, this year four. We're still at the start of this trend. Entertainment travels well. We follow the movie industry. We follow their distributors. We like pre-recorded music. Polygram, Thorn, Sony, Time Warner – they all have a global franchise.'

This positioning of the portfolio to benefit from global trends is combined with the core notion that a good stock-picker needs to buy stocks at a discount. Everything comes back to choosing a company where Gabelli can see some unrecognized value.

'We're buying American Brands because we get Gallagher's for free and we get their liquor business in the UK for free. Gallagher's, which is Benson and Hedges and Silk Cut, could be worth as much as $5 billion, and you're getting it for free when you buy the stock at these current levels. There are short run problems but we think these create vast opportunities to buy an undervalued asset. Media General owns newspapers in Tampa, Richmond and Winston-Salem. If you analyse the circulation and the value of their franchise and the TV stations in Tampa and Jacksonville and see what these are worth if you were to sell them, you get 220,000 cable subscribers for free. That is a $650 million value. Take BC Telecom in Vancouver. The traditional phone business is worth their stock price so you get their $1 billion cellular business for free.'

Like other great wealth creators, Gabelli has a very positive view of the future, as well as his own ideas of how individual investors can profit from global trends.

'Whether you are in the north of Italy or the South Bronx, you want to encourage entrepreneurs. Now the capitalist system has emerged as the winning system you start with capital formation. That means healthy stock markets. Certain industries in certain countries become particularly important to that development. Two that stand out are the telephone and the cable industries. To some extent, America is colonizing the world because we are imposing our standards in these industries. It is the most visible example of global conversion. Investors should look for businesses that travel well. MTV travels well. Newspapers can travel well. The *Wall Street Journal* and *Financial Times* do that. Some of the newspaper companies based in Hong Kong could be interesting.

One huge trend for the next 30 years or so which is fairly easy is "follow the Chinese". Wherever the Chinese expats are, whether they're in Vancouver, Toronto, New York or Singapore, you want to see what they are doing, because they know how to accumulate capital.

Ownership of businesses will be the way to make money over the next 20 years and, if you can't do that directly, you can do the same thing by owning a mix of good common stocks and looking at these through the eyes of an owner. You can buy stocks directly, which is not that hard, or buy packaged goods. Find out which mutual fund families have good no-load offerings, incur reasonable fees and expenses and allow you good information access, and then ask specific questions. Who is the manager? What is their record? Track that and see if are there any changes. There is a great service in the US called Morningstar which is a low cost database and allows you to compare all mutual funds.'

Inevitably the focus of discussion keeps coming back to the media industry. Gabelli is confident investors will continue to make a lot of money from buying the right stocks from within that sector. The trend is with him.

'In India five years ago there were 400,000 disks receiving cable or satellite entertainment. Today there are 10 million. In England you had the BBC and a couple of ITV channels. Now you have Sky. You can see everywhere that entertainment is proliferating. All over the world the number of channels that the consumer wants has proliferated and operators have responded by delivering more choice. If you are the software supplier, say the movie company, you have a much larger market. If you make *The Bodyguard* with Whitney Houston, the rentals grow with inflation, but the market grows as well, because you have other ways to reach the customer, and there are more of them on a global basis now able to access your product. We believe the people who own these databases, whether its Canal Plus, or Bertlesmann, or Sony, or TVB in Hong Kong, or Tokyo Broadcasting, will always have a market for their products. This is part of a major cultural revolution. It's happening globally.'

Key publications: *Security Analysis*: Graham and Dodd. 🖊

670

ROBERT LLOYD GEORGE

'Always Looking One Field Ahead'

Robert Lloyd George has a background which encapsulates the essence of the word 'global'. He has worked in London, Paris, New York, Sao Paolo and Hong Kong. He speaks French, Portuguese, some Japanese and a little Mandarin. Where he excels is in applying an analysis of global trends to the emerging markets in Asia. His first fund, launched in October 1984, rose by 870 per cent in its first ten years.

Part of his remarkable reputation arises from his decision to allow redemptions in the Asian Growth Fund during the four days the Hong Kong market closed after the crash in October 1987. His was the only fund to remain open.

When Lloyd George turned up in Shanghai in December 1990 for the re-opening of the Shanghai Stock Exchange asking to set up the first China fund for foreigners (the 'Shanghai Fund'), he was greeted with astonishment. He was ahead of his time, but not by much. The Lloyd George Standard Chartered China Fund was incorporated in July 1992 and promptly made a return of 62 per cent in its first year.

What marks Lloyd George out from the crowd is a capacity to combine macroanalysis of long-term, political and economic forces and Western analytical concepts in markets which still co-exist with significant differences and a cultural context that would not find favour on Wall Street. In reviewing his book *The East-West Pendulum*, Lloyd George makes one forecast, which he believes has to be carefully considered by every serious investor. 'My contention is that the leadership of Asia, in economic and cultural terms, will pass from Japan to the Chinese (including the overseas Chinese) during the next 20 years.'

Like so many successful investors, Lloyd George's first contact with the market was on the trading floor though, in his case, it was in the Corbeille in Paris.

'This initial experience in the trading ring has always stood me in good stead. I learnt how a market worked, what was the psychology of a market, which is true of all markets all around the world; how rumours and gossip and nervousness sweep through a trading room. How prices fluctuate, and how to buy and sell shares. Anyone who wants to get into the investment business should spend some time in a trading room or on a stock exchange, or at least learn the nuts and bolts of the brokerage business.'

Lloyd George's approach to investment differs from most traditional strategies because the market environment when he moved to Asia in the early 1980s was different. As the markets have developed, so his strategy has evolved.

'The fundamental principle of investing in Asia is to maintain a regional balance and diversification. Initially this was between Japan and the four Tigers (Taiwan, South Korea, Singapore and Hong Kong). Later the balance became between Hong Kong and the rest of the region. Now there are the new emerging markets – Thailand, Indonesia, Philippines, Malaysia and, of course, India, Pakistan, Sri Lanka and Bangladesh – which makes the equation more complex. We follow 15 countries and there are dramatic differences between Sri Lanka and Tokyo.

My investment philosophy varies, depending on the structure of the market. I have never been afraid to take trading profits in more liquid markets like Tokyo and Hong Kong. In new emerging markets like Jakarta or Bombay, where trading volumes are so much thinner, it is often better to take the long view.

This balance and diversification is a key element to success in Asia. Volatility is a constant and argues against making very large bets on small markets. During Tiananmen Square the Hong Kong market fell over 40 per cent in a six-week period. Our regional Asian fund had a larger exposure to Thailand at the time and the NAV (net asset value) actually rose 2 per cent. When the Manila market crashed 50 per cent in December 1989 (after the attempted coup d'etat) it had little effect on our fund, because other markets were performing well.'

Lloyd George has a systematic approach in assessing a market environment and making a specific allocation. As of February 1995 Table 7.1 gives a snapshot of how he views the main Asian economies:

672

Table 7.1: Risk and Reward Analysis

	Risk[1]			Reward[2]		
	Political	Inflation	Currency US $	Population[3]	GNP[4]	Capital market[5]
Japan	1	1	2	8	5	5
Singapore	2	2	1	7	3	3
Thailand	3	5	1	2	1	5
Malaysia	3	4	2	1	2	3
Taiwan	5	3	2	6	2	7
South Korea	5	6	3	5	1	4
Hong Kong	7	8	1	5	3	6
China	8	8	5	3	2	-
Indonesia	6	9	4	2	4	8
Philippines	3	10	5	2	7	9

1 1 = low risk, 10 = high risk.
2 1 = high potential, 10 - low potential.
3 Population growth can be looked at either as an economic problem and threat or as a marketing opportunity. For these purposes, demographic growth and personal income growth are multiplied in the overall equation to reach economic growth potential in each country.
4 GNP growth is based on the 25-year averages.
5 For the capital market we have calculated performance, volatility, turnover and liquidity as well as price earnings ratios, dividend yields and interest rates.

'Now I am moving more and more to a "bottom up" approach in selecting individual companies, to balance the 'top down' political risk and reward ratio type of approach. We used to be able to pick countries in the mid-'80s, now we have to pick stocks within countries. Indonesia is a good example. When I first went for Jakarta in 1988 there were seven stocks we could buy. Now there are 150. The value among individual stocks becomes more important and starts to influence the question of balance.

At the end of 1994 we did a screen of every stock in Asia to see where we could find companies selling on earnings multiples below 15 times and growing profits more than 25 per cent annually. There were no names in Malaysia, which led us to downweight Malaysia. There were a lot of names, obviously, in Hong Kong. There were also a lot of names in Korea. This led us to do more work in Korea and increase our Korean exposure.

The other market which clearly is a strong candidate for this "bottom up" approach is India. India, of course, meets many of the conditions which, for me, make it the most exciting of the emerging markets for 1995. As Thailand was in 1986, when I first went there, (a) there is no decent research written by any inter-

India, of course, meets many of the conditions which, for me, make it the most exciting of the emerging markets for 1995.

national brokerage house; (b) there are many Indian companies, the majority, indeed, which have never been visited by any foreign analyst; (c) it's an illogical, inefficient and thoroughly neglected market where the foreigner accounts for less than 3 per cent of the market cap and less than 10 per cent of the trading value. By visiting several hundred companies a year you can uncover a lot of value in smaller and medium-sized Indian companies. In Madras we found a company making artificial limbs, which sells on a multiple of only 10 times. The total market cap is only $12 million, but it's growing at 50 per cent per year. It's a huge market of small cap companies waiting to be discovered. This drives the overall asset allocation because there is so much value. In contrast, in Japan today it's very, very hard to find growth or value. The rewards are very few compared to the effort required to find it.'

Lloyd George has seen just how well things can work in disorganized markets first hand.

'In April 1987 George Soros called me at 1:00 a.m., Hong Kong time (noon in New York), and asked, "Have you noticed the Politburo changes in Hanoi?". His next words were, "Start buying stock in Bangkok". Soros, like the global chess player he is, had seen that the Vietnamese government would shift its policy from military adventurism in Cambodia and Laos, to economic recon-struction, and that this would profoundly affect the investor perception of risk, in buying shares in Thailand. He then asked me to go down to Bangkok, and bid in an auction for the Krung Thai Fund. We succeeded in buying a portfolio of 57 Thai securities for about US$ 65 million. The next morning I woke up to find that we were the owners of a ragbag of shares, including seven bankrupt companies, another ten which were actually untradeable, and some more which were pretty undesirable investments. More importantly, there was not a single English language report on any of the companies. None of the companies bothered to publish their annual reports in anything but the Thai language. I spent nearly two months in Thailand visiting every one of these companies, making our own earnings estimates and getting to know the management. It was my first in-depth experience of investing in a true emerg-ing market.

Subsequently, I have always taken the view that we must make first-hand company visits, form our own impression of management and make our own estimates and valuations, not depending too much on brokers.'

Asset allocation of the Lloyd George portfolios within Asia is one element. Total asset allocation for the individual investor has to consider other factors, but the right strategy may not be that different at the end of the day.

'We're always trying to correct people's Eurocentric or America-centric world view. It is my firm belief that the centre of the economic world is now somewhere between Tokyo and Singapore. Wherever is the centre of the Chinese world. The Chinese world, by virtue of its vastness, its population, its wealth and growth rates, is now becoming the locomotive of the world econ-omy as a whole. China and the Chinese world, represented by the diaspora of

Chinese people, is the main source of new demand and new wealth. You've got to see that Asia is where growth is going to be consistently higher for many years ahead, and therefore investment returns are also likely to be consistently higher. Fifty per cent of a portfolio would be a good weighting.'

At the same time, if manufacturing is moving East, the demand for commodities is going to soar. This will lead to very big investment opportunities in Africa and Australia. This concept is not in dispute. The magnitude involved is less well understood. In his book *The East-West Pendulum*, Lloyd George summarized the personal consumption statistics comparing the US and Japan with China. The contrasts are provocative and the implications awesome. What will happen if one quarter of the world increases its use of aluminium by over 20 times, or its consumption of sugar by nearly 15 times?

Table 7.2: How much does one person consume? (as of 1993)

	Chicago	*Tokyo*	*Shanghai*
Oil (gallons/day)	2.73	1.55	0.80
Copper (kg)	9.00	10.50	0.40
Aluminium (kg)	18.50	13.90	0.70
Rice (g)	7.00	204.00	343.00
Meat (g)	307.00	69.00	63.00
Sugar (g)	174.00	58.00	12.00
Television sets (per 1000 people)	885.00	795.00	8.00
Newsprint (kg)	57.00	28.00	1.30

Source: The Economist - The World in Figures

Finding value in specific stocks in Asia often requires a lot of leg work, a willingness to dig behind the publicly available data, and a willingness to recognize less tangible assets. Lloyd George explained how he got to grips with Siam Cement, perhaps the best single investment his funds ever made, with a return of over 20 times, after stock splits, since 1987.

'Siam Cement occupies a more important economic role in Thailand than any other company, comparable perhaps to Royal Dutch in Holland, or Deutsche Bank in Germany. It's 37 per cent owned by the Thai Royal Family. It has extraordinary connections. It has the best management of any company in the country. It has innumerable subsidiaries, in all the basic industrial sectors, not only cement and construction materials, but also steel and petrochemicals. Siam Cement also has high-tech businesses. For example, there is a joint venture with Matsushita to produce televisions.

There is also a huge depreciation charge, so the annual cash flow is more than twice as high as the reported earnings. Because it generally has this high depreciation charge, the consolidated value and true earnings of the company are consistently understated. It is a play on Thailand. If you want Thailand, which is achieving 8 per cent real GDP growth consistently year after year, with a steady currency, stable politics and corresponding growth in wealth and real estate values, Siam Cement must be the right choice.

Siam Cement has not been well understood. The company has not been particularly forthcoming with information. Many US analysts visited, but basically gave up trying to value it, and missed the fundamental value, which is a reflection of the whole Thai economy.'

Lloyd George applies all the analytical tools you would expect from someone who is exceptionally thorough.

'Everything we have learnt from Graham and Dodd is applicable in Asia. Techniques of security analysis are common to all markets, and fundamental to picking good shares. Cash flow per share is perhaps even more important. In Japan, in Korea, in Thailand, you have companies which consistently under-report earnings because of the consolidation of subsidiaries and because of high tax rates. For instance, Korean companies rarely report their true profit. While not unknown in Europe and America, this is particularly prevalent in Asia.'

Everything we have learnt from Graham and Dodd is applicable in Asia. Techniques of security analysis are common to all markets, and fundamental to picking good shares.

This investor, who has been able to reconcile separate strands in investing and uncover extraordinary values all across Asia, has a core philosophy.

'I would distil my investment style and approach as following five principles:

- a long-term vision in being "two jumps ahead", especially in emerging markets;
- conservative low risk diversification across Asia;
- an emphasis on first-hand research and making our own estimates of what a company can do;
- finding reasonably priced securities with long-term capital growth prospects. We do regular screening of all stocks in Asia to find P/Es well below earnings growth;
- flexibility.'

His greatest insight, however, is an intuitive understanding of what makes a company succeed in Asia. This often requires a departure from the purely quantitative tools of a Western analyst. An investor has to start by accepting that the dynamics which make a business work, and lead a company to create value for its shareholders, are not all the same in Lahore as in London. Here a sense of history, and a willingness to learn about another culture, stands Lloyd George in good stead. He has enormous respect for, and appreciation of, the Chinese contribution to the development of the world which allows him to listen, learn and understand.

'You have to go into the family factor in Asian companies. That cultural aspect is reflected both in management, and in reported earnings. There is frequently an overlap between the private and the public companies, which creates some unique conditions and can affect presentation. This is true, most of all, in companies run by Chinese families.'

In *The East West Pendulum*, Lloyd George further comments that:

'The Chinese race has a proven genius that spans three thousand years of continuous civilization. The accomplishments of the Chinese people in the field of scientific and technological invention as described by Joseph Needham in his book, *Science and Civilisation in China*, are further proof of the creativity and artistic brilliance exhibited in Chinese painting, ceramics and literature. China began to turn in on itself just after the voyages to Arabia and East Africa in the 1420s by the great admiral Zheng He. The faltering leadership of the later Qing Dynasty from 1800 onwards came as the West was accelerating its momentum in the age of scientific discovery. Now there is evidence that economic trends are converging. Hong Kong's personal income level overtook that of the United Kingdom in 1985, just as Japan's overtook the US in 1989.

Neither the nation, nor the company, but the family, is the basic unit of Chinese society. Just as if we want to understand the success of Japan, we must study the Japanese corporation, so, too, to understand Chinese business corporations we must study the Chinese family.

The main ideas preached by Confucius were the principles of hierarchy, order and harmony within the society. The loyalty owed by a subject to the emperor parallels that owed by a son to his father. Chinese stories are full of examples of filial piety. The hierarchy is based on generation, age, and sex. Father/son relationships are central to the success of a continuing family business. This is still valid in Chinese businesses today, where it is rare for a son to take any important decisions while his father is alive. Nothing is more misleading than to be told that the family patriarch has "retired". (And this is equally true in the political arena. Notable examples have been Deng Xiao Ping and Lee Kwan Yew.)

The individual within the Chinese family is of far less importance than in the West. It is not the family which exists in order to support the individual, but rather the individual that exists in order to continue the family. The reverse of Western thinking. In traditional China, the family has always come before the law. There is an almost universal Chinese aversion to lawsuits and arbitration. Personal relationships account for much more than contractual relationships. If we try to sum up the style and essence of Chinese business we can identify the following four characteristics:

1   Flexible decision-making by one strong individual.
2   Strong family control and connections to overseas cousins.
3   Highly informed financial planning (though unstructured in the Western sense).
4   Reliance on personal trust rather than legal contracts.

Parallel to the view that the family is more important than the individual is the very different Chinese idea of time. Because the individual's life is of less importance, so a longer-term view can be taken of investment decisions, which may be meditated for many years. These beliefs produce a rather different sense of the value of a business.'

It is essential to understand that stock markets have not developed in Asia in exactly the same way as they did in the US.

'Clearly, the extraordinary financial wealth which was created in Tokyo and Osaka in the past 20 years reflected the great economic success of Japan's exporters, but it is also true to say that it would not have grown as success-fully as it did over such a long period of time if it had not been for careful planning and institutional support. This involved the Ministry of Finance, the big banks, the four major brokerage houses and many of the large listed com-panies themselves, especially those of the trading houses or zaibatsu groups.

Korea and Taiwan were both former Japanese colonies with a strong Japanese cultural influence and their capital markets reflect much of the Japanese model. In Korea the chaebol performed much the same role as had the zaibatsu in Japan. Hyundai, Samsung, Daewoo and Lucky formed the core of the stock market as they did of the Korean economy, in much the same way as Mitsui, Mitsubishi, Yasuda and Fuji groups had represented the core of the Japanese market and economy. The close relationship between the banks and the trading and manufacturing houses both assisted and, to some extent, restrained the flexibility of those markets.'[1]

As might be expected, Lloyd George is excited about the long-term future potential in Asia, whatever the bumps along the road. The growth in the importance of Asia is the single greatest change in the investment environment of the 1990s versus the 1980s, but he is careful to put that in the context of other significant shifts.

'The environment in the 1990s is probably more difficult to make money in, not merely because there has been a whiff of deflation, but also because capi-tal flows are far bigger than they used to be. There is much more freedom to invest all over the world. Long term, a greater and greater percentage of US savings will go international. More of that will go into the emerging markets, namely Asia, whatever the year to year fluctuations. Both growth and inflation are likely to be lower and the high expectations of investment return may have to be reduced.

Having said that, there are still outstanding opportunities in Asia because of the spread of economic reform and the capitalist mentality to more countries,

678

but notably in China and India. Deregulation is now a fact of life in countries like India, and that does tend to produce better returns as those businesses are less shackled by governments and are more interested in making profits.

The free trade movement is also most important, even though it's hard to see the direct impact on share values. Had we gone down the path to protectionism, we would be in a long-term bear market. As long as we allow exports to flow from the newly industrialized countries to the developed countries, there is an overall rise in wealth and economic activity.

Another aspect which is not often commented on is **currency**. Those individuals who invested in Japan in the 1970s or early 1980s experienced not only the long-term growth in share values, but they also made a lot of money on the yen. What I would argue today in 1995 is that the Singapore dollar, the Malaysian ringit, perhaps the Thai baht, possibibly the Indonesian rupiah, and possibly one day the Chinese renimibi, which have all, to one extent or another, been linked to the American dollar, are now where the Japanese yen was in the late 1970s. They are undervalued. They are experiencing capital inflows, strong economic growth, large trade surpluses and, in some cases, lower inflation and interest rates. All these factors make me think that, if we look out ten years, these currencies should reflect their underlying economic strength and perform against the dollar as the Japanese yen did over the last 15 years. Individual investors in the West should focus more on this, even though it is a longer-term view.'

> **All these factors make me think that, if we look out ten years, these currencies should reflect their underlying economic strength and perform against the dollar as the Japanese yen did over the last 15 years.**

It is impossible to spend any time with Lloyd George without coming back to what is his key contribution to the development of global investing. He recognized early on the implications of what was happening in Asia and made investment decisions accordingly. Individual investors would be wise to follow his lead.

'Asia is once again on the move. During the next ten years it will again be the centre of the world economy. It has already replaced the United States. Within Asia the leadership is changing, too. Japan led in management, and in technology, and has maintained a stable political system. Now, however, it is the overseas Chinese of South East Asia which are taking up the baton. It is clear that the centre of gravity in the Chinese world has moved south. Today the centre of economic and, increasingly, cultural activity is the Pearl River and the coastal city of Hong Kong, which may be described as the nerve centre of the overseas Chinese world.

Since, perhaps, the first British embassy under Lord MaCartney to the Emperor Chien Lung in 1793, the insistent pressure in terms of trade, technology and ideas has been from West to East. In the twenty-first century the tide will be reversed. As a new century starts, leadership in economic and cultural terms will return to the Chinese.'

[1] Permission to quote from *The East West Pendulum*, Woodhead Faulkner, 1991 ♀

CHRISTOPHER MILLS

'Working with Management to Create Shareholder Value'

When Christopher Mills makes an investment he does not sit back and wait to see what happens. He gets involved with companies where he becomes a significant shareholder. This pro-active approach has proved very rewarding for his own investors.

Along the way, first at Invesco/MIM and now at J O Hambro, Mills has collected just about every prize that a fund manager in the UK can win. He was the 1995 winner of the *Sunday Telegraph* Best Investment Trust Group, which came on top of the same award in 1994, when he was also the *Sunday Telegraph* Best Investment Trust Manager. Other recent honours include:

- Best North American Investment Trust 1993 and 1994 (Micropal).
- Best Small Investment Trust and Best Single Country Fund 1991 (*Observer*).
- Best General Investment Trust 1990 (Chatterhouse Communications Ltd).

The performance is perhaps even more remarkable as it has been achieved through investing in a highly mature market, viz the United States, and in currency which has been weak most of the last ten years.

In addition to managing money for private clients, Mills is at the helm of two quoted investment trusts, North Atlantic Smaller Companies Investment

Trust (NASCIT) and American Opportunity Trust (AOT). Open your Saturday *Financial Times* to the performance tables and you will find NASCIT is top of its category over all relevant time periods. AOT is usually in second place. As of February 1995, NASCIT was 15 per cent ahead of its rivals over one year, and 70 per cent ahead over three years. Over the same period NASCIT was the sixth best performing UK investment trust. The first five were all Asia specialists. If you had purchased £1,000 of NASCIT at its original subscription price of 50p in August 1984, you would have an investment worth £5,500 today, despite a near 30 per cent fall in the value of the dollar. That is a compound annual rate of return of 21 per cent over the period.

Mills started making money while other students were struggling to master Latin declension.

'We formed an investment club at school in the late 1960s which caught the Australian mining boom. We were advised by one student, Robbie Lyle, whose father was a stockbroker. As a consequence, instead of buying sweets, I spent my pocket money acquiring shares in Tasminex, Australian Consolidated Coal, and a whole lot of other obscure Australian companies. The initial experience was extremely favourable. In our club you put up to £10 in the pot. We went home at the end of term in December. By the time we came back in late January the following year, Tasminex had gone from £2 to £60. Our £10 had increased to £40. This seemed a lot easier than most of the other ways of making money which we were hearing about in class.'

Mills classifies himself as a value investor, but he is willing to create the catalyst which will unlock the value. That marks him out from the crowd and gives him an enormous edge over more passive peers. Mills brings a remarkable multidimensional and multinational set of skills, often to companies where strong operating management has little experience or ability in dealing with the investment community. This gives him an opportunity to help them enhance the value of the business. The primary area to accomplish this has been through innovative financial restructuring.

'Once I have taken a position, what distinguishes me from most other investors is that, from time to time, I will work actively to promote the value that I perceive in a company.

In 1983–4 on the London Stock Exchange there were companies, primarily in the oil and gas businesses in the United States, which had effectively lost all their money but had accumulated very substantial tax loss carry forwards. I realized that the tax loss, which – in the United Kingdom – was relatively valueless, could be transferred in the US to another business. At the time, the IRS rules for introducing new shareholders were relatively lax. It was possible to take these shells, buy good businesses

what distinguishes me from most other investors is that, from time to time, I will work actively to promote the value that I perceive in a company.

and shelter their taxes for a considerable period of time. This enabled them to grow faster through extra cash generation and obtain a quote in London. The first was a company called American Electronic Components, which was bought by Burgess Products at a premium of over 150 per cent above the purchase price rather less than two years before. The most successful was Newcourt Natural Resources, which purchased Danka Business Systems, an office products distributor. That stock has risen approximately 30 times in eight years.

You have to look at the structure of these transactions. We were able to create value for the shareholders through translating goodwill into assets which could be depreciated for tax purposes, such as non-compete agreements. This further reduced tax and freed up more cash to be reinvested.

Another area of opportunity arises from arbitrage between the UK and US. When you have these cross-country corporate structures, you can create cash flow through recognizing the differences that exist in the tax codes and the treatment of group relationships such as inter-company loans. Designating those in different currencies can lead to notional losses which improve cash flow and have no adverse impact on earnings per share.

Overhauling the financial structure of a company can also create exceptional value. American Healthcare Management was a company which had been over leveraged and was run by a team who flew around in two corporate jets. As a consequence it went bankrupt. New management, led by Steve Volla, came in. He was an excellent hands-on manager, but inherited a financial nightmare. He was faced with $100 million of debt at 11 per cent rates, another $100 million at 14 per cent, and interest expense of $25 million against an EBITDA of $33 million. We, along with some other investors, bought control of the 14 per cent debt which was trading at 40 cents on the dollar current pay and yielding 35 per cent. We converted that debt into equity. This enabled the company to go from interest coverage of 1.2 to nearly 3.0. They were able to go to their banks and arrange cheaper medium-term finance. Interest expense fell. With the true earnings power clear, the share price went from $1 to $14.'

While Mills' primary focus is financial, he also contributes to the development of the business.

'Being involved with a number of companies, I can often introduce them to see if they can work together to enhance their business. A number of other companies I had invested in became photocopying clients of Danka. At Horace Small, for example, I was able to introduce Corrections Corporation of America, a private prison company in the US. Now Small provides the uniforms for all the guards employed by CCA.

In European Home Products we bought Singer Sewing Machines' European operation. Management had not been able to manage effectively. To fill up manufacturing plants, the distribution company had been forced to sell the mail order sector, which is solely influenced by price. Sterling was weak at the time. They had fixed price sterling contracts but were purchasing from factories in Italy and the United States. When the dollar and the lire rose, which it did for a while back in 1985, margins were wiped out. The first thing we did was to stop the mail order business. Then we changed all sourcing arrangements. Lastly we managed the currency mix differently. Within 12 months the company was profitable. Two years later we were able to have a very successful public offering.'

While Mills tries to work in tandem with management, his overriding concern is the shareholder. If a company where he is invested does not put shareholders first or pursues a course of action which undermines the stock price, he is willing to call for changes. Making sure management respects its responsibilities sometimes requires a willingness to stand up for shareholders' rights.

'Particularly in the United States this has led to a need to engage in a proxy fight or actions which entrenched management or stagnant Boards may consider hostile. In 1994 I was a Director of American Funeral Services. Shortly after we went public the company found itself under accumulation from one of its competitors, Service Corporation of America. The company announced a number of measures to deter Service Corporation. They adopted a poison pill. I started out as the only Director who was committed to seeing the shareholders get a fair deal. My view was that the Board should not stand in the way if there was going to be an attractive offer. Eventually the company agreed to enter into serious negotiations and a bid followed at a good premium to the public offering price.

In a company called Oak Industries some of the actions which management were proposing appeared potentially disastrous. With one outside director leading the charge, a new slate was put forward for election to the Board. The fight won, fresh management was brought in. The new team unlocked the earnings potential of the existing business, and also expanded the company through both organic growth and acquisition. We gave them full support. They made us five times our money in six years.'

In one final capacity Mills may also play an active role. If the business reaches a point in its evolution where the next logical step is sale to a larger entity or a public offering, he can guide the company through these processes.

Another aspect of Mills' philosophy is that you can never have too much of a good thing. As he knows his main holdings well, Mills often takes positions which would scare most managers, such as 24 per cent of Oak Industries, or 25 per cent of Danka. The more Mills owns of a company, the more time he can devote. Large concentrated stakes make sense if you know how to add and then extract value. Because of his activist approach, he can afford to make the big bet most managers shun. In some cases, over 10 per cent of an entire portfolio will be in one stock.

Once Mills is involved with a good company or a good management team he will try to invest in the same winning formula several times over.

'We made ten times our investment in four years backing a man called Ken White to build up Bristol Corporation in plumbing supplies. That was sold to an LBO Group and then to Wolseley. When Ken was looking to buy a business in environmental services, we put up most of the money. We expect to sell his new company at a good profit and would back him in his next venture. After Burgess bought American Electronics, they were acquired by Williams Holdings. Management wanted to buy back the original company. So we put up 20 per cent of the equity to do a leveraged buy-out in 1989 and in 1994 AEC went public on NASDAQ.'

One final common theme runs through Mills' approach. Almost every investment is in smaller companies.

'Smaller companies require us to meet with, talk with, and work with management. They involve us in a great deal of extra effort, but we will continue to focus on the area of the market which is less than £100 million in capitalization, perhaps in the US up to $200 million. That's where the bargains are. Companies are under-researched. Our idea of sheer bliss is a company with no broker, growing nicely, at a low multiple, and often with a complicated story. We can do our own research. Once we have bought a position we will often take that company to friends in the brokerage community and share our analysis. In some cases they will pick it up. Comdata went from no coverage to seven analysts in 18 months.'

> **Our idea of sheer bliss is a company with no broker, growing nicely, at a low multiple, and often with a complicated story.**

One unorthodox feature of Mills' investment portfolio is a large element of unquoted securities. In that sense he straddles the fence between venture capital and traditional investment management. That fits with his style of taking large positions and then helping a company fulfil its potential. The unquoted portfolio has typically been between 20 and 25 per cent of his holdings at any one time. Mills invests in leveraged buy-outs of established business and in development capital situations, but he seldom, if ever, invests in start-ups. Mills has made money in businesses as diverse as prison health care, regional savings banks, spice manufacturing and industrial pumps. The one common theme was backing a top flight team of managers with a well-thought-out plan to change some element of a market place.

'Of course it's critical when making any investment in an unquoted company to have a clearly defined exit strategy. That's one of the problems in investing in very small companies. We always discuss this in great detail beforehand because that's an area where disagreement can jeopardize the value of an investment.'

This focus also involves looking at businesses which have been in bankruptcy, and which are re-emerging following a financial reorganization.

'These are often very small companies, particularly the equity component. They have no natural sponsor. Usually management are hoping to get options at a low price. Brokers are once bitten, twice shy. There's no research. Creditors often have ended up as involuntary owners of stock. Basically they just want to sell as quickly as possible. The investment bank which signed off on the forecast is usually conservative, because why risk getting it wrong twice? Companies emerging from bankruptcy come out as orphan stocks. To pick winners requires a great deal of research, but the effort is often rewarded.'

Mills is a long-term investor by inclination. He believes holding over several years normally results in the best capital appreciation, but he will trade even his core holdings under certain circumstances.

'When we analyse a business we make a long-term forecast of its performance. Within that period it is likely that the company will, at times, be overvalued or undervalued relative to the objective. We may take the top off investments if we believe the price has been pushed up too far and we will add more when they are undervalued. We may sell if the future IRR is driven down by an expensive price, and buy back in if the level falls.'

Of course, the structure of the portfolio and the investment style, limits to some degree, market timing but, on occasions, Mills has taken a view.

'In 1987 we liquidated very heavily. We were 40 per cent liquid when the crash came. Markets were substantially overvalued on almost any basis; liquidity was drying up; indices were struggling on a technical basis to make new highs. There were increasing new lows to new highs among individual stocks.'

His main aim, however, is to make sure his portfolio is relatively market neutral, more dependent on events he can control or influence than exposed to forces he cannot predict or affect.

Mills has developed a number of investment guidelines which complement his unique style.

'We seldom, if ever, invest in technology stocks companies. The life cycles of their products do not conform well with our longer-term investment philosophy. We also stay away from businesses which are so complicated you have to be an expert to make a difference.

Our analysis tends to be old-fashioned nuts and bolts. We look at the product, the cash flow, and the financial structure. The one concept we have based our investment philosophy on is EBITDA, the enterprise value. Food-brands America, currently trading at $8, should earn 80¢ this year. Not an obviously cheap stock. However, the company is writing off 40¢ of goodwill for acquisitions made in the 1980s. The core business, under UK GAAP conventions, would earn $1.20 a share. There is a huge tax loss carry forward which means that actual earnings are closer to $2. So a stock which looks to be trading on a P/E of 10 is actually on a P/E of less than 4. Non-cash charges disguise a cash flow of about $25 million versus a market capitalization today (February 1995) of little more than $100 million.'

Mills sees the 1990s as placing more demands on investors to do thorough analyses, both macroeconomic and company specific.

'I see more investors abandoning P/E based valuations for EBITDA/ Enterprise Value analysis. A company with an old, dilapidated facility will, in the short-term, have higher earnings than a company with a brand new plant producing the same product and selling it at the same price. In the longer-term it will have to re-modernize. It is a nonsense that these two companies should trade on the same ratio when the one with lower earnings has higher cash flow and less future need. In a British context companies like Grand Metropolitan, which have substantial debt and whose profits depend, to some extent, on releasing reserves, will be downgraded relative to an industry comparable like Allied Lyons, which has less debt and more free cash flow. Grand Met may have a lower P/E but on cash flow measures which reflect the sustainable growth of the business, Allied Lyons looks cheaper.'

Mills does identify some trends which he believes investors can latch onto and expect to achieve above average returns. His own portfolio has been rejigged to reflect these new priorities.

'We are at the start of a major capital spending boom. Capacity utilization rates rose very rapidly in the last recovery. We are now at the point where, unless additional capacity is brought on-line, there will be a pick-up in inflation. Europe already has a capital goods-led boom rather than a consumer-led boom. That trend is likely to continue for at least the next three years. People who understand the technology sector can identify companies that benefit from spending by firms to increase their productivity. There are other, more basic businesses. We are buying Gardner Denver Machinery, one of the leading compressor companies in the US. We also have a large stake in Denison, a global pump manufacturer.

Companies no longer have the ability to raise prices as costs rise. Only companies which are able to improve productivity or where input costs are relatively unimportant are likely to achieve superior earnings growth over the next decade. If the price of copper goes up and you make copper pans, your margins will be squeezed.

In this environment the concept that brands have pricing flexibility because they are well known no longer works. If you look at the reverse, a company like McBride in the UK is growing very rapidly, because it provides generic pharmaceutical products under the store's own name, which are substantially cheaper than the branded alternatives; and the store makes more margin, so wants to push generics. McBride can increase its volume and its margins at the expense of branded competitors.

The focus of our portfolio has changed in the 1990s. We sold all our branded consumer product holdings which used to be a big percentage in one fund. We have replaced these with service businesses where there are strong recurring revenue streams as a core investment strategy. Credit card processing is just such a business. Fund management is another. I believe managing money is an outstanding business which should grow rapidly with increased savings from ageing populations. They are in a good position to control their costs, which are basically two: technology, which is coming down in price, and people, where a lot of compensation is variable because of the high bonus element. The industry itself is also going through consolidation. The number of companies will come down sharply.

> **The focus of our portfolio has changed in the 1990s. We sold all our branded consumer product holdings which used to be a big percentage in one fund. We have replaced these with service businesses where there are strong recurring revenue streams as a core investment strategy.**

Some sectors of the stock market should benefit from macro-population trends. Nursing companies should do well. Ageing means more demand, but also many nursing homes are emerging as an alternative provider of care to hospitals. Less ill patients can get basic treatment in nursing homes at half the cost of a hospital stay. The US nursing home industry is converting beds to accommodate this type of patient rather than the traditional inmate. This conversion helps governments control costs, which is another important area. Any business which reduces the cost of government services should do well. Information providers who reduce paperwork are in this category. The move to one-stop electronic processing is attractive.

The recent election in the US has shifted the policies of that country. That's good news for saving and investment. Capital gains tax should be cut. There are likely to be more programmes to encourage individual investment. The US economy has, for so long, been consumer driven. The climate is right to see a shift to being investment driven, which is where it needs to be. This has been one of its fundamental weaknesses over the last 20 years. All these changes should be very positive in the US over the next ten years.

We have seen some of these trends in the UK. The government has been pushing people to invest more through an increasing number of instruments. First the focus was on equities with PEPs. TESSAs encouraged bank accounts. The latest scheme allows corporate bonds. Household ownership of corporate bonds is virtually nil. This scheme could create a new class of long-term capital

for industry in the UK and give another choice to companies who have historically had to rely on the equity markets or their banks.'

These changes suggest some reappraisal of asset allocation may be needed to
achieve decent returns over the next decade.

'Equities in the US and the UK have a number of structural difficulties to over-
come. The ageing of the population is the main problem. While individuals
may invest more, traditional pension plans will be reaching maturity. They
will have to shift their equity/bond mix in favour of bonds. This shift will be
more pronounced in the UK because bond portfolios have typically been
around 15 per cent of assets whereas, in the US, the percentage is closer to
50 per cent.

Good companies growing at 13 to 20 per cent compound should still be the
best investment over the next decade but, when you come to the bigger blue
chips, bonds could perform better in that environment. You want a balance,
but with a different tilt.'

Mills believes markets are strongly stacked against the individual investor. The
time required to follow investments and dealing costs make direct investment
difficult. Most individuals should focus on finding managers with a superior
track record and back them for long periods. Chopping and changing is a certain recipe for reducing returns. For a UK-based individual, Mills advocates a
mix of holdings in investment and unit trusts as shown in Table 7.3.

Table 7.3

Recommended Asset Allocation	% of Total
United Kingdom (two-thirds stocks, one-third bonds)	45
Far East	12.5
Europe	10
High potential specialist funds	10
United States	7.5
Emerging markets	10
Property	5
Commodities (through equities)	5

Mills feels that talking with people in the investment business has been one
essential factor to his success. He has learnt from watching investors he
regards highly and absorbing elements of their approach which worked well
into his own. He notes in particular Ira Unschuldt at Schroders, Buzz Zeano at
Trust Company of the West and John Gildea of Gildea Asset Management. ♀

MICHAEL PRICE

'A Three-Pronged Approach to Finding Value'

1995 is the twentieth anniversary of Michael Price's arrival at Mutual Series. $1 invested in the flagship Mutual Share Fund then was worth $35 nineteen years later, a truly phenomenal performance. The hallmark is consistency. In twenty years there have only been three when the Fund did not notch up double digit gains. As the family of Funds expanded, far from diluting success Price has replicated his performance. All three main Funds have out-performed the S&P over ten, five and three year-periods.

In the most recent year the out-performance has accelerated with returns across his Funds more than triple the S&P. He won the Kiplinger personal finance award as top Fund Manager in 1994, attaining at the same time the lowest volatility ranking. No wonder he was recently called 'Priceless' by Mutual Fund magazine. All this performance comes without added risk. Rather the reverse. Morningstar recently ranked his funds as Nos 2, 5 and 6 for performance, yet they incur less than half the risk of the average equity fund. Not so surprising, then, that Mutual Series never has to advertise.

Michael Price has always been fascinated with stocks.

'I bought my first stock when I was thirteen. It was Bandag, the rubber retreading company. My dad's broker liked it. It was a growth stock which is quite the contrary of what I do today. Now I like to buy a dollar of assets for 50 cents. Anyway Bandag tripled and I was hooked.'

Price's introduction to the world of investing was typical of how his personal style has evolved. He gravitated to a part of the market which was not in vogue.

'When I was sixteen I started to meet people in the merger arbitrage business, which at that time was a little corner of Wall Street. No one knew much about it and no one much cared. The action was elsewhere. This was just a neglected niche but I was attracted to what they were doing. I just knew intuitively that this was the right way to make money and that I would enjoy doing it.'

Mutual Series already had developed an impressive record. Founded in 1950 under the guidance of Max Heine the Fund had achieved a cumulative return of 1,563 per cent over twenty-five years before Price joined. Heine was a purist stock picker who applied the Graham and Dodd approach to value with unmatched discipline. Price was his most ardent and most successful disciple. The Heine approach remains at the core of the philosophy which guides a business now with almost $8.5 billion under management.

'Two thirds of our investments are in cheap stocks. By cheap I mean we look at the intrinsic values. We want to fish in ponds where stocks trade at a large discount from real value. You can feel comfortable that if it's going to go down it can't go down much. We don't want to fish among stocks valued on multiples of future earnings. What if the earnings stop? We can't predict what these earnings are going to be three, four years from now.

We want to fish in ponds where stocks trade at a large discount from real value.

Don't show me numbers for 1998. They're meaningless. I want to know what a company is worth today and start from that. We like to own stocks that have a Margin of Safety. That's very important for us. That's why after the crash of '87 our Fund was the first to regain its high. These stocks bounce back more quickly than stocks trading at twice their intrinsic value. There are several ways to look at intrinsic value. Book is only a starting point. We try and look at value in a lot of different ways. There are companies being bought and sold every day. That's a good indicator of

Don't show me numbers for 1998. They're meaningless. I want to know what a company is worth today and start from that.

value. The market is always valuing comparable companies. We do look at replacement value or liquidation value. We are not tied to one way and this leads us to find value in some odd places. For example many conglomerates are often trading for a lot less than the value of the pieces. By buying a stock like that you get a lot of good businesses for less than someone who bought them separately.

> **many conglomerates are often trading for a lot less than the value of the pieces.**

Then we like to see if there is a chance of something happening. The thing that really makes an investment work well is when you get an event which brings out the value. It could be a company buy-back programme, or an acquisition, or a restructuring. When American Express spun out Lehman Brothers the market was finally able to put a proper value on that division which had been buried for so long. Events are really what move stock prices rather than earnings growth which may or may not happen. Litton was an event story. Their seismic surveying business was worth more than the total company. So you got

> **The thing that really makes an investment work well is when you get an event which brings out the value.**

the defence business for free. The value of Litton doubled when Western Atlas was spun out to shareholders and the defence business still could be a take-over target.'

Price is the first to say that value investing is not the same game it was in 1975. Even back then he wanted to redefine the concept. His first contribution was to introduce a new wrinkle, merger arbitrage, something extra to overlay over the traditional approach. Whenever the crowd caught up Price was ready to reappraise his style, move on to the next level and fine tune his thinking; but he never lost sight of the fundamentals.

'Max had been doing this in the '30s long before I got here. I added the arbitrage and we had a person interested in bankruptcies. That way we developed a three-pronged approach. The same thing works with stocks and bonds. You saw it with utilities in the thirties and then again with railroads in the fifties. The NYSE would come along and delist the investment but the value was still there. A lot of bonds were mortgage backed, collateralized on real assets, cars, track, rights of way. They held a value independent of what was happening to the company. Penn Central was a classic. In 1975 the bonds were trading at ten cents on the $. We had the confidence of the intrinsic value behind the assets and bought big. In 1979 they turned out to be worth par. There were quite a few of these like Erie, and Boston and Maine.

In the 1980s the focus shifted to a different sort of business but the story was still the same. The market missed the real value in the assets. We did very well with Itel in 1981, AM International in 1982 and Storage Technology in 1985. These were big winners and our purchases changed the business forever. A lot of other players were attracted by our success. Too much competition is bad for values.

So we took a fresh look at the capital structure of these problem companies. We found that most often the debt in there was four or five times the value of shares or even more. This was a much larger pool of merchandise; when things went wrong the banks holding the paper didn't have a lot of options. We started to offer them an option. Effectively we expanded the market by buying bank debt which was secured so the risk was not extreme. We were on our own in that for four to five years.

That's the way we found our very best deal, Allegheny International, which was renamed Sunbeam. Here was a company which had four nice divisions struggling to get out but submerged and stifled by a financial structure which was out of whack. We looked past the debt and the bad management. We were able to analyse the overhead and see where if you cut out some of the improper allocation you had profitable operations. $60 million invested was converted into $1.5 billion in five years.'

One-third of the portfolio is in special situations, announced mergers, arbitrage possibilities, bankruptcies and cash. Price likes to keep a cash reserve so he can move quickly if something particularly interesting comes his way. If this sounds like a strange mix it's actually very conservative.

'Roughly half the assets we're in aren't affected directly by the market but by the progress of unrelated events, restructurings, acquisitions, bankruptcy hearings, sales, spin offs. That's why our Funds tends to go down less than the market. In a good year we may go up less, but when the event closes we get a bounce up, whatever may be happening. That's why we get better performance overall.'

Price is not a trader. Buying on dips may be OK, but trading in and out of a stock is discouraged. Price is also not a macro-market timer and does not attempt to second guess broad brush trends. He focuses on value, one stock at a time.

'We don't do any top down analysis. We have no views of the overall market. We don't take a position on interest rates or the economy or the cycle or anything like that. You have to spend time looking at the accounts of individual companies not whether stocks in general are trading at high or low values. We do try and stay out of the way of any adverse trends which are obvious. And we do take notice and like to be on the right side of trends where we can participate. For example there are still way too many banks in the US. There are less today than there were in 1990 and I believe there will be a lot less around in five and ten years. We want to own the stocks that will be taken over. That call fits two of our three prongs, buying cheap stocks and merger arbitrage.

> **For example there are still way too many banks in the US. There are less today than there were in 1990 and I believe there will be a lot less around in five and ten years.**

We're in the business of bottom up stock analysis. We look at sectors which are weak and find the best values within the sector. We only buy after intense work. We don't buy sectors, but we do look at which sectors are down. Casinos are down now (comment made just before ITT bid for Caesar World) and utilities are off by 21 per cent. These are good places to go looking for value. We really like an event which causes the market price of a share to drop but does not damage the fundamentals of the company. If the business is intact and the intrinsic value is still there we can buy it cheaper that way. We look for things like a dividend omission or a lawsuit. The market often overreacts to these things. Problems lead to opportunities.'

A recent example of this philosophy at work was Philip Morris. When the company announced its intention to slash the price of Marlboro the stock price slid $15 wiping out a fourth of its market value. While others were bailing out Price was buying in. 'Sometimes bad news doesn't mean the value is gone.'

Price agrees that selling is tougher than buying.

'You never know what the buyer has in mind. If we think a stock is worth 20 we might start to sell down as it gets to 16 or 17. By 21 we're out. But there may be plenty of people who think it is worth 30 or 40 and so it may go on up to 28, 29. We have to stick with our own sense of values even if that means leaving something on the table. The other thing is that if we make a mistake we clean out the portfolio quickly. It's too easy to leave a loser and come up with excuses. You don't want to drive yourself crazy looking at losers. So it's best to sell and take the loss and move on.'

Looking to the end of the century Price is upbeat about a number of trends in the market, particularly as they pertain to his style of investing.

'There's a lot going on that's very positive for the US. We've addressed a lot of problems in industry in this country. We have made great productivity gains. We've opened up markets. Ten years ago barriers were higher and foreign sales were harder. NAFTA and GATT on the whole are very positive. We have a lower currency which makes us more competitive. The exports from the US are in areas which are growth markets. In effect America has a large market share in sectors where we are strong. Our big exports are trademarks, music, software. All around the world more and more people want to wear Levi's or eat at McDonald's. Buying Coca-Cola is sometimes said to be akin to investing in China even if it's based here (Warren Buffet owns a big stake). We're better placed to take advantage of that financially and many companies have made

> **The exports from the US are in areas which are growth markets. In effect America has a large market share in sectors where we are strong. Our big exports are trademarks, music, software.**

huge productivity gains over the last ten years so our competitive position is that much stronger.

A lot of people are chasing the global story overseas and buying foreign stocks. That makes it easier for someone like us as it frees up more opportunities in the US. We're also helped by the focus on growth as a proxy for value. The more people who pay attention to growth the less the asset approach is popular and that suits us. Derivatives will increase and that helps us too. Derivatives and synthetics increase overall market volatility which means there will be more opportunity to pick up stocks cheaper.'

Price is ambivalent about how far investors should go in getting involved with the companies they own. In his case ownership can be a big percentage. He recently bought 20 per cent of Van Melle, a Dutch candy maker, in a single trade and his funds own over 29 per cent of the Convertible Preferred of Ransomes plc, the oldest manufacturer of lawnmowers in the world.

'We are active in speaking with management and sharing ideas about how to make a business better. There's a perspective we have and in some ways we are closer to shareholder concerns. We must vote our proxies carefully. It's important to take a stand against management actions which are not in the interests of shareholders. If management is overreaching through too big an acquisition or voting themselves too much in stock options or adding shark repellent, we'd vote against them and we'll speak out. We have to be active but shareholders can't and shouldn't run the business.'

Price is confident his own company continues to offer a unique approach to investors.

'No one in mutual funds combines the cheap stock picking approach with risk arbitrage and bankruptcy plays. There are a few which do one or the other but not all three. The key to success is the people. I've built this team over fifteen years and each person is a specialist in a field. We aren't competing with the other mutual funds. My competition is Soros and the arbitrage department at Goldman Sachs. Only we do it for the average investor at a much lower fee, one or two per cent versus their twenty. We are much less risky. We have no leverage and we are more diversified as a Fund. That's why we can be so consistent.'

Most helpful books for investors to read: *Value Investing* by Graham & Dodd and a 1971 thesis on risk arbitrage written by Guy Wyser-Pratte at NYU.

'These two books are all you need to know to succeed at investing.'

SIR JOHN TEMPLETON

'The World is his Oyster'

Since the Second World War, Templeton has been synonymous with global investing. Though now retired from day-to-day involvement with the family of funds which bears his name, his guidance, vision and values not only permeate that organization but also influence a host of managers around the world who have adopted his investment style in an attempt to replicate his performance. The results speak for themselves. Since 1954 the value of a $10,000 investment in the Templeton Growth Fund has mushroomed to $2,168,343. That is an annual compound total rate of return of 14.6 per cent. Over 40 years! For a fund which is now over $5.5 billion. All the Templeton mutual funds now total over $35 billion.

His other funds, which started more recently, have all done extremely well. The World Fund has achieved a hair less than 16 per cent per annum over 17 years, the Foreign Fund, which excludes US stocks, 17.6 per cent per annum over 12 years, and the Smaller Companies Growth Fund managed 14.3 per cent over 13 years. Wherever you put your money at the start of the 1980s, you did very well if the Templeton name was on the fund. Now part of Franklin, Templeton's global emphasis remains. The firm has research offices in Edinburgh, Fort Lauderdale, Hong Kong, Melbourne, Nassau, Singapore and Toronto.

Unlike most people who entered the investment business because they wanted to make money, Sir John Templeton sort of slid in sideways, because he wanted to make other people money.

'Where I was reared in Franklin County, Tennessee, I honestly didn't know a single person who owned a share of anything. But in my second year at Yale (1931) I was studying elementary economics and became amazed at how widely share prices fluctuated. At that time the difference between the low for the year and the high for the year was averaging around 100 per cent in a single year. So it came to me that the market couldn't conceivably be always right about the true value of the company, and anyone who could make a reasonable estimate of the true value would have a useful way to help people get in at low prices and out at high prices . . . so I did a long period of thinking. God gives everyone some abilities, and what he'd given me seemed to be suitable for making estimates or judgements of values, and that if I was going to utilize these God-given abilities, investment counsel, which was then a new concept, and there were very few counsellors at that time, was a place where I could be useful.'

This combination of a desire to provide a superior service and a phenomenal ability to exploit the inefficiencies in the stock market became his hallmark. The other distinguishing attribute of the Templeton approach was a readiness to look globally for these inefficiencies at a time when lateral thinking was rare, if not heretical.

'To my mind it's simply common sense. My job as an investment counsellor was to find those stocks selling at the smallest price in relation to their value and if I limited myself to the United Kingdom or the United States I could find many; but I could surely find more if I looked around the world. To be more useful than other investment counsellors, it was necessary for me to be able to make those selections everywhere. Not only does it give you a broader selection, but you can also get better bargains looking in odd places. In London and New York share prices get out of line in value, but in other places they get even further out of line. You get better bargains in addition to more bargains by looking world-wide.'

> you can get better bargains looking in odd places. In London and New York share prices get out of line in value, but in other places they get even further out of line.

Sounds so simple stated that way!

'Another very important factor is that you reduce your risk. Every major market in the world has bear markets about twice every 12 years. They do not, however, occur at the same time in different places. Therefore, if you help your client to be invested in many nations, the client will not suffer as much in bear markets as if he would if the holding were all concentrated in one place.'

697

It is worth noting that Sir John Templeton's preparation for the investment business was not traditional, either. A combination of economics at Yale, followed by law at Oxford, 'but only because they didn't teach business', led to a period when he went walkabout.

'If I said I'm going to help people to invest all over the world, I decided I really ought to get acquainted with the variations in people and different nations. The trouble was I didn't have any money. I had saved up £90. I joined up with a Canadian and together we travelled for seven months through 35 nations. We learned a lot because we were living like the nationals in every country we went to. Our average cost for hotels was only a shilling (25¢) a night. That time of travel was the most valuable year of education.'

Looking around the world is only step one. The question of how to identify better bargains has undergone intensive scrutiny over the 54 years Templeton has been making money for his clients. Some recurring themes always contrive to come through and show superior investment results, however many more new ideas are tried and tested. The front line troops in this struggle to uncover value are the security analysts. Sir John places great emphasis on the importance of thorough analysis.

'For each corporation there is a set of specific things which apply to determine value. In most cases the important thing is how high is the price in relation to earnings. Now, of course, it's also important how high it is in relation to assets, how high in relation to dividends, how high in relation to other stocks.' (The emphasis is on the words 'in relation to'.) 'If you had to single it out in the majority of appraisals we make, the key question is "how high is the price in relation to earnings?" However, it's not necessarily the last reported earnings, because that may have been abnormal. You are more interested in how high is the price in relation to average earnings; but even that's not the best, because what you're really interested in is how high is the price in relation to **probable future earnings**.

We've specialized in judging what each corporation might be able to earn five years in the future. Then we compare that to today's market price. Eighty to ninety per cent of our competitors look out one year and they're wrong a high percentage of the time. We find we're wrong less looking out five years because you don't base your estimate on where we are in the business cycle. We just assume conditions are normal, which makes it easier to measure earnings power and not for today but based on what that corporation is likely to grow. That is the other important factor. Trying to estimate the rate of growth of each corporation.

To do that you need to know its competition and the future of the industry or industries it operates in. Of course you do look at its past growth rate, but it would be a mistake to project the past into the future. You have to study management's ability to continue that growth in earnings per share. Out of all the ways of looking at earnings, we still come back to reported earnings net after taxes. Audited. The other ways of measuring earnings power have just not proved as good.'

Templeton opened its doors in Radio City in New York in 1940. The pitch was world-wide investing, which attracted some interest, but it was two years before he was able to pay himself a salary. The first $20 million took 20 years to amass in his first investment mutual fund. Now the company takes in more than $20 million each day.

Sir John has had so many successes in his career, but a couple stand out. One is the classic contrarian play of all times which hopefully can never be replicated.

'In the late 1930s the world had gone through the greatest business recession ever. Then Stalin invaded Poland. Any knowledge of history will tell you that, during any major war, there is such demand that even the worst companies come back to life and have good earnings. So I bought $100 of every stock on both exchanges selling for no more than $1. There were 104 stocks in that category and I made a profit on 100 of them. The best of all was the $7 preferred stock of Missouri Pacific Railway. It had been issued about 15 years earlier, paying a cash dividend of $7 per year, but it was in bankruptcy, so the shares were available for 12¢. For $100 I bought 800 shares. Just what I expected happened. It started to make a profit and, in five years, it got up to $5, which was 40 times my money.'

The second shows that an enquiring mind has its own reward and you can never be sure where an interesting conversation might lead.

'Twelve years ago I was giving a speech in San Francisco. I was offered a ride to the airport by the sales manager of a mutual fund group called Franklin Resources. I had never heard of them. They were very small. As any security analyst always does, I kept asking a hundred questions and his answers were so interesting that I bought every share I could at $3 for four months. My average cost became 30¢ with stock splits and dividends. When I was ready to retire I selected them as my merger partner. One of the reasons was that I owned 122,000 shares which were then selling at $26. This caused me to think they were well managed. It's now over $37, which is over 120 times what I paid for it in 12 years.'

The Templeton approach to selling stock is rather idiosyncratic and difficult for others to follow. 'We sell any stock when we have found an alternative stock which is 50 per cent lower in relation to value. We have studied over a dozen different ways to sell. This is a common sense answer. It combines all the elements of when to make a change . . . when you're getting 50 per cent more for your money.'

Surprisingly, this methodology results in relatively low turnover. Templeton credits low turnover and a long average holding period as one of the keys to his outperformance of his industry. There is also a whiff of momentum philosophy which emerged from his experience.

'We have a holding period of more than four years: I don't know any major mutual fund group which holds stocks as long as we do. One of the things we've found over the years is not to act too soon. If a security has been going up steadily, don't think it's going to turn down quickly. We might hold a stock now to see how far up it's going to go even when we have found something better. I can't illustrate that better than with Missouri Railway. Two years after I sold it for $5 it was at $105. I remember that investment well.'

Sir John Templeton is highly sceptical about the value of market timing. It's one of those things which would be great, if only it worked in practice.

'Nobody can tell you when a bear or bull market will start or stop.' He points out that his own funds have prospered through seven bear markets. 'It's normal for share prices in North America to double every 11 years.'

Sir John Templeton has a very positive perspective on the investment climate over the next ten years. Fundamental to this view are the changes underway in the world. His book *Looking Forward - the Next Forty Years* talks about these trends and the potential to unlock the power of information in a free society.

'When history is written, I think the year 1989 will go down as a major turning point, maybe of the same significance as Columbus' discovery of the New World. His discovery led to an expansion in transportation and commerce and prosperity because of the greater knowledge.

In 1989 the world was relieved of the two most serious worries we had in my lifetime. One was the fear of nuclear war. The other one was that the Russians might be right in saying their system was going to dominate the world. When I was at Oxford (1934) the majority of the students thought it was the way of the future. We would all end up living under that system, and two-thirds of the teachers believed it, too. The Russians never captured a nation by voting, but they did capture 23 nations one by one and, up until 1989, no captured nation had ever become free. Even worse than that, they had captured the minds of some of the most important people in colleges, newspapers and the church. If that had gone on much further, the free enterprise minded people could have become intimidated, and not minded to speak up.

It was so serious it was having a depressing effect on almost everything in the world. Now that's been relieved. Consequently the world is going to prosper

> **'When history is written, I think the year 1989 will go down as a major turning point, maybe of the same significance as Columbus' discovery of the New World.**

much more quickly than it did before. There's going to be far more travel, far more transportation, far more commerce, far more international investing, far more production of goods in areas where production costs are lowest. The richness and variety of life will expand more rapidly. Now, in trying to decide what a corporation is worth, we can take into account that these opportunities may have improved the future growth rate and, therefore, its valuation.'

Sir John Templeton believes the rate of change also has a drawback for individuals because it makes the world of investment that much more difficult.

'There was an old saying when I was studying at Oxford: "The man who serves as his own lawyer has a fool for a client". Fifty-four years ago the profession of investment counsel had not developed much. Now, with over 22,000 professionals working at it every day, the chances of an amateur getting ahead of them is very small. The best step most people can take is to find a good manager.'

One other piece of advice shines through. On a global basis Sir John Templeton is as much a contrarian on countries as Michael Aronstein is on asset categories. The key to successful investing is to look for markets which have been performing badly. He looks for the best opportunities to be

'at the point of maximum pessimism. If you buy where the outlook is good, you're not likely to get a bargain. Other people can see that too. There are very few things selling for a small fraction of their true value. Look where the people are most pessimistic. That's the place to search.

Look where the people are most pessimistic. That's the place to search.

That changes from year to year . . . sometimes from month to month. In the last six years there have been bear markets greater than 50 per cent in Taiwan, Japan, Korea, Thailand, Austria, Finland, Brazil, Portugal, Spain, Italy and Turkey. In two nations there has been a 70 per cent bear market. Greece and New Zealand: now those were the places to find your opportunities.

This doesn't require a lot of technical analysis. You just have to ask yourself under what conditions can you get something for a small fraction of its value. The answer is clearly when people are desperately trying to sell. We accommodate them by buying. When they are desperately trying to buy, we accommodate them by selling.'

Sir John Templeton is convinced that his success can be attributed to his own personal beliefs, which have had more of an influence over the way he has conducted his business than any economic dogma or investment discipline. Sir John has a commitment to improving the world he lives in as a sincere but practical Christian.

'The thing which is fundamental is, if you pray you can think more clearly. We open every directors' meeting with prayer. We don't pray that what we bought yesterday will go up tomorrow. We pray for a clear mind. We pray that what we do will be to the advantage of everybody. We pray that we will not be too emotional. I really do believe it works. You are less likely to make stupid mistakes if you pray first. If you are doing very difficult analysis, praying helps a lot.'

Sir John has laid out the philosophy which he credits as the cornerstone of his phenomenal record in a book called *The Templeton Plan: '21 Steps to Personal Success and Real Happiness.'* His keys to success include:

- Helping Yourself by Helping Others
- Finding the Positive in Every Negative
- Investing Yourself in Your Work
- Giving the Extra Ounce
- Winning Through Humility
- Discovering New Frontiers.

I read this book starting out somewhat sceptical. There is so much truth and good sense in what he has to say that no one could help but be convinced if only they are open minded. I would urge everyone interested in improving their quality of life to track down a copy and read it cover to cover.

In this, as in so much else, Sir John Templeton has created a legacy to inspire not just the current generation of investors, but generations to come. ♟

DR. MARTIN ZWEIG

'Protecting Capital and Avoiding Icebergs'

No one has a better understanding about markets than Martin Zweig, and no one in the investment business is more involved with every aspect of the market. Zweig not only runs managed accounts and mutual funds amounting to more than $9 billion, but he also edits one of the top ranked weekly newsletters. Zweig is one of only twelve people selected to PBS Television's Wall Street Week with Louis Rykeyser's Hall of Fame.

These activities each contribute to, and reinforce, a record of almost unparalleled investment performance. The emphasis is on stocks, both short and long positions, but the mix also spans several different asset categories. There is a Zweig for every occasion and, in almost every case, the returns are comfortably better than the relevant benchmark index, often by huge margins. Zweig's Performance Ratings are the basis on which he buys and sells individual stocks. Each company in his universe of 3,000 is ranked on a scale of 1 (best) – the top 5 per cent – to 9 (worst). He revises these ratings monthly. From May 1976 to March 1995, his category one stocks achieved a return of 6,793 per cent versus the market's 822 per cent.

Best of all, Zweig achieves his high returns with less volatility than the market and considerably lower exposure to risk. Zweig's investors sleep well at night. Even in 1987 his funds were up. He was buying puts. His portfolio climbed 9 per cent on 'Black Monday', while the market plunged 22.6 per cent. As *Time* said, 'When Zweig talks, people listen.' When picking investment advisors, sometimes it pays to start at the end of the alphabet.

Zweig is another example of a pre-eminent investor who got fascinated by the markets early on, owned stock while still a teenager, and whose interest was crystallized by mooching around the trading floor with an open mind.

'I had an innate curiosity about the stock market starting from the time I was a kid. I remember when I was very young my father would talk about the stock market crash and the depression. This really intrigued me, but I could not understand. 'Where did all the money go?' When you are six or seven years old, you can't grasp the concept of demand deposits and bank failures.

In 1961, at the end of my freshman year at the Wharton School of Finance, I tried to get a job in a brokerage office, as a chalk boy, but couldn't even get that. Anyway, I sat in on one of the firms all summer watching the market and trying to learn, and the industry got to me.

My first investment was General Motors. Most people start off with blue chips. My uncle gave me six shares for my thirteenth birthday. I had a few thousand dollars saved up and decided to buy more stocks. I added to General Motors, buying 14 more shares, and paid a little over $40. Four years later, I sold them at about $109, and I think the high was $115. The second stock I bought was American Cynamid, which promptly went down four points. They lost some anti-trust suit. So I learned very quickly things can go down.'

Zweig is unambiguous in characterizing his investment style.

'Risk averse. It evolved out of my own psychological bent. I was a big poker player in college, and hated losing . . . not so much from losing the game. I don't care if I win or lose. It was the money.

In my early days in the stock market, whenever I lost money it would just rip me apart. Over the years I decided there had to be a way not to get hurt badly, so I developed a very defensive style. I never wanted to get caught up in another crash; and I figured there would be another one some day. Why not? People always said there would never be another 1929. The more I looked at the market, the more I felt there could be. Things always reappear.'

Zweig has a poster on his wall given to him by a client over 20 years ago. The caption reads, 'The Things which hurt Instruct'. These words are attributable to Benjamin Franklin. Zweig has converted the pain into a proprietory and rigorous quantitative approach to measuring the risk profile of markets. His aim is to eliminate repetition of mistakes.

'You are always reading in the newspaper interest rates do this to stocks or that to stocks, but you never see people go back and try and scientifically prove it. Or someone might allude to a past case, but not say how many times it had happened before. So I started to go back and search for how many times interest rates did go up x per cent and what the market did after that; and I began to quantify everything I could get my hands on and build up a big database.

I'm trying to measure risk. It's not so much a forecast of where the market is going to be, it's how much risk is there in the market right now. And if risk is relatively low, I can be fully invested, because how much can I lose? I don't know how much I can make, but I won't lose much. If risk gets very high, I want to retreat to the sidelines.

> **I'm trying to measure risk. It's not so much a forecast of where the market is going to be, it's how much risk is there in the market right now.**

I'm not trying to time the market and be all in or all out. The world is filled with grey and it's perfectly appropriate to move in small increments. I move the mix in small increments. We have averaged 65 per cent invested in our managed accounts. We have been 100 per cent at times, and literally zero at times. Very few institutional investors try to assess the market risk and then raise significant levels of cash. Twenty per cent is huge. We've even taken our mutual funds to 80 per cent cash. That reduced the client's risk but, as a manager, we have increased the manager's risk. When you are sitting with that much cash and the market goes up, you are guaranteed to be the worst performer in the universe. It's a risk I am willing to take.

I'm not trying to call tops or bottoms. I'm trying to get with the major trends and I'm trying to cut losses short. Say the market is up 20 per cent, if I'm 70 per cent invested and up 15 per cent, I can live with that, because I'm more interested in absolute returns. On the other hand, if the market is down 20 per cent and I were to be down 15 per cent, that is horrendous. Most money managers can live with that because they are going to be in the top quartile. I don't want to be down more than five. Down markets give me this performance gap. As much as we all like to see bull markets, bear markets are a fact of life. I cannot hold stocks through a bear market even in the greatest company in the world. The pain would kill me.

> **If you can protect the bulk of capital in bear markets you don't have to be a hero in bull markets. You just have to be there.**

If you can protect the bulk of capital in bear markets you don't have to be a hero in bull markets. You just have to be there.'

Consistent with a view that a good manager should make money on both sides of the market, when multiples appear excessive and prices seem detached from underlying values, Zweig will switch to the sell side. He buys put options on the indices and shorts stocks.

'We are always short in our private partnerships. It's probably averaged 30 per cent. It's never been less than 10 per cent, except in 1991, which was a good call. Even in our mutual funds, once in a while we'll have something short, but there are too many tax rules and regulations which really work against it. We frequently short stock index future to hedge our positions. That way we don't have to sell the stock.'

Intentions are admirable. What sets Zweig apart is that he makes them work. The question remains, 'how does he call the trend when no one else seems able to?' There is an absolute consensus among both academics and professional money managers that it is impossible to time the market. Zweig is adamant he is not a market timer. Yet, in a way, as the layman understands the term, he is. Zweig understands better than any other manager how to move between cash and stocks. The bedrock of his approach is a mind-boggling amount of quantitative analysis, similar to the style of that brilliant statistician and technician, Ned Davis, for whom Zweig has nothing but praise. If you can think of a possible relationship between any economic, fiscal, demographic or even whimsical indicator and the stock market, Zweig almost certainly has run the correlation.

'I am open to anything that works. I like to start with some clear theory as to why something might move the market. I can see why interest rates have an effect. Some sentiment indicators, some valuation indicators. I'm not sure about sun spots, though, believe it or not, I've even tested that relationship.

The indicators that test best get the most weight in my models. As it turns out, monetary conditions get the top spot. It's primarily the trend in interest rates. I look at the central banks. In a general sense, the Fed dominates the monetary indicators. We're measuring the financial system's overall liquidity. I look at changes in loan demand and in the money supply. Changes in interest rates are probably the most important of the pieces in the monetary model and my monetary model gets the most weight in the overall model. It all comes down to 'don't fight the Fed'.

I generally take things as far back as I can get reliable data. With the monetary indicators, I have been able to back test to 1919. On a cursory basis I have gone back 200 years with a couple of things. You have to look at the data because markets change over time. The basic elements of greed, fear and liquidity are the same, but we have moved to a much more institutional market now. If you go back too far, you may be looking at a different kind of market. Take odd lots. That's one of the indicators which used to work best 30 years ago. Not today. Now most of the odd lots are done by programme traders, which is different from the old odd loters. All the good economic indicators have changed. You used to look at street car traffic. Blast furnaces in blast was useful in the 1920s. Nowadays you look at semiconductor chip production.

Part of my process is consistently to try and keep up with these changes in the economy and the market and get better measurements. This is frustrating because, if you do find, say, a good sentiment measure, it may be new and you only have a few years of data. You start tracking it. When you've got 15 or 20 years and you have a good sense of what it says, suddenly it stops working. One of the things I do in my models to counter this is to use a lot of indicators. All the models are designed to allow the weight of the indicators to be changed, or I can drop one, and add a new indicator.'

In his excellent book, '*Winning on Wall Street*', Zweig reveals those indicators which he has found to provide the most reliable reading of market direction and risk. He contrasts the change in stock prices with the magnitude and direction of changes in these key indices:

- Prime Rate.
- Federal Reserve Discount Rate.
- Federal Reserve Reserve Requirements.
- Money Supply.
- Consumer Instalment Debt.

Zweig's monetary model has been an astonishingly powerful predictor of the stock market. Going back to 1954, if you followed the buy signals, $10,000 in the price index became $339,992 by 1993. If you ignored the sell signals, you turned $10,000 into $2,989. Quite a contrast. Anyone who still believes in the efficient market has a good second career as a tooth fairy. Maybe it's time for the Nobel committee to take a look at results rather than theory. If so, Zweig must be in line for the prize.

Other indicators Zweig follows are market related or sentiment related. Examples are:

- Advance/Decline Ratio.
- A 4 per cent Change in the Value Line Composite.
- Mutual Funds Cash/Assets.
- Investment Advisors Bullish/Bearish.
- Ads in Barrons Magazine.
- The Moving Average Number of Secondary Offerings.

The correlations are impressive and deserve serious study. Zweig believes in the value of seasonal indicators and has tracked market movements back to 1952 to evaluate patterns during the course of a year. His research has shattered the myth espoused by many academics that stock price movements are random. Following the optimal trading strategy between 1952 and 1985 would have produced a tally of 223 up days versus only 8 down! Zweig also looks at particular indicators to predict a bear market.

- Inflation versus Deflation.
- Price/Earnings Ratios for the Dow Jones and S&P.
- The Yield Curve.

Looking ahead remains the challenge. How will Zweig's model hold up in the next decade?

'I always feel that monetary conditions and interest rates are important. I expect to weight sentiment indicators more heavily, if only I can get good data.

Quantifying as many things as you can helps, because you're sorting out a lot of noise, but the one constant is change. What happened in the past is not always a good guide to the future. That's where judgement comes in. Is this indicator really still showing me the same results, or is there a structural change going on? No one rings a bell the day an indicator stops working.

If low employment is generally bearish for the bond market and the government starts screwing around with their data, which they do, and there are constant revisions to everything they put out, which there are, you have to be very careful with that indicator – either downgrade the weight or make some kind of adjustment. Price is the purest indicator of all. Hard to screw up. That's why I like the price of money. Interest rates tell you what the market thinks. The problem with just using price is that you'll find price trends tend to persist more often than not. Momentum tends to work but, at the top and bottom, the signal will be wrong, because you will still be following the trend.'

> **Price is the purest indicator of all. Hard to screw up. That's why I like the price of money. Interest rates tell you what the market thinks.**

As you would expect, Zweig's success stems from calling the direction of the market correctly on a consistent basis rather than by selecting specific stocks.

'What works is when I follow my model, particularly at extremes. We were quite bearish in 1990. In October we began to cover shorts and buy stocks because, in that period to January 1991, interest rates began to fall, and the Fed began to loosen up in order to protect the banking system. The increase in liquidity and the drop in interest rates turned us very bullish; and sentiment at the time was more pessimistic by far than even after the '87 crash. I've only seen that level of pessimism twice. It was comparable to 1982 and 1974. The valuations weren't particularly cheap, but most of the other stuff fell into place.

The war was overhanging the market. This was the first announced war in history. We were going to war on 16 January and everybody was afraid; but our indicators were extremely bullish by then. We had been buying for three months. We went from 35 per cent net short to 70 per cent net long. That day the market opened about 100 points higher. Every single trader who called our desk was saying to sell. And that convinced Joe Di Menna, my partner, and I to keep on buying, because I figured if that many people were saying one thing, they were probably going to be wrong. So we increased our exposure to 90 per cent net long within a day. I told one of my partners, Brenda Earl, 'we're going to make a pile of money this year'. Everything was in place so, when the momentum turned, it was going to be very good. We were up 47.2 per cent in 1991.

The key is not to let your ego get in the way of the indicators. I did that once in the summer of 1974 and I don't have much of an ego left after that. I discovered that sentiment indicators do not factor everything in. Sentiment was extremely pessimistic, which was why I had been bullish, but monetary conditions remained hostile and the market had one last breakdown.

In 1987 all the indicators turned negative. In August I started predicting the market would fall about 1,000 points. I was basing this off the similarities to 1929, 1946 and 1962, which were the three previous crashes. There were, in all three cases, a big rally, a sell off, then a small rally to the top. In all three cases they lost back almost the entire previous two rallies. The big rally I saw started in the fall of 1986 and the levels were in the mid 1700s then, so I thought we would go back there in a couple of months. We went down to 40 per cent invested in September in our closed-end fund and wound up the number one performing US closed-end fund that year. Our partnerships went to zero about Labour Day. We ended the year up 65.1 per cent.'

Zweig believes the next decade will see continued globalization. In keeping with his philosophy, he is cautious there, too. While confident over the long term, he is worried about whether investors will benefit, and he is decidedly downbeat about near term prospects for equities.

'American investors have not been that big about investing abroad until recently. Now they have poured a ton of money into global international mutual funds. I think at the wrong time (early December 1994: Ed).

I worry about why there is so much financial information around compared to what was available 20, even 10 years ago. At four o'clock in the morning on three different channels there is business news. Who is watching this stuff? There is so much written on mutual funds. Pages and pages. The increase is gargantuan. Is this part of a speculative bubble that's going to burst? We're in a decade in which the defensive style of investing will be more valuable.

I'm relatively negative on financial assets for the next five years or so. The world's markets are basically overvalued. I foresee a series of bear markets or, at least, an unpleasant period. Especially stock markets. We're going to have a period of five to eight years where stocks will underperform their long-term mean. You have to get back to a reasonable set of valuations again. The good news is that there will be another great buying opportunity at the end of that, with a lot more safety.

Only a year ago people were saying , "cash is trash". Rates are up a bit. Cash doesn't look like trash right now. At some point, rates will get high enough that people will only want to hold cash and that will be the mistake again, just as it was in 1982 in the US. In the last couple of years people have been buying mutual funds because they did not want that lousy 3 per cent on cash. They're down. So when will cash be king? That's the time to buy stocks again. You don't get really great buying opportuities very often. The key to success is restraint. Don't get frustrated. Wait for the time when all the signals line up and then make the big bet. Most of the time my indicators are somewhere in the middle – moderately bullish or moderately bearish. There's this tendency to want to go for it all the time, put all the money to work; but you have to be patient.

Sometimes the market goes mad. The only way to get an edge is to have people go wrong. It's often enough just to be the one-eyed man in the land of the blind. If people are buying stocks at fifty times earnings, and I personally think they are irrational, I have to remind myself that's OK. Maybe I get bearish a little too soon, but if the rest of the world were rational, then stocks would not have gotten to 50 times earnings or even 40 times, and we wouldn't have an overvalued market to work with.'

Sometimes the market goes mad. The only way to get an edge is to have people go wrong. It's often enough just to be the one-eyed man in the land of the blind.

The other key is to make sure you never make the same mistake twice. Which is where historical quantitiative analysis helps most, though, as Zweig points out.

'Even if you do get that part right, there's a whole bunch of mistakes waiting for you out there that you've never experienced. There's always new kinds of mistakes. So if you do make mistakes, it's important to get out of them as soon as you can. There's no way around making mistakes. If you are a stock picker and you get 60 per cent right, you're good. You can even be less than 50 per cent accurate and still beat the market, as long as you eliminate the losses quickly and let the good ones ride. Cut short your losses and let the profits run. It's hard to do that, but you have to keep the discipline.'

That's where the strategy begins and ends. Zweig is conservative, careful and constantly concerned not to lose money.

'You can beat the market over time if you don't lose too much in the bad markets. It only takes one iceberg to ruin your career as a ship's captain, and there are a whole lot of icebergs. Let some other guy cross the Atlantic a little bit faster. I want to be around for the return voyage.'

Zweig's recommended reading is *Reminiscences of a Stock Operator*, the history of that most famous of speculators, Jesse Livermore, first published in 1923, and now in its ninth printing. He gives a copy to all his new employees. The message is clear. You have got to be flexible and follow the trend. Turn to the second page and you can see why Zweig calls it 'The best book about the stock market'. Point one: 'There is nothing new on Wall Street'. Point two: 'Don't fight the tape'. ♀

GLOSSARY

Many technical terms used are explained in the relevant section in which they appear. Issues arising relative to warrants and options can be found on page 52; for a better understanding of annuities the reader should refer to page 49. *The Global Guide* has compiled a short list of some of the terminology most frequently employed by the investment community where words and phrases do not always have their everyday meaning.

Advance Decline Line A simple day-to-day accumulation that subtracts the total number of stocks closing each day with losses from the total closing with gains; if the differential is a positive number, it is added to the previous day's total: if a negative number, it is subtracted. Unchanged issues usually are ignored; so are prices. The A/D Line can tell you whether the stock market at large is moving the same way as indicated by the indices.

Balanced Fund A fund which buys a mix of equities, and income instruments such as bonds, but including preferred stock and convertibles. The objective is to achieve a higher yield than a pure stock fund with less market risk.

Bellweather A stock considered to be a proxy for the general mood of its market segment. When it rises, the direction should be bullish and when it falls, bearish. These securities are usually very liquid and widely held by large institutional investors.

Benchmark Bonds A particular bond whose price and yield will be representative of a whole section of the market or, in the case of UK Government, benchmark gilts. Benchmark bonds exist in all major bond markets such as US Treasuries and German Bunds. Each series will have benchmarks for separate time periods such as five, ten or fifteen years. A Benchmark bond also needs to be a highly liquid issue.

Beta Beta is a measurement of the volatility of the price of a given stock compared to an average composite. In the UK, that could be the FT-SE 100; in the US, the S&P 500. A beta of one means that the stock swings are about the same as the market movements. If the market rises or falls by 1 per cent, so will that stock price. Higher beta stocks are more volatile. High tech, high growth companies tend to have high betas. Betas less than one are less volatile. Usually high dividend stocks like utilities have betas below one.

Black Monday 19 October 1987, a day when most markets around the world experienced huge declines. The Dow Jones Industrial Average dropped a record 508 points.

Black-Scholes Options Pricing Model Used to assess whether an option contract is correctly priced. The model is driven by the volatility of the underlying equity, the relationship of the price of the stock to the strike or exercise price of the option, the time remaining until the option expires, and the prevailing interest rate.

Blue Chip Common stock of a well-known company in its particular market. Blue chip stocks usually have a long record of profit and growth, steady rather than spectacular, and a long standing and continuous dividend.

Breakout Chartists use this term to signify the change in a trading range of a stock. A breakout takes place when the price moves above a resistance level (often the previous high) or falls below a support level (normally the previous low). This is usually taken as a signal that the stock price will continue to move in the same direction for several trading sessions.

Break-up Value What a company would be worth if it could be broken up and sold, division by division, piece by piece.

Bulldog Loan stock issued by foreign borrowers in sterling. They are usually traded on the London market.

Buy and Write This is an option strategy whereby the owner of a common stock sells a covered call at a premium to obtain the dividend and the call price. This is a conservative approach which increases current income, but limits the potential for capital gain if the stock rises above the call price.

Call Option The right to buy shares or an index at a specified price on a specified date.

Call Protection The length of time during which the call feature in a bond or stock cannot be exercised by the issuer.

Capital Asset Pricing Model (CAP) This model quantifies the relationship between the expected return from an investment and its expected risk. The market is believed to require a risk-free rate of return such as the interest payable on a one-year government bond, plus a risk premium. The CAP model is used to price many fixed income securities.

Certificate of Deposit Debt instrument issued by a bank.

Consumer Spending Growth The growth in personal disposable income plus or minus any change in the savings ratio.

Contingent Liabilities Contingent liabilities is accountant-speak for problems which may come back to bite you under certain circumstances. The most common relate to leased assets and the residual risk should the lessee choose to return the equipment. There are plenty of other contingent liabilities. Building companies often give guarantees over work they have done, and many companies guarantee loans to their subsidiaries and joint ventures.

Contrarian Investing The contrarian philosophy is to buy when everyone else is selling and vice versa. The rationale is simple: 'When everyone is bearish, a market must go up because there are no sellers left; conversely, when everyone is bullish, a market must go down because there are no buyers left.'

Convergence One factor affecting option values is the amount of time remaining before expiry. As the time to expiration diminishes, the price of the futures contract will converge to the price of the underlying asset.

Conversion Premium or Discount The amount by which the convertible varies from the market price of the underlying stock. If the convertible trades above the conversion price it is at a premium and if below at a discount. See page 26.

Conversion Price or Ratio The fixed amount or formula which governs the conversion of a bond or preference share into common equity. There are usually clauses which set specific timing windows to a conversion right.

Covenant A condition in a debenture or bank loan such as a certain level of interest coverage or a minimum net worth.

Covered Option Option written against a stock already owned by the writer of the option.

Cum Dividend A stock that trades at a price which includes a dividend already declared. After the date on which a stock goes ex-dividend, the seller is entitled to claim that payment, even after selling the stock.

Depreciation An accounting convention which specifies the percentage by which a fixed asset should be reduced in value each year. Several methodologies are recognized and applied over different periods. A car might be written off by the straight line method over three years, which would mean by one-third each year. It is a non-cash charge against a company's taxable earnings.

Derivative It is a financial arrangement between two parties, derived from the future performance of an underlying asset, such as currencies, bonds, stocks and commodities. At its simplest it involves options and swaps giving the right, but not the obligation, to buy over a specific period. At its most complex, it can involve as many as five movable assets. At least 1,200 types are traded.

Dow Theory Some analysts state that a major stock market trend must be confirmed by similar direction and change in both the Industrial Average and the Transportation Average. Both averages have to make new highs or new lows to signal a trading breakout.

The Earnings Yield The inverse of the more commonly used price earnings (P/E) ratio, i.e. earnings divided by price. This can be based either on historical earnings or, more commonly, on the prospective earnings for the current year.

Earnings Per Share (EPS) The profit of a company divided by the average number of shares outstanding during the period. Normally the ratio will use post-tax profit as the numerator, but some analysts prefer to look at the pre-tax profit to even out distortions that can arise from unequal tax treatment. The average number of shares outstanding should include not only the common shares but also make some provision for any convertible preference shares or loan stock, outstanding warrants, or share option schemes. If shares under option exceed 5 per cent of the total common shares, a company will be required to report both regular earnings and fully diluted earnings per share. The fully diluted calculation assumes all options have been exercised and warrants converted.

Equivalent Taxable Yield The rate on tax free securities is grossed up by a notional tax charge to show a comparable yield to a taxable bond. For someone in the 40 per cent tax bracket, receiving 5 per cent tax free is the same as receiving 8.3 per cent if the income is taxed.

Escalator Bonds Bonds where the rates rise during the period they are held. The longer held, the higher the rate of interest received.

Eurobonds Bonds issued by a government or corporation traded in the Euro market. They are bearer bonds with no registered owner. Eurobonds can be traded in a number of currencies. The largest pool is $ denominated, but there are Eurosterling, Euro Deutsche marks and Euro francs.

FIFO or LIFO To calculate book value, an investor must know which accounting approach to inventory is used by a company. The Last In First Out method causes inventory on the books to be understated, relative to true value, as long as the price of the products rises. During inflation, companies using this method can accumulate a significant LIFO reserve. First In First Out has no such reserve and also will tend to produce a lower cost of goods sold and report a higher gross margin and profit versus a similar company using LIFO.

Federal Reserve System The core of the US banking system. 'The Fed' consists of 12 regional Federal Reserve banks, 25 branches and qualified commercial banks. The Governing Board has many critical responsibilities, of which the most important is to regulate the national money supply. In the US the Board is, under the constitution, set up to be independent of the President and the Congress. Similar systems in Asia and Europe tend to be under greater control from politicians though, in 1994, the Bank of England started to move towards the US model.

Financial Cannibals Companies with substantial buy-back programmes.

Financial Future A forward contract on a financial instrument often used to hedge against interest rate movements. Futures are also actively traded as leveraged bets on the future direction of interest rates.

GAAP Generally Accepted Accounting Principles.

Goodwill The amount by which assets are valued over and above their book value. Goodwill usually arises in the purchase of a business when the consideration paid exceeds the value of the assets acquired.

Graham & Dodd Classic value based method of investing. See section on Peter Cundill starting on page 643 and the Tweedy Browne analysis on page 240.

Head and Shoulders Chartist term which is used to call a change in direction for a market index. If the position, which resembles two small tops flanking a higher top, is reversed, it is taken to meant that the market will be going up. The normal pattern is read as a flag of future declines in the relevant benchmark.

Hedge Funds Originally funds which make money, or lock in gains via hedging indexes. Has become used more widely for Funds which have a broad brief trading multiple asset classes both short and long. The most famous is George Soros' Quantum Fund. See pages 45–49.

Intangible Asset A thing of value which is not a physical asset, such as a brand name, copyright, customer list, capitalized expenditure with future benefits such as advertising or software development, organization costs or a patent. Accounting treatment varies by country.

In the Money When applied to options, this means the strike or exercise price is below the market price of a call option at the time the option is purchased, or above the strike price of a put option.

Index Funds Often known as Tracker Funds, these hold shares selected on purely mathematical criteria in order to ensure that the resulting portfolio will mimic the performance of a particular stock market index. Turnover and costs are both unusually low. Such Funds always do slightly worse than the index they track but they do better than most managed funds concentrating on the same stock market. Points to watch here are which index the fund is designed to track, and what the costs are.

Investment Trusts See section starting on page 31.

Junk Bond Bond with a credit rating of BB or lower from the credit agencies.

Kicker Feature added to a financial instrument to increase the rate of return for an investor. This usually comes in the form of warrants or options over equity attached to debt.

LIBOR London Inter Bank Offered Rate: the rate the banks with the highest credit rating charge each other for loans.

Limit Order Order to buy or sell a security only at a specified price or better.

Load A sales charge paid by an investor when purchasing a collective investment scheme or insurance product.

Lock up Lock up agreements between the underwriters of a public stock and investors in a company preclude the pre-IPO investors, such as venture capitalists, from selling their shares for a period following the IPO which usually averages about six months. When lock ups expire, the stock often weakens as the venture investors realize gains.

Long Gilt/Equity Yield Ratio The ratio between the yield on the long dated bond and the dividend yield on equities. In the UK this ratio has averaged 2.2 over the last ten years.

Market Breadth The percentage of stocks moving the same way as the market on a given day.

Moving Average A measure of price momentum for an asset which takes the average of daily prices for a given period adjusted every day by adding the most recent and dropping the oldest in the series. Thirty-day and ninety-day periods are common. The longer-term trend is often compared to the daily chart.

Naked option Option on a stock that is not owned by the writer. This is also called an uncovered option.

Net Asset Value (NAV) The assets less all liabilities. In a company this is the same as book value, or the shareholder's equity. For a unit trust or mutual fund net assets means the market value of the portfolio of investments minus any margin loans. Net asset value is the sum quoted in most financial newspapers such as the *Financial Times*.

Net Present Value NPV represents all future cash payments discounted back using a factor, usually the required rate of return for an investment decision. The net present value of a projected dividend stream can be compared to the current market price of an equity.

Nifty Fifty Stocks favoured by institutions which tend to exhibit above average growth and be awarded higher P/E ratios.

Odd Lot A number of securities less than the normal trading unit, usually less than 100 shares.

Orphan Assets A fashionable name for the surplus assets in the life fund of a proprietary company. The DTI description is as those assets in a life fund 'whose allocation between shareholders and policy holders may not be clear-cut'.

Out of the Money See 'In the Money' – exact reverse of.

Overhang A block of securities held by a potential seller who wants to unload into the market. This situation often occurs after a rights issue when underwriters have had to take up a lot of stock. An overhang in a security tends to depress the price.

Pass-Through Security A security which represents some pool of debt obligations packaged to pass income from the debtors via some intermediary to investors. Commonly used for mortgages and auto loans, the category is expanding to embrace credit card receivables, student loans and other groups of marketable collateral.

Trailing P/E The P/E ratio for the company, based on the last four completed quarters, as opposed to the most recent financial year end.

P/E Ratio Price per share divided by earnings per share.

P/CF Ratio Price per share divided by operating cash flow per share.

Piggyback Registration A right of holders to sell shares in certain circumstances when others sell. Often demanded in private placements by minority investors as a prelude to liquidating their investment through an IPO.

PIK Payment in Kind is a security where the interest or dividend is paid by issuing additional securities of the same type rather than in cash.

PSR The market value of the company divided by the turnover. Ideally, this should be calculated using trailing 12-month sales. This ratio is especially relevant in high tech stocks with uneven earnings.

Pre-emptive Right Existing shareholders may have the right to purchase shares (or bonds) in a new issue before it is offered to outsiders. This is common practice in private companies and standard in some countries. In the UK, public companies are limited to 10 per cent open issues unless a shareholder vote at an EGM waives the right.

Premium The effective price of an option. With a call option, it includes the cost plus or minus the difference between the strike price and the market price at the date of purchase.

Prime Rate The interest rate that US banks charge their most creditworthy customers.

Producer Price Index (PPI) A basket of commodities at different stages of processing collected monthly and converted into an index.

RIP(X) The UK government's target measure of underlying inflation, which excludes mortgage interest payments.

Random Walk Theory that says the past price movement of a security is irrelevant in predicting future prices.

Repurchase Agreement (REPO) An agreement where the seller agrees to repurchase a security at an agreed price and often at a stated time. The most common underlying asset is some form of US Government security. Central banks can use repos to manage the domestic money supply by injecting and extracting liquidity into/from the banking system for specified periods.

Revolving Credit A loan which allows a borrower to reborrow under a line amounts previously repaid. This 'overdraft' arrangement is considered short-term but, in practice, is usually renewed over extended periods of time. Such an approach is particularly suitable for businesses with large seasonal working capital requirements.

Risk Free Rate of Return The yield on a 'riskless' investment. The relevant three-month government security is generally considered to be risk free.

Sentiment Indicators Measures of the level of bullish or bearish opinions among key groups whose opinions may affect markets. See page 188 for the Investor's Intelligence Sentiment Index, a key indicator.

Short Sale When an investor borrows a security to sell something not owned on the expectation the price will decline. See pages 264–272 for a detailed description.

Sinking Fund An amount borrowed each year for repayment of a debt obligation at some point in the future. Some debentures have mandatory schedules. The term is also used to designate special reserves set aside for replacing long-term assets such as oil tankers.

Spot Commodity A commodity traded with the expectation that the buyer will take delivery of the physical product as opposed to the futures market which is more of a financial market for speculating and hedging.

Spread The difference between the bid and ask price on a security.

Swap An exchange of securities.

Tangible Book Value Book value reduced to exclude intangible assets such as goodwill, patents and capitalized R&D.

Tick A single movement in the price of a security. Can be up or down.

Topping Out When an index or individual security has been rising in price and then plateaus.

Trading Pattern The longer-term trend of the day-to-day price changes in the market for a security.

Underwrite To insure.

Unit Trust Pricing Unit trusts are created at creation price and cancelled at the cancellation price. The difference between the two is known as the spread, which can sometimes be as much as 12 or 13 per cent. Because this spread is so unattractive, fund managers take a commercial decision to narrow the spread to 5 or 6 per cent. The result is published in the form of two prices: one is the price investors buy at (called the 'offer'); the other is the sell price ('bid'). If you were to buy units and then immediately sell them back to the manager, you would lose 5 or 6 per cent straight away, depending on how wide the bid-offer spread was. See section beginning on page 28.

Volatility The movement, up or down, of the price of a security or market. The longer the movement and the more rapid the movement the greater the volatility.

Widow and Orphan Stock A security generally considered to be very safe, paying a relatively high dividend to produce good current income.

Yield to Maturity A combination of the interest coupon and the difference between the purchase price and the redemption amount at the redemption date. This is the bond equivalent of the internal rate of return calculated over the remaining life of the instrument.

NAME INDEX

723

725

SUBJECT INDEX

More authoritative books for investors in the Financial Times/Pitman Publishing series

Investor's Guide to Technical Analysis
Predicting Price Action in the Markets

What drives share price movement? How do trends develop? How can you predict them for financial gain? The key to successful investment can rest as much in the timing of the decision to buy or sell as in the selection of the share in the first instance. To do this, this book shows you how to use charts and technical analysis more effectively, including a review of the great theorists such as Dow, and Elliot & Gann.

ISBN: 0-273-61068-6   Author: Elli Gifford

Investor's Guide to Emerging Markets
'clear, interesting and easy, accessible and enlightening' – Pensions World
'Mark Mobius, the reigning king of emerging market funds' – Wall Street Journal

As the economies of developed nations experience sluggish growth, much better returns can be gained from investing in emerging markets. But the inherent risk is much greater. Written by Mark Mobius, star of the Templeton Emerging Markets fund, this is a comprehensive guide to investing in emerging markets, including strategies and techniques, market research and selection, regulations and accounting issues, and a dedicated section – Mobius Emerging Market Casenotes.

ISBN: 0-273-60327-2   Author: Mark Mobius

Investor's Guide to Warrants, 2nd edition
How to capitalize on the fastest growing market on the stock exchange.

Warrants represent one of the most rewarding and exciting investment opportunities available. But the market is loaded with jargon and good information on warrants trading is limited. Step-by-step, this unique book outlines the remarkable growth of the market and takes the sophisticated investor through the process of investing with warrants, including their advantages, how to structure a warrant portfolio to suit your needs and exercising subscription rights.

An intruiging examination of warrants trading from the publisher of market-leading Warrant Alert.

ISBN: 0-273-61241-7   Author: Andrew McHattie

Investor's Guide to Traded Options
'Investors will welcome the examination of sophisticated trading strategies' – Stockbrokers Journal

Options are one of the most flexible investment vehicles available. They can be used for speculation, to hedge a position, or to save money. This book is a clear and concise introduction to traded options which covers the basics such as options pricing and performance, through to more advanced issues such as risk management, advanced pricing theory and derivitives trading.

ISBN: 0-273-60704-9   Author: David Ford

Investor's Guide to Selecting Shares That Perform
10 Ways that Work

Select the shares that will perform for you ... by developing your own investment approach from a variety of proven techniques described by a highly successful investor.

The key to success lies in matching your investment techniques to your own personality and skills. Most private investors fail to perform as well as the stock market index simply because they use techniques that are unsuitable for them as individuals. This book provides ten successful investment approaches and helps you select the best one for you.

This best-selling book demonstrates that investing can be fun as well as profitable.

ISBN: 0-273-60528-3   Author: Richard Koch

Investor's Guide to Offshore Investment
International Tactics for the Active Investor

This book will teach you how to discover the secrets of the offshore market and how to maximise investment earnings through tax havens and perfectly legal tax loopholes. Essential information for the serious investor, including a gazetter of over 30 tax havens and how to make the best use of them.

ISBN: 0-273-61593-9   Author: Leo Gough

Investor's Guide to Investing Abroad
Profit from the World's Equity Bargains

This book will help you to find the world's best value equities and manage a broader portfolio for greater profits. The author, Paul Melton, is the editor of The Outside Analyst, a successful investment newsletter based in Amsterdam.

ISBN: 0-273-61973-X   Author: Paul Melton

Investor's Guide to How the Stock Market Really Works

'Modern and thorough, it will answer all the questions that investors (experienced and otherwise) might have' – Securities and Investment Review

ISBN: 0-273-61070-8   Author: Leo Gough

Investor's Guide: Be Your Own Stockbroker

'Vintcent's book will transform the occasional shareowner into a serious DIY investor' – David L Jones, Chief Executive, Sharelink

ISBN: 0-273-61328-6   Author: Charles Vintcent

Investor's Guide: How to Use Company Accounts for Successful Investment Decisions

'A model of clarity – for anybody interested in investment and all its aspects' – James Capel & Co.

ISBN: 0-273-61082-1   Author: Michael Stead

Investor's Guide to Measuring Share Performance

ISBN: 0-273-60628-X   Author: Dan Macfie

Financial Times Guide to Using the Financial Pages, 2nd edition

The most comprehensive and prestigious guide to reading and understanding the financial pages, brought to you from the experts at the Financial Times. This new revised edition gives you the strategies and tips to get the most from the financial press.

ISBN: 0-273-61248-4   Author: Romesh Vaitilingham